Italian Readers of Ovid from the Origins to Petrarch

Medieval and Renaissance Authors and Texts

Editor-in-Chief

Francis G. Gentry (*Emeritus Professor of German, Penn State University*)

Editorial Board

Teodolinda Barolini (*Lorenzo Da Ponte Professor of Italian, Columbia University*)
Cynthia Brown (*Professor of French, University of California, Santa Barbara*)
Marina Brownlee (*Robert Schirmer Professor of Spanish and Professor of Comparative Literature, Princeton University*)
Keith Busby (*Douglas Kelly Professor of Medieval French, University of Wisconsin-Madison*)
Jason Harris (*Director of the Centre for Neo-Latin Studies, University College Cork*)
Alastair Minnis (*Professor of English, Yale University*)
Brian Murdoch (*Professor of German, Stirling University*)
Jan Ziolkowski (*Arthur Kingsley Porter Professor of Medieval Latin, Harvard University and Director, Dumbarton Oaks Research Library and Collection*)

VOLUME 24

The titles published in this series are listed at *brill.com/mrat*

Italian Readers of Ovid from the Origins to Petrarch

Responding to a Versatile Muse

By

Julie Van Peteghem

BRILL

LEIDEN | BOSTON

This publication was supported by the Book Completion Award Program, The Office of Research, The City University of New York (2019–2020) and the PSC-CUNY Research Award Program, The Research Foundation, The City University of New York (2015–2016, 2018–2019).

Parts of Chapters 2 and 4 have been published as "The Vernacular Roots of Dante's Reading of Ovid in the *Commedia*," *Italian Studies* 73, no. 3 (2018): 223–39.

Library of Congress Cataloging-in-Publication Data

Names: Van Peteghem, Julie, author.
Title: Italian readers of Ovid from the origins to Petrarch : responding to a versatile muse / Julie Van Peteghem.
Other titles: Medieval and Renaissance authors and texts ; v. 24.
Description: Leiden ; Boston : Brill, 2020. | Series: Medieval and Renaissance authors and texts, 09257683 ; vol. 24 | Includes bibliographical references and index.
Identifiers: LCCN 2020002052 (print) | LCCN 2020002053 (ebook) | ISBN 9789004421684 (hardback) | ISBN 9789004421691 (ebook)
Subjects: LCSH: Ovid, 43 B.C.–17 A.D. or 18 A.D.—Appreciation—Italy. | Italian literature—To 1400—History and criticism.
Classification: LCC PA6537 .V36 2020 (print) | LCC PA6537 (ebook) | DDC 873/.01—dc23
LC record available at https://lccn.loc.gov/2020002052
LC ebook record available at https://lccn.loc.gov/2020002053

Typeface for the Latin, Greek, and Cyrillic scripts: "Brill". See and download: brill.com/brill-typeface.

ISSN 0925-7683
ISBN 978-90-04-42168-4 (hardback)
ISBN 978-90-04-42169-1 (e-book)

Copyright 2020 by Koninklijke Brill NV, Leiden, The Netherlands.
Koninklijke Brill NV incorporates the imprints Brill, Brill Hes & De Graaf, Brill Nijhoff, Brill Rodopi, Brill Sense, Hotei Publishing, mentis Verlag, Verlag Ferdinand Schöningh and Wilhelm Fink Verlag.
All rights reserved. No part of this publication may be reproduced, translated, stored in a retrieval system, or transmitted in any form or by any means, electronic, mechanical, photocopying, recording or otherwise, without prior written permission from the publisher.
Authorization to photocopy items for internal or personal use is granted by Koninklijke Brill NV provided that the appropriate fees are paid directly to The Copyright Clearance Center, 222 Rosewood Drive, Suite 910, Danvers, MA 01923, USA. Fees are subject to change.

This book is printed on acid-free paper and produced in a sustainable manner.

Contents

Acknowledgments   VII
Abbreviations   IX
List of Figures and Tables   X

PART 1
Writers as Readers

Introduction: "Ovid, the philosopher who wrote books about love"   3

1 Ovidius – Ovidi – Ovide – Ovidio: A History of Reading Ovid in the Due- and Trecento   13
   1.1 Reading Ovid: The Material and Cultural Contexts   14
   1.2 The Italian Readers of Ovid Turned Writers   48
   1.3 Beyond Intertextuality? How to Think about Ovid's Influence   55

PART 2
Readers as Writers

2 Examples (Not) to Follow: The First Italian Ovidian Poems and Their Occitan Models   73
   2.1 Better and More: Ovidian Similes in Vernacular Poetry   74
   2.2 Ovid's Book that Does Not Lie (to Troubadours)   98
   2.3 Reading and Discussing *Ovidio*   107
   2.4 Conclusion   121

3 Something Old, Something New: Dante, Cino da Pistoia, and Ovid   124
   3.1 "Per Ovidio parla Amore": First, the *Vita nuova*   125
   3.2 Dante's *petrose*: Testing Out New Techniques   133
   3.3 Cino da Pistoia, Dante, and Ovid on Love, Myth, and Exile   144
   3.4 Conclusion   167

4 Ovid in Dante's *Commedia*   169
   4.1 In Search of Dante's (Copy of) Ovid   172
   4.2 Dante's *Ovidius*: Close Readings of the Latin Text   181
   4.3 Dante's *Ovidio*: The Vernacular Roots of Dante's Reading of Ovid   198

        4.3.1 *Ovidian Similes from Lyric Poetry to the* Commedia   199
        4.3.2 *Discussing Ovidian Poetics from Lyric Poetry to the*
              Commedia   209
    4.4 Conclusion   220

5 **Petrarch's Scattered Ovidian Verses**   223
    5.1 Petrarch's Ovid Found   224
    5.2 Just Like Apollo, Just Like Daphne: Similes and Identification   235
    5.3 Metamorphosis as a Narrative Principle   264
    5.4 Conclusion   286

Bibliography   289
Index Locorum   324
Index of Manuscripts   331
General Index   332

Acknowledgments

I want to thank the institutions and the people who supported me in writing this book. Two semesters of release time at Hunter College, CUNY, offered the necessary time for research and writing. Additional support came from two PSC-CUNY Research Awards and the CUNY Office of Research Book Completion Award. Parts of Chapters 2 and 4 have been published as "The Vernacular Roots of Dante's Reading of Ovid in the *Commedia*," *Italian Studies* 73, no. 3 (2018): 223–39. The Biblioteca Medicea Laurenziana and Biblioteca Riccardiana in Florence, Italy gave permission to reprint images from their collections in this book. I could not have written this book without the assistance of the Interlibrary Loan Office at Hunter College Libraries, Columbia University Libraries, and the MaRLI Program at the New York Public Library.

I thank Francis Gentry for accepting this book in the MRAT series, and for his most generous support throughout. At Brill, Irini Argirouli, Alessandra Giliberto, and Peter Buschman guided me expertly through the publication process. The anonymous reader comments have made this book better, and for that I am very grateful. Deborah Aschkenes was again the perfect editor, and Alberto Gelmi and Katherine Volkmer provided invaluable help with the translations and the index of this book. All remaining errors are my own.

I first started to write about Dante and Ovid in Teodolinda Barolini's seminar on Dante's *Divina Commedia*. Both the project and I have undergone quite the transformation since that first Dante course, and I thank Teo for her steadfast guidance and honest advice she has given me over the years, and the outstanding example as a scholar, mentor, and person she continues to be.

My digital humanities project *Intertextual Dante*, which functions as a companion site to especially Chapter 4 of this book, would not exist without Teodolinda Barolini, Rebecca Kennison, Mark Newton, and especially Jack Donovan, who coded and designed the project's reading tool. I thank Columbia University Libraries for their continued support.

Presenting on my research at Hunter and beyond and teaching some of the material in this book to the students in the Italian Program has been very helpful. At the Department of Romance Languages at Hunter I found the most welcoming and interesting colleagues and students. I especially thank Michael Taormina for his guidance during the final phase of this book, and Lucrecia Aviles and Michele Stetz for their cheer. Monica Calabritto and Paolo Fasoli, my colleagues in the Italian Program, are the most supportive and generous mentors, and have become dear friends.

Working with Teodolinda Barolini, Meredith Levin (my favorite librarian), Akash Kumar, and Grace Delmolino on *Digital Dante* perfectly complements the solitariness of writing. The ACERT community at Hunter also reminds me that there is more than Ovid and medieval Italian literature. I also thank Daniela D'Eugenio, Stefania Porcelli, Paola Ureni, and Gloria Yu Yang for their friendship and support.

Bedankt aan de families Van Peteghem en Oppeel voor het warme welkom dat jullie mij altijd geven. De vriendschap van Vincent en Evelyn, en Elisa en Pieter doet zoveel deugd. Mijn ouders hebben mij altijd gesteund en in mij geloofd. Ik kan hen niet genoeg bedanken.

My deepest thanks go to mijn lief Richard, the most versatile person I know, for his love and support in everything I do.

Abbreviations

Aen.	*Aeneid*
Am.	*Amores*
Ars am.	*Ars amatoria*
Conv.	*Convivio*
DM	*De monarchia*
DVE	*De vulgari eloquentia*
Ep.	*Epistles*
Ex Ponto	*Epistulae ex Ponto*
Fam.	*Familiares*
Georg.	*Georgics*
Inf.	*Inferno*
Met.	*Metamorphoses*
Par.	*Paradiso*
Phars.	*Pharsalia*
Purg.	*Purgatorio*
Rem. am.	*Remedia amoris*
Rvf	*Rerum vulgarium fragmenta*
Secr.	*Secretum*
Sen.	*Seniles*
Theb.	*Thebaid*
VN	*Vita nuova*

Figures and Tables

Figures

1. Brunetto Latini, *Il tesoretto*. Ser Burnetto encounters Ovidio. Florence, Biblioteca Medicea Laurenziana, MS Strozzi 146, fol. 21v (detail). Courtesy of the Ministero per i Beni e le Attività Culturali. Any further reproduction, by any means, is forbidden   4
2. Beginning of the story of Apollo and Daphne in the pseudo-Lactantian *Narrationes*. Florence, Biblioteca Medicea Laurenziana, MS San Marco 225, fol. 7v. Courtesy of the Ministero per i Beni e le Attività Culturali. Any further reproduction, by any means, is forbidden   64
3. Beginning of the story of Apollo and Daphne with Arnulf of Orléans's glosses. Florence, Biblioteca Medicea Laurenziana, MS Pluteo 36.18, fol. 6v. Courtesy of the Ministero per i Beni e le Attività Culturali. Any further reproduction, by any means, is forbidden   65
4. Beginning of the story of Apollo and Daphne in the Vulgate Commentary. Florence, Biblioteca Riccardiana, MS Riccardianus 624, fol. 85v. Courtesy of the Ministero per i Beni e le Attività Culturali. Any further reproduction, by any means, is forbidden   66
5. Conclusion of the story of Apollo and Daphne in the Vulgate Commentary. Florence, Biblioteca Riccardiana, MS Riccardianus 624, fol. 87r. Courtesy of the Ministero per i Beni e le Attività Culturali. Any further reproduction, by any means, is forbidden   67

Tables

1. Chiaro Davanzati, *Come Narcissi, in sua spera mirando*, and anonymous poet, *Guardando la fontana il buo·Narciso*   84
2. Onesto da Bologna, *Assai son certo che somenta in lidi*, and Cino da Pistoia, *Se mai leggesti versi de l'Ovidi*   113
3. Dante da Maiano, *Amor mi fa sì fedelmente amare*, and Dante Alighieri, *Savere e cortesia, ingegno ed arte*   115
4. Comparison between terms used by Dante da Maiano, *Amor mi fa sì fedelmente amare*, and Dante Alighieri, *Savere e cortesia, ingegno ed arte*   117
5. Guido Orlandi, *Per troppa sottiglianza il fil si rompe*, and Guido Cavalcanti, *Di vil matera mi conven parlare*   118

FIGURES AND TABLES

6   Cino da Pistoia, *Dante, quando per caso s'abbandona*, and Dante Alighieri, *Io sono stato con Amore insieme*   150
7   Comparison between Dante Alighieri, *Amor, da che convien pur ch'io mi doglia*, and Ovid's exile poetry   158
8   The sequence and names of the horses of the Sun   174
9   Virgilio and the pilgrim with Beatrice absent (*Purg.* 27)   205
10   Beatrice and the pilgrim with Virgilio absent (*Purg.* 30)   206
11   The six major transformations in *Nel dolce tempo de la prima etade* (*Rvf* 23)   252
12   The distribution of Ovid's story of Apollo and Daphne in the *Canzoniere*   268

PART 1

Writers as Readers

∴

INTRODUCTION

"Ovid, the philosopher who wrote books about love"

Toward the end of Brunetto Latini's *Tesoretto*, a hard-to-categorize Italian poem in which Latini (1220–94) combines autobiographical narrative with encyclopedic knowledge of the world, the protagonist Ser Burnetto encounters the Latin poet Ovid. Burnetto is finally nearing the end of a long journey: at the beginning of the poem, he had appeared lost in a strange wood (vv. 1–190); while finding his way back, he met and received extensive lessons from the personified Nature and the Virtues (vv. 191–2170).[1] At this point in the text, the winged god of love starts to chase Burnetto on a crowded meadow. While trying to escape, Burnetto sees Ovid (vv. 2358–62):

> E in un ricco manto
> Vidi ovidio maggiore,
> Chelgli atti del amore,
> Che son così diversi,
> Rassempra e mette in versi.
>
> [And in a rich mantle I saw great Ovid, who collects and puts into verse the acts of love, which are so diverse.]

When Burnetto asks Ovid for advice about the workings, both good and bad, of the god of love, Latini's Ovid responds in Italian — "mi rispuose in volgare" (v. 2373) — that the power of love remains unknown to those who do not try it, and he advises him to look inside his heart for both the good and bad stemming from love (vv. 2374–80). Then the god of love hits Burnetto, and it is Ovid's "art" that guides him back to the straight path: "... ovidio per arte / Mi diede maestria, / Sì ch'io trovai la via / Ond'io mi traffugai" ("Ovid through art gave me mastery, so that I found the way from which I had strayed" [vv. 2390–93]).

In the only extant illuminated manuscript of Brunetto Latini's *Tesoretto* (Florence, Biblioteca Medicea Laurenziana, MS Strozzi 146), the artist imagines this encounter between the protagonist Ser Burnetto and the Latin author Ovid as follows (*fig.* 1): on the left we see Burnetto, who abandons the tranquil

---

1 The *List of Editions* in the Bibliography provides the full references of all primary sources cited in this book.

FIGURE 1   Brunetto Latini, *Tesoretto*. Ser Burnetto encounters Ovidio. Florence, Biblioteca Medicea Laurenziana, MS Strozzi 146, fol. 21v (detail)

stance that he had maintained in most of the previous drawings, lifting his head and right hand as if in enthusiastic agreement with what he hears from Ovid; on the right Ovid is seated on a bench with in front of him an open book and a pot of ink with a quill, and seems to be in mid-explanation (MS Strozzi 146, fol. 21v).[2] The tag above Ovid's head reads, "Ovidio filosafo che fece libri d'amore" ("Ovid, the philosopher who wrote books about love").

Both this drawing and the narrative of the *Tesoretto* provide interesting insights into the characterization and interpretation of the classical Latin poet Publius Ovidius Naso (43 BCE–17/18 CE) in medieval and early Renaissance Italian poetry. Brunetto Latini is the first to feature Ovid as a character in an Italian poem, and he describes him as an authority in matters of love: Ovid is clad in a rich mantle, he possesses skill ("arte"), and shares his mastery ("maestria"). Also in the drawing, Ovid's attire is refined, and their meeting place is no longer a meadow, but now a study with a finely decorated bench and lectern,

---

2   Brunetto Latini, *Tesoretto: Riproduzione in facsimile del ms. Strozzi 146 conservato presso la Biblioteca Laurenziana* (Florence: Le Lettere, 2002). On this image, see also Brunetto Latini, *Il tesoretto (The Little Treasure)*, ed. and trans. Julia Bolton Holloway (New York: Garland Publishing, Inc., 1981), 152–53; and Catherine Harding, "Visualizing Brunetto Latini's *Tesoretto* in early Trecento Florence," *Word & Image* 19, no. 3 (2003): 230–46, especially at 240–42. Both scholars made the comparison between this illustration and the first in the manuscript, where Ser Burnetto is sitting behind a similar desk and hands over a book (his *Tesoretto*) to the reader.

featuring a book, ink, and quill, further suggesting the importance and seriousness of Ovid's words. In the *Tesoretto*, Ovid's teachings are actually much briefer than those of the previous teachers, the personified Nature and the Virtues: his teachings consist of general advice for self-reflection (vv. 2374–80) or are not disclosed at all (vv. 2390–91). But however short, general, or unrevealed, Ovid's teachings have a positive impact: after listening to Ovid, the protagonist returns to the straight path and confesses his sins, which concludes the poem (vv. 2402–6).

Ovid's words clearly hit their mark in the *Tesoretto*, but on what was this positive assessment of Ovid based? Ovid is at once the poet of love (*Amores, Ars amatoria, Remedia amoris, Heroides*), myth (*Metamorphoses, Fasti*), and exile (*Tristia, Epistulae ex Ponto, Ibis*), and the texts belonging to each aspect of Ovid's poetic persona are quite different.[3] In the centuries that separate Ovid and Brunetto Latini, the Latin poet's diverse oeuvre had become an important source of inspiration for commentators, translators, and writers of poetry and prose in Latin and the vernacular languages; many admired Ovid's work, others vehemently denounced it. Ovid contains multitudes: understanding which Ovid Brunetto Latini had in mind in the *Tesoretto* and which Ovid the artist of MS Strozzi 146 depicted is not that simple.

Unpacking the *Ovidio* created by Latini in the *Tesoretto* and the artist who illustrated the poem introduces us to the central concerns in this book. First, the difficulty in easily pinning down which Ovid Brunetto Latini and the illuminator are representing and responding to reveals the versatility Ovid offered to all his Italian readers. As I am beginning to suggest, both text and image point to the different meanings *Ovidio* could convey in medieval Italy. The artist's tag "Ovidio filosafo che fece libri d'amore" and Latini's description of the Latin poet as "ovidio maggiore" (v. 2359) underline the prolific character of Ovid as a writer. In fact, Latini's language to characterize Ovid evokes several works of the Ovidian tradition, a general term to indicate Ovid's Latin poems and all the subsequent works related to or inspired by these poems. In the *Tesoretto*, Latini simultaneously evokes Ovid's *Ars amatoria*, *Remedia amoris*, and *Metamorphoses*, and Italian translations of these works.

Latini's Ovid is first introduced as "ovidio maggiore" (v. 2359), a title used in the Middle Ages, often in its Latin variant *Ovidius maior*, to indicate the

---

[3] On this triple thematic divide of Ovid's poetic persona, see Ralph Hexter, "Ovid in the Middle Ages: Exile, Mythographer, Lover," in *Brill's Companion to Ovid*, ed. Barbara Weiden Boyd (Leiden: Brill, 2002), 413–42, at 413–16; and Michelangelo Picone, "Ovid and the *Exul Inmeritus*," in *Dante for the New Millennium*, ed. Teodolinda Barolini and H. Wayne Storey (New York: Fordham University Press, 2003), 389–407, at 389.

work for which Ovid up until this day is most famous: his epic poem the *Metamorphoses*.[4] However, the topics on which Ovid advises in the *Tesoretto* are much closer to those of Ovid's love poetry (vv. 2360–62). This perceived inconsistency has led to various interpretations of the title "ovidio maggiore" and the work intended by Latini: Elio Costa interpreted it to mean "Ovidio moralizzato," the allegorizing reading of Ovid's *Metamorphoses*; Michelangelo Picone read the passage as Latini's recognition that Ovid's major work, the *Metamorphoses*, is mainly about love; and Kevin Brownlee understood the title as a strategic choice attributing the prestige of the *Metamorphoses* to the *Remedia amoris*.[5] To these interpretations, I add another Ovidian work: Ovid's intervention in the *Tesoretto* is described with key terms from his *Ars amatoria*, "arte" (v. 2390) and "maestria" (v. 2391).[6] At first glance, the *Remedia amoris* may seem to fit the content of the passage in the *Tesoretto* better, but already in his initial question to Ovid, Latini had made the distinction between good and evil stemming from love (vv. 2366–68). Indeed, instead of curing the protagonist of love altogether (definitely a *Remedia amoris*-like undertaking), Latini's Ovid teaches him the art of good love. So which Ovidian work is it? In his introduction of Ovid in the *Tesoretto*, Latini himself acknowledged the variety of Ovid's writings, as if hinting that we might not have to settle on only one of his poems:

---

4 On the Italian title *Ovidio maggiore* and its Latin variant *Ovidius maior*, see Madison U. Sowell, "Ovid in the Middle Ages," in *Medieval Italy: An Encyclopedia*, ed. Christopher Kleinhenz, 2 vols. (New York: Routledge, 2004), 2: 813–14.

5 Elio Costa, "Il *Tesoretto* di Brunetto Latini e la tradizione allegorica medievale," in *Dante e le forme dell'allegoresi*, ed. Michelangelo Picone (Ravenna: Longo, 1987), 43–58, at 50; Michelangelo Picone, "L'Ovidio di Dante," in *Dante e la "bella scola" della poesia: autorità e sfida poetica*, ed. Amilcare A. Iannucci (Ravenna: Longo, 1993), 107–44, at 117; Kevin Brownlee, "The Practice of Cultural Authority: Italian Responses to French Cultural Dominance in *Il Tesoretto, Il Fiore*, and the *Commedia*," *Forum for Modern Language Studies* 33, no. 3 (1997): 258–69, at 258–61.

6 The opening distich of Book 1 of the *Ars amatoria* reads: "SI QUIS in hoc *artem* populo non nouit amandi, / hoc legat et lecto carmine doctus amet" ("If someone in this crowd does not know the *art* of loving, let him read this poem, and having read it, he will be a well-taught lover" [*Ars am.* 1.1–2; emphasis added]). Further on, Ovid presents himself as Love's teacher: "ego sum praeceptor Amoris" (*Ars am.* 1.17). This notion of mastery is repeated at the end of the sections dedicated to the teachings for men and women, respectively: "sed quicumque meo superarit Amazona ferro, / inscribat spoliis NASO MAGISTER ERAT" ("But whoever will overcome an Amazon with my sword, let him inscribe on his spoils: NASO WAS MY MASTER" [*Ars am.* 2.743–44; emphasis added]), and "ut quondam iuuenes, ita nunc, mea turba, puellae / inscribant spoliis NASO MAGISTER ERAT" ("As did the young men before, let now the girls, my crowd, inscribe on their spoils: NASO WAS MY MASTER" [*Ars am.* 3.811–12; emphasis added]). While the *Remedia amoris* constitutes a teaching project as well, Ovid does not present himself explicitly as a teacher in this poem.

the "acts of love" Ovid puts into verse, Latini wrote, "son così diversi," "are so diverse" (vv. 2360–62).

Latini further puts a spin on his characterization of Ovid in the *Tesoretto* by drawing our attention to the fact that Ovid answers in Italian: "mi rispuose in volgare" (v. 2373). An *Ovidio* who lectures in Italian, and not his original Latin, constitutes an act of translation that goes further than rendering some Ovidian Latin key terms ("ars" and "magister") into Italian. Latini was a writer who moved comfortably between the Latin, French, and Italian languages and cultures, and contributed to the ongoing process of translating Latin works into the vernacular languages, called *volgarizzamento* in Italian. While Latini focused in his work of *volgarizzatore* mainly on bringing Cicero's rhetorical writings to an Italian public, translations of Ovid's poems had started to appear in the vernacular, first in French and later in Italian: the creation of a fully Italian *Ovidio* had begun to take shape, as the passage in Latini's *Tesoretto* reminds us.[7] Kevin Brownlee, in fact, argued that Latini uses the authority of the Latin poet, the "ovidio maggiore," to legitimize his own poem in Italian, and to contrast his *Tesoretto* with another vernacular poem that engaged with Ovid's works, the French allegorical poem the *Roman de la Rose*.[8] The presence of Ovid in the *Tesoretto* takes on different layers, not only evoking several of Ovid's poems in Latin, but also their translations in the vernacular, and other medieval poems inspired by Ovid. To have Ovid speak Italian thus appears less a practical decision (to have all characters communicate in one language, ignoring linguistic difference, as literary texts often do) and more a deliberate choice (to which Latini draws our attention with the phrase "rispuose in volgare") signaling the desire to distinguish his writings in the vernacular from the Latin tradition.

Based on this multilayered portrayal of Ovid in the text, the artist of MS Strozzi 146 translated the encounter between Burnetto and Ovidio into the drawing that opens this chapter. All elements in both visual and literary depictions of Ovid point to his mastery: the most telling difference between text and image is that the artist replaced the meadow in the *Tesoretto* with the more serious indoor study space as the backdrop for Ovid's teachings. Moreover, the tag identifying Ovid — "Ovidio filosafo che fece libri d'amore" ("Ovid, the philosopher who wrote books about love") — recognizes the diversity of Ovid's oeuvre, which Latini evoked in the text, and further assigns seriousness and importance to the Latin poet: Ovid is the "philosopher," a word Latini does not

---

7   In Ch. 1.1, I describe in greater detail Latini's work as *volgarizzatore*, which in addition to his translations of Cicero, included the rendering of shorter passages from classical and medieval Latin works into French and Italian.
8   Brownlee, "The Practice of Cultural Authority," 261.

use in his poem to describe him, but corresponds to the positive evaluation of Ovid's thought in Latini's *Tesoretto* and beyond. The term "philosopher" brings to mind the *accessus ad auctores*, the common medieval introductions to classical texts used in education, explaining among other things the work's content and the branch of philosophy to which it belongs. Ovid's writings, from the *Remedia amoris* to the *Ars amatoria* and even the *Amores*, were consistently categorized under the branch of "ethics."[9] In moral and other treatises, well-chosen verses from Ovid's poems taken out of context were mentioned alongside citations of philosophers such as Seneca and Cicero. Latini himself inserted at various points Ovidian verses in translation in the *Tresor*, his encyclopedic work in French, to corroborate his point. (Moreover, the choice to write the *Tresor* in French and not in Latin, the usual language of encyclopedias, constitutes another example of Latini's desire to establish his worth as an author in the vernacular.)

The combination of the brief cameo of Ovid in the *Tesoretto* and the accompanying image in MS Strozzi 146 puzzled me at first — I wanted to find their one Ovidian source — until I understood that Latini and the artist's portrayals of Ovid were ambiguous, because at their time the Ovidian tradition was as "diverse" as Latini wrote Ovid's writings were (v. 2361). Their brief portraits of Ovid, in fact, contain many of the features of the Ovidian tradition in medieval and early modern Italy I will examine in this book: the recognition of the diversity of Ovid's oeuvre, the wide range of later texts in Latin and the vernacular that engage with Ovid's poems, the appeal to the authority of a classical author, the translation and adaptation of classical literature in the vernacular, the emergence of an authoritative voice in the vernacular, and the construction of a vernacular *Ovidio*. While no other poem packs all those features in one short passage as Latini did in the *Tesoretto*, in writing the reception history of Ovid in the Italian thirteenth and fourteenth centuries, these are central features that come to the foreground.

Keith Busby and Christopher Kleinhenz have recently pointed out that "[t]raditional literary histories of the Middle Ages, irrespective of the language areas and periods they cover, are largely based on the reading of texts in modern critical editions." Their intent was to direct medieval studies back to the manuscript tradition of the texts, which can lead to a "radically different vision."[10] In this book, not one but at least two texts are required to write the literary history of Ovid's reception in the Italian Middle Ages: the Italian poems

---

9   I discuss the practice of the medieval *accessus* in more detail in Ch. 1.1.
10 Keith Busby and Christopher Kleinhenz, "Medieval French and Italian literature: towards a manuscript history," in *The Medieval Manuscript Book: Cultural Approaches*, ed. Michael

and Ovid's. And what Busby and Kleinhenz pointed out about medieval texts is true for Ovid as well: we cannot simply look at our modern critical editions of Ovid's poems. A text of Ovid looked radically different to medieval readers (like Latini) than to readers today. The reception history of Ovid in medieval Italy starts with the history of *reading* Ovid: examining what exactly their copies of Ovid looked like and what it could mean to "read Ovid" in the Italian thirteenth and fourteenth centuries.

• • •

This is a book about medieval and early Renaissance Italian poetry from a historicized and culturally-embedded perspective. The connections between Ovid and the Italians are not unexplored territory, but often reduced to a few single authors: Dante's Ovid and Petrarch's Ovid, with a focus on the direct connections between the Latin poet and the Italians. Such an approach places Dante and Petrarch, both well-read authors, in a literary and historical vacuum, ignoring the multiplicity of the Ovidian tradition, to which Dante and Petrarch both contributed and responded. This limited approach leaves many other poets writing before and during Dante's lifetime out of the story, and presents Dante and Petrarch's readings of Ovid as isolated moments, unconnected to the unfolding history of reading and writing about Ovid in medieval Italy. While several aspects of the transmission, translation, and adaptation of Ovid's works (such as the commentary tradition of the *Metamorphoses*, or Ovid's presence in the *accessus ad auctores*) have been studied within their European context, this book includes an extensive account focused specifically on medieval Italy, and studies the dynamic interactions between reading and writing — activities that were and still are closely connected, but often treated separately in the scholarship.

I have structured this book as follows. In Part 1, I look at "Writers as Readers," focusing on the material forms and the cultural and intellectual environments in which Ovid was available and read. As many of Ovid's Italian readers wrote poetry themselves, Part 2 focuses on "Readers as Writers," examining how these forms and environments shaped the poetry of these readers turned writers.

In the first chapter, "Ovidius – Ovidi – Ovide – Ovidio: A History of Reading Ovid in the Due- and Trecento," I outline the broad cultural and material contexts of the reception of Ovid in Italy during the thirteenth and fourteenth centuries, describing in which formats (commentaries, translations, anthologies,

---

Johnston and Michael Van Dussen (Cambridge: Cambridge University Press, 2015), 215–42, at 215.

mentions in treatises, other works of literature) and contexts (schools, universities, courts, monasteries) Ovid's writings were available. In matching Italian readers with the different texts and contexts in which they could encounter Ovid, I show that many could read Ovid or Ovid-inspired poetry and prose in Latin and at least one vernacular language, and illustrate the coexistence of and dynamic relationships between Latin, Occitan, French, and Italian readings of Ovid. The understanding of this highly diversified reading of Ovid then forms the basis for the methodological framework of the book: the Italian poets who feature Ovidian material in their poetry will be studied as readers of their time.

Part 2, "Readers as Writers," follows a roughly chronological order, and examines — or, in the case of Dante and Petrarch, re-examines — Italian poetry as part of the medieval Italian history of reading and writing about Ovid, illustrating that the widely varying material forms and contexts in which the Italians encountered Ovid informed the Ovidian poems they wrote.

Chapter 2, "Examples (Not) to Follow: The First Italian Ovidian Poems and Their Occitan Models," focuses on a first group of Italian readers of Ovid from the first three poetic movements in Italian literature — the Sicilian poets, the Siculo-Tuscan poets, and the *dolce stil novo* poets — and the ways in which they include Ovidian material in their poetry. I argue that while these Italian poets read and wrote in environments where Ovid was also available in other formats, they mainly looked at how the troubadours worked with Ovidian material. I identify the specifics of the troubadours' approach — their preference for the simile, certain Ovidian characters, mentions of Ovid in their poems — and show close connections between their practices and those of Italian poets. I analyze how these Italian poets adopted but also altered their Occitan models, and how their mentions of Ovid at times became forceful statements about the status of vernacular literature.

Chapter 3, "Something Old, Something New: Dante, Cino da Pistoia, and Ovid," analyzes the presence of Ovid in the writings of Dante and Cino da Pistoia, identifying the innovations that distinguish them from the poets discussed in the previous chapter. I show that Dante and Cino moved beyond the Occitan models that so far had dominated the featuring of Ovidian material in Italian poetry, and worked more closely with Ovid's Latin texts. The chapter starts by looking at Dante's first mention and citation of Ovid in the prose of the *Vita nuova*, read as an early indicator of his interest in the classical world. I then turn to Dante's *rime petrose*, and illustrate Dante's closer reading of Ovid, finding both central and peripheral elements from his works in Dante's poems. Also Cino da Pistoia's poetry and his exchanges with Dante display a wider knowledge of Ovid's oeuvre, and rely on Ovidian material to explore their shared roles as lover, poet, and exile.

In Chapter 4, I turn to Ovid in Dante's *Commedia*, the poem in which his presence is most felt and most studied. I argue that Dante's Ovid is too often examined in a vacuum, and I instead closely tie Dante's Ovidian strategies in the *Commedia* to both his own earlier poetry and the vernacular lyric poetry written before and during his lifetime. I first relate the findings of the scholars who looked for Dante's actual copy or copies of Ovid to my discussion of the material and cultural contexts of reading Ovid in Ch. 1.1. I then make the case that Dante's two main Ovidian sources were *Ovidius* — all of Ovid's Latin texts — and *Ovidio* — the vernacular readings of Ovid in Italian lyric poetry. I show Dante's close engagement with Ovid's Latin poems in their entirety in the *Commedia*, rather than working with the many intermediary sources that presented isolated passages from Ovid's oeuvre. I also illustrate the vernacular roots of Dante's reading of Ovid, by connecting the practices of vernacular lyric poets to Dante's treatment of Ovidian material in the *Commedia*.

Like the previous chapter on Ovid in Dante's *Commedia*, Chapter 5, "Petrarch's Scattered Ovidian Verses," re-examines the traits of his treatment of Ovidian material that are considered distinctively "Petrarchan," and instead situates them in their Italian literary and cultural contexts. I start by documenting Petrarch's strong familiarity with the Italian Ovidian tradition, which included Ovid-inspired literature in Italian, Occitan, and French, in addition to Ovid's works in Latin and commentaries. I then examine Petrarch's interest in self-identification with Ovidian characters, a feature of vernacular lyric poetry from the very beginning, and connect Petrarch's frequent identification with the women in Ovid's stories in the *Canzoniere* to previous poems of Cino da Pistoia and Dante, where such gender reversals also occurred. I further argue that more than any Italian reader of Ovid before him, Petrarch understood that Ovid's concept of metamorphosis is also a narrative principle. Ovid created the stories in the *Metamorphoses* from different sources, often intertwined his stories and at times even rewrote them in his poem. In the *Canzoniere*, Petrarch applies this same principle not only when scattering fragments of Ovidian stories and themes in his poems, but also when rewriting his own story throughout the collection.

• • •

The meanings of "Ovid" expand in many directions — this is one of the central arguments of this book. While I set out to provide a much broader understanding of what reading and responding to Ovid meant in the Italian thirteenth and fourteenth centuries, I also discuss the Italian Ovidian tradition within certain parameters, as the previous breakdown of this book's chapters already indicated. My main focus is poetry, not prose; the vernacular, not Latin. And, as a result of those two emphases, Dante and Petrarch, not Boccaccio. Prose works in Latin and the vernacular and medieval Latin poetry were under Ovid's influence as well and I mention some of these works in this book. But my main focus is on tracing the development of Italian vernacular poetry through the lens of the Ovidian tradition. It is in vernacular Italian poetry that the versatility of Ovid becomes most apparent and where Italian poets repeatedly turn to Ovid to draw distinction between past and present, between Latin and the vernacular. Among these Italian readers of Ovid, Dante and Petrarch are arguably the two best known. (Boccaccio clearly was an avid reader of Ovid as well, and in many respects the Ovid to Dante's Vergil, but that is a different book altogether.) But this book is most definitely not only about Dante and Petrarch. It is incomplete and incorrect to treat them as readers who only turn their attention to what Ovid wrote and ignore the Ovidian tradition, which at their time already included several Italian works. Ovid made an appearance in some of the earliest poetry written in Italian, and remained a constant presence in Italian vernacular poetry as it developed over time. Including Ovid's Italian readers before Dante and Petrarch offers a more complete account of the reception history of Ovid in the Italian Middle Ages. And that history, as we will see in the chapters that follow, can be difficult to reconstruct due to the dynamic and versatile character of the Ovidian tradition.

CHAPTER 1

Ovidius – Ovidi – Ovide – Ovidio: A History of Reading Ovid in the Due- and Trecento

The Italian Middle Ages were not exclusively Italian. When the Italians started to compose poetry in the vernacular around the early thirteenth century, they came late to the European literary scene, and already had French and Occitan literature as models. In Italy, as in other parts of Europe, the writing of poetry and prose in the vernacular emerged against a long and ongoing Latin tradition, and the Latin, Occitan, French, and Italian literatures and cultures coexisted. The origin story of Italian literature cannot be told without reference to these different traditions.

Similarly, the reception history of Ovid's works in Italy does not exist in an exclusively Italian vacuum. In the more than a century that separates Ovid's writings and the Italian poetry studied in this book, a wide variety of poetry and prose in Latin and in the vernacular languages, in addition to Ovid's oeuvre in Latin, complemented and complicated the meaning of "reading Ovid." That will be the starting point of this book: a detailed history of what it could mean to read Ovid in the Italian Due- and Trecento, or the thirteenth and fourteenth centuries. As the title of this chapter already indicates, there existed dynamic relationships between Latin, Occitan, French, and Italian languages and cultures. The understanding of this highly diversified reading of Ovid is detailed in the first section, and sets up the following two sections of this chapter. After identifying the material contexts (the different formats in which one could read Ovid) and cultural contexts (the environments in which Ovid was read) in the first section, I then connect (to the extent possible) the Italian readers with their Ovidian texts and contexts. In the final section, I describe in more detail the methodological framework to study the Italian Ovidian poetry given this diverse Ovidian tradition.

1.1 Reading Ovid: The Material and Cultural Contexts

In a well-known passage from St. Bonaventure's prologue to Peter Lombard's *Book of Sentences*, the thirteenth-century Doctor of the Church breaks down the making of books ("modus faciendi librum") into four different roles:[1]

> Aliquis enim scribit aliena, nihil addendo vel mutando; et iste mere dicitur *scriptor*. Aliquis scribit aliena, addendo, sed non de suo; et iste *compilator* dicitur. Aliquis scribit et aliena et sua, sed aliena tamquam principalia, et sua tamquam annexa ad evidentiam; et iste dicitur *commentator*, non auctor. Aliquis scribit et sua et aliena, sed sua tamquam principalia, aliena tamquam annexa ad confirmationem; et talis debet dici *auctor*.

> [Sometimes a man writes others' words, adding nothing and changing nothing; and he is simply called a scribe [*scriptor*]. Sometimes a man writes others' words, putting together passages which are not his own; and he is called a compiler [*compilator*]. Sometimes a man writes both others' words and his own, but with the others' words in prime place and his own added only for purposes of clarification; and he is called not an author but a commentator [*commentator*]. Sometimes a man writes both his own words and others', but with his own in prime place and others' added only for purposes of confirmation; and he should be called an author [*auctor*].]

St. Bonaventure makes these distinctions to conclude that Peter Lombard is indeed the *auctor* of the *Sentences*, and not just collecting passages from Scripture and theological writings.[2] While these four roles — scribe, compiler, commentator, author — were once exclusively connected to the making of works on Scripture and theological writings, over time the same figures also turned to classical texts and poetry, and later works in the vernacular, both original

---

1 Text quoted from Philipp W. Rosemann, *Mediaeval Commentaries on the 'Sentences' of Peter Lombard*, Vol. 3 (Leiden: Brill, 2015), 5, n. 12. Translation quoted from J. A. Burrow, *Medieval Writers and their Work: Middle English Literature 1100–1500*, 2nd ed. (Oxford: Oxford University Press, 2008), 31.
2 As Philipp W. Rosemann pointed out in his edition of the *Sentences* (3: 5 and n. 14), it is important to include St. Bonaventure's reason for making these distinctions, as well as the following statement that further clarifies his point: "Et quod sunt ibi multa dicta aliorum, hoc non tollit Magistro auctoritatem, sed potius eius auctoritatem confirmat et humilitatem commendat" ("And that there are many words from others does not take away the authority of the Master [i.e., Peter Lombard], but rather confirms his authority and commends his humility").

compositions and translations.³ St. Bonaventure's description captures well that medieval writing is intrinsically connected with reading: all four "makers of books" rely on other books to do so, on "aliena," the words of others — from the obvious reading expected from the scribe, compiler, and commentator, to the author, who also uses the words of others in support of his own.⁴ When we replace the repeated "aliena" in St. Bonaventure's passage by "Ovidiana" (Ovid's works or words), his four different makers of books become our first identified readers of Ovid: *scriptores* read and copied Ovid's Latin works, *compilatores* excerpted Ovid's texts and collected them in anthologies and compendia, *commentatores* read and commented on them, and *auctores* used Ovid's words to confirm their own. Taking St. Bonaventure's different roles as a starting point, in this section I look closer at the books these readers of Ovid made and who, in turn, read those books. The first step in reconstructing these reading communities is sketching the material and cultural contexts of reading Ovid in thirteenth- and fourteenth-century Italy, examining in which environments and formats one could encounter Ovid, and how those environments and formats could condition their interpretation of the Latin poet.

Let us start with the scribes and their copying of Ovid's Latin texts. Extant manuscripts are an obvious place to begin.⁵ The general trend during the twelfth and thirteenth centuries in all of Europe, Italy being no exception, was

---

3   See Alastair Minnis's fundamental work on the topic: *Medieval Theory of Authorship: Scholastic Literary Attitudes in the Later Middle Ages*, 2nd ed. (Philadelphia: University of Pennsylvania Press, 1988); *Medieval Literary Theory and Criticism c.1100–c.1375: The Commentary Tradition, Revised Edition*, ed. Alastair J. Minnis and A. B. Scott, with the assistance of David Wallace (Oxford: Oxford University Press, 1992); *Magister amoris: The 'Roman de la Rose' and Vernacular Hermeneutics* (Oxford: Oxford University Press, 2001). Studies such as Albert Russell Ascoli, *Dante and the Making of a Modern Author* (Cambridge: Cambridge University Press, 2008), and Jelena Todorović, *Dante and the Dynamics of Textual Exchange: Authorship, Manuscript Culture, and the Making of the 'Vita Nova'* (New York: Fordham University Press, 2016) showed how Dante takes on all four roles identified by St. Bonaventure.

4   On the complementarity of the acts of reading and writing, see Armando Petrucci, "Le biblioteche antiche," in *Letteratura italiana*, ed. Alberto Asor Rosa, Vol. 2, *Produzione e consumo* (Turin: Einaudi, 1983), 527–54, at 528.

5   On the transmission of Ovid's works, see Richard J. Tarrant, "Ovid," in *Texts and Transmission: A Survey of the Latin Classics*, ed. L. D. Reynolds (Oxford: Clarendon Press, 1983), 257–86; and John Richmond, "Manuscript Traditions and the Transmission of Ovid's Works," in Boyd, *Brill's Companion to Ovid*, 443–83. Keith Busby and Christopher Kleinhenz redirected the attention of literary scholars of the Middle Ages back to the examination of manuscript transmission. The realization that "manuscripts ... in various genres survive in greater or fewer numbers, which may or may not provide insight on their popularity at the time" should not put a stop to discussion, Busby and Kleinhenz argued: "numbers *can be* important indicators and *should be* considered in any reassessment of the literary history of the period" ("Medieval French and Italian literature," 230).

an exponential increase in manuscripts of Ovid's oeuvre.[6] Throughout this period, the *Metamorphoses* remains the most popular text, but the manuscript numbers include almost all of Ovid's works.[7] Before 1200, Ovid's *opera omnia* were rarely collected in one manuscript; the amatory works, on the other hand, would often appear together as the *carmina amatoria*.[8] Moreover, the medieval conception of Ovid's complete works included a few texts whose authorship was later questioned: spurious poems that are now considered the work of Ovid's contemporaries (such as the *Consolatio ad Liviam de Morte Drusi*, *Nux*, and *Halieutica*), and the pseudo-autobiographical *De vetula*, which actually is a mid-thirteenth century creation.[9] Especially *De vetula* — the account of Ovid's last love story that ends with the poet's conversion to Christianity — circulated widely and attests to the medieval interest in the biography and writings of the Latin poet in general.

In fact, most historians studying the high and late Middle Ages (from the tenth to the fifteenth century) agree that the study of classical authors steadily increased from the twelfth century on — a general trend, as they describe, characterized by regional differences and shifts in preferences for certain Latin authors and genres over time. The scholars who deny such a continuously increasing interest in classical antiquity focus in particular on the thirteenth century in Italy, the century during which vernacular Italian poetry came into existence and also the starting point of this book.[10] The socio-political

---

6 Jean-Yves Tilliette, "Savants et poètes du moyen âge face à Ovide: les débuts de l'aetas Ovidiana (v. 1050–v. 1200)," in *Ovidius redivivus: Von Ovid zu Dante*, ed. Michelangelo Picone and Bernhard Zimmermann (Stuttgart: M&P, 1994), 63–104, at 70–71.

7 To be precise: the data mention the *Metamorphoses*, *Fasti*, *Epistulae ex Ponto*, *Tristia*, *Heroides*, *Remedia amoris*, *Ars amatoria*, *Amores*. There is no mention of the *Ibis* and *Medicamina faciei femineae*.

8 See Tilliette, "Savants et poètes du moyen âge face à Ovide," 72. In the Appendix of the *Incipitarium Ovidianum: A Finding Guide for Texts Related to the Study of Ovid in the Middle Ages and Renaissance* (Turnhout: Brepols, 2000), Frank T. Coulson and Bruno Roy identified all manuscripts that collect several of Ovid's texts: the most prevalent is a combination of several amatory works, but a few manuscripts also include the *opera omnia*. In the Appendix to *Ovid in the Middle Ages*, ed. James G. Clark, Frank T. Coulson, and Kathryn L. McKinley (Cambridge: Cambridge University Press, 2011), the editors listed some manuscripts that are prime examples of such collections.

9 Dorothy M. Robathan, *The Pseudo-Ovidian 'De Vetula': Text, Introduction, and Notes* (Amsterdam: A. M. Hakkert, 1968); *The Pseudo-Ovidian Ad Liviam de morte Drusi (Consolatio ad Liviam, Epicedium Drusi): A Critical Text with Introduction and Commentary*, ed. Henk Schoonhoven (Groningen: E. Forsten, 1992). On the genre, see Ralph Hexter, "Shades of Ovid: Pseudo- (and para-) Ovidiana in the Middle Ages," in Clark, Coulson, and McKinley, *Ovid in the Middle Ages*, 284–309.

10 Robert Black, *Humanism and Education in Medieval and Renaissance Italy: Tradition and Innovation in Latin Schools from the Twelfth to the Fifteenth Century* (Cambridge:

changes in the Italian cities, these scholars argue, created an increasing need for a faster, more practical method of teaching Latin to notaries, lawyers, and merchants — one that no longer required the study of Latin literature.[11] Moreover, key figures in the study and teaching of rhetoric at the time at Bologna, such as Boncompagno da Signa, teacher of rhetoric around the beginning of the thirteenth century, and his successor Guido Faba, opposed the use of pagan authors in the study of rhetoric and removed Cicero from the syllabus.[12] In his study of Italian schoolbook manuscripts from the twelfth to the fifteenth century, Robert Black found that during the thirteenth century fewer Latin authors appeared in comparison to the previous century,[13] suggesting that the interest in classical literature had decreased during that period. But increasing or decreasing numbers of extant manuscripts do not reveal the complete picture, especially when these numbers only include a specific kind of manuscript, in this case schoolbooks. During the thirteenth century, classical authors — Ovid not the least — were known and read both inside and outside the classroom, and not always in the format of the schoolbook. To get a fuller understanding of the Italian readers' knowledge of Ovid, we need to go beyond the classroom and look at all the possible sources that incorporated this classical author.

Parallel to the rising interest in the source texts, Ovid also became the main source of inspiration for translators, commentators, and writers of poetry and prose. This vast body of Ovid-inspired texts makes it easy to recognize the peak of Ovid's popularity, but to understand the fascination with the poet we need to "anatomize" it — to use Ralph J. Hexter's term for the task at hand — as there

Cambridge University Press, 2001) is the most recent monograph on education in Italy during this period. Black, one of the scholars who argue for a declined interest in the classics during the thirteenth century, provides an overview of both sides of the argument, with bibliographical references in the footnotes (193–94). See also Black's essay "Teaching techniques: the evidence of manuscript schoolbooks produced in Tuscany," in *The Classics in the Medieval and Renaissance Classroom: The Role of Ancient Texts in the Arts Curriculum as Revealed by Surviving Manuscripts and Early Printed Books*, ed. Juanita Feros Ruys, John O. Ward, and Melanie Heyworth (Turnhout: Brepols, 2013), 245–65. Especially Ronald G. Witt's work has challenged Black's account: *In the Footsteps of the Ancients: The Origins of Humanism from Lovato to Bruni* (Boston: Brill, 2000) and the subsequent study *The Two Latin Cultures and the Foundation of Renaissance Humanism in Medieval Italy* (Cambridge: Cambridge University Press, 2012).

11 Black, *Humanism and Education in Medieval and Renaissance Italy*, 197–98; Helene Wieruszowski, "Rhetoric and the Classics in Italian Education," in *Politics and Culture in Medieval Spain and Italy* (Rome: Edizioni di storia e letteratura, 1971), 589–627, at 590–92.
12 Wieruszowski, "Rhetoric and the Classics in Italian Education," 593–97.
13 Black, *Humanism and Education in Medieval and Renaissance Italy*, 192. Black defined his criteria to consider which manuscripts qualify as "schoolbooks" at 3–6, 10–11.

is not one, but several medieval Ovids.[14] The complexity of Ovid's influence in the Middle Ages is due in part to the complexity of his oeuvre: as pointed out in the introduction, Ovid wrote about a variety of themes (love, myth, and exile are often identified as the main ones), and he approached each theme in different forms and contexts. Not surprisingly, then, Ovid's works appealed to different readers in different ways. At the end of the *Metamorphoses* Ovid correctly predicted that he would be read through all the ages (*Met.* 15.877–79) and, as it turned out, the reception of his work became governed by the very principle that ruled his epic: constant change.

This principle of constant change applies foremost to the commentary tradition of Ovid's works.[15] In the broadest sense, "commentary" includes all interlinear and marginal glosses in the hand of the teacher, student, or more casual reader; short summaries and outlines inserted in between Ovid's texts or organized as separate texts; and *accessus*, short introductions on the subject of the work, the life of its author, the work's form, title, intention, and the branch of philosophy to which it belongs. But most often the term "Ovidian commentaries" refers to different established sets of notes to Ovid's writings, which will be discussed in more detail below. The nature of the notes in these commentaries ranges from grammatical explanations to literary analysis, comments on history, philosophy, and geography, and moral and allegorical interpretations. At times the principle of change also applies to the interpretation of Ovid's writings within the same work: a commentator often proposes different interpretations for one and the same story.[16] Moreover, the copying of commentaries was treated differently than the copying of Ovid's actual text: in contrast with the authoritative Latin text, the commentary format allowed

---

14   Ralph J. Hexter, *Ovid and Medieval Schooling: Studies in Medieval School Commentaries on Ovid's 'Ars Amatoria,' 'Epistulae Ex Ponto,' and 'Epistulae Heroidum'* (Munich: Arbeo-Gesellschaft, 1986), 3, 11.

15   In what follows, I focus on works that directly and specifically engage with Ovid's poems, and not those that discuss Greco-Roman mythology more broadly, often with a moralizing approach, such as Fulgentius's *Mythologiae* (late fifth–early sixth century) or the works of the three Vatican Mythographers, dated between the eighth and the thirteenth century. While especially the work of the Third Mythographer included citations from Ovid and is an example of the indirect, fragmented transmission of Ovid's poems (discussed further on in this chapter), Ovid is but one of his sources. For brief introductions to both works, see *Fulgentius the Mythographer*, trans. Leslie George Whitbread (Columbus: Ohio State University Press, 1971), 15–37; and *The Vatican Mythographers*, trans. Ronald E. Pepin (New York: Fordham University Press, 2008), 1–12. I mention these works again in Chapter 5 on Petrarch, who was familiar with both Fulgentius and the Mythographers.

16   Robert Levine, "Exploiting Ovid: Medieval Allegorizations of the *Metamorphoses*," *Medioevo Romanzo* 14 (1989): 197–213, at 207.

for small corrections, updates, and further comments.[17] Alison Cornish's description of the relationship between classical Latin texts and their vernacular Italian translations holds for commentaries as well: commentaries likewise "adapt an unchanging authoritative text to changing circumstances."[18] New readers of Ovid would at times leave additional notes to Ovid's verses or the commentary on their copies, already marked with sure signs that Ovid's text was being read. In short, the medieval Ovidian commentary tradition is not a monolith, but a diverse, varied, and changing corpus of texts.[19]

Thanks to the work of Fausto Ghisalberti, Frank T. Coulson, and Ralph J. Hexter, several medieval commentaries on Ovid's writings are also available to scholars today; yet, numerous other commentaries are still buried in unedited manuscripts. Thus, what follows offers merely a broad sketch, but nevertheless one that aims to highlight the diversity of approaches that characterizes the genre. This diversity, as pointed out earlier, manifests itself in two main ways: differences in the content and length of the comments on Ovid's works, and in the material presentation of Ovid's poetry and the prose or verse commentary in the manuscripts. The images included in this chapter (*figs.* 2–5) aim to visualize these different layouts and broaden and refine the image of an Italian reader of Ovid.[20] Before even attempting to assess how Italian readers in their own writings interpreted and reused the Ovid they read, we begin by looking at the format and content of their editions of Ovid, which are often far from alike.

---

17   Ralph Hexter, "Literary History as a Provocation to Reception Studies," in *Classics and the Uses of Reception*, ed. Charles Martindale and Richard F. Thomas (Oxford: Blackwell, 2006), 23–31, at 30–31.

18   Alison Cornish, *Vernacular Translation in Dante's Italy: Illiterate Literature* (Cambridge: Cambridge University Press, 2011), 5.

19   This is not a new insight, but a point made in many writings on the medieval commentary tradition on Ovid: see, for instance, Ralph J. Hexter's to-the-point comparison in "Medieval Articulations of Ovid's *Metamorphoses*: From Lactantian Segmentation to Arnulfian Allegory," *Mediaevalia* 13 (1987): 63–82; Jamie C. Fumo, "Commentary and Collaboration in the Medieval Allegorical Tradition," in *A Handbook to the Reception of Ovid*, ed. John F. Miller and Carole E. Newlands (Chichester: Wiley-Blackwell, 2014), 114–28; Amanda J. Gerber, "Rethinking Ovid: The Commentary Tradition," in *Medieval Ovid: Frame Narrative and Political Allegory* (New York: Palgrave Macmillan, 2015), 11–50. It is important, however, to keep emphasizing the diversity and variety of these commentaries, since still too often in the discussions of Ovid and medieval literature "The Commentary Tradition" is treated as the monolith it is not.

20   This method was used before in Hexter, "Medieval Articulations of Ovid's *Metamorphoses*," and Frank T. Coulson, "Ovid's *Metamorphoses* in the school tradition of France, 1180–1400: Texts, manuscript traditions, manuscript settings," in Clark, Coulson, and McKinley, *Ovid in the Middle Ages*, 48–82. In this chapter, I compare how the same passage in Ovid's *Metamorphoses* (the opening of the story of Apollo and Daphne) appears in different commentaries.

What emerges from such an approach is a nuanced description of what reading Ovid could look like: that the medieval reader would have a text edition of Ovid similar to our modern ones is not a statement anyone would call realistic when hearing or seeing it, but nevertheless a persistent and rarely questioned working assumption, when scholars use Ovid's Latin verses as found in the Oxford Classical Text or Loeb editions to compare the Latin or Italian text by a medieval author who is said to be inspired by Ovid. The other extreme is imagining that in medieval manuscripts each of Ovid's texts is accompanied by commentary and copious lengthy notes that take up more space on the page — and more attention of the reader — than Ovid's poetry. To describe the development of the Ovidian commentary tradition means to emphasize the distinct differences within.

Among the extant commentaries on Ovid, the earliest is the pseudo-Lactantius Placidus's *Metamorphoseon narrationes*, traditionally datable to the fifth or sixth century.[21] Similar to many modern translations of Ovid's *Metamorphoses*, this commentary breaks down Ovid's text into individual stories with numbered titles (*tituli*) and opens each of the fifteen books of the *Metamorphoses* with a list of all stories belonging to that book. As is clear in *fig.* 2, the *Narrationes* is not a free-standing text, but consists of short prose summaries (*argumenta*), which were inserted in between Ovid's stories. The indented prose of the *argumenta* is visually clearly separated from Ovid's poetry. Brooks Otis identified three types of additional material in these brief *argumenta*: extra background information on the myths (sometimes contradicting Ovid's version), quotations from other commentaries (e.g., on Statius's *Thebaid*), and scholiastic material.[22] That the exact dating of the commentary and its sources are still debated is of little importance for our discussion here; what is relevant is that this commentary survived in seven medieval manuscripts of Ovid's *Metamorphoses* (dating from the ninth to the twelfth century), the so-called "Lactantian" family of manuscripts.[23] Three of these manuscripts were written in Italy (Florence, Biblioteca Medicea Laurenziana, MS San Marco 225; Naples,

---

21 D. A. Slater, *Towards a Text of the Metamorphosis of Ovid* (Oxford: Clarendon Press, 1927), appendix; Hugo Magnus, ed., *Metamorphoseon libri XV, Lactanti Placidi qui dicitur narrationes fabularum Ovidianarum* (New York: Arno Press, 1979), 625–721. Alan Cameron argued to move the traditional dating of the commentary from the fifth or sixth century to the third or fourth century. See "An Anonymous Ancient Commentary on Ovid's *Metamorphoses*?" in *Greek Mythology in the Roman World* (Oxford: Oxford University Press, 2004), 3–32.

22 Brooks Otis, "The Argumenta of the So-Called Lactantius," *Harvard Studies in Classical Philology* 47 (1936): 131–63, at 134–40.

23 On the "Lactantian family," see Richard J. Tarrant, "The *Narrationes* of 'Lactantius' and the Transmission of Ovid's *Metamorphoses*," in *Formative Stages of Classical Traditions: Latin*

Biblioteca Nazionale di Napoli, MS IV.F.3; and London, British Library, MS Add. 11967). *Fig.* 2 shows a page from MS San Marco 225 (labeled a school-type manuscript by Robert Black) written around the turn of the twelfth century in central or southern Italy. In this particular manuscript (which, as we will see in Ch. 4.1, Alan Robson believed was Dante's source for Ovid's *Metamorphoses*), we also find some interlinear glosses and a few marginal notes that do not belong to the *Narrationes*, added by different hands around the time the text was copied.[24] These different kinds of commentary — the *tituli* and brief *argumenta* from the pseudo-Lactantian *Narrationes*, and the additional light interlinear and marginal glosses — do not really take the focus away from Ovid's poetry, presented in one text column. Some later manuscripts only copy the *tituli* and not the *argumenta*, which presents an even cleaner Ovidian text.[25]

A reader of Ovid's *Metamorphoses* in one of the Lactantian manuscripts literally encounters a different Ovid than the one who studies the same poem with the commentary of Arnulf of Orléans, a schoolmaster who in the second half of the twelfth century wrote commentaries on all of Ovid's works. Working at Orléans, at the time a flourishing center of classical studies in France, Arnulf was not the first to comment on Ovid's works, but the first to sign his commentary with his name.[26] Arnulf was familiar with the pseudo-Lactantian *Narrationes*,[27] but in contrast to the *Narrationes*, which consisted of brief

---

Texts from Antiquity to the Renaissance, ed. Oronzo Pecere and Michael D. Reeve (Spoleto: Centro italiano di studi sull'alto medioevo, 1995), 83–115.

24 Black, *Humanism and Education in Medieval and Renaissance Italy*, 134.
25 Coulson and Roy, *Incipitarium Ovidianum*, 37–38 (no. 52), which specifies which manuscripts only contain the *tituli*.
26 Wilken Engelbrecht described the reputation of Orléans as a center for classical learning during that period to introduce his discussion of three Orléans commentators on Ovid: Arnulf, Fulco, and William of Orléans. See "Fulco, Arnulf, and William: Twelfth-Century Views on Ovid in Orléans," *The Journal of Medieval Latin* 18 (2008): 52–73, at 52–57. On William of Orléans's commentary, see Wilken Engelbrecht, *Filologie in de Dertiende Eeuw: De 'Bursarii super Ovidios' van Magister Willem van Orléans (fl. 1200)* (PhD diss., Utrecht University, 2003). On Arnulf's commentaries, see Fausto Ghisalberti, "Arnolfo d'Orléans: Un cultore di Ovidio nel secolo XII," *Memorie del Reale Istituto Lombardo di Scienze e Lettere* 24 (1932): 157–234, with the text of Arnulf's allegories at 201–29. David T. Gura edited Arnulf's *accessus* and *glosulae* on Books 3, 7, 8, 11 of the *Metamorphoses* in *A Critical Edition and Study of Arnulf of Orleans' Philological Commentary to Ovid's 'Metamorphoses'* (PhD diss., The Ohio State University, 2010), 161–244. On the anonymous school commentators of the amatory works, see Hexter, *Ovid and Medieval Schooling*. He pointed out that "medieval Ovid commentaries were not by nature allegorizing or moralizing" (*Ovid and Medieval Schooling*, 11; "Medieval Articulations of Ovid's *Metamorphoses*," 77).
27 Hexter, "Medieval Articulations of Ovid's *Metamorphoses*," 70. The *Narrationes* was also among the sources of the Third Mythographer (Pepin, *The Vatican Mythographers*, 7).

comments or *argumenta* on each story inserted in between Ovid's poetry, Arnulf's commentary is much more substantial, providing three different kinds of comments for each book of the *Metamorphoses*. The first lengthy section of philological glosses or *glosulae* on the text of each book of the *Metamorphoses* is followed by a second that lists all the *mutationes* pertaining to that book, the feature that resembles the *Narrationes* the most. The third section of *allegoriae* consists of didactic, allegorical, but not necessarily Christian explanations of the stories — some just a few verses long, others more substantial in length. (Arnulf's commentaries on Ovid's other works consist of only glosses.)[28] Arnulf's commentary on the *Metamorphoses* is often associated with its allegorizing readings of Ovid's work, and while these readings are indeed Arnulf's innovation, clearly these allegories are only one part of his commentary. Originally Arnulf's *accessus* or introduction to the *Metamorphoses* and the three parts of his commentary (the *glosulae, mutationes, allegoriae*) were transmitted together, separated from the text of the *Metamorphoses*. From the thirteenth century on, the different parts of Arnulf's commentary were found as separate texts, and the glosses started to appear together with Ovid's Latin poem, as can been seen in *fig.* 3, a page from MS Pluteo 36.18, a fourteenth-century manuscript.[29]

John of Garland's *Integumenta Ovidii* responds to Arnulf's innovative allegorical interpretations. Educated in England, John of Garland was teaching in France around 1230 when he composed a 520-verse-long Latin commentary on Ovid's *Metamorphoses*. John of Garland focuses on select stories and reveals their true discourse ("sermo verus"), covered up under the veil ("integumentum") of historical discourse (vv. 57–62). These "true discourses" are short: about four verses dedicated to each selected story, so that they could be easily added next to Ovid's text or inserted into other commentaries.[30] As for their content, the *Integumenta*'s short verse comments provide straightforward allegorical explanations. For example, in the story of Narcissus and Echo, John simply explains that Narcissus is "an eager boy misled by the glory of material things" (vv. 163–64), while he describes Echo as the natural phenomenon

---

28 For example, see his commentary on Ovid's *Fasti, Arnulfi Aurelianensis Glosule Ovidii Fastorum*, ed. Jörg Rudolf Rieker (Florence: SISMEL-Edizioni del Galluzzo, 2005).
29 Gura, *A Critical Edition and Study of Arnulf of Orleans*, 22–26. When the glosses originally appeared as a free-standing text, they were presented in what is called the *catena* format: underlined snippets of Ovid's poem served to introduce and link the subsequent note to the corresponding passage in the *Metamorphoses*. For an example of a *catena* commentary, see Plate 4 (Munich, Bayerische Staatsbibliothek, MS clm 7205) in Hexter, "Medieval Articulations of Ovid's *Metamorphoses*," 74.
30 Coulson, "Ovid's *Metamorphoses* in the school tradition of France," 64.

where enclosed air repeats words (vv. 165–66). Like the *allegoriae* of Arnulf, John of Garland's explanations have mainly a moral tone; only at the very end of his poem in his description of the deification of Caesar (*Met.* 15.745–842) does he mention Christ (vv. 511–20).

John of Garland and Arnulf of Orléans's allegorical readings of Ovid's *Metamorphoses*, which during the thirteenth century also started to circulate together, seem to suggest that allegory was the prevailing interpretative approach to Ovid's poem.[31] While later in the fourteenth century commentators followed their example, the so-called "Vulgate" Commentary on the *Metamorphoses* illustrates that the allegorical reading of the *Metamorphoses* was just one of the kinds of comments on Ovid's work.[32] Created around 1250 in central France (perhaps at the school of Orléans), the anonymous Vulgate Commentary consists of interlinear and marginal glosses to the text of the *Metamorphoses*. Like the commentaries of Arnulf of Orléans, John of Garland, and those of other anonymous commentators, the Vulgate Commentary was intended for use in the classroom. While the Vulgate adopts material from these earlier commentaries, its unique feature is the close attention that the anonymous commentator pays to the literary qualities of Ovid's work: in addition to grammatical and lexical notes, he frequently points out intratextual connections between stories of the *Metamorphoses*, and is also attentive to Ovid's influence on contemporary medieval writers.[33] In 2015, Frank T. Coulson counted twenty-two manuscripts of the Vulgate Commentary, which he called the "single most important commentary on the *Metamorphoses* from the high

---

31 Gura, *A Critical Edition and Study of Arnulf of Orleans*, 24. On the circulation of John of Garland's *Integumenta*, see Coulson, "Ovid's *Metamorphoses* in the school tradition of France," 64.

32 Frank T. Coulson has published widely on the Vulgate Commentary. See his editions of parts of the commentary: *The 'Vulgate' Commentary on Ovid's 'Metamorphoses': The Creation Myth and the Story of Orpheus*, ed. Frank T. Coulson (Toronto: The Pontifical Institute of Mediaeval Studies, 1991); and *The Vulgate Commentary on Ovid's 'Metamorphoses' Book 1*, ed. and trans. Frank T. Coulson, TEAMS Secular Commentary (Kalamazoo: Medieval Institute Publications, 2015). See also his essays "The *Vulgate* Commentary on Ovid's *Metamorphoses*," *Mediaevalia* 13 (1987): 29–61; "Ovid's Transformations in Medieval France (ca. 1100–ca. 1350)," in *Metamorphosis: The Changing Face of Ovid in Medieval and Early Modern Europe*, ed. Alison Keith and Stephen Rupp (Toronto: Centre for Reformation and Renaissance Studies, 2007), 33–60; "Literary criticism in the Vulgate Commentary on Ovid's *Metamorphoses*," in *Medieval Textual Cultures: Agents of Transmission, Translation and Transformation*, ed. Faith Wallis and Robert Wisnovsky (Berlin: Walter de Gruyter, 2016), 121–32. See also Nicolette Zeeman, "In the Schoolroom with the *'Vulgate'* Commentary on Metamorphoses I," *New Medieval Literatures* 11 (2009): 1–18.

33 Coulson, "Literary criticism in the Vulgate Commentary on Ovid's *Metamorphoses*."

Middle Ages."[34] These manuscripts circulated widely in France and Italy,[35] and according to Fausto Ghisalberti, discoverer of Arnulf of Orléans's commentary and editor of several medieval texts on Ovid, this was the commentary Dante consulted (see Ch. 4.1). Not only the content of the Vulgate sets it apart from earlier commentaries, but also the format: Ovid's Latin verses appear in one or two text columns with copious interlinear glosses, and are surrounded by longer notes to the left and right of the text. Pages from a thirteenth-century manuscript (Florence, Biblioteca Riccardiana, MS Riccardianus 624), now identified as one of manuscripts containing the Vulgate Commentary, provide a good example (*figs.* 4 and 5).[36] At the center of the page we see Ovid's text with interlinear glosses, flanked by marginal notes on the left and the right. Looking more closely at the end of the story of Apollo and Daphne (*fig.* 5), we see that most of the glosses on the left appear in one column and refer to Ovid's language, with pilcrow signs indicating each new note. On the right the shorter lexical and syntactical notes are stacked next to each other. The longest note is featured more prominently in one block of text: it contains a detailed moral explanation of the Apollo and Daphne story (in brief: Apollo = wisdom; Daphne = chastity) and also includes the four verses from John of Garland's *Integumenta* on this Ovidian story (vv. 93–96). Especially compared with the page containing roughly the same Ovidian verses in the pseudo-Lactantian MS San Marco 225 (*fig.* 2), the experience of reading Ovid in the Vulgate Commentary is quite different.

The first commentaries of the fourteenth century — Giovanni del Virgilio's *Expositio* and *Allegorie librorum Ovidii Metamorphoseos* — are both dated around 1321, the year of Dante's death.[37] 1321 was also the year in which Giovanni del Virgilio, Dante's correspondent in the *Eclogues*, was appointed to teach the first course dedicated to the classics (Vergil, Statius, Lucan, and

---

34 Coulson, "Ovid's Transformations in Medieval France," 52. The complete list of the twenty-two manuscripts is found in Coulson, *The Vulgate Commentary on Ovid's 'Metamorphoses' Book 1*, 191–92. Coulson found that the text was "extremely stable for an anonymous commentary, revealing only minor variation amongst manuscript witnesses" (xv).
35 Coulson, "Ovid's Transformations in Medieval France," 42.
36 Fausto Ghisalberti listed MS Riccardianus 624 among the six copies of a "ricchissimo commento anonimo" in "Arnolfo d'Orléans," 177; and coined its name, "commentario 'vulgato'" in "Il commentario medioevale all' '*Ovidius maior*' consultato da Dante," *Rendiconti (Istituto lombardo di scienze e lettere, classe di lettere e scienze morali e politiche*) 100 (1966): 267–75, at 268. Frank T. Coulson later discovered several more copies of the Vulgate Commentary. See Coulson and Roy, *Incipitarium Ovidianum*, 123–25 (no. 421) for the full list.
37 Fausto Ghisalberti, *Giovanni del Virgilio espositore delle 'Metamorfosi'* (Florence: Leo S. Olschki, 1933), which includes the *accessus* to the *expositio* (3–19) and the text of the *allegorie* (43–107).

Ovid) at the University of Bologna. These classical authors were not included into the university curriculum until the fifteenth century, which makes Giovanni del Virgilio's two-year-long teachings "an uncharacteristic example in the Trecento."[38] The relationship between the two texts is not well understood (the manuscript tradition mostly keeps the two works separated), but the *Allegorie* probably grew out of the *Expositio*, and both were used in the university context.[39] In the *Allegorie*, Giovanni mixes poetry and prose: prose consisting of mainly moral or natural explanations of Ovid's "transformationes," as he calls them, and brief summaries of Ovid's poetry in elegiac couplets (which, as Giuseppe Rotondi has shown, came from another source).[40] In his explanations, Giovanni follows the example of Arnulf of Orléans and John of Garland, often referring to their interpretations without mentioning their names ("dicunt"). Similar to the two French schoolmasters, the only transformation Giovanni understands in truly Christianizing terms is the deification of Caesar. Explaining Caesar's deification as the "prenuntia Christi" ("foreteller of Christ" [v. 787]), Giovanni ends the *Allegorie* on a Christian note.

The anonymous *Ovide moralisé* (probably) and Pierre Bersuire's *Ovidius moralizatus* (definitely) postdate the conclusion of the *Commedia*; while at times used as reference points for Dante's reading of Ovid in his poem, these two texts belong firmly to Petrarch's possible Ovidian sources, and not Dante's. Composed between 1316 and 1328, the *Ovide moralisé* reworks the roughly 12,000 verses of the *Metamorphoses* into a 70,000-verse-long French text, adding extensive commentary to the translation. While the previous commentaries sporadically included Christianizing readings, the *Ovide moralisé* is the first work that offers this kind of reading in "a systematic and consistent fashion."[41] This explicitly Christianizing approach also characterizes the *Ovidius moralizatus*, a Latin commentary written in Avignon between 1337 and 1340 by the Benedictine prior Pierre Bersuire.[42] Originally the fifteenth book of Bersuire's

---

38 Black, *Humanism and Education in Medieval and Renaissance Italy*, 201. Witt noted that this was indeed the first documented teaching of the ancient authors, and added that earlier teachings during the second half of the thirteenth century in Padua, Arezzo, and Bologna were probable but not documented (*In the Footsteps of the Ancients*, 196).

39 On the manuscript tradition, see Ghisalberti, *Giovanni del Virgilio*, 39–42; Clark, Coulson, and McKinley, *Ovid in the Middle Ages*, 314.

40 Giuseppe Rotondi, "Ovidio nel medioevo," *Convivium* 6 (1934): 262–69.

41 Renate Blumenfeld-Kosinski, "The Hermeneutics of the *Ovide moralisé*," in *Reading Myth: Classical Mythology and Its Interpretations in Medieval French Literature* (Stanford: Stanford University Press, 1997), 90–136, at 91.

42 Ana Pairet, "Recasting the *Metamorphoses* in fourteenth-century France: The challenges of the *Ovide moralisé*," in Clark, Coulson, and McKinley, *Ovid in the Middle Ages*, 83–107, at 86. Grover A. Zinn placed the writing of this fifteenth book even later, in 1343. See

Reductorium morale (an encyclopedic work on morality for preachers), the *Ovidius moralizatus* soon circulated as a free-standing text. Thus, around or after the time Dante that finished the *Commedia*, two commentaries on the *Metamorphoses* offered for the first time consistently Christianizing readings of Ovid's work. While it seems quite impossible that Dante had direct contact with these commentaries, readers of Ovid during this period could encounter a truly Christianized Ovid. The fact that Bersuire and Petrarch were in correspondence underscores that Petrarch's Ovidian readings were essentially different from Dante's and other poets before him.

Regardless of whether Ovid's works were supplemented by one of these commentaries or not, manuscripts of Ovid's texts often also included *accessus Ovidii*: short introductions that covered the work's subject, form, title, and intention, a biographical introduction to Ovid, and the branch of philosophy to which his work belonged. The *accessus ad auctores*, the general term for such book prefaces, became self-standing texts around the beginning of the twelfth century, and soon became collected in handbooks (the earliest collection dates from the twelfth century: Munich, Bayerische Staatsbibliothek, MS clm 19475, also called the *Accessus ad auctores*).[43] These *accessus* served pedagogical purposes, for instance, rendering Ovid accessible and acceptable in the school context.[44] It was common to classify the works of Ovid, a favorite to include in the *accessus*, under the branch of ethics ("ethice supponitur") and interpret

---

Medieval France: An Encyclopedia, ed. William W. Kibler and Grover A. Zinn (New York: Garland Publications, Inc., 1995), 116.

43 See *Accessus ad auctores. Bernard D'Utrecht. Conrad D'Hirsau. Dialogus super auctores*, ed. R. B. C. Huygens (Leiden: Brill, 1970), and especially the more recent edition by Stephen M. Wheeler, *Accessus ad auctores: Medieval Introductions to the Authors (Codex latinus monacensis 19475)*, TEAMS Secular Commentary (Kalamazoo: Medieval Institute Publications, 2015). Ten of the twenty-nine *accessus* in MS clm 19475 are dedicated to Ovid, but it does not include an introduction to Ovid's *Metamorphoses* (Wheeler, *Accessus ad auctores*, 8, 9). Huygens's edition also includes the Benedictine monk Conrad of Hirsau's *Dialogus super auctores* (ca. 1130), a dialogue between a teacher and student about which Christian and pagan authors to read (Ovid was not a favorite). On this dialogue, see Leslie G. Whitbread, "Conrad of Hirsau as Literary Critic," *Speculum* 47, no. 2 (1972): 234–45. On the *accessus* in general, see Edwin Quain, "The Medieval Accessus Ad Auctores," *Traditio* 3 (1945): 214–64; on the *accessus Ovidii*, see Fausto Ghisalberti, "Mediaeval Biographies of Ovid," *Journal of the Warburg and Courtauld Institutes* 9 (1946): 44–59; Warren Ginsberg, "Ovidius ethicus? Ovid and the Medieval Commentary Tradition," in *Desiring Discourse: The Literature of Love, Ovid through Chaucer*, ed. James J. Paxson and Cynthia A. Gravlee (Selinsgrove: Susquehanna University Press, 1998), 62–71. Wheeler mentioned two manuscripts that anthologized the *accessus* on Ovid (*Accessus ad auctores*, 3).

44 Alison G. Elliott, "Accessus ad auctores: Twelfth-Century Introductions to Ovid," *Allegorica* 5 (1980): 6–48, at 7.

their intention in terms of morality, as in fact most classical texts were categorized.[45] For example, in his *accessus* Arnulf of Orléans described the intention of the *Metamorphoses* and its philosophical approach as follows:[46]

> Intencio est de mutacione diceret ut non intelligamus de mutacione que fit extrinsecus tantum in rebus corporeis bonis vel malis sed etiam de mutacione que fit intrinsecus ut in anima, ut reducat nos ab errore ad cognitionem veri creatoris.... Ethice supponitur quia docet nos ista temporalia, que transitoria et mutabilia, contempnere, quod pertinet ad moralitatem.

> [Ovid's intention is to describe transformation, not so that we may understand the change which takes place externally into good or bad corporeal forms, but rather so that we may understand that which takes place internally, in the soul, to lead us back from error to the knowledge of the true creator.... This work is to be considered ethics because it teaches us to spurn these temporal things, which are transitory and mutable, a subject which relates to morality.]

The *Accessus ad auctores* described the intention of Ovid's *Heroides* in similar terms, equating the author with his work: "Ethice subiacet quia bonorum morum est instructor, malorum uero exstirpator" ("He is classified under ethics because he is an instructor of good manners and an eradicator of evil"). The introduction to the *Amores* from the same collection just includes the bare minimum: "Ethice subponitur."

Anthony Grafton and Lisa Jardine found that Renaissance editions of classical authors, especially those used in classrooms, often do not incorporate moral instruction as thoroughly and consistently as their introductions may suggest.[47] In his study of medieval and Renaissance Italian schoolbooks, Robert Black reached the same conclusion. Calling the moralizing *accessus* "the ideal way to

---

45 Vincent Gillespie, "Part II: The Study of Classical Authors: From the twelfth century to c. 1450," in *The Cambridge History of Literary Criticism,* Vol. 2: *The Middle Ages,* ed. Alastair Minnis and Ian Johnson (Cambridge: Cambridge University Press, 2008), 145–235, at 161; Wheeler, *Accessus ad auctores,* 9–10.

46 The text and translation (with a slight revision) are quoted from Elliott, "Accessus ad auctores," 14–17. Arnulf's section on Ovid's life was long enough for Ghisalberti to consider it the "first true 'life'" of Ovid ("Mediaeval Biographies of Ovid," 18). The text in the following paragraph is taken from Wheeler, *Accessus ad auctores,* 26, 48.

47 Anthony Grafton and Lisa Jardine, *From Humanism to the Humanities: Education and the Liberal Arts in Fifteenth- and Sixteenth-Century Europe* (Cambridge: Harvard University Press, 1986), 24.

pay lip service to the moralistic arm of education," Black explains that "having got through the moral conventions of the *accessus* and so fulfilling any formal requirement of providing good morals in the classroom, teachers then felt free to turn to their real business: teaching Latin in a philological manner."[48] Edwin Quain concluded pointedly that "Ovid ... could be used for whatever purpose the teacher wished."[49] The example from Arnulf's teachings on Ovid illustrates these scholars' point: in the *accessus*, Arnulf emphasizes the moral reading of the *Metamorphoses*, while this is only one aspect of the actual content of his commentary.

Another recurrent feature of manuscripts containing the *Metamorphoses* was the inclusion of an index or table of contents for each book of Ovid's epic: the pseudo-Lactantian *tituli* and Arnulf's list of *mutationes* already functioned that way, dividing each book of Ovid's *Metamorphoses* into stories with a strong focus on the transformation occurring in each of them. Summaries of this kind were also written in hexameters (of the commentaries so far discussed, only John of Garland's *Integumenta* was entirely written in verse), such as Orico da Capriana's *Summa memorialis*, which dates as early as the first half of the fourteenth century. These verse summaries appeared on flyleaves or in the margins, and at times at the opening of each book of the *Metamorphoses*.[50]

Commentaries, *accessus*, and summaries were also added to the vernacular translations of Ovid's works, but those translations appeared relatively late on the Italian literary map.[51] At first Italian translators made Latin rhetorical treatises and prose works on history and politics available to a broader public,

---

48 Black, *Humanism and Education in Medieval and Renaissance Italy*, 315.
49 Quain, "The Medieval Accessus Ad Auctores," 225 (also quoted in Wheeler, *Accessus ad auctores*, 10).
50 The text of Orico da Capriana's *summa memorialis* is edited by Luigi Munzi in "Una inedita *Summa memorialis* delle *Metamorfosi* ovidiane," in *Dicti studiosus: scritti di filologia offerti a Scevola Mariotti dai suoi allievi* (Urbino: Edizioni QuattroVenti, 1990), 329–85. Munzi counted nineteen manuscripts, to which Frank T. Coulson added the "Newly Identified Manuscripts containing the *Summa Memorialis* on the *Metamorphoses* by Orico de Capriana," *Studi Medievali* 35 (1994): 817–22. Coulson mentioned Orico's verse summary and seven other authors of similar works in "Ovid's *Metamorphoses* in the school tradition of France," 64.
51 The Italian term for these texts is *volgarizzamento*, which I use in this book alongside the English terms "translation" and "vernacular translation." On the interchangeable use of these terms and its other equivalents (version, vulgarization, vernacularization), see Cornish, *Vernacular Translation in Dante's Italy*, 4. In the case of the *volgarizzamenti* of Ovid, the term always indicates the rendering of Ovid's Latin poems into Italian, sometimes in verse, sometimes in prose.

as there was a need for access to such writings in the vernacular.[52] The translations of French and medieval Latin works followed, and only later, toward the end of the thirteenth century, did Italian translators turn to Latin poetry.[53] Among the classical Latin poets, Ovid was a favorite author of translators.[54] Between the end of the thirteenth and the beginning of the fourteenth century, Ovid's *Ars amatoria* and *Remedia amoris* were translated three times into Tuscan and later accompanied by commentaries.[55] While the commentator of one of the *Ars amatoria* translations distinguishes himself as a "scolaio rozzo" ("rough scholar") from the "scienziato maestro" ("learned master") who had

---

52 On the development of vernacular translation in Italy, see Cesare Segre's introduction to *Volgarizzamenti del Due e Trecento* (Turin: Unione Tipografico-Editrice Torinese, 1953), 11–45; Bodo Guthmüller, "Die *volgarizzamenti*," in *Die Italienische Literatur im Zeitalter Dantes und am Übergang vom Mittelalter zur Renaissance*, Vol. 2: *Die Literatur bis zur Renaissance*, ed. August Buck (Heidelberg: C. Winter, 1989), 201–54; Witt's chapter on "Florence and Vernacular Learning," in *In the Footsteps of the Ancients*, 174–229; and Alison Cornish's most recent study *Vernacular Translation in Dante's Italy*. See also Ralph J. Hexter's overview "Ovid in translation in Medieval Europe," in *Übersetzung – Translation – Traduction: Ein internationales Handbuch zur Übersetzungsforschung / An international Encyclopedia of Translation Studies / Encyclopédie internationale de la recherche sur la traduction*, ed. Harald Kittel et al., 3 vols. (Berlin: Walter de Gruyter, 2004), 2: 1311–23.

53 Segre, *Volgarizzamenti del Due e Trecento*, 14–16; Cornish, *Vernacular Translation in Dante's Italy*, Chapter 1.

54 Segre, *Volgarizzamenti del Due e Trecento*, 19; Guthmüller, "Die *volgarizzamenti*," 248. Short overviews of the first Italian translations of Ovid are also found in Witt, *In the Footsteps of the Ancients*, 192; Carrie E. Beneš, *Urban Legends: Civic Identity and the Classical Past in Northern Italy, 1250–1350* (University Park: Penn State University Press, 2011), 157; Guthmüller, "Die *volgarizzamenti*," 342–44.

55 Vanna Lippi Bigazzi, *I volgarizzamenti trecenteschi dell'Ars amandi e dei Remedia amoris*, 2 vols. (Florence: Accademia della Crusca, 1987). Alison Cornish pointed out that these commentaries contain many citations from Dante (*Vernacular Translation in Dante's Italy*, 222, n. 3). Andrea Lancia, long-considered author and definitely copyist of the Ottimo Commento, is linked to several vernacular translations and often proposed as one of the translators of these *volgarizzamenti*, as is Giovanni Boccaccio. Cornish discussed Boccaccio's possible role as *volgarizzatore* of Ovid's works and, more generally, his attitude toward vernacularization in "Vernacularization in context (*Volgarizzamenti* of Livy, Valerius Maximus, and Ovid)," in *Boccaccio: A Critical Guide to the Complete Works*, ed. Victoria Kirkham, Michael Sherberg, and Janet Levarie Smarr (Chicago: University of Chicago Press, 2013), 255–61, at 255, 260–61. Cornish concluded that even given the uncertainty about his authorship, "Boccaccio's engagement with vernacular translations remains certain.... Use of a vernacularization, even by as accomplished a Latinist as Boccaccio, does not signify authorship. What it does signify is a readiness to use, or even a preference for, vernacularizations" (261). We possess Boccaccio's annotated copy of Ovid's *Tristia* and the pseudo-Ovidian *Nux*: Florence, Biblioteca Riccardiana, MS Riccardianus 489.

translated Ovid's Latin text,[56] the addition of *chiose* or glosses nevertheless shows that the translated text is deemed worthy of the same treatment as the original Latin.[57] All other translations of Ovid's work postdate 1321, the year of Dante's death. Between 1320 and 1330, Filippo Ceffi translated the *Heroides* as the *Pistole di Ovidio Nasone*, a popular text that circulated widely.[58] One manuscript of the *Pistole* included an Italian translation of the pseudo-Ovidian *De pulice*, also attributed to Ceffi.[59] (A slightly earlier, still unedited and incomplete translation of the *Heroides*, the "volgarizzamento Gaddiano" [Florence, Biblioteca Medicea Laurenziana, MS Gaddi rel. 71] was probably based on

---

56   For the full remarks of the commentator of the *Ars amatoria*, see the edition by Lippi Bigazzi, *I volgarizzamenti trecenteschi*, 1: 221. The comment is made in the second prologue to the so-called Volgarizzamento B of the *Ars amatoria*: originating in a Florentine environment, this was the translation that circulated most widely, and was linked to Andrea Lancia and Giovanni Boccaccio (see the previous note). Cornish placed the use of the adjective "rozzo" in its not necessarily negative or inferior context (*Vernacular Translation in Dante's Italy*, 32).

57   Claudia Villa, "I commenti ai classici fra XII e XV secolo," in *Medieval and Renaissance Scholarship: Proceedings of the Second European Science Foundation Workshop on the Classical Tradition in the Middle Ages and the Renaissance*, ed. Nicholas Mann and Birger Munk Olsen (Leiden: Brill, 1997), 19–32, at 27: "Il commento mantiene la sua autorità anche quando un autore classico è reso in volgare" ("The commentary maintains its authority also when a classical author is translated"). Examples of beautifully prepared manuscripts only containing vernacular texts further underline their status: see, for instance, Carrie E. Beneš's discussion and description of the illuminated manuscript with Ciampolo di Meo Ugurgieri's translation of the *Aeneid* and commentary from the mid-fourteenth century (Siena, Biblioteca Comunale degli Intronati, MS S.IV.11) in *Urban Legends*, 160–62, with an image of the opening page of Ciampolo's translation at 161.

58   Massimo Zaggia counted over fifty different fourteenth- and fifteenth-century manuscripts transmitting Ceffi's translation, including an autograph. See his extensive work on Ceffi's translation: *Heroides: volgarizzamento fiorentino trecentesco di Filippo Ceffi*, Vol. 1, *Introduzione, testo secondo l'autografo e glossario* (Florence: SISMEL-Edizioni del Galluzzo, 2009), Vol. 2, *I testimoni oltre l'autografo: ordinamento stemmatico e storia della tradizione* (Florence: SISMEL-Edizioni del Galluzzo, 2014), and Vol. 3, *Le varianti di una tradizione innovativa e le chiose aggiunte* (Florence: SISMEL-Edizioni del Galluzzo, 2015). Lauren McGuire Jennings studied the pairing of Ceffi's vernacular translations of Ovid's *Heroides* with fourteenth-century songs in the personal miscellany of a certain Florentine Amelio Bonaguisi. See "Ovid's *Heroides*, Florentine *Volgarizzamenti*, and Unnotated Song in Florence, Biblioteca Nazionale Centrale, II.II.61 and Magliabechiano VII 1040," in *Senza Vestimenta: The Literary Tradition of Trecento Song* (Surrey: Ashgate, 2014), 133–58. For an extensive overview of the illustrated manuscripts of Ceffi's translation, see Massimo Zaggia and Matteo Ceriana, *I manoscritti illustrati delle Eroidi ovidiane volgarizzate* (Pisa: Scuola normale superiore, 1996).

59   Zaggia, *Heroides*, 1: 208–15. Filippo Ceffi also translated Guido delle Colonne's *Historia destructionis Troiae*.

an Old French translation of the letters.)[60] The first Italian translation of the *Metamorphoses* by Arrigo Simintendi da Prato dates from 1333, followed by the *Metamorphoseos Vulgare* by Giovanni Bonsignori, written during the 1370s (1375–77).[61] Ovid's *Amores, Fasti, Ibis,* and exile letters were not translated into Italian during the period covered in this book. Petrarch's Latin translation of Boccaccio's novella of Griselda is a telling sign of the changing attitudes toward vernacular translations.[62]

As translators of Ovid are by default also readers of Ovid, our central questions return in a new formulation: who were these readers/translators and which texts were they reading and translating? Italian vernacular translators came from the world of professional studies and religion, but mostly from the lay elite, and predominantly from Tuscany.[63] The translators mentioned so far all fit this profile: Filippo Ceffi was a Florentine notary, who dedicated his translation of the *Heroides* to the wife of a rich Florentine merchant; Arrigo Simintendi was a notary in Prato; and Giovanni Bonsignori was involved in politics in his hometown of Città di Castello. The translations of the *Ars amatoria* and the *Remedia amoris* are anonymous, but another Florentine notary, Andrea Lancia has been linked (with Giovanni Boccaccio) to one of these translations, and at times cast in the roles of the "scienziato maestro" and "scolaio rozzo" from the earlier mentioned prologue to the *Ars amatoria*.

Italian translators were not necessarily working with the original Latin text: classical and medieval Latin writings also entered the Italian vernacular

---

60 Zaggia, *Heroides,* 1: 223–28, which specified that only *Her.* 1, 2, 3, 5 were translated (1: 224). Carrie Beneš also discussed this early fourteenth-century manuscript, which in addition to the four translated letters from the *Heroides* contains parts of Andrea Lancia's translation of the *Aeneid* and two Italian translations of medieval French romances — another example of a carefully prepared and extensively glossed manuscript with vernacular texts (*Urban Legends,* 160).

61 Arrigo's full translation is still only available in a three-volume nineteenth-century edition: *I primi V libri delle Metamorfosi d'Ovidio volgarizzate da Ser Arrigo Simintendi da Prato* (Prato: Ranieri Guasti, 1846); *Cinque altri libri delle Metamorfosi d'Ovidio volgarizzate da Ser Arrigo Simintendi* (Prato: Ranieri Guasti, 1848); *Gli ultimi V libri delle Metamorfosi d'Ovidio volgarizzate da Ser Arrigo Simintendi da Prato* (Prato: Ranieri Guasti, 1850). Selections are also included in Segre, *Volgarizzamenti del Due e Trecento,* 517–64. The modern edition of Giovanni Bonsignori da Città di Castello's *Metamorphoseos Vulgare* is edited by Erminia Ardissino (Bologna: Commissione per i testi di lingua, 2001). On both translations, see also Bodo Guthmüller's study *Ovidio metamorphoseos vulgare: Formen und Funktionen der volkssprachlichen Wiedergabe klassischer Dichtung in der italienischen Renaissance* (Boppard am Rhein: Boldt, 1981), 56–128.

62 Cornish, *Vernacular Translation in Dante's Italy,* Chapter 6.

63 Guthmüller, "Die *volgarizzamenti*," 212–15; Beneš, *Urban Legends,* 157; Cornish, *Vernacular Translation in Dante's Italy, passim.*

through French translations, but in general the Ovidian translations from this period do not fall under that category.[64] Ovid had been translated into French: the anonymous *Ovide moralisé*, mentioned earlier in the discussion of commentaries, conflates our modern labels of translation, adaptation, and commentary in a text about six times as long as Ovid's Latin epic; and the five anonymous French translations of Ovid's *Ars amatoria* (dating from between the first half of the thirteenth and the beginning of the fourteenth century) freely reworked Ovid's Latin verses.[65] In general, the Italians did not take such liberties in their translations, but only occasionally updated the ancient texts for their contemporary readers (adopting domesticating or familiarizing translation strategies, as translation theorists would say).[66] In fact, Ceffi followed the text of Ovid's *Heroides* closely, with few omissions and adjustments.[67] Arrigo Simintendi could be called a faithful translator of the *Metamorphoses*, only occasionally replacing Ovid's most unfamiliar terms with contemporary equivalents.[68] Giovanni Bonsignori's translation of Ovid's *Metamorphoses*, on the other hand, contains more drastic changes, paraphrasing or glossing over several passages from Ovid's poem. Nothing is known about Bonsignori's education, but he was clearly familiar with Giovanni del Virgilio's work on Ovid's *Metamorphoses*: in the judgment of modern critics, Bonsignori faithfully, if not slavishly, repeated del Virgilio's writings in the *Metamorphoseos Vulgare*, following Giovanni rather than Ovid.[69] As becomes clear from the "tavola delle

---

64   On the French-Italian translations during this time, see Cornish, *Vernacular Translation in Dante's Italy*, Chapter 3.
65   Witt, *In the Footsteps of the Ancients*, 181–82; Alastair J. Minnis, "Latin to Vernacular: Academic Prologues and the Medieval French Art of Love," in Mann and Munk Olsen, *Medieval and Renaissance Scholarship*, 153–86.
66   Without using this terminology from translation studies, Francesco Maggini provided some examples from the *Fiore di rettorica* (the translation of the *Rhetorica ad Herennium*), where Guidotto da Bologna's rendering had his contemporary readers in mind: the temple of Jupiter ("templum Jovis") became San Giovanni Laterano; the Latin "iudices" or judges were replaced by "podestà"; the "citharoedus," the singer and *cithara*-player, became a "giullare." See "Il 'Fiore di Rettorica,'" in *I primi volgarizzamenti dai classici latini* (Florence: F. Le Monnier, 1952), 1–15, at 11.
67   Zaggia, *Heroides*, 1: 183–85.
68   Guthmüller, "Die *volgarizzamenti*," 249–51; Zaggia, *Heroides*, 1: 43–44.
69   Ardissino quoted Concetto Marchesi, who called Bonsignori "un fedele, anzi un servile e avido ripetitore" ("a faithful, or, more accurately, a servile and ardent repeater") of Giovanni del Virgilio's *Allegoriae* and added that the same can be said of Bonsignori's use of del Virgilio's *Expositio* (*Ovidio Metamorphoseos Vulgare*, xiii). As Ardissino further pointed out, many of the sources Bonsignori cites were also found in his model (Giovanni del Virgilio's work on Ovid), making it hard to determine whether Bonsignori also had a direct knowledge of these sources (*Ovidio Metamorphoseos Vulgare*, xii–xiii). The references that do not match up with del Virgilio's writings come from the Scriptures,

rubriche" that lists the content of each book of the *Metamorphoseos Vulgare*, Bonsignori, like Giovanni, also breaks down the *Metamorphoses* into stories, and combines the prose translations of select stories with allegories that clarify the "trasmutazioni" (Bonsignori's Italian term for del Virgilio's "transmutationes") these stories contain.[70] Giovanni Bonsignori, who was said to have "vulgarizzato, allegorizzato e composto" ("translated, allegorized, and composed") the *Metamorphoseos Vulgare*,[71] in a sense synthesizes the Latin commentary tradition on Ovid's poem in the vernacular. Insofar as Bonsignori is a commentator on Ovid, he is also the translator of Giovanni del Virgilio's Latin commentary on the *Metamorphoses*. Vernacular translation sets into motion a new iteration of St. Bonaventure's four roles involved in the making of books (the scribe, compiler, commentator, and author): the "aliena" or words of others in St. Bonaventure's definition (that are transcribed, compiled, commented on, or used to confirm the author's own words) are now translated words. Vernacular translation also reveals how easily these roles are blurred.

The texts discussed up until this point treat Ovid's poems in their entirety, in the Latin original or in translation, sometimes with additional *accessus* and commentary. Through the work of *compilatores* and *auctores* the Latin poet's writings were also transmitted in fragmented, indirect ways. Isolated and decontextualized Ovidian passages or phrases were collected in anthologies, and reinserted into a wide variety of prose texts — works on history, moral treatises, *artes dictaminis*, dictionaries, encyclopedic works — used for educational purposes and for private use. Separated from the narrative to which they originally belonged, these Ovidian lines could take on surprising new meanings in their new contexts in prose; the anthologies that only list the decontextualized Ovidian passages often turn the Latin poet into "Ovidio filosofo" ("Ovid the philosopher"), the label that the artist of the illustrated *Tesoretto* manuscript assigned to Ovid (*fig.* 1).

In anthologies or *florilegia*, a *compilator* collected excerpts from Christian and classical writings and often organized them by genre, author, and work, sometimes introduced them through short summarizing titles, and

---

Aristotle, Fulgentius, the Vatican Mythographers, Dante, Guido delle Colonne's *Historia troiana*, Vergil's writings, Servius's commentary, the *Ilias latina*, Isidorus, Guida da Pisa, Ovid's *Metamorphoses, Heroides, Fasti, Ars amatoria*. On Giovanni del Virgilio as source for Bonsignori, see Matteo Ferretti, "Per la 'recensio' e la prima diffusione delle 'Allegorie' di Giovanni del Virgilio," *L'Ellisse* 2 (2007): 9–28.

70   The text of the "tavola delle rubriche" can be found in Ardissino, *Ovidio Metamorphoseos Vulgare*, 65–98.
71   Ardissino, *Ovidio Metamorphoseos Vulgare*, 101.

mostly replicated the order in which the passages appeared in the original text.[72] Mainly created with pedagogical purposes in mind, their selections focused heavily on passages that were most helpful — that offered *utilitas* to their medieval readers.[73] The *Florilegium Angelicum* and *Florilegium Gallicum*, two twelfth-century anthologies that were probably produced in the Orléans region and circulated widely, focused on classical writing and included large selections from Ovid's poems. In fact, Ovid is the most cited author in the *Florilegium Gallicum*;[74] many one- or two-verse-long quotations from the Latin poet's works appear together with longer passages of up to twenty verses long. Moreover, this anthology features some Ovidian texts that were rare at the time, such as *Her.* 15, 16, and 17. In these anthologies, well-chosen isolated phrases from Ovid's amatory works and the exile letters are transformed into wise words and aphorisms, and their sections with passages from the *Metamorphoses* and the *Fasti* become a reference work on Roman history and myth. The Ovidian works are cut and prepackaged to present an Ovid much different than the author of the works in their entirety — serious, wise, knowledgeable, and no longer risqué.

The judge and *causidicus* or legal counselor Albertano da Brescia (ca. 1190–1251), author of several moral and rhetorical treatises and a well-read man, features such an Ovid in his works.[75] At first glance Albertano displays

---

72 On the anthologies, see *Florilegium Gallicum: Prolegomena und Edition der Exzerpte von Petron bis Cicero, De oratore*, ed. Johannes Hamacher (Bern: Herbert Lang, 1975); Birger Munk Olsen, "Les classiques latins dans les florilèges médiévaux antérieurs au XIIIe siècle," *Revue d'histoire des textes* 9 (1979): 47–121 and 10 (1980): 115–64; R. H. Rouse, "Florilegia and Latin Classical Authors in Twelfth- and Thirteenth-Century Orléans," *Viator* 10 (1979): 131–60; Rosemary Burton, *Classical poets in the 'Florilegium Gallicum'* (Frankfurt am Main: P. Lang, 1983); Sally A. Rackley, "The Amatory Excerpts of Ovid in the *Florilegium Gallicum*: Evidence of the Knowledge of this Poet in the Twelfth Century," *Florilegium* 8 (1986): 71–112; and "The Excerpts from Ovid's *Heroides* in the *Florilegium gallicum*," *Manuscripta* 36, no. 2 (1992): 125–35; and Beatriz Fernández de la Cuesta González, *En la senda del 'Florilegium Gallicum': edición y estudio del florilegio del manuscrito Córdoba, Archivo Capitular 150* (Louvain-la-Neuve: Fédération internationale des instituts d'études médiévales, 2008). Modern editions of anthologies tend to add the corresponding verses next to passages from a certain author and work — a practice that reveals that at times the chronological order of the passages that the compiler followed differs from that in our modern editions of these authors and texts.

73 Burton, *Classical Poets in the 'Florilegium Gallicum,'* 6–7.

74 Burton, *Classical Poets in the 'Florilegium Gallicum,'* 14; Fernández de la Cuesta González, *En la senda del 'Florilegium Gallicum,'* 223.

75 James M. Powell defined the term causidicus in *Albertanus da Brescia: The Pursuit of Happiness in the Early Thirteenth Century* (Philadelphia: University of Pennsylvania Press, 1992), 11, n. 1. Angus Graham described Albertano's wide range of sources and his avid

a firm command of Ovid's works, but when, for instance, we look more closely at the Ovidian citations in his popular and often-translated treatise *Liber consolationis et consilii* (1246), it becomes clear that he could also have known these passages from anthologies.[76] The *Liber consolationis et consilii* takes the form of a long-spun dialogue between Melibeus and his wife Prudentia, who discuss how to respond to an attack on Prudentia and their daughter during Melibeus's absence.[77] In doing so, they cite many different sources, ranging from biblical wisdom literature to Cicero, (pseudo-)Seneca, and more contemporary writers such as Hugh of Saint Victor. Often, but not always, Melibeus and Prudentia name the author or title of their source, or introduce the words of others with the general statement, "it has been written" — a rhetorical move that follows St. Bonaventure's definition of an *auctor*: confirm one's own words with those of some else.

All the passages that Albertano da Brescia selected from Ovid's *Remedia amoris*, *Amores*, and *Heroides* express general truths; their content does not even remotely touch on Ovid's amatory themes. For instance, in the *Remedia amoris* Ovid referred to a mother's grieving process to illustrate the importance of timely reactions in dealing with lovesickness (*Rem. am.* 127–30); in Albertano's treatise, Ovid's example of the mourning mother becomes

---

book collecting — "a precursor of the Renaissance book collector" — in "Albertano da Brescia," in Kleinhenz, *Medieval Italy*, 1: 9–11, at 10. Paola Navone collected several quotations of modern scholars underlining Albertano's importance and intellectual stature, and his fame in Europe in Albertano da Brescia, *Liber de doctrina dicendi et tacendi. La parola del cittadino nell'Italia del Duecento*, ed. Paola Navone (Florence: SISMEL-Edizioni del Galluzzo, 1998), xi. Navone also signaled the work that remains to be done on Albertano's frequent invocations of *auctoritates*, raising the question whether these are the result of direct or indirect readings. For now, we can only be certain that he had direct knowledge of Seneca (xix–xx, and xix–xx, n. 2).

76 Cesare Segre described the wide circulation of the *Liber consolationis et consilii* and its vernacular translations in *La prosa del Duecento*, ed. Cesare Segre and Mario Marti (Milan: Riccardo Ricciardi, 1959), 203–4. Segre listed the Italian translations by Andrea da Grosseto and Soffredi del Grazia di Pistoia, and four anonymous translations. Selections from the Italian translations of the *Liber consolationis et consilii* are included in Segre and Marti, *La prosa del Duecento*, 205–16 (Andrea da Grosseto), and 217–26 (Soffredi del Grazia). For Andrea da Grosseto's translations of all of Albertano's treatises, see *Dei trattati morali di Albertano da Brescia volgarizzamento inedito fatto nel 1268 da Andrea da Grosseto*, ed. Francesco Selmi (Bologna: Gaetano Romagnoli, 1873). Witt noted that these translations were probably intended for Tuscan merchants in France, but circulated widely in Tuscany as well (*In the Footsteps of the Ancients*, 181).

77 On how the treatise debates and ultimately rejects the role of *vendetta* or personal revenge in Italian city life, see Powell's chapter "The Attack on the Vendetta," in *Albertanus da Brescia*, 74–89.

Prudentia's reminder to be patient with a distressed Melibeus (Chapter 1, p. 2, ll. 11–22).[78] The same decontextualized Ovidian passage (that is, without the reference to lovesickness) is also included in the *Florilegium Gallicum*.[79] Similarly, a line from Helen's letter to Paris (*Her.* 17.100) becomes in the *Liber consolationis et consilii* Ovid's authoritative claim that it is virtuous to refrain from what is pleasing (Chapter 45, p. 101, ll. 12–14)[80] — again, a verse that made the selection in the *Florilegium Gallicum*.[81] Twice Albertano uses the Ovidian verse, "impia sub dulci melle uenena latent" ("wicked poison hides underneath sweet honey" [*Am.* 1.8.104]). The first instance appears when Prudentia tries to convince her husband, whose initial impulse after the attack was to swear revenge, that one can or should change their promise when things are not what they seem to be (Chapter 29, quotation from the *Amores* at p. 62, ll. 14–15). This same verse appears for the second time (p. 84, ll. 2–3) when the same Prudentia discusses the reason of the attack (Chapter 37), linking the meaning of Melibeus's name — "he who drinks honey" — to his fault: drunk on the sweetness of this world, he had abandoned his maker. "Impia sub dulci melle uenena latent," somewhat of a favorite among Ovid's quotable verses,[82] shows

---

78 "Melibeus vero post modum reversus, hoc videns cœpit magno planctu flendo comas sibi dilaniare vestesque suas quasi more furiosi dilacerare. Uxor autem jam dicta, ut taceret, cœpit illum instanter ammonere. Ille vero semper plus clamabat; at illa distulit aliquantulum recordata de verbo Ovidii, De Remedio Amoris, qui dixit: 'Quis matrem, nisi mentis inops, in funere nati flere vetat? non hoc illa monenda loco est. / Cum dederit lacrimas animumque impleverit ægrum, / Ille dolor verbis emoderandus erit'" ("Yet when Melibeus returned shortly after and saw this, he started to cry and lament deeply, and tear his hair and his clothes almost furiously. But his wife started to pressingly urge him to be silent. He, however, always complained more; and she backed off a bit when she remembered the words of Ovid in the *Remedia amoris*, where he said: 'Who but a fool would forbid a mother to weep at the funeral of her son? That is not the place to give her advice. When she has shed her tears and her mind is no longer sad, then this pain may be restrained with words'"). Andrea da Grosseto and Soffredi del Grazia, the two identified Italian translators of the treatise, rendered this passage quite differently: Andrea da Grosseto adhered fairly closely to Albertano's Latin text (Segre and Marti, *La prosa del Duecento*, 205–6); Soffredi del Grazia, on the other hand, not only renamed Ovid "Uvedio" and the *Remedia amoris* "*D'amore*," but also left out half of the Ovidian quotation and modified the content of the remaining two verses (Segre and Marti, *La prosa del Duecento*, 217).
79 Rackley, "The Amatory Excerpts of Ovid in the *Florilegium Gallicum*," 100.
80 "Et Ovidius dixit: 'Est virtus placidis abstinuisse bonis'" ("And Ovid said: 'It is a virtue to abstain from what is delightful'").
81 Burton, *Classical Poets in the 'Florilegium Gallicum,'* 221; Fernández de la Cuesta González, *En la senda del 'Florilegium Gallicum,'* 334.
82 For instance, the verse is included in the *Florilegium Gallicum* (Fernández de la Cuesta González, *En la senda del 'Florilegium Gallicum,'* 340); and in Geremia da Montagnone's *Compendium moralium notabilium* (which I discuss further on) in Pars 2, Liber 2, rubric 4

not only its versatility in these two passages in the *Liber consolationis et consilii*, but also the remarkable distance that can arise between the original context of Ovid's verses and their later applications. In Ovid's poem *Am.* 1.8, this phrase is uttered by Dipsas, an old, ugly, drunk witch in the poet's description (vv. 1–20), a bawd who with a long speech (vv. 23–108) instructs a young girl how to win over a rich man. One of Dipsas's tricks was to use flattery; in its original context "impia sub dulci melle uenena latent" is an encouragement to tell a man whatever he wants to hear (vv. 103–4). The free-standing verse, in contrast, was used to convey a quite different sentiment: a caution to be wary of sweet talk. All these Ovidian citations in Albertano's *Liber consolationis et consilii* are also found in anthologies: if Albertano did not find them there, then he surely edited the Ovidian verses in the same way compilers of anthologies did.

These Ovidian verses stripped of their original from context were particularly vulnerable to wrong attributions, as all citations and aphorisms were and still are. It is hard to tell, for instance, at what point the attribution of an Ovidian quotation in the *Storie de Troia e de Roma* went wrong.[83] The *Storie de Troia e de Roma* (mid-thirteenth century) was among the earliest translations in Italy, translated from a Latin original dating from the first half of the twelfth century.[84] In writings on Roman history, Ovid is not the obvious or

"on flattery, praise, and approval" ("De adulatione, blandimento et assentione"). In addition to the double citation in the *Liber consolationis et consilii*, Albertano also included the verse in his earlier treatise *De amore et dilectione Dei* (1238), in Chapter 22 of Book 2 on false and dubious friends ("De amicis fictitiis et dubitatis"). Andrea da Grosseto, who translated all of Albertano's treatises into Italian, and thus translated this Ovidian quotation in all three occasions Albertano used it, rendered them considerably differently every time (Selmi, *Dei trattati morali di Albertano da Brescia*, 103, 129, 284) — a reminder of the instability of the translated text in the process of vernacularization. Albertano's treatises were among the sources for the *Fiore di virtù* (first quarter of the fourteenth century), and the same Ovidian verse is included there in Chapter 14 on the allurement suitable to Sirens ("Della lusinga appropriata alle Serene"), now in Italian: "Ovidio dice: Sotto il dolce mèle s'appiatta il malvagio veleno." Selections from the *Fiore di virtù* are also included in Segre and Marti, *La prosa del Duecento*, 886–99. See also Maria Corti, "Le fonti del *Fiore di virtù* e la teoria della 'nobilità' nel Duecento," *Giornale storico della letteratura italiana* 136 (1959): 1–82.

83   *Storie de Troja et de Roma, altrimenti dette Liber Ystoriarum Romanorum*, ed. Ernesto Monaci (Rome: Società Romana di Storia Patria, 1920). Monaci's edition includes the Latin text, and the Roman volgarizzamento as found in two manuscripts. Two other manuscripts contain heavily Tuscanized translations. Selections are included in Segre and Marti, *La prosa del Duecento*, 377–426.

84   Both the Latin text and the translations originated in or around Rome: see Ernesto Monaci, "Sul *Liber ystoriarum Romanorum*," in *Storie de Troja et de Roma*, xiii–lxxvi; Segre and Marti, *La prosa del Duecento*, 375–76, 1080–82.

most important source, but he is not absent from the text.[85] The *Storie de Troia e de Roma* turns to Ovid in the description of the Roman general Maximus Fabius's superior tactics during the Roman wars with Hannibal. The anonymous translator of the *Storie* concludes: "E como trovamo in Ovidio *De Ponto*, Massimo restitugìo molto la republica in quella ora" ("And as we find in Ovid's *Epistulae ex Ponto*, at that moment Maximus really restored the republic").[86] However, the Maximus who is frequently addressed in Ovid's exile letters is Paullus Fabius Maximus: related to the general but a good two hundred years younger. Yet the word choice in the *Storie* reveals the knowledge of an Ovidian passage — just not one from the *Epistulae ex Ponto*, but from the *Fasti*. In Book 2 of the *Fasti*, the general is addressed in words that closely resemble the Italian of the *Storie*: "scilicet ut posses olim tu, Maxime, nasci, / cui res cunctando restituenda foret" ("namely that you, Maximus, might be born one day to restore the state by delaying" [*Fasti* 2.241–42]).[87] The anonymous translator most likely was not reviewing the references, and translated the attribution to the wrong Ovidian poem together with the rest of the Latin text.

Another work that features passages from Ovid in translation is Brunetto Latini's *Tresor*.[88] Latini rendered Latin citations from Ovid — and many others — into French, the language of his encyclopedic work. (Over time, Latini's French translations of Latin citations were translated with the rest of the text into Italian and other vernacular languages, and even into Latin.)[89] With its focus on philosophy, logic, and rhetoric the *Tresor* is not the most obvious match even for a heavily edited Ovid, and the Ovidian phrases that Latini translated are mostly the kind of aphorisms found in anthologies. Latini was familiar with the practice of *volgarizzamento*: his *Rettorica* was a partial translation of Cicero's *De inventione*, with additional commentary, and he translated several Ciceronian orations. Also in the *Tresor*, Brunetto rendered

---

85 In addition to the example discussed below, Ovid is also named as a source in *Storie de Troja et de Roma*, 3–334, at 81 (*Fasti*), and 275 (Ovid's amatory works). The *Fasti* is a source on the architecture of Rome in the *Miracole de Roma*, also among the oldest vernacularizations in Italian: see Ernesto Monaci, "Le Miracole de Roma," *Archivio della Reale Società Romana di Storia Patria* 38 (1915): 551–90, at 565, 568.
86 Segre and Marti, *La prosa del Duecento*, 403.
87 Segre and Marti, *La prosa del Duecento*, 403, n. 7. On Paullus Fabius Maximus in Ovid's exile poetry, see Ovid, *The Poems of Exile*, trans. Peter Green (Berkeley: University of California Press, 2005), 296–97.
88 French was an unexpected language for an encyclopedic work — for that reason the colophon at times states that Latini "translated" the *Tresor* "from Latin into French."
89 In *Vernacular Translation in Dante's Italy*, 78–79, Cornish documented these various (re)translations of Latini's work.

extended passages from some of his Latin sources into French: for instance, from Albertano da Brescia's treatise *De arte loquendi et tacendi*, which, like his previously discussed *Liber consolationis et consilii*, contained several Ovidian quotations, some of which were translated in the *Tresor* as well.[90] (In this case, of course, the reliance on intermediary sources brings up the question how well Brunetto knew the Latin authors he was quoting.)[91] The *Tresor* also includes a snippet from Ovid's biography: in the chapter on the stork Latini describes the ibis, the stork's Egyptian relative, and its intestinal cleaning methods (1.160.5–6), concluding that when the "very good poet" Ovid was "imprisoned" by the emperor, Ovid called the emperor by the name of this "most filthy creature" — a reference to Ovid's curse poem *Ibis* (1.160.7).[92]

90   For instance, in the chapter on how to prepare for public speaking, Latini stresses the importance of controlling your emotions: "Ovide dit: Veinque ton coraige et ta ire, tu qui veinques toutes choses" ("Ovid says: 'Overcome your mind and your anger, you who overcome all things'" [2.62.2]) — the French translation of Ovid's Latin verse "Vince animos iramque tuam, qui cetera vincis!" (*Her.* 3.85), from the letter of Briseis to Achilles. Albertano da Brescia's treatise *De arte loquendi et tacendi* is an important source for Book 2 of the *Tresor*. Latini copied more than just this sentence with the quotation from Ovid's *Heroides* from *De arte loquendi et tacendi:* entire chapters of the *Tresor* (2.61–67) are translated from Albertano's treatise, without the mention of the source. See Powell, *Albertanus da Brescia*, 122; and Brunetto Latini, *Tresor*, ed. and trans. Pietro G. Beltrami, Paolo Squillacioti, Plinio Torri, and Sergio Vatteroni (Turin: Einaudi, 2007), where Pietro G. Beltrami noted that "si può parlare di un volgarizzamento completo dell'operetta mediolatina" ("this can be considered a full translation of the medieval Latin work" [xix]). Cesare Segre pointed out that parts of Albertano's treatise ended up in the *Fiore di virtù* (Segre and Marti, *La prosa del Duecento*, 204). The *De arte loquendi et tacendi* was also translated into Italian by Andrea da Grosseto and Soffredi del Grazia di Pistoia, the same translators of Albertano's *Liber consolationis et consilii*. Selections are included in Segre, *Volgarizzamenti del Due e Trecento*, 139–71.
91   On Latini's sources for the *Tresor*, see Aristide Marigo, "Cultura letteraria e preumanistica nelle maggiori enciclopedie del Dugento: Lo 'Speculum' e il 'Tresors,'" *Giornale storico della letteratura italiana* 68 (1916): 1–42, 289–326, at 309–26 (on the *Tresor*) and especially at 316 (on the Ovidian passages in the *Tresor*). In addition to the two Ovidian citations in the passage from Albertano's treatise that Latini translated into French (mentioned above), according to Marigo also the remaining references to Ovid come from intermediary works: for a citation from the *Heroides*, Marigo pointed to the existence of several French translations of the *Heroides*; and the reference to Ovid's *Ibis*, discussed in the remainder of this paragraph, is linked to the bestiary that Latini used for the *Tresor* (316 and nn. 2–3).
92   "Et sachiez que Ovide li tres bon poetes, quant li empereres le mist en prison, fist un livre ou il apeloit l'empereor par le nom de cel oisel, car il ne savoit penser plus orde cr[e]ature" ("And know that the very good poet Ovid, when the emperor put him into prison, wrote a book where he called the emperor by the name of that bird, because he could not think of a filthier creature").

Ovid's poems are also frequently cited in works intended solely for rhetorical education. The *Summa dictaminis* or *Candelabrum* by Bene da Firenze, a teacher of rhetoric in Bologna during the first decades of the thirteenth century, provides many examples. For instance, Bene names the letters of St. Paul and Ovid's elegies as representing the mediocre style between the sublime and the humble (1.6.4). He uses the opening verses of the pseudo-Ovidian *Nux* (VII.11.3) as an example of *prosopopoeia* or personification. Without mentioning Ovid's name or the title of the work, Bene cites the passage from the creation story in the *Metamorphoses* that distinguishes humans from animals for their upward posture and outlook (*Met.* 1.85–86) to remind his readers of this divine gift (11.1.7); in Bene's rhetorical manual, Ovid's creator or "opifex rerum" (*Met.* 1.79) becomes the "summus opifex" (11.1.6).[93] Bene da Firenze's frequent mentions of Ovidian passages nevertheless pale in comparison with the abundance of Ovidian material included in the *Compendium moralium notabilium* by the Paduan judge Geremia da Montagnone (ca. 1250–1320). The two men were writing at different times and in different milieus: Bene da Firenze, teacher of rhetoric at Bologna at the beginning of the thirteenth century — a time when the study of the classics was no longer considered indispensable for such instruction — insists on continuing to look at Latin authors, in opposition to his fellow teachers of rhetoric Boncompagno da Signa and Guido Faba, who push for the use of the vernacular. Geremia's *Compendium*, on the other hand,

---

[93] In the *Etymologiae*, Isidore of Seville turns to the same Ovidian passage (*Met.* 1.85–86) when he discusses the Greek word *anthropon* (XI.1.5). A list of quotations from Ovid (sixteen in total, significantly fewer than the almost two hundred from Vergil) is included in *The 'Etymologies' of Isidore of Seville*, trans. with introduction and notes by Stephen A. Barney, W. J. Lewis, J. A. Beach, and Oliver Berghof (Cambridge: Cambridge University Press, 2006), 471. Commenting on this quotation from Ovid's *Metamorphoses* in Isidore's *Etymologies*, Winthrop Wetherbee noted that "explicit citation is random and infrequent in the early-medieval period" ("The study of classical authors: From late Antiquity to the twelfth century," in Minnis and Johnson, *The Cambridge History of Literary Criticism*, 99–144, at 130). The creation story in the *Metamorphoses* also appealed to preachers: Siegfried Wenzel discussed how the English Dominican scholar Robert Holcot (d. 1333) integrated this story in one of his sermons ("Ovid from the pulpit," in Clark, Coulson, and McKinley, *Ovid in the Middle Ages*, 160–76, at 169). Robert Black also mentioned the citation from the pseudo-Ovidian *Nux* in Bene's *Candelabrum* in "Ovid in medieval Italy," in Clark, Coulson, and McKinley, *Ovid in the Middle Ages*, 123–42, at 124. The twelfth-century jurist Uguccione da Pisa wrote *Derivationes*, a lexicographical work that in its study of word roots and their derivations relied heavily on examples — brief citations — from a variety of Latin sources, including over a hundred passages from Ovid's complete oeuvre. A list of all Ovidian citations can be found in Uguccione da Pisa, *Derivationes*, ed. Enzo Cecchini and Guido Arbizzoni (Florence: SISMEL-Edizioni del Galluzzo, 2004), 256–67.

was written toward the end of the thirteenth century, in the (proto-)humanistic Paduan milieu best described by Ronald G. Witt, which included Lovato dei Lovati and Albertino Mussato, both Ovidians in their own right.[94] The *Compendium moralium notabilium* was a work of compilation different from the anthologies previously discussed. The *Florilegium Gallicum*, for instance, presented the excerpts from each author and work together, while in the *Compendium* Geremia organized his quotations by topic.[95] The included list of authors, organized chronologically and assigned labels such as "religiologus," "philosophus," and "poeta," documents the broad scope of Geremia's sources: Scripture, classical authors, theological writers and poets from late antiquity, medieval rhetoricians and grammarians, and even Italian proverbs. Ovid is treated as an authority on a wide variety of topics treated in the *Compendium*, such as anger, the naturalness of death, (women's) fidelity and infidelity, mental strength, and so on.[96] But not unexpectedly on matters of love he is a prevalent source, and much longer passages from Ovid's writings make it into the *Compendium* when such topics are treated. Geremia does not pretend that Ovid did not write about physical love — after all, he includes topics such as

---

94 Witt placed the origins of humanism in Padua, in the intellectual circles around Lovati and Mussato (two generations before Petrarch's Christian humanism) in *In the Footsteps of the Ancients,* Chapters 3 and 4. On the intellectual activity in Padua, see Remigio Sabbadini, *Le scoperte dei codici latini e greci ne' secoli XIV e XV: Nuove ricerche col riassunto filologico dei due volumi. Edizione anastatica con nuove aggiunte e correzioni dell'autore a cura di Eugenio Garin* (Florence: G. C. Sansoni Editore, 1967), 1: 105–21. I briefly discuss Lovati and Mussato's Latin poetry inspired by Ovid further on in this section.

95 There is no modern edition of the complete *Compendium moralium notabilium*; I work here with a digitized edition of an early-sixteenth-century print (Venice, 1505) with the title *Epytoma sapientiae*. The Catullus citations in the *Compendium*, which are among the earliest testimonies of the Latin poet, can be found in Berthold Louis Ullman, "Hieremias de Montagnone and his citations from Catullus," in *Studies in the Italian Renaissance* (Rome: Edizioni di Storia e Letteratura, 1955), 79–112. Also the vernacular proverbs have been edited in Andrea Gloria, *Volgare illustre nel 1100 e proverbi volgari del 1200* (Bologna: Forni, 1977). Chris L. Nighman is working on open access digital resources on the *Compendium*, including an index of the quotations by author and source. See the *Compendium moralium notabilium* Project, http://web.wlu.ca/history/cnighman/CMN/index.html.

96 See in the *Epytoma sapientiae* the citations on anger (p. 121; Pars 2, Liber 1, rubric 12), the naturalness of death (p. 144; Pars 5, Liber 4, rubric 3), (women's) fidelity and infidelity (p. 32; Pars 2, Liber 2, rubric 2), mental strength (p. 120; Pars 5, Liber 1, rubric 1). The Ovidian quotation included in the chapter on mental strength ("de fortitudine animi"; p. 119, Pars 5, Liber 1, rubric 1) is "Omne solum forti patria est: ut piscibus equor. / Ut volucri vacui quicquid in orbe patet" (*Fasti* 1.493–94). The first verse is also found in Dante's *De vulgari eloquentia* (see Ch. 3.3). The Ovidian verses are quoted as found in the *Compendium*.

"people fit to love in a sexual relationship" ("de eligibilibus personis amandis amore venereo"; Pars 4, Liber 5, rubric 2). But when we look at the content of the citations that document sexual love, Geremia's editing practices become clear. Ovid is by far the most important source on love, with short quotations appearing from the *Amores*, *Metamorphoses*, and *Medicamina faciei femineae*, and more than hundred verses appear from all three books of the *Ars amatoria*. The selections from Book 2, for instance, include some of Ovid's greatest hits — I am the teacher of the poor; flattering will do the trick; be patient and do not give up; do not rush but do not disappear either; money can buy you love — but Geremia leaves out all the mythological examples that Ovid used in Book 2 to make his points, as well as all explicit mentions about sex.[97] The reader of Geremia's *Compendium*, in other words, finds an edited Ovid, not detached from his amatory works, and also considered a relevant source on a wide variety of other topics.

The Dominican friar Bartolomeo da San Concordio (1264–1347) brings the same proverbial Ovid to yet another audience: preachers.[98] Educated in Bologna and Paris, the friar taught in Dominican schools in Tuscany and Rome. At the beginning of the fourteenth century, he translated his own Latin work, the *Documenta antiquorum*, into the vernacular as the *Ammaestramenti degli antichi*, a popular *volgarizzamento* at its time. At the opening of the work Bartolomeo explains that since the wisdom of the ancients cannot be contained in one book, he will collect their teachings on four main topics: natural dispositions, virtues, vices, and fortune. Bartolomeo further breaks down these topics in more manageable talking points, all illustrated with suitable quotations, chiming in from time to time as the "auctor" (Latin) or "autore" (Italian). The *Ammaestramenti* is dedicated to the Florentine banker Geri Spina (known to readers of Boccaccio's *Decameron* 6.2), but it is essentially a handbook for preachers — this is particularly clear when Bartolomeo provides quotations illustrating that one should not preach about lofty subjects to simple folks (pp. 224–25), or that the sins of a few should not disgrace the entire congregation (pp. 352–53). In Bartolomeo's view, there was much to learn from the *antichi*, so what precisely did Ovid have to offer?

---

97 Less than thirty verses from the second book (almost 750 verses long in the modern editions) are included in the *Compendium*: *Ars am.* 2.145, 152, 159–62, 177–78, 229, 241–42, 276–80, 289–90, 293–94, 329, 340, 351, 357–58, 511–512. Most passages are just one or two verses long.

98 See Cesare Segre, "Bartolomeo da San Concordio," in *Dizionario biografico degli Italiani*, ed. Alberto M. Ghisalberti (Rome: Istituto della Enciclopedia Italiana, 1964), 6: 768–70; David P. Bénéteau, "Bartolomeo da San Concordio," in Kleinhenz, *Medieval Italy*, 1: 99–100.

The Latin poet has a modest but not trivial presence in the *Ammaestramenti*, where Bartolomeo quotes more frequently from the Bible and the Church Fathers, and from Cicero and Seneca, among the classical authors. Bartolomeo always identifies his sources, and they include all of Ovid's poems, except for the *Ibis* and the *Medicamina faciei femineae*. Ovid provides wise words on topics such as physical beauty, the inevitability of death, one's natural attachment to the homeland, rest, the fact that we are all sinners, and so on. The organization of these quotations by subject brings compendia such as Geremia da Montagnone's to mind, and the Ovidian phrases Bartolomeo selected sound much like the ones found in compendia, anthologies, and treatises — in fact, with the exception of one, they are all found in one of the most popular anthologies, the *Florilegium Gallicum*. "No Italian before Petrarch," Ronald G. Witt noted, "extolled the importance of studying antiquity as a guide to life more clearly than did Bartolomeo da San Concordio."[99] But as Bartolomeo's study regarded Ovid, it seems that the lessons to learn from the Latin poet had already prepared by compilers before him.

In transmitting the wisdom of the ancients from a Latin-reading audience to an Italian one, Bartolomeo mainly remains faithful to the original text, but alters details here and there for his contemporary readers — the prevalent approach to Italian vernacularization during that time. The following passage illustrates this approach particularly well. In the chapter collecting citations on the topic that no one is without sin, Bartolomeo includes a passage from Book 2 of Ovid's *Tristia*: "Si quotiens peccant homines sua fulmina mittat Juppiter, exiguo tempore inermis erit" ("If anytime someone sinned Jupiter launched lightning bolts, he would be quickly out of ammunition").[100] Bartolomeo's Italian translation replaces the classical deity Jupiter with "Iddio," the Christian God of his audience: "Se quante volte gli uomini peccano Iddio mandasse le saette, in poco tempo rimarrebbe disarmato" ("If anytime anyone sinned God launched arrows, he would be quickly out of ammunition").[101] The lightning bolts, Jupiter's quintessential weapons and further indicators of the classical world to which the Ovidian citation belonged, become "saette," or arrows in Bartolomeo's Italian rendering: in that way, Bartolomeo adjusts the citation for his intended readers, as arrows were often God's weapon of choice in the Old

---

99 Witt, *In the Footsteps of the Ancients*, 187.
100 Bartolomeo da San Concordio, *Ammaestramenti degli antichi*, 356. The precise introduction of the quotation is "Ovidius 2. de tristib." The Ovidian verses (*Tristia* 2.33–34) are quoted as found in the *Documenta*.
101 Bartolomeo da San Concordio, *Ammaestramenti degli antichi*, 357.

Testament.[102] Moreover, while in the *Documenta* Bartolomeo gets the Ovidian attribution right (the citation is found in Book 2 of the *Tristia*), he places the translated Italian citation in the second book of the *Ars amatoria* — a reminder of how easily misattributions sneak into translations.[103]

In contrast to Bartolomeo's generous inclusion of Ovid's words among the teachings of the ancients, Giordano da Pisa (ca. 1260–1310), a fellow Dominican friar and teacher, found (limited) value in Aristotle, Plato, and Socrates, but not immediately in Ovid. In the only mention of the Latin poet in Giordano's more than 700 surviving sermons transcribed in the vernacular by his audience in Florence, he called Ovid lascivious and depraved ("omo carnale e vizioso"), a great sinner and bad example, and a very bad pagan ("pessimo pagano").[104] However, Giordano then turns to the story of Orpheus's descent into the underworld from Ovid's *Metamorphoses* ("l'*Ovidio maggiore*"), using the punishments of Tantalus, Ixion, and Sisyphus that Orpheus there witnesses (*Met.* 10.40–44) to illustrate that sinners will be punished for eternity (paragraphs 18–20). Giordano concludes that both the Holy Scriptures ("le Sante Scriture") and "the writings and the books of pagans" ("le scritture e i libri de' pagani") confirm this — only in this instance, Giordano finds that also the very bad pagan Ovid got it right.[105]

From the pulpit we return to the classroom and younger readers of Ovid, who could be introduced to the Latin poet indirectly and directly through the *Liber catonianus*, a collection of six Latin works used in elementary school education. (The commentaries on Ovid's works and the rhetorical manuals, with their occasional inclusion of Ovidian citations, were used at higher levels of education from grammar school to the university.) The *Liber catonianus*

---

102 See, for instance, the following two passages from the Psalms, which contain the same phrase "to launch arrows": "et misit sagittas et dissipavit eos et fulgora multiplicavit et conturbavit eos" ("and he sent arrows and scattered them and he multiplied the lightning and he disturbed them" [Psalm 17:15]), and "fulgora coruscationem et dissipabis eos emitte sagittas tuas et conturbabis eos" ("send lightning and you will scatter them, send your arrows and you disturb them" [Psalm 143:6]).

103 Bartolomeo da San Concordio, *Ammaestramenti degli antichi*, 356–57, at 357: "Ovidio, secondo de arte."

104 Sermon XXXII (March 3, 1305), paragraph 17: "E diremo pur di quegli che fu pessimo pagano, ch'ebbe nome Ovidio, e fu omo carnale e vizioso, e fa egli uno libro ove ammonisce le genti in quello ove egli fu molto peccatore, dando exemplo di sé."

105 Sermon XXXII (March 3, 1305), paragraph 22: "Ecco non solamente le Scritture Sante, ma le scritture e i libri de' pagani il dimostrano e dicono" ("Look, not only the Holy Scriptures, but also the writings and the books of the pagans show and tell this"). On the use of Ovid in preaching, with a focus on England, see Wenzel, "Ovid from the pulpit."

included Statius's *Achilleid*, several works of late antiquity (Claudian's *De raptu Proserpinae*, Avianus's *Fables*, Maximian's *Elegies*, and the *Disticha Catonis*), and the tenth-century *Ecloga* by Theodulus. Ovid's *Remedia amoris* and the medieval plays *Pamphilus* and *Geta* were frequent substitutes.[106] Three texts from the *Liber catonianus*, the *Disticha Catonis* and the two Latin comedies, are especially relevant to our discussion.

The *Disticha Catonis* consists of four books of proverbial knowledge written in the third or fourth century that were wrongly attributed to Cato the Elder during the Middle Ages. The original Latin text was sometimes accompanied by vernacular translations, while at other times these vernacular translations circulated independently.[107] While Ovid's role in the *Disticha* is limited, he is nevertheless presented as an authority on love, like in the *Remedia amoris* (another text often included in the *Liber catonianus*). In the preface to the second book, where the purpose of the work is explained most explicitly (vv. 7–10), the author of the *Disticha* associates certain authors with certain themes: he mentions Vergil as the source on how to work the earth, Macer to learn about the virtues of herbs, Lucan to understand the Roman and African wars (vv. 1–5). However, the author of the *Disticha* notes that "if you want to love, or learn about love through reading," one should "look for Ovid."[108] Students using the *Liber catonianus* were introduced to Ovid as the expert in matters of the heart.

The other works of interest included in the *Liber catonianus* are the two medieval Latin comedies, the *Pamphilus* and *Geta* (twelfth century).[109] Both plays are good examples of the kind of texts that I would call "filtered" Ovidian sources. Different from the indirect transmission of Ovid's poems, such sources do not literally transcribe or translate Ovidian verses but instead use Ovid's words, themes, and style as a starting point for original

---

106 See Gillespie, "The Study of Classical Authors," 153–59; and Jill Mann, "'He Knew Nat Catoun': Medieval School-Texts and Middle English Literature," in *The Text in the Community: Essays on Medieval Works, Manuscripts, Authors, and Readers*, ed. Jill Mann and Maura Nolan (Notre Dame: University of Notre Dame Press, 2006), 41–74, at 44–50.
107 Segre and Marti, *La Prosa del Duecento*, 187–88.
108 "Si quid amare libet, vel discere amare legendo, / Nasonem petito" (vv. 6–7); "S'el plas a ti amar alguna causa, o enprendre amar leçando, demandaràs Ovidio" (Venetian translation in Segre and Marti, *La Prosa del Duecento*, 189); "E se alcuna cosa ti piace amare uvero leggendo imparare ad amare, dimanda Ovidio se tu questa cura hai" (Tuscan translation in Segre and Marti, *La Prosa del Duecento*, 192).
109 For the Latin text of the *Pamphilus* and *Geta*, see *Three Latin Comedies*, ed. A. Keith Bate (Toronto: Pontifical Institute of Mediaeval Studies, 1976); for the English translation, see *Seven Medieval Latin Comedies*, trans. Alison Goddard Elliott (New York: Garland Publishing, Inc., 1984), 1–24 and 26–48.

creations.[110] Their writers could have a command of Ovid's Latin texts (in the case of the *Pamphilus* and *Geta*, the Ovidian imitations are well documented),[111] but are often also familiar with other Ovid-inspired texts in Latin or the vernacular (in the case of the *Pamphilus* and *Geta*, other medieval Latin comedies). Indeed, with the growing circulation of Ovid's texts came the production of new works of literature inspired by the Latin poet. In these works, writers intertwined their readings of Ovid's Latin texts with those of contemporary Latin or vernacular works that were similarly inspired by Ovid. Examples of such "filtered" Ovidian works include the Latin epistolary poems by the abbot and later bishop Baudri of Bourgueil (written during the second half of the eleventh century), certain French romances and troubadour lyric poems, Andreas Capellanus's Latin treatise *De amore* (second half of the twelfth century) and its anonymous Tuscan translation *Trattato d'amore* (first half of the fourteenth century), Henry of Settimello's Latin poem *Elegia* (end of the twelfth century) and its Tuscan translation (first half of the fourteenth century), the *Roman de la Rose* (written during the thirteenth century), and the Latin poetry from the Paduan scholars Lovato dei Lovati (1240–1309) and Albertino Mussato (1261–1329).[112]

Each of these "filtered" Ovidian texts tells a different story of how its author combined classical Latin and contemporary sources. As a result, readers of these works are exposed to Ovid not in literal wording but in spirit. Both the authors and the readers of these "filtered" Ovidian sources could be quite familiar with

---

110   Rita Copeland considered the *Ovide moralisé* an original creation in which its author wanted to highlight the status of vernacular writings compared to Latin. See *Rhetoric, Hermeneutics, and Translation in the Middle Ages: Academic Traditions and Vernacular Texts* (Cambridge: Cambridge University Press, 1991), Chapter 4. On this kind of translation, see the last section of this chapter.

111   Wilfred Blumenthal, "Untersuchungen zur pseudo-ovidianischen Komödie *Pamphilus*," *Mittellateinisches Jahrbuch* 11 (1976): 224–311, at 224–46. On the Ovidian influence on these Latin comedies, see also Stefano Pittaluga, "Le *De tribus puellis*, 'comédie Ovidienne,'" *Vita Latina* 61 (1976): 2–13, and *Vita Latina* 62 (1977): 2–14.

112   On the Ovidian inspiration in these works, see Peter L. Allen, *Art of Love: Amatory Fiction from Ovid to the Romance of the Rose* (Philadelphia: University of Pennsylvania Press, 1992); Michael L. Stapleton, *Harmful Eloquence: Ovid's 'Amores' from Antiquity to Shakespeare* (Ann Arbor: University of Michigan Press, 1996); Witt, *In the Footsteps of the Ancients*, 79, 99; Minnis, *Magister amoris*; Guthmüller, "Die *volgarizzamenti*," 334–35 (on the Italian translations of the *Elegia* and the *De amore*); Don A. Monson, *Andreas Capellanus, Scholasticism, and the Courtly Tradition* (Washington: The Catholic University of America Press, 2005); Giuseppe Billanovich, "'Veterum vestigia vatum' nei carmi dei preumanisti padovani: Lovato Lovati, Zambono di Andrea, Albertino Mussato e Lucrezio, Catullo, Orazio (*Carmina*), Tibullo, Properzio, Ovidio (*Ibis*), Marziale, Stazio (*Silvae*)," *Italia medioevale e umanistica* 1 (1958): 155–244.

Ovidian themes or characters without possessing a thorough knowledge of the Latin text. For instance, one does not need to know Ovid's opening words to his story of Apollo and Daphne, "Primus amor Phoebi Daphne Peneia" ("Phoebus's first love was Daphne, the daughter of Peneus" [*Met.* 1.452]), to refer to the story. Similarly, one does not need to know the Ovidian origin of Love's double arrows — introduced in the Apollo and Daphne story (*Met.* 1.466–71) — to use it in one's work. Therefore, these "filtered" Ovidian sources add numerous possibilities for readers to encounter the Latin poet's works, albeit in derived forms. They might not be reading *Ovidius*, Ovid's Latin poems, but were familiar with Ovidian material.

In conclusion, the Italian thirteenth century may have witnessed a drop in the number of schoolbook manuscripts of Ovid's works, as Robert Black showed, but the Latin poet was still omnipresent in and outside the classroom. Foremost, the general manuscript numbers of all his works steadily increase from the twelfth century on. In the classroom, Ovid's *Remedia amoris* was sometimes part of the *Liber catonianus*, a standard collection of Latin works used in elementary school education. While the origin of the pseudo-Lactantian *Narrationes* (the oldest extant commentary on the *Metamorphoses*) is not well understood, the numerous twelfth- and thirteenth-century Latin commentaries all undoubtedly originated in the school context. The context changes for commentaries produced in the fourteenth century: Giovanni del Virgilio's commentaries on Ovid's *Metamorphoses* were written for university students; the anonymous *Ovide moralisé* was a vernacular work and therefore appealed to a much broader public; Pierre Bersuire's *Ovidius moralizatus* was originally intended for preachers. While the *accessus* or introductions to these twelfth- and thirteenth-century commentaries indicate that all of Ovid's works should be understood in terms of morality ("ethice supponitur"), the actual content of the commentaries focuses on many aspects besides allegory (e.g., grammar, history, geography, literature). Moreover, while the fourteenth-century *Ovide moralisé* introduced a consistently Christianizing reading of the *Metamorphoses*, the allegorical readings included in the twelfth- and thirteenth-century commentaries only occasionally interpret Ovid's stories in an explicitly Christian key.

In the classroom, students also encountered fragments of Ovid's works in rhetorical texts, where passages from Ovid served as examples, and in anthologies, where Ovidian quotes were taken out of context and took on an aphoristic quality. Stripped of their original contexts, quotations from Ovid's works (with or without acknowledgment of the sources) were included in moral treatises and prose works on Roman history — works that circulated outside the classroom. When these Latin prose works were translated into the vernacular, as they often were, their reading public only broadened. Italian translations of entire Ovidian works, on the other hand, were only produced at the approximate time that Dante started to compose the *Commedia*, and thus could not have been sources for many poets included in this book. Finally, both Latin and vernacular literature, inspired by Ovid's words, themes, and style, were not only part of the educational system (e.g., the medieval Latin comedies that were included in the *Liber catonianus*), but also circulated widely outside that context. In short, it is not an exaggeration to state that it was impossible for a literate person not to encounter Ovid's works in some form.[113] By virtue of having learned the Latin language, a student would have encountered Ovid's works in either the original Latin (with or without accompanying commentary) or fragmented in anthologies; similarly, a reader of the vernacular would have been exposed to snippets from Ovid's works in the prose works of the time or one of the many works of vernacular literature that were inspired by the work of the Latin poet. To say that Ovid is everywhere is imprecise and unhelpful, but does capture the unwieldy, widespread presence of Ovidian works in their manifold shapes and forms described in this section. The coexistence of these wide varieties of texts and the dynamic relationships between them make the Ovidian tradition a complex puzzle. Having started with the texts and contexts where readers could encounter Ovid, I will in the following section move on to a specific group among Ovid's Italian readers: the poets who engage with the Ovidian tradition.

1.2 The Italian Readers of Ovid Turned Writers

In the sonnet *Assai son certo che somenta in lidi* (Marti CXXXVa), the thirteenth-century Bolognese poet Onesto da Bologna (also Onesto degli Onesti) lamented the cruelty of his lady and called his addressee, fellow poet Cino da Pistoia, inexperienced in this bitter aspect of love.[114] In his response sonnet, *Se mai*

---

[113] Elena Lombardi goes even further in her general discussion of reading practices during Dante's time: "one did not need to be literate in order to be a reader, since reading took place through the ears as well as with eyes." See *The Wings of the Doves: Love and Desire in Dante and Medieval Culture* (Montreal: McGill-Queen's University Press, 2012), 213. Her entire chapter on "Reading" (212–47) is an excellent overview on the topic.

[114] Instead of citing the full reference to the primary sources used in this book, I provide all this information in the *List of Editions* in the bibliography. At the first mention of a poem I provide the last name of the editor(s) and the number of the poem in the edition used, and, where relevant, the Pillet-Carstens (PC) or *Indice bibliografico degli autori e dei testi* (IBAT) numbers.

leggesti versi de l'Ovidi (Marti CXXXV), Cino defended his behavior with a reference to Ovid: "Se mai leggesti versi de l'Ovidi, / so c'hai trovato, sì come si dice, / che disdegnoso contra sdegnatrice / convien ch'Amore di mercede sfidi" ("If you ever read verses of Ovid, I know you found out that, as they say, Love inevitably takes away any hope for mercy to anyone who is haughty toward a haughty lady" [vv. 1–4]).[115] In those verses, Cino appealed to Ovid's authority to prove that Onesto only had himself to blame for his misfortune in love. Moreover, Cino implicitly acknowledged the existence of a community of Italian readers of the Latin poet, for whom "l'Ovidi" was a shared point of reference. In the preceding section, I described the texts and contexts in which Italians could encounter Ovid's works, basically finding that any reader of Latin and the vernacular was, in widely varying degrees, familiar with the Latin poet's writings — a familiarity that could range from being a regular reader of the Latin texts to one who merely happened upon one of Ovid's characters or themes in the vernacular literature of the time. Cino and Onesto, two Italian poets exposed to this ubiquitous Ovid, openly discussed "Ovid's verses" in their poetry. As we have also seen in the previous section, the acts of reading and writing are closely interconnected: many Ovidian sources were written by readers of Ovid's works — the commentaries, the translations, to name the most obvious ones, but also the "filtered" Ovidian sources. Many Italian poets, several of them self-declared readers of Ovid like Cino and Onesto, are readers of Ovid turned into writers about Ovid as well. How precisely can we describe their Ovidian readings?

Not until Petrarch (1304–74) do we find an Italian reader of Ovid whose copy of the *Metamorphoses*, with annotations, we still possess. Only Petrarch provided plenty of information about his own education with references to reading Ovid, and placed Ovid's *Metamorphoses* on the list of his favorite books (see Ch. 5.1). In the absence of such first-hand information and readers' copies and notes, and detailed biographical information about many Italian poets, the poetry often becomes the main witness of their engagement with Ovidian material. But while in most cases it is not possible to identify the precise Ovidian sources Italian poets were using, even limited biographical information can be sufficient to make general connections between certain groups of poets and their presumed sources.

In medieval Italy to hold a particular professional function or social status implied certain language skills and educational preparation. The first Italian poets, often referred to as the poets of the Sicilian School, were not professional poets or performers, but first and foremost court officials: most of them

---

115   This exchange between Onesto and Cino is discussed in more detail in Ch. 2.3.

occupied juridical and administrative positions (judges, notaries, chancellors) at the court of Emperor Frederick II.[116] While they wrote their occasional poetry in the vernacular, their professional (and more extensive) writing was in Latin. Moreover, these poets were working in an environment where the study of classical literature was not only possible but also encouraged.[117] The library of the Emperor contained, according to his own account, books on a wide range of topics not only in Latin and Greek, but also in Arabic, Hebrew, French, Occitan, and Italian.[118] The judge and poet Pier della Vigna, for instance, described himself as "fundatus" in "multa litteratura divina et humana et poetarum" ("grounded in divine and human literature and poetry").[119] Pier wrote many letters for the Emperor in Latin (as his *logotheta*, often rendered as chancellor in English), and a few poems in Italian (see Ch. 2.1). The primacy of their professional activities was reflected in later mentions of the Sicilian poets: for instance, when in a famous episode in *Purg.* 24 Dante refers to the poetry of Giacomo da Lentini, he does not use his name but simply calls him "'l Notaro" ("the Notary" [*Purg.* 24.56]); and in one of the three late-thirteenth-century *canzonieri* that contain most of the early Italian lyric poetry (Vatican City, Biblioteca Apostolica Vaticana, MS Vat. lat. 3793), the authors of the poems are first identified by their profession and then by their name (e.g., "il giudice Guido delle Colonne" ["the judge Guido delle Colonne"], "lo re Enzo" ["the king Enzo"]).[120]

While the next generations of Italian poets are no longer linked to the Sicilian court but rather to a city on the Italian mainland, their professional and social status continues to provide insights into their exposure to Latin literature. In Roberto Antonelli and Simonetta Bianchini's formulation, those Italian poets were well-off citizens — merchants, bankers, judges — important to the economic and political city life, often professionally trained in rhetoric,

---

116 On the Sicilians writing poetry as a secondary occupation or complementary activity, in contrast with the troubadours, their literary predecessors, who wrote poetry for a living, see, for instance, Karla Mallette, "Rereading *Le Origini*: Sicilian Romance Poetry and the Language of Natural Philosophy," in *The Kingdom of Sicily, 1100–1250: A Literary History* (Philadelphia: University of Pennsylvania Press, 2005), 65–83, at 75; and Roberto Antonelli and Simonetta Bianchini, "Dal *clericus* al Poeta," in Asor Rosa, *Produzione e consumo*, 171–229, especially at 182–83.

117 Wieruszowski, "Rhetoric and the Classics in Italian Education," 606–10; *I poeti della Scuola siciliana*. Vol. 1, *Giacomo da Lentini*, ed. Roberto Antonelli (Milan: Mondadori, 2008), xlvii–xlix.

118 Petrucci, "Le biblioteche antiche," 532 and n. 1.

119 Quoted in Wieruszowski, "Rhetoric and the Classics in Italian Education," 609.

120 Antonelli and Bianchini, "Dal *clericus* al Poeta," 186–87.

and writing poetry in the vernacular "for pleasure and prestige."[121] Antonelli and Bianchini listed Brunetto Latini as a prime example: Latini was indeed involved in both city politics and rhetoric, which intertwined in his functions as notary and magistrate. Notaries were often also active as private teachers,[122] and based on Dante's portrayal of Latini in *Inf.* 15, early commentators considered him Dante's teacher, even though no evidence exists that Latini was ever active as a teacher of rhetoric.[123] Latini also wrote poetry (his *Tesoretto* and its featuring of Ovid opened this book) but mostly prose: notable are his *Rettorica*, a partial translation of Cicero's *De inventione* in Italian, and the *Tresor*, his encyclopedic work in French. A familiar question returns: Were Latini's works based on their author's direct knowledge of Ovid's Latin poems, or were they based on rather fragmented Ovidian sources, such as anthologies, compendia, rhetorical and other treatises as well?[124] For a figure like Latini, involved in city politics or administration and writing in Latin and in the vernacular, the knowledge of the proverbial Ovid can be safely considered the lower bound of his familiarity with the Ovidian tradition.

In the cities of the Italian mainland also emerged the figure of the *giurista-poeta*, a figure with roots at Frederick's Sicilian court.[125] A thorough command of Latin was a prerequisite for the study of the law, and the education leading up to university could include Ovid's poems in a variety of forms. Guido Guinizzelli fits the profile of the jurist-poet, as does Cino da Pistoia, both trained in law in Bologna. A younger Cino is known to have studied with the grammarian Francesco da Colle, who "provided excellent instruction in grammar and the classics."[126] As Luigi Chiappelli has shown, Cino's legal writing contains several citations from classical authors.[127] Rustico Filippi, fellow poet

---

121 Antonelli and Bianchini, "Dal *clericus* al Poeta," 189: "Il poeta in volgare, complessivamente considerato, si qualifica come un cittadino benestante (mercante, finanziere, o dotato di qualche rendita, soprattutto uomo di legge), importante nella vita economica e politica cittadina, frequentatore per diletto e per prestigio, ma spesso con alte capacità retoriche di tipo professionale, della lirica volgare."
122 Ronald Witt, "What Did Giovannino Read and Write? Literacy in Early Renaissance Florence," *I Tatti Studies in the Italian Renaissance* 6 (1995): 83–114, at 89–91.
123 Robert Black, "Education," in *Dante in Context*, ed. Zygmunt G. Barański and Lino Pertile (Cambridge: Cambridge University Press, 2015), 260–76, at 271.
124 On Latini's familiarity with the classical authors found in his works, see also n. 91.
125 Antonelli and Bianchini, "Dal *clericus* al Poeta," 186.
126 Christopher Kleinhenz, "Cino da Pistoia," in Kleinhenz, *Medieval Italy*, 1: 225.
127 Luigi Chiappelli, "Appunti sul valore culturale dell'opera di Cino da Pistoia," *Bullettino Storico Pistoiese* 39 (1937): 31–39. See also Leyla M. G. Livraghi, "Due usi di Ovidio a confronto in Cino da Pistoia lirico (*Se mai leggesti versi de l'Ovidi* & *Amor, che viene armato a doppio dardo*)," *Arzanà* 19 (2017): 9–22, at 11.

and friend of Brunetto Latini, is known to have been the teacher of Jacopo da Leona, an Arretine notary, jurist, and poet.[128] In *Comune perta fa comune dolore* (Egidi XLVI), a poem Guittone d'Arezzo wrote after Jacopo's death, Guittone praised all his talents: Jacopo was truly a "good poet" (v. 17), who wrote also in French and Occitan (v. 20), a gifted singer and player (v. 23), and an excellent speaker (vv. 24–25).[129]

The writings of Dante more firmly establish his familiarity with classical literature than his professional or political involvement. Other than some brief comments by Dante himself and his biographers, we possess no further documentation on his educational background or access to the classics. The state of education in Dante's Florence is better understood: there was no university in the city, but at least three monastic *studia* or schools of higher learning (Santa Croce, Santa Maria Novella, and Santo Spirito) were operational, in addition to the elementary and secondary schools.[130] While Charles T. Davis noted that a widespread interest in the classics came late to Florence compared to other Italian cities,[131] several classical authors were available at these schools' libraries

---

128 Joan H. Levin, "Rustico Filippi," in Kleinhenz, *Medieval Italy*, 2: 992–93.

129 *Comune perta fa comune dolore*, vv. 17–28: "Tu, frate mio, vero bon trovatore / in piana e 'n sottile rima e 'n cara / e in soavi e saggi e cari motti, / francesca lingua e proenzal labore / piú dell'artina è bene in te, che chiara / la parlasti e trovasti in modi totti. / Tu sonatore e cantator gradivo, / sentitor bono e parlador piacente, / dittator chiaro e avenente, eretto / adorno e bello spetto, / cortese lingua e costumi avenenti / piacenteri e piacenti."

130 On education in Florence during Dante's time and on Dante's education and library, see especially Charles T. Davis, "Education in Dante's Florence," in *Dante's Italy, and Other Essays* (Philadelphia: University of Pennsylvania Press, 1984), 137–65; Davis, "The Florentine *Studia* and Dante's 'Library,'" in *'The Divine Comedy' and the Encyclopedia of Arts and Sciences: Acta of the International Dante Symposium, 13–16 November 1983, Hunter College, New York*, ed. Giuseppe Di Scipio and Aldo Scaglione (Amsterdam: John Benjamins Publishing Company, 1988), 339–66; Luciano Gargan, "Per la biblioteca di Dante," *Giornale storico della letteratura italiana* 186 (2009): 161–93; also in Gargan, *Dante, la sua biblioteca e lo Studio di Bologna* (Rome: Antenore, 2014), 3–36; Raffaella Zanni, "Una ricognizione per la biblioteca di Dante in margine ad alcuni contributi recenti," *Critica del testo* 17, no. 2 (2014): 161–204; and Black, "Education." On education practices in Italy in the Middle Ages and Renaissance, see Paul F. Grendler, *Schooling in Renaissance Italy: Literacy and Learning, 1300–1600* (Baltimore: Johns Hopkins University Press, 1989); and Black, *Humanism and Education in Medieval and Renaissance Italy*.

131 A common point of comparison is Padua, already mentioned a few times as a center of classical learning, and scholars such as Lovato dei Lovati, Albertino Mussato, and Geremia da Montagnone, all roughly contemporaries of Dante, who manifested their interest in the classical world and Ovid specifically in manuscript collecting (Lovati uncovered Ovid's *Ibis*), the writing of Latin poetry (Lovati and Mussato's poetry shows the influence of Ovid), or compilation of knowledge from the classics (Geremia's *Compendium* included several citations from Ovid's works).

and at private libraries.[132] Inventories of the libraries at Santa Croce and Santa Maria Novella document a wide range of books, but little or no Latin poetry.[133] Davis already cautioned that the presence of certain books in Florentine libraries did not mean that Dante, a layman, would have access to them — their use was restricted to the monks, often even to individual monks.[134] At the same time, we know that the monastic schools were open to laymen, who could attend the *disputationes* or structured theological debates, and of course listen to the sermons, where, as we have seen before, a rare quotation from Ovid could appear.[135] Based on Dante's own words in his treatise *Convivio*, he probably attended debates at these schools, places to be introduced to and schooled in biblical exegesis, theology, philosophy, and Aristotle — but not Ovid.[136]

Dante was a reader of classical authors, as he tells us himself in the *Convivio*: after Beatrice's death (in 1290) he turned to Boethius's *Consolation of Philosophy* (a widely circulating and very popular school text, even though Dante claims otherwise)[137] and Cicero's *De amicitia*. At first he read these texts with difficulty, but "finally got into them as much as [his] command of Latin and a small

---

132 Davis, "Education in Dante's Florence," 141, 143, and 146.
133 Giuseppina Brunetti and Sonia Gentili, "Una biblioteca nella Firenze di Dante: i manoscritti di Santa Croce," in *Testimoni del vero: Su alcuni libri in biblioteche d'autore*, ed. Emilio Russo (Rome: Bulzoni, 2000), 21–55; Sonia Gentili and Sylvain Piron, "La bibliothèque de Santa Croce," in *Frontières des savoirs en Italie à l'époque des premières universités (XIIIe–XIVe siècles)*, ed. Joël Chandelier and Aurélien Robert (Rome: École française de Rome, 2015), 481–507, at 491–507; Davis, "The Florentine *Studia*," 352–53; Gabriella Pomaro, "Censimento dei manoscritti della Biblioteca di S. Maria Novella, Parte I, Origini e Trecento," *Memorie Domenicane*, n.s. 11 (1980): 325–470.
134 See, for instance, Davis, "The Florentine *Studia*," 343–44, 353.
135 See, for instance, Davis, "The Florentine *Studia*," 339, 353.
136 In the *Convivio*, Dante wrote that after Beatrice's death (in 1290) he started to go to the schools of the religious orders and the disputations of the philosophers ("[le] scuole delli religiosi e … [le] disputazioni delli filosofanti") for a period of perhaps thirty months (*Conv.* II XII 7). This sentence continues to spark critical debate about the location of these schools (in Florence or Bologna), the meaning of "filosofanti" and the identity of the teachers, the precise nature of this "schooling," and its influence on Dante's thinking: Zygmunt Barański deplored that "few other passages in Dante … occasioned as much unsatisfactory scholarship as this phrase" in "On Dante's Trail," *Italian Studies* 72 (2017): 1–15, at 11.
137 "quello non conosciuto da molti libro di Boezio" ("that book of Boethius, not known by many" [*Conv.* II XII 2]). On Dante's statement, see Black, "Education," 269–70. On the use of Boethius's *Consolation* in the Florentine classrooms, see Robert Black and Gabriella Pomaro, *La 'Consolazione della filosofia' nel Medioevo e nel Rinascimento italiano: libri di scuola e glosse nei manoscritti fiorentini / Boethius's 'Consolation of Philosophy' in Italian Medieval and Renaissance Education: Schoolbooks and Their Glosses in Florentine Manuscripts* (Florence: SISMEL-Edizioni del Galluzzo, 2000).

part of his intellect allowed [him] to" ("finalmente v'entrai tanto entro, quanto l'arte di gramatica ch'io avea e un poco di mio ingegno potea fare" [*Conv.* II XII 4]). That Dante would read Boethius and Cicero only in his twenties and initially with difficulty suggests that he did not go through sustained formal education in reading and writing Latin as a young boy.[138] And since Dante does not provide more information about his readings or schooling, the references to Latin authors in his works become the main guide. At first glance, there is a marked difference between the *Vita nuova* and the poetry written before 1302, the year of his exile from Florence, and the works Dante wrote in exile, the *Commedia* and especially the treatises *Convivio, De vulgari eloquentia,* and *De monarchia* (which Luciano Gargan aptly described as "books written with other books").[139] In the following chapters, I will analyze what precisely these works can tell us about Dante's reading of Ovid. But it is clear that Dante's wanderings in exile meant increased access and contact with the northern Italian world and its well-stocked libraries.[140]

Interest in Dante's life greatly exceeds the biographizing of the other Italian poets mentioned thus far.[141] And yet only Petrarch truly ends the need to mainly make assumptions and speculations about Italian poets' education and exposure to Ovidian sources based on biographical information (their professional and social status) or any available textual witnesses (their poetry). As I will disucss in detail in Ch. 5.1, Petrarch volunteers all this information himself, revealing, for instance, when and where he first read Ovid and which poems, and annotating part of the *Metamorphoses* in his own hand. But this remarkable difference between Petrarch and the Italian poets before him does not mean our focus on reading is misguided or misplaced. As we already saw in the exchange between Cino and Onesto and will see repeatedly from Chapter 2 on, the Italian poets themselves lead us to such questions: when they do not mention reading *Ovidio*, their poems do so for them. In the following section, then, I turn to the question of what makes a poem "Ovidian" and how the Italian readers of Ovid turned writers will be studied in this book.

---

138   Black, "Education," 267.
139   Gargan, "Per la biblioteca di Dante," 174 ("libri scritti con i libri"), 181 ("libro costruito in gran parte con altri libri").
140   A point frequently made, for instance in Gargan, "Per la biblioteca di Dante," 161; Witt, *In the Footsteps of the Ancients*, 214, 219; Zanni, "Una ricognizione per la biblioteca di Dante," 164; Barański, "On Dante's Trail," 14.
141   On the recent biographical and historicizing turn in Dante Studies, see the Forum on this topic in *Dante Studies* 136 (2018) with Elisa Brilli's introduction "Dante's Biographies and Historical Studies: An *Ouverture*" (122–43) and contributions from Manuele Gragnolati, Elena Lombardi, Giorgio Inglese, Giuliano Milani, Paolo Pellegrini, Jean-Claude Schmitt, Mirko Tavoni, and David Wallace (143–231).

1.3 Beyond Intertextuality? How to Think about Ovid's Influence

Influence, inspiration, imitation, emulation. Intertextuality, allusions, references, translation, rewriting, and adaptation. There is no shortage of terms to label the many instances when one author does something with the work of another in his writing, when one text has something to do with another. The road from author A to author B, from text A to text B, is hardly ever linear, and all the more meandering when author B is composing text B during the Middle Ages, and the contours of author A and text A — in our case, Ovid and the Ovidian tradition — are blurry, to say the least. There is only so much linking we can do between Italian poets and their Ovidian sources, as pointed out in the previous section, and this exercise is complicated by the always-changing and ubiquitous nature of the Ovidian tradition: in theory, an Italian poet could be responding to Ovid's Latin poems and the many Ovid-inspired works in Latin or in the vernacular, dating from late antiquity up to his own times. Moreover, as Mary Carruthers has argued, the role of memory is significant in the life of the medieval reader, who is, to put it in contemporary phrasing, not concerned with correct citation practices or plagiarism.[142] Thus, if we can determine only to some degree of certainty what the sources of a certain poet were and whether he was working with Ovid's original Latin texts or not, what is the added value of formulating precise definitions to explain the relationship between the source text (text A) and target text (text B)? And if there are different Ovidian sources in play, how can we determine which of these are more important or relevant than others?[143]

While this book's ultimate goal is to formulate an approach for the study of Ovid in the Italian Due- and Trecento, it is helpful to start with Dante: only Dante's extensive use of Ovid, which greatly exceeds that of any other medieval Italian poet before him, prompted the formulations of several approaches and methods to organize and define this vast amount of Ovidian material.[144] The most structured way to do so is in the form of a concordance: Gioachino

---

142 Mary Carruthers, *The Book of Memory: A Study of Memory in Medieval Culture*, 2nd ed. (Cambridge: Cambridge University Press, 2008).

143 Don Fowler described these two questions as traditional controversies in the study of allusion in classical literature. These questions basically are: How can one say that the author of text A when writing a passage of text A had text B in mind? And how can we determine whether in a particular passage source text A is more important than source text B? See "On the Shoulders of Giants: Intertextuality and Classical Studies," *Materiali e discussioni per l'analisi dei testi classici* 39 (1997): 13–34, at 15–16.

144 I discussed the history of studying Dante's Ovid in "Digital Readers of Allusive Texts: Ovidian Intertextuality in the *Commedia* and the Digital Concordance on *Intertextual Dante*," *Humanist Studies & the Digital Age* 4 (2015): 39–59.

Szombathely (1888), Edward Moore (1896), and Steno Vazzana (2002) all compiled such lists of corresponding passages, but only Moore discussed the rationale behind his system of organization.[145] In his introduction to *Scripture and Classical Authors in Dante*, he set out to define the nature of intertextuality in Dante's works, identifying three categories: "direct citations," "obvious references or imitations," and "allusions and reminiscences."[146] At the same time, Moore was also the first to temper the importance of this system of classification, admitting that he himself had often hesitated when classifying an entry.[147] Indeed, the added value of these categories is limited in the case of Ovid: with hardly any direct citations,[148] almost all Ovid-inspired lines in Moore's concordance fall under the category of "obvious references or imitations," a broad definition that covers many different uses of Ovid's texts. The category "allusions and reminiscences" is the perfect label for cases of doubt (because it is both general and generous), where Ovid's text is but one of the sources that features a certain classical character or motif. While thinking about such categories might make sense when considering Dante (who frequently translates or paraphrases Ovid's Latin verses in the *Commedia*) and also for Petrarch (who did the same in his *Canzoniere*), it is hard to find Italian poets before them who worked so closely with the Latin source text.

Themes have been another organizing principle for the study of Dante's Ovidian allusions: for instance, Michelangelo Picone characterized Ovidian myths in the *Commedia* as "objective" (i.e., explaining historical facts) or "subjective" (i.e., explaining the experience of the pilgrim); Madison U. Sowell identified Ovidian myths that run "horizontally" through the cantos and "vertically" through the canticles of the *Commedia*.[149] Other scholars focused on the use of a particular Ovidian character or on the influence of Ovid on a specific canto or series of cantos in the *Commedia*.[150] A common feature in such essays are

---

145 Gioachino Szombathely, *Dante e Ovidio: Studio* (Trieste: Lloyd Austro-Ungarico, 1888); Edward Moore, *Studies in Dante. First series: Scripture and Classical Authors in Dante* (Oxford: Clarendon, 1896), 349–51; Steno Vazzana, *Dante e "la bella scola"* (Rome: Edizioni dell'Ateneo, 2002), 148–51.
146 Moore, *Studies in Dante*, 4, 45–46.
147 Moore, *Studies in Dante*, 46.
148 Moreover, almost all of these "direct citations" are found in Dante's Latin treatises, especially the *Convivio*. Moore only counts one direct citation in the *Commedia*: for *Inf.* 25.97–98 he lists the passage from *Met.* 5.572–88 (*Studies in Dante*, 349, 350, 363).
149 Picone, "L'Ovidio di Dante," 126; Madison U. Sowell, "Introduction," in *Dante and Ovid: Essays in Intertextuality*, ed. Sowell (Binghamton: Medieval & Renaissance Texts & Studies, 1991), 1–14, at 10.
150 See, for instance, the essays collected in Rachel Jacoff and Jeffrey T. Schnapp, ed., *The Poetry of Allusion: Virgil and Ovid in Dante's 'Commedia'* (Stanford: Stanford University

comparisons with the allegorical readings in earlier commentaries on Ovid's *Metamorphoses*. There are two reasons to be cautious about this approach. First, as we have seen the first section of this chapter, there is no such thing as "The Allegorical Reading of Ovid." The approaches in these commentaries vary widely and while the *accessus* or introductions present all of Ovid's works as "belonging to ethics" ("ethice supponitur"), in reality this classification often does not correspond to the actual content of the commentaries. Moreover, some of the commentaries used as point of comparison in these essays are simply not part of the Italian cultural context at Dante's time. For instance, Giovanni del Virgilio's prose commentary and allegories, the anonymous *Ovide moralisé*, and Pierre Bersuire's *Ovidius moralizatus* were all created around or postdate 1321, the year of Dante's death. Nevertheless, these three later commentaries are frequent points of comparison for the study of Dante's Ovid, because they interpret the *Metamorphoses* in a Christian key — especially the *Ovide moralisé*, which introduces this kind of reading for the first time in a consistent manner. But Dante could not have been a reader of the *Ovide moralisé* and the other commentaries, and neither could the Italian poets writing before him.

Lastly, scholars have applied ancient and modern theories of reception in their study of Dante's Ovid and the afterlife of classical poetry in general. One of the first students of Dante to be interested in the relationship between Dante's writings and his readings of classical authors was Giovanni Boccaccio (1313–75).[151] In his *Trattatello in laude di Dante*, he clearly tells us that Dante's education included the study of Ovid. Boccaccio mentioned that Dante not only enjoyed studying Ovid and the classics, but also strived to imitate them, as his works reveal.[152] Boccaccio's notion of "ingegnarsi di imitare" ("strive to

---

Press, 1991), and Sowell, *Dante and Ovid*. For the thematic discussion of Ovid in the Middle Ages, see, for instance, Louise Vinge, *The Narcissus Theme in Western European Literature up to the Early 19th Century* (Lund: Gleerups, 1967), 42–115; Kenneth J. Knoespel, *Narcissus and the Invention of Personal History* (New York: Garland Publishing, 1985); John Block Friedman, *Orpheus in the Middle Ages* (Cambridge: Harvard University Press, 1970); and the essays from "Ovid in Medieval Culture," ed. Marilynn Desmond, *Mediaevalia* 13 (1987).

151   On Giovanni Boccaccio as editor, copyist, and biographer of Dante, see especially Martin G. Eisner's study *Boccaccio and the Invention of Italian Literature: Dante, Petrarch, Cavalcanti, and the Authority of the Vernacular* (Cambridge: Cambridge University Press, 2013).

152   "non solamente avendo caro il conoscergli, ma ancora, altamente cantando, s'ingegnò d'imitarli, come le sue opere mostrano" (1.22). In the second redaction of the *Trattatello*, which was less favorable to Dante's achievements in the vernacular, Boccaccio left out this sentence and only mentions that Dante became "very familiar" ("familiarissimo") with poetry (2.18).

imitate") reads as a definition of "aemulari," used in classical Latin to describe when one poet strives to rival another and imitates him with the goal of surpassing the original. Dante himself had paired the Latin terms "imitari" and "aemulari" in his treatise *De vulgari eloquentia*. Comparing vernacular poets to their classical predecessors, Dante stated that the more closely they imitate ("imitemur") those great Latin poets, the more correctly they write poetry; vernacular poets should emulate ("emulari oportet") their learned poetics, he concludes (*DVE* II IV 3). Should we take Dante and Boccaccio's statements on imitation as prescriptive? Not entirely: as Martin L. McLaughlin pointed out, the notions of imitation and emulation as used by Dante and Boccaccio are not as precisely defined as later in the Renaissance, and overall, Dante is not the kind of poet whose general theoretical reflections always apply to his own poetry.[153] In any case, these two authors, much more practitioners than theorists of imitation, presented notions that are still central to modern scholars' theoretical reflections on how to describe the relationship between two texts.

The first way in which "imitation" is used in modern theories is mainly to distinguish between different degrees of closeness between source and target texts. I already mentioned one such system of categorization earlier in this section: Moore's differentiation between citations, obvious references or imitations, and allusions and reminiscences. The classicist Giorgio Pasquali proposed another system: the "art of allusion" ("arte allusiva"), which distinguishes between allusions, imitations, and reminiscences.[154] While not organizing their systems of categorization in the same manner, Moore and Pasquali's systems share the same basic assumption. Both scholars assume that the citing, alluding, imitating, or reminiscing author of the target text possesses a thorough knowledge of the source text. To be fair, Pasquali wrote about classical, not medieval literature, and Moore developed his system specifically for Dante, for

---

153   Martin L. McLaughlin, *Literary Imitation in the Italian Renaissance: The Theory and Practice of Literary Imitation in Italy from Dante to Bembo* (Oxford: Clarendon Press, 1995), 14–15, 19. On the classical origin of these notions, see G. W. Pigman III, "Versions of Imitation in the Renaissance," *Renaissance Quarterly* 33 (1980): 1–32; and Thomas M. Greene, "Themes of Ancient Theory," in *The Light in Troy: Imitation and Discovery in Renaissance Poetry* (New Haven: Yale University Press, 1982), 54–80.

154   Giorgio Pasquali, "Arte allusiva," in *Pagine stravaganti di un filologo*, 2 vols. (Florence: Le Lettere, 1994), 2: 275–82. Pasquali defined these three notions as follows (275): "Le reminiscenze possono essere inconsapevoli; le imitazioni, il poeta può desiderare che sfuggono al pubblico; le allusioni non producono l'effetto voluto che non su un lettore che si ricordi chiaramente del testo cui si riferiscono" ("Reminiscences could be unconscious, the poet could wish that imitations escape the reader's notice, and allusions do not produce the desired effect unless the reader clearly remembers to which text they refer").

whom this assumption generally stands. But for many medieval poets included in this study, we do not possess the same certainty that they were working with Ovid's Latin text. Moreover, this kind of approach does not take into consideration the possibility that all of them, including Dante and later Petrarch, were working with more than one Ovidian source, including "filtered" Ovidian sources as well. It is hard to define "closeness" between two texts if one of these texts ("Ovid") in fact consists of many works.

The focus on defining the relationship between source and target texts as precisely as possible could turn the search for the source text into the ultimate goal of the research process instead of the starting point for further discussion. Opposing this detective-like approach to the study of imitation, the classicist Gian Biagio Conte proposed that we examine instead how imitation of the source text creates new poetic meaning in the target text.[155] Considering imitation to function as a rhetorical trope, Conte distinguished two modes of imitation: integration, where the allusion to the source text blends into the new text (imitation as a metaphor), and reflection, which instead explicitly calls attention to the presence of the imitation (imitation as a simile).[156] Conte's approach to imitation shifts the focus from the citing, alluding, or imitating author to the text. The text, Conte explained, simply cannot be read outside the context of other texts ("poetic memory," as he calls it); its meaning can only be understood in reference to these other texts. In short, intertexuality is an essential feature of literature. Conte found this to be a more helpful starting point for discussion than the focus on the author, which in his view depends too much on reconstructing authorial intention at the moment of writing.[157] While mainly developed for the study of classical literature, Conte's approach

---

155 Gian Biagio Conte, *The Rhetoric of Imitation: Genre and Poetic Memory in Virgil and Other Latin Poets* (Ithaca: Cornell University Press, 1986). Conte aptly summarized the skepticism toward approaches such as Moore and Pasquali's, calling them "comparisonitis" (23). To be sure, Conte's criticism is not directed to Pasquali; while distinguishing his own approach from Pasquali's, Conte is also indebted to his work on the art of allusion (23–27).
156 Conte, *The Rhetoric of Imitation*, 52–95.
157 Conte considered Harold Bloom's theory of "anxiety of influence" an extreme example of such an author-based interpretation (*The Rhetoric of Imitation*, 26–27). Poetic influence, Bloom explained, is not the transmission of ideas and images — that is just something that inevitably happens — but what occurs instead when a writer intentionally misreads his predecessors' work and offers a creative correction. See *The Anxiety of Influence: A Theory of Poetry*, 2nd ed. (Oxford: Oxford University Press, 1997). While Bloom's theory formally excluded poets writing before the eighteenth century, some Dante scholars have explored whether canto 25 of the *Inferno*, where Dante explicitly silences his predecessors Ovid and Lucan, could be read as an example of the literary "anxiety" Bloom described: see Robert J. Ellrich, "Envy, Identity, and Creativity: *Inferno* XXIV–XXV," *Dante Studies* 102 (1984): 61–80, at 80, n. 24; and Caron Ann Cioffi, "The Anxieties of Ovidian

should, in theory, translate to other fields. But when applied to medieval literature, we encounter the same problem as with Moore and Pasquali's approaches. When attempting to reconstruct the previous texts that would create the meaning of a classical Latin text, the classics scholar works with a well-defined corpus; the poetic memory of the medieval author, on the other hand, is not that easy to define and confine.[158] As we have seen in the first section of this chapter, in the case of Ovid in the Italian Due- and Trecento, this is a rather complex and sometimes puzzling exercise.

Some medievalists have looked at Thomas M. Greene's theory of imitation in an attempt to address the uncertainty about sources.[159] Greene's theory may not seem to lend itself to such an end: it was developed for the study of Renaissance literature and clearly contrasts imitation in the Middle Ages and the Renaissance. Greene argued that while both medieval and Renaissance authors imitate and alter their classical sources, the medieval writer nevertheless considers himself part of an enduring community of writers. (One of his examples to illustrate this point is the episode in Dante's *Commedia* where the thirteenth-century poet Sordello, writing in Occitan and Italian but not in Latin, greets Virgilio as the "glory of the Latins" and talks with him about "our" language [*Purg.* 7.16–17].)[160] The Renaissance author, on the other hand, is fully aware of the distance that separates him from his classical past and turns imitation into strategies to reflect the rupture that the passing of time has created between himself and his predecessors. Greene divides these strategies into "reproductive or sacramental imitation" (i.e., reverent rewriting), "eclectic or exploitative imitation" (i.e., the combination of different allusions), "heuristic imitation" (i.e., when the Renaissance text defines itself through the rewriting

---

Influence: Theft in *Inferno* XXIV and XXV," *Dante Studies* 112 (1994): 77–100, with explicit references to Bloom's paradigm at 78–79, 96–97, n. 6.

158   Stefano Pittaluga discussed the issues that arise from applying Conte's "rhetoric of imitation" to medieval literature in "Memoria letteraria e modi della ricezione di Seneca tragico nel medioevo e nell'umanesimo," in *Mediaeval Antiquity*, ed. Andries Welkenhuysen, Herman Braet, and Werner Verbeke (Leuven: Leuven University Press, 1995), 45–58, at 47–48. More recent work on allusion and intertextuality in Roman poetry has provided further breathing room and nuance: see especially Stephen Hinds, *Allusion and Intertextuality: Dynamics of Appropriation in Roman Poetry* (Cambridge: Cambridge University Press, 1998); Alessandro Barchiesi, *Speaking Volumes: Narrative and Intertext in Ovid and Other Latin Poets* (London: Duckworth, 2001); and Lowell Edmunds, *Intertextuality and the Reading of Roman Poetry* (Baltimore: Johns Hopkins University Press, 2001). But the issue remains the same: theories developed for Latin poetry and poets are difficult to apply on medieval vernacular and Latin literature.

159   Greene, *The Light in Troy*, 38–51.
160   Greene, *The Light in Troy*, 28.

of its source text), and "dialectical imitation" (i.e., the strongest expression of the conflict between the two "mundi significantes," the past and the present).

Some medievalists, however, have argued that medieval poets also wanted to address the difference between themselves and their classical predecessors and applied Greene's theory of imitation to do so. For instance, Leslie Cahoon argued that early troubadour poets engaged in dialectical imitation with Ovid.[161] Her work offers a good example of how Greene's notion can mitigate the problem of uncertainty about sources — a problem central to my discussion. Uncertain whether troubadour poets knew the exact verses of Ovid's Latin poems or not, Cahoon instead described how distinct Ovidian themes and rhetorical strategies were used by three early troubadours. By focusing on larger themes and strategies and not on imitation at the sentence level, Cahoon offered a model for scholars to look at larger passages or even entire poems. In that way, scholars can avoid the analysis of isolated sentences — an exercise that promises little return, given the uncertainty about what the precise sources were — and instead develop a more general discussion of the medieval writers' poetics and the ways in which they depart from Ovid's.

Alastair Minnis's work on medieval authorship set up an even clearer formulation of how medieval authors distinguish themselves from the texts of the past.[162] First working with the commentary tradition on the Bible, Minnis illustrated how medieval commentators evolved into authors in their own right. (Recall St. Bonaventure's conclusion that Peter Lombard was indeed the *auctor* of his *Book of Sentences,* discussed at the beginning of this chapter.) Where commentators first established themselves as authors in their writing on biblical texts, Minnis explained, they later did the same for classical literature, and eventually turned to writing about vernacular authors. Rita Copeland further developed this argument by looking specifically at medieval vernacular translation from Latin.[163] Her Ovidian case study of the French *Ovide moralisé* described but one of the instances where the vernacular author abandoned the role of faithful translator and instead took up the position of an author of a new literary creation. In doing so, the vernacular author placed himself on the literary map, confirming the value of the vernacular over Latin. As mentioned in the first section, Ovid was not translated into Italian until the turn of the thirteenth century, but the relationship between vernacular poets and

---

161 Leslie Cahoon, "The Anxieties of Influence: Ovid's Reception by the Early Troubadours," *Mediaevalia* 13 (1987): 119–55.
162 Minnis, *Medieval Theory of Authorship*; Minnis, Scott, and Wallace, *Medieval Literary Theory and Criticism*; and Minnis, *Magister amoris*.
163 Copeland, *Rhetoric, Hermeneutics, and Translation in the Middle Ages.*

Latin literature should not be limited only to the act of translating Ovid. In this book, I identify other ways in which vernacular poets distinguished themselves from their Latin predecessors, such as mentioning and commenting on Ovid or featuring his stories.

The question nevertheless remains: from which "Ovid" are medieval authors distinguishing themselves? The Ovid of the Latin texts, the Ovid of one of the many commentaries, the fragmented Ovid from the anthologies and other prose works, the Ovid of one of the "filtered" Ovidian sources, or a combination of all of the above? Why does reconstructing this "Ovid" matter? In a theoretical essay on the study of Ovid in the Middle Ages, Ralph J. Hexter argued that the intertextual study that compares one single Ovidian text and one single Ovid-inspired medieval text ignores the literary context in which the medieval text was created — a context that consisted of much more than only the direct encounter with the Latin text.[164] To reconstruct the literary context, scholars need to consider the medieval author of the Ovid-inspired text as a reader and describe his "horizon of expectation." This horizon of expectation — a term Hexter borrows from Hans Robert Jauss's reception theory — consists of all his previous readings, everything the reader already understood about the literary tradition when he encountered a new text. When a reader then became a writer, his work in turn became part of the cultural context for future readers.

As a scholar who worked extensively on the influence of Ovid in the Middle Ages, Hexter fully realized the particular difficulties that the "horizon of expectation" approach may pose. One obstacle lies in determining how precise a description of the elements that make up a literary context ought to be. For example, each manuscript with its particular textual differences, small and large, creates a different instance of reception with potentially no end. How thick should the textual description be? Moreover, since these writers are reading and responding to several literary traditions at the same time, it can be difficult to determine which elements of the literary context are most relevant. In addition to the challenges Hexter acknowledges, we are of course limited in how much of the reading history of each individual poet we can feasibly reconstruct. Thus, we must accept that our efforts will be inevitably incomplete: as Hexter put it, we must "write despite the worries."[165]

---

164   Hexter, "Literary History as a Provocation to Reception Studies," 23–31. Part of the collection of essays *Classics and the Uses of Reception*, Hexter's essay actually set out to discuss the study of the afterlife of classical literature in general, but all his examples and methodological reflections focused on the study of Ovid in the Middle Ages.
165   Hexter, "Literary History as a Provocation to Reception Studies," 30.

To that end, the material, cultural, and historical contexts established in this chapter will serve to inform my discussion of the Italian readers of Ovid turned writers in the following chapters. I will first and foremost use their writings as testimonies to determine which elements of these contexts they considered worth responding to. The most succinct description of this approach is to treat the poets included in this study as readers of their times — the Ovidian tradition, as we have seen, encompasses many different languages, genres, and styles; all the Italian poets included in this book operate in at least two languages, Latin and Italian (and often other vernacular languages and cultures). To establish the most relevant points of intersection, I will look at the sentence level, rhetorical strategies, and overall themes. I am less interested in tropes and motifs, as so many lyric common places are Ovidian in name only. Instead, I examine the Italian poets' choices for certain characters, themes, and elements from the Ovidian tradition as ways to create and further establish their authority as vernacular Italian poets. Central in this approach in the crucial understanding that no Italian reader of Ovid can be studied in isolation: the Italian poets included in this book do not only respond to a highly diversified Ovidian tradition, but also to their fellow Italian readers of Ovid. Dante and Petrarch have been extensively studied as readers of Ovid, but mainly as discrete moments in the history of Ovid's reception in Italy. My perspective in this book is to underline how these moments are deeply connected: Dante and Petrarch were part of an Italian tradition of reading and writing about Ovid. The intertextual approach, where only Ovid's original Latin text and the later poem are taken into consideration, is not sufficient to analyze these Italian poems. I replace this anachronistic one-on-one comparison with a truly historicizing and comparative approach. And only by placing the Italian poetry discussed in this book within the history of reading Ovid in the Italian Due- and Trecento, can we view the wide variety of and versatility in Ovid's works, life, and characters, and in the Ovidian tradition — crucial features to the understanding why Ovid and no other (Latin) poet became a means for Italian poets to explore fundamental questions about their identity and art.

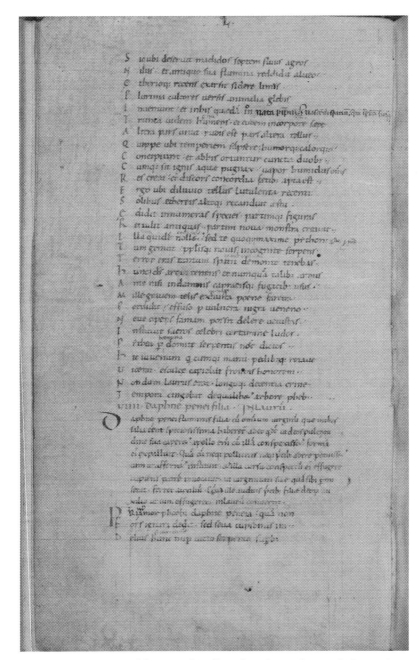

FIGURE 2 Beginning of the story of Apollo and Daphne in the pseudo-Lactantian *Narrationes*. Florence, Biblioteca Medicea Laurenziana, MS San Marco 225, fol. 7v

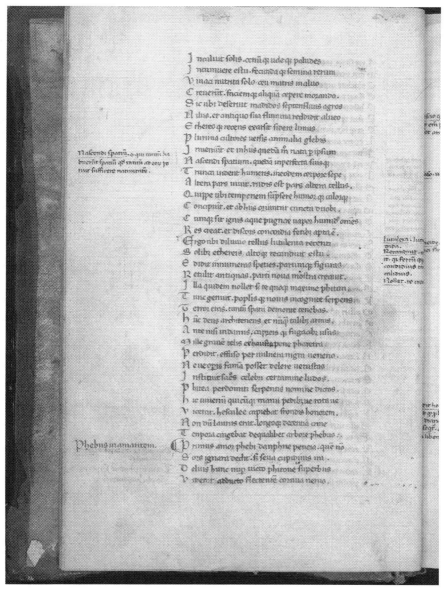

FIGURE 3   Beginning of the story of Apollo and Daphne with Arnulf of Orléans's glosses. Florence, Biblioteca Medicea Laurenziana, MS Pluteo 36.18, fol. 6v

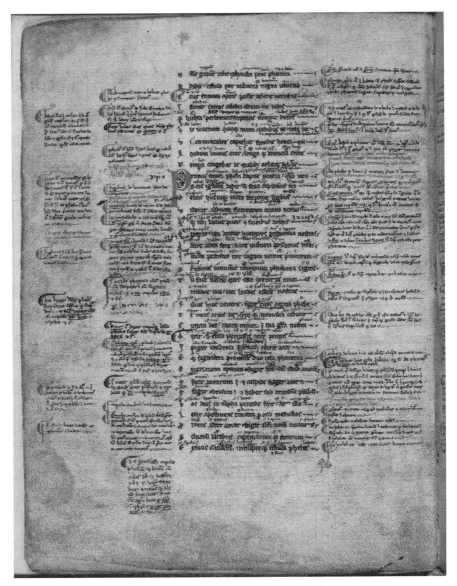

FIGURE 4   Beginning of the story of Apollo and Daphne in the Vulgate Commentary. Florence, Biblioteca Riccardiana, MS Riccardianus 624, fol. 85v

FIGURE 5   Conclusion of the story of Apollo and Daphne in the Vulgate Commentary. Florence, Biblioteca Riccardiana, MS Riccardianus 624, fol. 87r

Description *fig.* 2

In this manuscript, written around the turn of the twelfth century in central or southern Italy, the text of the *Metamorphoses* appears front and central in one wide column with just a few interlinear glosses. Also the commentary, the pseudo-Lactantian *Narrationes*, is not relegated to the margins of the page, but placed in between the stories, visually separated from Ovid's text. After the final verse from the story of Apollo and Python, we see the *titulus* (in red) indicating the number of the transformation (the ninth of Book 1), the name of who undergoes the change ("Daphne, the daughter of Peneus"), and her transformation into a laurel tree ("in laurem"). What follows are eight lines of prose from the *argumenta*, with slightly-indented prose filling the entire lines. The beginning of Ovid's story of Apollo and Daphne is marked with the first letter of the opening verse in a red large capital P. As also noted earlier in this chapter, the prose commentary and minimal glosses do not really take the focus away from Ovid's verses.

Description *fig.* 3

This fourteenth-century manuscript contains the philological glosses of Arnulf of Orléans's commentary on the *Metamorphoses*. Like in MS San Marco 225 (*fig.* 2), one of the manuscripts with the pseudo-Lactantian commentary, the text of Ovid's poem appears in one column, dominating the page. A red paragraph sign next to the verse "Primus amor phebi ..." marks the beginning of the story, as well as the marginal note, also in red, which summarizes the transformation told in this story: "Phebus in amantem" ("Phoebus [transformed] into a lover"). Arnulf of Orléans's commentary appeared in different ways in manuscripts: the glosses that appear on this page in the margins — underlined phrases from Ovid's poem introducing a brief note on the passage in question — were in other manuscripts all collected in a separate section (see n. 29). Each of these formats creates a different reading experience. In this particular manuscript, the minimal glosses barely distract from the main feature: Ovid's Latin verse.

Description *fig.* 4

This manuscript contains the Vulgate Commentary on the *Metamorphoses*. Among the three manuscripts here discussed, this thirteenth-century copy of the Vulgate has by far the "busiest" *mise-en-page* or layout. The text of Ovid's poem appears in the middle of the page with copious interlinear glosses, and is flanked by columns of longer glosses on the left and the right. The beginning of the story of Apollo and Daphne is marked with a large capital P.

Description *fig.* 5

In the same manuscript containing the Vulgate Commentary on the *Metamorphoses* (*fig.* 4), the moral explanation of Apollo and Daphne appears toward the end of the story, placed to the right of Ovid's text, as part of the columns with glosses to the poem. This particular gloss is longer and appears more prominently on the page: in contrast to the shorter notes above and beneath, presented in smaller text blocks next to each other, this longer note appears in one block of text, occupying the entire marginal space to the right of Ovid's poem.

PART 2

Readers as Writers

∴

CHAPTER 2

Examples (Not) to Follow: The First Italian Ovidian Poems and Their Occitan Models

Ovid was widely read in medieval Italy. The previous chapter discussed the cultural and intellectual milieus in which this occurred and the different forms Ovidian texts could take. Reading Ovid, for instance, could mean learning Latin using his poems, or finding Ovidian excerpts in *florilegia* and prose writings, or reading other poetic works, Ovidian in inspiration, and so on — the thematic and generic variety of Ovid's works and the even greater variety and range of their medieval artistic afterlives (in different languages, genres, modes of interpretation) mean that the intertwined paths of transmission and inspiration are often hard to untangle. While the previous chapter provided an introduction to these texts and contexts, in the present chapter I shift the focus from reading to writing: from "Italian readers of Ovid" to "Italian writers about Ovid." In the previous chapter, we have seen that the acts of reading and writing are closely connected: the scribe, compiler, commentator, and author (the four different "makers of books" in St. Bonaventure's definition) are first and foremost readers of the works they transmit; and among the many texts where Italian readers could encounter Ovid were medieval works of poetry in Latin, Occitan, and Old French, considered "Ovidian" because of some kind of contact with or inspiration from Ovid's works. Thus, when we ask how important Ovid was as a model and source of inspiration for the Italian poets writing poetry in the vernacular for the first time, this question needs to be accompanied by another: which Ovid are we talking about?

In addressing these questions for the first generations of Italian poets, in this chapter I identify the crucial role of Occitan poetry — another vernacular literature which flourished before the birth of Italian literature, and which in many ways offered the Italian poets an example to adopt and alter Ovidian material. Because many Italian poets had access to Ovid's writings in Latin, their choices of which Ovidian sources to follow thus reflect artistic preferences, and at times become forceful statements about the status of vernacular poetry. The previously used phrase "Italian writers about Ovid" is to be taken literally: several among the first Italian poets are self-declared readers of *Ovidio* (the Italian name of the Latin poet) who write about these readings in their poems. In this chapter, I explore the poetic implications of including Ovid in Italian verse, how it is similar to and differs from their Occitan models, and how *Ovidio* became a shared point of reference for a wide variety of poetic concerns.

Ovid's Latin love poetry had long been an example for later love poets. As we will see in this chapter, medieval Italian poets mention *Ovidio* in their discussions about how to write poetry, held in sonnet exchanges, and feature him as the emblem of the kind of poetry they write or no longer wish to write. They treat Ovid's *Metamorphoses* similarly. By means of the simile, Italian poets feature a select group of Ovidian characters to underline their own exceptionality: the poet is similar to the male Ovidian character (but better), his lady to the female (but more beautiful), and he loves this lady like the male Ovidian character loved his (but more). In this chapter, I trace these ways of integrating Ovidian material in Italian verse, roughly covering the first three Italian poetic movements: from the Sicilian poets, who started to write poetry in Italian during the first decades of the thirteenth century at the court of Frederick II; to the Siculo-Tuscan poets, their followers on the Italian mainland; and the *dolce stil novo* poets, the innovators of the "sweet new style," with figures such as Guido Guinizzelli, Guido Cavalcanti, Cino da Pistoia, and Dante. Instead of treating each Italian poet and poem as separate moments in the history of Ovid's reception, in this chapter and the following I underline how these moments are connected. Medieval Italian readers of Ovid not only looked at the Occitan models, but also responded to the ways in which their Italian predecessors read and responded to Ovid.

2.1 Better and More: Ovidian Similes in Vernacular Poetry

Ovid was not the first to write about mythological figures, but many times his account in the *Metamorphoses* became the standard version. Yet how "Ovidian" is a character when we find this character centuries later in a medieval text? Certain stories of the *Metamorphoses* greatly inspired readers and writers and reappeared in later writings in multiple languages and genres. As these stories lived on, they were — to use the plainest image in this Ovidian context — inevitably and deeply *transformed*. The two Ovidian stories that are most frequently featured in medieval Italian lyric poetry, the stories of Narcissus and Echo and of Pyramus and Thisbe, have long literary afterlives. In the twelfth century, when interest in all of Ovid's work flourished, the Narcissus theme began to appear more frequently in literature: Narcissus is featured in the French poems *Roman de Troie* and *Roman d'Alexandre*, in the *Roman de la Rose* (vv. 1437–1508), as well as in several troubadour poems, and is the sole subject of the *Lai de Narcisse* (mid-twelfth century).[1] Pyramus and Thisbe also became the subject of vernacular and Latin texts: the French poem *Piramus et Tisbé* circulated independently in the thirteenth century before it was included in its entirety in the *Ovide moralisé*; short Latin poems about the two Ovidian lovers were frequently used in medieval classrooms.[2] At the same time, the Latin text of the *Metamorphoses* was available, often accompanied by Latin commentaries.

And still, with all this Ovidian and Ovid-inspired literature circulating, most Italian vernacular poets mainly looked at the example of the troubadours. They favor the same Ovidian characters, adopt the troubadours' repeated use of the simile to feature these characters in their poetry, focus on the same aspects of Ovid's stories the troubadours focused on, and at times even borrow the troubadours' phrasing. While in most cases it is possible to find affinities between the Italian poems and Ovid's Latin texts, these affinities are often so general that the Latin text of the *Metamorphoses* should not necessarily be considered the source of these characteristics. In contrast, the specifics of the troubadours' treatment of these Ovidian characters are closely connected to the Italian poems, as this section will illustrate. (This Italian adherence to features of Occitan verse is, as a matter of fact, not limited to Ovidian material, or even only classical figures: biblical figures, characters from classical history and romance receive a similar treatment.)[3] Many Italian poets, writing

---

1   On the figure of Narcissus, see especially Vinge, *The Narcissus Theme in Western Literature*; Frederick Goldin, *The Mirror of Narcissus in the Courtly Love Lyric* (Ithaca: Cornell University Press, 1967); Knoespel, *Narcissus and the Invention of Personal History*. For the French poem, see *Narcisus et Dané*, ed. and trans. Penny Eley (Liverpool: University of Liverpool, 2002).
2   For the French poem, see *Piramus et Tisbé*, ed. and trans. Penny Eley (Liverpool: University of Liverpool, 2001); for the short Latin poems, see Robert Glendinning, "Pyramus and Thisbe in the Medieval Classroom," *Speculum* 61 (1986): 51–78. On the afterlife of the Pyramus and Thisbe story, see the bibliographical overviews in Eley, *Piramus et Tisbé*, 80–83; *Piramo e Tisbe*, ed. Cristina Noacco (Rome: Carocci, 2005), 41–45; and Franz Schmitt-von Mühlenfels's study *Pyramus und Thisbe: Rezeptionstypen eines Ovidischen Stoffes in Literatur, Kunst und Musik* (Heidelberg: C. Winter, 1972). K. Sarah-Jane Murray studied how the poets of *Piramus et Tisbé* and *Narcisse* imitated their Ovidian sources in "Rewritings of Ovid," in *From Plato to Lancelot: A Preface to Chrétien de Troyes* (Syracuse: Syracuse University Press, 2008), 48–83.
3   A comprehensive history and study of this practice of comparison from antiquity to the Renaissance is found in Olive Sayce, *Exemplary Comparison from Homer to Petrarch* (Woodbridge: D. S. Brewer, 2008); Oriana Scarpati studied the same phenomenon in troubadour poetry in *Retorica del trobar: Le comparazioni nella lirica occitana* (Rome: Viella, 2008). For Italian inspiration from the Arthurian tradition, see Roberta Capelli, "Presenze arturiane nella lirica italiana delle origini (Pt. I)," *Quaderni di lingue e letterature* 31 (2006): 43–56; "Presenze arturiane nella lirica italiana delle origini (Pt. II)," *Quaderni di*

vernacular verse for the first time, found inspiration in troubadour lyrics — an older and more established vernacular tradition — to write about Ovidian stories for which plenty of Latin sources existed. In other words, when it comes to Ovid, the Italian lyric poets prefer the Occitan *Ovidis* as a source over the Latin *Ovidius*.

The poem *Tant m'abellis e.m plaz* (Bec III, PC 60.23α) by the troubadour Arnaut de Mareuil (fl. 1195) offers a good starting point to analyze this close connection between the two vernacular traditions.[4] The poem is a *salut* or love letter in verse, in which the poet tries to convince his lady of his love for her. In a final tour de force, Arnaut wants to make it clear that no one loves her more than he does — "Q'anc, Domna, ço sapchaz, / Non fo neguns amans / Qe tant be, ses engans, / Ames com eu am vos" ("Because you should know, Lady, that there never existed a lover who loved so much and so deeply as I love you" [vv. 146–49]) — listing a long series of famous lovers that he outdoes (vv. 150–75). This list includes mainly classical figures (Leander and Hero, Paris and Helen, Pyramus and Thisbe, to name the first three couples), characters from romance literature (Floris and Blanchefleur, Tristan and Iseult), and perhaps even biblical figures (the still puzzling couple "Absalon" and "Florissen" [v. 168]). The featuring of famous lovers, the combining of references to different literary traditions, the use of the simile in the form of a comparison between the poet who is or does something more than someone else famous — these are all features that categorize both the Occitan and Italian traditions, although with certain adjustments by the later poets.

The *salut*, the poetic form of Arnaut's *Tant m'abellis*, is one of the many genres used by the troubadours, but not by the Italian poets. Because of its length and its inclusion of a significant amount of learned material (the references to the famous couples take up almost thirty verses in a 201-verse-long poem), Arnaut's *salut* also resembles the *ensenhamen* or didactic poem, a genre

---

lingue e letterature 32 (2007): 17–27; "The Arthurian Presence in Early Italian Lyric," in *The Arthur of the Italians: The Arthurian Legend in Medieval Italian Literature and Culture*, ed. Gloria Allaire and F. Regina Psaki (Cardiff: University of Wales Press, 2014), 133–44. A useful overview of the influence of the troubadours in Italy is Ronald Martinez, "Italy," in *A Handbook of the Troubadours*, ed. F. R. P. Akehurst and Judith M. Davis (Berkeley: University of California Press, 1995), 279–94, with ample bibliographical references.

4 The full reference to the edition used for Arnaut de Mareuil's poem and all other poems cited in this book can be found in the *List of Editions* in the bibliography. At the first mention of a poem, I provide the last name of the editor and the number of the poem in the edition used, and, where relevant, the Pillet-Carstens (PC) or *Indice bibliografico degli autori e dei testi* (IBAT) numbers.

where references to the Bible, the classical world, and romances are common.[5] Italian didactic poems, such as the *Proverbia quae dicuntur super natura feminarum* (written between 1152 and 1160) and *L'Intelligenza* (late thirteenth–early fourteenth century), and longer poems, such as the *Mare amoroso* (1270–80), feature the same kind of learned knowledge and wide range of classical material. But as much as the Italian poets greatly reduced the number of genres and themes they took over from the troubadours in their vernacular poetry writing, they also restricted the amount of classical material. In general, the Occitan poets are more inclined to include a wider variety of biblical, historical, mythological figures and characters from romances, even in their shorter poems. Such richness is not found in the sonnets and *canzoni* written by the Sicilian poets, the Siculo-Tuscans poets, Guittone and his followers, and even most of the *stilnovisti*. Only later poets, such as Cino da Pistoia, Dante Alighieri, and Petrarch, include more references to other literary traditions in their poems.

Thus, in the first decades of Italian vernacular poetry, mythological material is limited and closely linked to the Occitan example. With a few exceptions, the Italian poets' focus is entirely on the stories of Narcissus and of Pyramus and Thisbe, which are also the two favorites of the troubadours. While each Ovidian story has its own distinctive entry point to the vernacular poets, the folly of both Narcissus and Pyramus is a shared feature that allows the poets to explore the nature and effects of love — central questions in their poetry. To think about these two lovers together in this way is not uncommon: in the French romance *Florimont* (1188), the poet Aimon de Varennes explicitly unites both figures in folly in the question, "Volez vos sembler Narcisus / De folie ou Piramus?" ("Do you want to resemble Narcissus in folly or Pyramus?") [vv. 3959–60]).[6]

The story of Narcissus as told by Ovid in the *Metamorphoses* (3.339–510) is actually the story of Narcissus and the nymph Echo. Echo was one of the many admirers of the beautiful young boy, who rejected them all. One of these suitors wished Narcissus would fall in love with himself and then be rejected to experience what he had done to them; Nemesis, the goddess of revenge, granted this plea. Narcissus fell for his own reflection in a fountain, and when he realized what was happening, his madness and despair literally consumed him. The story concludes with his transformation into a narcissus flower near the fountain.

---

5 Pierre Bec noted that *Tant m'abellis* could also be considered an *ensenhamen* because of its high number of learned allusions. See *Les saluts d'amour du troubadour Arnaud de Mareuil*, ed. Pierre Bec (Toulouse: Edouard Privat, 1961), 66, n. 61.
6 Quoted in Vinge, *The Narcissus Theme in Western Literature*, 70.

The Occitan poets who feature Narcissus in their poetry find common points of interest in the story: the moment that the gazing Narcissus falls in love with his own reflection in the water, his madness, and his death.[7] The troubadour Bernart de Ventadorn (fl. 1147–70), a poet known for his negative view on love and misogynistic ideas about women, introduces the figure of Narcissus in his *canso Can vei la lauzeta mover* (Lazar 31, PC 70.43).[8] Bernart features Narcissus in the way most vernacular poets work with material from other literary traditions: in a simile. In the first two stanzas of the *canso*, the poet envies the simple happiness of the lark ("la lauzeta") flying in the sun, which starkly contrasts with the sense of hopelessness that entered his life the moment that his lady stopped showing herself to him, and left him with only a longing heart. The third stanza opens with a further explanation: this loss of control originated from the first time that she let him look into her eyes, that "miralh" or mirror that pleases him so greatly (vv. 17–20).[9] The image of the lady's eyes as a mirror

---

[7] The mentions of Narcissus in troubadour poetry are listed in Frank M. Chambers, *Proper Names in the Lyrics of the Troubadours* (Chapel Hill: University of North Carolina Press, 1971), 195; Scarpati, *Retorica del trobar*, 216; and Sayce, *Exemplary Comparison*, 398–99 (both in the troubadour and Italian poems). Ramiro Ortiz studied Ovidian echoes in the Italian poetry of this period, identifying the stories of Pyramus and Thisbe, Narcissus and Echo, and Daedalus and Icarus as the three Ovidian stories that inspired the Italian poets, in "La materia epica di ciclo classico nella lirica italiana delle origini," *Giornale storico della letteratura italiana* 85 (1925): 1–93, at 1–40. As we will see in Chapter 3, more Ovidian stories can be added. A more recent and complete study of the same classical (not necessarily Ovidian) material is found in Matteo Giancotti, "La poesia del Duecento: 'Se Narcisso fosse vivo,'" in *Il mito nella letteratura italiana*, ed. Pietro Gibellini, Vol. I, *Dal Medioevo al Rinascimento*, ed. Gian Carlo Alessio (Brescia: Morcelliana, 2005), 97–123. Eugenio Savona listed the *stilnovisti*'s references to the classical world in *Repertorio tematico del Dolce stil nuovo* (Bari: Adriatica Editrice, 1973), 398–401. On the figure of Narcissus in Italian poetry, see also Roberto Crespo, "Narciso nella lirica italiana del Duecento," *Studi di filologia italiana* 47 (1989): 5–10. Louise Vinge studied the medieval versions of the Narcissus story in Latin and the vernacular languages in *The Narcissus Theme in Western Literature*, 42–115.

[8] Bernart's *canso* is a classic example of an Occitan poem translated and transformed by later Italian poets. In the *canzone Madonna, m'è avenuto simigliante* (Coluccia 41.2, IBAT 9.5), the Siculo-Tuscan poet Bondie Dietaiuti translates the first two stanzas of Bernart's *Can vei la lauzeta mover*, but replaces Bernart's reference to Narcissus with one to a basilisk (vv. 31–36). On the relationship between Bernart's and Bondie's poems, see the notes of Sergio Lubello, editor of Bondie Dietaiuti's poems, in *I poeti della Scuola siciliana*. Vol. 3, *Poeti siculo-toscani*, ed. Rosario Coluccia (Milan: Mondadori, 2008), 327, 329–32; Aniello Fratta, *Le fonti provenzali dei poeti della scuola siciliana. I postillati del Torraca e altri contributi* (Florence: Le Lettere, 1996), 20–21; and Nathaniel B. Smith, "The Lark Image in Bondie Dietaiuti and Dante," *Forum Italicum* 12 (1978): 233–42, which also discussed Dante's later reuse of Bernart's lark comparison in *Par.* 20.

[9] On the image of the lady's eyes as a mirror and its connections to the myth of Narcissus, see Goldin, *The Mirror of Narcissus*, 92–106; and Sarah Kay, "Love in a Mirror: An Aspect of

in which the poet sees his reflection sets up the remaining verses of the stanza, dedicated to the comparison between the poet and Narcissus (vv. 21–24):

> Miralhs, pus me mirei en te,
> m'an mort li sospir de preon,
> c'aissi·m perdei com perdet se
> lo bels Narcisus en la fon.

[Mirror, since I stared at myself in you, deep sighs have caused my death, so that I lost myself, just as beautiful Narcissus did in the fountain.]

All three main points of interest from the Narcissus story — staring at his reflection in the water, madness, death — are present in Bernart's *canso* to underline the destructive power of love. The creation of a shared experience between the poet and that famous lover Narcissus is one of the ways in which the *canso* moves from the personal to the general and back. We also see this in the following stanza, which opens with an attack on all women, "De las domnas me dezesper" ("I despair of women" [v. 25]), and then moves from the general statement — all women are bad — back to the specific case of his lady, who acts just like them (vv. 33–36). In line with these negative views on love in *Can vei la lauzeta mover*, Bernart's only other reference to literary figures in his poetry again focuses on the pain that loving his lady causes: in *Tant ai mo cor ple de joya* (Lazar 4, PC 70.44), he declares that he suffered more "pena d'amor" than Tristan, heartbroken for Iseult (vv. 45–48).[10]

---

the Imagery of Bernart de Ventadorn," *Medium Aevum* 52 (1983): 272–85. Pointing out the repeated use of the words "mirror" ("miralh" [v. 20] and "miralhs" [v. 21]) and "lost" ("perdet" [v. 23] and "perdei" [v. 23]), applied to Narcissus and the poet, Kay proposed that these parallels in the language act like a reflection in a mirror (277–78). I am following here the text and stanza sequence as established in the 1966 Lazar edition, which takes over the order first found in Carl Appel's 1934 edition of Bernart's poetry. Simon Gaunt suggested a rearranging of the stanzas to better reflect the manuscript tradition ("Discourse Desired: Desire, Subjectivity, and *Mouvance* in *Can vei la lauzeta mover*," in Paxson and Gravlee, *Desiring Discourse*, 89–110). While this rearrangement changes the overall tone of the *canso*, the consequences for our reading of Bernart's use of Narcissus are minimal.

10   Bernart also mentions Tristan in the *tornada* of *Can vei la lauzeta mover*. There, the name is to be understood as a *senhal* (a secret nickname), and not a reference to the Arthurian knight and lover of Iseult mentioned in *Tant ai mo cor ple de joya*. Gaunt provided an overview of the debate on the identification of the *senhal* Tristan in "Discourse Desired," 107–8, n. 4.

The troubadour Peirol (fl. 1188–1222), writing slightly later than Bernart de Ventadorn, also includes Narcissus as a reference point in his *canso Mout m'entremis de chantar voluntiers* (Aston XV, PC 366.21). Just like Bernart, Peirol mentions the same three elements from the Narcissus story: in order of appearance in Peirol's *canso*, Narcissus's love for his own reflection, his madness, and his death. But for Peirol the point of comparison lies primarily in the intensity of their madness — death is what separates Narcissus's story from his own. To underscore that his madness was even greater than Narcissus's, Peirol uses *polyptoton*, the repetition of words with the same root, in the phrase "folley follamen" (v. 19), declaring he was "foolishly foolish" and that Narcissus was not "plus fols," "more foolish" than he was (v. 21). The entire comparison reads as follows (vv. 19–21):

> Mal o ai dig, ans folley follamen,
> quar anc Narcis, qu'amet l'ombra de se,
> si be·s mori, non fo plus fols de me.
>
> [I have said it wrongly, rather I am foolishly foolish, for never was Narcissus, who loved his own reflection, even though he died, more foolish than I.]

Peirol, taking syntactic and stylistic clues from Bernart de Ventadorn,[11] also mentions only the literary figures Narcissus and Tristan and Iseult in his poetry. The Arthurian lovers are included in the *partimen* (a debate poem about a dilemma) with Dalfi d'Auvergne, *Dalfi, sabriatz me vos* (Aston XXVIII, PC 366.10), to help settle the question whether the lover loves more before or after a sexual encounter with his lady. Dalfi claims that love brings "great anxiety" ("grant esmai") after joy: "e membre vos de Tristan / c'ab Yzeut morit aman" ("and remember Tristan, who died of love for Iseult" [vv. 29–32]). Peirol replies that Tristan's feelings of desire came from the potion that Brangain, Iseult's maid, gave them to drink (vv. 34–35), continuing Dalfi's reference to the Arthurian lovers. In the *partimen*, the literary figures are mentioned to corroborate Dalfi's claim that a sexual encounter intensifies all feelings — "membre vos" (v. 31), Peirol tells us: just think of the famous story of Tristan and Iseult.

In both poems, Peirol refers to other literary traditions, but the rhetorical device he uses to feature Narcissus in *Mout m'entremis de chantar voluntiers* is by far the more common way to do so: the simile in the form of a comparison between the poet and a famous literary lover that focuses on one characteristic

---

11 S. C. Aston, *Peirol: Troubadour of Auvergne* (Cambridge: Cambridge University Press, 1953), 23.

of the literary figure (often the one that made him so well known) that the poet possesses more strongly. As pointed out before, through the simile Peirol makes the point that his folly is greater than Narcissus's.

One more Occitan poem features Narcissus, the anonymous *canso Aissi m'ave cum a l'enfan petit* (Gambino XIV, PC 461.9a).[12] Its poet joins Bernart de Ventadorn in fearing for his own life, and Peirol in equating love with folly. Besides these thematic similarities, we also find in the poet's four-verse comparison between himself and Narcissus a stylistic feature that returns in Italian poetry: the placement of the preposition "com" ("like") to introduce the comparison at the beginning of the verse (vv. 12–16):

> car la bela tan m'a vencut e·m lia
> que per mos olhs tem que perda la via
> com Narcisi, que dedins lo potz cler
> vi sa ombra e l'amet tot entier
> e per fol'amor mori d'aital guia.

> [For the beautiful lady has so defeated and fettered me that I fear to lose my life because of my eyes, just as Narcissus, who saw his shadow in the clear well and loved it completely, and in that way he died of mad love.]

This is not the moralistic reading of the Narcissus story that we find in the Latin commentaries on the *Metamorphoses*.[13] Bernart de Ventadorn, Peirol, and the anonymous poet of *Aissi m'ave cum a l'enfan petit* are not interested in the destructive power of self-love or in exploring whether it stands for

---

12   As documented most recently in Francesca Gambino's edition of the *Canzoni anonime di trovatori e trobairitz* (Alessandria: Edizioni dell'Orso, 2003), 147–48, the transmission of this *canso* is peculiar: the Occitan poem seems a source for the German Lied *Mirst geschên als eime kindelîne* by the Minnesinger Heinrich von Morungen (d. 1222), and was first included in the 1858 edition of von Morungen's poetry by Karl Bartsch. The Occitan poem, however, is not found in the manuscript from which Bartsch claimed he transcribed it.

13   There is no consensus among commentators about what Ovid's stories mean. Arnulf of Orléans, for instance, interprets Narcissus as arrogance and Echo as good reputation: Narcissus rejecting Echo then becomes an arrogant person not wanting to have a good name. Narcissus's self-love means that he prefers his own excellence to anything else; his death and transformation into a flower made this arrogance person useless like a flower (Ghisalberti, "Arnolfo d'Orléans," 219). John of Garland, on the other hand, interprets Narcissus's self-love as love for glory in the world, which, like the flower he turned into, will not last forever (vv. 163–66). Giovanni del Virgilio takes a similar stance: Narcissus is a famous person whose love for his own shadow means that he relies too much on fame, and his transformation into a flower turns him into a fleeting object as well (Ghisalberti, *Giovanni del Virgilio*, 53). See also Ch. 1.1.

something else. They simply see the Ovidian boy as the strongest representative of "fol'amor," mad love: in Narcissus's case, mad love of himself; in their case, mad love of their ladies. If this love is vain, it is not because it is directed to oneself, but because of the cruelty of the lady who drives the poet to despair and ultimately his death. These vernacular poets find common ground with Narcissus in the devastating effects of love on the lover.

Moving on to Italian poetry, we first find Narcissus featured in the *canzone Poi li piace ch'avanzi suo valore* (Di Girolamo 7.3, IBAT 60.14) by the Sicilian poet Rinaldo d'Aquino (thirteenth century).[14] Rinaldo's poetic oeuvre, consisting of ten *canzoni* and one sonnet, shows close connections with Occitan lyrics.[15] The *canzone Poi li piace* in particular translates in part Folquet de Marselha's *canso Chantan volgra mon fin cor descobrir* (Squillacioti XVII, PC 155.6), as Antonella Ramazzina has shown in great detail.[16] Rinaldo included his comparison with Narcissus (one of the few literary references in his eleven poems)[17] in the last stanza of his *canzone*, which, together with the third stanza, contains the fewest links with Folquet's *canso*.[18] But the influence of previous renditions of the Narcissus story in Occitan poetry is clear (vv. 31–36):

> altresì finamente
> come Narciso in sua spera vedere
> per sé s'innamorao
> quando in l'aigua isguardao,
> così poss'io ben dire
> che eo son preso de la più avenente.

[just as Narcissus fell so finely in love with himself, when he looked at the water and saw himself in the mirror, so I am sure that I am taken by the most beautiful woman.]

---

14 Ortiz, "La materia epica di ciclo classico," 25, 29.
15 Fratta, *Le fonti provenzali*, 75–82.
16 Antonella Miriam Ramazzina, "'Chantan volgra mon fin cor descobrir' e 'Poi li piace c'avanzi suo valore': due testi a confronto,'" *Medioevo Romanzo* 22, no. 3 (1998): 352–72. Ramazzina called Rinaldo's *canzone* an example of "traduzioni-rielaborazioni di testi provenzali" (352). See also Fratta, *Le fonti provenzali*, 80–81.
17 The two other literary figures, the famous classical couple Paris and Helen, are included in the *canzone In gioia mi tegno tuta la mia pena* (Di Girolamo 7.7, IBAT 60.8): "sì com' Parigi quando amav'Alena / così fac'io" ("just like Paris when he loved Helen, so do I" [vv. 3–4]). Two features of the poem further suggest the Occitan influence on Rinaldo's poetry: the spelling of Helen's name ("Alena"), and the fact that Paris and Helen are featured in a simile comparing them to the poet and his lady.
18 Ramazzina, "'Chantan volgra mon fin cor descobrir,'" 363.

Rinaldo features Narcissus in a simile (as the troubadours Bernart de Ventadorn, Peirol, and the anonymous poet of *Aissi m'ave cum a l'enfan petit* did), which compares the Ovidian boy and the poet. Just like the anonymous poet of *Aissi m'ave cum a l'enfan petit*, Rinaldo places the preposition "come" at the beginning of the verse (v. 32). The manuscripts Vat. lat. 3793 and Laur. Redi 9, two of the three late-thirteenth-century *canzonieri* that contain most of the early Italian lyric poetry, have "Narcisi" instead of "Narciso" (v. 32), a form several editors found suggestive of a French transmission of the Narcissus story via the *Lai de Narcisse*.[19] However, the form is actually closer to the Occitan spellings of the Latin name and exactly how the anonymous poet of *Aissi m'ave cum a l'enfan petit* wrote his name.[20]

Even with all these similarities between the Occitan and Rinaldo's featuring of Narcissus, there also exists one clear difference: Rinaldo's comparison is remarkably different in tone. While the Occitan poets focused on the destructive power of love, turning Narcissus into a poster boy for the devastating effects of "fol'amor," Rinaldo's Narcissus falls in love "finamente" (v. 31), suggesting that the poet's love for his lady is equally "fine."[21] Rinaldo d'Aquino often writes about "fin amore" and the "fin amadore," and in the *canzone Venuto m'è in talento* (Di Girolamo 7.1, IBAT 60.16), he even uses the same adverb "finamente" to directly describe his own love for his lady.[22] This different description of

---

19 *I poeti della Scuola siciliana*. Vol. 2, *Poeti della corte di Federico II*, ed. Costanzo Di Girolamo (Milan: Mondadori, 2008), 171, note to v. 32.

20 In fact, Aldo Menichetti noted regarding the spelling "Narcissi" and "Narcisi" in Chiaro Davanzati's sonnet *Come Narcissi, in sua spera mirando* (a sonnet discussed further on in this section) that these are Occitan rather than Italian forms and referred to the spelling of Narcissus's name in Rinaldo's *canzone*. See Chiaro Davanzati, *Rime*, ed. Aldo Menichetti (Bologna: Commissione per i testi di lingua, 1965), 244.

21 Editors of Rinaldo's poem have commented differently on the meaning of the adverb "finamente." Annalisa Comes, who edited the text of the *canzone* here used, glossed the adverb as "completamente" in Di Girolamo, *Poeti della corte di Federico II*, 171, note to v. 31. Bruno Panvini paraphrased the adverb as "sinceramente" in *La scuola poetica siciliana. Le canzoni dei rimatori non siciliani. Testo critico, interpretazione e note* (Florence: Leo S. Olschki, 1957), 1: 29; and *Poeti italiani della corte di Federico II* (Naples: Liguori Editore, 1994), 155. Rinaldo's use of the adverb "finamente" could be another textual link with Folquet's *canso*, which includes the phrases "fin cor" (v. 1) and "lo plus fin amador" (v. 18), a connection not noted in the discussions of the poems in Ramazzina, "'Chantan volgra mon fin cor descobrir'"; and Fratta, *Le fonti provenzali*, 80–81.

22 "per zo ch'i' l'amo tanto finemente" ("therefore I love her so finely" [v. 39]). The *Tesoro della lingua Italiana delle Origini* (http://tlio.ovi.cnr.it/TLIO/) defines one meaning of the adverb "finamente" as "con purezza di cuore e completa dedicazione (secondo i canoni dell'amor cortese)" ("with a pure heart and complete dedication, according to the canons of courtly love") and uses this verse from Rinaldo's *Venuto m'è in talento* as an example of that meaning. Rinaldo also mentions "fin amor" in the same *canzone* (v. 17). Other instances of the phrase, used to describe love, the lover, and his heart, are found in *Per fin*

love affects the poet in a manner that varies from the Occitan poems: leaving out Narcissus's tragic outcome, Rinaldo is only "preso," "taken" by his lady (*Poi li piace ch'avanzi suo valore*, v. 36). In the Occitan precedents, on the other hand, Peirol turned mad (*Mout m'entremis de chantar voluntiers*, vv. 19–21); the anonymous poet of *Aissi m'ave cum a l'enfan petit* feared to lose his life (v. 13); and Bernart de Ventadorn described that he lost himself and how deep sighs caused his death (*Can vei la lauzeta mover*, vv. 23, 22).

Rinaldo's *canzone Poi li piace ch'avanzi suo valore* is an important intermediary between Occitan poetry and two Siculo-Tuscan poems, Chiaro Davanzati's sonnet *Come Narcissi, in sua spera mirando* (Menichetti 26) and the anonymous sonnet *Guardando la fontana il buo-Narciso* (Coluccia 49.72, IBAT 72.49). The textual and stylistic connections between Rinaldo's *canzone* and these two sonnets, included in their entirety below, are undeniable; in content the Siculo-Tuscan poems rather resemble the Occitan treatments of the Narcissus story in their focus on its tragic outcome.

TABLE 1   Chiaro Davanzati, *Come Narcissi, in sua spera mirando*, and anonymous poet, *Guardando la fontana il buo-Narciso*

Come Narcissi, in sua spera mirando,	Guardando la fontana il buo-Narciso
s'inamorao per ombra a la fontana;	de lo suo viso forte 'namorao,
veg[g]endo se medesimo pensando,	e 'ntanto che lo vide, fue conquiso
ferìssi il core e la sua mente vana;	ed ismarito sì che s'oblidao,
gittòvisi entro per l'ombrìa pigliando,	pensando che 'nfra l'aqua foss'asiso
di quello amor lo prese morte strana;	ed incarnato ciò ch'alor mirao:
ed io, vostra bielta[te] rimembrando	vogliendolo tenere fue diviso
l'ora ch'io vidi voi, donna sovrana,	da tutte gioie, e sua vita finao.
inamorato son sì feramente	Così cred'eo fenir similemente
che, poi ch'io voglia, non poria partire,	poi son venuto a la dolze fontana
sì m'ha l'amor compreso strettamente;	dov'è la spèra di tutte bellezze.
tormentami lo giorno e fa languire:	Volendol'abrazzar, trovo neiente,
com'a Narcis[s]i paràmi piagente,	piango e sospir la fresca cera umana
veg[g]endo voi, la morte soferire.	per cui follezo e pero in gran matezze.

---

amore vao sì allegramente, v. 1, v. 28 (Di Girolamo 7.4, IBAT 60.13); *Amor, che m'à 'n comando*, v. 11, v. 30 (Di Girolamo 7.5, IBAT 60.1); and *Amorosa donna fina*, v. 47 (Di Girolamo 7.8, IBAT 60.2).

[As Narcissus, looking in his mirror, fell in love with the shadow in the fountain; thinking that he was seeing himself, he hurt his own heart and vain mind; he threw himself into the fountain to catch the shadow, and a strange death took him, following that love; and I, remembering your beauty, supreme lady, that time I saw you, am so wildly in love that I could not leave you, even if I wanted to, so tightly has love taken a hold of me. The day makes me suffer and sigh: as it was to Narcissus, it seems a pleasure to me to suffer death, while looking at you.]

[Looking at the fountain, good Narcissus fell deeply in love with his own face and, while he was staring at it, became so won over that he lost himself, thinking that what he saw in the water was a person in the flesh. Wanting to hold this person, he was taken away from all other joys of life and his life was over. I believe I will end in the same manner, when I came to the sweet fountain where the mirror of all beauty lies. While I wish to embrace it, I find nothing; I weep and long for her fresh human face, for which I go insane and suffer in great madness.]

Especially the opening verse of Davanzati's sonnet, "Come Narcissi, in sua spera mirando" (v. 1) seems modeled on a verse in Rinaldo's short Narcissus comparison, "come Narciso in sua spera vedere" (*Poi li piace ch'avanzi suo valore*, v. 32). In addition, the following verse in Davanzati's sonnet, "s'inamorao per ombra a la fontana" (v. 2), stays close to the subsequent verses in Rinaldo's *canzone*, "per sé s'innamorao / quando in l'aigua isguardao" (*Poi li piace ch'avanzi suo valore*, vv. 33–34). The imitation of the Sicilian model is particularly clear in Davanzati's use of "s'inamorao" (v. 2), with the Sicilian verb ending –ao, rarely used by Davanzati.[23] The anonymous sonnet has the same verb " 'namorao" in its second verse as well, placed in the rhyme position, just like in Rinaldo's *canzone*.[24]

While the textual and stylistic connections between these two Siculo-Tuscan sonnets and Rinaldo's poem are clear, their visions on love are firmly in line with the Occitan precedents. Narcissus's example is seen as a tragic one — love can, also for these Italian poets, lead to death: Chiaro Davanzati ends his

---

23 Davanzati, *Rime*, ed. Menichetti, 245.
24 The relationship between Davanzati's *Come Narcissi, in sua spera mirando* and *Guardando la fontana il buo-Narciso* is not clear. The editors of the three volumes of *I poeti della Scuola Siciliana* included the anonymous sonnet in the volume dedicated to the Siculo-Tuscan poets, and Riccardo Gualdo, who edited this anonymous sonnet, noted that while Ramiro Ortiz considered this sonnet later than Davanzati's (Ortiz, "La materia epica di ciclo classico," 23–24), this cannot be confirmed with certainty (Coluccia, *Poeti siculo-toscani*, 989).

sonnet with "la morte soferire" (v. 14), and the anonymous poet concludes by describing his madness, two sentiments heavily emphasized in the comparisons with Narcissus in Occitan poetry. The two Italian poets both construct an entire sonnet around the comparison,[25] which leaves plenty of textual space to explore both the experience of the Ovidian boy and the poet. The two poets go about this slightly differently. The poet of *Guardando la fontana il buo·Narciso* dedicates the quatrains of his sonnet to the description of Narcissus, and the tercets to his own situation, following the traditional structural and content divide between the first eight and following six verses of the sonnet.[26] Not following this traditional division, Chiaro Davanzati instead first dedicates six verses to Narcissus, then six verses to his own situation — in this way their experiences are literally mirrored in the structure of the poem — and unites Narcissus and the poet in a brief concluding comparison in the last two verses of the sonnet. The two poems construct an ample semantic field of pain, despair, folly, and death: "ferìssi," "morte," "inamorato ... feramente," "tormentami," "languire," "la morte soferire" (*Come Narcissi, in sua spera mirando*, vv. 4, 6, 9, 12, 14), "ismarito," "sua vita finao," "fenir," "piango," "sospir," "follezo," "pero in gran matezze" (*Guardando la fontana il buo·Narciso*, vv. 4, 8, 9, 13, 14).

The lengthy treatment of the Narcissus story (at least for lyric poetry) in these two sonnets also invites a closer comparison with the Latin source text. It is not difficult to find similarities. Davanzati's Narcissi and the anonymous poet's Narciso stare at their reflection — "in sua spera mirando" (v. 1) / "guardando la fontana" (v. 1) — just as Ovid's Narcissus did: while alive, everything that others admired in him, Narcissus adored himself ("cunctaque *miratur*, quibus est *mirabilis* ipse" (*Met.* 3.424; emphasis added), and in the Underworld he kept staring at himself in the river Styx ("quoque *se* ... / in Stygia *spectabat* aqua" (*Met.* 3.504–5; emphasis added). Both Narcissi and Narciso fall in love with their own "ombra" (v. 2) / "viso" (v. 2) and try to seize it (v. 5 / v. 7), while

---

25 The extended simile is considered one of the defining characteristics of Chiaro Davanzati's poetry. Even though he uses them both in the longer *canzoni* and in sonnets, the most famous examples are found in his sonnets, which are often entirely constructed around the comparisons, mainly with animals. Aldo Menichetti discussed Chiaro Davanzati's sources, ranging from bestiaries to Occitan poets with a similar taste for animal similes such as Rigaut de Berbezilh, in his edition of Davanzati, *Rime*, xlv–lxi. In fact, the sonnet *Come Narcissi, in sua spera mirando* is nested in a series of sonnets (Menichetti 24–31) that except for the Narcissus sonnet all make comparisons with animals.

26 Teodolinda Barolini illustrated this classic divide in structure and content with the example of Giacomo da Lentini's sonnet *Io m'aggio posto in core a Dio servire* in "Dante and the Lyric Past," in *The Cambridge Companion to Dante*, ed. Rachel Jacoff (Cambridge: Cambridge University Press, 1993), 14–33, at 14–16; also in *Dante and the Origins of Italian Literary Culture* (New York: Fordham University Press, 2006), 23–45, at 23–25.

Narcissus, taken by a vision of beauty ("uisae correptus imagine formae"), thinks he loves a body, but it is only the water ("corpus putat esse quod unda est" [*Met.* 3.416–17]). But while Davanzati and the anonymous poet attribute to Narcissus several qualities that stand out in Ovid's text, by the time these medieval Italian poets were writing, those qualities had become emblematic of the young boy, who was, as we saw before, included in many Latin and vernacular writings.

Ramiro Ortiz has argued that Davanzati's description of the torment and languish that the poet believes to share with Narcissus (vv. 12–14) contains an Ovidian echo of the verses, "nec mihi mors grauis est posituro morte dolores; / hic qui diligitur uellem diuturnior esset. / nunc duo concordes anima moriemur in una" ("death will not be hard for me, as death will take away my pain; I wish my beloved could have lived longer. Now we will die, two souls as one" [*Met.* 3.471–73]).[27] But these affinities between the Latin text of the *Metamorphoses* and Davanzati's sonnet are rather general, and do not necessarily lead to Ortiz's conclusion that Davanzati had direct knowledge of the Latin source. It is much more compelling to read Davanzati's *Come Narcissi, in sua spera mirando* as well as *Guardando la fontana il buo·Narciso* alongside the treatment of the Narcissus theme by Occitan poets, who also feature him in similes and compare his "fol'amor" with theirs, and with Rinaldo d'Aquino's *canzone*, which offers a linguistic and stylistic model. These are concrete and specific similarities, and strongly point to the influence from both Occitan and Sicilian vernacular poetry rather than from Ovid's Latin account of the tale.

Another poem by Chiaro Davanzati also suggests that he was looking at earlier vernacular poems in Occitan and Italian that featured Narcissus rather than Ovid's Latin text. The sonnet *Come 'l fantin ca ne lo speglio smira* (Menichetti 115), a response to Monte Andrea's *Sì come ciascun om può sua figura* (Menichetti 115ª), opens with one of Davanzati's characteristic extended similes, describing how a "fantin" or young boy looked into a mirror and wanted to grab this pleasing image. When he failed to do this, he angrily broke the mirror (vv. 1–8). Scholars have pointed out the textual similarities between this first half of Davanzati's sonnet and the first stanza of the anonymous *canso Aissi m'ave cum a l'enfan petit*.[28] But the second stanza of the anonymous

---

27   Ortiz, "La materia epica di ciclo classico," 29–31.
28   Aldo Menichetti gave an overview in his edition of Davanzati, *Rime*, 355. Menichetti does not identify this young boy as Narcissus nor does he make the connection with Davanzati's sonnet *Come Narcissi, in sua spera mirando*. Francesca Gambino has found metrical reasons in support of István Frank's suggestion that the author of *Aissi m'ave cum a l'enfan petit* could have been a North-Italian troubadour (*Canzoni anonime di trovatori e trobairitz*, 145, 149).

Occitan poem could have been equally interesting to Davanzati: it includes a comparison with Narcissus (vv. 12–16), which, as discussed earlier, shares several thematic and stylistic characteristics found in other Occitan and Italian poems, including *Aissi m'ave cum a l'enfan petit*.

A similar pattern of influence is seen in the treatment of the Ovidian lovers Pyramus and Thisbe.[29] In *Met.* 4.55–166, Ovid tells the story of two young lovers who communicate through a crack in the wall after their parents prohibited their love. The plan for a secret nighttime meeting leads to their deaths: Pyramus, who arrives later at the meeting place, believes Thisbe was killed by a lion and commits suicide; Thisbe, who was actually hiding in a cave after the lion showed up, finds her lover's lifeless body and also kills herself. But rather than with Ovid's Latin original version, the Italian poets engage with the troubadours' treatment of this tragic love story. They highlight different aspects of this story in their poems; for each aspect, we find Occitan and Italian examples.

The main way in which Occitan and Italian poets feature Pyramus and Thisbe is again in similes. They focus on Thisbe's beauty and the depth of Pyramus and Thisbe's love, which several Occitan and Italian poets compare to their own love for their lady. These are somewhat common comparisons in Occitan and Italian lyrics, which feature other famous lovers and other legendarily beautiful women.[30] The purpose of these comparisons is always to stress how the poet's lady is even more beautiful than the women famously praised for their beauty, and to demonstrate that the poet loves his lady even "better and more" than that famous lover. That is exactly how the troubadour Giraut de Salignac declares to love his lady in the *canso En atretal esperansa* (Strempel Appendix 1, PC 249.5): "miels e may / No fes Piramus Tibe" ("better and more than Pyramus loved Thisbe" [vv. 26–27]). The *canso Era·m requier sa costum' e son us* (Linskill X, PC 392.2) by Raimbaut de Vaqueiras (fl. 1180–1205) is one of those poems that include several learned comparisons with legendary figures from different literary traditions — in the case of Raimbaut's *canso*, from the classical world and contemporary romances.[31] One of these references is to

---

29 I base my discussion of troubadour poetry on the list provided in Chambers, *Proper Names in the Lyrics of the Troubadours*, 212, 253; Scarpati, *Retorica del trobar*, 217, 221; and Sayce, *Exemplary Comparison*, 402, 405. For the Italian poets, I follow most of the examples from Ortiz, "La materia epica di ciclo classico," but not his analysis. A similar list of examples is also found in Gianfranco Contini, "Alcuni appunti su 'Purgatorio' XXVII," in *Un'idea di Dante: Saggi danteschi* (Turin: Einaudi, 1976), 171–90, at 185–86.

30 Sayce, *Exemplary Comparison*, 191.

31 Joseph Linskill, *The Poems of the Troubadour Raimbaut de Vaqueiras. With an English Translation of the Poems and an Introductory Study* (The Hague: Mouton, 1964), 151.

Pyramus and Thisbe, and also here the poet claims to love his lady more than the famous lover Pyramus (vv. 9–12):

> Anc non amet tan aut cum eu negus
> ni tant pro dompn', e car no·i trob pareill
> m'enten en lieis e l'am al sieu conseill
> mais que Tisbe non amet Pyramus.

> [Never did someone love in such a high place as I, or love such an outstanding lady, and because I do not find her equal, I set my mind on her and love her, according to her counsel, more than Pyramus loved Thisbe.]

Following this Occitan example in the Italian language, the Sicilian poet Pier della Vigna claims to outdo Pyramus and Thisbe in the *canzone Amore, in cui disio ed ò speranza* (Di Girolamo 10.2, IBAT 55.3). Even though the actual comparison with the Ovidian lovers is limited to the three last verses of the second stanza, the entire stanza can be read with their story in mind (vv. 9–16):

> Or potess'eo venire a voi, amorosa,
> com' lo larone ascoso, e non paresse:
> be·l mi teria in gioia aventurusa,
> se l'Amore tanto ben mi facesse.
> Sì bel parlante, donna, con voi fora,
> e direi como v'amai lungiamente,
> più ca Prïamo Tisbia dolzemente,
> ed ameraggio infin ch'eo vivo ancora.

> [Now if I could come to you, my love, like a thief hidden and not be seen: I would consider it a joy and good luck, if Love granted me such goodness. I would be so eloquent with you, my lady, and I would tell you how I loved you for a long time, more than Pyramus loved Thisbe dearly, and I will love you as long as I live.]

The poet's wish to approach his lady unseen — "like a thief hidden" — resembles Pyramus and Thisbe's plan to sneak past the guards at nighttime for a secret meeting (*Met.* 4.83–92), but perhaps evokes a biblical passage or an episode from the Tristan and Iseult romance at the same time.[32] Pier della

---

32   Gianfranco Contini considered the biblical verse "Dies Domini, sicut fur in nocte, ita veniet" ("the day of the Lord will come like a thief in the night" [1 Thess. 5:2]) a source for

Vigna introduces the actual comparison between the poet's love for his lady and Pyramus's love for Thisbe with "più ca" at the beginning of the verse (v. 15), which follows Raimbaut de Vaqueiras's phrasing in *Era·m requier sa costum' e son us*: Raimbaut had started his comparison with the Occitan equivalent "mais que" (v. 12).[33] Pier della Vigna modified the comparison between the two men loving their ladies somewhat clumsily with two adverbs: "lungiamente" (v. 14) and "dolzemente" (v. 15). He could of course not apply the adverb he used to qualify his own love ("lungiamente") to Pyramus, who died young and tragically; rather, to describe Pyramus's love for Thisbe, Pier uses "dolzemente." In the last verse of the stanza, the poet claims that he will love his lady all the while he lives (v. 16): this statement brings the tragic end of the Ovidian lovers to mind, which, as we will see later, is the focus of several other Occitan and Italian poems that feature Pyramus and Thisbe.

Pier della Vigna's treatment of Pyramus and Thisbe in this *canzone* thus shows close similarities with Occitan poetry, even though his familiarity with Ovid's original Latin story is actually documented. As chancellor of Emperor Frederick II, Pier della Vigna was a prolific letter writer: his *epistolario* consists of 365 letters in Latin, compared to his limited lyric production of four *canzoni*, one *canzonetta*, and one sonnet. In one of these letters (Huillard-Bréholles 104), Pier included the verse "quoque magis tegitur, tectus magis aestuat ignis" ("the more they kept it hidden, the more the fire burned" [*Met.* 4.64]) — a verse in which Ovid described how Pyramus and Thisbe's love only grew stronger after their parents prohibited their love. In his analysis of Pier's letter, Ettore Paratore convincingly has demonstrated Pier's direct knowledge of Ovid's

---

these verses in Pier's *canzone*. See *Poeti del Duecento*, 2 vols. (Milan: Riccardo Ricciardi, 1960), 1: 121, note to v. 10. Contini further referred to Giacomo da Lentini's *discordo* (an irregular poem of Occitan origin) *Dal core mi vene* (Antonelli 1.5, IBAT 27.15), where the poet expresses a similar wish to come to his lady: "Or potess'eo, / o amore meo, / come romeo / venire ascoso" ("If I could come now, my love, hidden as a pilgrim" [vv. 27–30]) — possibly a reference to Tristan, who, disguised as a pilgrim, met up with Iseult (*Poeti del Duecento*, 1: 69, note to vv. 29–30). Tristan and Iseult are also mentioned further on in the second strophe of Giacomo's *discordo*: "Tristano Isalda / non amau sì forte; / ben mi par morte / non vedervi fiore" ("Tristan did not love Iseult that much; not seeing you at all sure feels like death to me" [vv. 39–42]). If Pier della Vigna is referencing Tristan in this *canzone*, this would be another example of the vernacular practice to mix exemplary figures from different literary traditions.

33   Fratta also listed the Pyramus and Thisbe comparisons in both Giraut de Salignac and Raimbaut de Vaqueiras's poems among the Occitan sources for Pier della Vigna's *canzone* (*Le fonti provenzali*, 71), but Pier della Vigna's phrasing resembles Raimbaut's wording much more closely than Giraut's.

writings: he excluded an intermediate source for the Ovidian verse from the Pyramus and Thisbe story and pointed out other quotations from Ovid's *Ars amatoria* in the same letter.[34] But this knowledge of the Latin original source does not enter Pier's lyric poetry in the vernacular: rather than translating or paraphrasing verses from Ovid's text, he opts to follow the Occitan ways of featuring Ovidian characters in lyric poetry. This was a writer familiar with the original Latin texts, who had read *Ovidius*,[35] but in featuring mythological material in his lyric poetry in Italian, he chose an Ovidian story popular in Occitan lyrics and followed the example of previous treatments of this Ovidian story in the vernacular.

The Florentine poet Rustico Filippi (thirteenth century), more known for his comic-realistic poetry, also features Pyramus and Thisbe in *Oi amoroso e mio fedele amante* (Buzzetti Gallarati XVII), the first sonnet of a series of imagined exchanges between the poet and his lady.[36] The connections between Rustico's poem and its vernacular precedents appear similar to those between Chiaro Davanzati's *Come Narcissi, in sua spera mirando* and *Guardando la fontana il buo-Narciso* and previous treatments of the Narcissus theme in Occitan and Italian lyrics. As we have seen there, those two Siculo-Tuscan poets were clearly influenced by a Sicilian precedent (i.e., the language and syntax of Rinaldo d'Aquino's *canzone Poi li piace ch'avanzi suo valore*) as well as by some specific features that were only found in the Occitan poems (i.e., the focus on Narcissus's folly and his death). Rustico Filippi's sonnet similarly shows influences from both Occitan and Sicilian poetry. He makes the same claim to

---

34   Ettore Paratore, "Alcuni caratteri dello stile della cancelleria federiciana," in *Antico e nuovo* (Caltanissetta: Salvatore Sciascia Editore, 1965), 117–63, at 128, 133, 133–34, n. 12.

35   Alessandro Boccia found more Ovidian allusions in Pier's letter collection, calling Ovid "una delle presenze più costanti nell'intera opera di Piero" ("one of the most constant presences in Pier's entire oeuvre"). See "Stile allusivo e interpretazione testuale nell'epistolario di Pier della Vigna," in *Author and Authorship in Medieval Latin Literature: Proceedings of the VIth Congress of the International Medieval Latin Committee* (*Benevento-Naples, November 9–13, 2010*), ed. Edoardo D'Angelo and Jan Ziolkowski (Florence: SISMEL-Edizioni del Galluzzo, 2014), 85–100, at 98.

36   More precisely, *Oi amoroso e mio fedele amante* is the first in the "piccola corona" of five sonnets: the first four are dialogues between the lady (the first and third sonnet) and the poet (the second and fourth sonnet), and the fifth is a dialogue between the lady and the poet in the quatrains, and between the poet and Love in the tercets. See Rustico Filippi, *Sonetti amorosi e tenzone*, ed. Silvia Buzzetti Gallarati (Rome: Carocci, 2009), 165. Silvia Buzzetti Gallarati further called the reference to Pyramus and Thisbe "[r]icercata, e inusuale per Rustico" (166). As indeed Joan H. Levin's concordance confirmed, "Prïamo" and "Tisbïa" are the only two proper names that appear in Rustico's love sonnets. See *Rustico di Filippo and the Florentine Lyric Tradition* (New York: Peter Lang, 1986), 147.

surpass Pyramus and Thisbe's deep love that we found in the Occitan poems and Pier's *canzone*, but this time from the standpoint of the lady (vv. 9–11):

> Amore meo, cui più coralmente amo
> ch'amasse già mai donna suo servente,
> e che non fece Tisbïa Prïamo.

> [My love, whom I love more deeply than ever a lady loved her servant and Thisbe loved Pyramus.]

While the general structure of the comparison is found in both the Occitan precedents and Pier della Vigna's *canzone* in Italian, Rustico's phrasing shows specific influences from both languages. The lady's declaration that she loves the poet more "che non fece Tisbïa Prïamo" (v. 11) translates the language of the Occitan poets (Giraut de Salignac: "No fes Piramus Tibe" [*En atretal esperansa*, v. 27], Raimbaut de Vaqueiras: "que Tisbe non amet Pyramus" [*Era·m requier sa costum' e son us*, v. 12]), although Pier della Vigna did not phrase his comparison with a negation. At the same time, Rustico's use of the adverb "coralmente" to qualify the verb "amare" (v. 9) points in the direction of Pier della Vigna's *canzone*: Rustico's "coralmente" replaces the two adverbs "lungiamente" (v. 14) and "dolzemente" (v. 15) that Pier had used to describe Pyramus's and his own loving in *Amore, in cui disio ed ò speranza*.

    The Siculo-Tuscan poet Chiaro Davanzati, whose sonnet *Come Narcissi, in sua spera mirando* I discussed earlier, also includes the story of Pyramus and Thisbe in his poetry. He highlights another aspect of the story, Thisbe's beauty, which he compares to his lady's beauty in five different poems. Ovid only briefly describes Thisbe as the most desirable girl in the East (*Met.* 4.56), and no Occitan poet praises her appearance (as Olive Sayce noted, comparisons in Occitan poetry rarely focus on the lady's looks).[37] But this does not make Chiaro's featuring of Thisbe less connected to his Occitan models. The Ovidian girl never appears alone in these comparisons: Davanzati pairs her with other women from the classical world and Arthurian legends — the practice of combining literary traditions that we already identified in Raimbaut de Vaqueiras's *canso Era·m requier sa costum' e son us*, and in Arnaut de Mareuil's *salut Tant m'abellis e.m plaz*.[38] In these brief comparisons, Davanzati pairs

---

37 Sayce, *Exemplary Comparison*, 188.
38 The anonymous sonnet *Lo gran valor di voi, donna sovrana* (Coluccia 49.56, IBAT 72.69) offers another Italian example of this combining of legendary beautiful women from different literary traditions: "né Blanziflor né Isaotta, Morgana / non eber quanto voi di

Thisbe with Morgana in *Ringrazzo amore de l'aventurosa* (Menichetti 2, v. 4) and *Madonna, lungiamente ag[g]io portato* (Menichetti XXXIX, v. 8); he mentions her together with both Morgana and Helen in the *canzone Di lontana riviera* (Menichetti LVII, vv. 20–21); and links her with Iseult in *Lo disïoso core e la speranza* (Menichetti 13, v. 7). As in the poems previously discussed, the purpose of these comparisons in Chiaro's poems is to highlight exceptionality: Thisbe and these other women may be classic examples of great beauty, but Davanzati's lady surpasses all.

In all other poems that feature Pyramus and Thisbe, the Ovidian characters are employed to make a statement about the effects and nature of love. We already saw earlier how vernacular poets represented two opposing views on love through the comparison with Narcissus: Rinaldo d'Aquino wrote that Narcissus loved "finamente" and he believed to be an equally "fin amador," while for the other Occitan and Italian poets Narcissus represented "fol'amor." Pyramus and Thisbe are also cast in these two opposing roles.

In the camp of "fin amore," we find the sonnet *Disidero lo pome ne lo fiore* (Menichetti D. 1), whose authorship is uncertain but attributed to Chiaro Davanzati. Part of a *tenzone* or exchange with two unnamed correspondents, this sonnet responds to the opening sonnet *Chi giudica lo pome ne lo fiore* (Menichetti D. 1ª). This opening sonnet states that the inexperienced lover would think love, "amore," is sweet, but soon he will discover that it really is "amarore," "bitterness" (vv. 9–14) — a point illustrated with examples from the natural world where danger also often hides under a pleasant appearance. Refuting these statements and examples in *Disidero lo pome* (vv. 1–8), Davanzati (or the anonymous poet) evokes the Ovidian lovers to settle the matter (vv. 9–14):

> Chi nonn-ha de l'amore 'sperïenza,
> già de l'amore briga non si dea
> e con fini amador' nonn-ag[g]ia intenza,
> ché 'n tut[t]e parti il piato perderia
> e non poria apellar de la sentenza,
> se ne domandi Prïamo e Tisbia.

[Those who do not understand love should not be bothered to experience it, and should not have a case against fine lovers, because in every

piacimento" ("Blanchefleur, Iseult, or Morgana do not possess as much pleasantness as you" [vv. 7–8]).

respect they would lose the dispute and would not be able to appeal the decision, if Pyramus and Thisbe were interrogated on the matter.]

Neglecting the tragic outcome of the story, Davanzati features Pyramus and Thisbe here as judges who make the case for a positive view of love.[39] Davanzati teams up the Ovidian lovers with the "fini amador[i]" (v. 11) — a combination earlier found in the troubadour Peire Cardenal's *ensenhamen Sel que fes tot cant és* (Lavaud LXXI, PC 335.14); in this didactic poem the Ovidian lovers are the first to be named in the list of "li fin aimadór" (vv. 83–84).

The Occitan and Italian poets who do acknowledge the tragic ending of Pyramus and Thisbe focus on the pain and the folly that characterized their love. In the brief mention of Pyramus and Thisbe in Giraut de Cabreira's *ensenhamen Cabra juglar* (de Riquer), Giraut only describes the pain of the separated lovers: "de Piramus / qui for lo murs / sofri per Tibes passion" ("of Pyramus who through the wall suffers in passion for Thisbe" [vv. 166–68]). In the *tenso* or debate poem *Vos qe amatz cuenda donn'e plazen* (Harvey and Paterson, PC 425.1), the troubadours Isarn and Rofian discuss the fate of Jaufre Rudel who had died, like Pyramus, out of love for his lady. Rofian claims that Pyramus, just like Jaufre, acted "with great courage" when he killed himself for Thisbe's sake (vv. 39–40). Isarn counters that Pyramus's love was madness ("follaje" [v. 48]): his suicide was a mistake ("failhimens" [v. 46]) and a more patient Pyramus would have enjoyed a happy life with his Thisbe (vv. 47–48).[40]

In the anonymous Sicilian *canzone L'amoroso conforto e lo disdotto* (Di Girolamo 25.20, IBAT 72.63), the poet does not frame Thisbe's love in terms of madness, but instead focuses on her suicide in an attempt to soften his lady's behavior. The poet's initial feelings of comfort and delight turned into tears and pain after his lady failed on her promise (vv. 1–7). In the third stanza, he features Thisbe's suicide as an extreme commitment to love — she was willing to die for Pyramus — in the hope that his lady at least would offer him some comfort (vv. 15–21):

> Non mi deggia fallir la più cortese,
> né metere in dottanza lo suo core;
> che Tisbïa per Prïamo s'aucise
> e lasciausi perire per amore.

---

39 Ramiro Ortiz pointed out the legal language in the last tercet: "il piato perderia" (v. 11) and "non poria apellar de la sentenza" (v. 12) — a response to the legal language used in the opening verse of *Chi giudica lo pome ne lo fiore*. See "La materia epica di ciclo classico," 9, n. 1.

40 Ortiz, "La materia epica di ciclo classico," 9.

THE FIRST ITALIAN OVIDIAN POEMS AND THEIR OCCITAN MODELS 95

> Adunqua ben poria madonna mia
> un poco tormentare in cortesia,
> per confortare lo suo fino amore.

[May the most courteous woman not abandon me, may her heart not be in fear, because Thisbe killed herself for Pyramus and let herself die for love. Therefore, my lady could easily suffer a bit out of kindness to comfort her fine lover.]

The anonymous poet is not as straightforward with the identification between Pyramus and Thisbe and the "fini amador[i]" (v. 11) as the poet of *Disidero lo pome ne lo fiore* was, but he nevertheless firmly places himself in that category in the last verse of the stanza, calling himself a "fino amore" (v. 21).

If the view on Thisbe's suicide in this Sicilian *canzone* is in line with Rofian's praise for Pyramus's in the *tenso Vos qe amatz cuenda donn'e plazen*, then the Florentine poet Schiatta di Messer Albizo clearly sides with Rofian's discussant Isarn. In the sonnet *Poi che vi piace ch'io deg[g]ia treguare* (Minetti 46ᵇ), part of a long *tenzone* with Monte Andrea, suicide and madness open and close the same verse (v. 14) in the following passage (vv. 12–14):

> (ché 'l vano dir mi mise 'n esta via!)
> sì come Ania, — a Prïamo laudato,
> c'aucise lui per sé. Fec'e' follia!

[So my vain speech led me this way, just as Ania, praised by Priamo, caused his suicide, as love was madness.][41]

The name "Ania" (v. 13) may seem unrecognizable, but the presence of "Prïamo," a spelling of Pyramus found in several Italian poems, and especially the mention of suicide and folly in the same verse make this passage another example of how some vernacular poets feature the Ovidian lovers to express a negative view of love.

That the Italian lyric poets only include Pyramus and Thisbe and Narcissus in their poetry should not necessarily be seen as an indication of their limited knowledge of Ovid's writings, but rather as an artistic choice to follow the Occitan model instead. In one of his letters written in Latin, we saw that the Sicilian poet Pier della Vigna quoted a verse from the story of Pyramus and

---

41   Like the poem, my translation is ambiguous about who or what was madness: Love, Ania (Thisbe), or Prïamo (Pyramus).

Thisbe in Ovid's *Metamorphoses*; in his Italian *canzone Amore, in cui disio ed ò speranza* he featured the Ovidian lovers in ways closely related to Occitan precedents. In fact, longer Italian poetic texts further demonstrate a more extensive familiarity with Ovidian material than the limited featuring of only the stories of Narcissus and of Pyramus and Thisbe in sonnets and *canzoni* would suggest. The anonymous poet of the 334-verse-long Tuscan poem *Il mare amoroso* (1270–80), for instance, still frequently uses the simile — the main rhetorical device used to include Ovidian characters in troubadour and Italian lyric poems — to describe his unrequited love for a beautiful lady. At the same time, he also includes comparisons with animals, Arthurian characters, and the classical figures Peleus (v. 103), Cicero, Orpheus (v. 152), and Daedalus (v. 236). With this wider range of literary material to draw upon, it is not a surprise that the poet of *Il mare amoroso* features Narcissus differently than how the Occitan and Italian lyric poets did. Replacing the use of the simile with a counterfactual conditional, he highlights an aspect of the story that was not covered in the lyric tradition. In *Met.* 3.353–55, Ovid narrates how Narcissus categorically rejected all his suitors; the poet of *Il mare amoroso*, however, believes that if Narcissus were still alive, he would have fallen for his lady (vv. 87–89):

> ch'io penso, se Narcisso fosse vivo,
> sì 'ntendereb[b]e in voi, a mia credenza,
> e non in sé medesmo come fece.

> [So that I think, if Narcissus were alive, he would be in love with you, in my opinion, and not with himself, as he was.]

In the much earlier *Proverbia quae dicuntur super natura feminarum*, a poem with a completely different form and content, we find a similarly wide range of Ovidian characters. The anonymous *Proverbia*, written between 1152 and 1160, contains over one hundred four-verse stanzas of misogynist proverbs, making it the oldest misogynist text in Italian. The poet names Ovid as one of the sources for the many examples that illustrate the mischievous character traits of women, together with Cato (as the supposed writer of the *Disticha Catonis*), Panfilo (after the twelfth-century comedy *Pamphilus*), and Cicero (vv. 71–72). Instead of launching immediately into the actual proverbs, the poet first justifies his misogynist stance by listing the examples of wicked biblical, classical, historical, and contemporary women of which he had heard (e.g., "audito avé contare" [v. 133]) or read (e.g., "en scrito trovato l'aio" [v. 105].[42]

---

42   The majority of the references is to written sources: fourteen references to books and reading (vv. 69–72, 86, 98, 105, 126, 129, 145, 149–52, 161–62, 169–70, 197, 245, 269–76, 347)

Several of the mentioned classical characters are carefully linked to Ovid. This is how Myrrha is included: "La fii[ol]a d'un re, c'Amirai l'om apela, / ço q'ela fe' al pare, Ovidio ne favela" ("Ovid narrates what a king's daughter, named Myrrha, did to her father" [vv. 169–70]). Referring to what seems to be a familiar story to his readers, the writer of the *Proverbia* finds it unnecessary to specify the girl's actions (i.e., pretending to be a concubine in order to sleep with her father) or the name of the Ovidian work where this story is told (i.e., the *Metamorphoses* at 10.298–502). He applies a similar approach when mentioning Tiresias: "Lo fato de le femene volì saver qual este? / Demandai 'nde Terrisia, qé quela sì 'nd'è teste, / qé fo masclo e femena, com' se truova en le geste" ("You want to know the nature of women? Ask Tiresias, since she can testify, having been both a man and a woman, as we find in the books" [vv. 345–47]). In this instance, in addition to omitting the story's source (*Met.* 3.316–38), the poet does not even mention Ovid's name.

At one point the *Proverbia* writer confuses his Ovidian sources: he claims that Ovid tells the story of the Tracian queen Procne in the *Heroides*, while her story is told in the *Metamorphoses*.[43] But even with this one imprecise citation,

---

against only three references to oral transmission (vv. 133, 157, 243). The writer's justification of his misogyny on the basis of these sources is most explicit in vv. 269–76:
"Asai son qe reprendeme   e dis c'ai vilanato
perq'eu quisti proverbii   de femen' ai trovato.
S'eu a lo dì çudisio   stëa dal destro lato,
çascun d'isti proverbii   en libri ai trovato.

En libri ancïani,   qu li poeti fese,
stratute 'ste paravole   ò trovate et entese:
cui à empreso en scola,   se ad altri mostra e dise,
non li pò dar reproço.   vilano ni cortese."
("Many of those who reproach me say that I was rude to write these proverbs about women. May I sit on the right side at Judgment Day, because I have found each of these proverbs in books. In old books, written by poets, I have found and understood all these parables; no rude or polite person can reproach someone who learned in school and shows and tells to others.")

43 The verses read: "La raina Trïesta como lo fiio aucise, / Ovidio ['n]dele Pistole ben lo conta e 'l dise" ("Ovid tells in great detail in his Letters [i.e., the *Heroides*] how the queen Trïesta killed her son" [vv. 161–62]). This is the only instance where the writer of the *Proverbia* mentions both Ovid's name and the title of one of his works, but unfortunately the title and the content are impossible to combine. Adolf Tobler identified "the queen Trïesta" as the Tracian Procne, who killed her son Itys and served him to her husband Tereus to revenge the rape of her sister Philomela, in "Proverbia que dicuntur super natura feminarum," *Zeitschrift für Romanische Philologie* 9 (1885): 287–331, at 302, n. 41. But, as Gianfranco Contini pointed out, there is no mention of the sisters in Ovid's *Heroides*. Instead, Contini suggested the alternative reading "Tieste" or Thyestes, whose sons got served to him in a dish by his brother Atreus as revenge for Thyestes's affair with Atreus's wife (*Poeti del Duecento*, 1: 530, note to v. 161). That story, however, is not included in the

the writer of the *Proverbia* shows a much greater basic knowledge of Ovid's complete oeuvre than any of the later Italian sonnets and *canzoni* that feature just Narcissus and Pyramus and Thisbe would make us believe. That the *Proverbia* poet often refers to Ovidian stories without mentioning Ovid's name or the title of the Ovidian work that contains it suggests that his readers would be familiar with these characters and stories and did not require this complete information. As the many excerpts from Ovid's writings in prose works (treatises, didactic materials, anthologies, and so on) discussed in Ch. 1.1 showed, not only the Ovidian stories of Narcissus and Pyramus and Thisbe were known. But those three Ovidian characters were the ones that the Occitan poets repeatedly featured in their poetry, and the Italian lyric poets, who presumably would have had no problem understanding the references to the many Ovidian characters in the *Proverbia*, decided to follow the literary example of the Occitan poets when writing their own poems in Italian.

2.2   Ovid's Book that Does Not Lie (to Troubadours)

In *Amics Marchabrun, car digam* (Harvey and Paterson, PC 451.1), probably the oldest *tenso* or debate poem in Occitan poetry, the troubadour Marcabru and Uc Catola discuss the nature of love. Marcabru, the moralistic voice in the debate, objects to every positive statement on love from the much lesser-known Uc Catola, identified in other sources as a monk and an addressee of Peter the Venerable — Catola's enthusiastic remarks about love, in fact, date the *tenso*

Heroides either. Moreover, in contrast to the Procne story that is narrated at great length in the *Metamorphoses* (6.424–674), the Thyestes tale can hardly be called an Ovidian story at all, as it gets only the briefest mention at the end of the *Metamorphoses* (15.462). Cono A. Mangieri read the line alternatively as "la raina trista" ("the wicked queen") and identifies her as Phaedra — the queen who falsely accuses her stepson Hippolytus of rape, which leads to the boy's death. See Giuseppe Bonghi and Cono A. Mangieri, trans. and notes to the *Proverbia quae dicuntur super naturam feminarum* (Biblioteca dei classici italiani, 2003), 14, n. 88. http://www.classicitaliani.it/duecento/Proverbia_Contini.pdf. Phaedra is indeed one of the letter writers of the *Heroides* (*Her.* 4), but her letter is a declaration of love to Hippolytus and does not contain the detailed account of his death to which the writer of the *Proverbia* refers ("Ovidio ... ben lo conta e 'l dise" [v. 162]). Therefore, I believe that the Thracian Procne is intended here (the murder of her son is described at great length in *Met.* 6.619–49) and that the *Proverbia* writer is confusing sources. Not referring to this particular passage, Matteo Giancotti also mentioned several instances where the *Proverbia* writer presents different versions of classical stories in "La poesia del Duecento," 108.

before his entry into monastic life.[44] Using first biblical figures to support their claims (an allusion to Eve in the second stanza, a mention of Samson in the fifth, and Solomon and David in the eighth), the discussant Marcabru then turns to a Latin authority, Ovid (vv. 37–40):

Catola, Ovides mostra chai
– e l'ambladura o retrai –
qe non soana brun ni bai,
anz se trai plus aus achaïz.

[Catola, Ovid shows (and goes out of his way to prove it) that love does not disdain blondes or brunettes, but rather clings to the most wretched.]

Marcabru's way of mentioning the Latin poet in this *tenso*, most likely the first occurrence of his name in Occitan poetry,[45] is indicative of all later uses of Ovid's name. Marcabru, not a love poet but a writer of moral and satirical verse, goes after "faus'amistat" ("false love" [v. 6]) in this *tenso* and firmly places the kind of love and lover that Ovid describes in that category, while the troubadours writing after Marcabru are more enthusiastic about the content of the Latin poet's writings.[46] But in every other aspect, Marcabru's featuring of the Latin poet can be seen as the blueprint for his Occitan successors and later the Italian poets. Marcabru's verses become a sort of template for featuring Ovid in poems, consisting of the following elements: (1) the name of the Latin poet placed at the opening of the verse;[47] (2) the use of a verb of affirmation after Ovid's name, such as Marcabru's "mostra" ("shows") or "retrai" ("confirms"), "declina" ("explains"), "dis" ("says"); followed by (3) a general statement about love that at times can be traced back to specific passages in the Latin poet's writings.

---

44   Aurelio Roncaglia, "La tenzone fra Ugo Catola e Marcabruno," in *Linguistica e Filologia: Omaggio a Benvenuto Terracini*, ed. Cesare Segre (Milan: Il Saggiatore, 1968), 203–54, at 212. Ruth Harvey and Linda Paterson were more cautious about the dating and the identification in *The Troubadour 'Tensos' and 'Partimens': A Critical Edition*, 3 vols. (Woodbridge: D. S. Brewer, 2010), 1260.
45   Roncaglia, "La tenzone fra Ugo Catola e Marcabruno," 240.
46   Maria Luisa Meneghetti discussed the exchange between Marcabru and Uc Catola in *Il pubblico dei trovatori: ricenzione e riuso dei testi lirici cortesi fino al XIV secolo* (Modena: Mucchi, 1984), 149–56, and included the text of the *tenso*, identifying in a few words the theme of each stanza (150–52).
47   "Ovides" is strictly speaking the second word of the verse, but each stanza opens with Catola's name, which serves to remind us that this is a dialogue between poets, and has further nothing to do with the content of the stanzas.

For Marcabru's claim that love does not discriminate against blondes or brunettes but simply prefers the wretched, Jean Marie Lucien Dejeanne referred to Ovid's *Ars am.* 1.769–70: "inde fit ut, quae se timuit committere honesto, / uilis ad amplexus inferioris eat" ("Then it happens that a girl who was afraid to commit to an honest guy, gets cheap and walks into the arms of a lesser one");[48] James J. Wilhelm and Luciano Rossi cited *Am.* 2.4.39–40: "candida me capiet, capiet me flaua puella; / est etiam in fusco grata colore uenus" ("A fair-skinned girl will capture me, a blond girl will capture me, and Venus is still pleasing in her dark color").[49] In discussing this passage and its potential sources, Leslie Cahoon has rightly raised the question whether the Latin poet's oeuvre was an actual source for Marcabru — whether Ovid was "anything more ... than a name to be revered as Dante and Chaucer, for instance, revered Homer."[50] Indeed, the connections between Marcabru's verses and the passages from Ovid's *Ars amatoria* and *Amores* can be made, but are not very convincing. How did Marcabru read Ovid's texts, if he read them at all? This is the question that extends to all Occitan poets further discussed in this section, and one that we encountered before in the previous section dedicated to the presence of Ovidian characters in vernacular lyrics — with one important difference. When vernacular poets include Narcissus and Pyramus and Thisbe in their lyrics, we modern readers are well aware of the long and rich literary traditions of these characters, of which Ovid's original Latin account is only one part, and as a result do not consider Ovid's text the first or most obvious source. In Marcabru's case, as well as in the poems that follow in this section, the poets themselves point our attention directly and unambiguously to Ovid by citing him as their source, even though we cannot always easily find that precise Ovidian passage that the vernacular poets seem to have in mind.

But instead of mainly focusing on the vernacular poets' sources — something these mentions of Ovid in Occitan poems surely invite us to do — an additional approach is needed. Whether any of these Occitan poets had consulted Ovid's texts in their entirety or found excerpts in anthologies, memorized and

---

48   The reference is quoted in Roncaglia, "La tenzone fra Ugo Catola e Marcabruno," 241.
49   James J. Wilhelm, *Seven Troubadours: The Creators of Modern Verse* (University Park: The Pennsylvania State University, 1970), 77; and Luciano Rossi, "Ovidio," in *Lo spazio letterario del Medioevo, 2. Il Medioevo volgare, Vol. 3, La ricezione del testo*, ed. Piero Boitani, Mario Mancini, and Alberto Varvaro (Rome: Salerno, 2003), 259–301, at 268.
50   Cahoon, "The Anxieties of Influence," 120. In the introduction essay to a special journal issue on Dante and the troubadours, Teodolinda Barolini raised a similar question: "To what extent can the bookishness of [Dante] ... be ascribed to the more oral world in which the troubadours composed?" in "Dante and the Troubadours: An Overview," *Tenso* 5, no. 1 (1989): 3–10, at 7.

internalized passages and incorporated them into their own writings or not, they can still declare Ovid's authority on a certain matter without necessarily having had direct contact with his writings. *Ovides* or *Ovidis*, as the Occitan poets call the Latin author, could be constructed from very precise and attentive readings or from just impressions about the kind of poet Ovid was, and anything in between. It is true that aspects of the troubadours' professional and educational backgrounds suggest contact with classical literature; manuscripts of Ovid's writings circulated, as did *florilegia* that collected fragments from his poems; in the *vidas* (lives) of several troubadours we read that they were trained in "letras."[51] But a focus on how the image of the Latin poet is constructed could be more informative than the hunt for the precise Ovidian citations that match general, somewhat vague statements about love following the Latin poet's name in Occitan poems.[52]

Take two other mentions of Ovid in Occitan poetry that raise similar questions about the poets' familiarity with the source texts: the discussion about love and nobility in Arnaut de Mareuil's *canso Mout eron doutz miei cossir* (Johnston xxv, PC 30.19) and Azalais de Porcairagues's *Ar em al freg temps vengut* (de Riquer 75, PC 43.1). Luciano Rossi has studied these two poems together for their similar themes and references to Ovid.[53] Arnaut de Mareuil (fl. 1195) writes, "Mas Ovidis retrais / qu'entre·ls corals amadors / no paratgeia ricors" ("But Ovid confirms that for true lovers wealth does not matter" [vv. 28–30]); Azalais de Porcairagues (fl. 1173) points out, "Que Ovidis o retrai / Qu'amors per ricor non vai" ("That Ovid confirms that love does not work

---

51   Pietro G. Beltrami, "Lirons-nous encore les troubadours, et comment?" in *L'Occitanie invitée de l'Euregio. Liège 1981 – Aix-la-Chapelle 2008: Bilan et perspectives, Actes du Neuvième Congrès International de l'Association Internationale d'Études Occitanes, Aix-la-Chapelle, 24–31 Août 2008*, ed. Angelica Rieger and Domergue Sumien (Aix-la-Chapelle: Shaker Verlag, 2011), 101–20, at 106–7, 107, n. 36. Also Wendy Pfeffer mentioned several passages from the *vidas* mentioning that the troubadours learned "letras" in her study *Proverbs in Medieval Occitan Literature* (Gainesville: University Press of Florida, 1997), 27–30.

52   Also when Ovid's name is not mentioned, similar questions about the troubadours' sources are posed. For instance, while the *vida* of Folquet de Marselha does not mention his study of "letras," he is clearly familiar with classical authors (Pfeffer, *Proverbs in Medieval Occitan Literature*, 29–30, 44–52). Stanisław Stroński, who edited Folquet's poetry and counted twelve Ovidian passages in his poems, concluded that direct contact with Ovid's texts, which were widely read in schools, was possible, but the aphoristic quality of the Ovidian passages included in Folquet's poetry points rather to *florilegia*, which Stroński considered without any doubt the source for other Latin authors that Folquet included in his poems. See *Le troubadour Folquet de Marseille* (Kraków: Académie des Sciences: 1910), 77–81.

53   Luciano Rossi, "I trovatori e l'esempio ovidiano," in Picone and Zimmermann, *Ovidius redivivus*, 105–49, at 116–20.

through wealth" [vv. 21–22]).[54] All the elements from Marcabru's first mention of Ovid are also present in Arnaut and Azalais's poems: Ovid's name is placed at the beginning of the verse, followed by a verb of affirmation ("retrais" in Arnaut's poem, "retrai" in Azalais's) and a statement about love that, as Rossi pointed out, can be brought back to Ovid's words in *Ars am.* 2.161–65:

> non ego diuitibus uenio praeceptor amandi;
> nil opus est illi, qui dabit, arte mea.
> secum habet ingenium qui, cum libet, 'accipe' dicit;
> cedimus, inuentis plus placet ille meis.
> pauperibus uates ego sum, quia pauper amaui.

> [I come not to teach the rich how to love; those who can give, do not need my art. Someone who says "take this," as he pleases, has enough wit. I give up; he is more pleasing than my inventions. I am the poet of the poor, because I was poor when I loved.]

As was the case for Marcabru's verses about Ovid in the *tenso* with Uc Catola, the connection between the statements in Arnaut de Mareuil and Azalais de Porcairagues's poems and the passage in Ovid's *Ars amatoria* can be made; but this is not necessarily where their knowledge of Ovid came from. The Ovidian passage that Rossi mentioned is also found, for instance, in the *Florilegium Gallicum* (mid-twelfth century), an anthology collecting excerpts of classical authors, with Ovid's writings well represented (see Ch. 1.1).[55] Other troubadours made similar statements about love and riches, without reference to Ovid.[56] We do not know if Arnaut and Azalais read or heard these exact words from Ovid's *Ars amatoria*, but based on the way in which Ovid is mentioned in their poems, they had clearly internalized their meaning: they considered

---

54 I quote here the alternative reading included in Martín de Riquer, *Los trovadores: Historia literaria y textos* (Barcelona: Editorial Ariel, 1975), 1: 461, note to v. 21. In most editions the text reads, "car so dis om en Veillai / que ges per ricor non vai" ("Since they say in Velay that riches and love do not go together"), replacing Ovid with the Velay region in France. This replacement suggests that the statement about love and wealth, while indeed found in Ovid's poetry, functioned as a general truth or proverb, not necessarily connected to the Latin poet. On the use of this statement by other troubadour poets, see below, n. 56.
55 Fernández de la Cuesta González, *En la senda del 'Florilegium Gallicum,'* 348.
56 Eugen Cnyrim, *Sprichwörter, sprichwörtliche Redensarten und Sentenzen bei den Provenzalischen Lyrikern* (Marburg: N. G. Elwertsche Verlagsbuchhandlung, 1888), 25, especially numbers 17–22 (numbers 17 and 18 are Arnaut de Mareuil and Azalais de Porcairagues's mentions, which include Ovid's name).

Ovidis an authority on matters of love, the love poet of the poor, and presented him as such in their poetry.

Some Occitan poets connect their mentions of Ovid more closely with the act of reading. Bertran Carbonel (fl. 1252–65), like Marcabru more a moralist than a love poet, offers a first such example. In the *canso Aisi m'a dat fin'amor conoissensa* (Routledge VI, PC 82.6), Bertran declares that "fin'amor" led him to love his lady, but he withholds telling her. He explains that his behavior was inspired by Ovid's writings: "no·n parlera; qu'ieu truep en l'escriptura / c'Ovidis dis qu'ieu feira desmezura" ("I would not speak about it, since I found in the writings that Ovid says that I would exaggerate" [vv. 29–30]). At first, not confessing his love to his lady seemed the right thing to do (Ovid's writings would refer to a passage in *Her.* 4, Phaedra's letter to Hippolytus), but then Love urged him to tell her anyway: "Pero ar vol qu'ieu vos o deya dir / e vos preguar que vos dey'abelir" ("But now Love wants me to tell you and request that it would please you" [vv. 31–32]). The sequence of attitudes in Bertran Carbonel's *canso* follows those expressed in Phaedra's letter, who in a matter of a few verses went from silently enduring her love for Hippolytus to being compelled by Love to write and tell him (*Her.* 4.7–14):

> Ter tecum conata loqui, ter inutilis haesit
> lingua, ter in primo restitit ore sonus.
> Qua licet et sequitur, pudor est miscendus amori;
> dicere quae puduit, scribere iussit amor.
> Quidquid Amor iussit, non est contemnere tutum;
> regnat et in dominos ius habet ille deos.
> Ille mihi primo dubitanti scribere dixit:
> "Scribe! Dabit victas ferreus ille manus."

> [Three times I have tried to speak to you, three times my tongue was worthless, three times the words got stuck on the tip of my tongue. As much as it is possible, modesty should be mixed with love; love ordered me to write what is shameful to say. Whatever Love ordered, it is not safe to condemn; he rules and holds the law over the gods, our lords. He said to me when I first was in doubt to write: "Write! That cruel one will be overcome and surrender."]

The mention of Ovid in Bertran's poem contains all the usual elements: we find Ovid's name at the beginning of the verse (v. 30), followed by the verb of affirmation "dis" (v. 30), and a reference to Ovid's writings that ends up being convincing enough for a mention to an actual Ovidian passage in a footnote in the discussion of Bertran Carbonel's poems (vv. 30–32).[57] But the Occitan poet's own words make the case for his familiarity with this passage in Ovid's *Her.* 4: Bertran notes that he found this passage in Ovid's writings — "ieu truep en l'escriptura" (v. 29) — and decided to follow the Latin poet's advice; he presents himself as a poet familiar with literature ("escriptura"), one who would search his books to find guidance.[58] As Bertran states it, his readings of Ovid informed his actions.

Ovid's name is not always directly included in these citations; sometimes, the poet merely refers to the act of consulting previous literature. For instance, Bernart de Ventadorn, the troubadour who also featured Narcissus in his poetry, simply introduces a likely Ovidian passage with the words "eu ai be trobat legen" ("I have discovered while reading" [v. 36]). In the *canso Conortz, era sai eu be* (Lazar 15, PC 70.16), the poet writes that he will serve his lady until her "wild, hard, and angry" heart ("fers ... durs et iratz" [v. 34]) is softened. This approach, he explains, was inspired by his readings: "qu'eu ai be trobat legen / que gota d'aiga que chai, / fer en un loc tan soven, / tro chava la peira dura" ("that I found in my readings that a falling drop of water hits a spot so often that it carves a hard rock" [vv. 37–40]). Carl Appel proposed a passage from Ovid's *Ars amatoria* (1.475–76), where the Latin author uses the same image also in discussing how to deal with an uninterested and stubborn love interest: "quid magis est saxo durum, quid mollius unda? / dura tamen molli saxa cauantur aqua" ("What is harder than a rock, what is softer than water? But soft water hollows out the hard rock").[59] Patience and perseverance is also Ovid's

---

57 Rossi, "I trovatori e l'esempio ovidiano," 121–22.
58 In discussing the level and nature of familiarity troubadours had with written texts, Wendy Pfeffer cited another example from Guillem de l'Olivier (PC 246.23), who introduces a proverb with the statement "escrig truep en un nostr'actor" ("I find it written in one of our authors"). Also here the reference to writing ("escrig") points clearly to a written and not an oral source. See *Proverbs in Medieval Occitan Literature*, 32.
59 Quoted in *Bernard de Ventadour, troubadour du XIIe siècle: Chansons d'amour*, ed. Moshé Lazar (Paris: C. Klincksieck, 1966), 253. Appel also mentioned a verse from one of Ovid's exile letters as a possible source: "gutta cauat lapidem" ("a drop of water hollows out a stone" [*Ex Ponto* 4.10.5]). But the similar context in which Ovid uses the expression in the *Ars amatoria* makes it a much more likely source for this passage in Bernart de Ventadorn's *canso*. In contrast, in the *Ex Ponto* letter written to a friend, the exiled Ovid uses the expression to stress his perseverance now that he has been away from Rome for six summers. Both Ovidian passages on water carving stone from the *Ars amatoria* and the *Epistulae ex Ponto* are found in the *Lexikon der Sprichwörter des romanisch-germanischen Mittelalters* (Berlin: Walter de Gruyter, 2001), where Samuel Singer traced the proverb in its different variants from classical Greek and Latin literature to writings in medieval Latin and the vernacular languages (11: 129–32). This suggests that Bertran could be making a reference to a common expression (but still one he found while reading, "eu

advice, and the reward will eventually follow (*Ars am.* 1.478): "capta uides sero Pergama, capta tamen" ("Late you will see Pergamos captured, but captured nevertheless").

Rigaut de Berbezilh (fl. 1141–60) is another troubadour who indicates that his familiarity with Ovid is actual book knowledge. His *canso Tuit demandon qu'es devengud'Amors* (Varvaro IX, PC 421.10) is a poem that, like Marcabru and Uc Catola's *tenso*, sets out to describe the truth about love ("dirai·ne la vertat" [v. 2]): Rigaut gives us a series of statements on what "Amors" is and does, also describing his own experience as a lover. The mention of Ovid occurs in the stanza that marks the transition from a general to a personal discourse. Rigaut explains he is willing to endure suffering because "Ovidis dis el libre que no men / que per soffrir a hom d'amor son grat, / e per soffrir son maint tort perdonat / e sofrirs fai maint amoros iausen" ("Ovid says in the book that does not lie that through suffering one reaches his goal, and through suffering many mistakes are forgiven, and suffering has made many lovers happy" [vv. 29–32]). In Rigaut's mention of Ovid, we find once again the same pattern: Ovid's name (v. 29), the verb of affirmation "dis" (v. 29), and the Ovidian statement (vv. 30–32). Several corresponding passages have been found that identify different Ovidian works as the "book that does not lie." Willibald Schrötter, Stanisław Stroński, and Dimitri Scheludko mentioned the *Amores*, and specifically the verse "sperando certe gaudia magna feram" ("by hoping I will certainly obtain great joy" [*Am.* 2.9*b*.21, noted by Schrötter as *Am.* 2.9.44]) and "perfer et obdura: dolor hic tibi proderit olim" ("Put up with it and persist: one day this pain will prove useful to you" [*Am.* 3.11.7]). Scheludko and Alberto Varvaro proposed another candidate for Ovid's "book that does not lie": the *Ars amatoria*, where the corresponding verses read: "si nec blanda satis nec erit tibi comis amanti, / perfer et obdura: postmodo mitis erit" ("If she is not pleasant or gracious about your loving, put up with it and persevere: she will be kind soon" [*Ars am.* 2.177–78]).[60]

It must be Rigaut's mention of Ovid's book that drives this scholarly search for a corresponding passage in the Latin poet's writings, since otherwise this reported statement from Ovid could easily be deemed too general to match up with a specific passage in Ovid's poetry, like the ones in Marcabru, Arnaut de

---

ai be trobat legen" [v. 36]). The two verses from the *Ars amatoria* as well as the verse from the *Ex Ponto* letter are among the excerpts included in the *Florilegium Gallicum*, one of the fragmented and intermediary Ovidian sources (Fernández de la Cuesta González, *En la senda del 'Florilegium Gallicum,'* 345, 377).

60 *Rigaut de Berbezilh: Liriche*, ed. Alberto Varvaro (Bari: Adriatica Editrice, 1960), 211.

Mareuil, Azalais de Porcairagues, and Bertran Carbonel's poems.[61] And more forceful than those previous examples, Rigaut de Berbezilh unabashedly praises Ovid's work — in his *canso* that sets out to tell the truth about love, he only refers to one other text, "Ovid's book that does not lie." Probably the strongest confirmation of the Latin poet's authority in matters of love, Rigaut's mention of Ovid becomes a reference to a concrete, material object: a book that Rigaut read approvingly and now writes about.

According to the Occitan poets (with the exception of Marcabru), *Ovidis* says all the right things about love, whether they actually read Ovid's words of advice for lovers in his Latin works, as excerpts in *florilegia*, or had otherwise learned to associate them with the Latin poet. The ways in which Ovid is presented in these poems show how he was perceived: for the moralist Marcabru, he was a promotor of amoral behavior; for the other troubadours, an authority in matters of love. But the formula to invoke Ovid's authority found in these Occitan poems is not limited to the genre of poetry. In prose writing, statements are often backed up by passages from classical texts, or simply the author's name. Indeed, an *auctor*, as St. Bonaventure stated in his passage on book making discussed in Ch. 1.1, will add someone else's words to confirm his own — in the same chapter, I discussed several *auctores* using Ovid's words in confirmation of their own. The poetic version of this practice is found in phrases like "As Vergil / Ovid / Seneca / Tully / ... says," quite frequently used in Occitan poetry, making Ovid but one of the many classical authors troubadours feature in their poetry.[62] In other words, Marcabru is working with a common rhetorical device, originating in prose writing, to bolster one's claim with a reference to a perceived authority on the matter — Marcabru happened to be the first to do so with Ovid in Occitan verse.[63]

One more aspect of Marcabru's first mention of Ovid in Occitan poetry is important to point out. This mention was found in a *tenso*, a debate poem, a recorded dialogue between two poets. The text leaves little to question whether

---

61   At least one of the corresponding passages from Ovid's writings (the verse from *Am.* 3.11), is also found as an excerpt in the *Florilegium Gallicum* (Rackley, "The Amatory Excerpts of Ovid in the *Florilegium Gallicum*," 83).

62   Andrea Balbo and Giuseppe Noto, "I nomi dei classici latini nella poesia dei trovatori," in *'Tanti affetti in tal momento': Studi in onore di Giovanna Garbarino*, ed. Andrea Balbo, Federica Bessone, and Ermanno Malaspina (Alessandria: Edizioni dell'Orso, 2011), 11–40, at 17–22.

63   Proverbs were also introduced with certain fixed phrases: Claude Buridant identified three sets of "termes introducteurs" with which Old French poets would insert proverbs in *jeux-partis*, their version of the *tenso* or debate poem. See "Nature and function of proverbs in jeux-partis," *Revue des sciences humaines* 163, no. 3 (1976): 377–418, at 398–400. See also Pfeffer, *Proverbs in Medieval Occitan Literature*, 9, *passim*.

this was an actual conversation: in the opening stanza, Catola makes it clear that the words he and Marcabru now speak will be later recorded: "q'a l'hora qe nos partiram / en sia loing lo chanz auziz" ("so that from the moment we separate, the song version becomes widely distributed" [vv. 3–4]). Maria Luisa Meneghetti has pointed out that intertextuality and dialogism are two tendencies intrinsic to many Occitan poems, finding them present in the four most popular poetic genres, the *canso*, *sirventes*, *tenso*, and the *partimen*,[64] with the last two genres "dialogic in actuality (and not, or not only, metaphorically)."[65] Among the examples in Occitan poetry that feature Ovid's name, Marcabru and Uc Catola's is the only *tenso*; as we will see in the next section, it is this dialogic feature that will be maintained in the Italian poems about Ovid.

2.3   Reading and Discussing *Ovidio*

The sonnet exchange, a more general term to include all correspondence poems with a *proposta* and at least one *risposta*, becomes in Italian lyric poetry the preferred format to discuss Ovid's authority in matters of love.[66] In some cases, the discussion focuses on the question whether or not Ovid's writings are still of use for the contemporary lover; in others, the Italian poets debate whether or not Ovid's poetry should be an example for their own. These Italian poets take over the basic Occitan formula to mention the Latin poet, discussed in the previous section, as well as the poetic format in which this formula was first used: the debate poem or *tenso*, in Italian the *tenzone*. Different from the Occitan *tensos*, Italian *tenzoni* do not record the two or more voices of the

---

64   Maria Luisa Meneghetti, "Intertextuality and Dialogism in the Troubadours," in *Troubadours: An Introduction*, ed. Simon Gaunt and Sarah Kay (Cambridge: Cambridge University Press, 1999), 181–96, at 185.

65   Meneghetti, "Intertextuality and Dialogism in the Troubadours," 195, n. 9.

66   Christopher Kleinhenz made the distinction between the *tenzoni vere* and exchanges of sonnets or *rime di corrispondenza*, finding they each serve different ends: *tenzoni* seem intrinsically related to the desire to communicate about a topic, while poets would exchange sonnets for a variety of reasons: "the gaining of friendship, a personal request, and so on." See "Adventures in Textuality: Lyric Poetry, the 'Tenzone', and Cino da Pistoia," in *Textual Cultures of Medieval Italy*, ed. William Robins (Toronto: Toronto University Press, 2011), 81–111, at 85. For more on the different topics of the *tenzone*, see Claudio Giunta's chapter "Le rime di corrispondenza," in his study on the genre *Versi a un destinatario. Saggio sulla poesia italiana del Medioevo* (Bologna: Il Mulino, 2002), 167–266. On the *tenzone* as invective, see Fabian Alfie's chapter "*La debita correzione:* The Poetics of Insult in the *Duecento*," in *Dante's 'Tenzone' with Forese Donati: The Reprehension of Vice* (Toronto: Toronto University Press, 2011), 17–32.

poets in the same poem: *tenzoni* are sonnet exchanges where each participant composes their separate contribution (i.e., a sonnet) to the debate. As we will see in this section, virtually all mentions of Ovid in early Italian lyrics are part of such exchanges.

Even though the first century of Italian lyric poetry includes only a few poems featuring Ovid's name, it is important to note that Ovid is by far the most mentioned Latin poet in Italian lyric poetry, which already features significantly fewer proper names than Occitan poetry, and that authors of the past are rarely mentioned in sonnet exchanges. If Italian poets mention other poets in their poetry, they mainly talk about their contemporaries, or, more precisely, directly to them, often discussing features of each other's poetry. The vernacular poets mentioned in Italian poems are mainly Italians. Only in a *tenzone* between an unnamed poet and the Siculo-Tuscan poet Bonagiunta Orbicciani, do the poets mention several troubadours as a point of comparison. In the *proposta Poi di tutte bontà ben se' dispàri* (Contini IX), the anonymous poet praises Bonagiunta, claiming that "Di ciausir motti Folchetto tu' pari / non fu, né Pier Vidal né 'l buon di 'Smondo" ("In writing Folquet or Peire Vidal or the good Osmondo were no equal to you" [vv. 5–6]). But in this exchange featuring Occitan poets, the literary references remain within the realm of vernacular poetry.[67]

Latin poets do not receive much attention in early Italian lyrics. Vergil is mentioned a few times, but these mentions are not related to his writings, but to his legendary "arts" and love life.[68] In the anonymous *canzone Giamai null'om nonn-à sì gra·richezze* (Coluccia 49.4, IBAT 72.46), a poem-long series of opposing statements that all seem to apply at the same time, the poet declares: "Aggio poco senno a la stagione / e saccio tute l'arti di Vergilio" ("I have at times little understanding and I know all of Vergil's skills" [vv. 11–12]). In Chiaro Davanzati's misogynistic poem *Or tornate in usanza, buona gente* (Menichetti XXIX), Vergil is one of the wise men fooled by women: "Vergilio, ch'era tanto sapïente, / per falso amore si trovò ingannato" ("Vergil, who was so wise, found himself fooled by false love" [vv. 21–22]). Cino da Pistoia most explicitly

---

67 Gianfranco Contini mentioned Francesco Torraca's identification of "'l buon di 'Smondo" as l'Osmondo da Verona or also lo Schiavo da Bari (*Poeti del Duecento*, 1: 275).

68 Aurelio Roncaglia reached the same conclusion about the Occitan poets' interest in Vergil: "ils s'intéressent, à ce qu'il semble, surtout aux anecdotes de la légende qu'autour du nom de Virgilie le moyen âge avait bâtie" ("they are mostly interested, so it seems, in the legendary anecdotes that during the Middle Ages were formed around the name of Vergil"). See "Les Troubadours et Virgile," in *Lectures médiévales de Virgile. Actes du colloque de Rome (25–28 Octobre 1982)*, ed. École française de Rome (Rome: École française de Rome, 1985), 267–83, at 274.

features the medieval Vergil of the legends, and not Vergil the poet, in his *canzone Deh, quando rivedrò 'l dolce paese* (Marti CLXV). Calling him "sommo vate" (v. 13) in a clear nod to his magical powers,[69] he recounts the legendary story about Vergil's fly that kept all other flies out of Naples. Finally, Lucan is referred to once in the sonnet *La pena che sentí Cato di Roma* (Scariati 50) by the so-called Amico di Dante.[70] Writing about "serpente" (v. 7), the poet clearly thinks of Lucan's catalogue of snakes in *Phars.* 9.700–33, when he adds "come Lucan li noma" (v. 8).[71]

Compared to these few mentions of other Latin poets, Ovid is featured frequently and always as an author, and the Italian poets who mention him do so precisely to discuss the content and evaluate the worth of his writings. They are not only interested in assessing Ovid as a teacher of love, but also as a poet of love poetry. That we find his name mentioned mainly in sonnet exchanges, then, is not a surprise: *tenzoni* and *rime di corrispondenza* are natural places for such discussions. The genre often includes metapoetic discussions, moments of reflection by the poets on the changes in style and themes of their poems; often we hear the voices of the "old way" in conversation with those of the new guard.[72] The most notable examples are probably Bonagiunta Orbicciani's sonnet *Voi c'avete mutata la mainera* and Guido Guinizzelli's reply *Omo ch' è saggio non corre leggero*, and Guinizzelli's sonnet addressed to Guittone d'Arezzo *Caro padre mëo, de vostra laude* and Guittone's response *Figlio mio dilettoso, in faccia laude*. Not every metapoetic sonnet exchange features Ovid, but the Latin poet turns out to be a useful point of reference in such discussions.

Looking closer, then, at how these mentions of *Ovidio* are constructed in the Italian poems, we notice again the influence of Occitan poetry. But the troubadours' careful construction of an authoritative *Ovidis* undergoes several systematic changes in the writings of the Italian poets. They mainly give up the troubadours' use of verbs of affirmation that underlined the Latin poet's authoritative status (Ovid says, declares, shows, and so on). They also seem

---

69 Teodolinda Barolini, "Canto XX: True and False See-ers," in *Lectura Dantis: Inferno: A Canto-by-Canto Commentary*, ed. Allen Mandelbaum, Anthony Oldcorn, and Charles Ross (Berkeley: University of California Press, 1998), 275–86, at 280, who further pointed out that Dante never called Virgilio "vate" in the *Commedia*.

70 The Amico di Dante is the unidentified author of a series of poems included in one of the three late-thirteenth-century *canzonieri* that contain most of early Italian poetry (MS Vat. lat. 3793).

71 See also Sayce, *Exemplary Comparison*, 319.

72 On the metapoetic aspect of sonnet exchanges, see Kleinhenz, "Adventures in Textuality," 89; and especially Simone Marcenaro, "Polemiche letterarie nella lirica del Duecento," *Revista de Filología Románica* 27 (2010): 77–99, who illustrated how poetic polemics had been an integral part of the lyrical production from the Sicilian to the *dolce stil novo* poets.

less interested in featuring the specific content of Ovid's works that the troubadours repeatedly referred to in their poems, shifting the emphasis to the act of reading Ovid in general instead. The result is a series of passages in Italian verse that all contain Ovid's name and a form of the verb "leggere," to read (emphasis added):

> "ed *aggio letto* verso de *l'on Vidio*."
> [and *I have read* verses of *Ovid*.]
> > Anonymous poet, *Giamai null'om nonn-à sì gra·richezze*, v. 16

> "D'*Ovidio* ciò mi son miso a provare
> ....
> E ben conosco omai veracemente
> che 'nverso Amor non val forza ned arte,
> ingegno né *leggenda* ch'omo trovi."
> [I have set out to test what *Ovid* prescribed ... And I know well by now that against Love neither strength nor skill, intelligence nor *any available readings* are worth anything.]
> > DANTE DA MAIANO, *Amor mi fa sì fedelmente amare*, vv. 5–11

> "*Ovidio leggi*: più di te ne vide!"
> [*Read Ovid*: He understands this better than you!]
> > GUIDO ORLANDI, *Per troppo sottiglianza il fil si rompe*, v. 11

> "e certe fiate *aggiate Ovidio letto* ..."
> [and you *have read Ovid* a few times ...]
> > GUIDO CAVALCANTI, *Di vil matera mi conven parlar*, v. 7

> "Se mai *leggesti* versi de l'*Ovidi* ..."
> [If you ever *read* verses of *Ovid* ...]
> > CINO DA PISTOIA, *Se mai leggesti versi de l'Ovidi*, v. 1

This more general approach makes it easier for his Italian readers to turn *Ovidio* into the kind of lover or poet they want or need him to be, and his writings into an emblem of either the kind of love poetry they write in Italian, or no longer wish to write. The troubadours' repeated positive evaluation of the Latin poet's writings is now up for debate, and the Italian poets extend the discussion to include both the experience of the lover and the love poet. The troubadour Rigaut de Berbezilh may have referred to Ovid's work as a "book that does not lie," but his Italian readers find that the Latin poet sometimes gets it wrong.

At first glance, two Italian poems still seem to adhere closely to the troubadours' ways of mentioning Ovid, one probably among the earliest Italian poems to include Ovid's name, and the other by Cino da Pistoia, writing significantly later; both poets refer to Ovid as an authority in matters of love, as we repeatedly found in the Occitan examples. The first to do so is the anonymous Sicilian or Siculo-Tuscan poet of the *canzone Giamai null'om nonn-à sì gra·richezze* (Coluccia 49.4, IBAT 72.46), discussed earlier because of its mention of Vergil.[73] Ovid is mentioned (as is Vergil) in a pair of opposing statements that according to the poet occur at the same time. A closer reading of the entire second stanza, where we find Vergil and Ovid's names, gives a good idea of the poet's approach (vv. 11–20):

> Aggio poco senno a la stagione
> e saccio tute l'arti di Vergilio;
> e son sacente più che Salamone,
> con tuti folli vo' tener congilio;
> e de l'amor no sacio dir ragione
> ed aggio letto verso de l'on Vidio.
> E dico il vero e no ne son creduto
> e facio bene e son tutor perduto,
> e sanza fede son leal tenuto
> ed ardo tuto a gelo fortemente.

[And I have at times little understanding, but know all of Vergil's skills. And I am wiser than Solomon, but want to meet up with all the fools. And I cannot say anything reasonable about love, but have read verses of Ovid. And I say the truth, but am not believed, and I do well, but am still ruined, and I am not worthy of trust, but am considered loyal, and I am completely burning in ice.]

---

73   Bruno Panvini included this *canzone* in his 1962 edition of *Le rime della scuola siciliana* (Florence: Leo S. Olschki) with other anonymous poems (1: 485–87), while in the Mondadori three-volume series *I poeti della Scuola siciliana* (2008), the editors included it in the volume dedicated to the Siculo-Tuscan poets (Vol. 3), and not the poets at the court of Frederick II (Vol. 2). The *canzone Giamai null'om* is only found in MS Vat. lat. 3793, where it is preceded by *Al cor tanta alegranza* and followed by *Amor, non saccio a cui di voi mi chiami*. The editors of the Mondadori series included these among the anonymous Sicilian poems (Di Girolamo 25.5 and 25.6 respectively). Aniello Fratta, who edited the *Giamai null'om* in the Mondadori edition, found a few Senese forms in the *canzone*, signs of the probable Senese origin of the author (Coluccia, *Poeti siculo-toscani*, 639, note to v. 17, 640, note to v. 47).

The *sirma* or second part of this stanza (vv. 17–20) contains four pairs of opposite statements in the same verse: for instance, the poet claims that he is feeling burning hot and ice cold at the same time (v. 20). The *fronte* or first part of the stanza (vv. 11–16) is structured in a similar way, but each pair takes up two verses and features famous men: Vergil, Solomon, and Ovid. The poet connects each famous man with the quality that made him famous: Vergil is mentioned for his "arts," Solomon as the wisest man, and Ovid ("l'on Vidio") knows everything about love. The poet claims to simultaneously not possess these qualities at all *and* possess them even more.[74] In the verses dedicated to love, he first mentions his complete inability to "dir ragione" (v. 15), to reason or to discourse about love — "de l'amor no sacio dir ragione" (v. 15); and then achieves the opposite by reading Ovid — "ed aggio letto verso de l'on Vidio" (v. 16). The best-informed discussant about love, following this poet's reasoning, is the one who read Ovid. This is the same positive assessment of the Latin poet's writings that we found in the Occitan poets. But while the troubadours referred in their poems to concrete passages in Ovid's writings to corroborate a specific point about love, the anonymous poet of *Giamai null'om nonn-à sì gra·richezze* makes a general claim about reading Ovid, a distinctively Italian feature.[75]

Cino da Pistoia's sonnet *Se mai leggesti versi de l'Ovidi* (Marti CXXXV) draws closely on the troubadours' way of praising Ovid by referring to specific Ovidian viewpoints that are considered helpful for the lover. That Cino, a *stil novo* poet and roughly a contemporary of Dante, still adheres to this Occitan template should be seen more as evidence that later Italian poets also looked at and followed the example of their vernacular predecessors, rather than the

---

74   Bruno Panvini has corrected the verse mentioning Ovid (v. 16) as "ed agio letto verso de l'Ovidio" (*Le rime della scuola siciliana*, 1: 485). The manuscript has "delonvidio" (MS Vat. lat. 3793, fol. 20v), which the edition here used transcribed as "de l'on Vidio." There is no doubt that this reading refers to the Latin author. Fratta added that the use of "on" brings the Occitan particle "en" in mind (Coluccia, *Poeti siculo-toscani*, 639, note to v. 16).

75   The connections with Occitan poetry have not escaped the editors of this anonymous *canzone*; see Fratta, *Le fonti provenzali*, 110–11, and his comments in Coluccia, *Poeti siculo-toscani*, 638–42, which identified several connections with Occitan poems (especially Giraut de Borneil's *Un sonet*), placing this Italian *canzone* within the Occitan genre of the *devinalh*, a riddle-poem often constructed from contrasting statements. Contini also connected it to the Sicilian poet Ruggieri Apugliese's *canzone Umile sono ed orgoglioso* (Contini I), of which the *incipit* already reveals Ruggieri's similar reliance on opposing claims (*Poeti del Duecento*, 1: 885). The mention of Ovid in this *canzone* and its connections with similar passages in Occitan poetry has, to my knowledge, gone unnoticed so far. Another connection could be made with the opening verses of the second book of the *Disticha Catonis* (see Ch. 1.1), which contains a similar message: "If you want to love, or learn about love through reading, look for Ovid" ("Si quid amare libet, vel discere amare legendo, / Nasonem petito" [vv. 6–7]).

defining trait of Cino's engagement with Ovid's works. (The following chapter draws a much more complete picture of Cino as reader of Ovid, one who works with Ovidian material more frequently and in more complex ways than the poets discussed in this chapter.) Cino's sonnet is a reply to *Assai son certo che somenta in lidi* (Marti CXXXVa) by the Bolognese poet Onesto da Bologna, a frequent correspondent of Cino.[76] In *Assai son certo che somenta in lidi,* the opening sonnet of the exchange, Onesto describes Love's cruelty and calls Cino inexperienced in this bitter aspect of love:

TABLE 2   Onesto da Bologna, *Assai son certo che somenta in lidi*, and Cino da Pistoia, *Se mai leggesti versi de l'Ovidi*

Assai son certo che somenta in lidi	Se mai leggesti versi de l'Ovidi,
e pon lo so color senza vernice	so c'hai trovato, sì come si dice,
qualunque crede che la calcatrice	che disdegnoso contra sdegnatrice
prender si possa dentro in le miei redi;	convien ch'Amore di mercede sfidi;
e già non son sì nato infra gli abidi,	però tu stesso, amico, ti conquidi,
che mai la pensi trovare amatrice,	e la cornacchia sta 'n su la cornice,
quella ch'è stata di me traditrice,	alta, gentile e bella salvatrice
né spero 'l dì veder, sol ch'eo m'affidi;	del suo onor: chi vòle, in foco sidi.
merzé d'Amor, che sotterra Rachele,	D'Amor puoi dire, se lo ver non cele,
non già Martino, Giovanni né parte,	ch'egli è di nobil core dottrina ed arte
c'ha del servire prescrizione e carte;	e sue virtù son con le tue scomparte.
né te, che non conosci acqua di fele	Io sol conosco lo contrar del mele,
nel mar dove ha' tutte allegrezze sparte,	che l'assaporo ed honne pien le quarte:
che val ciascuna più ch'amor di parte.	così stess'io con Martino in disparte!

---

[76] In Ch. 1.2, I referred to this exchange between Onesto and Cino to introduce the shared reading experience of Ovid among Italian poets. Onesto's sonnet *Mente ed umile e più di mille sporte* (Marti CXXXIIIa) and Cino's reply *Amor che vien per le più dolci porte* (Marti CXXXIII) are another prime example of the metapoetic debates that Italian poets often held in sonnet exchanges: in his sonnet, Onesto mocks the lexicon and the philosophizing of the *stilnovisti*, and in his reply, Cino ardently defends these poetic choices. On this sonnet exchange, see also the introduction of Chapter 3 and Ch. 4.3. On the exchanges between Onesto and Cino, see Simone Marcenaro, "Polemica letteraria e ironia nella lirica italiana del Duecento. Il caso di Cino da Pistoia," in *Parodia y debate metaliterarios en la Edad Media*, ed. Mercedes Brea, Esther Corral Díaz, and Miguel A. Pousada Cruz (Alessandria: Edizioni dell'Orso, 2013), 277–90, at 279–84; Furio Brugnolo, "Cino (e Onesto) dentro e fuori la *Commedia*," in *Omaggio a Gianfranco Folena*, 3 vols. (Padua: Editoriale Programma, 1993), 1: 369–86, and "Appendice a Cino (e Onesto) dentro e fuori la *Commedia*: Ancora sull'intertesto di *Purgatorio* XXIV 49–63," in *Leggere Dante*, ed. Lucia Battaglia Ricci (Ravenna: Longo, 2003), 153–70.

[I am quite sure that everyone who believes that the crocodile can be caught in my nets, sows on the shores and adds color without varnish; and I was not born between the pine trees, too crude to think I might one day find a lover in her, the one who has betrayed me; but I do not fear to see her every day, provided I have the strength to do so, with the mercy of Love, who buried Rachel, but has not yet buried Martino, and in part Giovanni, who knows the rules of the service well, and not you, for you do not know the water of bile in the sea where you have all pleasures available and each of them is worth more than love in part.]

[If you ever read verses of Ovid, I know you found out that, as they say, Love inevitably takes away any hope for mercy to anyone who is haughty toward a haughty lady. Therefore, my friend, it is you who destroys yourself, and the crow stands on the ledge, the tall, gentle, and beautiful keeper of her honor; may whoever desires it, be aflame. Of Love you can say, if you do not hide the truth, that he possesses a noble heart, teachings, and skill, and his virtues are quite different from yours. I alone know the opposite of honey because I have tasted it and had plenty of it. Therefore, may I step aside with Martino.]

In his response sonnet, Cino corrects Onesto on the basis of Ovid's work, thus confirming Ovid's authority in these matters: "Se mai leggesti versi de l'Ovidi," he writes, "so c'hai trovato, sì come si dice, / che disdegnoso contra sdegnatrice / convien ch'Amore di mercede sfidi" (vv. 1–4). Indeed, in the first two books of the *Ars amatoria*, Ovid advises his reader to remain friendly and compliant with an arrogant woman (1.715–16; 2.145–46; 2.177–96).[77] Like the troubadours, Cino points to specific content of Ovid's works. He further praises Love's virtues (vv. 9–11), but since he did experience love's bitterness, he hopes not to be wounded by Love (vv. 12–14).

Despite Cino's concluding wish to escape Love's attacks, the poet nevertheless believes the lover possesses free will in the face of Love: the lover can decide how to respond to the haughty lady. If he (against Ovid's advice) opts to act "disdegnoso contra sdegnatrice" (v. 3), then let him be in flames, if that is what he wants: "*chi vòle*, in foco sidi" (v. 8; emphasis added).[78] The Florentine poet Dante da Maiano puts forward a contrasting sentiment in his sonnet *Amor mi fa sì fedelmente amare* (Bettarini LI), sent to Dante Alighieri: nothing can

---

77   Mario Marti further referred to *Ars am.* 2.109–250 or the twelfth-century comedy *Pamphilus* in *Poeti del Dolce stil nuovo* (Florence: F. Le Monnier, 1969), 762, n. 1.
78   Marti, *Poeti del Dolce stil nuovo*, 762, n. 5.

be done against Love. Suffering from lovesickness, Dante da Maiano had read Ovid and followed his advice — something that the Occitan poets Arnaut de Mareuil, Azalais de Porcairagues, Bertran Carbonel, and Rigaut de Berbezilh all wrote they successfully did. But for Dante da Maiano, Ovid's words are all lies. Like the exchange between Onesto da Bologna and Cino da Pistoia, the sonnets of the two Dantes feature Ovid in a larger debate on what love is and can do:

TABLE 3   Dante da Maiano, *Amor mi fa sì fedelmente amare*, and Dante Alighieri, *Savere e cortesia, ingegno ed arte*

Amor mi fa sì fedelmente amare	Savere e cortesia, ingegno ed arte,
e sì distretto m'ave en suo disire,	nobilitate, bellezza e riccore,
che solo un'ora non porria partire	fortezza e umilitate e largo core,
lo meo coraggio da lo suo pensare.	prodezza ed eccellenza, giunte e sparte,
D'Ovidio ciò mi son miso a provare	este grazie e vertuti in onne parte
che disse per lo mal d'Amor guarire,	con lo piacer di lor vincono Amore:
e ciò ver' me non val mai che mentire:	una più ch'altra ben ha più valore
per ch'eo mi rendo a sol mercé chiamare.	inverso lui, ma ciascuna n'ha parte.
E ben conosco omai veracemente	Onde se voli, amico, che ti vaglia
che 'nverso Amor non val forza ned arte,	vertute naturale od accidente,
ingegno né leggenda ch'omo trovi,	con lealtà in piacer d'Amor l'adovra,
mai che merzede ed esser sofferente	e non a contastar sua graziosa ovra;
e ben servir: così n'ave omo parte.	ché nulla cosa gli è incontro possente,
Provvedi, amico saggio, se l'approvi.	volendo prender om con lui battaglia.

[Love makes me love so faithfully and has me so bound to his will that my heart could not even pass an hour without thinking of him. I have set out to test what Ovid prescribed to cure lovesickness, and according to me it is all lies: for I end up crying for help. And I know well by now that against Love neither strength nor skill, intelligence nor any available readings are worth anything, but only mercy and undergoing the suffering and loyal service: that is the way one deals with him. Take note, wise friend, if you agree.]

[Knowledge and courtesy, wisdom and skill, nobility, beauty, and wealth; strength and gentleness and generosity, courage and excellence: these graces and virtues, taken together or separate, conquer Love in all cases for the pleasure they bring: one may have more value to Love than another, but all partake in it. Therefore, my friend, if you want to make the most out of natural or additional virtue, put them to work with loyalty at the pleasure of Love, and let them not oppose his gracious work. For nothing has power against Love, if one wants to start a fight against him.]

Dante da Maiano's mention of Ovid clearly refers to the *Remedia amoris,* the book that sets out to cure "lo mal d'Amor" (v. 6). Medical language was also used in the *accessus* to the *Remedia amoris*: for instance, Ovid was said to offer a "medicine for love" in the poem "like a good doctor."[79] The verses dedicated to the reading of the Latin poet in da Maiano's sonnet start out in line with what we found in Occitan lyrics: Ovid's name is mentioned at the beginning of the verse (v. 5) and the content of his works described with the verb of affirmation "disse" (v. 6). But there is also a clear break: Dante da Maiano does not simply accept what Ovid says: he questions and tests Ovid's advice — "mi son miso a provare" (v. 5) — and concludes from his own experience — "ver' me" (v. 7) — that his advice is ill-given. His conclusion about the *Remedia amoris* that "non val mai che mentire" (v. 7) is the exact opposite of Rigaut de Berbezilh's description of Ovid's *Amores* or *Ars amatoria* as "the book that does not lie."

Dante da Maiano's sonnet describes Love as a force the lover cannot battle with: Love has him bound — "distretto" (v. 2) — at his desire. Nothing is of use against Love: not "forza ned arte, / ingegno né leggenda" (vv. 10–11). Dante Alighieri's response sonnet *Savere e cortesia, ingegno ed arte* reaches the same conclusion: "nulla cosa gli è incontro possente, / volendo prender om con lui battaglia" (vv. 13–14).[80] Dante Alighieri, however, claims that certain graces and virtues can win Love over, or better, conquer the lady's love (vv. 1–11). Among these "grazie e vertuti" (v. 5), we find, only slightly reformulated, the same four weapons that Dante da Maiano considered worthless against love:

---

79 The entire passage with the medical language reads (in the translation of Wheeler, *Accessus ad auctores*, 50–51): "uidens hoc non melius posse fieri quam si dato amori medicinam adinueniret, hunc librum scribere aggressus est ... Instruit enim ad medici similitudinem; bonus uero medicus infirmis ut sanentur medicinam tribuit, et etiam sanis ut ab infirmitate non capiantur" ("because he saw that this could not be better done than if he discovered a medicine for the love he had given, he started to write his book ... He gives instruction, in fact, according to the analogy of a doctor; indeed, a good doctor gives medicine to the sick so that they may be cured and also to the healthy so that they may not be seized by sickness").

80 For the development of Dante Alighieri's thinking on the lover's free will, see the discussion on *Savere e cortesia* in *Rime giovanili e della 'Vita Nuova,'* ed. Teodolinda Barolini (Milan: Rizzoli, 2009), 73–75. For a discussion of this theme in Dante's later sonnet *Io sono stato con Amore insieme*, see Ch. 3.3.

TABLE 4 Comparison between terms used in Dante da Maiano, *Amor mi fa sì fedelmente amare*, and Dante Alighieri, *Savere e cortesia, ingegno ed arte*

Dante da Maiano	Dante Alighieri
"forza" (v. 10)	"fortezza" (v. 3)
"arte" (v. 10)	"arte" (v. 1)
"ingegno" (v. 11)	"ingegno" (v. 1)
"leggenda" (v. 11)	"savere" (v. 1)

Of these corresponding terms, only Dante Alighieri's "savere" does not entirely correspond with Dante da Maiano's "leggenda." Da Maiano's "leggenda" indicates literally things to be read, or knowledge coming from books.[81] Earlier in the sonnet, he clarified which precise book and knowledge he had in mind when he declares "leggenda" useless against Love: Ovid's advice from the *Remedia amoris* (vv. 5–8), which he tested out and failed. The type of knowledge Dante Alighieri intends with the term "savere," on the other hand, remains unspecified. But given the close parallels Dante Alighieri sets up in his response sonnet between Dante da Maiano's worthless weapons and the mention of the virtues and graces that can win Love over, we can at least surmise that Dante Alighieri would include Ovid's writings in this general category of "knowledge." With the help of the Latin poet's writings, Dante's poem suggests, he might be able to conquer his lady's love.

Guido Cavalcanti follows Dante da Maiano's example of rejecting Ovid's writings in an exchange with Guido Orlandi. But while Dante da Maiano's focus was the experience of the lover, Guido Cavalcanti's rejection concerns the poetics of love. The exchange between the two Guidos contains three poems: Guido Orlandi's twelve-verse poem, *Per troppa sottiglianza il fil si rompe* (Rea La); Guido Cavalcanti's response sonnet with coda or *sonetto caudato*, *Di vil matera mi conven parlare* (Rea Lb); and Orlandi's response *sonetto caudato*, *Amico, i' saccio ben che sa' limare* (Rea Lc).[82] The first two poems in particular discuss Ovidian poetics:

---

81 *Rime della 'Vita Nuova' e della giovinezza*, ed. Michele Barbi and Francesco Maggini (Florence: F. Le Monnier, 1956), 171, n. 11. The editors did not exclude "leggenda" might also mean "spells," but I believe the sonnet's mention of Ovid favors their first interpretation.

82 On the formal aspects of this exchange, see Corrado Calenda, "'Di vil matera': ipotesi esplicativa di una ipertrofia strutturale," in *Appartenenze metriche ed esegesi: Dante, Cavalcanti, Guittone* (Naples: Bibliopolis, 1995), 61–71.

TABLE 5   Guido Orlandi, *Per troppa sottiglianza il fil si rompe*, and Guido Cavalcanti, *Di vil matera mi conven parlare*

Per troppa sottiglianza il fil si rompe,	Di vil matera mi conven parlare
e 'l grosso ferma l'arcone al tenèro;	[e] perder rime, silabe e sonetto,
e se la sguarda non dirizz'al vero,	sì ch'a me ste[sso] giuro ed imprometto
in te forse t'avèn, cheri pompe;	a tal voler per modo legge dare.
e qual non pon ben diritto lo son pe'	Perché sacciate balestra legare
traballa spesso, non loquendo intero;	e coglier con isquadra arcale in tetto
ch'Amor sincero – non piange né ride:	e certe fiate aggiate Ovidio letto
in ciò conduce spesso omo o fema,	e trar quadrelli e false rime usare,
per segnoraggio prende e divide.	non pò venire per la vostra mente,
E tu 'l feristi? e no·lli par la sema?	là dove insegna, Amor, sottile e piano,
Ovidio leggi: più di te ne vide!	di sua maner' a dire e di su' stato.
Dal mio balestro guarda ed aggi tema.	Già non è cosa che si porti in mano:
	qual che voi siate, egli è d'un'altra gente:
	sol al parlar si vide chi v'è stato.
	Già non vi toccò lo sonetto primo:
	Amore ha fabricato ciò ch'io limo.

[When a thread is too thin, it breaks, and a thick thread blocks the bow at the grip, and if you do not aim at the right target, the arrow might turn toward you, when you try to speak pompously; and one who does not put his feet straight, often wobbles, leaving his speech incomplete; because true love does not cry or laugh (since that is what love makes men and women do); as a master, Love conquers and divides. And you say that you wounded Love? But we do not see a scar on him? Read Ovid: he understands this better than you. Watch out for my bow and be afraid.]

[I must speak of a vile subject, wasting rhymes, syllables, and sonnet, so that I swear and promise to myself to set some reasonable rules for this plan. Just because you can string a crossbow and hit a simple target, and you have read Ovid a few times, you can throw a spear and use false rhymes, Love cannot come to your mind, where he teaches, subtle and clear, to speak about his ways and his state. It is not something that you can carry in your hand: whoever you are, Love is of a different ilk: by their way of speaking one understands who has been there. My first sonnet to you did not move you: Love has created what I polish.]

In the opening poem of the exchange, Orlandi's language is boastful: he attacks poetry that is too subtle — that possesses "troppa sottiglianza" (v. 1) and is "non ... intero" (v. 6) — and uses the language of archery to express his viewpoints. True love ("Amor sincero" [v. 7]), he continues, does not cry or laugh: a clear dig at Cavalcanti's personification of love, often linked to the verse "fare'ne di pietà pianger Amore" ("I would make Love cry out of pity" [v. 8]) in Cavalcanti's single-stanza *canzone Poi che di doglia cor conven ch'i' porti* (Rea XI), and an attack that Orlandi repeats in the final poem of the exchange, "faresti Amore piangere in tuo stato" ("you would make Love cry in your state" [*Amico, i' saccio ben che sa' limare*, v. 10]).[83] Orlandi's aggressive language culminates in the last tercet, which personally addresses Cavalcanti with two imperatives. The first is a command to read Ovid, who is said to understand love better than Cavalcanti does; the second translates the previously used imagery of archery into a concrete threat to watch out for his bow.

Guido Cavalcanti responds to both imperatives in *Di vil matera mi conven parlare*. But first he sets out the two fronts on which he will attack Orlandi: on content — "vil matera" (v. 1) — and on style — "rime, silabe e sonetto" (v. 2). Then referring to the concluding imperatives of *Per troppa sottiglianza*, Cavalcanti counters Orlandi. His skills in archery and his readings of Ovid (vv. 5–8) do not render Orlandi the kind of poet who can be receptive to Amor's teachings, "sottile e piano" (v. 10): Amor is "d'un'altra gente" (v. 13) than Orlandi. These teachings, Cavalcanti specifies, regard both the style — "sua maner'" (v. 11) — and content — "su' stato" (v. 11) — of poetry. Concretely, Cavalcanti rejects the use of false rhymes (v. 8) and the content of Ovid's writings.

The exchange between the two Guidos then reads as an attack and subsequent defense of poetics. Guido Orlandi, representing the old Siculo-Tuscan tradition, considers Ovid a point of reference; Guido Cavalcanti, rehearsing key terms of the *dolce stil novo*, makes Ovid the emblem of the themes that his own poetry does not treat.[84] This reading may seem at first to overemphasize the weight of their mentions of Ovid.[85] Then again, the Orlandi-Cavalcanti

---

83   On this verse (*Per troppa sottiglianza il fil si rompe*, v. 7), see Roberto Rea's note in Guido Cavalcanti, *Rime*, ed. Roberto Rea and Giorgio Inglese (Rome: Carocci, 2011), 263, which summarized the commentary on Orlandi's attack.

84   Guido Favati, "Contributo alla determinazione del problema dello Stil nuovo," *Studi mediolatini e volgari* 4 (1956): 57–70; and Teodolinda Barolini, *Dante's Poets: Textuality and Truth in the Comedy* (Princeton: Princeton University Press, 1984), 177–78.

85   While most editors of Guido Cavalcanti and Guido Orlandi linked the mentions of Ovid to the Latin poet's authority in matters of love, they did not say much more about the presence of Ovid in the exchange; only Domenico De Robertis explicitly denied the poems' metapoetic implications in Guido Cavalcanti, *Rime. Con le rime di Iacopo Cavalcanti*, ed. Domenico De Robertis (Turin: Einaudi, 1986), 201. Often placed in the later pages of

exchange clearly resembles another exchange between two poets that explicitly addresses differences in poetics: *Voi c'avete mutata la mainera* (Rossi 14ª), in which the Tuscan poet Bonagiunta Orbicciani attacks Guido Guinizzelli's poetic inventions, and Guido responds with *Omo ch' è saggio non corre leggero* (Rossi 14). Besides the shared metapoetic subject matter of both the Orlandi-Cavalcanti and the Bonagiunta-Guinizzelli exchanges, the connection between the two sets of exchanges is further strengthened by the repeated use of the term "sottiglianza" / "sottigliansa." As we just saw, Orlandi opened his attack on Cavalcanti's poetics with the image of a thread breaking "per troppa sottiglianza" (v. 1); in doing so, he adopted Bonagiunta's term "sottigliansa," which was one aspect of Guido Guinizzelli's poetry he attacked in *Voi c'avete mutata la mainera* (v. 9).[86]

What unites these mentions of Ovid in the exchanges between Guido Orlandi and Guido Cavalcanti, Dante da Maiano and Dante Alighieri, and Cino da Pistoia and Onesto da Bologna, is the opportunity that the Latin poet offers to discuss their central topic (love) and their craft (love poetry). Ovid is of course not needed to hold such discussions that have taken place in Italian verse from its beginnings (the exchange about the nature of love between Iacopo Mostacci, Pier della Vigna, and Giacomo da Lentini is an early Sicilian example of such discussions).[87] While it may be too strong to state definitively

---

editions of Cavalcanti's poetry together with the other *tenzoni*, the exchange between the two Guidos did receive some more critical attention in Calenda's before-mentioned article ("'Di vil matera'"); in Donato Pirovano, *Il Dolce stil novo* (Rome: Salerno, 2014), 129–34; and by Luciano Rossi, who pointed out the sexual double meaning of the expressions used by Orlandi and Cavalcanti in "Maestria poetica e 'grivoiserie' nelle tenzoni Orlandi-Cavalcanti," in *Studi di filologia e letteratura italiana in onore di Gianvito Resta*, ed. Vitilio Masiello (Rome: Salerno, 2000), 27–42.

86   Valentina Pollidori, "Le rime di Guido Orlandi," *Studi di filologia italiana* 53 (1995): 55–202, at 125, 127; Emilio Pasquini, "Il mito dell'amore: Dante fra i due Guidi," in *Dante: Mito e poesia: Atti del secondo Seminario dantesco internazionale: Monte Verità, Ascona, 23–27 giugno 1997*, ed. Michelangelo Picone and Tatiana Crivelli (Florence: Franco Cesati, 1999), 283–95, at 286; Pirovano, *Il Dolce stil novo*, 129–30; Claudio Giunta, *La poesia italiana nell'età di Dante: La linea Bonagiunta-Guinizzelli* (Bologna: Il Mulino, 1998), 75–77. Stefano Carrai discussed both the exchanges between Bonagiunta and Guinizzelli and between Orlandi and Cavalcanti together under the heading "Polemiche sulla nuova maniera" in *La lirica toscana del Duecento* (Rome: Laterza, 1997), 70–72. Roberto Rea connected Cavalcanti's *Di vil matera* to another famous metapoetic debate, the exchange between Guido Guinizzelli (*Caro padre mëo, de vostra laude*) and Guittone d'Arezzo (*Figlio mio dilettoso, in faccia laude*) in "Guinizzelli *praised and explained* (da [O] caro padre meo al XXVI del *Purgatorio*)," *The Italianist* 30 (2010): 1–17, at 6: both Cavalcanti and Guinizzelli, Rea pointed out, use the verb "limare" in the concluding verse of their poems.

87   The *tenzone* consists of the sonnets *Solicitando un poco meo savere* by Iacopo Mostacci (Antonelli 1.19a), *Però ch'Amore non si pò vedere* by Pier della Vigna (Antonelli 1.19b),

that these Italian poets had a shared, well-defined Ovidian agenda when including the Latin poet's name in their poetry is probably too strong, that does not mean that their mentions of Ovid are mere intertextual flourishes. After all, we find Ovid featured in poems that address larger questions, such as what love truly is and does, how the lover should behave, and about what and how the love poet should write. *Ovidio* is not a blank canvas on which just any statement about love and love poetry can be projected, but a figure that may be modeled into the shape needed at the occasion. For Cino da Pistoia, *Ovidio* was the expert author of verses that proved Onesto da Bologna only had himself to blame for his misfortune in love — reading Ovid (i.e., passages in the *Ars amatoria*) could have avoided that outcome. For Dante da Maiano, reading *Ovidio*, now the Ovid of the *Remedia amoris*, was one of the strategies to deal with lovesickness, but it was, as all other remedies, an unsuccessful one. Guido Orlandi questions Guido Cavalcanti's descriptions of love and his writing of love poetry. "Ovidio leggi," "read Ovid," Orlandi writes, implying that Ovid understands love and love poetry better. Cavalcanti in his turn sees *Ovidio* as a poet who treated the themes of love too crudely, and concludes that reading Ovid a few times does not lead to a deeper and finer understanding of love. These widely differing interpretations and evaluations of Ovid's worth as teacher of love and love poet can easily overshadow the poetic implications of mentioning him. In exchanges between Italian poets, *Ovidio* served as a far from infallible reference point: love poetry in the vernacular no longer had to rely on the example of the Latin love poet *par excellence*. In starting to debate and question Ovid's authority as a teacher of and writer about love, the most innovative among the Italian readers of Ovid want to establish their own authority as vernacular love poets.

2.4 Conclusion

When it comes to including Ovid in vernacular verse, there are distinct ways in which the Italian poets depart from the example set by the troubadours: first (and most importantly), by questioning Ovid as a reliable source, and second, by reducing the mentions of classical authors all together. But most of them still mainly stick to the Occitan playbook: the Italians take over the Occitan

---

and *Amor è uno disio che ven da core* by Giacomo da Lentini (Antonelli 1.19c). On this exchange, see Michelangelo Picone, "La tenzone 'de amore' fra Jacopo Mostacci, Pier della Vigna e il Notaio," in *Il genere 'tenzone' nelle letterature romanze delle Origini*, ed. Matteo Pedroni and Antonio Stäuble (Ravenna: Longo, 1999), 13–31.

poets' formula for featuring Ovid, and their choice of which mythological figures to include in their similes is heavily inspired by their Occitan predecessors. As much as *Ovidius*, the Latin author who we can assume was part of the educational background of many troubadour and Italian lyric poets, was available to the Italian poets here discussed, the troubadours' way of featuring the Latin poet was the more important reference point. This chapter broadly adhered to a chronological structure in order to emphasize this close relationship between the Occitan tradition and the Italian response, by showing how the language and the phrasing of the Italians poets often closely resembles those of the Occitan poets.

While we might like to identify certain changes in the Italian attitudes toward the Latin poet along the broad lines of the development of Italian poetry, from the Sicilian to the Siculo-Tuscan poets to the *stilnovisti*, the Italian poems discussed in this chapter are more similar in their treatment of Ovid than different, and their differences do not correspond to traditional divisions into poetic schools and movements. The *stilnovo* poet Cino da Pistoia, the most recent Italian poet included in this chapter, still features Ovid in a quintessential Occitan manner, appealing to the Latin poet's authority in matters of love in the sonnet *Se mai leggesti versi de l'Ovidi*, while the older Siculo-Tuscan poet Dante da Maiano has serious questions about the value of Ovid's verses. The Sicilian poet Rinaldo d'Aquino is the only one who sees Narcissus and himself as a "fin amador," while Occitan poets before him and Italians after him found Narcissus representative of the opposite "fol'amor." The other Ovidian favorites of the vernacular poets, Pyramus and Thisbe, are seen as examples of both fine and foolish love. In that sense, a plasticity similar to the one we identified in the Italian debates about love and love poetry featuring *Ovidio* also applies to the Ovidian characters found in vernacular verse: the same characters easily fit opposing views.

The main feature that unites rather than distinguishes these poems is their reliance on comparison. This aspect was the most visible in the vernacular poems discussed in the first section of this chapter, many of which used the rhetorical device of the simile to include Ovidian characters. The troubadours led the way: in their poetry the Italians found the repeated use of the simile in the form of a comparison between the poet who possesses or does something more and/or better than someone else famous for that particular characteristic. Borrowing the Ovidian favorite characters of the troubadours' similes, Narcissus and Pyramus and Thisbe, the Italian poets feature this select group of Ovidian characters to underline their own exceptionality: the poet is similar to the male Ovidian character (but better), his lady to the female (but more beautiful). By means of the simile the Italian poets can mark a clear distance and divide between two (literary) worlds: between the past of Ovid's characters and their own contemporary world — the better one. In these poems, the sentiment of outdoing what came before is not necessarily poetically charged; that is much more the case for the Italian poets who singled out Ovid's poetry as an emblem to talk about their own in the *tenzoni* discussed in the latter part of this chapter. Love and love poetry unites the two literary traditions: classical Latin poetry, represented by Ovid's characters and the mentions of his name, and their own Italian vernacular poetry in the making. The Italian poets often made comparisons, and in general they argued that they were both better lovers *and* better love poets.

CHAPTER 3

Something Old, Something New: Dante, Cino da Pistoia, and Ovid

The identification of changes and innovations in the literary production over time is a task not only undertaken by scholars looking for patterns in the literature of the past, but also by much closer witnesses: contemporary readers and writers, often with their own stakes in declaring what makes a poem traditional (or perhaps outdated), or what makes it innovative and novel. As we have seen in the metapoetic sonnet exchanges discussed in the previous chapter, Italian medieval poets eagerly took part in labeling their contemporaries, criticizing fellow poets for their stale verse and praising their own innovative poetic choices. Scholars and contemporaries alike placed Dante and Cino da Pistoia consistently among the innovators. As we will start to see in this chapter, Dante was often the first to emphasize the novelty of his own writing. Cino da Pistoia participated during his lifetime in many sonnet exchanges, several of them about poetics, and was the recipient of perhaps the harshest criticism of the poetic novelties of his time, as formulated in Onesto da Bologna's sonnet *Mente ed umìle e più di mille sporte* [Marti CXXXIIIa]. Onesto attacked all the features that modern scholars now assign to the *dolce stil novo*: the use of a selective lexicon (vv. 1–2), the reliance on dreams (v. 2), the philosophizing (v. 6), and the use of personification (v. 10). In his reply *Amor che vien per le più dolci porte* (Marti CXXXIII), Cino defends these poetic innovations.

In this chapter, I illustrate that Dante and Cino da Pistoia were also innovative in their treatment of Ovidian material. Dante and Cino's "Ovidian" poems are mostly characterized by new features that clearly separate them from the poets discussed in the previous chapter.[1] Dante and Cino moved beyond the Occitan models that had dominated the featuring of Ovidian material in Italian poetry, and worked more closely with Ovid's Latin texts. This chapter starts by looking at Dante's first mention of Ovid in the prose of the *Vita nuova*, read as an early indicator of his interest in the classical world. I then turn to Dante's *rime petrose*, a series of four poems written toward the end of the thirteenth century, and illustrate Dante's closer reading of Ovid, finding

---

1 The traditional elements of Cino's sonnet *Se mai leggesti versi de l'Ovidi* and the exchange between Dante da Maiano and Dante Alighieri, which referenced reading Ovid, are discussed in Ch. 2.3.

both central and peripheral elements from Ovid's works in Dante's poems. In the *petrose*, Dante also starts to find different ways to identify with Ovid's characters from the *Metamorphoses*, no longer relying on the simile, so commonly used in Occitan and Italian poetry. In the final section, I show how also Cino da Pistoia's poetry and his exchanges with Dante display a greater knowledge of Ovid's oeuvre, and how both poets rely on Ovidian material to explore their identities as lover, poet, and exile. These poetic choices and innovations in Dante and Cino's poetry provide the starting point to understand Dante's reliance on Ovidian material in the *Commedia* (Chapter 4) and Petrarch's use of Ovid's poems in the *Canzoniere* (Chapter 5).

3.1   "Per Ovidio parla Amore": First, the *Vita nuova*

Dante's first work the *Vita nuova* (1292–93) centers on his own poetry in the vernacular, but also provides the first clear indication of his interest in the classical world. In his self-described "libello" or "little book" (first at *VN* 1.1), Dante collects and organizes his own poems written from 1283 on, reconstructing in the accompanying prose commentary a storyline about his love for Beatrice and his own development as a love poet. As Jelena Todorović argued, in the *Vita nuova* Dante takes on all four roles that St. Bonaventure identified in the making of books, uniquely uniting the tasks of author, commentator, compiler, and scribe in one and the same person.[2] As pointed out in Ch. 1.1, these four roles of writing are intrinsically linked to the act of reading, making Dante the interpreter of his own poetry, one who also dictates to others how to read his poems.[3] Dante takes control over the narrative about each poem — describing the circumstances from which they arose, stressing their new content and form — and draws the big picture — carving out a space for his poetry in literary history. It is in such literary discussions that classical poetry and Ovid, otherwise in the shadow of vernacular poetry in the *Vita nuova*, come to the foreground.

Dante turns to the example of the classical poets in a metanarrative reflection placed in the middle of the work (*VN* 25). After the sonnet *Io mi senti' svegliar dentr'a lo core* (*VN* 24), in which Love (Amore) walks, talks, and laughs,

---

2   Todorović, *Dante and the Dynamics of Textual Exchange*. See also Michelangelo Picone, "La Vita Nova come *prosimetrum*," in *Percorsi della lirica duecentesca: Dai Siciliani alla 'Vita Nova'* (Florence: Cadmo, 2003), 237–48, at 245–47.
3   Albert Russell Ascoli stressed the novelty of the author (Dante) taking on the role of the reader in the *Vita nuova* in *Dante and the Making of a Modern Author*, 178–201, especially at 190.

Dante addresses this personification of Amore in the *Vita nuova*. Clarifying that Amore may appear as a substance ("sustanzia," i.e., a body), but actually is an accident in substance ("uno accidente in sustanzia," i.e., passion) (*VN* 25.1), Dante explains that this personification of Love is justified because the classical poets ("litterati poete") used it before him (*VN* 25.3). Poets are given greater creative license than prose writers, he further explains, and what classical poets are allowed to do, vernacular poets can do as well (*VN* 25.7). Dante then provides concrete examples from classical poetry: he refers to the moments in Vergil's *Aeneid* when Juno talks to the winds and when the oracle of Delphi addresses the Trojans; and to the opening of the *Pharsalia* when Lucan addresses the city of Rome. In addition, Dante quotes Horace quoting Homer's opening verse of the *Odyssey*, an example of the poet talking to his own knowledge as to another person; and he concludes with an example from Ovid (*VN* 25.9):

> Per Ovidio parla Amore, sí come se fosse persona umana, nel principio del libro c'ha nome *Remedio d'Amore*, quivi: « Bella mihi, video, bella parantur, ait ». E per questo puote essere manifesto a chi dubita in alcuna parte di questo mio libello.
>
> [For Ovid Love speaks as if he were a human being, at the beginning of the book that has the name *Remedy of Love*: "Wars, I see, wars are being prepared against me, he says." And this may render things clear to those with doubts about some part of this little book of mine.]

With this first canon of classical poets in Dante's works — the same five poets later reappear in the *Commedia* in Limbo (*Inf.* 4.88–90) — Dante stresses the continuity between classical and vernacular poetry, transferring the seriousness and authority of the former to the latter. Perhaps that is the reason that most examples are taken from epic poetry, the more "serious" genre of poetry, as Ovid has often discussed (for instance, in *Am.* 1.1.1–4). Out of all the examples Dante lists, only the one from Ovid belongs to the genre of (didactic) love poetry and not epic poetry. It is nevertheless the most relevant example to Dante's discussion of the personification of love in his poetry, as also Ovid featured love talking like a human.

Through these citations, Dante could be providing a glimpse into the practical and material aspects of his study of the classical world. The order of the classical authors in the *Vita nuova*, as Domenico De Robertis pointed out, brings to mind the preface to Book 2 of the *Disticha Catonis*, a collection of proverbial wisdom, where Vergil, Lucan, and Ovid are introduced as authorities on agriculture, Roman history, and love, respectively (see Ch. 1.1).[4] Dante's examples, moreover, closely resemble those one would find in rhetorical manuals to illustrate *prosopopoeia* or personification.[5] Ronald G. Witt was not able to find Dante's exact examples in the rhetorical manuals that circulated in Italy during Dante's time.[6] While Dante could be citing examples after having read these Latin poems in their entirety,[7] the language he uses points to works that transmit classical literature in fragmented ways (see Ch. 1.1). Several medieval treatises and rhetorical manuals collected isolated and fragmented phrases from classical authors.

Dante further evokes the rhetorical tradition by using the technical terms "figura" ("figure") and "colore rettorico" ("rhetorical use of tropes") (*VN* 25.10). Giuseppe Mazzotta pointed out that Dante's descriptions of prose writers and poets, "prosaici dittatori" and "dicitori per rima" (*VN* 25.7), come from Brunetto Latini's *Rettorica*.[8] Dante never uses the technical rhetorical term *prosopopoeia* in the *Vita nuova*, but his definitions — when an inanimate object talks to animate objects ("parla la cosa che non è animata a le cose animate") or the other way around ("parla la cosa animata a la cosa inanimata") (*VN* 25.9) — translate the language typically used to define the term, including in the *accessus* or medieval introductions to classical texts (see Ch. 1.1). For instance, in this *accessus* on Ovid's *Amores*, the Latin poet's use of personification is described as follows: "Facit hic prosopopeiam, id est libros loquentes ut rationales, [in]inanimatos ut animatos" ("Ovid creates a *prosopopoeia*, that is, books speaking as if they were rational beings, inanimate as if they were animate").[9] In the rhetorical manual *Ars versificatoria*, Matthew of Vendôme (twelfth century) defines the

---

4   Domenico De Robertis, *Il libro della 'Vita nuova'* (Florence: G. C. Sansoni, 1970), 150–51, n. 1.
5   For instance, Geoffrey of Vinsauf, *Poetria nova*, vv. 461–66, which lists as examples the earth complaining to Jupiter about the mess made by Phaethon driving around in the Sun's chariot (from Ovid's *Metamorphoses*) and Rome lamenting Caesar's death (from Lucan's *Pharsalia*), both examples paraphrased and without naming the authors or their works. In the *Ars versificatoria*, Matthew of Vendôme gives concrete examples, citing passages from Statius's *Thebaid* and Ovid's *Tristia* (3.23). In his edition of the *Vita nuova* (Milan: Riccardo Ricciardi, 1980), 176–77, Domenico De Robertis noted a similar Latin definition in the grammatical work *Catholicon* (1286) by the Dominican priest John of Genoa.
6   Witt, *In the Footsteps of the Ancients*, 217–18, n. 127.
7   Also Zygmunt G. Barański only found the citations Dante used in separate works, never all together, and concluded that these citations could be very well Dante's selection in "The Roots of Dante's Plurilingualism: "Hybridity" and Language in the *Vita nova*," in *Dante's Plurilingualism: Authority, Knowledge, Subjectivity*, ed. Sara Fortuna, Manuele Gragnolati, and Jürgen Trabant (Oxford: Legenda, 2010), 98–121, at 110–11.
8   Giuseppe Mazzotta, *Dante's Vision and the Circle of Knowledge* (Princeton: Princeton University Press, 1993), 63, and 247, n. 29.
9   Wheeler, *Accessus ad auctores*, 86.

prosopopoeia as "metaphora ab animato ad inanimatum" ("a metaphor from an animate object to an inanimate one" [3.23]). Whether or not Dante handpicked the classical examples included in the *Vita nuova* directly from Vergil's *Aeneid*, Lucan's *Pharsalia*, Horace's *Ars poetica*, and Ovid's *Remedia amoris* to illustrate the use of *prosopopoeia* in Latin poetry, he presented these Latin citations using the same language found in rhetorical treatises and other Latin works that collect such excerpts from Latin authors. In this way Dante created continuity between the Latin tradition and his writing of the *Vita nuova* in the vernacular.

There is no shortage of talking, walking, and laughing Amors in Ovid's amatory works (the *Amores, Ars amatoria, Remedia amoris*, and the *Heroides*), so Dante's choice of the *Remedia amoris* is worth a further look. Moreover, throughout his oeuvre Dante draws on this Ovidian work only a few times: he translates a verse from the *Remedia amoris* in the *Commedia* (see Ch. 4.2), and Ovid's didactic poem also features in an early sonnet exchange with Dante da Maiano. Dante da Maiano claimed to have unsuccessfully tried out "what Ovid said would cure lovesickness" (*Amor mi fa sì fedelemente amare*, vv. 5–6) (undoubtedly the *Remedia amoris*) and Dante Alighieri replied without mentioning Ovid's name in *Savere e cortesia, ingegno ed arte* that "knowledge" ("savere" [v. 1]) could make the difference (see Ch. 2.3). The *Remedia amoris* was definitely the "safest" choice among Ovid's amatory works. The poem was sometimes included in the *Liber catonianus*, a collection of six Latin works used in elementary school education (see Ch. 1.1). And while some *accessus* managed to turn even the *Ars amatoria* into a work that "deals with the morals of girls,"[10] the *Remedia amoris* did not need such a forgiving introduction to make the work acceptable, as its project was to steer the lusty (perhaps too well instructed by the *Ars amatoria*) away from love. In that vein, Warren Ginsberg concluded that there was no place for the "pornographic Ovid" of the *Ars amatoria* in the *Vita nuova*, making the choice for the *Remedia amoris* obvious.[11]

According to several scholars, in the *Vita nuova* Dante rewrites and corrects Ovid's *Remedia amoris* — a narrative we recognize from the previous chapter, where some medieval poets found that their poems in the vernacular outdid

---

10   The full sentence reads (Wheeler, *Accessus ad auctores*, 48, 50): "Ethice subponitur, quia de moribus puellarum loquitur, id est quos mores habeant, quibus modis retineri ualeant" ("This works belongs to ethics, because it deals with the morals of girls, that is, what kind of morals they have, and in which ways they can be held in check").

11   Warren Ginsberg, "Dante's Ovids," in Clark, Coulson, and McKinley, *Ovid in the Middle Ages*, 143–59, at 146.

the century-old poetry of Ovid.[12] But if rewriting and correcting Ovid is the task at hand in the *Vita nuova*, then there is no need for the Ovidian model to be the *Remedia*, as all other Ovidian poems can be corrected as well, and many are much more corrigible. Rather than a poet writing on a specific aspect of love, Dante is featuring Ovid as the quintessential Latin love poet. Ovid occupies a unique position in the *Vita nuova*: among the classical authors mentioned in the work, he is the only love poet, and among all the love poets included, the only one writing in Latin.[13] In the same non-specific way that Ovid stood for "Latin love poetry" in the metapoetic debates in Italian sonnet exchanges, Dante features Ovid as the counterpoint to his own love poetry in the vernacular. After all, vernacular poetry, Dante writes, "was from the very beginning invented for writing about love" ("fosse dal principio trovato per dire d'amore" [*VN* 25.6]).

The *Remedia amoris* did provide a unique model for Dante's "libello" in its formal features. Among Ovid's amatory works, the *Remedia amoris* is the only one that consists of just one book, and also Ovid referred to the work as his "libellus" or "little book."[14] In fact, in the verse that preceded the Ovidian quotation that Dante selected from the *Remedia amoris,* the Latin poet used this precise term (vv. 1–2):

LEGERAT huius Amor titulum nomenque libelli:
'bella mihi, uideo, bella parantur' ait.

[Love has read the title and the name of this little book of mine: "Wars, I see, wars are being prepared against me," he says.]

---

12   Michelangelo Picone formulated this interpretation most strongly in "La teoria dell'*Auctoritas* nella *Vita nova*," *Tenzone* 6 (2005): 173–91, especially at 181–87; and in "La *Vita Nova* come *prosimetrum*," 244–48. Also Maria Ann Roglieri, who illustrated that the presence of Ovid's Amor goes beyond the citation from the *Remedia amoris* in *VN* 25, saw the *Vita nuova* as Dante's correction of the *Remedia amoris* in "*Per Ovidio parla Amore, sì come se fosse persona umana* (V.N. xxv): The case for Ovid's figure of Amore in Dante's *Vita Nuova*," *Carte italiane* 2, nos. 2–3 (2007): 1–22.

13   Vergil, Homer, Horace, and even Lucan have all treated the theme of love in their poetry, but the works from which the citations selected by Dante in the *Vita nuova* belong to different genres than love poetry. Fellow Italian love poets are present but remain unnamed in the *Vita nuova*: Dante mentions the "fedeli d'Amore" (*VN* 3), whom he asked to explain his vision described in *A ciascun'alma presa e gentil core* (*VN* 3.9), and throughout the work he mentions his "primo amico," Guido Cavalcanti (*VN* 3, 24, 25, 30).

14   On what the term "libello" would have evoked in Dante's time, see Todorović, *Dante and the Dynamics of Textual Exchange*, 147–51, with reference to Ovid's use of the term "libellus" at 147–48.

With the complete opening couplet of the *Remedia amoris* before us, it is worth looking again at the passage in the *Vita nuova* where Dante included its second verse (*VN* 25.9):

> Per Ovidio parla Amore, sí come se fosse persona umana, nel principio del libro c'ha nome *Remedio d'Amore*, quivi: « Bella mihi, video, bella parantur, ait ». E per questo puote essere manifesto a chi dubita in alcuna parte di questo mio libello.

There is no room for two "libelli" in the *Vita nuova*: Dante upgrades Ovid's Latin "libellus" to "libro" status (in the Latin *accessus* tradition, the *Remedia amoris* is called a "liber"),[15] before he mentions his own "libello."[16] Situating the Ovidian citation within the *Remedia amoris*, Dante specifies that it is found at the beginning ("ne lo principio") of the work, where its title and name are announced: his phrase "libro c'ha nome *Remedio d'Amore*" retakes Ovid's "huius ... nomen ... libelli" in the *Remedia amoris* (v. 1). Moreover, Dante transfers the Latin demonstrative adjective "huius" ("that"), which Ovid used to refer to his *Remedia amoris*, to his own "libello": "*questo* mio libello" (emphasis added). In this chapter of the *Vita nuova* (*VN* 25), Dante cites examples of *prosopopoeia* from Ovid's and other Latin poetry as a way to elevate the status of his own poetry in the vernacular; by transferring the language that Ovid used to describe his *Remedia amoris* to his own *Vita nuova* in the vernacular, Dante aims for the same.

At the beginning of the *Vita nuova* Dante relies on the language of the same opening couplet of Ovid's *Remedia amoris* (*VN* 1; emphasis added):

> In quella parte del libro de la mia memoria dinanzi a la quale poco si potrebbe *leggere*, si trova una rubrica la qual dice: *Incipit vita nova*. Sotto la qual rubrica io trovo scritte le parole le quali è mio intendimento d'assemprare in questo *libello*; e se non tutte, almeno la loro sentenzia.

---

15   See, for instance, Wheeler, *Accessus ad auctores*, 50.

16   Dante also connects both works through the word "libro." As Michelangelo Picone also pointed out, Dante mentions only two books in the *Vita nuova*: his metaphorical "libro de la mia memoria," "book of my memory" (*VN* 1) and Ovid's "book," the "libro c'ha nome *Remedio d'Amore*," "the book that has the name *Remedy of Love*" (*VN* 25.9). See "La *Vita Nova* come macrotesto," in *Percorsi della letteratura duecentesca*, 219–35, at 222; and "La *Vita Nova* come *prosimetrum*," 247. For Picone's views on the *Remedia amoris* as model and archetype for the *Vita nuova*, see n. 12. These are the only occurrences of the word "libro" in the *Vita nuova*. Dante uses "libello" four times, and always to refer to the *Vita nuova* (*VN* 1, 12.17, 25.9, 28.2).

[In that part of the book of my memory, before which there is little *to read*, there is a heading that says "Incipit vita nova." I intend to copy the words that I find written under this heading in this *little book*; if not all, then at least their meaning.]

At the beginning of the *Vita nuova* Dante restages the act of reading that opened the *Remedia amoris*, replacing Ovid's Amor with himself. Ovid's Amor who had read ("legerat" [v. 1]) the title and name of his work ("libelli" [v. 1]) becomes Dante who reads ("leggere") what is written under the rubric "Incipit vita nova" in the book of his memory, which offers the material for his "libello" (*VN* 1). While Love plays quite a different role in the *Vita nuova*, the similar phrasing at the opening of both works is striking.[17] By transferring language from Ovid's Latin poem to his own Italian "little book," at the beginning of the *Vita nuova* Dante signals for the first time the poetic concerns formulated explicitly in the metapoetic *VN* 25. The following chapter on Dante's reading of Ovid in the *Commedia* includes several passages where Dante relies on metapoetic language in Ovid's works to make statements about his own poetry in the vernacular. In this earlier instance in the *Vita nuova*, we encounter Dante as a reader of Ovid who is already attentive to such passages in the Latin poet's work.

Dante concludes his metapoetic digression by returning to the greater creative license that he earlier granted to poets. While poets have this advantage over writers of prose, he adds one caveat: those who use figurative speech should always be able to explain it. The classical poets are once again the model: they did not use figurative language without reason ("sanza ragione"), and it would be quite shameful, Dante continues, to dress up your poetry without being able to explain how and why (*VN* 25.10).[18] In the final sentence of the chapter, Dante indicates that he and his best friend, the unnamed Guido Cavalcanti, know many who wrote such "stupid" poetry: "E questo mio primo amico e io ne sapemo bene di quelli che cosí rimano stoltamente" ("And my first true friend and I know well those who write poetry in such a stupid way"

---

17   While my focus here is on Ovid, these opening sentences of the *Vita nuova* are packed with references to several other religious and secular texts and literary traditions, in Latin and in the vernacular.

18   This is yet another way in which Dante creates a narrative of continuity between Latin and Italian literature. See especially Ascoli, *Dante and the Making of a Modern Author*, on this Dantean program in the *Vita nuova* (184–85), on how Dante realizes this in *VN* 25 (193–97), best summarized in the following description: "the chapter follows what becomes the typical Dantean oscillation between an ambitious rapprochement of ancient and modern, and a humble, or at least mock humble, deference to the great *auctores* and *auctoritates*" (195).

[*VN* 25.10]). Guittone d'Arezzo is often considered the target of Dante's criticism here.[19] Guido Orlandi is another possible candidate.[20]

With these concluding words Dante not only brings back to mind the sonnet that had inspired this metapoetic digression in the first place — the personified Amor in *Io mi senti' svegliar dentr'a lo core* (*VN* 24), which also featured Monna Vanna and Monna Bice, Guido Cavalcanti and Dante's ladies — but also alludes again to Ovid and the personified Amor. As we have seen in Ch. 2.3, Guido Orlandi attacks Cavalcanti, among other things, for his representation of love in a series of metapoetic poems.[21] In those poems, both Guidos mention Ovid to draw the distinction between one another's poetry.[22] Guido Orlandi writes that "Amor sincero – non piange né ride" ("true love does not cry or laugh" [*Per troppa sottiglianza il fil si rompe*, v. 7]), alluding to the personification of Love in Cavalcanti's poetry. (These are the same human qualities that Dante mentioned in his description of Amor at the opening of *VN* 25.) Orlandi repeats this mocking attack in the final sonnet of the exchange: "faresti Amore piangere in tuo stato" ("you would make Love cry in your state" [*Amico, i' saccio ben che sa' limare*, v. 10]). Metapoetics, Ovid, and the personification of love tie Dante's *VN* 25 to the exchanges between Guido Orlandi and Guido Cavalcanti. Orlandi attacks in Cavalcanti's poetry precisely what Dante here in the *Vita nuova* defends: featuring Love as a person in a meaningful way. Orlandi tells Cavalcanti to read Ovid because he understood love better ("Ovidio leggi: più di te ne vide" [*Per troppa sottiglianza il fil si rompe*, v. 11]); in the *Vita nuova*, Dante defends his personification of love (which Orlandi attacked in Cavalcanti's

---

19   Not all editors of the *Vita nuova* identify "quelli che cosí rimano stoltamente." Marcello Ciccuto (Milan: Rizzoli, 1984), for instance, named Guittone as Dante's target here (199, n. 64), as did Stefano Carrai (Milan: Rizzoli, 2009) at 125. Readers of Dante's entire oeuvre know that he continues to criticize Guittone in his writing, culminating in *Purg*. 26. There, Guido Guinizzelli delivers a direct attack on Guittone (*Purg*. 26.124–26), preceded by a phrase similar to Dante's comment in the *Vita nuova*: "lascia dir li stolti" ("let the stupid ones talk" [*Purg*. 26.119]). Guglielmo Gorni pointed out this connection in Dante, *Opere*, Vol. 1, *Rime, Vita Nova, De vulgari eloquentia*, ed. Claudio Giunta, Guglielmo Gorni, and Mirko Tavoni (Milan: Mondadori, 2011), 972–73. On Dante's Guittone, see especially Barolini, *Dante's Poets*, 94–112; Tristan Kay, "Redefining the 'matera amorosa': Dante's *Vita nova* and Guittone's (anti-)courtly 'canzoniere,'" *The Italianist* 29, no. 3 (2009): 369–99, especially at 372–76; and *Dante's Lyric Redemption: Eros, Salvation, Vernacular Tradition* (Oxford: Oxford University Press, 2016), 93–154.

20   Guido Orlandi is mentioned as possible target together with Guittone d'Arezzo in *Vita nova*, ed. Gorni, 972–73.

21   The exchange consists of three poems: Guido Orlandi's *Per troppa sottiglianza il fil si rompe*, Guido Cavalcanti's reply *Di vil matera mi conven parlare*, and Guido Orlandi's final reply, *Amico, i' saccio ben che sa' limare*.

22   For a more detailed discussion of this *tenzone*, see the Ch. 2.3.

poetry) through the example of Ovid, since the Latin poet had featured Amor in a similar way. Such different uses of Ovid remind us again, as we have seen at various points in Chapter 2, how easily *Ovidio* can be molded into the shape needed for the occasion.

In the *Vita nuova*, the example of Ovid — a classical poet — mainly serves to validate a central feature of Dante's poetry in the vernacular: a personified Amor. Italian poetry, not classical poetry, is at the center of Dante's first work. The limited references to Latin and Greek poets as points of comparison raise the status of the vernacular in his own poetry. Dante is most explicit about this vernacular agenda in his metapoetic digression in *VN* 25, where Ovid is one of the classical poets mentioned among the examples of personification in Greek and Latin poetry. Ovid is not only the most important classical poet mentioned in that chapter, but the influence of his language and example also extend to other parts of Dante's "libello." The *Vita nuova* thus marks Dante's first interest in the classics in general, and in Ovid in particular. While this interest in classical literature manifests itself in language reminiscent of anthologies and other sources that feature classical citations out of context, Dante goes beyond simply citing Ovid's example from the *Remedia amoris* (v. 2) in the prose of the *Vita nuova*: he shows awareness of the larger passage in the Ovidian poem from which the citation was taken and of its metapoetic potential. In the following section, we will see how also Dante's poetry from the 1290s further reveals his reading of Ovid.

3.2   Dante's *petrose*: Testing Out New Techniques

The *rime petrose* stand out in Dante's lyric oeuvre because of the presence of the "donna Petra," who gave her name to the poems; their return to *trobar clus*, the learned and opaque poetry first championed by the troubadours Marcabru and Arnaut Daniel; and Dante's experimentation with form. But this series of four poems (*Io son venuto al punto della rota, Al poco giorno ed al gran cerchio d'ombra, Amor, tu vedi ben che questa donna,* and *Così nel mio parlar vogli'esser aspro*) also marks the more distinct turn that Dante made toward classical literature as source of literary influence after the *Vita nuova*.[23] This

---

23   Among the numerous readings of the *petrose*, the following in particular focused on their classical sources: Enrico Fenzi, "Le rime per la donna pietra," in *Miscellanea di studi danteschi* (Genoa: Mario Bozzi, 1966), 229–309; Vanni Bartolozzi, "Ambiguità e metamorfosi nella sestina dantesca," *Romance Philology* 36 (1982): 1–17; and Robert Durling and Ronald Martinez, *Time and the Crystal: Studies in Dante's 'Rime petrose'* (Berkeley: University of California Press, 1990). Durling and Martinez's study on the *petrose* has been crucial to

moment can even be traced precisely in time, as the astronomic periphrasis from the opening stanza of *Io son venuto al punto della rota* dates the *canzone* to December 1296. In the previous chapter, we found Dante's first, indirect expression of interest in Ovid in the early sonnet *Savere e cortesia, ingegno ed arte*, in response to Dante da Maiano's *Amor mi fa sì fedelmente amare*. As noted there and earlier in this chapter, Dante da Maiano considered the knowledge ("leggenda" [v. 11]) from Ovid's *Remedia amoris* useless against the power of love. Dante Alighieri indirectly discussed the value of this kind of knowledge when he includes "savere" (v. 1) as one of the graces and virtues that can win over the lady's heart. Moreover, as we have seen in the previous section, Dante's interest in the classics, and in Ovid in particular, emerged explicitly in prose writings dating slightly earlier than the *petrose*: in the prose commentary in the *Vita nuova*, Dante mentioned examples from the "litterati poete" (*VN* 25.3) Vergil, Lucan, Horace, and Ovid, and quoted the second verse of Ovid's *Remedia amoris* (*VN* 25.9). In the *petrose*, Dante does not use direct quotations from Ovid's work nor the techniques earlier Italian poets used to feature classical sources. Instead, Dante introduces some new approaches to Ovidian material: the introduction of other Ovidian myths besides the stories of Narcissus and Pyramus and Thisbe, the re-creation of the world of the *Metamorphoses*, and gender reversals in his comparisons with Ovidian characters. (In the following section, I will also discuss these innovations in Cino da Pistoia and Dante's later lyric poetry.) Moreover, Dante integrates both central and peripheral elements from Ovidian stories in his *petrose*, and combines several different Ovidian sources at once — testing out some techniques to integrate Ovidian material that he will use more frequently in the *Commedia*.

One of the *petrose*'s "basic ideas," as Robert Durling and Ronald Martinez put it, is the figure of Medusa.[24] Never mentioned by name, the Gorgon with the petrifying glance indeed oversees all four *petrose*. Dante does not strictly replicate the story as he could have known it from Lucan's *Pharsalia* (9.619–99) and Ovid's *Metamorphoses* (4.612–20; 4.772–803). Instead, he combines his classical sources and selects both central and peripheral elements from the stories, scattering them throughout the poems — techniques new to Dante's poetry. In the *canzone Io son venuto al punto della rota*, for example, the description of the winds rising from the sand of Ethiopia (vv. 14–16) recalls details from Lucan's

---

my thinking about these four poems. While I do not always agree with their conclusions about the role of Ovid in the *petrose* (as noted throughout this section), my engagement with this material is clearly indebted to their analysis (as also documented in the footnotes of this section).

24   Durling and Martinez, *Time and the Crystal*, 105.

DANTE, CINO DA PISTOIA, AND OVID   135

description of the Libyan desert lands (*Phars.* 9.338–40; 9.488–89), leading up to the story of Medusa in the *Pharsalia*.[25] Ovid's version in the *Metamorphoses* mentions the "Libycas ... harenas" ("the Libyan sands" [*Met.* 4.617]), turned into a snake pit by the blood dripping from Medusa's cut off head (*Met.* 4.618–20). This passage in Ovid's *Metamorphoses* is immediately followed by a description of Perseus's travel (*Met.* 4.621–26) that shares several meteorological elements with the second stanza of *Io son venuto*. For instance, Dante mentions the clashing winds (vv. 14–15), comparing them to a raincloud (v. 21) that crosses the sea (v. 17) and passes several times the extremities of the world (v. 19) — the northern hemisphere represented by the Bear constellations, the southern by the Crab constellation. All these elements mirror elements of the description of Perseus's journey in the *Metamorphoses*.[26] Furthermore, Ovid's "gelidas Arctos" ("the Bears in the north" [*Met.* 4.625], or the seven-star constellation Ursa Major) return in the third stanza of *Io son venuto* as "le sette stelle gelide" ("the seven freezing stars" [v. 29]). A third classical source for the description is

---

25   Dante, *Io son venuto*, vv. 14–16: "Lèvasi della rena d'Etïopia / il vento peregrin che l'aere turba, / per la spera del sol ch'ora la scalda" ("The pilgrim wind that darkens the air rises up from the sands of Ethiopia, through the sphere of the sun, which now warms it up"); Lucan, *Phars.* 9.338–40; 9.488–89: "tum magis impactis brevius mare terraque saepe / obvia consurgens: quamvis elisus ab Austro, / saepe tamen cumulos fluctus non vincit harenae" ("then the more the ship was pushed around, the less the sea became deep, and the land rose up often: even though the Auster made the waves larger, they nevertheless did not often conquer the heaps of sand"); "alligat et stantis affusae magnus harenae / agger, et immoti terra surgente tenentur" ("a great bulwark of accumulated sand hindered even those who were standing, and they were held immobile as the earth rose up"). The *canzone*'s mention of the "rena d'Etïopia" ("sands of Ethiopia" [v. 14]) becomes "Libia con sua rena" ("Libya with her sands") in *Inf.* 24.85 in a larger passage (*Inf.* 24.85–90) that is also inspired by the same book of the *Pharsalia*.

26   Dante, *Io son venuto*, vv. 14–21: "Lèvasi della rena d'Etïopia / il vento peregrin che l'aere turba, / ... / e passa 'l mare ... / ... / questo emisperio chiude e tutto salda; / ... e cade in bianca falda / di fredda neve ed i· noiosa pioggia" ("The pilgrim wind that darkens the air rises from the sands of Ethiopia, ... and crosses the sea, ... with a fog so thick that it shuts and seals this hemisphere completely ... and falls down in white flakes of cold snow and vexing rain"); Ovid, *Met.* 4.621–26: "Inde per immensum uentis discordibus actus / nunc huc, nunc illuc exemplo nubis aquosae / fertur et ex alto seductas aequore longe / despectat terras totumque superuolat orbem. / ter gelidas Arctos, ter Cancri bracchia uidit, / saepe sub occasus, saepe est ablatus in ortus") ("From there he was pushed by clashing winds through the big sky, this way and that way, just like a raincloud. From high up he looked down on distant lands and flew around the entire world. Three times he saw the icy Bears in the north, three times the claws of the Cancer constellation; he was often dragged to the west, often to the east").

found in Seneca's *Quaestiones naturales*, in the passage where the philosopher discusses the winds (V 18.2).[27]

In these few verses, Dante combines elements from different classical sources in a highly selective manner. Both Lucan and Ovid, for example, describe the desert sands of Libya, not Ethiopia as Dante does. But Ethiopia is mentioned in the surrounding passages: in Ovid's *Metamorphoses*, it is Perseus's next stop (*Met.* 4.668–69) and the place where Perseus narrates how he decapitated Medusa; Lucan describes Medusa's petrification of entire Ethiopian tribes (*Phars.* 9.650–51).[28] Dante's technique here consists in not only featuring the most prominent aspects of Ovidian stories, but also peripheral elements.

Medusa's essential trait is of course her petrifying glance. In the *petrose*, the poet oscillates between the fear of being turned into stone (e.g., *Io son venuto*, vv. 71–72) and the painful realization that he was already petrified (e.g., *Amor, tu vedi ben che questa donna*, v. 18). Enrico Fenzi listed numerous lines from the Medusa story and other stories in the *Metamorphoses* that could have inspired several verses of the four *petrose*.[29] Indeed, petrification is one of the most common transformations in the *Metamorphoses*,[30] and Ovid's poem offers a comprehensive lexicon to describe this kind of metamorphosis: the sensation of wintry cold and frost, the mentions of marble, stones, rocks, paleness, whiteness, and stoniness. However, it has not been noted enough that Ovid's exile

---

27 "deinde ut imbres terris subministrarent, idemque nimios compescerent. nam modo adducunt niues modo deducunt, ut per totum orbem pluuiae diuidi possint: in Italiam auster impellit, aquilo in Africam reicit, etesiae non patiuntur apud nos nubes consistere; idem totam Indiam et Aethiopiam continuis per id tempus aquis inrigant" ("next, so that the winds deliver rainclouds to the earth and curb excessive wetness as well. Because the winds sometimes collect clouds, other times disperse them, to distribute rain over the entire world. The Auster pushes rain to Italy, the Aquilo sends it back to Africa; the Etesian winds do not allow clouds to stay near us; they irrigate all of India and Ethiopia during their season with continuous rain"). See Kenelm Foster and Patrick Boyde, *Dante's Lyric Poetry* (Oxford: Oxford University Press, 1967), 2: 262, notes 14–16. See also Fenzi, "Le rime per la donna Pietra," 301, nn. 77–80. For a more detailed discussion of the connections between Seneca's *Quaestiones naturales* and Dante's *Io son venuto*, see Robert M. Durling, "'Io son venuto': Seneca, Plato, and the Microcosm," *Dante Studies* 93 (1975): 95–129.

28 Ovid, *Met.* 4.668–69: "gentibus innumeris circumque infraque relictis / Aethiopum populos Cepheaque conspicit arua" ("leaving many nations behind, around and below, he finally noticed the Ethiopian people and the lands of Cepheus"); Lucan, *Phars.* 9.650–51: "vicina colentes / Aethiopum totae riguerunt marmore gentes" ("entire tribes of Ethiopians living nearby turned into hard marble").

29 Fenzi, "Le rime per la donna Pietra," 244–45.

30 Gilles Tronchet listed all thirty-five instances in *La métamorphose à l'oeuvre: recherches sur la poétique d'Ovide dans les 'Métamorphoses'* (Leuven: Peeters, 1998), 578.

poetry even more closely conforms to the images of the *petrose*.[31] For instance, the following passage from the *Epistulae ex Ponto* (1.2.23–36) sounds like a miniature *petrosa*:

> adde loci faciem nec fronde nec arbore tecti,
> et quod iners hiemi continuatur hiems.
> hic me pugnantem cum frigore cumque sagittis
> cumque meo fato quarta fatigat hiems.
> fine carent lacrimae, nisi cum stupor obstitit illis,
> et similis morti pectora torpor habet.
> felicem Nioben, quamuis tot funera uidit,
> quae posuit sensum saxea facta mali.
> uos quoque felices, quarum clamantia fratrem
> cortice uelauit populus ora nouo.
> ille ego sum, lignum qui non admittor in ullum;
> ille ego sum, frustra qui lapis esse uelim.
> ipsa Medusa oculis ueniat licet obuia nostris,
> amittet uires ipsa Medusa suas.

> [Add that the face of this place is not covered by leaves or trees, and that idle winter turns into another winter. I am worn out by my fourth winter here, fighting against cold, against arrows, against my own fate. There are endless tears, unless a stupor blocks them; and a lethargy that feels like death fills my chest. Lucky Niobe, even though she saw so many deaths, that she lost the ability to feel and turned into a stone! You, too, are lucky, whose mouths the poplar covered with a strange new bark, when you were calling your brother! I am one who is not allowed to turn into a tree; I am one who in vain wants to be a rock. Should Medusa herself come before my eyes, Medusa would lose her powers.]

Written in the first person, this fragment from Ovid's *Epistulae ex Ponto* shares with the *petrose* the personal tone that is absent from the *Metamorphoses* fragments. These fourteen verses unite the very basic ideas of the *petrose* — only the amorous aspect is missing. First, Ovid describes the harsh climate and the barren winter (one of his main complaints about the location of his exile),

---

31   Giuseppe Velli focused on the images and verses from Ovid's exile letters in *Io son venuto* in "Petrarca, Dante, la poesia classica: 'Ne la stagion che 'l ciel rapido inchina' (RVF, L) 'Io son venuto al punto de la rota' (*Rime*, C)," *Studi petrarcheschi* 15 (2002): 81–98, especially at 88–94.

and their effects on both the landscape and the poet's mood. In that sense, the external "frigor" (v. 25) leads to the internal experience of "stupor" (v. 27) and "torpor" (v. 28). The poet of change is stuck in an unchangeable world where the finality of metamorphosis seems the only imaginable escape. He considers his own characters from the *Metamorphoses* fortunate — the named Niobe (vv. 29–30) and the unnamed sisters of Phaethon (vv. 31–32) — and hopes in vain to be the inanimate objects they had become (vv. 33–34). The futile desire to be a stone brings to mind Niobe's metamorphosis (vv. 29–30) and also anticipates the mention of Medusa (vv. 35–36): the poet imagines himself to be the only person who would remain unaffected by Medusa's powers. This fragment from Ovid's exile letters thus combines several motifs, starting with the winter weather and ending with Medusa, going from external cold to internal cold, from external freezing to petrification by Medusa. As these same motifs are fundamental to the *petrose*, this connection marks the beginning of Dante's interest in Ovid's exile poetry.[32]

While Medusa's presence is felt in the four *petrose*, in the *sestina Al poco giorno ed al gran cerchio d'ombra*, the central classical figure is the unnamed Clytie, the nymph abandoned by Apollo (in Ovid's account referred to with his other name Sol), when he had fallen in love with her sister Leucothoë (*Met.* 4.190–273). Vanni Bartolozzi has pointed out how in the fourth stanza the lover's flight "per piani e per colli" ("over plains and hills" [v. 21]) recalls Perseus's flight to Medusa's dwelling place "per agros / perque uias" ("over the fields and the roads" [*Met.* 4.779–80]). The majority of references, however, come from Ovid's description of Clytie's death, her slow transformation into a heliotrope or sunflower, forever following Sol's every move (*Met.* 4.256–70).[33] Already in the first stanza, for example, the description of the poet's desire as "barbato nella dura pietra" ("rooted in the hard stone" [v. 5]) recalls the description of Clytie slowly rooting in the ground (*Met.* 4.266, 4.269).[34] The mention in the same stanza that "si perde lo color nell' erba" ("the color gets lost in the grass" [v. 3]) recalls how Clytie's limbs lose color and change into bloodless

---

32   In the following section, I will identify the influence of Ovid's exile letters on Dante's later poetry, and in Ch. 4.3, I refer to a few passages in the *Commedia* that were clearly written with those letters in mind.

33   Bartolozzi briefly discusses the reference to Medusa and discusses the Clytie passage (*Met.* 4.256–70) in more detail in "Ambiguità e metamorfosi," 11, and 15–16.

34   "membra ferunt haesisse solo" ("they say that her limbs were stuck in the ground"); "illa ... quamuis radice tenetur" ("even though she was held back by her roots"). Contini pointed out that the word "barbato" is used in one of Guittone's letters and in Brunetto Latini's *Tesoretto* (*Rime*, 158, note to v. 5). I add the later occurrence in "[e]llera abbarbicata" ("ivy clung") in *Inf.* 25.58, a connection also noted in Sara Sturm-Maddox, "The 'Rime Petrose' and the Purgatorial Palinode," *Studies in Philology* 84, no. 2 (1987): 119–33, at 132, n. 31.

"herbas" (*Met.* 4.266–67).[35] In this *sestina*, Dante experiences and expresses rejection through language from Ovid's story about the nymph Clytie — the first instance where the male poet identifies with the female character of an Ovidian story.

Durling and Martinez revisited Bartolozzi's reading of the connections between the Ovidian Clytie and the poet of *Al poco giorno*,[36] and interpreted the flower in which she changes as an emblem for the *sestina*, calling both Ovid's story and Dante's *sestina* "heliotropic in structure and theme."[37] Indeed, Ovid sometimes mimics the kind of metamorphosis that a character undergoes in the structural aspects of his text. For instance, in the story of Narcissus and Echo (*Met.* 3.339–510), the nymph Echo's transformation consists of losing her voice and being turned into an echo. Ovid cleverly applies the principle of echo sounds to the passage's metrical scheme: when talking to her love interest Narcissus, Echo just repeats the last word(s) of his sentences, which are so well chosen that her "answers" create different sentences in their own right.[38] Durling and Martinez identified a similar mimetic practice in the story of Sol and Clytie, viewing the structure of the passage to be like that of the sunflower. But applied to Dante's *sestina*, the notions of heliotropic structure and theme pose some issues. Starting with the structure of the poem, what does it really mean that this *sestina*'s "formal principles ... follow the movement and tropic turns of the sun"?[39] The organization of the *sestina*'s rhyme words, the *retrogradatio cruciata*, is indeed undeniably cyclic, but this formal

---

35   "partemque coloris / luridus exsangues pallor conuertit in herbas" ("a ghastly pallor turned her complexion partially into the color of pale leaves"). Besides these two instances, Bartolozzi singled out five more Ovidian verses he considers of particular interest for *Al poco giorno* ("Ambiguità e metamorfosi," 15–16): *Met.* 4.260 // *Al poco giorno*, vv. 35–36; *Met.* 4.264 // *Al poco giorno*, v. 17; *Met.* 4.264–65, 4.260 // *Al poco giorno*, v. 14; *Met.* 4.265 // *Al poco giorno*, v. 23. I do not exclude that these verses might have contributed in conceptualizing certain images of the *sestina*, but do not find substantial overlap in the language, or even the content of the passages. Furthermore, Bartolozzi at no point indicated from which edition of the *Metamorphoses* he is quoting, which is problematic for *Met.* 4.260: Bartolozzi read "nympharum impatiens" and connected it with "trae della mente nostra ogni altra donna" ("she takes every other woman from our mind" [v. 14]), while "impatiens" is a later correction of the reading "patiens" that most manuscripts have. The most recent Tarrant edition (2004) has the Bentley correction "nimborum patiens."
36   Durling and Martinez, *Time and the Crystal*, 121.
37   Durling and Martinez, *Time and the Crystal*, 113.
38   For example, when the nymph Echo only repeats the last words of Narcissus's sentence "ante ... emoriar, quam sit tibi copia nostri" ("may I die before you get a piece of my body" [*Met.* 3.391]), her reply "sit tibi copia nostri" actually means "get a piece of my body " (*Met.* 3.392).
39   Durling and Martinez, *Time and the Crystal*, 113.

aspect characterizes every *sestina*. Even when combining the formal and thematic aspects of this *sestina*, *Al poco giorno* does not consistently connect to the movement of the sun. Out of the six words that are shuffled around in the *sestina*'s fixed rhyme scheme, "ombra" is the only rhyme word that is related to this movement. In that respect, Petrarch's first *sestina A qualunque animale alberga in terra* (*Rvf* 22) is far more "heliotropic" with the rhyme words "sole" ("sun"), "giorno" ("day"), "stelle" ("stars"), and "alba" ("dawn").

The movements of the sun are not completely absent from this *sestina*, but their importance is not felt over the entire poem. Doubling in Ovid's story as both star and god in love, in *Al poco giorno* the sun is initially the star whose light is seen more or less over the course of the seasons. Especially in the first two stanzas of the *sestina*, it is through the sun that the cycle of seasons is described: the lack of sunlight in the winter in the first stanza — "Al poco giorno ed al gran cerchio d'ombra" ("To the shorter days and the great circle of shadow" [v. 1]) — and the return of warm sunrays in the spring in the second — "il dolce tempo che riscalda i colli" ("the nice weather that warms up the hills" [v. 10]). Moreover, the movement from winter (vv. 1–3) to spring (vv. 10–12) at the extremities of the first two stanzas encircles the verses that describe the stability of the poet's desire (vv. 4–6) and the immovability of the lady (vv. 7–9). But the rest of the *sestina* stays set in the spring and the attention shifts almost entirely to the poet and the lady, with nature figuring in the background.[40] Except for the rhyme word "ombra," the sun almost entirely disappears from the *sestina*.

Only in one instance does the sun reappear in its double Ovidian meaning of star and lover. As pointed out before, the poet identifies with the female character Clytie whose love for Sol remains unaltered, even though it is unrequited. This turns the lady of the *sestina* into the counterpart of the Ovidian Sol: it is in this respect that we should read the verse "dal *suo lume* non mi può far ombra" ("from *her light* I cannot find shadow" [v. 23; emphasis added]),

---

40 I propose the following breakdown:
    Stanza 1: vv. 1–3: nature
                vv. 4–6: poet
    Stanza 2: vv. 7–9: donna
                vv. 10–12: nature
    Stanza 3: poet and donna
    Stanza 4: poet and donna
    Stanza 5: poet and donna
    Stanza 6: vv. 31–33: nature
                vv. 34–36: poet
    Envoy: v. 37: nature
                vv. 38–39: donna and poet

where the lady is also both star and lover.[41] Moreover, a previous verse from the same stanza also seems to indicate that Ovid was on Dante's mind. Describing the lady's incurable wounds, Dante writes that " 'l colpo suo non può sanar per erba" ("her blows cannot be healed with herbs" [v. 20]). This description reprises "quod nullis amor est sanabilis herbis" ("there exists no herb that cures love" [*Met.* 1.523]), taken from the story of Apollo and Daphne — the first love story starring Sol and also the very first love story of the *Metamorphoses*.[42]

Taking all these elements into account, I thus temper Durling and Martinez's "heliotropic" reading of *Al poco giorno*, because the formal argument is based on features that are present in every *sestina*. While some of the Ovidian motifs or thematic connections that Durling and Martinez and Bartolozzi establish between Ovid's story of Sol and Clytie and Dante's *sestina* are not only present in Ovid's poetry (for instance, the theme of unaltered love after rejection is not exclusively found in Clytie's story), they identified in the *sestina* several close textual connections with this Ovidian story as well as with the story of Apollo and Daphne. These connections illustrate again Dante's technique of incorporating central and peripheral elements from different sources.

The third classical character of importance in the *petrose* is Dido. As the only classical character mentioned by name in all of Dante's *rime*, she appears in the *canzone Così nel mio parlar vogli'esser aspro*, where Love threatens the poet "con quella spada ond'elli ancise Dido" ("with the sword with which he killed Dido" [v. 36]).[43] Dido is mainly a Vergilian character and, as Durling and Martinez showed, the structure of the *canzone* somewhat parallels the narra-

---

41   The previous verse, "per potere scampar da cotal donna" ("to be able to escape such a woman" [v. 22]), makes it clear that Dante is talking about the lady. However, the way possessive adjectives are used in the Italian language — the adjective takes the gender of the noun it modifies, not the gender of the person who possesses the noun, as is the case in English — makes that "suo lume" is inherently ambiguous, as it could mean both "his light" and "her light."

42   Durling and Martinez, *Time and the Crystal*, 120.

43   As this particular moment is not discussed in the following chapter on the *Commedia*, I note here that in the *Inferno* Dante introduces Dido in the circle of lust with a similar description, "colei che s'ancise amorosa" ("she who killed herself for love" [*Inf.* 5.61]). In a larger discussion of how Dante, through Dido, casts himself in the role of the lustful woman, Carolynn Lund-Mead pointed out, following Giuseppe Mazzotta who first made the connection, that Dante's description of Dido retakes St. Augustine's in the *Confessions* (1.13): "quia se occidit ab amore," "because she killed herself for love." See "Dido Alighieri: Gender Inversion in the Francesca Episode," in *Dante & the Unorthodox: The Aesthetics of Transgression*, ed. James Miller (Waterloo: Wilfrid Laurier University Press, 2005), 121–50, at 124. Also Tristan Kay focused on the Vergilian connection in this *canzone*, as part of an essay that traces Dante's changing identification with the Vergilian lovers throughout his work: Aeneas in the *Convivio*; Dido in *Così nel mio parlar vogli'esser aspro*; Dido and

tive line of Book 4 of the *Aeneid*.[44] Furthermore, Vergil's opening description of the night during which Dido dies (*Aen.* 4.522–32) contains the same contrast between the external tranquility of nature and the internal agitation of the lover that we found in the opening stanza of *Io son venuto*.[45]

Dido, however, is also an Ovidian character, one of the letter-writing heroines of the *Heroides*. (In the *Metamorphoses*, her story is reduced to four verses [*Met.* 14.78–81] and, instead of Dido, she is called obscurely the "Sidonian" [*Met.* 14.80].) Small but distinct elements from Dido's letter to Aeneas (*Her.* 7) are found in the *petrose*. In *Così nel mio parlar*, Love attacks with the sword that killed Dido (v. 36), which is essentially a rewriting of the letter's epitaph: "Praebuit Aeneas et causam mortis et ensem. / Ipsa sua Dido concidit usa manu" ("Aeneas provided both the cause of her death and the sword; Dido died by her own hand" [*Her.* 7.195–96]).[46] In her letter, Dido accuses Aeneas of stony-heartedness, which made him act as if he were brought up by wild animals: "te saevae progenuere ferae" ("wild animals produced you" [*Her.* 7.38]). In *Amor, tu vedi ben che questa donna*, the poet attributes a similar origin to the lady's harsh behavior: "sì che non par ch'ell'abbia cuor di donna / ma di qual fiera l'ha d'amor più freddo" ("so that it does not seem that she has the heart of a woman, but of some wild animal, most insensitive to love" [vv. 7–8]).[47]

This third and last example from the *petrose* showcases again Dante's technique of incorporating central and peripheral elements from Ovid's stories. Just like Medusa and Clytie, Dido's presence is a patchwork of different sources scattered throughout the *petrose*. Also in the case of Dido, Dante reverses gender roles and associates himself with the female classical character, based on their shared experience as rejected lover. Inversion, contrast, and reversal are important notions in the *petrose*. Dante is hot for an icy lady; he burns for

    Aeneas in the *Commedia*. See "Dido, Aeneas, and the Evolution of Dante's Poetics," *Dante Studies* 129 (2011): 135–60.
44 Durling and Martinez, *Time and the Crystal*, 182–83.
45 Dante later reprises the description of these tensions in *Inf.* 2.1–4, as does Petrarch in the sestina *A qualunque animale alberga in terra* (*Rvf* 22.1–12). See Andrea Battistini, "Lo stile della Medusa. I processi di pietrificazione in 'Io son venuto al punto de la rota,'" *Letture classensi* 26 (1997): 93–110, at 93–94; and Durling and Martinez, *Time and the Crystal*, 408, n. 77.
46 Durling and Martinez, *Time and the Crystal*, 182, 407, n. 69.
47 In her accusations in the *Heroides*, Dido describes Aeneas's birthplace as a harsh environment, with rocks, mountains, and oaks (*Her.* 7.37). In *Aen.* 4.365–67, she explains Aeneas's harsh character as the result of an upbringing by wild animals in a tough natural setting. Also in the *Tristia*, Ovid attacks friends and enemies with similar accusations (1.8.37–46; 3.11.3–4) and calls them literally stony-hearted (1.8.41; 3.11.4). On Ovid's poems with this image, see Green, *The Poems of Exile*, 217.

love during the cold winter season; he fears petrification as if his lady were Medusa (but imagines her with golden curls instead of writhing snakes); he wants to switch the power dynamics and dominate her physically; he draws analogies between himself and the female Ovidian characters Dido and Clytie. Durling and Martinez carefully analyzed these elements, as did Chiara Ferrari through the lens of the Freudian concept of wishful reversal.[48] As readers of the *Commedia* know, Dante will compare Virgilio, Beatrice, and himself to both male and female characters, continuing to switch between the genders where it seemed apt.[49] In the *petrose*, however, gender reversals are only found in comparisons that treat the poet's experience of frustration and rejection in love: Ovid's *Metamorphoses* offers many stories of rejected female lovers to explore those experiences.

In the *petrose*, then, Dante distinguishes himself from the Italian poets discussed in Chapter 2, whose engagement with Ovidian material followed certain patterns, much in the mold of how the Occitan poets featured Ovid in their poetry. Dante is interested in other Ovidian characters besides the favorites of the Occitan and Italian poets, Narcissus and Pyramus and Thisbe; in the *petrose*, we found elements from the stories of Medusa and Perseus, Clytie and Sol (Apollo), Daphne and Apollo from the *Metamorphoses*, Dido as featured in the *Heroides*, and one of the *Epistulae ex Ponto*. Different from the troubadours and Italian poets who spelled out the comparisons between their situation and Narcissus or Pyramus and Thisbe in similes, Dante evokes those Ovidian characters (with the exception of Dido, all unnamed) via central and peripheral phrases from Ovid's accounts. The fact that also minor details from their stories appear into his poetry, makes Dante's reliance on out-of-context phrases in anthologies and other intermediary sources much less likely. Also the neat gender parallels to which earlier vernacular poets adhered in their comparisons (the poet is like the male Ovidian lover, his lady is like the female Ovidian beloved) disappear in the *petrose*: Dante features his lady as cruel as Medusa throughout the *petrose*, shares Apollo's hopelessness against love and

---

48 Chiara Ferrari, "Gender Reversals: Inversions and Conversions in Dante's *Rime Petrose*," *Italica* 90, no. 2 (2013): 153–75.

49 On gender reversal in the *Commedia*, see especially Rachel Jacoff, "Models of Literary Influence in the *Commedia*," in *Medieval Texts & Contemporary Readers*, ed. Laurie A. Finke and Martin B. Shichtman (Ithaca: Cornell University Press, 1987), 158–76; Jeffrey T. Schnapp, "Dante's Sexual Solecisms: Gender and Genre in the *Commedia*," in *The New Medievalism*, ed. Marina S. Brownlee, Kevin Brownlee, and Stephen G. Nichols (Baltimore: Johns Hopkins University Press, 1991), 201–25; Lund-Mead, "Dido Alighieri"; Kay, "Dido, Aeneas, and the Evolution of Dante's Poetics"; Ferrari, "Gender Reversals," 162–71.

the physical and emotional isolation Ovid described in his exile letters, but also identifies several times with the female characters Clytie and Dido as fellow rejected lovers. Compared to his poetic predecessors and contemporaries, Dante engages with Ovidian material in the *petrose* in more extensive and novel ways. In the following section, I will discuss these and other innovations in Cino da Pistoia and Dante's later lyric poetry.

3.3 Cino da Pistoia, Dante, and Ovid on Love, Myth, and Exile

The poetry of Cino da Pistoia (1270–1336/37) is often a point of comparison and contrast with better-known and studied poets, namely Dante and Petrarch. While Cino's poems can stand on their own, this comparative approach is especially insightful in discussing the treatment of Ovidian material. Cino's poetry shares some of the features identified in Dante's *petrose*, and his interest in the story of Apollo and Daphne makes his poetry an important intertext for Petrarch's, which I will further discuss in Chapter 5. Cino da Pistoia, like Dante and Petrarch, displays a wider knowledge of Ovid's oeuvre than earlier Italian poets. This section looks at Cino da Pistoia's poetry and his exchanges with Dante, showing how they both rely on Ovidian material to explore their shared roles as lover, poet, and exile.

Cino da Pistoia integrates Ovidian material most clearly in the sonnets *Se mai leggesti versi de l'Ovidi* (Marti CXXXV), *Amor, che viene armato a doppio dardo* (Marti CXLVI), *Se conceduto mi fosse da Giove* (Marti LXII), and *Dante, quando per caso s'abbandona* (Marti CXXVIII), which is part of a sonnet and letter exchange with Dante Alighieri.[50] *Se mai leggesti versi de l'Ovidi* adhered to

---

50   These particular sonnets of Cino have received minimal scholarly attention, with the small exception of Cino and Dante's sonnet and letter exchange (see n. 56). Leyla M. G. Livraghi also focused on two "Ovidian" sonnets, *Amor, che viene armato a doppio dardo* (included in this chapter) and *Se mai leggesti versi de l'Ovidi* (discussed in the previous chapter) in "Due usi di Ovidio a confronto in Cino da Pistoia lirico." Livraghi and I reached the same conclusion about the two sonnets: *Se mai leggesti versi de l'Ovidi* shows the traditional use of Ovidian material, and *Amor, che viene armato a doppio dardo* is the more innovative and personal sonnet. Her reasons are slightly different: Livraghi focused on the traditional citational practice in her discussion of *Se mai leggesti versi*, while I consider the sonnet traditional because of its connections with Occitan poetry, of which citing verses attributed to Ovid is only one aspect (see Ch. 2.3). Giuseppina Brunetti discussed Cino's sonnet *Se conceduto mi fosse da Giove* in "All'ombra del lauro: nota per Cino e Petrarca," in *La lirica romanza del medioevo: Storia, tradizioni, interpretazioni. Atti del VI Convegno triennale della Società Italiana di Filologia Romanza*, ed. Furio Brugnolo and Francesca Gambino (Padua: Unipress, 2009), 825–50, at 834–37. The relationship

the Occitan model to confirm Ovid's authority in matters of love (see Ch. 2.3). In the three "Ovidian" sonnets analyzed in this chapter, Cino does not feature Narcissus and Pyramus and Thisbe (the common Ovidian characters included in vernacular poetry), but instead introduces new characters and finds ways to associate himself with both the men and women in Ovid's tales, like Dante in the *petrose*. Ovidian characters only sporadically appear in Cino's sonnets, but these occasional moments surpass the brief mentions of Pyramus and Thisbe and Narcissus in Italian poetry before him, or even the sonnet-long comparisons with Narcissus by Chiaro Davanzati and an anonymous poet. In those poems, the Ovidian characters served as an external reference point and the second element of the comparison; in Cino's "Ovidian" sonnets, these characters are at the same level as the poet, and the world of the *Metamorphoses* is part of the poet's world — or at least a world that he imagines to recreate.

This kind of direct interaction between the poet and Ovid's characters is first found in Cino's sonnet *Amor, che viene armato a doppio dardo* (Marti CXLVI).

Amor, che viene armato a doppio dardo
del più levato monte che si' al mondo,
e de l'auro ferìo il nostro, Gherardo,
e 'l bel soggetto del piombo ritondo.

between Dante and Cino, on the other hand, has been studied more extensively. See in particular, Domenico De Robertis, "Cino e le 'imitazioni' dalle rime di Dante," *Studi Danteschi* 29 (1950): 103–76; Guglielmo Gorni, "Cino 'Vil ladro': Parola data e parola rubata," in *Il nodo della lingua e il verbo d'amore. Studi su Dante e altri duecentisti* (Florence: Leo S. Olschki, 1981), 125–39; Robert Hollander, "Dante and Cino da Pistoia," *Dante Studies* 110 (1992): 201–31; Brugnolo, "Cino (e Onesto) dentro e fuori la *Commedia*," and "Appendice a Cino (e Onesto) dentro e fuori la *Commedia*"; Michelangelo Picone, "Dante e Cino: Una lunga amicizia. Prima parte: I tempi della *Vita Nova*," *Dante* 1 (2004): 39–53; Emilio Pasquini, "Appunti sul carteggio Cino – Dante," in *Le rime di Dante. Gargnano del Garda (25–27 settembre 2008)*, ed. Claudia Berra and Paolo Borsa (Milan: Cisalpino Istituto Editoriale Universitario, 2010), 1–16. While De Robertis argued that the inspiration only went one way with Cino imitating Dante's poetry, more recent studies have redefined the poets' relationship as one of reciprocity. Picone looked at the reciprocal influence in their poetry written around the time of the *Vita nuova*; Gorni, Hollander, and Brugnolo found echoes from Cino's *rime* in the *Commedia* and vice versa. The second part of Hollander's essay is highly speculative in nature, suggesting Dante's intention to first feature Cino in *Paradiso* and later cancel his appearance — something that cannot be documented, as even Hollander admitted. John A. Scott summarized the main arguments of these studies in "Cino da Pistoia and Dante Alighieri," *Flinders Dante Conferences 2002–2004*, ed. Margaret Baker, Flavia Coassin, and Diana Glenn (Adelaide: Lythrum Press, 2005), 26–37. On the relationship between the poetry of Cino and Petrarch, see especially Aurelio Roncaglia, "Cino tra Dante e Petrarca," in *Colloquio Cino da Pistoia (Roma 25 ottobre 1975)* (Rome: Accademia nazionale dei Lincei, 1976), 7–32; and Brunetti, "All'ombra del lauro."

Fu, quel che fece così duro e tardo
lo core a quella di Peneo, il secondo,
del qual poscia che fue il dolce sguardo,
in lei trasmutò sé. Sì ti rispondo:
che dé da noi ricever onor degno
per l'imagine sua, ch'ancor dimora
lo spirto intorno a lei, come a suo segno.
E se d'Amor non semo amanti, fôra
come Dafne del Sol: esser benegno
così vuol questo; onde perciò l'onora.

[Love, armed with two arrows, arrives from the highest mountain that exists in the world and wounds us, Gherardo, with the golden arrow, and our beautiful ladies with the blunt arrow of lead. The second arrow was the one that rendered the heart of the daughter of Peneus so harsh and stern. After she gave her father a sweet look, he transformed her into a laurel. Such an answer I give to you, that she deserves to receive from us the honor worthy of her image, since her spirit still moves around her, as around her sign. And if we are not lovers of Love, what happened to Apollo's Daphne will happen to us; only if we are, Love wants to be gentle with us; therefore, honor your lady.]

In Cino's sonnet, Love is armed with two kinds of arrows: he wounds the poet and the addressee Gherardo da Reggio (named in v. 3) with his golden arrow, and wounds their ladies with an arrow of lead (vv. 1–4). The origin of Love's double ammunition goes back to the myth of Apollo and Daphne, the first love story in the *Metamorphoses* (1.466–71). There, Ovid explains that the golden pointed arrow induces love, something that goes without saying in Cino's sonnet. On the other hand, the round arrow of lead, an Ovidian invention, drives love away.[51] In the verses 5–8, Cino explains this feature of Love's arrows by means of its first victim, "quella di Peneo" (v. 6), or the later named Daphne (v. 13). Italian poets had been wounded many times before by Love's arrow: for

---

51   *Ovidio. Metamorfosi: Volume I* (*Libri I–II*), ed. Alessandro Barchiesi, trans. Ludovica Koch (Milan: Fondazione Lorenzo Valla / Arnoldo Mondadori Editore, 2005), 207. In his notes to Cino's sonnet, Mario Marti is puzzled by the arrow "ritondo" (*Poeti del Dolce stil nuovo*, 798, note to v. 3), while Cino is simply following Ovid's text (*Met.* 1.470–71): "quod facit auratum est et cuspide fulget acuta; / quod fugat obtusum est et habet sub harundine plumbum" ("the arrow that makes you fall in love is made of gold and has a shiny, sharp point; while the one that drives you away is blunt with lead below the reed").

example, in Guido Guinizzelli's sonnet *Lo vostro bel saluto e 'l gentil sguardo* (Rossi 1, vv. 5–8). Even the double arrow had made its appearance in Italian poetry before Cino: for instance, in the Sicilian poet Abate di Tivoli's *Ai deo d'amore, a te faccio preghera* (Antonelli 1.18a, IBAT 1.2, vv. 9–14), and in Guido Cavalcanti's sonnet *O tu, che porti nelli occhi sovente* (Rea XX), where the second arrow would make the enamored poet desirous of a third arrow that cures love (vv. 12–14). Also in Dante's exile *canzone Tre donne intorno al cor mi son venute*, Amor appears armed with two arrows (v. 59).

While these other poets focused on the arrow's effect on themselves, Cino constructs the sonnet around the effect on Daphne, the first woman ever hurt by the arrow of lead. After explaining the effect of the arrow (vv. 5–6), Cino shifts his attention to Daphne's transformation in the last line of the octave (v. 8). In the first tercet of the sestet, Cino gives us a quick lesson in Ovidian metamorphosis; yes, Daphne's form has altered, but her spirit still lives on (vv. 9–11). This quality can also be seen in Ovid's verses when the laurel tree refuses Apollo's embraces and the tree waves and nods her branches (*Met.* 1.553–56; 1.566–67). In line with the conclusion of Ovid's story (*Met.* 1.565), in Cino's sonnet the laurel also becomes the sign to be honored (vv. 9–11). In an alternative reading of the same tercet (vv. 9–11), the poet returns his focus to his and Gherardo's lady. The tercet then states that even though their ladies are driven away from love, some residue — "lo spirto" of Love (v. 11) — remained and therefore they should be treated with respect, or "onor" (v. 9). My translation follows the first interpretation, and while it is unclear whether this tercet (vv. 9–11) focuses on the Ovidian or contemporary lovers, the sonnet's concluding tercet (vv. 12–14) unambiguously features both. In these last verses, the world of Apollo and Daphne and that of Cino and Gherardo clearly coincide: what happened in the world of the *Metamorphoses* to Daphne can also happen to them.

Besides the conflation of the poet's contemporary world with the world of the *Metamorphoses*, Cino's sonnet differs from the poems discussed in Ch. 2.1 in another aspect. In those earlier poems, the poet always likened himself to a male Ovidian character and the woman to a female character: the poet is more in love than Narcissus ever was, the poet loves his lady more than Pyramus loved Thisbe; the poet's lady is more beautiful than Thisbe. Already in the *petrose*, Dante started to revise this common lyric practice, identifying at times with the female rejected Ovidian lovers. In *Amor, che viene armato a doppio dardo*, Cino goes even further, switching back and forth between the two Ovidian characters Apollo and Daphne within the same poem. In the octave, Cino still respects the gender roles: Cino and Gherardo were hit by Love's golden arrow just like Apollo, and their ladies were wounded by the arrow of lead just like Daphne. In the sestet, on the other hand, the male poets Cino and

Gherardo should avoid becoming like Daphne. Since Cino applies the gender reversal to Apollo and Daphne, Petrarch's main Ovidian story of interest, *Amor, che viene armato a doppio dardo* becomes an important intertext for Petrarch's similar fluid identifications with these and other Ovidian characters in the *Canzoniere*, as we will see in Chapter 5.

In *Amor, che viene armato a doppio dardo*, Cino, Gherardo, and their ladies actually dwell in the world of the *Metamorphoses*; in *Se conceduto mi fosse da Giove* (Marti LXII), Cino's second "Ovidian" poem, the poet only imagines himself part of that world:

> Se conceduto mi fosse da Giove,
> io no[n] potrei vestir quel[l]a figura
> che questa bel[l]a don[n]a fred[d]a e dura
> mutar facesse de l'usate prove.
> Adunque, 'l pianto che dagl[i] occhi piove,
> e 'l continuo sospiro e la rancura,
> con la pietà de la mia vita oscura,
> nient'è da mirar se lei no[n] move.
> Ma s'i' potesse far come quel dio,
> 'sta donna muterei in bella faggia,
> e vi farei un'el[l]era d'intorno;
> ed un ch'i' taccio, per simil desio,
> muterei in uccel ched onni giorno
> cantereb[b]e sull'el[l]era selvaggia.

[Even if Jupiter allowed it, I could not put on a shape that would make this beautiful, cold, and harsh lady alter her usual resistance. Therefore, it is no surprise that the tears streaming from my eyes and my continuous sighing and pain, with the misery of my hidden life, do not move her. But if I could act like that god, I would change that lady into a beautiful beech and I would add ivy around it, and, by the same token, I would change one whose name I do not mention into a bird and every day it would sing on the wild ivy.]

The sonnet expresses in Ovidian language ("mutar facesse" [v. 4] and "nient'è da mirar" [v. 8]) that nothing could change his lady's harshness and usual resistance: not his tears (v. 5), not his constant sighing or worrying (v. 6), not even Jupiter's permission to take up a shape like his (v. 2). But if the poet had the god's powers, the sestet contrasts, he would then change her ("muterei" [v. 10]) into a beech, surrounded by ivy, and change himself ("un ch'i' taccio" [v. 11]) into a bird that would sing every day on that ivy. The sonnet thus shifts from the reality of the lady's immutability in the octave to Cino's imagination in the sestet: there the poet imagines himself in the role of a god, creating outward change.

Because of the transformation theme in the sestet, critics have linked the poem to specific Ovidian stories. In particular, Gianfranco Contini, Mario Marti, Eugenio Savona, and Giuseppina Brunetti referenced the story of Philemon and Baucis, and Philomela and Procne. With the exception of Brunetti, however, these critics did not further elaborate on the reasons for the connections, but it seems that Contini, Marti, and Savona were connecting the lady's change into a "bella faggia" (v. 10) to the mention of a beech in Ovid's story of Philemon and Baucis (*Met.* 8.669) and their metamorphosis into a linden and an oak (*Met.* 8.620–21).[52] Likewise, the poet's change into a singing "uccel" (v. 13) would parallel the presence of transformed birds in the story of Philomela and Procne (*Met.* 6.667–70).[53] But in this sonnet of transformation there is nothing that links it directly to Ovid's text. No names of Ovidian characters are mentioned, and the tree species do not match. Rather than recreating certain Ovidian stories, I suggest that in this sonnet Cino imagines to recreate the world of the *Metamorphoses*: his transformations refer to no specific Ovidian stories but could nevertheless fit perfectly into the world that Ovid created. These transformations, moreover, are influenced by Ovid but are also undeniably Cino's: the poet would change himself into a bird singing on the "el[l]era selvaggia" (v. 14) — an obvious reference to Selvaggia, his lady's name.[54]

"Trasmutò" was the verb Cino used in *Amor, che viene armato a doppio dardo* to describe Daphne's metamorphosis (v. 8), a *hapax* in his poetry. While it is not clear whether Cino was thinking of the Latin poet of change when he used the similar "trasformar" (also used only once in his poems) in *Dante, quando per caso s'abbandona* (Marti CXXVIII, v. 8), his addressee Dante Alighieri surely made the connection. Here are Cino's poem and Dante's subsequent response:

---

52 Contini, *Poeti del Duecento*, 2: 666, note to v. 9; Marti, *Poeti del Dolce stil nuovo*, 571, n. 1; Savona, *Repertorio tematico del Dolce stil nuovo*, 399. Brunetti compared Cino's sonnet with Ovid's text of the *Metamorphoses* ("All'ombra del lauro," 834–36).
53 Marti, *Poeti del Dolce stil nuovo*, 571, n. 4; Savona, *Repertorio tematico del Dolce stil nuovo*, 399. Brunetti did not make the connection with the story of Philomela and Procne.
54 Brunetti made a similar point, also comparing Cino's pun on his lady's name with Petrarch's extensive play on Laura/l'aura/lauro/alloro in the *Canzoniere* ("All'ombra del lauro," 837).

TABLE 6   Cino da Pistoia, *Dante, quando per caso s'abbandona*, and Dante Alighieri, *Io sono stato con Amore insieme*

Dante, quando per caso s'abbandona	Io sono stato con Amore insieme
lo disio amoroso de la speme	dalla circulazion del sol mia nona,
che nascer fanno gli occhi del bel seme	e so com'egli afrena e come sprona
di quel piacer che dentro si ragiona,	e come sotto lui si ride e geme.
i' dico, poi se morte le perdona	Chi ragione o virtù contra gli sprieme
e Amore tienla più de le due estreme,	fa come que' che ['n] la tempesta suona
che l'alma sola, la qual più non teme,	credendo far colà dove si tuona
si può ben trasformar d'altra persona.	esser le guerre de' vapori sceme.
E ciò mi fa dir quella ch'è maestra	Però nel cerchio della sua palestra
di tutte cose, per quel ch'i' sent'anco	libero arbitrio già mai non fu franco,
entrato, lasso, per la mia fenestra.	sì che consiglio invan vi si balestra.
Ma prima che m'uccida il nero e il bianco,	Ben può co· nuovi spron punger lo fianco;
da te che sei stato dentro ed extra,	e qual che sia 'l piacer ch'ora n'adestra,
vorre' saper se 'l mi' creder è manco.	seguitar si convien, se l'altro è stanco.

[Dante, when by chance we are abandoned by the desire of love, the desire of hope, which the eyes cause to grow from the beautiful seed of that pleasure that we reflect upon in our minds, I say that, if death allows that hope and Love holds it firmer than the two extremes, the soul by itself, no longer fearing anything, could easily change to another person. And she who is master of everything makes me say this, because of that feeling that I sense entered again at my window, alas. But before the black and the white kill me, I would like to know if my beliefs are faulty, from you, who has been inside and out.]

[I have been together with Love since my ninth turn around the sun, and I know how he constrains and incites, and how under his reign one laughs and sighs. He who relies on reason or virtue against him acts like one who rings the warning bell, believing that this would reduce the battle of the steam clouds where it thunders. Therefore, within reach of his arena free will was never free, so that one has no use of reason. He can easily hit us in the flank with new spurs, and we must follow whatever pleasure is now at our side, if the other one is exhausted.]

In his sonnet to Dante, Cino wonders whether the soul can transform love by moving from one person to another. In a letter that accompanied his response sonnet, Dante similarly asks "utrum de passione in passionem possit anima transformari" ("whether the soul can pass from passion to passion" [*Ep.* III 1]). In Dante's sonnet *Io sono stato con Amore insieme*, this transformation is not explained in Ovidian language: his discourse is rather one of "libero arbitrio" (v. 10), the lack of free will that one has in the face of Love's power, as Love can change one's love interest.[55]

In the letter that accompanies the sonnet, however, Dante approaches the matter differently. The obvious connection between the letter and the sonnet is the notion of experience. In the letter, Dante offers "experientia" ("experience" [*Ep.* III 3]) as the first proof that leads him to accept Cino's claim. In the sonnet, the octave is dedicated to the poet's personal experience with Love: the long time that the poet spent with Love has made him an expert in Love's powers. But the rest of Dante's argument in the letter relies on "ratio" and "auctoritas" ("reason" and "authority" [*Ep.* III 3]).[56] The reason Dante cites to accept Cino's claim is that "every faculty ("potentia") not destroyed after consummation is naturally reserved for another" (*Ep.* III 3). Therefore, also the seat of love ("potentia concupiscibilis" [*Ep.* III 3]) could be receptive to another passion. Dante cites Ovid as the authority on this matter, more precisely a passage that "directly and literally" regards the matter and is located in the fourth book of the *Metamorphoses*, or, as Dante calls it, "De Rerum Transformatione" (*Ep.* III 4):

> equidem in fabula trium sororum contemtricium in semine Semeles, ad Solem loquens, qui, nymphis aliis derelictis atque neglectis in quas prius exarserat, noviter Leucothoen diligebat: « Quid nunc, Yperione nate », et reliqua.

> [indeed in the story of the three sisters who were scornful of the son of Semele, [Ovid] addressed the Sun, who, after he had abandoned and neglected other nymphs with whom he had been obsessed before, was

---

55   For the discussion of the powerlessness against Love in the sonnet exchange between Dante Alighieri and Dante da Maiano (which also featured a reference to Ovid), see Ch. 2.3.

56   For a detailed reading of the letter that focuses on the notion of authority, see Ascoli, *Dante and the Making of a Modern Author*, 122–29, and 124, n. 90 for the very limited bibliography on the letter. Recent additions are Leyla M. G. Livraghi, "Eros e dottrina nel sonetto dantesco *Io sono stato con amore insieme*," in *AlmaDante. Seminario Dantesco 2013*, ed. Giuseppe Ledda and Filippo Zanini (Bologna: Edizioni Aspasia, 2015), 67–85; and Sabrina Ferrara, "*Io mi credea del tutto esser partito:* il distacco di Dante da Cino," in *Cino da Pistoia nella storia della poesia italiana*, ed. Rossend Arqués Corominas and Silvia Tranfaglia (Florence: Franco Cesati, 2016), 99–112.

newly in love with Leucothoë, and said: "What now, son of Hyperion," and what follows.]

Before discussing the relevance of the Ovidian story of Leucothoë, Dante first locates it within the frame story of the *Metamorphoses*: the three daughters of Minyas refused to participate in the festivities for Bacchus and passed their time telling each other stories. Leucippe, the second storyteller, narrated the story of Sol (Apollo, the son of Hyperion), who often changed his love interest. This reference to the storytelling sisters is perhaps the earliest clear indication that Dante is truly familiar with the structural organization of Ovid's epic poem. Furthermore, Dante also explicitly refers to the text of the *Metamorphoses*: he quotes the half-verse "Quid nunc, Yperione nate" ("What now, son of Hyperion" [*Met.* 4.192]), adding "et reliqua" ("and what follows"), assuming that Cino knows how the rest of the passage continues.[57] And indeed, in what follows in the *Metamorphoses*, we read what Dante summarized in the letter: how the son of Hyperion (Sol or Apollo) was burning "with a new flame" ("ureris igne nouo" [*Met.* 4.195]) for Leucothoë, and forgot all his previous love interests, including Clytie, Leucothoë's sister (*Met.* 4.204–8):

> diligis hanc unam, nec te Clymeneque Rhodosque
> nec tenet Aeaeae genetrix pulcherrima Circes,
> quaeque tuos Clytie quamuis despecta petebat
> concubitus ipsoque illo graue uulnus habebat
> tempore; Leucothoe multarum obliuia fecit.

> [You only love that one girl. Neither Clymene nor Rhodos nor the stunning mother of Aeaean Circe attracts you anymore. Nor does Clytie, who, even though you looked down on her, still wanted to have her way with you, and was deeply hurt at that moment. Leucothoë made you forget many women.]

---

57 In Ch. 4.1, I mention Christopher Kleinhenz's discussion of a similar passage in the *Commedia*. In Dante's description of the singing souls on a boat approaching Mount Purgatory, he points out that the souls were singing the psalm *In exitu Israel de Aegypto* "con quanto di quel salmo è poscia scripto" ("with as much of that psalm that is written after" [*Purg.* 2.48]) — the Italian equivalent of "et reliqua." Also there Dante assumes his readers know how the rest of the text continues.

This explicit reference and the rare quotation from the story of Sol and Leucothoë in Dante's letter has been used as an argument to accept the Dantean authorship of the sonnet *Nulla mi parve mai piú crudel cosa*.[58]

> Nulla mi parve mai piú crudel cosa
> di lei per cui servir la vita lago,
> ché 'l suo desio nel congelato lago,
> ed in foco d'amore il mio si posa.
> Di cosí dispietata e disdegnosa
> la gran bellezza di veder m'appago;
> e tanto son del mio tormento vago
> ch'altro piacere a li occhi miei non osa.
> Né quella ch'a veder lo sol si gira,
> e 'l non mutato amor mutata serba,
> ebbe quant'io già mai fortuna acerba.
> Dunque, Giannin, quando questa superba
> convegno amar fin che la vita spira,
> alquanto per pietà con me sospira.

[Nothing seems to be more cruel to me than the lady for whose service I abandon life, since her desire rests in a frozen lake, and mine in the fire of love. I am pleased to see the great beauty of such a cruel and scornful woman; and I am so much yearning for my agony, that nothing else attempts to be pleasing to my eyes. The girl who turns herself toward the sun and in her changed form preserves her unchanged love, did not have a fortune as ungrateful as mine. Therefore, Giannin, since I have to love this arrogant woman until the end of my life, have some pity on me.]

This sonnet stands out within the corpus of medieval Italian lyric poetry for several reasons. First, the anonymous poet does not feature the stock Ovidian characters of Italian verse: Narcissus or Pyramus and Thisbe. He laments his lady's extreme harshness and believes to suffer more than "that girl who turns herself toward the sun and in her changed form preserves her unchanged love" (vv. 9–10). That girl is Clytie, who, abandoned by Sol for Leucothoë, fails to win her lover back and languishes away as a heliotrope (*Met.* 4.234–70) — one of

---

58   After its exclusion from Domenico De Robertis's five-volume edition of Dante's *Rime* (Florence: Le Lettere, 2002), we can consider the matter of attribution closed (2: 949, 954, 1112, 1116, 1120, 1130–31, 1138, 1190). Gianfranco Contini summarized the earlier discussions on the sonnet's authorship in Dante Alighieri, *Rime* (Turin: Einaudi, 1939; rpt. 1995), 266.

the "abandoned and neglected" nymphs Dante mentioned in his letter to Cino (*Ep.* III 4). Similar to Cino and Dante in the *petrose*, the poet reverses gender roles, comparing himself to the female victim of the cruel Sol. But unlike the transformations in Cino's sonnet *Se conceduto mi fosse da Giove*, here the identification with the Ovidian character is explicitly related to the text of the *Metamorphoses*. The verses "Né quella ch'a veder lo sol si gira, / e 'l non mutato amor mutata serba" (vv. 9–10) bear an undeniable resemblance to Ovid's words "uertitur ad Solem mutataque seruat amorem" ("she turns toward the Sun and, transformed, preserves her love" [*Met.* 4.270]).

A sonnet that translates so literally an entire verse from Ovid's epic poem into Italian is exceptional in the lyric poetry of this period. It is tempting to consider it Dante's, since Dante employs the story of Sol and Clytie in his sestina *Al poco giorno ed al gran cerchio d'ombra* (discussed in the previous section) and turns more than once to its surrounding stories in the *Metamorphoses* (the stories of Pyramus and Thisbe, Salmacis and Hermaphroditus, and Cadmus return in the *Commedia*,[59] and Dante mentioned the story of Sol and Leucothoë in the letter to Cino da Pistoia). However, for its un-Dantean rhyme scheme and its placement in a separate folio, *Nulla mi parve mai piú crudel cosa* is rightly excluded from Dante's canon; the thematic connection with other Dantean texts, and especially the letter to Cino, is compelling but far from sufficient.

Thus far I have discussed how Dante and Cino turned to Ovid's texts and authority to address matters of love and transformation — through Dante's quotation from the story of Sol and Leucothoë in the *Metamorphoses* in the letter, and Cino and Dante's Ovidian language of transformation in their sonnets. Exile, the third main theme of Ovid's oeuvre, is also crucial to the exchange.[60] Dante addresses their shared exile in the salutation (*Ep.* III) and mentions it explicitly in his concluding words of consolation (*Ep.* III 5). However, the letter's main discussion about love (*Ep.* III 2–4) can also be read through the lens of exile because of a reference to Ovid's first, programmatic letter of the *Tristia*. In his opening words to Cino, Dante draws upon this Ovidian letter written in exile, which immediately puts the discussion in a broader perspective than one simply concerning love. Thanking Cino for making him the arbiter on the question as to whether the soul can pass from passion to passion (*Ep.* III 1),

---

59 In both Moore and Vazzana's concordances, Book 4 of the *Metamorphoses* — the book to which all these stories belong — is the most frequently mentioned (eleven times). See Moore, *Scripture and Classical Authors in Dante*, 349; and Vazzana, *Dante e "la bella scola,"* 149.

60 For an overview of all instances in Dante's oeuvre where he refers to his exile, see Giuseppe De Marco, "L'esperienza di Dante *exul immeritus* quale autobiografia universale," *Annali d'Italianistica* 20 (2002): 21–54.

Dante foresees how his answer could enhance "the renown of [his] name" ("titulum mei nominis" [*Ep.* III 1]). In those words, he echoes two Ovidian distichs (*Tristia* 1.1.53–54, 1.1.63–64; emphasis added):[61]

> donec eram sospes, *tituli* tangebar amore,
> quaerendique *mihi nominis* ardor erat:
> ....
> clam tamen intrato, ne te mea carmina laedant:
> non sunt ut quondam plena fauoris erant.
>
> [As long as I was safe, I was touched by the love of *renown*, and I burned to win *a name for myself*.... But enter in secret, so that my poems do not hurt you; they are not as popular as they once were.]

The phrase "titulum mei nominis" seems particularly well chosen, given Ovid's further reflections on "titulus" in this opening letter of the *Tristia*. Ovid explains how he has moved away from one genre (love poetry as the "praeceptor amoris") to another (the current exile letters): "'inspice ... titulum: non sum praeceptor amoris; / quas meruit poenas iam dedit illud opus'" ["Look at the title: I am not the teacher of love; that work has already received the punishment it deserved" [1.1.67–68]). By that token, the central question of Dante's letter — whether the soul can pass from one passion to another — can be extended beyond the realm of love. Catherine Keen has shown how Cino da Pistoia and other exiled poets mapped the language of exclusion, captivity, and exile on their love poetry, and addressed their lost cities with the language of desire.[62] In Dante's letter, the loss of a beloved woman, as also Albert Russell Ascoli suggested,[63] can be understood as the loss of a beloved city, or even, I would add, the loss of a public. By referencing Ovid's first exile letter, Dante connects his concerns about his waning poetic fame with those of Ovid, creating a shared experience of exile — with Ovid, and with Cino. Moreover, in exile Dante was exploring how to successfully move from the passion for one genre

---

61   Dante Alighieri, *Epistole*, ed. Arsenio Frugoni and Giorgio Brugnoli, in *Opere minori*, ed. Pier Vincenzo Mengaldo et al. (Milan: Riccardo Ricciardi, 1979), 2: 533; and Ascoli, *Dante and the Making of a Modern Author*, 124.

62   Catherine Keen, "Cino da Pistoia and the Otherness of Exile," *Annali d'Italianistica* 20 (2002): 89–112; and "Sex and the Medieval City: Viewing the Body Politic from Exile in Early Italian Verse," in *Troubled Vision: Gender, Sexuality and Sight in Medieval Text and Image*, ed. Emma Campbell and Robert Mills (New York: Palgrave Macmillan, 2004), 155–71.

63   Ascoli, *Dante and the Making of a Modern Author*, 126.

to another. Or in Dante's own words from his letter to Moroello Malaspina (*Ep.* IV): how to move from "women and the songs about women" to "constant meditations" about "heavenly and earthly matters" (*Ep.* IV 2) — a transition, as the lyrics from this time show, that was not an easy one.

The opening letter of the first book of the *Tristia* inspired Dante in other ways as well.[64] In the envoy of the *canzone Amor, da che convien pur ch'io mi doglia*, linked to Dante's exile through its content and the accompanying letter to Moroello (*Ep.* IV), Dante takes over two other elements from Ovid's letter: (1) both Ovid and Dante send their book / *canzone* off to the city from where they were exiled; and (2) both poets call their poems little and unpolished. Ovid calls his book "parue" ("little" [v. 1]), "incultus" ("unadorned" [v. 3]), literally with rough edges (vv. 11–12). Dante comprises all this information in the adjective "montanina" (v. 76), literally "little mountain dweller."[65]

> Parue – nec inuideo – sine me, liber, ibis in urbem,
> ei mihi! quo domino non licet ire tuo.
> uade, sed incultus, qualem decet exulis esse;
> infelix, habitum temporis huius habe.
> ....
> nec fragili geminae poliantur pumice frontes,
> hirsutus passis sed uideare comis.
> (*Tristia* 1.1.1–4, 1.1.11–12)

[Little book, you will go without me — I do not hold a grudge — to the city, where, alas, I, your master, am not allowed to go! Go, but do so unadorned, befitting the book of an exile; unhappy book, wear the dress that matches this moment.... Do not let fragile pumice polish your two edges, so that you are seen all rough and with messy hair.]

> O montanina mia canzon, tu, vai:
> forse vedrai Fiorenza, la mia terra,

---

64 On the use of the *congedo* or envoy in Italian *canzoni*, and its particular meaning for exiled poets, see Catherine Keen, "'Va', mia canzone': Textual Transmission and the Congedo in Medieval Exile Lyrics," *Italian Studies* 64, no. 2 (2009): 183–97. For a more general discussion, see Joan H. Levin, "Sweet, New Endings: A Look at the Tornada in the Stilnovistic and Petrarchan Canzone," *Italica* 61, no. 4 (1984): 297–311.

65 Dante Alighieri, *La canzone montanina*, ed. Paola Allegretti (Verbania: Tararà, 2001), 43–44, note to v. 76. For a discussion of the appearance of Ovid's books and its poetic implications, see Gareth D. Williams, "Representations of the Book-Roll in Latin Poetry: Ovid, *Tr.* 1, 1, 3–14 and related texts," *Mnemosyne* 45 (1992): 178–89.

> che fuor di sé mi serra,
> vota d'amore e nuda di pietate.
> Se vi vai dentro, va' dicendo ...
> (*Amor, da che convien*, vv. 76–80)

> [Oh my little mountain song, you go your way: maybe you will see Florence, my homeland, that shuts me out of her, void of love and stripped of compassion. If you enter, tell ...]

In the envoy of *Io sento sì d'Amor la gran possanza*, another *canzone* written in exile, Dante also addresses and sends off his *canzone*. This time, he gives specific instructions about whom to greet (vv. 97–100):

> Canzone, a' tre men rei di nostra terra
> te n'anderai prima che vadi altrove:
> li due saluta e 'l terzo fa' che prove
> di trarlo fuor di mala setta in pria.

> [My song, you will go to the three least bad men in our homeland, before you go elsewhere: greet two of them, and for the third, make sure that you first pull him away from bad company.]

The mention of the "tre men rei" and "li due ... e 'l terzo" not only anticipates Ciacco's prophecy in the *Commedia*, where he describes the remaining two "giusti" ("just men") in Florence (*Inf.* 6.73),[66] but it also reprises a passage from Ovid's *Tristia* (1.5.33–34):[67]

> uix duo tresue mihi de tot superestis amici:
> cetera Fortunae, non mea turba fuit.

> [There are barely two or three of you left, friends, and you were once so many; the rest followed Fortune, not me.]

---

66 Dante, *Rime*, ed. Contini, 131, notes to vv. 97–106; Dante Alighieri, *Rime della maturità e dell'esilio*, ed. Michele Barbi and Vincenzo Pernicone (Florence: F. Le Monnier, 1969), 513, note to v. 97; and Dante Alighieri, *Rime*, ed. Domenico De Robertis (Florence: SISMEL-Edizioni del Galluzzo, 2005), 101, note to v. 97.

67 Paola Allegretti, "La canzone 'montanina': Dante tra Ovidio e Melibeo," *Dante Studies* 124 (2006): 119–36, at 130.

As these examples start to show, Ovid's exile letters provide fellow poets in exile with a language to describe their state of being. The *canzone Amor, da che convien pur ch'io mi doglia* contains several more verses Dante formulated with the exile letters clearly in mind. The desperation of not knowing what to do, the feeling of being dead and alive at the same time, the absence of intelligent interlocutors: all these sentiments expressed in *Amor, da che convien* can be traced back to Ovid's *Tristia* and the *Epistulae ex Ponto*. Paola Allegretti has identified several corresponding passages in her edition of the *canzone*; I list the most notable here below:[68]

TABLE 7 Comparison between Dante Alighieri, *Amor, da che convien pur ch'io mi doglia*, and Ovid's exile poetry

Dante, *Amor, da che convien*	Ovid's exile poetry
"ma più non posso" [but more I cannot do] (*Amor, da che convien*, v. 38)	"sed nunc quid faciam?" [But now, what should I do?] (*Tristia* 4.1.29)
"qui vivo e morto come vuoi mi palpi" [here, alive and dead, I feel your touch, as you want] (*Amor, da che convien*, v. 64)	"non aliter stupui quam qui Iouis ignibus ictus uiuit et est uitae nescius ipse suae." [I was as stunned as someone who was struck by the fire of Jove and was still alive, unaware that he still was.] (*Tristia* 1.3.11–12)
	"si uita est mortis habenda genus" [if a kind of death must be considered life] (*Ex Ponto* 1.7.10)

---

[68] For the first example (*Amor, da che convien*, v. 38) and the third (*Amor, da che convien*, vv. 67–68), see Allegretti, *La canzone montanina*, 33, note to v. 38, and 41–42, note to v. 68. For the latter example, Allegretti added *Tristia* 3.11.9 and *Tristia* 3.11.13–14 among Dante's sources, which I find less convincing parallels. More intertextual connections between *Amor, da che convien* and Ovid's works are found in Allegretti's edition at 17–18, note to v. 3; 18, note to v. 4; 19–20, note to v. 7; 21–22, note to v. 11; 28–29, note to v. 28; 30–31, note to v. 32; 32–33, note to v. 37; 42–43, note to v. 73; 46–47, note to v. 83; 47–48, note to v. 84.

TABLE 7   Comparison between Dante Alighieri, *Amor, da che convien pur ch'io mi doglia*, and Ovid's exile poetry (*cont.*)

Dante, *Amor, da che convien*	Ovid's exile poetry
"Lasso!, non donne qui, non genti accorte veggio a cui mi lamenti del mio male" [Alas! I see no women here, no wise people to whom I can complain about my misery] (*Amor, da che convien*, vv. 67–68)	"nullus in hac terra, recitem si carmina, cuius / intellecturis auribus utar, adest." [There is nobody in this land who could understand my verse, if I read it to them.] (*Tristia* 3.14.39–40)
	"hic ego sollicitae iaceo nouus incola sedis: heu nimium fati tempora lenta mei!" [This is where I lie, a newcomer in a troubled place: oh, too slow passes the time of my sentence!] (*Tristia* 4.1.85–86)
	"quod quamquam nemo est, cuius referatur ad aures" [although there is no one who could listen] (*Tristia* 4.10.113)

Moreover, in the letter to Moroello Malaspina that accompanies the *canzone Amor, da che convien* (*Ep.* IV), Dante highlights the *canzone*'s theme of exile even further.[69] Introducing the *canzone* in the letter, Dante describes his reunion with Love after he left Moroello's court and arrived at the banks of the Arno.[70] Although he was "enrolled in the service of liberty" (*Ep.* IV 2) and had resolved to "stay away from women and songs about women" (*Ep.* IV 2), he finds himself nevertheless again powerless against Love's attack. In this description, Dante does not emphasize his own exile but explicitly casts Love as

---

69 On this letter and the accompanying *canzone*, see also Enrico Fenzi, "Ancora sulla *Epistola* a Moroello e sulla 'montanina' di Dante (*Rime*, 15)," *Tenzone* 4 (2003): 43–84.

70 On the dating of the letter, see Foster and Boyde, *Dante's Lyric Poetry*, 2: 330, who briefly discussed the generally accepted 1307–08 dating in favor of the alternative 1310–11 dating, suggested by Francesco Torraca, in his review of Oddone Zenatti's *Dante e Firenze: Prose antiche con note illustrative ed appendici* in *Bullettino della Società Dantesca Italiana*, n.s. 10 (1903): 139–60.

the exile. Dante involves himself only implicitly by describing how Love exiles his free will (*Ep.* IV 2; emphasis added):[71]

> atque hic [Amor] ferox, tanquam dominus *pulsus a patria post longum exilium sola in sua repatrians*, quicquid enim[72] contrarium fuerat intra me, vel occidit vel *expulit* vel ligavit. Occidit ergo propositum illud laudabile quo a mulieribus suisque cantibus abstinebam; ac meditationes assiduas, quibus tam celestia quam terrestria intuebar, quasi suspectas, *impie relegavit*; et denique, ne contra se amplius anima rebellaret, *liberum meum ligavit arbitrium*, ut non quo ego, sed quo ille vult, me verti oporteat.
>
> [But there Love, as a ruthless ruler *driven from his fatherland and returning after a long exile to his native soil*, killed or *expelled* or tied up

---

[71] On the appearance of Love as exile in this letter, see Michelangelo Picone, "Sulla canzone 'montanina' di Dante," *L'Alighieri* 42 (2002): 105–12, at 111–12; and Paola Allegretti, "La canzone 'montanina': Dante tra Ovidio e Melibeo," 126. Picone focused in particular on Dante's use of "relegavit" (v. 24) in reference to his "constant meditations" on "heavenly and earthly matters" (vv. 22–23), which Picone took as a clear allusion to the *Commedia*. A classical Latin judicial term, "relegare" indicates the sending away of a person to a place relatively close to Rome for a limited period of time without the loss of citizenship (see Oxford Latin Dictionary, s. v. "relegare"), which was a less serious and definite punishment than "exilium." As Picone correctly pointed out, Dante could have encountered this distinction in Ovid's exile letters, where Ovid indeed repeatedly stresses that he was not an "exul" but a "relegatus" (e.g., *Tristia* 2.137, 5.11.21–22). According to Picone, Dante then implies that his "unceasing meditations" were only temporarily sent away, not definitely exiled, which would offer an interesting insight into the genesis of the *Commedia*. However, strictly adhering to the different meanings of "exul" and "relegatus," one would have to go as far as to state that Dante had already given up the hope of ever returning to Florence, since in the letters, Dante presents himself explicitly as an "exul" and never a "relegatus" (see the salutations of *Ep.* III, V, VI, and VII, where Dante calls himself an "[Florentinus] exul immeritus" and *Ep.* II 1 where he repeats the same formulation). Sabrina Ferrara showed that Dante used "exul immeritus" and "relegatio," terms originating from classical law and literature, rather than the (milder) terminology used in the registers of the Florence Chancellery in "Tra pena giuridica e diritto morale: l'esilio di Dante nelle *epistole*," *L'Alighieri* 40 (2012): 45–65; and "D'un bannissement subi à un exil revendiqué: la construction de l' 'exul' dans les *Épîtres* de Dante," *Arzanà* 16–17 (2013): 199–213. Colin G. Hardie argued that the donna of the *canzone* is Beatrice in "Dante's 'canzone montanina,'" *The Modern Language Review* 55 (1960): 359–70, but that hypothesis is convincingly refuted by Foster and Boyde in *Dante's Lyric Poetry*, 2: 338–40.

[72] Toynbee reads and translates "eius contrarium" instead of "enim contrarium," but, as Manlio Pastore Stocchi noted, this correction, also accepted by other editors of Dante's letters, makes little difference to the meaning of the sentence. See *Epistole · Ecloge · Questio de situ et forma aque et terre*, ed. Manlio Pastore Stocchi (Rome: Antenore, 2012), 26–27.

everything within me that was against him. He thus killed the praiseworthy plan with which I held myself away from women and songs about them; and he *wickedly banned* the constant meditations, in which I used to contemplate heavenly and earthly matters, as if they were suspect; and finally, in order that my soul would not rebel against him again, *he tied up my free will*, so that I was forced to turn myself not where I want, but where he wants.]

As already noted in the discussion of Dante's letter to Cino da Pistoia, Dante inserts the language of exclusion, captivity, and exile into his discussions about love. Both his letter to Cino (*Ep.* III) and to Moroello Malaspina (*Ep.* IV) introduce and comment on a love poem (*Io sono stato con Amore insieme* and *Amor, da che convien pur ch'io mi doglia*, respectively), suggesting a parallel reading in which matters of love can become reflections on Dante's exile.[73] Dante sets up this parallel in the letter to Moroello by repeatedly using exile as a metaphor and switching roles between the one who exiles and the one who is exiled. On the figurative level, the explicit comparison of Love with an exile returning to his homeland (*Ep.* IV 2) implies that Dante actually exiled Love, since he was determined to cease writing love poetry and instead write about matters of heaven and of earth (*Ep.* IV 2). Love, the returned exile, then becomes the one who exiles, explicitly banishing Dante's serious meditations (*Ep.* IV 2). In short, once-exiled Love in turn "exiles" the thoughts of Dante, who was the one who exiled him in the first place.

The importance of this figurative exile narrative becomes clear when comparing it to one of the moments where Dante talks about his physical exile. In the letter to Moroello, Dante describes Love with the apposition "pulsus a patria" (*Ep.* IV 2), which is almost identical to the apposition he used to describe himself in his letter to the counts Oberto and Guido da Romena ("a patria pulsus" [*Ep.* II 1]). By paralleling his actual exile so explicitly with Love's figurative exile, he sets up his own expectations that one day, just like Love in the figurative narrative, he too will "return after a long exile to his native soil" ("post longum exilium sola in sua repatrians" [*Ep.* IV 2]).

In his letters, Dante treats the theme of exile both directly and indirectly. There are several moments where Dante explicitly addresses his exile: in the salutations of *Ep.* III, V, VI, and VII, where he calls himself a "(Florentinus)

---

73   These two poems (and letters) are also connected by their shared discussion and vision of the theme of free will: both present a lover who seems powerless against Love (see, for instance, Foster and Boyde, *Dante's Lyric Poetry*, 2: 331). On the two letters, see also Ferrara, "*Io mi credea del tutto esser partito*."

exul immeritus" ("a (Florentine) undeserved exile"); in his lament on his poverty in exile in *Ep.* II (2, 3); in his words of consolation directed to Cino da Pistoia, but also to himself in *Ep.* III (5); and in the most personal letter to a friend in Florence where he rejects the conditions for his return (*Ep.* IX). At the same time, Dante also addresses his personal experience indirectly through a more general discussion of the effects of exile. The letter to Moroello already furnished an example of this practice. Another comment on exile is found in Dante's letter to the princes and peoples of Italy (*Ep.* V), where he compares the state in which Italy finds itself to the oppression of the tribe of Judah in Egypt. But the "lamentations of the universal captivity" ("ullulatum universalis captivitatis" [*Ep.* V 1]) are heard,[74] and a hopeful Dante announces to the people of Italy the arrival of "another Moses" ("Moysen alium" [*Ep.* V 1]), who will "lead them to a land flowing with milk and honey" ("ad terram lacte ac melle manantem perducens" [*Ep.* V 1]). Dante repeats this biblical exile narrative in the letter to the Emperor Henry VII (*Ep.* VII) — the other Moses of *Ep.* V — concluding his plea to the emperor with a comparison between the current state of the Italian people and the Babylonian captivity: "remembering the most holy Jerusalem, we lament as exiles in Babylon" ("sacrosancte Ierusalem memores, exules in Babilone gemiscimus" [*Ep.* VII 8]).[75] In these two instances, Dante attributes to the people of Italy a metaphorical state of exile, thus including his own literal experience of exile in all of Italy's figurative one.

Featuring other exiles as a way to address one's own is a technique Ovid himself practiced.[76] For instance, in the story of the Greek hero Evander, narrated in the *Fasti* and considered one of the passages that Ovid reworked during his own exile, the goddess Carmentis's words of consolation to her exiled

---

74   Paget Toynbee suggested that this clause echoes a verse from *Jeremiah*, "a voce captivitatis Babylonis commota est terra" (50:46). I would add that the second half of the verse is equally relevant: "et clamor inter gentes auditus est" ("At the sound of the capture of Babylon the earth will tremble, and its cry will be heard among the people"). In that sense Dante further emphasizes his discussion of exile with a verse from biblical exile literature. See *Dantis Alagherii Epistolae: The Letters of Dante* (Oxford: Clarendon Press, 1920), 48, n. 5.

75   In this passage, Dante again emphasizes the theme of exile with echoes from biblical exile poetry: "super flumina Babylonis ibi sedimus et flevimus cum recordaremur Sion" ("by the rivers of Babylon, there we sat down and wept when we remembered Zion" [Psalm 137:1–3]). See Toynbee, *Dantis Alagherii Epistolae*, 100, n. 6.

76   Mary H. T. Davisson, "'Quid Moror Exemplis'?: Mythological "Exempla" in Ovid's Pre-Exilic Poems and the Elegies from Exile," *Phoenix* 47, no. 3 (1993): 213–37, at 228–32; and Gareth D. Williams, *Banished Voices: Readings in Ovid's Exile Poetry* (Cambridge: Cambridge University Press, 1994), 108–15.

son seem directed to the exiled poet as well (*Fasti* 1.479–96).[77] Dante inserted a verse from this consolation speech into the first of two reflections on his exile in his unfinished treatise *De vulgari eloquentia*.[78] In his discussion of the origin of language, Dante mentions the town of Pietramala whose inhabitants believe they speak the language Adam spoke. Referring to people's tendency to consider their hometown the birthplace of everything good, Dante is determined not to fall into that narrow-minded trap (*DVE* I VI 3):[79]

> Nos autem, cui mundus est patria velut piscibus equor, quanquam Sarnum biberimus ante dentes et Florentiam adeo diligamus ut, quia dileximus, exilium patiamur iniuste, rationi magis quam sensui spatulas nostri iudicii podiamus.

> [The world is my homeland, like the sea is to the fish. And even though I drank from the Arno before I had teeth and I love Florence so much that, because of that love, I am suffering an unjust exile, I place the shoulders of my judgment under reason rather than feelings.]

Dante's feelings about his hometown are strong — so strong that they led to his "exilium ... iniuste" ("unjust exile") — but he suggests that reason rather than emotional attachment should prevail in serious matters such as the origin of language. In this context, the quotation of Carmentis's words that "omne solum forti patria est, ut piscibus aequor" ("every land is home to the strong, like the sea to the fish" [*Fasti* 1.493]) seems to rationalize the emotional experience of exile. In his commentary to *De vulgari eloquentia*, Pier Vincenzo

---

77 Even though, as Elaine Fantham noted, "Ovid in exile exploits for Evander the topoi which his personal poems admit to be no comfort." See "The Role of Evander in Ovid's *Fasti*," *Arethusa* 25 (1992): 155–72, at 168. The most direct commentary on Ovid's own exile in the Evander episode is the interjection "felix, exilium cui locus ille fuit!" ("lucky to have that place as the location of exile!" [*Fasti* 1.540]): in his letters, Ovid often complains about the location of his exile and repeatedly requests to be at least relocated, if he cannot return to Rome.

78 For a reading of the *Fasti* as a programmatic text of choice in the *De vulgari eloquentia*, see Simone Marchesi, "Distilling Ovid: Dante's Exile and Some Metamorphic Nomenclature in Hell," in *Writers Reading Writers: Intertextual Studies in Medieval and Early Modern Literature in Honor of Robert Hollander*, ed. Janet L. Smarr (Newark: University of Delaware Press, 2007), 21–39, at 21–25. Marchesi mentioned the *Fasti* quotation, but did not relate it to the content of Ovid's work (24–25).

79 On this passage, see especially Gary P. Cestaro, "'... quanquam Sarnum biberimus ante dentes ...': The Primal Scene of Suckling in Dante's *De vulgari eloquentia*," *Dante Studies* 109 (1991): 119–47, at 130–36.

Mengaldo has pointed out that this Ovidian phrase was commonly used.[80] Indeed, it is found in anthologies (e.g., in the *Florilegium Gallicum*),[81] compendia (e.g., in Geremia da Montagnone's *Compendia* in the chapters on moral strength, and in Bartolomeo da San Concordio's *Ammaestramenti* under the heading on one's attachment to the homeland),[82] and in other treatises such as Brunetto Latini's *Tresor* (2.84.11). In Dante's letters and his poems written in exile, we have found close and repeated connections to Ovid's exilic poetry. While in *De vulgari eloquentia* he uses the Ovidian verse "omne solum forti patria est, ut piscibus aequor" in the same context it had in the original passage in the *Fasti* (exile), the frequent use of the verse as a free-standing expression, including in some works that were on Dante's radar, suggests that its inclusion in the *De vulgari eloquentia* was more likely the result of a fragmented reading of Ovid's work. Dante seamlessly nestled the emotional verses describing Ovid's despair and isolation in exile into the fabric of his own poems written in exile. On the other hand, for his rational approach to the exile experience in *De vulgari eloquentia* Dante turned to one of the many verses from Ovid's poetry that came to stand on their own and took on more moral weight than they ever had in the original — such expressions were frequently found in treatises and other prose works (see Ch. 1.1), and Dante seems to adhere to this practice in his own treatise.

Brunetto Latini's citation of the Ovidian expression in the *Tresor* is worth a further look, as he too places it in its original context of exile: he inserted the phrase into a longer discussion on the topic (2.84.11), translated from the *De remediis fortuitorum* (section VIII). A short dialogue between Ratio (Reason) and Sensus (Feeling) about a variety of issues including exile, *De remediis fortuitorum* was considered during Latini's time (and Dante and Petrarch's) the work of the Latin philosopher Seneca, but actually dates from the sixth century.[83] Like in the pseudo-Senecan dialogue, when in the *Tresor* Paour ("fear," Brunetto's translation of "Sensus") brings up the worry caused by

---

80   Dante Alighieri, *De vulgari eloquentia*, ed. Pier Vincenzo Mengaldo (Padua: Antenore, 1968), 51.
81   Fernández de la Cuesta González, *En la senda del 'Florilegium Gallicum,'* 325.
82   Geremia da Montagnone, *Compendium moralium notabilium*, Pars 5, Liber 1, rubric 1, p. 120; Bartolomeo da San Concordio, *Ammaestramenti degli antichi latini e toscani raccolti e volgarizzati*, 60 (Latin), 61 (Italian).
83   As we have seen in Ch. 1.1, Latini included other unattributed translations of Latin treatises in his *Tresor*: Chapters 61–67 of Book 2 were Latini's translation of Albertano da Brescia's *De arte loquendi et tacendi*, and the entire Chapter 84 ("Ci parole de seurté contre paor") translates the short pseudo-Senecan *De remediis fortuitorum*. As noted a little further on, Dante will mention the *De remediis fortuitorum* in one of his letters, and Petrarch includes the treatise in the list of his favorite books (see Ch. 5.1).

impending exile, Seurté ("security," Brunetto's translation of "Ratio") dispenses comfort by saying that one can only be denied a place and not a home (cf. *De remediis fortuitorum*, VIII.1). Before continuing to translate the remainder of Ratio's words in *De remediis fortuitorum* (VIII.1–2), Latini includes Ovid's expression in French translation: "Toutes terres sont païs au preudome autresi comme la mers as poissons" ("All lands are home to the strong like the sea to the fish").[84] This pairing of Ovid and Seneca in the context of exile is also found in Dante's previously discussed letter to Cino da Pistoia (Ep. III), where Dante evoked Ovid's exile by citing verses from his *Tristia*. In the concluding words of consolation to his fellow exile Cino, Dante writes (*Ep.* III 5):

> Sub hoc, frater carissime, ad potentiam, qua contra Rhamnusie spicula sis patiens, te exhortor. Perlege, deprecor, Fortuitorum Remedia, que ab inclitissimo phylosophorum Seneca nobis velut a patre filiis ministrantur, et illud de memoria sane tua non defluat: « Si de mundo fuissetis, mundus quod suum erat diligeret ».

> [Therefore, my dearest brother, I recommend strength, with which you could endure the spears of Rhamnusia. Read carefully, I beg you, the *Remedies against Fortune*, which are delivered to us by the most famous philosopher Seneca, as by a father to his sons, and may this saying really not disappear from your memory: "If you belong to the world, the world will love what is his."]

In these final words of consolation, Dante further broadens the community of exiles, which up until this point in the letter included Cino, himself, and Ovid. In between the mention of the wrath of the classical goddess Rhamnusia and the consolation of Christ's words (John 15:19), Dante prescribes a thorough reading ("perlege") of the *De remediis fortuitorum*, here too considered to be the work of Seneca — he must be referring to the section on exile that Latini translated in the *Tresor*. Enrico Fenzi has called Seneca a "container" ("contenitore")

---

84 Dante Della Terza discussed this section on exile in the *Tresor* and its inclusion of the Ovidian citation in relation to Brunetto's appearance in *Inf.* 15. See "The Canto of Brunetto Latini," in *Lectura Dantis: Inferno,* ed. Allen Mandelbaum, Anthony Oldcorn, and Charles Ross (Berkeley: University of California Press, 1998), 197–212, at 204–6. Enrico Fenzi noted the connections between Dante's citation of the Ovidian sentence in the *De vulgari eloquentia* and Latini's *Tresor* and Dante's letter to Cino da Pistoia in Dante, *De vulgari eloquentia*, ed. Enrico Fenzi, with the collaboration of Luciano Formisano and Francesco Montuori (Rome: Salerno, 2012), 38; and "Il mondo come patria: Da Seneca a Dante, *De vulgari eloquentia* I 6, 3," *Letture Classensi* 44 (2015): 85–95, at 91–92.

of idioms and expressions for Dante, more a name than an actual source.[85] Phrases from Seneca and the pseudo-Senecan works are indeed, like Ovid, well represented in anthologies, compendia, and treatises. In his reading assignment to Cino in this letter, however, Dante sounds more thorough: he does not point to just one sentence, as he does with the biblical quotation at the end of the letter, but recommends to read through ("perlege") the *De remediis fortuitorum*. Dante combines the two main reading practices of his time — the use of free-standing citations and the reference to works in their entirety — in a thematic mini-collection of biblical phrases and classical references to exile, overall acting more like a *compilator*. While the fellow exiled poet Ovid was only evoked at the beginning of the letter via an allusion to Ovid's preoccupations about his fame in exile (*Tristia* 1.1), in the final paragraph of the letter, Dante turns explicitly to the experience and words of others to offer words of consolation to his fellow exile Cino — and to himself.

As we have seen in the poems and prose discussed in this section, the main themes of Ovid's poetry — love, myth, and exile — resonated with Dante and Cino da Pistoia. In the sonnets *Amor, che viene armato a doppio dardo*, *Se conceduto mi fosse da Giove*, and *Dante, quando per caso s'abbandona*, Cino went beyond the traditional treatment of Ovidian material, abandoning the usual comparisons between the poets (or their ladies) and Ovidian characters, common among Italian vernacular poets (see Ch. 2.1). Instead he recreated the world of the *Metamorphoses* in his poetry and explored more in depth the identifications with Ovidian characters, both male and female. This duality in identification, coupled with his interest in the Ovidian story of Apollo and Daphne, makes Cino's poetry an important intertext for Petrarch's *Canzoniere*. Whereas Cino links the Ovidian themes of transformation and love in his sonnet exchange with Dante, Dante goes even further, also inserting the Ovidian theme of exile, a shared reality for Cino and Dante, into his writing. Dante cites or alludes to Ovidian sentences about exile in his poetry and prose, and identifies with fellow exiles, just as Ovid himself did. Whereas the Italian poets discussed in the previous chapter looked at the example of their vernacular literary predecessors, the Occitan poets, for their Ovidian inspiration, Cino and Dante abandon their fixed choices for certain characters (Narcissus and Pyramus and Thisbe) and rhetorical figures (the simile). Adding more Ovidian characters and themes to their poetry, Cino and especially Dante no longer compartmentalize their Ovidian sources, weaving different Ovidian thematic threads into their poems. Cino and Dante were not necessarily better read in

---

85   Fenzi, "Il mondo come patria," 86.

DANTE, CINO DA PISTOIA, AND OVID 167

Ovid's works than their Italian predecessors, but, different from them, they let this familiarity with the Latin poet's works clearly stand out in their poetry.

3.4 Conclusion

As we have seen in Cino da Pistoia's poems and Dante's pre-*Commedia* poetry and prose, both poets distinguish themselves from their Italian predecessors and contemporaries as readers of Ovid: both Dante and Cino integrate Ovidian material into their poetry with more complexity than those other vernacular poets ever did. They show interest in a more diverse set of Ovidian characters, beyond the vernacular regulars, and turn to Ovid's entire oeuvre and its themes of love, myth, and exile. Dante and Cino also radically revise one of the hallmarks of Ovidian poems — the use of simile — by associating themselves with the female Ovidian character rather than the male; or by identifying with both men and women within the same poem. Gender switching within the poet's identification with Ovidian characters is a feature that Petrarch later will adopt. Both Dante and Cino also go beyond comparing their present world and experiences with those of the *Metamorphoses* (as the poets discussed in Ch. 2.1), and truly integrate Ovidian material into their poetry, blending Ovid's world into theirs. This fluidity in time and space is a characteristic often noted in Petrarch's treatment of Ovidian material in the *Canzoniere*, but the roots of such poetic choices are to be found in Cino and Dante's earlier poetry.

Finding such attention to Ovid's works in Dante's poetry before 1302 resists the narrative that his interest in the classics corresponds to his life after exile, when more classical texts became available to him. As we have seen in Ch. 1.2, Florence was not a thriving center of classicism during Dante's time in the city, but Ovid — in his various formats — was far from absent. While I cannot completely disagree with statements that before his exile "it does not seem that [Dante's] knowledge of ancient poets was extensive"[86] or that Dante "only began to read more widely during the early years of his exile,"[87] in this chapter I proposed to look beyond the rare quotations of classical poets in the *Vita nuova*, and more importantly to also consider the poems written during that period, which are often left out in the discussion of Dante's classical readings before his exile. Which Ovid was Dante reading in his twenties and thirties? The Ovidian citations found in Dante's prose writings could easily come from

---

86   Witt, *In the Footsteps of the Ancients*, 216.
87   Barański, "On Dante's Trail," 14. On the increased access to libraries and knowledge provided by Dante's exile, see also Ch. 1.2.

anthologies, compendia, or treatises that included many such sentences. (Only the *Vita nuova* predates his exile; the *De vulgari eloquentia* and the letters were all written after 1302.) When only looking at Chapter 25 of the *Vita nuova*, the inclusion of a verse from Ovid's *Remedia amoris* alone cannot make the case for a more thorough and global reading of Ovid's works during the early 1290s. But Dante's allusions in the *Vita nuova* to the entire passage in the *Remedia amoris* to which that verse belonged start to suggest this line of thought. Moreover, Dante's use of Ovidian material in the *petrose*, written in the late 1290s, further show Dante's attention to longer passages in Ovid's poems — longer than the one- or two-verse citations included in anthologies, compendia, and other intermediary sources. Dante's pre-*Commedia* poetry especially testifies to a finer understanding of Ovid's oeuvre.

Something old, something new: Dante and Cino explored several new ways to integrate Ovid's Latin verses into their Italian poetry, but, as documented in the previous chapter, they also adhered to the more common practices of vernacular poets. Cino da Pistoia's sonnet *Se mai leggesti versi de l'Ovidi* was the Italian poem most similar to the Occitan model, appealing to the authority of Ovid in matters of love. Dante was the recipient of Dante da Maiano's sonnet *Amor mi fa sì fedelmente amare*, which questioned the worth of Ovid's writings, but in his reply Dante Alighieri had little to say about reading Ovid. The poems and prose excerpts discussed in this chapter, on the other hand, illustrate Cino and Dante's experimentation with Ovidian material: their new ways to feature Ovidian characters and themes in their poetry will be crucial to understand Dante's reading of Ovid in the *Commedia* and Petrarch's use of Ovidian material in the *Canzoniere*.

CHAPTER 4

Ovid in Dante's *Commedia*

"Dante's Ovid" is the subject of several essays and book chapters that describe the presence and role of the Latin poet Ovid in Dante's poem where it is most felt: the *Commedia*.[1] While Dante's tribute to Virgil (through his guide Virgilio) may be more explicit, Ovid's presence is evident in the many Ovidian characters Dante mentions, for example, as souls the pilgrim encounters in hell and in the poem's numerous similes from the beginning of *Inferno* to the end of *Paradiso*.[2]

---

1 The following essays, book chapters, and dictionary entries focus on Dante's Ovid: Szombathely, *Dante e Ovidio*; Edward Moore, "Dante and Ovid," in *Scripture and Classical Authors in Dante*, 206–28; Rudolf Palgen, "Dante e Ovidio," *Convivium* 27 (1959): 277–87; Ettore Paratore, "Ovidio," *Enciclopedia dantesca*, ed. Umberto Bosco (Rome: Istituto dell'Enciclopedia Italiana, 1970–78), 4: 225–36; Paratore, "Ovidio e Dante," *Nuovi saggi danteschi* (Rome: A. Signorelli, 1973), 47–100; Peter S. Hawkins, "Dante's Ovid," *Literature and Belief* 5 (1985): 1–12; Picone, "L'Ovidio di Dante" ; Giorgio Brugnoli, "Forme ovidiane in Dante," in *Aetates Ovidianae: Lettori di Ovidio dall'Antichità al Rinascimento*, ed. Italo Gallo and Luciano Nicastri (Naples: Edizioni scientifiche italiane, 1995), 239–59; Michelangelo Picone, "Dante e i miti," in Picone and Crivelli, *Dante: Mito e poesia*, 21–32; Diskin Clay, "The Metamorphosis of Ovid in Dante's *Divine Comedy*," in Picone and Crivelli, *Dante: Mito e poesia*, 69–85, also in Miller and Newlands, *A Handbook to the Reception of Ovid*, 174–86; Kevin Brownlee, "Ovid" in *Dante Encyclopedia*, ed. Richard Lansing, Teodolinda Barolini, et al. (New York: Garland Publishing, 2000), 666–68; Vazzana, "Ovidio è il terzo," in *Dante e "la bella scola,"* 123–47; Warren Ginsberg, "Dante's Ovids: Allegory, Irony, and the Poet as Translation," in *Chaucer's Italian Tradition* (Ann Arbor: University of Michigan Press, 2002), 29–57, also as "Dante's Ovids"; Winthrop Wetherbee, "Ovid and Virgil in Purgatory," in *The Ancient Flame: Dante and the Poets* (Notre Dame: University of Notre Dame Press, 2008), 117–58; Maggie Kilgour, "Dante's Ovidian Doubling," in *Dantean Dialogues: Engaging with the Legacy of Amilcare Iannucci*, ed. Maggie Kilgour and Elena Lombardi (Toronto: University of Toronto Press, 2013), 174–214. This list does not include the many close readings of specific Ovidian passages in the *Commedia*. Two prominent collections of such essays are Jacoff and Schnapp, *The Poetry of Allusion*, and Sowell, *Dante and Ovid: Essays in Intertextuality*. Other essays will be mentioned in the notes where relevant to our discussion.

2 The first simile with an Ovidian character is found in *Inf.* 7.22–24, where Dante compares the movement of the avaricious souls to the breaking waves above the sea monster Charybdis: "Come fa l'onda là sovra Cariddi, / che si frange con quella in cui s'intoppa, / così convien che qui la gente riddi" ("As does the wave there over Charybdis, colliding and shattering the other wave it encounters, so must the people whirl around as they dance"). In Book 7 of the *Metamorphoses*, Ovid's Medea also described these breaking waves of Charybdis and Scylla (*Met.* 7.62–65). The last simile with Ovidian characters is found in *Par.* 33.94–96, where the pilgrim's startledness and confusion about the final vision of the Trinity is compared to Neptune seeing the Argo, the very first ship: "Un punto solo m'è maggior letargo / che venticinque secoli a la 'mpresa / che fé Nettuno ammirar l'ombra d'Argo" ("Only one

Finding this Ovidian material in a Christian poem invited comparisons with the moralizing and allegorizing readings of Ovid's myths in the medieval commentaries on the *Metamorphoses*: it is common to describe Dante's relationship with the Latin poet in terms of rewriting, reinventing, or even correcting the pagan stories within the Christian context of the *Commedia*.[3] But such readings only address Dante's debt to Ovid in part. Teodolinda Barolini warned that *in malo/in bono* readings, where the emphasis is on how Dante corrects Ovid's pagan tales in the *Commedia*, paint a too black-and-white picture of Dante's engagement with the Latin poet.[4] "Dante's Ovids" and "Dante's Ovidian Doubling," the titles of Warren Ginsberg and Maggie Kilgour's most recent general overviews of the topic, highlight the need to address the multitudes that Ovid also can contain for a medieval reader.[5] Aligning myself with such approaches, in this chapter I also find that Ovid provides Dante with more than just characters and stories from the *Metamorphoses* to be reinterpreted in a Christian key; Dante translates, paraphrases, loosely imitates numerous sentences and phrases from Ovid's entire oeuvre, from the amatory works

---

    moment brings me more lethargy than twenty-five centuries have brought to the endeavor that made Neptune marvel at the shadow of the Argo"). Ovid described the first sea voyage of the Argonauts in *Met.* 6.720–21. While this passage on Neptune and the Argo in the final canto of the *Commedia* is the last time that Dante uses Ovidian material in the *Commedia*, the Charybdis simile in *Inf.* 7 is preceded by several other passages inspired by Ovid, including another simile. In *Inf.* 1.46–48 Dante compares the arrival of the furious lion, one of the three beasts the pilgrim encountered in the dark wood, to trembling air: "Questi parea che contra me venisse / con la test' alta e con rabbiosa fame, / sì che parea che l'aere ne tremesse" ("It seemed as if he were coming my way with his head high and with ravenous hunger, and that the air was trembling because of him"). Dante's simile can be traced back to the *Metamorphoses*, where in Book 13 Ovid described the transformation of Hecuba, the queen of Troy who lost everything and everyone she loved during the capture of the city. Hecuba turned into a barking dog that made the air tremble: "externasque nouo latratu terruit auras" ("she made the foreign air tremble with her strange sound" [*Met.* 13.406]). This simile is one of the many examples where the presence of Ovid's text is not immediately noticed.

3 Scholars such as Kevin Brownlee, Madison M. Sowell, Rachel Jacoff, and Jeffrey T. Schnapp shifted in 1990s the focus from Ovidian intertextuality in Dante's *Inferno* to the other two canticles, arguing that Ovid's influence is equally present in *Purgatorio* and *Paradiso* — if not more. However, with only one exception, all essays in Sowell, *Dante and Ovid* and Jacoff and Schnapp, *The Poetry of Allusion* still work exclusively with Ovid's *Metamorphoses* and Dante's *Commedia*. The exception is Janet Levarie Smarr's essay "Poets of Love and Exile" (Sowell, *Dante and Ovid*, 139–51), which discusses the influence of Ovid's love and exile poetry on Dante's *Commedia*.

4 Teodolinda Barolini, "Arachne, Argus and St. John: Transgressive Art in Dante and Ovid," *Mediaevalia* 13 (1989): 207–26, at 208; also in *Dante and the Origins of Italian Literary Culture*, 158–71, at 159.

5 Ginsberg, "Dante's Ovids"; Kilgour, "Dante's Ovidian Doubling."

to the exile letters, in the text of the *Commedia*. As we have begun to see in Chapter 3 in the discussion of Dante's *petrose* and his exchange with Cino da Pistoia, Dante is an attentive reader of Ovid. For the citations of Ovid's works in his treatises, Dante could have worked with anthologies, which collected such isolated passages of classical authors.[6] But in his poetry, Dante reveals a knowledge of Ovid's texts that goes beyond having read and reused one or two verses taken out of context. We already saw in the previous chapter that in the *petrose* Dante worked with central and peripheral elements from the Ovidian passages that he selected to feature in his poems. In the *Commedia*, Dante fine-tunes this technique, which means that we need to pay close attention to the broader textual context of the Latin passages that Dante carefully selected to use, just as Dante himself did.

This chapter closely ties Dante's Ovidian strategies in the *Commedia* not only to his earlier writings but also to the Ovidian vernacular lyric poems written before and during his lifetime: the Latin texts of *Ovidius* were among Dante's sources for writing the *Commedia*, but so was the *Ovidio* constructed by the vernacular poets. In the *Commedia*, Dante often combines classical, theological, and vernacular sources. Although we are used to firmly placing Ovid among Dante's classical sources, Dante's Ovidian sources consist of both Ovid's Latin texts and Ovidian readings in vernacular lyric poetry.

Even though he is never explicitly identified as such, Dante is often treated as the first Italian reader of Ovid. He is the first Italian author for whom scholars have tried to find the manuscript(s) in which he read Ovid's texts, while of course the Latin poet had Italian readers before that. Even though Dante's readings of Ovid in the *Commedia* have at times been compared to the moralizations of Ovidian stories in the medieval commentaries on the *Metamorphoses* (that is, compared to the readings of Latin schoolmasters), too often they are read in an Italian vacuum and not placed in the community of medieval Italian readers of Ovid, who both read and wrote about the Latin poet before or during Dante's lifetime. In this chapter, I present such a contextualized discussion of Dante as reader of Ovid in the *Commedia*, in a league of his own in several respects, rooted in the Italian tradition of reading and writing about Ovid in others. In the first section, I take up the question of Dante's sources, relating the scholarship on this issue to previous discussions of the

---

6 In Ch. 1.1, I discussed the frequent inclusion of verses from Ovid's works in the medieval *florilegia* and the reliance of prose writers on such Ovidian phrases, aphorisms once detached from their original context. In Ch. 3.1 and 3.3, I looked at two such phrases in Dante's writing: the citation of a verse from Ovid's *Remedia amoris* in one of the prose chapters of the *Vita nuova* (*VN* 25), and the citation of a verse from the *Fasti* in *DVE* I VI 3.

material and cultural contexts of reading Ovid in medieval Italy described in Ch. 1.1. In the following two sections, I turn to Dante's Ovidian passages in the *Commedia*, illustrating their Latin and vernacular roots, respectively.

4.1 In Search of Dante's (Copy of) Ovid

In the long history of discussing Dante's Ovid, it is considered a given that Dante read Ovid, but only a few scholars have focused on the material object: what Dante's copy or copies of Ovid actually looked like.[7] Fausto Ghisalberti, Ettore Paratore, and Alan Robson have identified specific manuscripts and commentaries as Dante's source; Michelangelo Picone has thought more generally about the format and context in which Dante would have read Ovid's works; and Zygmunt G. Barański has extended these questions to all of Dante's reading. That the arguments of Ghisalberti, Paratore, and Robson focus on the actual text found in specific manuscripts is not surprising. Dante's relationship with the Latin author is often very textual; his working closely with Ovid's Latin texts becomes hard to deny given the Ovidian quotations in his prose works and the tight connections between Ovid's Latin and Dante's Italian poetry. At the same time, their approach does not yield conclusive results: Ghisalberti, Paratore, and Robson explained Dante's word choice at various points in the *Commedia* as the result of having read Ovid's text in a specific manuscript, but in all cases this does not lead to an unquestionable source. Moreover, they just are interested in Dante's copy of the *Metamorphoses*, and not Ovid's other works. Picone and Barański's more general approach — to think about formats and contexts rather than specific manuscripts — reminds us of the importance of placing any acts of reading Ovid within their material and cultural contexts.

Fausto Ghisalberti, editor of several Latin commentaries on Ovid's works (discussed in Ch. 1.1), was the first to propose a specific commentary and a concrete manuscript as Dante's Ovid. In a 1966 essay, Ghisalberti claimed that at least in two instances, Dante "certainly" used the Vulgate Commentary on the *Metamorphoses*, found in a thirteenth-century manuscript at the Biblioteca Ambrosiana in Milan (MS P 43 sup.) and several other codices.[8] These instances are actually explained in more detail in two previous essays, in which

---

7 In Ch. 1.2, I discussed the little we know about Dante's education — from his own limited comments, the information given by his biographer Boccaccio, and our understanding of the educational practices in Florence during Dante's time. Teodolinda Barolini highlighted the importance of studying material culture (including books and the history of textuality) in "'Only Historicize': History, Material Culture (Food, Clothes, Books), and the Future of Dante Studies," *Dante Studies* 127 (2009): 37–54.
8 Ghisalberti, "Il commentario medioevale," 267.

Ghisalberti argued that Dante's mention of the riddle-solving Naiades (in *Purg.* 33.46–51) and the names of the four horses of the Sun (in *Conv.* IV XXIII 14) suggested his use of the Vulgate Commentary on the *Metamorphoses*.[9] In both cases, however, the Vulgate Commentary on those Ovidian passages neither proves that Dante was actually using the Vulgate, nor excludes his use of other commentaries. Moreover, Ghisalberti's evidence does not rule out the possibility that Dante would have worked directly with the text of the *Metamorphoses*.

The first case of the riddle-solving Naiades (*Purg.* 33.46–51) is a particularly interesting one, because it offers insights in both the manuscript and commentary tradition on the *Metamorphoses*. For a long time, Dante scholars and commentators had been puzzled or uneasy about Dante's different rendition of the Sphinx's riddle in the *Commedia* where the Naiades (and not the expected Oedipus) solve the riddle.[10] The manuscript tradition of the *Metamorphoses* easily explains this choice. One of the passages in Ovid's epic poem that mentions Oedipus solving the riddle was transmitted with the reading "Naiades" instead of "Laiades," the son of Laius or Oedipus: the verses "Carmina *Naiades* non intellecta priorum / *soluerant* ingeniis" ("The *Naiades had solved* the riddle that smart people previously failed to understand"; emphasis added) were only corrected in the sixteenth century to "Carmina *Laiades* non intellecta priorum / *soluerat* ingeniis" ("*The son of Laius had solved* the riddle that smart people previously failed to understand" [*Met.* 7.759–60]; emphasis added).[11] Given that "Naiades ... soluerant" is the consensus reading of the oldest fragments and a group of twelve manuscripts dating from the tenth to the twelfth century, Dante most likely read that the Naiades had solved the riddle in whatever text of the *Metamorphoses* he consulted. Moreover, as Ghisalberti further illustrated, medieval commentators on the *Metamorphoses* also had to make sense of the riddle-solving Naiades, and came up with stories about their prophetic qualities. Ghisalberti singled out the Vulgate Commentary as Dante's certain source for this passage,[12] but since "Naiades ... soluerant" was a common reading during Dante's time (other commentaries remarked on the passage in similar ways), it is hard to share Ghisalberti's certainty.

Dante's list of the names of the horses of the Sun mentioned in the *Convivio* (*Conv.* IV XXIII 14) is the other passage central to Ghisaberti's case for the

---

9   Fausto Ghisalberti, "L'enigma delle Naiadi," *Studi Danteschi* 16 (1932): 105–25; and "La quadriga del sole nel 'Convivio,'" *Studi Danteschi* 18 (1934): 69–77.
10 Ghisalberti documented the discomfort several scholars had about Dante's "mistake," including their explanations of why Dante would have featured the Naiades instead of Oedipus in "L'enigma delle Naiadi," 108–11.
11 Ghisalberti, "L'enigma delle Naiadi," 112; Ovid, *Metamorphoses*, ed. R. J. Tarrant (Oxford: Oxford University Press, 2004), xlvi, 210: "Laiades *Jac. Taurellus* (*teste Ciofano*)."
12 Ghisalberti, "Il commentario medioevale," 269.

Vulgate. Dante refers to the horses when he draws a parallel between the four periods of the day and the four horses of the Sun (Eous, Pyrois, Aethon, and Phlegon), and cites Ovid as his source. While Ovid does not attach any further meaning to these names, medieval commentators on the *Metamorphoses* did. Ghisalberti identified the Vulgate as Dante's source based on the sequence and interpretations of their names.[13] In the *Convivio*, Dante switches the names of the first two horses in respect to Ovid's passage ("Eoo" and "Pirroi" instead of Ovid's Pyrois and Eous). As the following table illustrates, only Arnulf of Orléans's commentary on the *Metamorphoses* could explain mentioning Eoo first:[14]

TABLE 8   The names and sequence of the horses of the Sun

Source	Names and order of the horses			
Ovid, *Met.* 2.153–54	Pyrois	Eous	Aethon	Phlegon
Arnulf of Orléans	Pirous	Eous	Flegon	Ethon
	Eous	Ethon	Lampas	Philogeus
Vulgate Commentary	Pyrous	Eous	Ethon	Phlegon
Dante, *Conv.* IV XXIII 14	Eoo	Pirroi	Eton	Flegon

Arnulf's gloss on the horses contains two sets of names: the first lists the names as they appear in Ovid, and the second list of alternative names starts with Eous. Ghisalberti's belief that the Vulgate was Dante's source stems from the way the Vulgate commentator explains Pyrous's name, calling him "rubeus" or red, which is also how Arnulf explained Eous's name.[15] In other words, Dante

---

13 Ghisalberti either simply stated this conclusion ("Il commentario medioevale," 269–70, n. 4) or mentioned the Vulgate only briefly ("La quadriga del sole nel 'Convivio,'" 74–75, n. 3), focusing more on Arnulf of Orléans. Ghisalberti also correctly excluded the sources suggested by H. Theodore Silverstein for the passage in the *Convivio* ("La quadriga del sole nel 'Convivio,'" 69–70).

14 I copied the text of Arnulf of Orléans's commentary as transcribed by Ghisalberti from Paris, Bibliothèque nationale de France, MS lat. 14135, fol. 59r ("La quadriga del sole nel 'Convivio,'" 75, n. 3; "Arnolfo d'Orléans," 186, with slight variation), and the text of the Vulgate Commentary as transcribed from Milan, Biblioteca Ambrosiana, MS P 43 sup., fol. 12v ("La quadriga del sole nel 'Convivio,'" 75, n. 3). The edition of the *Convivio* here used (Fioravanti) has "Filogeo" instead of "Flegon," but I refer to the alternative (attested) reading Ghisalberti uses.

15 Arnulf's commentary read, "Eous id est rubeus propter auroram" ("Eous, or red, because of dawn") (Ghisalberti, "Arnolfo d'Orléans," 186), and the Vulgate Commentary read

would have read the Vulgate commentator's explanation, which incorporated Arnulf's comments. But as the table above shows, the switch of names occurs in Arnulf, not the Vulgate, which makes Arnulf's commentary a more likely source. Then again, none of the sources has the four names in the exact order of the *Convivio*; even when using Arnulf's commentaries, Dante would have had to combine the names of Arnulf's first set (Pirous, Eous, Flegon, Ethon) with the second list of names (Eous, Ethon, Lampas, Philogeus). This is no more probable than the possibility that Dante, instead of consulting commentaries or glosses, simply read the text of the *Metamorphoses* and changed the sequence and names of Ovid's horses. In fact, Dante explicitly identified Ovid's *Metamorphoses* as his source ("secondo che scrive Ovidio nel secondo del Metamorfoseos" [*Conv.* IV XXIII 14]). It is difficult to call the Vulgate Commentary the text that Dante certainly consulted, but Ghisalberti again rightfully called attention to the richness of the Ovidian tradition and the various forms reading Ovid could take on.

A few years later, Ettore Paratore suggested that Dante might have consulted another manuscript (Florence, Biblioteca Medicea Laurenziana, MS Pluteo 36.12) based on the similarities between the textual variants in this manuscript and certain passages in the *Commedia*.[16] One of these passages is Dante's opening comparison in *Inf.* 30.1–12, which includes the king Athamas. Turned insane by Juno, Athamas had killed his son Learchus, and his wife jumped off a cliff to save their other son, holding him in her arms. Athamas's words in *Met.* 4.513–14 are "io, comites, his retia tendite siluis! / hic modo cum gemina uisa est mihi prole leaena" ("Friends, spread out your nets right here in the woods! I just saw a lioness with two cubs"). These words are slightly modified in MS Pluteo 36.12, which has "pandite" instead of "tendite."[17] According to Paratore, this rare textual variant would explain Dante's rendition of Athamas's words: "Tendiam le reti, sì ch'io pigli / la leonessa e ' leoncini al varco" ("Let us spread our nets,

---

"Pirous ... quia sol summo mane igneus et rubeus" ("Pirous ... because the sun is fiery and red at the very early dawn" (Ghisalberti, "La quadriga del sole nel 'Convivio,'" 75, n. 3).

16   Paratore, "Ovidio e Dante," 69–70 (an echo from the story of Phaethon in *Inf.* 17), 74 (Pyramus and Thisbe in *Purg.* 27), 80 (Athamas in *Inf.* 30), 88–89 (the Naiades in *Purg.* 33, also discussed above), 90 (Narcissus in *Par.* 3). I focus on the example of Athamas in *Inf.* 30, since it best illustrates how this particular manuscript could not be Dante's sole source for the *Metamorphoses*. For a description of the manuscript, see Franco Munari, *Catalogue of the MSS of Ovid's Metamorphoses* (London: Institute of Classical Studies in Conjunction with the Warburg Institute, 1957), 30 (no. 131). Munari noted that the manuscript contains "copious glosses and corrections." See also Frank T. Coulson, "A Bibliographical update and corrigenda minora to Munari's catalogues of the manuscripts of Ovid's *Metamorphoses*," *Manuscripta* 38 (1994): 3–22, at 7.

17   Magnus, *Metamorphoses*, 151.

so that I can seize the lioness and her cubs along the pass" [*Inf.* 30.7–8]). But Dante's wording still includes "tendiam" after Ovid's "tendite" (which all other manuscripts feature instead of "pandite"). Moreover, MS Pluteo 36.12, an eleventh- or twelfth-century manuscript, breaks off at *Met.* 12.298 and therefore could not have been Dante's sole source, as Dante also inserts material from the last three books of the *Metamorphoses* in the *Commedia*.[18] A fitting example here is the story of Hecuba, Polyxena, and Polydorus (*Met.* 13.429–575), which is the second comparison of the canto and immediately follows the Athamas story (*Inf.* 30.13–21).

Alan Robson added several more possible sources to the list in his 1980 essay "Dante's Reading of the Latin Poets and the Structure of the *Commedia*."[19] Robson first introduced the possibility that Dante knew quotations from Ovid and other Latin poets through intermediate sources: for example, Brunetto Latini's *Tresor* or other works that compiled quotations from several sources (described in Ch. 1.1).[20] As for Ovid's *Metamorphoses*, he suggested three types of manuscripts that Dante might have known, based on the extant manuscripts now held at the Florentine Medicea Laurenziana and Riccardiana libraries. These include large manuscripts from the eleventh and twelfth centuries, some containing the prose summaries of the pseudo-Lactantian *Narrationes*; smaller thirteenth-century copies with marginal notes; and manuscripts from the thirteenth and fourteenth centuries containing more extended commentaries (e.g., Arnulf of Orléans or Giovanni del Virgilio's commentaries).

Notwithstanding the different commentary formats that Robson listed, he is extremely focused on the idea that Dante read the *Metamorphoses* in the pseudo-Lactantian *Narrationes* and conjectured that Dante might even have made a "workbook of his own in which he noted passages of Ovid omitted by Lactantius," because he quotes passages from Book 7 of the *Metamorphoses* that are absent in the pseudo-Lactantian *Narrationes*.[21] Concluding from that instance that Dante is eager to explain connections between passages that are

---

18   Munari, *Catalogue of the MSS of Ovid's Metamorphoses*, 30; Ovid, *Metamorphoses*, ed. Tarrant, xiii.
19   Alan Robson, "Dante's Reading of the Latin Poets and the Structure of the *Commedia*," in *The World of Dante: Essays on Dante and His Times*, ed. Cecil Grayson (Oxford: Clarendon Press, 1980), 81–122. The article's main focus, Dante's intended expansions of *Paradiso*, is highly speculative in nature. Critical responses to this essay are found in Robert Hollander, *Allegory in Dante's 'Commedia'* (Princeton: Princeton University Press, 1969), 202–14, and Kenelm Foster's review in "Dante in Great Britain, 1965," *Dante Studies* 84 (1966): 69–71.
20   Robson, "Dante's Reading of the Latin Poets," 84–85.
21   Robson, "Dante's Reading of the Latin Poets," 88.

absent in the *Narrationes*, Robson added the example of *Ep.* III, the letter to Cino da Pistoia, where Dante indeed places the story of Leucothoë correctly within its context in Book 4 of the *Metamorphoses* (see Ch. 3.3). However, the pseudo-Lactantian commentary does not completely ignore the context to which Dante refers in his letter.[22] Robson's arguments that Dante was reading the pseudo-Lactantian commentary and not another commentary or focusing solely on Ovid's text are not fully convincing. It seems more likely that Dante was actually interested in reading and mastering the text of the *Metamorphoses* than showing off his awareness that the commentary failed to make some connections between Ovid's stories.

In the introduction to his 1993 essay "L'Ovidio di Dante,"[23] Michelangelo Picone explicitly raised questions that have appeared in the previous discussion of Ghisalberti, Paratore, and Robson's arguments: Did Dante read Ovid directly or through medieval commentaries? Did he read Ovid's text in its entirety or as fragments and quotations in anthologies or other works?[24] While the three previous scholars singled out one text as Dante's source — a choice that in all cases was not irrefutable — Picone departed from them in two important ways. First, instead of indicating a specific commentary or manuscript that Dante must have consulted (as Ghisalberti, Paratore, and Robson did), Picone offered a more general discussion of the format in which Dante would have encountered Ovid's writings. He stated that Dante did not read in the modern way (with only the text of Ovid's poem in front of him) but "in the only manner in which someone in the Middle Ages could read Ovid": in a heavily annotated manuscript that places the Latin text, "the expression of ancient wisdom," in the center and fills the rest of the page with "the *inveramento* of the Christian sense which was only understood by the *auctor*."[25]

---

22 In *Ep.* III, Dante refers to the story of Leucothoë as one of the stories the daughters of Minyas told each other to entertain themselves while weaving, an activity they preferred to participating in the city's festivities for Bacchus. The writer of the *Narrationes* refers to this frame story in Magnus, *Metamorphoses*, 646, lines 22–24–647, lines 1–6 and 649, lines 14–21.

23 Picone, "L'Ovidio di Dante," 107–44.

24 Picone, "L'Ovidio di Dante," 107.

25 Picone, "L'Ovidio di Dante," 112: "Dante leggeva quindi Ovidio non in modo moderno, avendo davanti il solo testo poetico, ma nell'unico modo in cui poteva leggerlo un uomo del Medioevo: in un manoscritto cioè che disponeva al centro della pagina il testo poetico, l'espressione della sapienza antica, e che ammassava ai quattro margini, oltre che nell'interlinea, il testo prosastico, l'inveramento del senso cristiano solo intuito dall'*auctor*. In un siffatto manoscritto è da additare il modello letterario e l'archetipo culturale del *prosimetrum* dantesco." ("Therefore, Dante did not read Ovid in the modern way, having only Ovid's text in front of him, but in the only manner in which someone in the Middle

Picone rightfully brought the discussion back to the medieval context of reading, and given the inconclusive results of Ghisalberti, Paratore, and Robson's close comparisons between Ovidian manuscripts and Dante's text, his general approach to the question is probably more realistic. But Picone's answer overlooks two distinct features of Ovid's reception: not all manuscripts are heavily annotated and not all commentaries moralize and allegorize the stories. Manuscripts and commentaries on the *Metamorphoses* take on very different formats: some commentaries contain only the Latin text with minimal interlinear glosses, some combine Ovid's text with more extensive notes in the left or right margins, others have the notes as a separate text. In other words, not every manuscript of the *Metamorphoses* is filled to the corners with comments, as Picone stated. The pseudo-Lactantian *Narrationes*, which Robson proposed as Dante's Ovidian source, places the limited prose commentary before and after Ovid's verse (see *fig.* 2 and the more detailed description of the *Narrationes* in Ch. 1.1). Arnulf's commentary on the *Metamorphoses* (consisting of separate sections of glosses, lists of the stories belonging to each book, and allegorical explanations) at times appeared as a free-standing text, but in other manuscripts the glosses were placed in the margins (see *fig.* 3). The Vulgate Commentary, the Ovidian text Ghisalberti believed Dante used, most resembles the kind of manuscript Picone described: copies of this commentary have the text of Ovid's *Metamorphoses* in one or two columns and the remaining space filled with the commentary (see *figs.* 4 and 5). In addition to these different layouts, we saw that the content of the commentaries varied greatly, ranging from notes on history, natural phenomena, literary references, to moral allegories of the stories, many of which were not overtly Christian. Not every commentary contains "the *inveramento* of the Christian sense which was only understood by the *auctor*," as Picone put in his description.

But that particular mode of interpreting Ovid, Picone found, also applies to Dante's own reading of Ovid. This is the second point of difference between Picone's approach and that of Ghisalberti, Paratore, and Robson: Picone connected the format and layout of Dante's Ovidian source text with his way of interpreting Ovid. However, the format and content of the medieval manuscripts of Ovid's *Metamorphoses* are more varied than Picone presented; that Dante read the text of the *Metamorphoses* surrounded by allegories of Ovid's stories

Ages could read Ovid: that is, in a manuscript that placed the poetic text, the expression of ancient wisdom, in the center of the page, and filled the four margins and the space in between the lines with prose text, the *inveramento* of the Christian sense which was only understood by the *auctor*. In such a manuscript we find the literary model and the cultural archetype of the Dantean *prosimetrum*.")

is but one possible scenario. And even if he did, that does not mean that Dante necessarily approaches Ovidian material in the same manner as the author of these allegorizing readings: Dante has proven himself to be a reader against the grain in other cases. Moreover, what could apply to Dante's featuring of Ovidian myths does not cover his entire engagement with the Latin poet's writings, which, as we will see in this chapter, goes beyond including selected characters and stories from the *Metamorphoses*.

Discussing Dante's reading in general, not just of Ovid, Zygmunt Barański took a similar position as Picone. In the opening chapter of *Dante e i segni*, he advocated strongly — and rightfully — for a less anachronistic portrayal of Dante as a reader. His plea that we cannot treat Dante as a modern reader with modern text editions, but instead must study him as a reader of his time, has been the guiding methodological principle for my own discussion of Ovid's medieval readers.[26] His description of the medieval context of Dante's reading includes several aspects which I drew upon in earlier chapters: the fluidity of the text and its translations in medieval times; the collection and inclusion of isolated, fragmented passages in anthologies and other medieval works that provide indirect, intermediary access to an author; and the *accessus*, biographies, glosses, and commentaries that accompany medieval texts, but not their modern editions. Like Picone, Barański imagines any text surrounded by such glosses and comments,[27] and its interpretation necessarily rooted in the exegetical tradition: a medieval reader was mainly influenced by the commentary and not the commented text.[28] But if Picone's statement that Dante could have read Ovid only in such a context was too general, can we really apply the same yardstick to all of Dante's reading?

Barański considered close comparisons between Dante's words and the text of another author in the modern editions of his work a main manifestation of wrongly treating Dante as "one of us." Barański questioned the conclusions of

---

26   Zygmunt G. Barański, "L'*iter* ideologico di Dante," in *Dante e i segni: Saggi per una storia intellettuale di Dante Alighieri* (Naples: Liguori, 2000), 9–39, especially at 9–22.

27   Barański, "L'*iter* ideologico di Dante," 18: "Nel Medioevo, i testi non solo avevano forme fluide, ma ... era impossibile leggerli in modo indipendente, essendo essi inevitabilmente circondati da commenti e glosse più o meno canonici che ne condizionavano la ricenzione." ("In the Middle Ages, texts did not only have fluid forms, but it was impossible to read them independently, since they were inevitably surrounded by more or less canonical comments and glosses that conditioned their reception.")

28   Barański, "L'*iter* ideologico di Dante," 19–20: "Il punto chiave di questo rapporto, come per tutti i contemporanei del poeta, è che l'influsso determinante su di lui fu esercitato dal *commentum*, e non dal testo commentato." ("The key aspect of this relationship [i.e., between the poet and the exegetical tradition], as for all his contemporaries, is the defining influence the commentary had on him, and not the commented text").

intertextual readings in which Dante allegedly had direct knowledge of this author or text based on one or a few close similarities.[29] However, the instances where Dante works closely with the text of Ovid's writings are numerous, and taken together do strongly suggest a direct knowledge of the Latin author's writings. To work with Ovid's Latin text from a modern edition is mostly a practical choice then: it does not stem from a lack of awareness about the cultural context of Dante's reading Ovid — a context that includes not only the highly annotated manuscripts Picone and Barański singled out, but all the texts and contexts in which he could find the Latin poet, including the many Ovid-inspired writings in Latin and the vernacular languages. A modern text edition of Ovid is not likely to render the exact same text Dante had before his eyes, but since we find example after example where Dante's language in the *Commedia* closely resembles Ovid's Latin (in modern text editions), as opposed to any other medieval Ovidian source, it remains our best point of comparison. Within a culture of fragmented, isolated readings of *auctoritates*, textual variations in manuscripts, and the commentary tradition, we also find instances where Dante did read his texts "contextually" and "globally," as Albert Russell Ascoli pointed out.[30] In the following section, I will show that Dante read Ovid's verses contextually (that is, in their original context) more often than not.

In an essay on Dante's citational practices in the *Commedia*, Christopher Kleinhenz argued convincingly that Dante intended his interpretations to include the larger passages from which the citations were selected. Kleinhenz illustrated this view most clearly with the passage from *Purg.* 2 that describes the souls on a boat nearing Mount Purgatory. In his description, Dante points out that the souls were singing the psalm *In exitu Israel de Aegypto* "con quanto di quel salmo è poscia scripto" ("with as much of that psalm that is written after" [*Purg.* 2.48]). In other words, Dante indicates that the entire text of the psalm is relevant to the passage in *Purgatorio*. In his essay, Kleinhenz focused on the citation, a form of including source texts that is more direct than the intertextual passages in the *Commedia* where Dante does not cite his sources or instead translates or paraphrases them. But in interpreting such passages we should also look at the broader textual context, at what is "written after" and before.[31]

---

29 Barański, "L'*iter* ideologico di Dante," 13–14.
30 Albert Russell Ascoli, "Reading Dante's Readings: What? When? Where? How?" in *Dante and Heterodoxy: The Temptations of 13th Century Radical Thought*, ed. Maria Luisa Ardizzone (Newcastle upon Tyne: Cambridge Scholars Publishing, 2014), 126–43, at 140.
31 Christopher Kleinhenz, "Perspectives on Intertextuality in Dante's *Divina Commedia*," *Romance Quarterly* 54, no. 3 (2007): 183–94, especially at 184–85.

4.2 Dante's *Ovidius*: Close Readings of the Latin Text

From Orpheus, the first Ovidian character mentioned in *Inferno* (*Inf.* 4.140), to Neptune, the last Ovidian character in the *Commedia* (*Par.* 33.96), the instances where Dante works with Ovidian characters and stories from the *Metamorphoses* in the *Commedia* are extremely numerous.[32] In this section, I will show how these obvious borrowings from Ovid often appear together with less evident Ovidian passages, and how Dante works with almost all of Ovid's works, at times even combining them — Ovidian strategies that Dante started to use in the *petrose* (see Ch. 3.2) and now distinctly characterize his reading of Ovid in the *Commedia*. I will illustrate these reading strategies through the discussion of the Cacciaguida episode in *Paradiso* (*Par.* 15.13–18.51). This episode shows the breadth of Dante's Ovidian sources (from the amatory works to the *Metamorphoses* and the exile letters), and how closely Dante works with the Latin text: often the verses that make it into the text of the *Commedia* are strategically chosen from Ovidian narratives that address the broader themes and concerns of the episode. In the *Commedia*, the verbal similarities between Ovid's Latin and Dante's Italian verses are often so close that they must have come from more thorough contact with the text instead of with isolated Ovidian citations read in anthologies or other intermediary sources.[33]

In assembling the full list of Ovidian passages in the *Commedia*, I have included only those with at least one lexical connection between Dante's and Ovid's texts.[34] This list of corresponding passages can be consulted in my Digital Humanities project *Intertextual Dante*, part of the *Digital Dante* website.[35]

---

32 For the full list of the Ovidian characters Dante includes in the *Commedia*, see the "character" category on the *Intertextual Dante* site, discussed below.

33 I have mainly excluded such close textual similarities for earlier Italian poems, especially those discussed in Chapter 2, showing that the connections were too general to consider Ovid's Latin text the undeniable source.

34 For this list, I worked with entries found in concordances and commentaries, and own findings. The main sources were Szombathely, *Dante e Ovidio*; Moore, *Studies in Dante*; Paratore, "Ovidio e Dante"; Vazzana, "Ovidio è il terzo." In Ch. 1.3, I discussed Moore's criteria for compiling his concordance (Szombathely and Vazzana do not expand on the reasons for inclusion for their lists). My insistence on at least one lexical connection between Dante's and Ovid's texts excludes those passages where Ovid is but one of the many authors who wrote about a character or event and nothing about Ovid's account ties it to the passage in the *Commedia*.

35 The project can be consulted at https://digitaldante.columbia.edu/intertexual-dante-vanpeteghem/. The limitations of print concordances I encountered while working on my own list of corresponding passages in Dante and Ovid's texts led me to conceptualize the idea of a digital concordance, which would build on and exceed the capabilities of

Intertextual Dante is a digital edition of Dante's *Commedia* that visualizes its Ovidian intertextual passages: it transforms the print concordance, a static list of corresponding passages, into an interactive digital tool that allows users to read the intertextual passages side by side and in context. All intertextual passages in the texts are indicated with the icon of a pointing finger (a nod to the *manicula* in medieval and Renaissance manuscripts, the little drawings of a hand with a finger literally pointing out that a specific passage is noteworthy). Clicking on this icon brings up the two corresponding passages in Dante and Ovid, highlighted and side by side. The *Intertextual Dante* interface, where Dante's *Commedia* and his source texts appear together in their entirety, fosters the kind of reading and research that the intertextual passages in the *Commedia* often require: not restricted to only the obviously corresponding verses in Dante's poem and his sources, but attentive to the broader passages from which Dante selected those verses.[36]

The instances where Dante translates or paraphrases Ovid's language in the *Commedia* are varied, and for that reason I further divided them into categories that are more attentive to Dante's specific use of his Ovidian sources: word choice, characters/places/events, and similes. These categories, which can be searched separately on *Intertextual Dante*, provide more information about specific stylistic, structural, and rhetorical aspects of Dante's textual borrowings — features that the total number of Ovidian passages easily masks.[37] It is also possible to search for the intertextual passages in specific cantos in the *Commedia* or works by Ovid: as the icons of the pointing finger mark each intertextual passage, it becomes easy to see which are the Ovidian cantos in the *Commedia* and to which Ovidian works Dante was most drawn. The intertextual passages from the Cacciaguida episode in *Paradiso*, which can also be consulted on *Intertextual Dante*, serve in what follows to illustrate in more depth the ways in which Dante works with his Ovidian sources.

---

print. I then worked with the Columbia University Libraries to develop *Intertextual Dante*. The reading tool, which aligns passages from Dante's *Commedia* with his source texts, was coded and designed by Jack Donovan at the Libraries.

36 On this project, see my essay "Digital Readers of Allusive Texts: Ovidian Intertextuality in the 'Commedia' and the Digital Concordance on *Intertextual Dante*," *Humanist Studies & the Digital Age* 4 (2015): 39–59. For a detailed introduction to *Intertextual Dante*, including instructions on how to use the site, see "What is *Intertextual Dante*?" *Intertextual Dante*, Digital Dante (New York: Columbia University Libraries, 2017), https://digitaldante.columbia.edu/intertexual-dante-vanpeteghem/.

37 For instance, the compiling of a "simile" category revealed that *Inferno*, *Purgatorio*, and *Paradiso* roughly contain the same number of similes of Ovidian inspiration, while the latter two canticles have fewer Ovidian references than *Inferno*.

The pilgrim's encounter with his great-great-grandfather Cacciaguida in the heaven of Mars, a narrative unit that runs over four cantos mid-way *Paradiso* (*Par.* 15.13–18.51), forms the emotional core of the third canticle. Throughout *Inferno* and *Purgatorio* different characters had anticipated Dante's exile from Florence: in *Inferno*, Ciacco (*Inf.* 6.64–75), Farinata (*Inf.* 10.79–81), Brunetto Latini (*Inf.* 15.55–57), and Vanni Fucci (*Inf.* 24.143–50), and in *Purgatorio*, Currado Malaspina (*Purg.* 8.133–39), Oderisi da Gubbio (*Purg.* 11.139–41), Bonagiunta Orbicciani (*Purg.* 24.37–39), and Forese Donati (*Purg.* 24.82–90).[38] After these earlier predictions Cacciaguida discusses Dante's exile from Florence in the clearest formulations, closely connecting it to the writing of the *Commedia*. Dante's personal history is placed within the history of the city of Florence and its families. This is not an episode that is typically read from an Ovidian angle, even though it contains two notable and clearly noticeable Ovidian moments: in *Par.* 17, the pilgrim compares himself to Phaethon, who also wanted to establish a family connection, and to Hippolytus, a fellow undeserved exile. I read these two Ovidian similes alongside other less obvious Ovidian passages (often considered intertextual flourishes more than anything else), identifying Dante's meaningful engagement with Ovid's works and themes.

Already in Cacciaguida's first appearance Dante uses language similar to Ovid's. The souls in the heaven of Mars, those who fought for faith, form a cross together; when Cacciaguida moves down from this shining cross to talk with the pilgrim and Beatrice, his descend is compared to a shooting star (*Par.* 15.13–18):

> Quale per li seren tranquilli e puri
> discorre ad ora ad or sùbito foco,
> movendo li occhi che stavan sicuri,
> e pare stella che tramuti loco,
> se non che da la parte ond' e' s'accende
> nulla sen perde, ed esso dura poco:

> [Just as through the calm and clear evening from time to time a sudden fire spreads rapidly across the sky, moving eyes that had been at rest, and it seems a star that changes location, except that in the part where it catches fire, nothing is lost, and it lasts only a little while.]

---

38   Robert Hollander listed all predictions of Dante's exile (four in *Inferno*, four in *Purgatorio*) leading up to Cacciaguida's final prophecy in *Paradiso* in Dante Alighieri, *Paradiso*, a verse translation by Jean Hollander and Robert Hollander, introduction and notes by Robert Hollander (New York: Anchor Books, 2007), 420–21.

As several commentators have noted, both Vergil's *Aeneid* (2.692–704) and Ovid's *Metamorphoses* (2.319–24) contain similar passages. The Vergilian source often gets preference because immediately after this comparison between Cacciaguida and a shooting star, Dante inserts a Vergilian simile — Cacciaguida affectionately recognizing the pilgrim is compared to the reunion between Aeneas and his father Anchises's soul in the classical underworld (*Par.* 15.25–27). But the passage in Ovid's *Metamorphoses* more closely resembles Dante's comparison (the passage in Vergil is about a falling star that Aeneas and Anchises take to be an omen), and is taken from the story of Phaethon (*Met.* 2.319–24):

> At Phaethon rutilos flamma populante capillos
> uoluitur in praeceps longoque per aera tractu
> fertur, ut interdum de caelo stella sereno,
> etsi non cecidit, potuit cecidisse uideri.
> quem procul a patria diuerso maximus orbe
> excipit Eridanus flagrantiaque abluit ora.

> [But Phaethon spiraled down head first, while flames burned his reddish hair, and he was dragged through the air in a long trail, like sometimes a star in a clear sky appears to fall, even though it has not fallen. Far away from home, in a distant part of the world, the long Eridanus river caught him and washed his burning face.]

The verse describing a star that only appears to be falling (*Met.* 2.322) comes especially close to Dante's comparison in the *Commedia*. Dante is sampling the story of Phaethon at the beginning of the Cacciaguida episode: Phaethon will play a more substantial role later on in the episode when Dante features him in a simile, comparing their experiences (*Par.* 17.1–3). In the Ovidian passage that inspired Dante here at the beginning of the Cacciaguida episode, Phaethon is described as "procul a patria," far away from home (*Met.* 2.323). In that way, Dante introduces the theme of exile: a theme he will treat most explicitly in *Par.* 17 — the canto that opens with the Phaethon simile and includes Cacciaguida's prophecy of Dante's own exile.

The next Ovidian source is a passage from the amatory works: in Cacciaguida's first long speech, which praises Florence's glorious past and criticizes the present, Dante reuses verses from Ovid's *Remedia amoris*. During his lifetime, Cacciaguida explains, the city "si stava in pace, sobria e pudica" ("lived in peace, sober and chaste" [*Par.* 15.99]). To illustrate the difference between past and present, he inserts a series of negations: a list of all the bad habits and practices that did not exist when he was alive. When discussing women's appearance, he notes that during his lifetime (*Par.* 15.100–2):

> Non avea catenella, non corona,
> non gonne contigiate, non cintura
> che fosse a veder più che la persona.

> [There were no necklaces, nor crowns, no embellished gowns, nor belts that were more visible than the person wearing them.]

In the corresponding passage in the *Remedia amoris*, Ovid addresses the heartbroken lover, warning him not to be impressed by a girl's appearance — clothing makes her more beautiful than she really is (vv. 343–44):

> auferimur cultu; gemmis auroque teguntur
> omnia; pars minima est ipsa puella sui.

> [We are carried away by appearances; gems and gold cover up everything; the girl herself is the least part of it.]

Dante reuses Ovid's language of love to write a moralizing discourse that criticizes the abundance of women's finery.[39] Similar to writers of moral treatises and compilers of anthologies, he took the statement from Ovid's *Remedia amoris* out of its amatory context and attributed a moral quality to Ovid's words — a common medieval practice, discussed in detail in Ch. 1.1. In this particular case, it is even possible that Dante had found this Ovidian passage in such intermediary sources, already prepackaged for a moralistic reading.[40]

The following Ovidian passage works in a similar way. To describe the light that Cacciaguida sends out, Dante uses the following Ovid-inspired comparison (*Par.* 16.28–30):

---

[39] By connecting Cacciaguida's words with Ovid's verses on female dress, I interpret this passage in *Par.* 15 to be about women. Kristina Olson has raised questions about this gendered reading of the tercet, included in Cacciaguida's larger critique of both men and women in Florence, and traced its origins to the commentary tradition on the canto. See "Shoes, Gowns and Turncoats: Reconsidering Cacciaguida's History of Florentine Fashion and Politics," *Dante Studies* 134 (2016): 26–47.

[40] These two verses from the *Remedia amoris* are included in the *Florilegium Gallicum*, see Rackley, "The Amatory Excerpts of Ovid in the *Florilegium Gallicum*," 102; and Fernández de la Cuesta González, *En la senda del 'Florilegium Gallicum,'* 355.

Come s'avviva a lo spirar d'i venti
carbone in fiamma, così vid' io quella
luce risplendere a' miei blandimenti

[As at the blowing of the winds a piece of coal becomes aflame, so I saw that light shine at my charming words.]

Several commentaries referred to the following simile in the corresponding passage in the *Metamorphoses* (*Met.* 7.79–81):

utque solet uentis alimenta adsumere quaeque
parua sub inducta latuit scintilla fauilla
crescere et in ueteres agitata resurgere uires

[Just as a tiny spark hidden under the ashes, when fed by the wind, grows and regains its previous strength]

Most comments only pointed to the clear similarities at the sentence level: both passages describe how winds spark flames. But the broader context from which the Ovidian simile is taken also deserves a closer look: Ovid compares the growing spark to the passion Medea felt for Jason (*Met.* 7.82–83).[41] In that sense, this passage is another instance where Dante strips Ovid's language from the erotic desire it describes in the original context to make it fit in the *Commedia*, in a reinterpreting move similar to the one applied to the verses from the *Remedia amoris* earlier on in the Cacciaguida episode. In this instance, Dante uses Ovid's language of sexual attraction to describe the sparkling light of the saints in *Paradiso*. This is a reinterpretation, and not a decontextualization, of the Ovidian simile. Like in the first simile where Cacciaguida was compared to the shooting star in Ovid's story of Phaethon, Dante again selects an Ovidian simile from a passage whose broader context also fits the themes he is concerned with: separation from one's family and hometown. In the *Metamorphoses*, the description of Medea's growing passion for Jason immediately follows her monologue (*Met.* 7.11–71). In that monologue, she is torn between staying with her family or leaving her hometown to follow Jason

---

41 An exception is Robert Hollander, who did discuss the content of the passage in Ovid's *Metamorphoses* in his edition and commentary on the *Paradiso*, finding it odd that Dante would compare the affection between the pilgrim and his great-great-grandfather to Medea's feelings for Jason (442). In what follows, I suggest how the broader context and the themes of this Ovidian myth can explain Dante's choice.

(*Met.* 7.22, 39, 53, and repeated at *Met.* 7.90) — a thought that both excites and horrifies her. In this subtler Ovidian reference, Dante carefully chose a simile taken from a larger passage in the *Metamorphoses* that addresses the same themes as the episode in the *Commedia*.

But before Cacciaguida turns to the pilgrim's future separation from his family and hometown, he first continues to describe Florence's history from his time (the end of the eleventh century) to the pilgrim's (the year 1300, the fictional date of his journey). Cacciaguida's portrayal of Florence's golden age in *Par.* 15 is followed in the next canto by his analysis of its decline and current state of corruption and decadence. While pointing to families from outside immigrating to the city as the specific root of the problem, Cacciaguida also takes a more general and philosophical stance: nothing can and will last forever; time, as Dante pointedly puts it at the beginning of *Par.* 16, goes around with her scissors ("lo tempo va dintorno con le force" [*Par.* 16.9]). Applying this general principle to the inevitable extinction of cities and races, Cacciaguida explains to the pilgrim that the noble Florentine families will eventually become extinct, in the same way that cities disappear. We mortals just do not live long enough to perceive this inescapable change (*Par.* 16.79–81):

> Le vostre cose tutte hanno lor morte,
> sì come voi; ma celasi in alcuna
> che dura molto, e le vite son corte.

> [All things have a death, just like you; but death conceals itself in some things that last a long time, and lives are short.]

A few Ovidian phrases and ideas made their way into Cacciaguida's speech. The most notable is the phrase "tempus edax rerum" ("time, devourer of things" [*Met.* 15.234]), equally succinct in Dante's "time with her scissors" (*Par.* 16.9) — those three Latin words aptly summarize Cacciaguida's entire speech on Florence's decline. "Tempus edax rerum" had become an aphorism by Dante's time, included in collections of proverbs and *sententiae*.[42] But already the commentator of the Ottimo Commento (1333–38) considered the Ovidian passage in which this phrase was found meaningful, citing a long excerpt in Italian translation (*Met.* 15.234–80), starting with "O tempo

---

42 See Paolo Roos, *Sentenza e proverbio nell'antichità e i 'Distici di Catone,'* (Brescia: Morcelliana, 1984), 119; a longer Ovidian excerpt starting with "tempus edax rerum" (*Met.* 15.234–53, 15.247–53, 15.259–61) is also included in the *Florilegium Gallicum* (Fernández de la Cuesta González, *En la senda del 'Florilegium Gallicum,'* 322–23).

consumatore delle cose."[43] The passage that the Ottimo commentator selected are thirty-six verses from the long speech by the Greek philosopher Pythagoras in the final book of the *Metamorphoses*, a speech that theorizes change (*Met*. 15.60–478). "Tempus edax rerum" is the pithy expression of its content; somewhat longer, but equally representative is Pythagoras's phrase "nihil est tot quod perstet in orbe" ("there is nothing in the whole world that can last" [*Met*. 15.177]). Pythagoras's speech illustrates this principle of constant change with many examples, including cities (*Met*. 15.287–306) and races (*Met*. 15.418–52). Dante's Cacciaguida focuses in his speech on these two entities, the ones that are most relevant to the pilgrim: family and city, both of which his exile forced him to abandon.

In the next canto, *Par*. 17, Dante finally turns to this personal history, and already from the first verses we learn that Ovid will be a close companion in this exile narrative.[44] In those opening verses, Dante inserts the first of two similes that compare the pilgrim to an Ovidian character. To express the pilgrim's curiosity to hear about his future from Cacciaguida, Dante works with an episode from the story of Phaethon (*Met*. 1.747–79, 2.1–400). The pilgrim is compared with the equally curious Phaethon who wants his mother Clymene to finally identify his father (*Par*. 17.1–4):

> Qual venne a Climenè, per accertarsi
> di ciò ch'avëa incontro a sé udito,
> quei ch'ancor fa li padri ai figli scarsi;
> tal era io …

---

43   *L'Ottimo commento della Divina Commedia*, ed. Alessandro Torri (Bologna: Arnaldo Forni, 1995), 3: 372–73. This translation is not the same as Arrigo Simintendi's translation of the *Metamorphoses* (see Ch. 1.1), dated to the same year of the first redaction of the Ottimo Commento (1333), as found in *Gli ultimi V libri delle Metamorfosi d'Ovidio volgarizzate da Ser Arrigo Simintendi da Prato*, 217–20. In the third and final 1338 version of the Ottimo Commento, Arrigo's translation of the *Metamorphoses* is mentioned in the introductory note to *Inf*. 18 (the 1333 edition does not include this remark). Giuliana De' Medici, who studied the sources of the Ottimo Commento, included Arrigo's translation of the *Metamorphoses*, but did not address this difference in translation. See "Le fonti dell'Ottimo commento alla *Divina Commedia*," *Italia medioevale e umanistica* 26 (1983): 71–125, at 83–84.

44   Giuseppe Ledda's *lectura* of *Par*. 17 paid particular attention to Dante's use of Ovidian myths in this canto, closely connecting them to the central themes of the canto: Dante's autobiography and his prophetic and poetic mission. See "*Paradiso*, XVII," in *Il trittico di Cacciaguida: lectura Dantis Scaligera, 2008–2009*, ed. Ennio Sandal (Rome: Antenore, 2011), 107–46. In his reading, the opening simile featuring Phaethon is Dante's way to immediately announce the importance of issues of identity (109).

[Like the boy, who still makes fathers wary of sons, came to Clymene to be sure of what he had heard about himself, so was I ...]

This passage is but one of several instances where the Phaethon story appears in the *Commedia*.[45] Here Dante works with Phaethon's search for family and identity (*Met.* 1.747–79): his mother Clymene's revelation that the Sun (or Apollo) is indeed his father, as rumor had it, leads to Phaethon's visit to the Palace of the Sun, his borrowing of his father's chariot, and his fatal ride.[46] When Phaethon lost control over the reins and started to set the world on fire, only Jupiter's lightning bolt could stop him. Dante features Phaethon's misguided decision to drive his father's chariot — painfully clear at that moment when he loses control over the reins — several times in the *Commedia*, from its first mention in *Inf.* 17.106–8 (where the pilgrim's fear to fly down to the eighth circle on Geryon's back is compared to Phaethon's fear when he lost control during his flight) to its final mention in *Par.* 31.125 (where Dante reminds us one last time of Phaethon's bad driving). In the Cacciaguida cantos, Dante is drawn to both the beginning and the end of the Phaethon story: Phaethon's questioning his mother about his father's identity (featured at the opening of *Par.* 17) sets into motion the entire story in the *Metamorphoses*, and the story concludes with Phaethon's death far away from home, fading out like a shooting star (*Met.* 2.319–24), the passage that inspired Dante at the beginning of the Cacciaguida episode (*Par.* 15.13–18).[47]

To point out that Dante works with both the beginning and ending of the Phaethon story in the Cacciaguida episode is not an anachronistic representation of Dante as a reader of Ovid. Many modern bilingual editions and translations of Ovid's *Metamorphoses* break down the poem into books and stories,

---

45 On Dante's use of the Phaethon myth throughout the *Commedia*, see especially Kevin Brownlee, "Phaeton's Fall and Dante's Ascent," *Dante Studies* 102 (1984): 135–44; Jeffrey T. Schnapp, "Dante's Ovidian Self-Correction in *Paradiso* 17," in Jacoff and Schnapp, *The Poetry of Allusion*, 214–23, at 218–20; and Ledda, "*Paradiso*, XVII," 109–10. On the *Intertextual Dante* site, one can read through Ovid's story of Phaethon and find the various points in the Latin text that inspired Dante in the *Commedia*.

46 As Ledda has shown ("*Paradiso*, XVII," 109–16), the theme of paternity, introduced in this canto through the myth of Phaethon, runs through the Cacciaguida cantos. Ledda analyzed the father figures leading up to Cacciaguida, both positive (Virgilio, Beatrice to some extent), and negative (Apollo as Phaethon's father, Daedulus as Icarus's father) and their classical and biblical models.

47 In his reading of the Cacciaguida episode, Warren Ginsberg also connected these two intertextual moments from Ovid's story of Phaethon, focusing more on the themes of paternity and identity. See *Dante's Aesthetics of Being* (Ann Arbor: University of Michigan Press, 1999), 109–10.

often with brief titles for the stories (critical text editions normally only divide the text into books), but, as we have seen in Ch. 1.1, that is also how the medieval text of the *Metamorphoses* is presented in manuscripts. While in a typical modern copy of the *Metamorphoses*, the story of Phaethon runs from the end of Book 1 (*Met.* 1.747–79) to about mid-way Book 2 (*Met.* 2.1–400), many medieval manuscripts end the story with Phaethon's death (at *Met.* 2.328) and consider the transformation of his grieving sisters into poplars (*Met.* 2.329–400) to be the next story, indicated by its own title.[48] Dante is thinking about the structure of the Phaethon story in similar terms, using both its beginning and ending in the Cacciaguida cantos in *Paradiso*. That does not make him a cursory reader of the Phaethon story: the verbal similarities discussed earlier exclude Dante solely relying on a summary of the story, as does the repeated featuring of other elements from the story at various points in the *Commedia*. Taken together, all references to the Phaethon story in the *Commedia* can be read as a cautionary tale, an example not to follow for Dante,[49] but Dante provides a different kind of completeness: including both the beginning and the end of the story becomes a way to emphasize its conclusion, only used by Dante here in the Cacciaguida cantos — that Phaethon ended by dying "far away from home" (*Met.* 2.323).

Dante inserts one more comparison between the pilgrim and an Ovidian character in this canto, in the most famous part of Cacciaguida's speech: the prophecy of the pilgrim's exile. Cacciaguida compares the pilgrim with

---

48   An excellent example of the attention given to the narrative structure of Ovid's poem in medieval manuscripts is provided by MS San Marco 225, one of the Italian copies of the pseudo-Lactantian *Narrationes* (see also *fig.* 2). The layout of this manuscript presents the verses from *Met.* 1.747–79 (end of Book 1) to *Met.* 2.1–328 as the "narratio" or story of Phaethon. Ovid had smartly divided this story over two books in the *Metamorphoses*: he ends Book 1 with Phaethon's questions to his mother and the beginning of his journey to the Palace of the Sun (*Met.* 1.747–79), and opens Book 2 with the description of the Palace — in that way, the break between the end of one book and the beginning of another covers Phaethon's movement in time and space. But MS San Marco 225 treats the story as one continuous narrative unit, even ignoring the textual break between Book 1 and 2, normally marked with a title in red indicating the beginning of the new book and a larger initial for its first verse. (The beginning of all other books in this manuscript are marked that way.) In contrast, there is only a small note in the left margin indicating the end of Book 1 and the beginning of Book 2 (on fol. 11v), and the first verse of Book 2, "REGIA Solis erat sublimibus alta columnis," simply follows the last verse of Book 1. Moreover, the pseudo-Lactantian *Narrationes* opens each book of the *Metamorphoses* with a list of titles of the stories belonging to that book. In this particular manuscript, the list of titles of Book 2 is placed at the beginning of the story of Phaethon (technically still *Met.* 1), at v. 747 (fols. 11v and 12r).

49   See in particular Brownlee's essay "Phaeton's Fall and Dante's Ascent" for such a reading.

Hippolytus, who also suffered an undeserved exile. The young prince was forced to leave his home when his stepmother Phaedra falsely accused him of rape as punishment for refusing her advances (*Met.* 15.497–546). In Cacciaguida's words, the comparison between the two exiles goes as follows (*Par.* 17.46–48):

> Qual si partio Ipolito d'Atene
> per la spietata e perfida noverca,
> tal di Fiorenza partir ti convene.

[Just as Hippolytus left Athens because of his cruel and treacherous stepmother, so you should leave Florence.]

The entire Ovidian passage is of interest here, as Marguerite Mills Chiarenza and Jeffrey Schnapp have shown.[50] What happens after Hippolytus's exile from Athens, his rebirth in Italy as Virbius (literally: twice a man, or a man reborn), must be the happy ending Dante liked to envision — the opposite of Phaethon, mentioned earlier in the canto, who died far away from home. Hippolytus's rebirth as Virbius was often discussed in the medieval commentaries on Ovidian stories,[51] but Dante's "spietata e perfida noverca" (*Par.* 17.47) — almost literally translating Ovid's description of Phaedra as the "sceleratae ... nouercae" (*Met.* 15.498) — reminds us again that Dante was working closely with Ovid's text.[52]

---

50 See Marguerite Mills Chiarenza, "Hippolytus' Exile: *Paradiso* XVII, vv. 46–48," *Dante Studies* 84 (1966): 65–68; Chiarenza, "Time and Eternity in the Myths of *Paradiso* XVII," in *Dante, Petrarch, Boccaccio: Studies in the Italian Trecento in Honor of Charles S. Singleton*, ed. Aldo S. Bernardo and Anthony L. Pellegrini (Binghamton: Center for Medieval & Early Renaissance Studies, State University of New York at Binghamton, 1983), 133–50; Schnapp, "Dante's Ovidian Self-Correction"; Schnapp, "Trasfigurazione e metamorfosi nel *Paradiso* dantesco," in *Dante e la Bibbia: Atti del convegno internazionale promosso da "Biblia," Firenze, 26–27–28 settembre 1986*, ed. Giovanni Barblan (Florence: Leo S. Olschki, 1988), 273–94; Michelangelo Picone, "Dante, Ovidio e la poesia dell'esilio," *Rassegna europea di letteratura italiana* 14, no. 2 (1999): 7–23, at 20–21; and Picone, "Ovid and the *Exul Inmeritus*," 402–4.

51 On these discussions of Hippolytus – Virbius in medieval commentaries on the *Metamorphoses* as well as in other texts, such as Servius's commentary on the *Aeneid* and St. Jerome's commentary on *Ephesians*, see especially Chiarenza, "Hippolytus' Exile," 65–66.

52 Another phrase in Ovid's account of Hippolytus in the *Metamorphoses* stands out: Hippolytus's exile, we read, is "meritum ... nihil" ("entirely undeserving" [*Met.* 15.504]). In his letters, Dante presents himself in similar terms, calling himself a "(Florentinus) exul inmeritus" ("a (Florentine) undeserved exile") in the salutations of *Ep.* III, V, VI, and VII. On this connection, see, for instance, the commentary by Enrico Mestica (Florence:

In addition to the exile narratives from Ovid's *Metamorphoses*, Dante also draws on the letters Ovid wrote during his own exile. Early readers of Cacciaguida's prophecy of Dante's exile already noted the strong connections between the experiences of the two poets. In his commentary on these verses, the writer of the Ottimo Commento pointed to "Ovidio, libro *de Ponto*, assai chiaro testimonia di questa piaga, la quale non li lasciòe amico, nè parente" ("Ovid's *Epistulae ex Ponto*, a clear testimony of this curse, which leaves one without friends and relatives" [3: 397]); in the first version of his commentary, Dante's son Pietro Alighieri cited passages from the *Epistulae* that express similar sentiments.[53] But as Michelangelo Picone has shown, Dante actually works closely with the text of Ovid's *Tristia*.[54] In the key passage of Cacciaguida's prophecy, he echoes Ovid's language (*Par.* 17.55–57):

> Tu lascerai ogne cosa diletta
> più caramente; e questo è quello strale
> che l'arco de lo essilio pria saetta.

[You will leave everything you love most dearly; and this is the arrow that the bow of exile shoots first.]

The language Cacciaguida uses to describe the pilgrim's future (Dante's present reality) almost literally translates a half-verse from Ovid's letter that recounts in detail the night that the poet was forced to leave his city and abandon his family (*Tristia* 1.3).[55] In the opening of that letter, Ovid describes that night as

---

R. Bemporad, 1921–22), and Tommaso Casini and S. A. Barbi (Florence: G. C. Sansoni, 1944) on these verses. Both commentaries are consulted on the Dartmouth Dante Project, https://dante.dartmouth.edu.

53 "Unde Ovidius de Ponto: *Dulcis amor patriae ... allicit omnes*. Item: *Nescio qua natale solum dulcedine cuntos / Ducit, et immemores non sinit esse sui ... / Felicem dicas quem sua terra tenet*" (668). On Pietro's Ovidian sources, see Sabbadini, *Le scoperte dei codici latini e greci ne' secoli XIV e XV*, 1: 97–105, at 100 (his knowledge of Ovid's works), 104 (on the wrong attribution of "Dulcis amore patriae allicit omnes"). Sabbadini provided the following explanations for this and other mistakes (he listed several more at 103–4): not enough diligence in the collecting of the passages, the use of indirect and incorrect sources, relying too much on memory (104) — aspects of the fragmentary and indirect transmission of Ovid also discussed in Ch. 1.1.

54 Giorgio Brugnoli charted the Dantean passages inspired by Ovid's exile works in "L'Ovidio dell'esilio nell'esilio di Dante," *Linguistica e letteratura* 41, nos. 1–2 (2016): 13–35.

55 Picone, "Dante, Ovidio e la poesia dell'esilio," 21–22; Picone, "Ovid and the *Exul Inmeritus*," 404. See also Niccolò Tommaseo's commentary to the *Commedia* (Turin: Unione Tipografico-Editrice Torinese, 1944), 3: 267, which discussed the same connection.

the moment "tot mihi cara reliqui" ("I left so many things dear to me" [v. 3]). The connection with Ovid's exile letters is reinforced fifty-some verses later, when the pilgrim, having taken in Cacciaguida's words, replies (*Par.* 17.106–11):

> Ben veggio, padre mio, sì come sprona
> lo tempo verso me, per colpo darmi
> tal, ch'è più grave a chi più s'abbandona;
> per che di provedenza è buon ch'io m'armi,
> sì che, se loco m'è tolto più caro,
> io non perdessi li altri per miei carmi.

[I clearly see, my father, how time is running fast against me, to deliver me such a blow that is felt more gravely by one who is unprepared; therefore, it is good that I arm myself with foresight, so that, if the place most dear to me is taken away from me, I would not lose the rest because of my poems.]

It turns out that Dante was familiar with one of the verses from Ovid's exile letters most famous to us today. As Giorgio Brugnoli pointed out, the pilgrim's last verse, "[che] io non perdessi li altri per miei carmi" (*Par.* 17.111), translates in part Ovid's well-known, deliberately vague remark on the reason of his exile in *Tristia* 2: "perdiderint ... me duo crimina, carmen et error" ("two crimes, a poem and a mistake, have ruined me" [v. 207]).[56] The most outrageous interpretations of Ovid's error circulated during the Middle Ages (the "carmen" was easily identified as the *Ars amatoria*).[57] But Dante is not interested in juicy stories about what Ovid might have done or seen. Both Ovid and Dante link losing everything in exile to their writing, but both continue to write. As Cacciaguida assures the pilgrim in his reply: he must write to make manifest what he has seen ("tutta tua visïon fa manifesta" [*Par.* 17.128]). And also from another letter of Ovid, *Tristia* 4.10, Dante knows that in writing lies the exile's only solace, rest, and medicine: to his Muse, his guide and comrade, Ovid writes, "tu solacia praebes, / tu curae requies, tu medicina mali; / tu dux et comes es" (vv. 117–19).

---

56   Giorgio Brugnoli, "Paradiso XVII," *L'Alighieri* 5 (1995): 47–58, at 56–57; and "L'Ovidio dell'esilio nell'esilio di Dante," 17.
57   On these interpretations, see Huygens, *Accessus ad auctores*; Wheeler, *Accessus ad auctores* (which both include several lives of Ovid); Elliott, "Accessus ad auctores"; Hexter, "Ovid in the Middle Ages"; and "Shades of Ovid."

In the Cacciaguida episode, Dante thus turns to Ovid's writing in two main ways in order to reinforce the theme of exile: by drawing upon Ovid's own statements about the experience from his letters written in exile, and by adopting his exile narratives in the *Metamorphoses*. The presence of some passages from the *Metamorphoses* is obvious (especially when Dante mentions the names of Ovidian characters); the Ovidian origin of the other passages is perhaps less clear. Dante's description of Cacciaguida's moving toward the pilgrim and Beatrice like a shooting star (from the Phaethon story), or the comparison between a growing spark and the light Cacciaguida emits (from the Medea story) may appear at first mere intertextual flourishes, but in both cases, Dante was inspired by the concerns underneath these Ovidian verses.

Dante incorporates passages from Ovid's complete oeuvre in the Cacciaguida episode: he covers the Latin poet's works of love (*Remedia amoris*), myth (*Metamorphoses*), and exile (*Tristia* and exile narratives in the *Metamorphoses*), all in the same narrative episode. Dante combines his Ovidian sources, working with both central and peripheral elements of the stories he chose to include. He turns passages with a distinct amorous tone into moralistic statements. Ovid's consoling words from the *Remedia amoris* to the heartbroken lover that a girl's splendid dress is mere appearance become Cacciaguida's moral disapproval of contemporary excessive dress in Florence. Dante reuses a simile that described Medea's passionate desire for Jason for the brilliance of the light that the saints emit in paradise. When Dante includes less identifiable passages from Ovid's writings (such as the growing spark simile from the Medea story, or the shooting star simile from the Phaethon story), they are taken from larger narratives that address themes relevant to the passage in the *Commedia*: separation from family and city. Ovid is also present in Cacciaguida's crudest description of Dante's departure from Florence, "Tu lascerai ogne cosa diletta / più caramente" (*Par.* 17.55–56), a sentence modeled on the Latin poet's description of his own exit from Rome. The pilgrim's fear that he would lose everything because of his writing (*Par.* 17.110–11) was the reality that Ovid described in his exile letters. In all these ways Dante connects his own fate with that of the fellow exiled writer Ovid.

How representative is the Cacciaguida episode of Dante's engagement with Ovid's Latin texts in the *Commedia*? In the *Commedia*, I count over 150 passages inspired by Ovid's writings, which share many of the features I have described in detail in the Cacciaguida episode. These passages, available on the *Intertextual Dante* site, are characterized by the following: (1) while the *Metamorphoses* is the most important Ovidian source text, providing over half of all instances, the passages come from all of Ovid's works; (2) similes are the most common place for Ovidian borrowings in the *Commedia*, totaling more than a third of all passages; (3) the number of Ovidian passages decreases as the poem moves from *Inferno* to *Purgatorio* and *Paradiso* — mainly because we find so many Ovidian characters in *Inferno*, their natural habitat — but the numbers of similes remain roughly the same in each canticle; (4) Ovidian passages are not equally distributed over the *Commedia*: in each canticle, there are clear Ovidian moments and Ovidian silences.

Dante signals his close readings of Ovid's text through his word choice. As we have seen in the Cacciaguida cantos, Dante's selection of a particular Ovidian sentence or phrase is not always part of a contextualized reading of the entire passage in Ovid, but in all instances there were verbal similarities between Dante's Italian and Ovid's Latin verses. A few more examples can illustrate this approach. In *Inf.* 27, Dante compares the confused sound coming from the flame of Guido da Montefeltro to the sound made by Perillos, the creator and first victim of the torture device called the Sicilian bull (*Inf.* 27.7–15). When looking at Dante's Ovidian source text (*Ars am.* 1.653–58), we see that both Ovid and Dante found that Perillos's punishment was "right" (in Ovid: "iustus ... fuit" [*Ars am.* 1.655]; in Dante: "fu dritto" [*Inf.* 27.8]). When Dante features Myrrha among the falsifiers (she pretended to be just a young girl willing to share the bed with the king, her father), he calls her "scellerata" ("wicked" [*Inf.* 30.38]), while Ovid described Myrrha's love for her father as a "scelus" (*Met.* 10.314, 10.315). In *Purg.* 28, Matelda described Earthly Paradise as the place that the classical poets had in mind when they wrote about the Golden Age (*Purg.* 28.139–44). Matelda explains that the land there needed no seed to produce flowers ("l'alta terra sanza seme gitta" [*Purg.* 28.69]), which uses Ovid's description of the Golden Age, a time when flowers also grew without being seeded ("natos sine semine flores" [*Met.* 1.108]). Dante's description of the gluttonous souls (*Purg.* 23.22–24) contains several elements from Ovid's portrayal of Fames (Hunger), sent by the goddess Ceres to punish Erysichthon, the king of Thessaly who had the trees in Ceres's sacred grove cut down: both have hollow eyes, pale faces, and protruding bones (*Met.* 8.801–8). Dante mentions Erysichthon's name in the following verses (*Purg.* 23.25–27) to further signal the connection. But in the following canto, Ovidian language from the Erysichthon story also appears in the description of the gluttonous souls Ubaldin da la Pila and Boniface. For hunger they bit the empty air (*Purg.* 24.28), while Ovid's Erysichthon, punished with constant hunger, did exactly the same (*Met.* 8.825–26). Given these close similarities, it becomes difficult to reduce Dante's Ovidian sources to only summaries in the commentaries on the *Metamorphoses*, or other intermediary, fragmented Ovidian sources. This close engagement with the Latin text of course does not exclude other sources; in the following section, I propose the earlier Ovidian readings in vernacular poetry to be included among those.

But before turning to these vernacular readings of Ovid, let us consider one final example of Dante's engagement with the Latin text of Ovid's poems, which perhaps best exemplifies the appeal of the Latin poet to the Italian one. This example takes us to the opening of *Paradiso*, where Dante announces the challenges and difficulties that the topic of the third and last canticle poses, stating that he will describe "quant' io del regno santo / ne la mia mente potei far tesoro" ("as much as I can treasure the holy kingdom in my mind" [*Par.* 1.10–11]). One such difficulty is putting into words how his mortal body could enter paradise. In his attempt to do so, Dante turns to the Ovidian story of Glaucus, the mortal who became an immortal sea god after eating a magical herb (*Met.* 13.898–968). Dante then describes his own transition in paradise, which occurs while watching Beatrice, as follows (*Par.* 1.67–72):

> Nel suo aspetto tal dentro mi fei,
> qual si fé Glauco nel gustar de l'erba
> che 'l fé consorto in mar de li altri dèi.
> Trasumanar significar *per verba*
> non si poria; però l'essemplo basti
> a cui esperïenza grazia serba.

> [While I looked at her, I was changed within, as Glaucus changed when he tasted the grass that made him a companion of the other gods in the sea. One could not put into words what it means to become beyond human; therefore, let his example be enough for whom grace reserves this experience.]

This is the first simile in which Dante compares the pilgrim's situation in paradise to that of an Ovidian character (four more comparisons follow, including those with Phaethon and Hippolytus, discussed earlier in this section). Dante finds Ovid's Glaucus as valid an "example" ("essemplo" [*Par.* 1.71]) to verbalize the experience as his self-coined term "[t]rasumanar" (*Par.* 1.70), a term that, especially when introduced immediately after the Ovidian simile, brings the transformations of the *Metamorphoses* to mind.[58]

---

58 In fact, as we have seen in Ch. 3.3, Dante calls Ovid's epic poem *De Rerum Transformatione* (*Ep.* III 4) in the letter in which he refers to the Ovidian story of Sol and Leucothoë (*Ep.* III).

Not entirely satisfied with this description, Dante returns to the concept of "[t]rasumanar" in the second canto (*Par.* 2.37–42):

> S'io era corpo, e qui non si concepe
> com' una dimensione altra patio,
> ch'esser convien se corpo in corpo repe,
> accender ne dovria più il disio
> di veder quella essenza in che si vede
> come nostra natura e Dio s'unio.

[If I were in body, and we here cannot conceive how one dimension can tolerate another, which must happen when body enters body, then our desire should be even more kindled to see that essence in which we can see how our nature and God became united.]

Dante again does not entirely succeed in putting the experience into words: he recognizes that understanding how his mortal body (the first "corpo") could enter the sphere of the Moon (the second "corpo" [*Par.* 2.39]) is not something that can be understood "qui" (*Par.* 2.37), here on earth. This mystery, he continues, would kindle an even greater desire to see the double nature of Christ (*Par.* 2.40–42). This language, too, is Ovidian, but in ways less apparent than the previous reference to the Ovidian character Glaucus in *Par.* 1. Focusing on the body in his formulation of change ("corpo in corpo repe" [*Par.* 2.39]), Dante offers, after *De Rerum Transformatione* in *Ep.* III, another alternative title or the pithiest summary of the *Metamorphoses*: ultimately a collection of hundreds of stories of how bodies enter other bodies. At the opening of the *Metamorphoses*, Ovid announces its topic as "IN NOVA ... mutatas ... formas / corpora" ("forms changed into new bodies" [*Met.* 1.1–2]), and in his formulation of paradisal change in *Par.* 2, Dante gets to the core of Ovid's poem. Also "repe" (*Par.* 2.39), the verb Dante uses to describe this transformation — the body does not just enter another body, but "crawls" into it — is distinctively Ovidian. The word "repe" appears only once in the *Commedia*, but it evokes the transformations of thieves into slithering and crawling snakes in *Inf.* 25, undoubtedly the most Ovidian canto of the *Commedia*: *Inf.* 25 contains the highest number of Ovidian borrowings (the transformations, the infernal punishment of the thieves, are all modeled after Ovid's *Metamorphoses*), and toward the end of the canto, Dante explicitly silences Ovid (*Inf.* 25.97), telling him that his own stories in Italian outdo the Latin poet's transformations. But as we see here at the opening of *Paradiso*, Ovid continues to provide characters, language, and imagery to Dante. This will be the case until the very end of the *Commedia*, until Neptune gazes at the first ship the Argo (*Par.* 33.96), the last time Dante turns to Ovid's Latin verses in his poem.

4.3   Dante's *Ovidio*: The Vernacular Roots of Dante's Reading of Ovid

As we have seen in Chapter 2, the first generations of Italian poets, broadly speaking, looked at the example of the troubadours for including Ovid in their poems, and not at Ovid's Latin texts or other Ovidian sources. The Italian poets favored the same Ovidian characters that the Occitan poets did (Narcissus and Pyramus and Thisbe), and wrote about them in similar ways. The Italians also found in Occitan poetry the formula to discuss Ovid's authority in matters of love, which, often in sonnet exchanges, they questioned more than their Occitan predecessors did. While Dante participated in such discussions (in the sonnet exchange between Dante da Maiano and himself), I showed in Chapter 3 how his poetry written before the *Commedia* started to move beyond these common ways to feature Ovid in Italian poetry, and reveal much closer attention to Ovid's Latin texts. Dante's reading of Ovid in the *Commedia* can be seen as a continuation of these innovations in his pre-*Commedia* poetry. But Dante's very close engagement with Ovid's Latin text does not exclude a vernacular reading of Ovid. In this section, I return to the distinctive features of earlier Occitan and Italian mentions of Ovid and look at how they inform certain passages in the *Commedia*. I first reconsider Narcissus and Pyramus and Thisbe, the Ovidian characters featured prominently in vernacular lyric poetry. While in the *Commedia* Narcissus and Pyramus and Thisbe are only three among the many Ovidian characters that Dante includes in his poem, the passages where Dante features them are better understood when read alongside the vernacular lyric context. I also revisit the role of Ovid in poetic debates among vernacular poets, their practice of discussing Ovid's poetics in *tenzoni*. In the *Commedia*, Dante transforms poetic debates found in sonnet exchanges into a verbal exchange between vernacular poets: the encounter between Dante and Bonagiunta Orbicciani in *Purg.* 24. In all these passages in the *Commedia*, Dante's text closely resembles Ovid's Latin writings — some of these borrowings are well established and discussed, others received much less critical attention. At the same time, these passages are also rooted in earlier vernacular readings of Ovid: Dante reflects on Ovid's poetics and includes Ovidian characters in ways similar to those found in Occitan and Italian lyric poetry.

4.3.1 *Ovidian Similes from Lyric Poetry to the* Commedia

In Chapters 2 and 3 we have identified the simile as the rhetorical device that the vernacular lyric poets used the most to feature a selected group of Ovidian characters. This simile often took on a particular form: the poet compared himself or his lady with the Ovidian character, focusing on the characteristic that made him or her so famous, and claiming that the poet or his lady possessed this characteristic more. In the *Commedia*, the simile is also a highly distinguishing trait of Dante's writing, mainly influenced by the frequent use of the simile in the epic tradition, not lyric poems.[59] Dante features similes with characters from these Latin epics — Vergil's *Aeneid* and Ovid's *Metamorphoses* are the main providers of such material — or reworks similes from the natural world or daily life from those Latin epics in the *Commedia*.[60] But there is also something quintessentially vernacular about comparisons. Cino da Pistoia recognized this in his reply to Onesto da Bologna, who expressed his skepticism about the new features of Cino's poetry in the sonnet *Mente ed umìle e più di mille sporte* (Marti CXXXIIIa). In Cino's reply *Amor che vien per le più dolci porte* (Marti CXXXIII), he defended their way of writing and distinguished it from Onesto's: "senza essempro di fera o di nave, / parliam sovente" ("we often write without the example of beasts or ships" [vv. 12–13]), a dig at the frequent use of the comparison in earlier Sicilian and Siculo-Tuscan poetry. While Cino zooms in on examples coming from the animal and nautical world, the Ovidian characters Narcissus and Pyramus and Thisbe were common points of comparison for the vernacular poets, as we have seen in Ch. 2.1. When Dante in the *Commedia* sets up comparisons with the most featured Ovidian characters in those vernacular lyric poems, a reading attentive to the vernacular and not just epic background of the simile is needed.

4.3.1.1 Pyramus and Thisbe

The story of the Ovidian lovers Pyramus and Thisbe was a favorite of Occitan and Italian poets: Giraut de Salignac, Raimbaut de Vaqueiras, Giraut de Cabreira, Isarn, Rofian, Pier della Vigna, an anonymous Sicilian poet, Rustico Filippi, Chiaro Davanzati, and Schiatta Pallavillani all included them in their poetry. As we have seen in Ch. 2.3, at least one of the Italian poets, Pier della Vigna,

---

59   On the simile in Dante's *Commedia*, see Luigi Venturi's compilation in *Le similitudini dantesche ordinate, illustrate e confrontate*, 3rd ed. (Florence: G. C. Sansoni, 1911), and Richard H. Lansing's study *From Image to Idea: A Study of the Simile in Dante's 'Commedia'* (Ravenna: Longo, 1977).

60   For the full list of the Ovidian similes Dante includes in the *Commedia*, see the "simile" category on the *Intertextual Dante* site.

showed familiarity with Ovid's Latin account in *Met.* 4 in one of his letters. But such Latin readings of Ovid did not enter Italian lyric poetry: I identified close thematic, stylistic, and linguistic connections between the Occitan and Italian poetic mentions of Pyramus and Thisbe, which together formed a distinctly vernacular approach to the story. Both the Occitan and Italian poets were greatly interested in Pyramus and Thisbe's deep love, a mad love that eventually led to their deaths; most mentions of the lovers occurred in similes (they loved more and better than Pyramus, and their lady was more beautiful than Thisbe); and the Italian poets' word choice and placement was often similar to the troubadours'. Thus, when Dante includes the two Ovidian lovers in the *Commedia*, there is already a long vernacular tradition of featuring Pyramus and Thisbe. As we will see in this section, Dante's choice for this very common lyric material becomes especially meaningful given the context in which he uses it: in the last cantos of *Purgatorio* where the guide Virgilio prepares the pilgrim for the arrival of Beatrice and later disappears, and Beatrice rebukes the pilgrim for his vain love.[61] In other words, I connect Dante's use of this quintessential lyric material in the last cantos of *Purgatorio* (*Purg.* 27.37–39, 30.49–54, and 33.67–72) to the content of those cantos: the transition from Virgilio to Beatrice as the pilgrim's guide and Beatrice's reproach of Dante's lyric past.

The names of Pyramus and Thisbe are first uttered on the terrace of lust in *Purgatorio*, but Dante also added a quick nod to their story in the circle of lust in *Inferno*, as to make sure that his aligning of the Ovidian lovers with the kind of love and love poetry at stake in these cantos is not missed.[62] The Ovidian reference is tucked into Virgilio's identification of the Assyrian queen Semiramis

---

61   My reading of Pyramus and Thisbe in *Purgatorio* is indebted to Christian Moevs's thorough analysis of *Purg.* 27 and 33 in "Pyramus at the Mulberry Tree: De-petrifying Dante's Tinted Mind" in *Imagining Heaven in the Middle Ages*, ed. Jan Swango Emerson and Hugh Feiss, O.S.B. (New York: Garland Publishing, Inc., 2000), 211–44, as well as his slightly longer version in the chapter "Form," in *The Metaphysics of Dante's 'Comedy'* (Oxford: Oxford University Press, 2005), 49–106. While not neglecting the vernacular sources, Moevs's emphasis is on the theological sources and medieval allegorizations of the *Metamorphoses*. My focus here is precisely on those vernacular sources and how they informed Dante's reading of the Pyramus and Thisbe story.

62   Moreover, as Christian Moevs noted in *The Metaphysics of Dante's 'Comedy,'* 105, the protagonists of the mid-thirteenth-century French romance *Floris et Liriopé* fell in love while reading the story of Pyramus and Thisbe, like Francesca and Paolo during their reading of the romance of Lancelot and Guinevere, as Francesca reports in *Inf.* 5. Moevs also reminded us of St. Augustine's mention of Pyramus and Thisbe in *De ordine*, first discussed by Salvatore Battaglia in "Piramo e Tisbe in una pagina di Sant'Agostino," in *La coscienza letteraria del Medioevo* (Naples: Liguori, 1965), 51–61.

as the first among the lustful souls (*Inf.* 5.52–60). In the opening verses of Ovid's story of Pyramus and Thisbe, the Latin poet does not mention the location of Babylon directly, instead calling it "the elevated city, which Semiramis is said to have enclosed with brick walls" ("dicitur altam / coctilibus muris cinxisse Semiramis urbem" [*Met.* 4.57–58]). Virgilio's description of Semiramis in *Inf.* 5 is actually much closer to Orosius's account of her reign and reputation (and that of her late husband Ninus) in his *Historiae adversus paganos* — Ovid is not the obvious source here.[63] But when Dante in his treatise *De monarchia* turns to the Assyrian rulers Semiramis and Ninus, the first to seek world domination (*DM* II VIII 3), he not only mentions his source Orosius ("ut Orosius refert") but also makes the connection with the Ovidian tale (*DM* II VIII 4):[64] "Horum amborum Ovidius memoriam fecit in quarto, ubi dicit in *Piramo*: 'Coctilibus muris cinxisse Semiramis urbem' et infra: 'Conveniant ad busta Nini lateantque sub umbra'" ("Ovid remembered both of them in the fourth book of the *Metamorphoses*, where he says in the story of Pyramus, 'Semiramis had enclosed the city with brick walls' and further on, 'They met up at the grave of Ninus and hid in the shadow'"). In other words, while we do not find Pyramus and Thisbe among the list of lustful souls that started with Semiramis (*Inf.* 5.52–72), Dante does seem to associate them with it.

Toward the end of *Purgatorio,* the Latin and vernacular readings of this Ovidian story intertwine in the pilgrim's salute to his guide Virgilio and in his expression of regret for his wrong ways of loving during the first interactions with his new guide Beatrice. In the first mention of Pyramus and Thisbe on the terrace of lust, Virgilio sets up the comparison by describing the flames that separate the pilgrim and Beatrice as "questo muro" ("this wall" [*Purg.* 27.36]) — a reference to the wall that separated the two Ovidian lovers: "inuide ... paries," Pyramus and Thisbe whispered through the crack in the wall, "quid

---

63 As several commentators pointed out, the verse "libito fé licito" ("she made license licit" [*Inf.* 5.56]) translates Orosius's line "ut cuique libitum esset liberum fieret" ("so that everyone should be free to act as he pleased" [*Hist.* I, 4, 8]). Also the verses "si legge / che succedette a Nino e fu sua sposa" ("we have read that she succeeded Ninus and was his wife" [*Inf.* 5.58–59]) are to be read together with Orosius's "mortuo Semiramis uxor successit" ("on his death, his wife, Semiramis, succeeded him" [*Hist.* I, 4, 4]). The latter passage in Dante compares with Bono Giamboni's *volgarizzamento* of Orosius's *Historiae adversus paganos:* "Costui morto, Semiramis sua moglie gli succedette nel regno" (30). However, Giamboni's rendering of "ut cuique libitum esset liberum fieret" as "secondo che piacesse a catuno, si potessero [congiungere]" (31) excludes that Dante solely relied on Giamboni's vernacular translation. See *Delle storie contra i pagani di Paolo Orosio libri VII: Volgarizzamento di Bono Giamboni*, ed. Francesco Tassi (Florence: T. Baracchi, 1849).

64 On this connection, see Charles S. Singleton, *The Divine Comedy. Inferno, 2: Commentary* (Princeton: Princeton University Press, 1990), 77–79.

amantibus obstas?" ("Jealous wall, why do you stand in the way of lovers?" [*Met.* 4.73]). This element of the story immediately leads to another: the moment the dying Pyramus lifts his eyes when Thisbe calls him (*Met.* 4.142–46). Dante introduces this material in a simile, comparing his reaction to Beatrice's name to Pyramus's reaction when he heard Thisbe's (*Purg.* 27.37–42):

> Come al nome di Tisbe aperse il ciglio
> Piramo in su la morte, e riguardolla,
> allor che 'l gelso diventò vermiglio;
> così, la mia durezza fatta solla,
> mi volsi al savio duca, udendo il nome
> che ne la mente sempre mi rampolla.

> [Just as at the name of Thisbe Pyramus near death opened his eyes and looked at her, at that time when the mulberry tree became bright red, so, when my stubbornness had softened, I turned toward my wise guide, hearing the name that in my mind always blossoms.]

With this comparison to Pyramus, one of the fourteen times in the *Commedia* that the pilgrim is compared with an Ovidian character, Dante connects the episode with vernacular lyric poetry, where such comparisons with the Ovidian lover are common.[65] But why this particular moment from the Pyramus and Thisbe story: Pyramus's reaction to Thisbe's name? Several scholars have pointed out how little the two compared situations actually have in common, and how Dante turns Ovid's story of "love and death" into a story of "love and life" in the *Commedia*.[66] I propose that Dante's choice to feature this specific moment

---

65   A brief overview of the comparisons with Pyramus, discussed in more detail in Ch. 2.1: Giraut de Salignac (*En atretal esperansa*, vv. 26–27), Raimbaut de Vaqueiras (*Era·m requier sa costum' e son us*, vv. 11–12), Pier della Vigna (*Amor, in cui disio ed ò speranza*, vv. 14–15) all declare to love their ladies more than Pyramus loved Thisbe; and Rustico Filippi, who imagined an exchange of several sonnets between himself and his lady, wrote in one of her sonnets that she loved him more than Thisbe loved Pyramus (*Oi amoroso e mio fedele amante*, vv. 9–11).

66   Maristella Lorch and Lavinia Lorch, "Metaphor and Metamorphosis: *Purgatorio* 27 and *Metamorphoses* 4," in Sowell, *Dante and Ovid*, 112–21, at 115. On this simile, see also Lansing, *From Image to Idea*, 89–92. Robert M. Durling's note on "Dante and Ovid's Pyramus (Canto 27)" paid close attention to several aspects of Ovid's account of Pyramus and Thisbe in the *Metamorphoses* (e.g., the wall that separates the lovers, Thisbe's veil, the misreading of signs, the lion, and so on). See *Purgatorio*, ed. and trans. Robert M. Durling, introduction and notes Ronald L. Martinez and Robert M. Durling (New York: Oxford University Press, 2003), 618–20. Durling further showed the metaphorical significance of Pyramus

should be read as the first step toward the pilgrim's reunion with Beatrice and Virgilio's disappearance.

The emphasis on calling out names connects the Pyramus simile in *Purg.* 27.37–42 to the moment when Beatrice first speaks to the pilgrim in *Purg.* 30. Between those two moments, the pilgrim crosses the wall of flames, the last obstacle between him and Beatrice, and witnesses the mystic procession in the Garden of Eden. Gazing at Beatrice, the pilgrim turns to Virgilio only to find out that his guide has disappeared (*Purg.* 30.40–54); at this moment, Beatrice addresses him for the first time. As her first word is the name "Dante" (*Purg.* 30.55), the poet restages for a second time the Ovidian scene where Thisbe calls her lover Pyramus.

Moreover, also the tercet in which Dante laments the disappearance of his guide Virgilio can be read alongside the Pyramus and Thisbe story (*Purg.* 30.49–51):

> Ma Virgilio n'avea lasciati scemi
> di sé, Virgilio dolcissimo patre,
> Virgilio a cui per mia salute die'mi.

> [But Virgilio had deprived us of himself, Virgilio, the sweetest father, Virgilio, to whom I gave myself for my salvation.]

These verses are intertextually rich: the most commonly cited verses are Orpheus's parting words at Eurydice's final disappearance in Vergil's *Georg.* 4.525–27:

> ... Eurydicen uox ipsa et frigida lingua,
> a miseram Eurydicen! anima fugiente vocabat:
> Eurydicen toto referebant flumine ripae.

> [his voice alone and his cold tongue with fleeting breath cried, "Eurydice! Ah, poor Eurydice!" "Eurydice" the riverbanks repeated, all along the stream.]

The connection with Vergil's text is indeed strong: Dante's triple repetition of the name "Virgilio" more or less corresponds to the position of Eurydice's

---

and Thisbe not only to *Purg.* 27 but the entire *Commedia*, which "involves a metaphorical reversal of the tale of Pyramus and Thisbe ... : it moves from confrontation with a lion and other beasts in the Dark Wood to the safety of home" (620).

name in the Latin, both passages describe an emotional goodbye, and Dante uses Vergil's words to salute his guide.[67] Rachel Jacoff has found similar passages in Statius's *Thebaid* and Bruce Holsinger in the *Achilleid*.[68] Ovid's poetry contains several triple name or word repetitions that have been brought up in connection with the Dantean tercet.[69] But here I propose Ovid's rendition of Pyramus and Thisbe's farewell (*Met.* 4.142–46) as the extra source of Dante's verses in *Purgatorio*:

---

67 On this passage, see, for instance, Robert Hollander, "Le opere di Virgilio nella *Commedia* di Dante," in Iannucci, *Dante e la "bella scola" della poesia*, 247–343, at 317–18, and his discussion in his commentary on *Purgatorio* (New York: Anchor Books, 2004), 680–81, which includes a bibliographical overview of the interpretation of this Vergilian citation.

68 Rachel Jacoff read the tercet as a layered allusion to the passage in Vergil's *Georgics* and the ending of Statius's *Thebaid*, specifically the lament for the fallen Arcadian Parthenopaeus, one of the seven against Thebes (*Theb.* 12.805–7, similar to Vergil's lament for Eurydice in the *Georgics*, with "Arcada" placed three times at the beginning of the verse) and the praise for Vergil's "divine" *Aeneid* (*Theb.* 12.816–19, of course also to be read in connection with Statius's expressions of admiration for Vergil in *Purg.* 21). In brief, Jacoff read Dante's farewell to Vergil as a final salute to Statius in the poem as well. See "Intertextualities in Arcadia: *Purgatorio* 30.49–51," in Jacoff and Schnapp, *The Poetry of Allusion*, 131–44. Bruce W. Holsinger turned to *Purg.* 30 in his discussion of Dante's homoeroticism in the *Commedia*. In addition to Orpheus's lament in Vergil's *Georgics*, he found a second classical source for Dante's salute to Virgilio in Statius's *Achilleid* (1.473–75): in this passage, Greek warriors, preparing to leave for Troy, lament the missing Achilles (his name is repeated three times in these verses). In Holsinger's reading, by placing his own text between Vergil's and Statius's, Dante mourns the loss of Vergil, Statius, and his own "momentary identity" as Achilles, soon to be reproached by Beatrice for his tears over this loss. See "Sodomy and Resurrection: The Homoerotic Subject of the *Divine Comedy*," in *Premodern Sexualities*, ed. Louise Fradenburg and Carla Freccero (New York: Routledge, 1996), 243–74, at 263–64.

69 In Ovid's rendition of the Orpheus story (*Met.* 10.1–85, 11.1–66), he imitates Vergil's account, repeating the word "flebile" three times to describe Orpheus's mourning after Eurydice's disappearance: "et (mirum!) medio dum labitur amne, / flebile nescioquid queritur lyra, flebile lingua / murmurat exanimis, respondent flebile ripae" ("and (a miracle!) while the lyre was sadly floating in the middle of the stream to an unclear destination, the lifeless tongue sadly mumbled and the riverbanks answered" [*Met.* 11.51–53]). Most recently, Simone Marchesi stated that this Ovidian passage complements the Vergilian echo in Dante's goodbye to his guide, in *Dante and Augustine: Linguistics, Poetics, Hermeneutics* (Toronto: University of Toronto Press, 2011), 179. Also Rachel Jacoff, overall more focused on the Vergilian and Statian intertexts in this canto, discussed this passage and found two more examples of triple name repetition in Ovid's writings: Daedalus's emotional cry after his son Icarus's fall and death (three almost identical verses in *Ars am.* 2.93–95 and *Met.* 8.231–33), which places the boy's name in vocative at the penultimate foot of the first verse, and at the beginning of the two subsequent verses ("Intertextualities in Arcadia," 134–35, 138).

"Pyrame," clamauit, "quis te mihi casus ademit?
Pyrame, responde! tua te, carissime, Thisbe
nominat; exaudi uultusque attolle iacentes."
ad nomen Thisbes oculos a morte grauatos
Pyramus erexit uisaque recondidit illa.

["Pyramus," she cried, "what misfortune has taken you away from me? Pyramus, answer! It is me, your dearest Thisbe calling; listen and raise your fallen head." At the name of Thisbe, Pyramus lifted his eyes, heavy with death, and when he saw her, he closed them again.]

The similarities between the passages in Ovid and Dante are striking — not surprisingly, given that Ovid's rendition of Pyramus and Thisbe's farewell is modeled after Vergil's verses in the *Georgics*.[70] But the connection between Ovid's and Dante's verses goes beyond the triple repetition of Pyramus's name. As we saw before, these verses from the *Metamorphoses* were already important in describing the transition from Virgilio to Beatrice as the pilgrim's guide: Dante explicitly referred to these verses when Virgilio, in one of his last interventions in the *Commedia*, mentions Beatrice's name to convince the pilgrim to cross the fire and enter the Garden of Eden (*Purg.* 27.34–42). Later Dante implicitly restages this Ovidian scene when Beatrice addresses the pilgrim with the name Dante (*Purg.* 30.55). To summarize, these are the two re-enactments of the Pyramus and Thisbe naming episode (*Met.* 4.142–46) at the conclusion of *Purgatorio*:

TABLE 9   Virgilio and the pilgrim with Beatrice absent (*Purg.* 27)

Dante	Ovid
Purg. 27.36	*Met.* 4.73
Virgilio: "questo muro" of flames separates you from Beatrice	a wall separates Pyramus and Thisbe
Purg. 27.37–42	*Met.* 4.145–46
the pilgrim's strong reaction when he hears Virgilio saying Beatrice's name	Pyramus's reaction when he hears Thisbe saying his name

70   See Alessandro Barchiesi's notes to this passage in *Metamorfosi: Volume II* (*Libri III–IV*), ed. Alessandro Barchiesi and Gianpiero Rosati, trans. Ludovica Koch (Milan: Fondazione Lorenzo Valla / Arnoldo Mondadori Editore, 2007), 267–68.

TABLE 10 Beatrice and the pilgrim with Virgilio absent (*Purg.* 30)

Dante	Ovid
Purg. 30.49–51 the pilgrim laments Virgilio's disappearance by repeating his name three times	*Met.* 4.142–46 Pyramus's reaction when he hears Thisbe saying his name three times
Purg. 30.55 Beatrice calling "Dante"	*Met.* 4.145–46 Pyramus's reaction when he hears Thisbe saying his name

The transition from one guide to another is thus also marked by the change in who is taking up the role of the calling Thisbe: the first time it is Virgilio who calls out the name, the second time it is Beatrice. The importance of this Ovidian story is reinforced by the fact that the salute to the disappeared guide Virgilio immediately precedes Beatrice's calling Dante's name and that this salute is also modeled after the same verses in Ovid.

Dante repeatedly introduces elements from an Ovidian story favored by the vernacular lyric poets to highlight the turning point that these cantos constitute: in order to move on to paradise, the pilgrim first needs to leave his guide Virgilio behind, break with his past, confess his wrong ways of loving, and repent. The last reference to the story of Pyramus and Thisbe in the *Commedia* further confirms this reading. To stress how vain thoughts obscured the pilgrim's understanding that it is God's justice prohibiting him from the Tree of Knowledge of Good and Evil, Beatrice features Pyramus one last time in the following metaphor (*Purg.* 33.67–72):

> E se stati non fossero acqua d'Elsa
> li pensier vani intorno a la tua mente,
> e 'l piacer loro un Piramo a la gelsa,
> per tante circostanze solamente
> la giustizia di Dio, ne l'interdetto,
> conosceresti a l'arbor moralmente.

> [And if the vain thoughts in your mind had not been like waters of the Elsa, and their pleasure a Pyramus by the mulberry tree, by so many circumstances alone you would recognize the moral sense and the justice of God's interdict of the tree.]

In just a few words Beatrice evokes the ending of the Pyramus and Thisbe story in the *Metamorphoses*: the gods grant Thisbe's request to turn the white mulberry fruits into red berries in order to always remember the death of both lovers (*Met.* 4.147–66). To explain to the pilgrim one last time how far he was removed from God, Beatrice features Pyramus's death as the extreme example of how the "delight in vain pleasures" distracts from God, as the ultimate symbol of the wrong way of loving. To make this point in cantos where the emphasis is on correcting the pilgrim to love in a different way and to write poetry in a different way, Dante could not have chosen a better Ovidian character than the one the vernacular lyric poets favored. The Occitan and Italian poets featured Pyramus and Thisbe in similes to underline their own and their ladies' exceptionality: they claimed to outdo the famous Ovidian lovers. And now at this point in the *Commedia*, the lyric past — signaled by Dante's use of this very common vernacular lyric material — is outdone. Along with these vernacular Ovidian strategies, Dante also draws closely on Ovid's Latin text: as we have seen, the connections between Dante's and Ovid's verses are clear. As many other Ovidian moments in the *Commedia*, the Pyramus and Thisbe episode in *Purgatorio* has been defined as a Christian rewriting of Ovid, most explicitly by Michelangelo Picone, who described how Dante through the use of this classical myth in *Purg.* 27 became the new Ovid, the Christian poet of love.[71] But while Dante continues to rewrite Ovidian stories until the end of *Paradiso*, his featuring of this quintessential vernacular reading of Pyramus and Thisbe more specifically addresses the themes and concerns of the last cantos of *Purgatorio*.

4.3.1.2 Narcissus

The second Ovidian myth favored by both Occitan and Italian vernacular poets is the story of Narcissus, whose vain self-love is often compared to their own futile quest for their ladies' love. Poets repeatedly represent the moment when Narcissus gazes at his own reflection in the water and, to a lesser extent, include elements of Narcissus's following madness and eventual death. However, as we have seen in Ch. 2.1, nothing about the way in which these vernacular poets include the boy's story into their poetry revealed their actual knowledge of Ovid's

---

71 Michelangelo Picone, "Purgatorio XXVII: Passaggio rituale e *translatio* poetica," *Medioevo romanzo* 12, no. 2 (1987): 389–402, at 397: "Dante ... imita, ma al tempo stesso rinnova, il mito classico; e così facendo diventa egli stesso il 'nuovo' Ovidio, il 'nuovo' *auctor* della poesia d'amore" ("Dante imitates the classical myth, but at the same time renews it; and in doing so, he himself becomes the 'new' Ovid, the 'new' *auctor* of love poetry").

Latin text — Narcissus's story circulated widely for centuries in both Latin and vernacular rewritings. Dante also favored the story and featured it prominently in the *Commedia*. Students of Dante's Ovid have paid careful attention to Narcissus's presence in Dante's poem, focusing mostly on the fragmentation of the myth over the three canticles, and the parallels between Dante's reading and earlier moralizing interpretations of the myth.[72] Placing *Narciso* back into his vernacular lyric context, I instead illustrate the connections between the vernacular lyric poets' treatment and Dante's. As was also the case for Dante's featuring of Pyramus and Thisbe in the *Commedia*, the traces of the vernacular lyric reading of the Ovidian myth appear simultaneously with other Ovidian influences. The fact that scholars often contextualized the Narcissus passages in the *Commedia* through comparisons with the medieval commentaries on Ovid's *Metamorphoses* is indicative of the moralizing and correcting tone that Dante takes on in featuring this particular Ovidian story. But the focus on the vernacular roots of Dante's reading of Narcissus reveals that Dante also uses this lyric material to clearly mark the distinction between the vernacular lyric tradition and his writing of the *Commedia*.

Glimpses of Ovid's Narcissus first appear in the concluding cantos of the *Inferno*. In Dante's description of Satan in Lake Cocytus, the shiny surface of the icy lake (*Inf.* 32.22–24, *Inf.* 34.52) and Satan's stare (*Inf.* 34.53–54), as Robert McMahon illustrated, reprise the reflecting surface of the pool in which Ovid's Narcissus admires himself (*Met.* 3.424, 504–5) — called "lo specchio di Narcisso" ("the mirror of Narcissus") in *Inf.* 30.128.[73] Dante thus immediately works with the main features of the vernacular lyric poets' version of the myth: the mirror-like water, the fixed stare, and the use of analogy. While in the *Inferno* Dante finds similarities between Narcissus and Satan, in *Purgatorio*

---

72   The Narcissus story is perhaps the most studied Ovidian myth in the *Commedia*, and definitely received more critical attention than the Pyramus and Thisbe story. The main studies are: Roger Dragonetti, "Dante et Narcisse ou les faux-monnayeurs de l'image," *Revue des études italiennes* 11 (1965): 85–146; Michelangelo Picone, "Dante e il mito di Narciso: Dal *Roman de la Rose* alla *Commedia*," *Romanische Forschungen* 89, no. 4 (1977): 382–97; Kevin Brownlee, "Dante and Narcissus (*Purg.* XXX, 76–99)," *Dante Studies* 96 (1978): 201–6; Robert McMahon, "The Christian Scripture of Ovid's Narcissus in the 'Commedia,'" *Pacific Coast Philology* 20 (1985): 65–69; McMahon, "Satan as Infernal Narcissus: Interpretative Translation in the *Commedia*," in Sowell, *Dante and Ovid*, 65–86; Edward Peter Nolan, "Dante's Comedic Displacements of Ovid's Narcissus," in *The Influence of the Classical World on Medieval Literature, Architecture, Music, and Culture: A Collection of Interdisciplinary Studies*, ed. Fidel Fajardo-Acosta (Lewiston: The Edwin Mellen Press, 1992), 105–21; Caroline Stark, "Dante's Narcissus," *Classical Outlook* 86, no. 4 (2009): 132–38; and Stark, "Reflections of Narcissus," in *The Afterlife of Ovid*, ed. Peter Mack and John North (London: Institute of Classical Studies, School of Advanced Study, University of London, 2015), 23–41.

73   McMahon, "Satan as Infernal Narcissus."

and *Paradiso* he draws upon the most characteristic aspect of the vernacular poets' use of the Narcissus story: the comparison between the poet and Narcissus. The first instance of this practice is particularly interesting in light of our previous discussion of Dante's use of the Pyramus and Thisbe myth in the Garden of Eden. In these cantos, where the pilgrim leaves his guide Virgilio behind and is reunited with his new guide Beatrice, the transition from one guide to another is marked by Beatrice's rebuke of the pilgrim's old ways of loving and writing. The Pyramus and Thisbe story, highly popular in the vernacular love poetry of the time, represented the old choices that the pilgrim had to denounce before entering paradise. Dante completes his salute to vernacular love poetry with references to the Narcissus story, that other Ovidian favorite of the lyric poets. In *Purg.* 30, the canto where we found the second re-enactment of Thisbe's calling out of Pyramus's name, Dante also inserts some details from Narcissus's story. For instance, he describes the river Lethe as a "chiaro fonte" ("clear stream" [*Purg.* 30.76]) — a phrase found both in Ovid's Latin and in vernacular love poetry to indicate the setting of the Narcissus tale. The effect of Beatrice's harsh words on the pilgrim is described as "lo gel che m'era intorno al cor ristretto" ("the ice that had hardened around my heart" [*Purg.* 30.97]), which is the opposite reaction of Narcissus in the *Metamorphoses*, who melted away during his transformation (*Met.* 3.486–90). In a short essay on this specific passage, Kevin Brownlee described how Dante's text presents the pilgrim as a reversed Narcissus.[74] While the vernacular poets included Narcissus to point out the similarities between his situation and theirs, Dante uses Narcissus to distinguish himself from the character.

In *Purgatorio*, the difference between the pilgrim and Narcissus is subtle; in *Paradiso*, on the other hand, Dante marks this difference explicitly. There, when the pilgrim mistakes the saints for reflections, he explains that he is making the opposite "error" the unnamed Narcissus once made: "per ch'io dentro a l'error contrario corsi / a quel ch'accese amor tra l'omo e 'l fonte" ("so that I ran against the mistake opposite to the one that sparked the love between a man and a fountain" [*Par.* 3.17–18]). In disassociating himself from Narcissus, Dante also distinguishes himself from the ways in which his predecessors featured this quintessential vernacular figure.

4.3.2   *Discussing Ovidian Poetics from Lyric Poetry to the* Commedia

When the Italian vernacular lyric poets mentioned "Ovidio" in their poems, as we have seen in Ch. 2.3, they did so to discuss — mainly in sonnet exchanges — the worth of his advice for lovers and his writing of love poetry. The young Dante was even a participant in such a discussion, replying in the sonnet

---

[74]   Brownlee, "Dante and Narcissus (*Purg.* xxx, 76–99)."

Savere e cortesia, ingegno ed arte to Dante's da Maiano's complaint that Ovid's words, among other things, did not help him against lovesickness. Not addressing Ovid's works in particular, Dante's response countered that knowledge, "savere" (v. 1), was one of the gifts and virtues that could win Love over. The continuation of such reflections about Ovid in the *Commedia* is most apparent in Dante's two mentions of the Latin poet's name: first in *Inf.* 4.90, where "Ovidio" appears as the third member of the "bella scola" (*Inf.* 4.94) of poets housed in limbo (marking the second time that Ovid is featured as a character in an Italian poem, after Brunetto Latini's *Tesoretto*, discussed in the Introduction); and in the bolgia of theft where Dante tells the Latin poet to be silent ("Taccia ... Ovidio") about his characters Cadmus and Arethusa (*Inf.* 25.97), because his own poetry of transformation outdoes Ovid's. It is now well understood that Dante used several Ovidian stories to shape his transformations in this bolgia, and also the featuring of Ovid and the other classical poets in *Inf.* 4 has an Ovidian precedent.[75] While in both passages in the *Commedia* the influence of Dante's Latin readings of Ovid is strongly felt, reflections about vernacular poetry are far from absent. In *Inf.* 4, Dante self-consciously includes himself as the only vernacular poet in a group of classical poets, consisting of Homer, Horace, Ovid, Lucan, and Vergil.[76] In *Inf.* 25, Dante draws the distinction between Ovid's

---

75 The importance of Ovid's *Metamorphoses* in *Inf.* 25 is strikingly clear in the digital edition of the *Commedia* on *Intertextual Dante*, where every Ovidian intertextual passage is marked in Dante's text, and the corresponding passages in Dante and Ovid can be read side by side on its digital interface. Ovid's story of Salmacis and Hermaphroditus (*Met.* 4.274–388) shaped Dante's transformation of a man and a serpent becoming one (*Inf.* 25.34–78) and the double transformation from man to serpent and from serpent to man (*Inf.* 25.79–141) should be read alongside the story of Cadmus and Harmonia (*Met.* 4.563–603). On Dante's use of this Ovidian material, see also Umberto Bosco, "La gara coi classici latini (canti XXIV–XXV dell'*Inferno*)," in *Altre pagine dantesche* (Rome: Salvatore Sciascia Editore, 1987), 93–108; Ettore Paratore, "Il canto XXV dell'*Inferno*," in *Tradizione e struttura in Dante* (Florence: G. C. Sansoni, 1968), 250–80; Ellrich, "Envy, Identity, and Creativity"; Cioffi, "The Anxieties of Ovidian Influence." Dante's self-inclusion in a group of poets finds a precedent in Ovid's autobiographical letter (*Tristia* 4.10), where Ovid called himself the fourth of the group of prominent Latin love poets, after Tibullus, Gallus, and Propertius (vv. 51–58). See Vazzana, "Ovidio è il terzo," 151, and for similar passages in vernacular literature, see the following footnote. I discussed how in several metapoetic episodes in the *Commedia*, including the passages in *Inf.* 4 and 25 mentioned above, Dante's sources include metapoetic passages in Ovid's writings, showing Dante's particular attention for moments where Ovid addresses the topics, style, and genre of his writing, and what that can mean for his own poetic choices. See "Dante lettore di Ovidio: Influssi ovidiani e riflessioni metaletterarie nella *Commedia*," *Studi Danteschi* 83 (2018): 149–71.

76 David Wallace called this "the sixth of sixth topos," and provided other instances where vernacular poets present themselves together with the greats of classical literature (Jean de Meun in the *Roman de la Rose*, Boccaccio in the *Filocolo*, Chaucer in *Troilus and*

Latin stories of transformation and his own in Italian, considering the latter as better and innovative. But my focus here is not on these two mentions of Ovid — two instances where Dante speaks directly to Ovid, two famous metapoetic episodes in the *Commedia* that are arguably the most discussed Ovidian passages in Dante's poem. In what follows, I turn to another great metapoetic moment in the *Commedia*, the pilgrim's encounter with fellow vernacular poet Bonagiunta Orbicciani in *Purg.* 24.34–63, illustrating how closely that passage adheres to the vernacular practice of discussing Ovid in sonnet exchanges.

4.3.2.1   From Sonnet Exchanges to Dante and Bonagiunta's Exchange in *Purg.* 24

The vernacular lyric tradition, and not classical poetry, is central in Canto 24 of *Purgatorio*, where the encounter with fellow vernacular poet Bonagiunta Orbicciani also constitutes an Italian literary history lesson (*Purg.* 24.34–63). At the heart of their conversation Dante defines himself as "I' mi son un che, quando / Amor mi spira, noto, e a quel modo / ch'e' ditta dentro vo significando" ("I am one who, when Love breathes in me, takes note, and in that way he dictates within, I give it meaning" [*Purg.* 24.52–54]). Scholars have mainly discussed the vernacular and theological intertextual layers of Dante's verses, focusing on the concept of inspiration by Amor as found in the vernacular poets Arnaut Daniel and Guido Cavalcanti, and the use of "spira," which adds a divine connotation to the statement.[77] But fewer have noted that this tercet should be read from a classical intertextual angle as well, as Latin love poetry provides several examples of a dictating Amor.[78] Among those Latin sources,

Criseyde) in "Chaucer and Boccaccio's Early Writings," in *Chaucer and the Italian Trecento*, ed. Piero Boitani (Cambridge, Cambridge University Press, 1983), 141–62, at 150–51; "Chaucer's Continental Inheritance: The Early Poems and *Troilus and Criseyde*," in *The Cambridge Chaucer Companion*, ed. Piero Boitani and Jill Mann (Cambridge: Cambridge University Press, 1986), 19–37, at 29–30; and *Chaucerian Polity: Absolutist Lineages and Associational Forms in England and Italy* (Stanford: Stanford University Press, 1997), 80–82.

77 Simone Marchesi provided the most recent bibliography on this episode in "Epic Ironies: Poetics, Metapoetics, Self-translation (*Inferno* 18.1, *Purgatorio* 24.52, *Paradiso* 1.13)," *Dante Studies* 131 (2013): 101–17, at 114, n. 2, 115–16, n. 11.

78 Niccolò Tommaseo and Giuseppe Campi are two nineteenth-century commentators who mentioned the image of the dictating Amor in Ovid's *Am.* 2.1 in their commentaries to *Purg.* 24, and Campi added the example of the same image found in an inscription on the walls of Pompeii. See *La Divina commedia*, ed. Tommaseo and *La Divina commedia di Dante Alighieri*, ed. Giuseppe Campi (Turin: Unione Tipografico-Editrice Torinese, 1888–93), both consulted on the Dartmouth Dante Project, http://dante.dartmouth.edu. Vazzana mentioned the connection in his concordance in *Dante e "la bella scola,"* 140, 148. Aurelio Roncaglia discussed three Ovidian citations and the Pompeian inscription as

Ovid's poem *Am.* 2.1 deserves a closer look: in addition to featuring Amor who dictates poems to him, Ovid opens the poem with a strong self-defining statement that has the same metapoetic tone as Dante's tercet in *Purg.* 24.

In this programmatic opening poem of Book 2 of the *Amores*, Ovid confidently announces his writing of a different genre. The poem does not include the conventional classical apology for not writing the more acclaimed genre of epic (as found, for instance, in Vergil's *Ecloga* 6.3–8 or Propertius's elegy 3.3), but instead praises love poetry and its superiority.[79] Ovid declares the gigantomachy and epic heroes topics of the past; light and flattering elegies are now his weapons (*Am.* 2.1.11–22).[80] Like Dante in the tercet in *Purg.* 24, Ovid defines what kind of poet he is. In the first two distichs of the poem, he writes (*Am.* 2.1.1–4):

> HOC quoque composui Paelignis natus aquosis
> ille ego nequitiae Naso poeta meae;
> hoc quoque iussit Amor; procul hinc, procul este, seueri:
> non estis teneris apta theatra modis.
>
> [I, Naso, poet of my own worthlessness, born by the Pelignian waters, also composed this. Love commanded it too; stay far, far away, serious people: you are no fit audience for my tender ways.]

In the *Commedia*, Dante comes close to translating Ovid's self-description "ille ego" (*Am.* 2.1.2) as "I' mi son un" (*Purg.* 24.52). To be complete, this is not the only time Ovid uses the expression "ille ego (qui)": it is also found in a later

---

Dante's sources for *Purg.* 24.52–54 in "Precedenti e significato dello 'stil novo' dantesco," in *Dante e Bologna nei tempi di Dante*, ed. Facoltà di lettere e filosofia, Università di Bologna (Bologna: Commissione per i testi di lingua, 1967), 13–34, at 29, later referenced by Guido Favati in *Inchiesta sul Dolce stil nuovo* (Florence: F. Le Monnier, 1975), 133–34. These and other instances in Latin poetry are also mentioned in Lino Pertile, "Canto XXIV: Of Poetry and Politics," in *Lectura Dantis: Purgatorio. A Canto-by-Canto Commentary*, ed. Allen Mandelbaum, Anthony Oldcorn, and Charles Ross (Berkeley: University of California Press, 2008), 262–76, at 269; and Luciano Rossi, "Canto XXIV," in *Lectura Dantis Turicensis: Purgatorio*, ed. Georges Güntert and Michelangelo Picone (Florence: Franco Cesati, 2001), 373–87, at 380, n. 20.

79 Ovid, *The Second Book of 'Amores,'* ed. with translation and commentary by Joan Booth (Warminster: Aris & Phillips, 1991), 24–25; James C. McKeown, *Ovid: Amores, Volume III. A Commentary on Book 2* (Leeds: Francis Cairns, 1998), 1–4.

80 Ovid opens the first book of the *Amores* with a similar sentiment, using "arma" as his first word (1.1.1), a clear nod to the first half-verse of Vergil's epic poem the *Aeneid*: "Arma uirumque cano" (1.1).

poem in the *Amores*, and in four letters written in exile.[81] As Joseph Farrell has noted, there always is, in varying degrees of intensity, a metapoetic tone in the use of this Latin expression.[82] In fact, several classicists have suggested that Ovid's repeated use of this phrase is a citation of the so-called *preproemium* to Vergil's *Aeneid*.[83] The Vergilian commentators Servius and Donatus cited the following verses as the original opening lines of the *Aeneid* that were later cancelled:

> Ille ego qui quondam gracili modulatus avena
> carmen et egressus silvis vicina coegi
> ut quamvis avido parerent arva colono,
> gratum opus agricolis, at nunc horrentia Martis
> (arma virumque cano)

> [I am the one who once tuned his song on a slender reed, and, coming out of the woods, forced the neighboring fields to obey the tenant farmer, however greedy, a work pleasing to farmers, but now of Mars's trembling (arms and the man I sing)]

In these verses, the expression "ille ego qui" is used to indicate the different phases in Vergil's writing. In the past ("quondam") he wrote bucolic poems and about agriculture, but now ("at nunc") he is writing epic poetry, the *Aeneid*. Dante could have been familiar with Servius and Donatus's writings.[84] He could have found the expression in several passages in Ovid's *Amores* and exile letters. But I consider the four opening verses from Ovid's *Am.* 2.1 the more likely classical source for the Dantean tercet for two reasons. First, of all the times that Ovid uses the expression, this is the only time that we find "ille ego" together with "poeta," which makes it the clearest metapoetic statement

---

81 The expression is found also in *Am.* 3.8.23, in *Tristia* 4.10.1, 5.7b.55, and in *Ex Ponto* 1.2.34, 1.2.35, 1.2.129, 1.2.131; 4.3.11, 4.3.13, 4.3.15, 4.3.16, 4.3.17.

82 Joseph Farrell called the phrase "a marker of posthumous literary fame" in "Ovid's Virgilian Career," *Materiali e discussioni per l'analisi dei testi classici* 52 (2004): 41–55, at 51.

83 For an overview of the scholarship on the *preproemium*, see *The Virgilian Tradition: The First Fifteen Hundred Years*, ed. Jan M. Ziolkowski and Michael C. J. Putnam (New Haven: Yale University Press, 2008), 22–23; and Katharina Volk, "*Ille ego*: (Mis)Reading Ovid's Elegiac Persona," *Antike und Abendland* 51 (2005): 86, n. 15. Simone Marchesi also discussed the importance of the so-called *preproemium* for Dante's self-definition in *Purg.* 24.52–54 ("Epic Ironies," 106–11). Marchesi focused mainly on the relationship between the pseudo-Vergilian statement and Dante's formulation, and Ovid's use of the idiom "ille ego" in two passages from the *Tristia* to evoke the theme of exile.

84 On Dante and Servius, see Edward K. Rand, "Dante and Servius," *Annual Reports of the Dante Society* 33 (1914): 1–11.

among them. Moreover, in the same opening verses of *Am.* 2.1, Amor is described as one who "iussit" or gives orders (*Am.* 2.1.3), an active role for Amor in the poet's activities. Ovid describes his role again at the end of the poem, specifying in the last distich that this same Amor dictates ("dictat") poems to him (*Am.* 2.1.37–38):

> ad mea formosos uultus adhibete puellae
> carmina, purpureus quae mihi dictat Amor.
>
> [Turn your pretty faces, young girls, to the songs that rosy Love dictates to me.]

In other words, in Dante's tercet in *Purg.* 24 we find several phrases from the beginning and the end of the same Ovidian poem — a programmatic, metapoetic poem. The textual similarities are clear: both passages start with the phrase "I am one who" to make a strong statement about the novelty of their writing (in Ovid: "ille ego"; in Dante: "I' mi son un che"), and both passages end with the image of Love dictating poems (in Ovid: "carmina... quae mihi dictat Amor"; in Dante: "quando / Amor mi spira, noto, e a quel modo / ch'e' ditta dentro vo significando"). As indicated earlier, these Dantean verses are traditionally read together with other vernacular sources: the role Dante assigns to Amor in his poetic creation is similar to the one described by the vernacular lyric poets Arnaut Daniel and Guido Cavalcanti in the verses "obre e lim / motz de valor / ab art d'Amor" ("I work and polish words of worth with art of Love" [Toja II; *Chansson do·ill mot son plan e prim*, vv. 12–14]) and "Amore ha fabricato ciò ch'io limo" ("Love has made what I polish" [*Di vil matera mi conven parlare*, v. 16]). Arnaut Daniel, Guido Cavalcanti, and Dante all consider Love the starting point of their poetry: Cavalcanti calls it an Amore who creates — "ha fabricato" (v. 16) — and teaches — "insegna" (v. 10); Dante's Amor inspires — "spira" (*Purg.* 24.53) — and dictates — "ditta" (*Purg.* 24.54). The theologically charged "spira" and passages that place dictation in a religious context have raised the question whether or not to interpret Amor as God, as in *Par.* 10.27 where the poet declares himself God's "scriba." The two passages, however, refer to different kinds of writing: the verse in *Paradiso* to the writing of the *Commedia*, the tercet in *Purgatorio* to the writing of lyric poetry. The passage in *Paradiso* leaves no doubt that it is God who inspires and dictates, while the tercet in *Purgatorio*, informed by theological, vernacular, and classical sources, is constructed in a more complex manner.[85] The classical source Ovid's *Am.* 2.1

---

85   In the long debate on this tercet, most critics interpreted "Amor" of *Purg.* 24.53 as the god of love from the lyric tradition; others do not separate this statement from the passage in

is more than just one of the mentions of a dictating Amor in Latin love poetry. More importantly it provides the language to formulate a strong statement about the exceptionality of one's poetry: in verses conventionally read from an almost exclusively vernacular and theological angle, it brings the connection between vernacular poetry and its classical precedents to the foreground.

By drawing on Ovid to formulate what and how he writes in this passage in *Purg.* 24, Dante inscribes himself into the vernacular tradition of discussing the writing of love poetry through the Latin poet's work. As we have seen in Ch. 2.2, the origin of this practice can be traced back to Occitan poetry, to troubadours who explicitly mention Ovid in their poems and confirm his authority as teacher of love. The Italian poets, at their turn, broke with this consistently positive view on Ovid's work and started to question the value of Ovid's writings. We should read this passage in *Purg.* 24 — where Dante defines his love poetry and its place in the Italian literary tradition by using language that resembles a programmatic poem by Ovid — alongside these earlier mentions of the Latin poet in vernacular poetry.

In Chapter 2, I explored the Occitan and Italian practice of discussing Ovidian poetics in lyric poetry. In troubadour poetry, the confirmation of Ovid's authority was often constructed through the following pattern: the poems mentioned Ovid's name (almost always as the first or second word of the verse), followed by a verb of affirmation (e.g., "retrai" ["confirms"], "dis" ["says"], "declina" ["explains"]), and a statement that could be traced back to Ovid's *Amores*, *Ars amatoria*, or *Heroides*.[86] For example, we read in Bertran

---

Par. 10.27 and read the tercet in *Purg.* 24 exclusively in theological terms. A useful entry point into the bibliography of the former point of view is Robert Hollander, "Dante's 'dolce stil novo' and the *Comedy*," in Picone and Crivelli, *Dante: Mito e poesia*, 263–81, at 265–66, n. 6. For a reading that unites both points, see Barolini, *Dante's Poets*, 90, and, more recently, Kay, *Dante's Lyric Redemption*, 89–90. Defenders of the exclusively theological reading, such as Hollander in "Dante's 'dolce stil novo,'" refer to the line "qui secundum quod cor dictat verba componit" ("he who writes words according to what the heart dictates") from Frate Ivo's letter on charity (previously attributed to Richard of St. Victor in his *Tractatus de gradibus charitatis*). This verse indeed places dictation in a religious context, but the tercet's well-established connection with the vernacular tradition (Arnaut Daniel, Guido Cavalcanti) and the less-considered classical connection, especially with Ovid, problematize this exclusively theological reading. The text from Frate Ivo's letter is quoted from Mira Mocan, *L'arca della mente. Riccardo di San Vittore nella 'Commedia' di Dante* (Florence: Leo S. Olschki, 2012), 50. For an overview of the scholarship of the attribution to Frate Ivo, see vii–viii, especially n. 2.

86   A brief list of the three examples discussed in more detail in this paragraph clearly shows this pattern (emphasis added):
"… qu'ieu truep en l'escriptura / c'*Ovidis dis* qu'ieu feira desmezura."
(Bertran Carbonel, *Aisi m'a dat fin'amor conoissensa*, vv. 29–30)
"Mas *Ovidis retrais* / qu'entre·ls corals amadors / no paratgeia ricors."

Carbonel's *canso Aisi m'a dat fin'amor conoissensa* that the poet knew that not confessing his love to his lady was the right thing to do, because he found "in the writings" (a passage in the *Heroides*) that Ovid said that he would exaggerate. But then Love urged him to tell her anyway, which is also how the passage in Ovid's *Heroides* continued. Or when the troubadour Arnaut de Mareuil discussed love and nobility, he considered Ovid the authority who confirmed that sincere love did not go together with wealth. These verses in his *canso Mout eron doutz miei cossir* corresponded to Ovid's statement in *Ars am.* 2.161–65. We found the strongest confirmation of Ovid's authority in Rigaut de Berbezilh's *canso Tuit demandon qu'es devengud'Amors*: the poet wrote that the lover should be patient and persevere, just as Ovid said "in the book that does not lie" ("el libre que no men" [v. 29]), in a passage from the *Ars amatoria* or the *Amores* with such a message for the lover.

Italian readers of Ovid, however, found that Ovid's books could indeed lie. In the Italian poems that discussed reading Ovid — the anonymous Sicilian or Siculo-Tuscan *canzone Giamai null'om nonn-à sì gra·richezze*, Dante da Maiano's *Amor mi fa sì fedelmente amare*, Guido Orlandi's *Per troppa sottiglianza il fil si rompe*, Guido Cavalcanti's *Di vil matera mi conven parlare*, and Cino da Pistoia's *Se mai leggesti versi de l'Ovidi* — we saw that the Italian poets no longer consistently accepted the authority of Ovid's works.[87] Moreover, most of these mentions of Ovid were found in *tenzoni* or sonnet exchanges, a genre that often includes metapoetic reflections. While of course not every metapoetic sonnet exchange featured Ovid, the poets who mentioned Ovid in sonnet exchanges did so to discuss the content and evaluate the worth of his writings. They were not only interested in assessing Ovid as a teacher of love, but also as a poet. In some cases, the discussion focused on the question whether or not Ovid's writings were still of use for the contemporary lover.[88] In other cases, Italian poets debated whether or not Ovid's poetry should be an example for their own.[89] Italian poets rarely mention non-contemporary poets, and Ovid is by far the most mentioned Latin poet in the Italian lyric poetry of the time.

(Arnaut de Mareuil, *Mout eron doutz miei cossir*, vv. 28–30)
"c'*Ovidis dis* el libre que no men / que ..."
(Rigaut de Berbezilh, *Tuit demandon qu'es devengud'Amors*, vv. 29–30)
These and other Occitan poets who feature Ovid in such a manner in their poems are discussed in more detail in Ch. 2.2.

87   See the more detailed discussion in Ch. 2.3.
88   Cino da Pistoia still found worth in Ovid's writings, and Dante da Maiano declared that the remedies against lovesickness he read about in Ovid "were all lies."
89   In the exchange between Guido Orlandi and Guido Cavalcanti, Orlandi considered Ovid's work a point of reference, while for Cavalcanti Ovid represented the themes his own poetry did not treat.

Especially the *tenzone* between Guido Orlandi and Guido Cavalcanti is of interest in the context of Dante's *Commedia*. Orlandi and Cavalcanti's exchange closely resembles, in both conceptual and verbal connections, the metapoetic debate between Bonagiunta Orbicciani and Guido Guinizzelli (*Voi c'avete mutata la mainera* and *Omo ch' è saggio non corre leggero*, respectively).[90] In both exchanges, two Italian poetic schools were opposed: Bonagiunta and Orlandi's Siculo-Tuscan poetry against Guinizzelli and Cavalcanti's early "dolce stil novo," to use the term Dante introduces in the exchange with Bonagiunta in *Purg.* 24.57. Orlandi and Cavalcanti used Ovid to mark the clear departure from the earlier poets in their methods of writing poetry. In *Per troppa sottiglianza il fil si rompe*, Orlandi questioned Cavalcanti's descriptions of love and argued that he had a deeper understanding of love through his reading of Ovid, advising Orlandi to read Ovid ("Ovidio leggi" [v. 11]). Cavalcanti, on the other hand, considered *Ovidio* a poet who treated those themes too crudely, contending that reading him a few times will not result in a deeper and finer understanding of love. And Ovid further leads their poetic discussion to Dante's metapoetic tercet in *Purg.* 24. Among the vernacular sources for Dante's self-definition in *Purg.* 24.52–54 is Cavalanti's verse "Amore ha fabricato ciò ch'io limo" (v. 16). This verse belongs from *Di vil matera mi conven parlare,* Cavalcanti's contribution to the poetic debate with Orlandi, where both vernacular poets use Ovid as an emblem of the poetry they write or no longer wish to write.

Against this backdrop of metapoetic discussions featuring Ovid in Italian vernacular poetry, I read the encounter between Dante and Bonagiunta in *Purg.* 24 as such a discussion: an encounter between two poets to exchange ideas about their craft. In other words, the traditional correspondence becomes direct conversation in the *Commedia*. A discussion about what constitutes good poetry and what not, what topics are suited for it and which not, is now orchestrated in the narrative of the *Commedia*, in a conversation between the vernacular poets Dante Alighieri and Bonagiunta Orbicciani — two poets who during their lifetimes participated in several sonnet exchanges of this kind,[91] two poets who clearly represent different poetic schools. What sets

---

90   In the opening verse of Guido Orlandi's *Per troppa sottiglianza il fil si rompe*, Orlandi retakes Bonagiunta Orbicciani's term "sottigliansa" from his attack to Guido Guinizzelli in *Voi c'avete mutata la mainera*: "Cosí passate voi di sottigliansa" ("At the same time you exceed in subtlety" [v. 9]). See Ch. 2, n. 86 for bibliographical references on this connection.

91   A few early commentators wanted to imagine that Dante and Bonagiunta actually exchanged poems. For instance, Benvenuto da Imola wrote: "Bonagiunta de Urbisanis ... qui noverat autorem in vita, et aliquando scripserat sibi" ("Bonagiunta Orbicciani, who knew the author during his life and at times had written to him" [note to *Purg.* 24.34–39]). The text from Giacomo Filippo Lacaita's 1887 edition of Benvenuto's commentary is quoted

this episode in the *Commedia* apart from the exchanges in correspondence is that Dante writes both parts of the conversation. As a result, Bonagiunta, who in the sonnet *Voi c'avete mutata la mainera* was attacking the novelty of Guinizzelli's writing, now appears to be convinced and approving of poetic innovation, praising Dante's "nove rime" ("new rhymes" [*Purg.* 24.50]) and "dolce stil novo" ("sweet new style" [*Purg.* 24.57]). With Dante putting words in his mouth, Bonagiunta easily sees the knot that separated the present from the past, signaled in the text by Giacomo da Lentini, Guittone d'Arezzo, and himself (*Purg.* 24.55–57). Dante controls the narrative in this episode that outlines Italian literary history; his character, the respondent in this discussion on poetry, does not need to strongly defend innovative choices, as participants in metapoetic debates in sonnet exchanges often did. Here in *Purgatorio*, Dante effectively erases the mocking and harsh words that Bonagiunta wrote to Guinizzelli in *Voi c'avete mutata la mainera*, and, by extension, all criticism of the "new style," including Guido Orlandi's similar accusations to Guido Cavalcanti in the earlier mentioned *Per troppa sottiglianza il fil si rompe*, and especially Onesto da Bologna's sonnet *Mente e umile e più di mille sporte* sent to Cino da Pistoia, which summarizes the main complaints the old guard launched in metapoetic sonnet exchanges to the poets we now thanks to Dante call the *stilnovisti*: the use of a selective lexicon (vv. 1–2), the reliance on dreams (v. 2), the philosophizing (v. 6), and the use of personification (v. 10). In this episode in *Purg.* 24, Dante writes a reply-to-all of sorts.[92]

The role of Ovid in this poetic discussion in *Purgatorio* is subtler than the previous sonnet exchanges that mentioned Ovid openly by name — this is not the canto where Dante explicitly silences Ovid (*Inf.* 25.97). But by translating

---

from the Dartmouth Dante Project, https://dante.dartmouth.edu. On these early testimonies, see Michelangelo Zaccarello, "Rimatori e poetiche 'da l'uno a l'altro stilo,'" in *Lectura Dantis Romana, Cento canti per centi anni, II. Purgatorio, 2. Canti XVIII–XXXIII*, ed. Enrico Malato and Andrea Mazzucchi (Rome: Salerno, 2014), 712–44, at 720, n. 15. Also Fabian Alfie referred to the early commentator Jacopo della Lana's mention of the exchanges between Dante and Bonagiunta, concluding that while many poets engaged in *tenzoni*, Dante appears to have chosen Forese and Bonagiunta to represent poetic correspondence at this point in the *Commedia*. See his chapter "The Terrace of the *Tenzone: Purgatorio* XXIII and XXIV," in *Dante's 'Tenzone' with Forese Donati*, 82–99, at 82–83. In his discussion of the exchange between Dante and Bonagiunta in *Purg.* 24, Alfie is more interested in the elements from that conversation that tie it to the *tenzone* between Dante and Forese Donati (especially at 93–97).

92 For a similar interpretation, see Furio Brugnolo, "Il "nodo" di Bonagiunta e il "modo" di Dante: Per un'interpretazione di *Purgatorio* XXIV," *Rivista di studi danteschi* 9 (2009): 3–28, at 14–15, 22. See also Brugnolo's earlier essays on the *tenzoni* between Cino da Pistoia and Onesto da Bologna and their presence in *Purg.* 24: "Cino (e Onesto) dentro e fuori la *Commedia*" and "Appendice a Cino (e Onesto) dentro e fuori la *Commedia*."

key phrases from Ovid's metapoetic poem *Am.* 2.1, and transforming the vernacular lyric poets' metapoetic sonnet exchanges, which often featured Ovid, into an actual exchange between two Italian poets about poetry in *Purg.* 24, Dante draws on both Latin and vernacular readings of Ovid in this episode. Put differently, Dante defines his own writing by drawing upon Ovid's imagery (his programmatic statements on writing love poetry in *Am.* 2.1) and by using the Italian vernacular poetic form (the sonnet exchange) where Ovid was most mentioned in discussing love and love poetry.

It is important, however, not to overlook the clear differences between Dante's words and his Ovidian model: Dante's poetics of love and love poetry are far from Ovid's self-declared "worthlessness" or "naughtiness" ("nequitiae" [*Am.* 2.1.2]), and Amor dictates poems to Dante other than the ones "rosy Love" dictated to Ovid (*Am.* 2.1.37–38). Ovid's announcement in *Am.* 2.1 was triumphant: unlike the traditional apology for not writing the more acclaimed genre of epic, Ovid was confident and self-assured in his announcement to write love poetry instead, praising the worth of his naughty love poems. The tone and content of these Ovidian poems are mostly absent from the *Commedia* and from the love poetry Dante describes in *Purg.* 24.52–54. Already in the *Vita nuova* — invoked in this episode by Bonagiunta's mention of its central *canzone Donne ch'avete intelletto d'amore* (*Purg.* 24.51; *VN* 19) — Dante had forgone the examples of the walking, laughing, and talking Amors in Ovid's *Amores, Ars amatoria,* and *Heroides,* and selected an example from the *Remedia amoris* to justify his use of personification (see Ch. 3.1). Not the content of Ovid's statement in *Am.* 2.1, then, but the spirit resonated, the proud formulation of one's poetic worth. In *Purg.* 24, Dante distinguishes himself and the "sweet new style" from Giacomo da Lentini, Guittone d'Arezzo, and Bonagiunta, and others who wrote poetry like them; through his use of Ovidian language and imagery in this canto, Dante evokes the classical poet Ovid as well, only to distinguish his own poetry in Italian from Ovid's Latin verses. In *Inf.* 25, Dante told Ovid to be silent about his characters Cadmus and Arethusa, claiming that he is more skilled when writing about change than the poet of the *Metamorphoses* (*Inf.* 25.97–102). The Latin poet, however, stays omnipresent in the *Commedia*: until the end of *Paradiso* Dante translates or paraphrases verses from Ovid's poem. Likewise, "naughty" poems like Ovid's *Amores* are far removed from the Italian poetry Dante writes, but traces — the verbal echoes of certain verses — remain. Dante's message to Ovid in *Inf.* 25 was loud and clear; here in *Purg.* 24 it is implicit, but essentially the same: his poetry in Italian is superior. Relying on Ovid to convey that message is ultimately a vernacular lyric practice.

4.4 Conclusion

This chapter's version of the "Dante's Ovid" essay placed Dante's reading of Ovid within its Italian literary and cultural contexts. No specific manuscript or even commentary could be identified as Dante's copy (or copies) of Ovid's texts, but I argued that we ought to think about Dante's reading of Ovid as mainly an engagement with Ovid's Latin works in their entirety, mostly undisturbed by the glosses and comments that may have accompanied these texts, and not in the many intermediary sources that presented isolated passages from Ovid's oeuvre. Moreover, Dante often features Ovidian verses but departs from the context in which Ovid wrote them, which is basically how anthologies operate: taking passages out of context. However, I read these instances not as undeniable evidence of Dante's reading of anthologies but, based on verbal, stylistic, or thematic connections, as examples of his reinterpretation of the Ovidian passages. At the local level, the comparison between Ovid's Latin and Dante's Italian verses revealed close textual similarities. Read more globally, the Ovidian verses that made it into the text of the *Commedia* were strategically chosen from stories that address the broader themes and concerns of the episode in which Dante uses these Ovidian verses. In that way, I fleshed out Dante's *Ovidius*: an impressive and important collection of Latin sources, ranging from Ovid's amatory works to the *Metamorphoses* and the exile letters, which Dante read closely and attentively.

The vernacular roots of Dante's readings of Ovid are a different story. The presence of the *Ovidio* of the Italian lyric poets is less straightforward than that of Dante's Latin Ovidian sources. The passages featuring Pyramus and Thisbe and Narcissus in the *Commedia* do not contain verses that obviously correspond to the Italian lyric poems on these Ovidian characters (as a matter of fact, verbal links with Ovid's Latin version of the tales are more easily established). The connections with the lyric tradition reveal themselves through rhetorical features — the use of the simile — and especially the specific points in the poem where Dante turns to these characters: the distinctively vernacular lyric pedigree of Pyramus and Thisbe and Narcissus means that when Dante features them in the *Commedia* their mentions cannot be separated from that tradition — Dante's accounts of Pyramus and Thisbe and Narcissus in the *Commedia* always comment on or contrast with the vernacular lyric focus on madness and death in their love stories.

The discussions of Ovid's works and poetics in sonnet exchanges can be traced from vernacular lyric poetry to the *Commedia*. As a poetic genre, the *tenzone* enters the text of the *Commedia* a few times, most noticeably in the biting exchange between Maestro Adamo and Sinone in *Inf.* 30 and the *tenzone* between Dante and Forese Donati that serves as intertext to their encounter in *Purg.* 23. Italian poets do not only hone the art of the insult in *tenzoni*, but also use the poetic form to discuss poetry itself. When in *Purg.* 24 Dante discusses poetry (his own and Italian lyric verse in general) with fellow Italian poet Bonagiunta Orbicciani, I read this episode as the performance of a *tenzone*: Dante literally stages an exchange between poets on poetry, normally held in correspondence, in the text of the *Commedia*. Since such metapoetic sonnet exchanges were the main place where Italian poets brought up Ovid to discuss love and love poetry, the Ovidian undertones in this Dantean episode do not surprise. Like the Italian lyric poets who featured Ovid in their poems to contrast Latin love poetry with their own vernacular verse, in *Purg.* 24 Dante reflects on Ovid's poetics in similar ways. But Dante's praise for his own poetry in the vernacular is part of an intertextually rich episode, where the poet of the *Commedia* also draws on theological sources, other vernacular poems by Guido Cavalcanti and Arnaut Daniel, and assertive phrases from Ovid's programmatic and equally metapoetic poem *Am.* 2.1 to formulate the kind of poetry he writes. In this passage packed with references to the words of others, the fact that Dante also adopts the *tenzone*, the poetic form used in vernacular lyric poetry to discuss Ovid, should not be overlooked.

In the much longer poetic form that the *Commedia* offered, Dante could of course feature Ovid in ways the poets of short lyric compositions could not. While the extent to which Ovid's Latin words in translation and paraphrase entered the Italian text of the *Commedia* is unparalleled (nothing Italian lyric poets before Dante ever did), the core of their treatment of Ovid — one of poetic comparison — resonated with Dante. Common narratives in the scholarship on Dante's Ovid are that Dante corrected Ovid's stories in the *Commedia*, or that Dante himself becomes the corrected Ovid in the *Commedia*, the Christian poet of love.[93] The striking biographical similarities between Dante and Ovid — both love poets who later in their poetic careers turned to more serious matters and considered themselves undeserved exiles — lend themselves easily to such readings. But the shared topics of love, myth, and exile are not the only things that bind them: to write about poetry is another important one.[94] Ovid knew how to underscore the novelty of his writing; the proem to the *Metamorphoses* (1.1–4) provides perhaps the best example:

---

93 A noteworthy example is Picone, "Purgatorio XXVII: Passaggio rituale e *translatio* poetica," briefly discussed in n. 71.

94 On this shared interest, see my essay "Dante lettore di Ovidio." On the theme of poetry, and more broadly art, in Ovid's writings, see in particular Barbara Pavlock's recent study, *The Image of the Poet in Ovid's 'Metamorphoses'* (Madison: University of Wisconsin Press, 2009); Eleanor Winsor Leach, "Ekphrasis and the Theme of Artistic Failure in Ovid's

IN NOVA fert animus mutatas dicere formas
corpora; di, coeptis (nam uos mutastis et illa)
aspirate meis primaque ab origine mundi
ad mea perpetuum deducite tempora carmen.

[My mind pushes me to speak of forms changed into new bodies; gods, inspire this undertaking (since you have changed it as well) and unfold an uninterrupted poem from the very beginning of the world up until my own time.]

For a long time readers of Ovid's proem have found "illas" and not "illa" at the end of its second verse — something that puzzled or bothered them. It seemed redundant to evoke the "formas" of the opening verse again by mentioning "illas," and the placement of "et" made little sense: how could Ovid be so clumsy at the very opening of his poem? While most manuscripts and older editions had "illas," the most recent Teubner and Oxford Classical Text editions have replaced it with "illa," attested in only a few manuscripts.[95] With "illa" referring to the "coeptis ... / ... meis" (*Met.* 1.2–3), Ovid's request for divine inspiration includes the acknowledgement that the gods also changed his beginnings, his poetic undertaking. In other words, at the opening of the *Metamorphoses* Ovid declares that he is embarking on a new kind of writing, one that pushes genre boundaries. As Mark Possanza noted, in these verses the gods are both "*causing the transformations that are the subject of the poem and transforming the maker of the poem himself*" (emphasis added).[96] Even if Dante did not read Ovid's text with "illa," he surely understood this Ovidian statement about the transformative power of writing.

Metamorphoses," *Ramus* 3, no. 2 (1974): 102–42; Donald Lateiner, "Mythic and Non-Mythic Artists in Ovid's *Metamorphoses*," *Ramus* 13 (1984): 1–30.

95 The case for "illa" was first laid out in E. J. Kenney, "Ovidius Prooemians," *Proceedings of the Cambridge Philological Society* 22 (1976): 46–53, and further elaborated in David Kovacs, "Ovid, *Metamorphoses* 1.2," *The Classical Quarterly* 37, no. 2 (1987): 458–65. See also James J. O'Hara, *Inconsistency in Roman Epic: Studies in Catullus, Lucretius, Vergil, Ovid and Lucan* (Cambridge: Cambridge University Press, 2007), 105–7, with further bibliographical references on the issue.

96 Mark Possanza, "Editing Ovid: Immortal Works and Material Texts," in *A Companion to Ovid*, ed. Peter E. Knox (Chichester: Wiley-Blackwell, 2009), 311–26, at 314.

CHAPTER 5

Petrarch's Scattered Ovidian Verses

Dante and Petrarch are often played off against each other in narratives that find Dante signaling the end and Petrarch the beginning of certain literary practices, tastes, and movements.[1] This chapter aims to erode such sharp divides: while not downplaying what distinguishes the two poets, in what follows I illustrate in which aspects Petrarch is an integral part of a longer Italian tradition of reading Ovid. Focusing on their shared approaches to Ovidian material brings Dante closer to Petrarch, and Petrarch closer to Dante. Like in the previous chapter on Ovid in Dante's *Commedia*, in this chapter on Petrarch I re-examine traits of his treatment of Ovidian material that are considered unique and idiosyncratic — distinctively "Petrarchan" — and instead situate them in their Italian literary and cultural contexts. In the first section, I document Petrarch's strong familiarity with the Italian Ovidian tradition, which included Ovid-inspired literature in Italian, Occitan, and French, in addition to Ovid's works in Latin and commentaries. I then examine Petrarch's interest in self-identification with Ovidian characters, a feature characterizing vernacular lyric poetry from the very beginning, and I connect Petrarch's frequent identification with the women in Ovid's stories in the *Canzoniere* to poems of Cino da Pistoia and Dante, where such gender reversals also occurred. In the chapter's last section, I argue that more than any Italian reader of Ovid before him, Petrarch understood that Ovid's concept of metamorphosis is also a narrative principle. Ovid created the stories in the *Metamorphoses* from different sources, often intertwined his stories and at times even rewrote them in his poem. In the *Canzoniere*, Petrarch applies this principle of scattering fragments of Ovidian stories and themes in his poems in order to rewrite his own story throughout the collection. From these discussions, which focus mainly on Petrarch's Italian poetry in the *Canzoniere*, emerges a portrait of Petrarch as a close reader of Ovid, and, more than any prior Italian poet, of the Ovidian tradition.

---

1   The most recent publication that takes this approach is *Petrarch & Dante: Anti-Dantism, Metaphysics, Tradition*, ed. Zygmunt G. Barański and Theodore J. Cachey, Jr. (Notre Dame: University of Notre Dame Press, 2009).

5.1 Petrarch's Ovid Found

Petrarch is different from the Italian readers of Ovid discussed up until this point in several ways. The first way is simple: rather than reconstructing a reading history from their education, profession, and especially their poetry, Petrarch himself provides us with plenty information about his Ovidian readings. Throughout his life (1304–74), Petrarch commented repeatedly on the books he reads, offering an unprecedentedly clear picture of which Ovidian texts he read and how he read them.[2] These texts are not limited to Ovid's Latin works, but include broad readings in the Ovidian tradition. And the works that make up this tradition had increased significantly during Petrarch's lifetime — another crucial difference between Petrarch and his predecessors. Before turning to Petrarch's Ovidian library, I give a quick overview of the changing cultures of reading Ovid during Petrarch's lifetime.

Toward the end of the thirteenth century (close to Petrarch's birth in 1304), Italian translators turned their attention to Latin poetry. The first translations of Ovid's works had started to appear around the time that Dante was writing the *Commedia*: first, the *Ars amatoria* and the *Remedia amoris* around the turn of the fourteenth century, followed by Filippo Ceffi's popular translation of the *Heroides* between 1320 and 1330. After Dante's death (1321) and during Petrarch's lifetime, Arrigo Simintendi da Prato (1333) composed the first Italian translation of the *Metamorphoses*; excerpts from this translation made their way into the commentaries on the *Commedia*. Giovanni Bonsignori's *volgarizzamento* of the *Metamorphoses* (1375–77), which drew heavily on Giovanni del Virgilio's writings on Ovid's poem, dates slightly after Petrarch's death in 1374. But Giovanni del Virgilio's *Expositio* and *Allegorie*, which had come out of his teaching of the *Metamorphoses* at the university of Bologna in 1321, still relied much on the Ovidian commentaries of the previous centuries: Arnulf of Orléans's commentary (second half of the twelfth century) and John of Garland's *Integumenta Ovidii* (around 1230). Petrarch was in Bologna during this time, and some scholars placed him in del Virgilio's audience.[3] The fourteenth-century commentaries that take the most allegorizing and

---

2 The most recent and complete account on Petrarch as reader of Ovid is Luca Marcozzi's "Petrarca lettore di Ovidio," in Russo, *Testimoni del vero*, 57–104. On Petrarch's library and reading practices, see *La bibliothèque de Pétrarque: Livres et auteurs autour d'un humaniste*, ed. Maurice Brock, Francesco Furlan, and Frank La Brasca (Turnhout: Brepols, 2011); *Petrarca lettore: pratiche e rappresentazioni della lettura nelle opere dell'umanista*, ed. Luca Marcozzi (Florence: Franco Cesati, 2016).

3 Witt considered the possibility that Petrarch attended Giovanni del Virgilio's lectures in Bologna (*In the Footsteps of the Ancients*, 236–38).

Christianizing approach to the *Metamorphoses* — the anonymous French *Ovide moralisé* (between 1316 and 1328) and Pierre Bersuire's *Ovidius moralizatus* (between 1337 and 1340) — belonged to Petrarch's and not Dante's literary context.[4] However, as we will see in this chapter, Petrarch was not interested in reading entire poems of Ovid in translation, and while Bersuire, the author of the *Ovidius moralizatus*, thanked his friend and correspondent Petrarch in the introduction, there are few traces of Bersuire's strongly allegorized readings of the *Metamorphoses* in Petrarch's writings.[5]

Petrarch himself provides the starting point of his Ovidian education. In a letter on the fleeting passing of time, written to his friend and longtime correspondent Philippe de Cabassole, bishop of Cavaillon (*Fam.* XXIV.1), he compiles a little anthology of Latin passages, and indicates where he first heard these: as a young student, some thirty years earlier.[6] In Petrarch's own account, he was a precocious student who understood hidden meanings ("abditum intelligens") of the excerpts used in class to teach Latin, while his fellow students (and even his teacher) focused only on the grammar and the strangeness of the words ("soli inhians grammatice et verborum artificio" [*Fam.* XXIV.1.5]).[7] Petrarch introduces the passages from Ovid, first heard in this context, as follows: "Audiebam Ovidium, cuius quo lascivior Musa eo michi severior graviorque confessio et incorruptius testimonium veri erat" ("I used to listen to Ovid; the more licentious his Muse, the more he was serious and profound evidence to me, and an uncorrupted testimony of the truth" [*Fam.* XXIV.1.6]). While Petrarch glosses reading Ovid with the poet's own words — in *Tristia* 2.313, for instance, Ovid lamented the trouble his "lasciuia Musa" had caused him — the included Ovidian passages in Petrarch's letter are far from the verses such a Muse would have inspired.[8] As we have seen in Ch. 1.1, if Ovid was not taught in his entirety at school, the educational works that contained excerpts of his texts turned the Latin poet into a philosopher, one who was as good a source on topics such as the fleeting passing of time as Seneca, Cicero, and St. Augustine,

---

4   Philippe de Vitry, bishop of Meaux, and correspondent of Petrarch, has been considered the author of the *Ovide moralisé*. On his correspondence with Petrarch, see Roberta Antognini, *Il progetto autobiografico delle 'Familiares' di Petrarca* (Milan: LED Edizioni Universitarie di Lettere Economia Diritto, 2008), 377.
5   Petrus Berchorius, *Reductorium morale, Liber XV: cap. i.*, fol. 1v, vv. 7–14 (p. 3).
6   For an overview of all letters written to Philippe de Cabassole, see Antognini, *Il progetto autobiografico delle 'Familiares' di Petrarca*, 421. Philippe de Cabassole was the dedicatee of Petrarch's *De vita solitaria*.
7   This teacher was Convenevole da Prato, who between 1312 and 1316 taught Petrarch and his younger brother Gherardo the *trivium*, or grammar, logic, and rhetoric. See Emilio Pasquini, "Convenevole da Prato," *Dizionario biografico degli Italiani* 28: 563–68.
8   The passages are *Met.* 10.519–20 and *Fasti* 6.771–72.

some of the other authors quoted in Petrarch's letter. Petrarch both applies and distances himself from the collecting of passages, or picking of flowers ("flosculos decerpere" [*Fam.* XXIV.1.9]) — calling it something a young boy does and not an old man (*Fam.* XXIV.1.9). Such excerpts from Ovid's works, however, are frequent in Petrarch's writings throughout his life, and a good indicator of the scope of his Ovidian readings.

In fact, Pierre de Nolhac found so many citations of Ovid's works in Petrarch's prose and poetry that he concluded that he must have possessed the *Metamorphoses* and the *Fasti*, the exile letters (the *Tristia* and *Epistulae ex Ponto*), and the amatory works (*Amores, Ars amatoria, Remedia amoris, Heroides*), perhaps the *Medicamina faciei femineae*, and possibly the *Ibis* and the spurious *Halieutica*.[9] In Petrarch's "libri mei peculiares," the list of his favorite books that he wrote down on a flyleaf in his copy of Cassiodorus's *De anima* and St. Augustine's *De vera religione* (Paris, Bibliothèque nationale de France, MS lat. 2201), he includes "Ovidius p(re)s(er)t(im) in maiori," or Ovid, especially the *Metamorphoses*.[10] (Petrarch refers to the *Metamorphoses* with the common label "Ovidius maior.")[11] In terms of physical evidence, however, there is not much to report. One manuscript (London, British Library, MS Harley 3754), containing the incomplete *Metamorphoses* (Books 1–4), is now considered to have been owned and glossed by Petrarch.[12] Another miscellany manuscript that belonged to Petrarch (Paris, Bibliothèque nationale de France, MS lat. 8500) contained one commentary on Ovid, and two other works on myth: Fulgentius's *Mythologiae*, an unglossed pseudo-Lactantian *Narrationes*, the oldest commentary on Ovid's *Metamorphoses* (see Ch. 1.1), and

---

9   Pierre de Nolhac, *Pétrarque et l'humanisme*, 2 vols., 2nd ed. (Paris, Champion, 1907), 1: 176–80 (on Petrarch and Ovid), and the citation at 1: 176: "Il les [=les oeuvres d'Ovide] cite même assez souvent pour qu'on puisse être sûr qu'il les possédât" (also in Marcozzi, "Petrarca lettore di Ovidio," 60–61).

10 Berthold Louis Ullman, "Petrarch's Favorite Books," in *Studies in the Italian Renaissance*, 113–33. Ovid is included in the first of three lists Petrarch wrote down on the flyleaf, under the heading "Poet(ica)." The title of Ullman's essay indicates how to read this list: as a collection of favorites, and not a comprehensive tally. Moreover, as Ullman specified in the essay, this list refers to readings before 1337.

11 See the Introduction, n. 4 on the labels "Ovidius maior" and "Ovidio maggiore."

12 London, British Library, MS Harley 3754, fols. 160–73. See Marcozzi, "Petrarca lettore di Ovidio," 61–63; and Maurizio Fiorilla, *I classici nel 'Canzoniere': Note di lettura e scrittura poetica in Petrarca* (Padua: Antenore, 2012), 4–5. The manuscript is lightly glossed throughout (except for the *Metamorphoses*), and has been connected with Petrarch's stay in Bologna (1320–26). On Fulgentius's *Mythologiae* and the Vatican Mythographers, see Ch. 1, n. 15.

the Third Vatican Mythographer.[13] Like the frequent citations of Ovid's works in Petrarch's own writings, the glosses with Ovidian verses in the margins of other manuscripts owned by Petrarch also document the range of his Ovidian readings. Luca Marcozzi pointed out that such glosses appear in Petrarch's manuscripts both from his young age and later in life.[14] For instance, in the Ambrosian Vergil (Codex Ambrosianus S.P. 10/27, *olim* A. 49 *inf.*), Petrarch's personal copy of Vergil's works with Simone Martini's famous frontispiece illustration, the citations of the *Metamorphoses* in the margins are frequent,[15] and several of Ovid's other works are mentioned one or two times each.[16]

While excerpts from Ovid's works in Petrarch's writings are thus our best indicators to gauge the breadth of his engagement with the Latin poet's oeuvre, Petrarch speaks out against fragmented reading of *auctores* at several occasions. *Fam.* IV.15, an attack on an unnamed "famous man," guilty of relying too much on the words of others, is often cited in this context. Also in the *Secretum*, his dialogue with St. Augustine, Petrarch criticized the practice. He claimed to find no delight in excerpts once he was past childhood, and called compilers "choppers of literature" ("literarum laceratores").[17] Consistent with this repeated rejection of learning from excerpts, Petrarch crafted an image of himself as a constant, attentive, and repeat reader of texts in their entirety, one

13 Paris, Bibliothèque nationale de France, MS lat. 8500, fols. 57–70. In this manuscript, the *Narrationes* is a free-standing text, in contrast with other manuscripts, where the *Narrationes* appeared together with the text of Ovid's *Metamorphoses* (for instance, MS San Marco 225 [*fig.* 2]). On this manuscript, see Marcozzi, "Petrarca lettore di Ovidio," 64; and *La biblioteca di Febo: Mitologia e allegoria in Petrarca* (Florence: Franco Cesati, 2003), 132–39.

14 Marcozzi, "Petrarca lettore di Ovidio," 65–66, with discussion of the Ovidian glosses on Petrarch's manuscripts at 63–66.

15 These are mostly notes specifying that Ovid also tells the story of this or that character, as well as linguistic comments, pointing out similar phrases in Ovid's poem.

16 Francesco Petrarca, *Le postille del Virgilio Ambrosiano*, ed. Marco Baglio, Antonietta Nebuloni Testa, and Marco Petoletti, 2 vols. (Padua: Antenore, 2006). The editors listed all passages from Ovid's works (which, in addition to the *Metamorphoses*, included the *Amores, Ars amatoria, Heroides, Fasti*, and the *Remedia amoris*, and the *Fasti*) at 2: 1011–12.

17 The entire passage (*Secr.* III.14.8) reads: "Nunquam, ex quo pueritiam excessi, scientiarum flosculis delectatus sum; multa enim adversus literarum laceratores, eleganter a Cicerone dicta notavi, et a Seneca illud in primis: 'Viro captare flosculos turpe est, et notissimis se fulcire vocibus ac memoria stare'" ("From the moment I stopped being a child, I never found pleasure in the wisdom of excerpts; in fact, I noted mainy elegant passages by Cicero against the choppers of literature, and above all, this passage by Seneca; 'it is shameful for a man to collect excerpts, and then to praise himself for remembering the most obvious and well-known sayings'").

who memorized and internalized his readings over time.[18] Dennis Dutschke noted that among Petrarch's possessions there are several miscellanies, books that contained multiple authors and texts, and the occasional anthology and collection of *exempla*.[19] In general, though, Petrarch preferred to own single authors and entire works, as indicated by the list of his "libri peculiares," where these "books" refer to authors and not to specific manuscripts (that often contained different authors or works). Moreover, in his correspondence, Petrarch indicates his pleasure in owning such books and his desire to get more.[20] But despite his obvious disapproval of the concept of fragmented reading and learning, the proverbial Ovid — the result of such decontextualized readings of the Latin poet — is not absent in Petrarch. For instance, in the previously mentioned *Fam.* XXIV.1 Petrarch dismissed the practice of collecting passages and, like in the *Secretum*, associated it with youth, but the two Ovidian passages that he cites in the letter on the fleeting passage of time (*Met.* 10.519–20 and *Fasti* 6.771–72) come straight out of the anthologies.[21]

---

18   Especially the following passage forged that image in the minds of Petrarch's readers and scholars, who cite it frequently in discussing Petrarch's reading practices (*Fam.* XXII.2.12–13): "Legi apud Virgilium apud Flaccum apud Severinum apud Tullium; nec semel legi sed milies, nec cucurri sed incubui, et totis ingenii nisibus immoratus sum; mane comedi quod sero digererem, hausi puer quod senior ruminarem. Hec se michi tam familiariter ingessere et non modo memorie sed medullis affixa sunt unumque cum ingenio facta sunt meo, ut etsi per omnem vitam amplius non legantur, ipsa quidem hereant, actis in intima animi parte radicibus, sed interdum obliviscar auctorem, quippe qui longo usu et possessione continua quasi illa prescripserim diuque pro meis habuerim, et turba talium obsessus, nec cuius sint certe nec aliena meminerim" ("I have read Vergil, Horace, Severinus, Cicero; I have read them not once but a thousand times; I did not rush but took all the time, and I dwelled on my readings, fully applying my intellect; I ate in the morning what I would digest at night, I swallowed as a boy what I would ruminate as an older man. These readings have become so familiar and internalized, fixed not only in my mind but also in my marrow, and they have become one with my mind, so that if I should stop reading them, they would still cling to me, having taken root in the intimate part of my mind. But when sometimes I would forget the author, since through long usage and uninterrupted possession I may adopt them as if they were my own words and for a long time consider them mine; surrounded by the amount of such readings, I may not remember for sure if they are mine or of others").

19   Dennis Dutschke, "Il libro miscellaneo: Problemi di metodo tra Boccaccio e Petrarca," in *Gli Zibaldoni di Boccaccio: Memoria, scrittura, riscrittura. Atti del Seminario internazionale di Firenze-Certaldo (26–28 aprile 1996)*, ed. Michelangelo Picone and Claude Cazalé Bérard (Florence: Franco Cesati, 1998), 95–112.

20   Dutschke, "Il libro miscellaneo," 99–100.

21   Both passages are included in the *Florilegium Gallicum*, where excerpts are organized by work. Fernández de la Cuesta González, *En la senda del "Florilegium Gallicum,"* 320 (*Met.* 10.519–20), 327 (*Fasti* 6.771–72). They are also found in Geremia da Montagnone's

Another Ovidian verse with proverbial qualities found several times in Petrarch's writings is "omne solum forti patria est" ("every land is home to the strong" [*Fasti* 1.493]).[22] Already in Ch. 3.3 we have seen the various new contexts in which this quotation took root: in anthologies and compendia, such as the *Florilegium Gallicum*, Geremia da Montagnone's *Compendium moralium notabilium* (under the heading on mental strength), and Bartolomeo da San Concordio's *Ammaestramenti* (under the heading on one's attachment to the homeland), and in prose writings, such as Brunetto Latini's *Tresor* and Dante's *De vulgari eloquentia* (in one of the few mentions of his exile in the treatise, and the closest fit to the verse's original context: the goddess Carmentis's words of consolation to her exiled son Evander). While in *De remediis utriusque fortune* Petrarch similarly places the passage from the *Fasti* in its exile context (II.67.10), in his letters he also turns to this Ovidian citation to use it as the idiomatic expression it had become. In a letter to Philippe de Cabassole (*Fam.* 11.1), the same addressee of the previously discussed letter *Fam.* XXIV.1, Petrarch cites the Ovidian expression "every land is home to the strong" — introduced with the phrase "as the Poet has said" — to console Philippe after his brother died away from home, reminding him that, if the whole world is indeed one's "patria" or homeland, his brother *did* die at home. Petrarch immediately follows the Ovidian quotation with one from St. Paul's letters (*Ad Hebr.* 13:14), stating that we all die outside our homeland, to eventually return to our true homeland. Petrarch goes out of his way to point out that the two quotations — and two traditions — only appear to contradict each other and can coexist.[23] This passage is one of Carol E. Quillen's examples of how

---

Compendium moralium notabilium, where both citations appear under the same heading "on the pressure of time" (p. 139; Pars 5, Liber 3, rubric 5).

22 Fabio Stok, "I *Fasti* di Ovidio tra Petrarca e Boccaccio," in *Ou pan ephemeron: scritti in memoria di Roberto Pretagostini offerti da colleghi, dottori e dottorandi di ricerca della Facoltà di Lettere e Filosofia (Vol. 1–2)*, ed. Cecilia Braidotti, Emanuele Dettori, and Eugenio Lanzillotta (Rome: Edizioni Quasar, 2009), 489–504, at 490.

23 *Fam.* 11.1.14–15: "Videntur hec sibi invicem adversa, sed non sunt; quisque pro diversitate loquentium satis breviter quod sentiebat expressit, et quamvis aliter atque aliter, uterque tamen vere. Si Poetam sequeris, non potuit frater tuus extra patriam suam mori; at si credis Apostolo, omnes extra patriam morimur, ut sic tandem in patriam revertamur. Et sane, utramvis sententiam sequaris, nichil invenies cur de fatalis zone distantia conqueraris" ("These two expressions may seem contradictory, but they are not; both men succinctly and sufficiently expressed their thoughts in the diversity of their speech, but even though they did so differently, they both spoke the truth. If you follow the Poet, your brother could not die outside his homeland; but if you believe the Apostle, we all die outside our homeland so that we can return to our homeland. And indeed, if you follow the words of either, you will find nothing to complain about because of the distant place of death"). Petrarch uses the same quotation in his plea to Pope Urban V to return the Holy

Petrarch blends pagan and Christian works in his letters. Quillen argued that such "harmonization suggests a range of topics on which Petrarch could use both pagan and Christian authors without focusing on the distinction."[24] On other occasions, Petrarch felt the need to defend the study of secular letters, as did some Church Fathers before him.[25] But the seamless joining of Christian and classical sources found in this letter is far from an exclusive hallmark of Petrarch's writings. Ovid has long been given similar standing as pagan philosophers, Christian authors, and biblical sources; in anthologies and compendia they could all, without distinction, weigh in a wide range of topics.

Take also the Ovidian phrase, "uideo meliora proboque, / deteriora sequor" ("I see and understand what is best, but pursue what is worse" [*Met.* 7.20–21]). These verses come from Medea's inner monologue at the opening of Book 7 of the *Metamorphoses* (7.11–71), in which she realizes she has many good reasons not to leave home and abandon her family for the stranger Jason, but finally decides otherwise. It is easy to see how the phrase "uideo meliora proboque, / deteriora sequor," taken by itself, can be applied in a variety of new contexts.[26] Petrarch uses the phrase, more paraphrasing than literally quoting it, in two letters, one to Andrea Dandolo, the doge of Venice, to dissuade a smart man from engaging in a stupid war with Genoa (*Fam.* XVIII.16), and one to Galeotto Spinola, a high-ranking official in Genoa, to convince him that Genoa should take the high road in the conflict (*Fam.* XX.3), making both instances straightforward applications of the Ovidian phrase in all its proverbial potential.[27] More remarkable is Petrarch's translation of the Ovidian expression in

---

See to Rome (*Sen.* VII 1), there coupled with Statius's phrase "Omne homini natale solum" (*Theb.* 8.320), but followed by a comment that echoes the content of St. Paul's quotation in *Fam.* 11.1: "Spero quod, dum terram aspicis, totus tibi orbis est patria, at dum celum, totus tibi hic mundus exilium est" ("I hope that, when you look at the earth, you see that the whole world is your homeland, or that the whole world is an exile" [*Sen.* VII 1, 96]).

24 Carol Everhart Quillen, *Rereading the Renaissance: Petrarch, Augustine, and the Language of Humanism* (Ann Arbor: University of Michigan Press, 1998), 124–25, with the citation at 124.

25 On this topic, see, for instance, Brenda Deen Schildgen, "Petrarch's Defense of Secular Letters, the Latin Fathers, and Ancient Roman Rhetoric," *Rhetorica* 11, no. 2 (1993): 119–34.

26 Even centuries later the phrase is still used: for instance, in Jean-Paul Sartre, *War Diaries: Notebooks from a Phoney War, November 1939–March 1940*, trans. Quintin Hoare (New York: Verso, 1999), 39.

27 *Fam.* XVIII.16.28–29: "Nam quid he litere profuerint, quid studia hec artium honestarum – quibus te pre cuntis etatis nostre ducibus abundantissimum fama predicat, nec mentitur – si cum meliora provideris, deteriora secteris?" ("What would be the advantage of these writings, or of the study of liberal arts, that fame, which does not lie, commends you for possessing more than all other doges of our age, if while you foresee what is best, will pursue the worst?"); *Fam.* XX.3.4: "dissoluta patrie membra componere,

the final verse of the *canzone I' vo pensando* (*Rvf* 264.136), the opening poem of the second part of the *Canzoniere*: "et veggio 'l meglio, et al peggior m'appiglio" ("and I see what is best, and I cling to what is the worst"). Here we can lay the context of Medea's story over Petrarch's use of the phrase, pointing to their shared feelings as conflicted lovers.[28] After all, Petrarch had already used another verse from Ovid's story of Medea in the same *canzone*. He opened the sixth stanza with the statement "Quel ch'i' fo veggio, et non m'inganna il vero / mal conosciuto, anzi mi sforza Amore" ("I see what I am doing, and the imperfect knowledge of the truth does not fool me, rather Love compels me" [*Rvf* 264.91–92]), which again translates the words of Ovid's Medea, this time in reply to Jason's promise of marriage: "quid faciam uideo, nec me ignorantia ueri / decipiet, sed amor" ("I see what I should do, and not ignorance of the truth would deceive me, but love" [*Met.* 7.92–93]). But while Petrarch turns twice to Medea's monologue in Ovid's *Metamorphoses* in this *canzone*, the two Ovidian quotations that he translated are of the kind included in anthologies.[29] Moreover, Marco Santagata has found several verses in Italian poetry similar to Petrarch's "et veggio 'l meglio, et al peggior m'appiglio": in a sonnet by Guittone d'Arezzo, in the anonymous didactic poem *Intelligenza*, and in Cecco d'Ascoli's *Acerba*.[30] Rather than concluding that these were all necessarily intertexts for Petrarch, to me this suggests that the Ovidian phrase had also entered the vernacular as an idiomatic expression.[31] In the previous chapter on the *Commedia*, I argued that Dante at times drew on Latin and vernacular readings of Ovid in

---

      ut meliora deterioribus imperent" ("put together the broken pieces of your homeland so that what is better rules over what is worse"). Roberta Antognini discussed Petrarch's use of the Ovidian quotation in *Fam.* XX.3 in *Il progetto autobiografico delle 'Familiares' di Petrarca*, 262–63, with reference to *Fam.* XVIII.16 and *Rvf* 264 at 263, n. 402.

28 Even though editors of Petrarch's *Canzoniere* without a fail cite the passage in Ovid's *Metamorphoses*, sometimes adding that these words belonged to Medea, a more in-depth comparison between the two texts is generally lacking.

29 Fernández de la Cuesta González, *En la senda del 'Florilegium Gallicum,'* 317.

30 Marco Santagata, *Per moderne carte: La biblioteca volgare di Petrarca* (Bologna: Il Mulino, 1990), 135–36, 229–30, n. 39. Compare Petrarch's "et veggio 'l meglio, et al peggior m'appiglio" (*Rvf* 264.136) with Guittone d'Arezzo, *De lui, cui di' ch'è morte*, v. 8: "ch'al peggio 'n tutto cum orbo s'appiglia"; *Intelligenza* 115.7–8: "e Brutto si ne tenne al su' consiglio, / e parvegli pigliar dal peggio 'l meglio"; Cecco d'Ascoli's *Acerba*, vv. 4296–97: "più non me ne impiglio, / salvando sempre lo miglior consiglio." (The citations are from *Per moderne carte*.)

31 As we have seen in Ch. 1.1, several Latin works that included citations from Ovid were translated into Italian (for instance the treatises of Albertano da Brescia and Bartolomeo da San Concordio's *Ammaestramenti*). Brunetto Latini's *Tresor*, written in French with plenty citations from Latin sources, already presented Ovid's words in the vernacular.

the same passage; here we might see an example of these different sources at work in Petrarch's poetry.

While both Latin and vernacular sources can be found for several passages in Petrarch's writings, these two traditions are often kept separate — in Petrarch's works and in scholarly writings about him. When scholars discuss Petrarch's library ("the first modern personal library"),[32] they mainly intend his Latin library: his possession and knowledge of Latin works, based on the Latin books he owned, the ones mentioned in his list of favorite books, and those he must have known or possessed.[33] Marco Santagata has pointed out that, in contrast, Petrarch's "modern library" (his "biblioteca volgare" of writings in Italian and other vernacular languages) was not an actual collection of texts, but mostly a "memorized treasure."[34] The reconstruction of such a library is thus an exercise very similar to the one undertaken in the previous chapters of this book, where the poetry itself becomes the best witness of influence. Scholars have identified many traces of memorized vernacular poetry in Petrarch's writings, coming from troubadour poetry, the *stil novo* poets, Dante's *Commedia* and lyric poetry, and other Italian poets.[35] What is of particular interest here, and will be discussed in the following sections, are the instances where these vernacular poets mentioned Ovid and included Ovidian material into their poetry, and how such passages entered Petrarch's poetry.

Ovid is an important source and reference point for Petrarch; and yet, a certain elusiveness about Ovid characterizes Petrarch's writings, similar to the way in which Dante heavily relies on Ovid's poems in the *Commedia*, but only mentions him twice (see Ch. 4.2 and 4.3). Petrarch includes Ovid in lists where he obviously belongs. In the *Rerum memorandarum libri*, Petrarch lists Ovid among the great minds of Latin antiquity, all alive at the same time: Varro, Cicero, Sallust, Livy, Seneca, Asinius Pollio, Vergil, Horace, and "innumerable others" (I 13, 7). In the *Triumphus Cupidinis*, Ovid represents the Latin love

---

32   Michelangelo Picone, "Dentro la biblioteca di Petrarca," in Brock, Furlan, and La Brasca, *La bibliothèque de Pétrarque*, 21–34, at 23: "la prima biblioteca personale moderna."

33   The main studies on Petrarch's Latin library are De Nolhac, *Pétrarque et l'humanisme*; Sabbadini, *Le scoperte dei codici latini e greci ne' secoli XIV e XV*.

34   Santagata, *Per moderne carte*, 12–13: "Con l'eccezione di pocchissimi esemplari, non fu una biblioteca materialmente posseduta: fu invece, quasi per intero, un tesoro memorizzato."

35   In addition to Santagata, *Per moderne carte*, on Petrarch and Dante's *Commedia*, see Peter Kuon, *L'aura dantesca: metamorfosi intertestuali nei 'Rerum vulgarium fragmenta'* (Florence: Franco Cesati, 2004); and Sara Sturm-Maddox, *Petrarch's Metamorphoses: Text and Subtext in the 'Rime sparse'* (Columbia: University of Missouri Press, 1985), which also discussed the influence of the *stil novo* poets. On the troubadours, see Maurizio Perugi, *Trovatori a Valchiusa: Un frammento della cultura provenzale del Petrarca* (Padua: Antenore, 1985).

poets, together with Catullus, Propertius, and Tibullus (IV.22–24), followed by the vernacular love poets (IV.28–60), a response of sorts to Dante's "bella scola" of six poets in Limbo (*Inf.* 4.94), in which he included himself. (Both Dante and Petrarch's passages ultimately go back to Ovid's autobiographical letter *Tristia* 4.10, the first such list.)[36] In the *Rerum memorandarum libri*, Petrarch calls Ovid "nostrorum secundus poetarum" ("the second among our poets" [III 73, 2]), but that honor is not really reflected in his writings, other than Ovid's inclusion in the above-mentioned lists. In the last book of the *Familiares* (XXIV), Petrarch composes letters for the famous classical authors to which he is indebted, but he does not include a letter to Ovid. Similarly, even though Ovid's poems (especially the *Metamorphoses*) are important sources in the *Canzoniere*, Petrarch names several classical poets directly by name (Catullus, Ennius, and Cicero; Vergil and Homer repeatedly), but never Ovid.

Some statements about Ovid can thus be found in Petrarch's writings, but taken together they fail to draw a precise and consistent picture. In his choice of which Ovidian poems to mention, Petrarch is not vastly different from the vernacular poets before him, who relied on Ovid's *Metamorphoses* (and, to a lesser extent, his exile letters) for content and phrases to imitate without much mention of their Ovidian sources, but openly and explicitly discussed his amatory works (see Ch. 2.3). Ovid and his "lascivious Muse" (the phrase used in the previously discussed letter to Philippe de Cabassole [*Fam.* XXIV.1.6]) sparked a few more statements from Petrarch, who is most vocal about Ovid's love poetry. In *De vita solitaria*, he first praises Ovid's great mind ("magni vir ingenii"), but then launches in an attack on his work and his person (lascivious, deceitful, a womanizer, desperate, and ruined). Petrarch calls the *Ars amatoria* an "insane" work ("insanum opus") and the right cause of his exile (II.XII).[37] Clearly referring to the *Remedia amoris*, Petrarch writes in the *De remediis utriusque fortune*

---

36   On this Ovidian letter and poets making lists of poets, see Ch. 4.2., and nn. 75 and 76 of the same chapter.

37   "Ille michi quidem magni vir ingenii videtur, sed lascivi et lubrici et prorsus mulierosi anime fuisse, quem conventus feminei delectarent usque adeo, ut in illus felicitatis sue apicem summamque reponeret. Itaque *Amatoriam artem* scribens, insanum opus et meritam (nisi fallor) exilii sui causam, non modo urbem Romam ceu matronarum puellarumque prefertilem querendam docet ab his qui ad illam insaniam, preter naturalem stimulum, artis quoque cuiusdam calcar adiciunt, sed loca etiam urbis et festa distinguit, quibus uberior materia sit furori" ("It seems to me that he was a man of great intellect, but of a lascivious and deceitful mind and certainly an effeminate one, who enjoyed meeting up with women so much that he placed in them the apex and sum of his happiness. And thus, in writing the *Ars amatoria*, an insane work and rightly (unless I am mistaken) the cause of his exile, he does not only teach that the city of Rome, overflowing with matrons and young girls, should be sought after by those who, in addition to the natural urge for

that Ovid is a "a curious doctor who is more in love with the disease than with the cure, and whose prescriptions are sometimes trivial and sometimes obscene, but nevertheless not ineffective" (1.69.40).[38] Petrarch assesses the efficacy of the *Remedia amoris*, like the Florentine poet Dante da Maiano (see Ch. 2.3), who wrote that "D'Ovidio ciò mi son miso a provare / che disse per lo mal d'Amor guarire, / e ciò ver' me non val mai che mentire" ("I have set out to test what Ovid prescribed to cure lovesickness, and according to me it is all lies" [*Amor mi fa sì fedelmente amare*, vv. 5–7]). Like vernacular poets before him, Petrarch evaluates Ovid's authority in matters of love. In the same work, Petrarch describes the *Ars amatoria* as the book in which Ovid teaches "a dishonest and superfluous art," adding, however, "something useful once in a while" (1.27.26).[39] Petrarch's admittance that something useful is to be found in the *Ars amatoria* brings to mind the Latin *accessus* tradition, where some writers of such introduction essays were keen to find something — anything — useful in Ovid's love poetry to make it accessible to its readers. Also in the *Rerum memorandarum libri*, Petrarch has words of praise for Ovid: he singles out his remarkable ability to write, a compliment that Petrarch had found in Seneca (II 20, 2).[40]

What to make of these inconsistent opinions and evaluations of Ovid, and of the silence with which Petrarch treats him at times? The passing of time

  this insanity, add the excitement of a certain art, but also lists the places and the occasions that provide even richer material for fury").
38 "Naso, mirus medicus, morbi amantior quam salutis, cuius quedam levia, quedam feda, nec inefficacia tamen est advertere."
39 "Meministi ut Naso — in eo libro quo inhonestam quidem ac supervacuam artem docet, utile tamen interdum aliquid interserit — amatrices monet, ut ob animi vitia celanda ludo hoc aut simili abstineant, ne conspecte ira tumide aut avaritia exhauste amatoribus displiceant suis. Quanto id viris dignius precipitur, ne non modo hominum sed Dei oculos omnia videntis et bonos animos moresque ingenuos amantis offendant!" ("As you know, Ovid, in that book in which he teaches a dishonest and superfluous art, nevertheless adds once in a while something useful; he advises women in love to stay away from games and similar activities in order to hide their vices of the mind, and so that they would not be seen around swollen with anger and worn out by greed, thus becoming unpleasant to their lovers. This is an even more dignified piece of advice for men so that they would avoid offense, not only to the eyes of men but also of God, who sees everything and loves honest minds and sincere manners.")
40 "puto nullum equari posse Nasoni poeti, qui — ut est apud Senecam — hoc seculum amatoriis non artibus tantum sed sententiis implevit. De exundanti quidem facultate carminum Ovidius ipse gloriatur, nec mendaciter" ("I think that no one can equal the poet Ovid, who, as we find in Seneca, greatly provided his times not only with the arts of love but also with *sententiae*. Ovid himself boasted about his excessive facility with poetry, and he was not mistaken"). On the passages discussed in this paragraph, see also Marcozzi, "Petrarca lettore di Ovidio," 74–79.

and changing tastes and intellectual interests alone cannot suffice as answer. Rather, with his comments and silences Petrarch seems to respond to the versatility of Ovid's poems: Petrarch compartmentalizes the Latin poet's works, making his judgments on the basis of the genre and the subject of his own writing. For instance, there is no place and praise for Ovid's love poetry in a treatise on contemplation as the *De vita solitaria*; the back-and-forth dialogue format of the *De remediis utriusque fortune* easily allows for different assessments of Ovid's poetry. Rather than being ambivalent about Ovid, Petrarch seems to recognize the versatility of Ovid, a poet who is hard to pin down and covers a lot of generic and thematic ground. And, as Luca Marcozzi has also argued, in that lies the fascination with the Latin poet: the "ambiguity" of Ovid offers a model for Petrarch's own writing.[41] It is worth repeating, though, as we have seen at various points in this section, that Petrarch's comments only mention the Latin poet and his works: while Petrarch's "Ovidian" library includes much more than only Ovid's poems in Latin, Petrarch does not explicitly recognize those other Ovidian works. In the following sections, the central question is how all of these Ovidian readings — by Ovid and by Ovid's readers, in Latin and in the vernacular languages — informed Petrarch's writing of the *Canzoniere*.

5.2 Just Like Apollo, Just Like Daphne: Similes and Identification

The story of Apollo and Daphne is the most visible and important Ovidian story in Petrarch's *Canzoniere*. Apollo's "primus amor" or "first love" — Ovid emphatically placed those two words at the beginning of the story's opening verse (*Met.* 1.452) — is the first love story in the *Metamorphoses* (1.452–567) and also the first story from Ovid's poem that enters into the *Canzoniere*. Petrarch introduces Amor with his arrows in *Per fare una leggiadra sua vendetta* (*Rvf* 2), and Apollo and the laurel, the post-transformation form of Daphne, in *Quando io movo i sospiri a chiamar voi* (*Rvf* 5), initiating a close engagement and identification with this Ovidian story that runs through the entire *Canzoniere*. Other Ovidian characters and stories make their appearance along the way. In this section and the next, I connect Petrarch's writing of the *Canzoniere* with his broad readings in the Ovidian tradition. The focus in this section is on the *Metamorphoses* and Petrarch's ways to identify with its characters (exploring different characters, from lover to beloved, from man to woman, but always

---

41 Marcozzi, "Petrarca lettore di Ovidio," 79.

returning to Apollo and Daphne) and how these identifications relate to the commentary tradition and previous readings of Ovidian stories in vernacular poetry and in Dante's *Commedia*.

Luca Marcozzi has studied more generally how Petrarch's readings on myth (Fulgentius, the Vatican Mythographers, and the pseudo-Lactantian *Narrationes*) have influenced his treatment of mythological material in the *Canzoniere*.[42] Especially the interpretations proposed in those prose writings about the laurel, the tree in which Daphne turns, are found in Petrarch's featuring of Apollo and Daphne. For instance, Petrarch gives great importance to the enduring quality of the laurel, often symbol for his literary career: the fact that the laurel cannot be destroyed, not even by Jupiter's thunderbolts, is a notion missing in Ovid's account in the *Metamorphoses*, but featured in other writings about the myth.[43] Albert Russell Ascoli has pointed out that "favola," the word Petrarch uses in the *Canzoniere*'s opening sonnet *Voi ch'ascoltate in rime sparse il suono* to describe himself — "Ma ben veggio or sì come al popol tutto / favola fui gran tempo" ("But now I see clearly how for a long time I was *the talk of the town*" [vv. 9–10; emphasis added]) — can also mean "exemplary fable."[44] As we have seen in Ch. 1.1, "fabula" is precisely the Latin word used in the commentary tradition to indicate Ovid's stories, and the first Italian translators of the *Metamorphoses* (Arrigo Simintendi and Giovanni Bonsignori) all use the Italian "favola," like Petrarch. But while Petrarch had several Ovidian commentaries in his possession or on his radar and his treatment of Ovidian material in the *Canzoniere* contains traces of such readings, he does not present consistent and comprehensive moral interpretations of Ovid's myths.[45] Marco Santagata has rightly warned against giving too much weight to the previous moralizing readings of Ovid's *Metamorphoses* in assessing Petrarch's treatment of Ovidian stories, cautioning not to create a *Petrarca moralizatus* after the *Ovidius moralizatus*.[46] While the connection with the commentary tradition is never completely absent, in what follows I instead suggest stronger ties between Petrarch's *Canzoniere* and vernacular poetry, and highlight Petrarch's

---

42   Marcozzi, *La biblioteca di Febo*.
43   On the passages in Pliny's *Natural History* and Pierre Bersuire's *Ovidius moralizatus* that describe this quality of the laurel, see Valerio Giovanelli, "Il mito di Apollo e Dafne e la tradizione esegetica delle moralizzazioni di Ovidio nel Canzoniere di Petrarca," *Carte italiane* 2, nos. 2–3 (2007): 23–34, at 29–30.
44   Albert Russell Ascoli, *"Favola fui": Petrarch Writes His Readers*, Bernardo Lecture Series, No. 17 (Binghamton: Center for Medieval & Renaissance Studies, State University of New York at Binghamton, 2010), 5–6, 19–20, n. 23.
45   Marcozzi, *La biblioteca di Febo*, 205–12, especially at 206–7, 258.
46   Santagata, *Per moderne carte*, 298, n. 34.

closer attention to the actual text of the *Metamorphoses* than to the surrounding commentary.

Like Dante in the *Commedia*, in the *Canzoniere* Petrarch works with the stories from Ovid's *Metamorphoses* in two main ways: there are the obvious, direct references, when Petrarch mentions an Ovidian character's name or provides enough details about their story that the identification is unmistakable; and then there are the more obscure, indirect passages, when Petrarch translates or paraphrases phrases from Ovidian stories without names or obvious clues that immediately give away the Ovidian origin of Petrarch's Italian verses. As Giuseppe Velli has noted, the *Canzoniere* is "a dense forest of word-for-word transfers from classical material."[47] Indeed, Ovidian material is found throughout the *Canzoniere*, with about half of the passages coming from the *Metamorphoses*. Among the many Ovidian characters with which Petrarch identifies himself or his lady, we find first and foremost Apollo and Daphne (*Met.* 1.452–567), followed by Phaethon and Cygnus (*Met.* 1.747–79, 2.1–400), Battus and Mercury (*Met.* 2.680–707), Diana and Actaeon (*Met.* 3.138–252), Echo and Narcissus (*Met.* 3.339–510), Perseus and Medusa (*Met.* 4.772–803), Tereus, Procne and Philomela (*Met.* 6.424–674), Medea and Jason (*Met.* 7.1–403), Byblis and Caunus (*Met.* 9.450–665), Orpheus and Eurydice (*Met.* 10.1–85), and Pygmalion (*Met.* 10.243–97).

These identifications with Ovidian characters and the dominating presence of Apollo and Daphne — the obvious links to Ovid's Latin poem — easily overshadow other connections with the vernacular Ovidian tradition, which are less discernable but not at all absent. In the *Canzoniere*, Narcissus and Pyramus and Thisbe, the beloved Ovidian characters of the troubadours and the first generations of Italian poets, fade into the background (Narcissus) or virtually disappear (Pyramus and Thisbe). In the previous chapter, we have seen how Dante used them as signposts of the lyric tradition in the *Commedia*. Petrarch, however, grants these Ovidian characters very little attention, as if he is unwilling to explicitly reveal his debt to the vernacular tradition.

Petrarch does not feature Pyramus and Thisbe in the *Canzoniere* in the same way that vernacular poets did before him: in similes explicitly comparing themselves with the Ovidian lovers. Instead, he embeds translated and paraphrased verses from their story in Ovid's *Metamorphoses* much less noticeably into his poems. But is the verse "quoque magis tegitur, tectus magis aestuat ignis" ("the more they kept it hidden, the more the fire burned" [*Met.* 4.64]),

---

47   Giuseppe Velli, "La memoria poetica del Petrarca," *Italia medioevale e umanistica* 19 (1976): 173–207, at 199: "una fitta selva di trasferimenti *mot à mot* di materiali classici." This citation is also included in Santagata, *Per moderne carte*, 303. See Petrarca, *Canzoniere*, ed. Santagata, 1566–67, for his list of Ovidian passages in the *Canzoniere*.

which describes the growing intensity of Pyramus and Thisbe's hidden love, still Ovid's? This exact verse was paraphrased in the popular twelfth-century comedy *Pamphilus* (see Ch. 1.1).[48] In the *canzone Ben mi credea passar mio tempo omai* (*Rvf* 207), Petrarch's rendition of the phrase in Italian — not a literal translation, but unmistakably modeled after the Latin verse — amounts to not much more than an intertextual flourish: "Chiusa fiamma è più ardente; et se pur cresce, / in alcun modo più non pò celarsi" ("A hidden flame burns the most; and if it grows, it can no longer conceal itself in any way" [*Rvf* 207.66–67]). Ovid's original verse demonstrates its wide applicability: to those in the know, Pyramus and Thisbe are lurking in the background, but first and foremost the expression is a recognizable sentiment well suited to Petrarch's *canzone* about his own enduring love pain and concealed suffering.

Petrarch illustrates the wide application of this Ovidian phrase also in the *ballata Quel foco ch'i' pensai che fosse spento* (*Rvf* 55), where he renders it as "Non fur mai tutte spente, a quel ch'i' veggio, / ma ricoperte alquanto le faville" ("They were never completely extinguished, as I see it, but the sparks somewhat re-covered" [*Rvf* 55.4–5]).[49] While in this *ballata* Petrarch draws on several thematic threads of the *Canzoniere* (his "error," his intense and long suffering, the trickster Love who ensnared him again in his traps), ultimately the entire poem is constructed around the image of the rekindling flame. The verse from Ovid's story of Pyramus and Thisbe expresses that sentiment, as does this comparison from the story of Medea and Jason (*Met.* 7.79–81):

> utque solet uentis alimenta adsumere quaeque
> parua sub inducta latuit scintilla fauilla
> crescere et in ueteres agitata resurgere uires
>
> [Just as a tiny spark hidden under the ashes, when fed by the wind, grows and regains its previous strength]

Petrarch implicitly places himself in Medea's situation, a story not unfamiliar to him. (In *I' vo pensando* [*Rvf* 264], Petrarch translates two phrases from Medea's

---

48 *Pamphilus*, vv. 21–22: "Exstimo mostrari melius; iam conditus ignis / acrior; effusus partior esse solet" ("I believe it is better to show it; a hidden fire normally becomes stronger, while it is weaker when spread out"). Gustave Cohen did not point to Ovid, but called it "a common idea in courtly romances ("[i]dée fréquente chez les romanciers courtois") in *La 'comédie' latine en France au XIIe siècle*, ed. Gustave Cohen, 2 vols. (Paris: Société d'édition Les Belles-lettres, 1931), 2: 195, n. 1.

49 On Petrarch's use of this phrase, see, for instance, Francesco Petrarca, *Canzoniere*, ed. Marco Santagata, rev. ed. (Milan: Mondadori, 2004), 295–96.

monologue and turns them into his own.) The same spark comparison from the Medea story had also interested Dante, who used it in the Cacciaguida episode in *Paradiso* (see Ch. 4.2). While Petrarch maintains the amorous context of the comparison in the *Canzoniere*, Dante stripped this connotation from the passage, comparing the light that Cacciaguida, a saint in paradise, emits to the growing spark (*Par.* 16.28–30):

> Come s'avviva a lo spirar d'i venti
> carbone in fiamma, così vid' io quella
> luce risplendere a' miei blandimenti

> [As at the blowing of the winds a piece of coal becomes aflame, so I saw that light shine at my charming words.]

Petrarch, like Dante and others before him, can take an Ovidian phrase about love out of its original context and give it a different meaning. But in his treatment of the Medea story, all the sentences that Petrarch selected to include into the *Canzoniere* maintain a close conceptual connection with Ovid's account. Also the verse from the Pyramus and Thisbe story that appears twice in the *Canzoniere* expresses the same idea as it did in the *Metamorphoses*: a reflection on the nature of love. But in the end, the vernacular darlings Pyramus and Thisbe are only evoked, and never seen.

While Petrarch is not interested in granting Pyramus and Thisbe any recognizable presence in the *Canzoniere*, the Ovidian lovers were on the poet's radar. Petrarch included them in the *Triumphus Cupidinis*: "vedi Piramo e Tisbe inseme a l'ombra" ("See Pyramus and Thisbe in the shade" [III.20]). In his Latin epic poem *Africa* (VI.65–70), the two lovers appear walking together in Hades in the field of dead lovers, bringing Dante's couple Francesca and Paolo to mind: "mediaque duos in valle videres / Solivagos lateri herentes alternaque collo / Brachia tendentes" ("and you could see the two of them in the middle of the valley, wandering around together both with their arms draped around the neck of the other" [VI.65–67]).[50] But it is in the *rime estravaganti* (the poems that did not make the cut in the *Canzoniere*) that we see Petrarch's willingness to engage much more openly with Ovidian material.[51] In *Sì come il padre del*

---

50 For the connection between Pyramus and Thisbe in the *Africa* and Dante's Francesca and Paolo, see Michele Feo, "Petrarca," *Enciclopedia Dantesca* (Rome: Istituto della Enciclopedia Italiana, 1973), consulted at http://www.treccani.it/enciclopedia/francesco-petrarca_(Enciclopedia-Dantesca)/.

51 On Petrarch's *rime estravaganti*, see Justin Steinberg, "Petrarch's Damned Poetry and the Poetics of Exclusion · *Rime disperse*," in *Petrarch: A Critical Guide to the Complete Works*,

folle Fetonte (Paolino 10), Petrarch features a parade of named Ovidian characters (including Pyramus and Thisbe) and builds his poem around several similes, which for a long time was the most common way to feature Ovidian characters in vernacular lyric poetry. The addressee is Sennuccio del Bene, fellow poet and long-time friend of Petrarch, who is mentioned several times in the *Canzoniere* (*Rvf* 108.13, 112.1, 113.1, 144.12, 287.1): Petrarch includes his name in the final two verses (vv. 15–16), the additional verses that turn this poem into a *sonetto caudato*, a sonnet with a "cauda" or tail. This poem lends itself well to draw distinctions between Petrarch's use of Ovidian material in the *rime estravaganti* and in the *Canzoniere*. Scholars have often reflected on why certain poems did not make Petrarch's selection in the *Canzoniere*.[52] And at first sight *Sì come il padre del folle Fetonte* seems to provide some good reasons. Petrarch infused a shot of Ovidian material in this poem, in contrast with the more constrained trickle of such material in the *Canzoniere*. He also relies heavily on the simile to feature Ovid's characters, a rhetorical device not often used in the *Canzoniere*. At the same time, a careful reading of *Sì come il padre del folle Fetonte* (included in full below) reveals more connections with previous Ovidian readings in vernacular lyric poetry and Dante's *Commedia*, as well as with other passages in the *Canzoniere*.

> Sì come il padre del folle Fetonte
> quando prima sentì la punta d'oro
> per quella Dafne che divenne alloro,
> de le cui fronde poi si ornò la fronte;
>
> e come il sommo Giove nel bel monte
> per Europa trasformossi in toro;
> e com' per Tisbe tinse il bianco moro
> Piramo del suo sangue innanzi al fonte;

---

ed. Victoria Kirkham and Armando Maggi (Chicago: Chicago University Press, 2009), 85–100. On this particular exchange with Sennuccio, see Joseph A. Barber, "Il sonetto CXIII e gli altri sonetti a Sennuccio," *Lectura Petrarce* 2 (1982): 21–39; Marcozzi, *La biblioteca di Febo*, 234, n. 177. On the dating of the poem, see Petrarca, *Trionfi, Rime estravaganti, Codice degli abbozzi*, ed. Vinicio Pacca and Laura Paolino (Milan: Mondadori, 1996), 688–89.

52 On the general tenor in the discussions of Petrarch's *rime estravaganti* (that is, the idea that they were excluded from the *Canzoniere* because they were inferior or work in progress), see Steinberg, "Petrarch's Damned Poetry and the Poetics of Exclusion," 92. On Petrarch's Ovidian poems in and outside the *Canzoniere*, see, for instance, Sara Sturm-Maddox, *Petrarch's Laurels* (University Park: Pennsylvania University Press, 1992), 4–6.

PETRARCH'S SCATTERED OVIDIAN VERSES 241

> così son vago de la bella Aurora,
> unica del sol figlia in atto e in forma;
> s'ella seguisse del suo padre l'orma!
>
> Ma tutti i miei pensier' convien che dorma
> finché la notte non si discolora:
> così, perdendo il tempo, aspetto l'ora.
>
> E se innanzi di me tu la vedesti,
> io ti prego, Sennuccio, che mi desti.

[Just as the father of the foolish Phaethon, when he first felt the point of the golden arrow for Daphne, who became a laurel with whose leaves he later adorned his face; and as the mighty Jupiter on the beautiful mountain was transformed into a bull; and as for Thisbe Pyramus tainted the white mulberry with his blood in front of a spring; so do I desire the beautiful Aurora, the only daughter of the sun in her movements and beauty; may she follow her father's footsteps. But all my thoughts need to rest until the night does not fade: so, letting the time go by, I wait for the right moment. And if you see her before me, I beg of you, Sennuccio, to wake me.]

Sì come il padre del folle Fetonte starts out following the traditional structure of the fourteen-verse-long sonnet, where the first eight verses (two quatrains or the octave) and the following six verses (two tercets or the sextet) belong together, both in form and content.[53] Petrarch features three very similar comparisons with Ovidian couples in the first eight verses of his poem: he introduces each simile with the preposition "like" ("come") in the same metrical position ("Sì come ... / e come ... / e com' ..." [vv. 1, 5, 7]); he mentions both the male and female Ovidian characters by name in all three similes; and he includes the transformations that occurred during their encounters. The first is the longest and most complex comparison (vv. 1–4), a mini-retelling of the story of Apollo and Daphne, from the arrow that made Apollo fall in love to Daphne's transformation into a laurel tree and the laurel leaves adorning his head, with a reference-within-the-reference, identifying Apollo as "the father of the foolish Phaethon" (v. 1);[54] next, a comparison with Jupiter, who transformed himself

---

53   On this classic divide in structure and content, see Ch. 2, n. 26.
54   In these first verses about Apollo and Daphne, Petrarch stays most closely to Ovid's Latin text: the golden point ("punta d'oro" [v. 2]) refers to Love's golden arrow that makes one

("trasformossi") into a bull for Europa (vv. 5–6);[55] and last, a comparison featuring Pyramus and Thisbe, describing how the blood that Pyramus spilled for Thisbe colored the white mulberry tree in front of a fountain (vv. 7–8).

In *Sì come il padre del folle Fetonte*, Petrarch draws on both the content and the language of Ovid's story of Pyramus and Thisbe: the two verses dedicated to the couple (vv. 7–8) translate a verse from Ovid's poem: "morus … gelido contermina fonti" ("a mulberry … bordering an ice-cold spring" [*Met.* 4.90]). Dante had also included the Ovidian lovers in the *Commedia*, featuring them at a crucial point in his poem, in the Earthly Paradise: first, in a simile comparing the pilgrim's reaction to hearing Beatrice's name to Thisbe calling Pyramus's name before he dies (*Purg.* 27.37–42); further on Beatrice brings up Pyramus again, also mentioning the mulberry tree (*Purg.* 33.67–72) (see Ch. 4.2). Moreover, Dante had also slipped a more concealed reference to the Ovidian lovers into *Inf.* 5, the circle of lustful souls, where the pilgrim encountered Francesca and Paolo (*Inf.* 5.73–142).[56] In *Sì come il padre del folle Fetonte*, Petrarch at his turn verbally links Pyramus and Thisbe with the Dantean lovers: his phrase "tinse … / … del suo sangue" (vv. 7–8) retakes Dante's verse from Francesca's speech, "noi che tignemmo il mondo di sanguigno" ("we, who stained the world with blood" [*Inf.* 5.90]).[57] If Dante in *Inf.* 5 wanted to signal a connection between the two pairs of tragic lovers whose love led to death, Petrarch certainly got the message.

After three vignettes of Ovidian transformation in the first eight verses in *Sì come il padre del folle Fetonte*, the poem's formal break initially marks the

---

    fall in love (*Met.* 1.466–71); the use of "prima" in the verse "quando prima sentì la punta d'oro" (v. 2) echoes the introductory verse of the story in Ovid's *Metamorphoses*, "Primus amor Phoebi" (*Met.* 1.452; emphasis added); the laurel crown framing Apollo's head (v. 4) is also mentioned in Ovid's account (*Met.* 1.558–59).

55 Ovid tells the story of Jupiter and Europa in *Met.* 2.836–75, 3.1–27. In this second comparison, Petrarch mainly follows the content, and not the language, of Ovid's account.

56 Dante opens the catalogue of lustful souls in *Inf.* 5 with the Babylonian queen Semiramis. While Dante draws on Paulus Orosius's account in the *Historia* to describe Semiramis in the *Inferno*, in the *De monarchia* he explicitly links Semiramis and her husband to Pyramus and Thisbe, citing the opening verse from Ovid's story about the two lovers, which identifies Babylonia as their hometown. See also Ch. 4.3.

57 There is another verbal connection between Petrarch's poem and the episode in Dante's *Inferno*: Petrarch describes how Aurora (as the light at night) loses color ("si discolora" [*Sì come il padre del folle Fetonte*, v. 13]), just like Francesca recounts how reading with Paolo "scolorocci il viso" ("drained the color from our faces" [*Inf.* 5.131]). As Paolino pointed out, Petrarch also describes this experience in the *Canzoniere*: "mi discoloro" (e.g., *Rvf* 291.3, *Rvf* 362.6). See *Trionfi, Rime estravaganti, Codice degli abbozzi*, ed. Pacca and Paolino, 691, note to v. 13. Ultimately, the pale lover is a very Ovidian concept, as Ovid wrote in the *Ars amatoria*: "palleat omnis amans" ("every lover should be pale" [1.729]).

transition from the world of Ovid's characters to the poet's own contemporary situation.[58] At verse nine, Petrarch moves on from Apollo and Daphne, Jupiter and Europa, and Pyramus and Thisbe to his own situation with his lady: "così son vago." This approach to Ovidian material is most similar to the sonnet *Guardando la fontana il buo-Narciso*, where the anonymous poet dedicated the quatrains to the description of Narcissus, and in the tercets turned to his own situation, stating, "Così cred'eo fenir similemente" ("I believe I will end in the same manner" [v. 9]) (see Ch. 2.1). Moreover, in both poems we find "così" at the beginning of the verse and the verb tense changes from past to present: "cred'" (*Guardando la fontana il buo-Narciso*, v. 9); "son" (*Sì come il padre del folle Fetonte*, v. 9). But while the anonymous poet of *Guardando la fontana il buo-Narciso* used the formal break in the sonnet structure to conclusively move from the classical world inhabited by the Ovidian character Narcissus to his own contemporary situation, in Petrarch's poem this division is less straightforward.

In *Sì come il padre del folle Fetonte*, Petrarch blurs the sharp lines that similes with Ovidian characters in vernacular poetry often drew between the world (the past) of the *Metamorphoses* and the contemporary, present situation of the vernacular poets. At first, Petrarch continues the poem in the present tense ("son" [v. 9], "aspetto" [v. 14]), distancing himself in time from the Ovidian characters with which he compares himself and whose actions all occurred in the past ("sentì," "divenne," "si ornò," "trasformossi," "tinse" [vv. 2, 3, 4, 6, 7]). He also announces, after having identified three pairs of Ovidian lovers in the quatrains, the name of his lady: Aurora ("così son vago de la bella Aurora" [v. 9]). Vernacular poets often employ *senhals* or code names to mask the true identity of their ladies. Aurora here takes the place of Laura in the *Canzoniere*, a name mentioned only four times in the entire collection, but often alluded to through the puns on her name.[59] (Aurora also appears a few times in the *Canzoniere*, most notably in the sonnet *Quand'io veggio dal ciel scender l'Aurora*, where "l'Aurora" [*Rvf* 291.1] rhymes with "Ivi è Laura ora" [*Rvf* 291.4]).[60]

---

58   The formal break in sonnets occurs at verse nine, where the quatrains becom tercets and the rhyme scheme changes.

59   Laura's name is found in *Rvf* 239.8, *Rvf* 239.23, *Rvf* 291.4, and *Rvf* 332.50. The poem that mentions Laura's name twice, the *sestina Là ver' l'aurora, che sì dolce l'aura* (*Rvf* 239), has both Aurora and "l'aura," the pun on Laura's name, in its opening verse. In the sonnet *Quando 'l sol bagna in mar l'aurato carro* (*Rvf* 223), Petrarch does not mention their names, but combines the puns on both Aurora and Laura in the verse "Vien poi l'aurora, et l'aura fosca inalba" ("Then dawn arrives and lights up the dark air" [*Rvf* 223.12]).

60   Petrarca, *Trionfi, Rime estravaganti, Codice degli abbozzi*, ed. Pacca and Paolino, 691, note to v. 9. While not mentioning Sennuccio, the addressee of several other poems in the

But as the poem continues, it becomes clear that Aurora is not a simple *senhal*: Petrarch describes her as the "only daughter of the sun" ("unica del sol figlia" [v. 10]), thus placing her back into the Ovidian world that he extensively described in the quatrains. He also expresses the desire that she follow her father's example (v. 11), that is, to arrive at sunrise. Cino da Pistoia's sonnet *Amor, che viene armato a doppio dardo* comes to mind, where Cino also drew on the story of Apollo and Daphne (see Ch. 3.3). In that poem, Cino mixed the classical past and the present: he described how Love hit Apollo, his addressee Gherardo, and himself (all three of them) with the arrow of gold, and likewise, Daphne and the poets' ladies with the arrow of lead that pushes love away.[61] Sennuccio del Bene's reply *La bella Aurora, nel mio orizonte* (Paolino 10a) contains the same blending of both worlds: Aurora does not simply appear to him, but "emerges from the mountain" ("uscire del monte" [v. 4]).

This blending of the world of the *Metamorphoses* and his own is a feature that Petrarch carried over into the *Canzoniere*. In the sonnet *In mezzo di duo amanti honesta altera* (*Rvf* 115), for instance, the poet delays the identification of the two lovers who appear side by side in the opening verse, clarifying later that they are Sol (Apollo's other name) and the poet himself, also operating on the same level (*Rvf* 115.1–4):

> In mezzo di duo amanti honesta altera
> vidi una donna, et quel signor co lei
> che fra gli uomini regna et fra li dèi;
> et da l'un lato il Sole, io da l'altro era.

> [In between the two lovers I saw an honest and haughty lady, and with her that lord who rules over men and gods; and on one side was the Sun, I on the other.]

Also in the sonnet *Apollo, s'anchor vive il bel desio* (*Rvf* 34), another poem in the *Canzoniere* that deals explicitly with the story of Apollo and Daphne, the two lovers appear together. The poet first addresses Apollo, asking him to "now defend your honored and sacred leaves" ("difendi or l'onorata et sacra fronde" [*Rvf* 34.7]), a reference to Ovid's story (*Met.* 1.565). Petrarch then features them

---

Canzoniere, Petrarch probably also wrote the sonnet *Quand'io veggio dal ciel scender l'Aurora* (*Rvf* 291) for Sennuccio.

61 As also pointed out in Ch. 3.3, the description of Love's double ammunition comes straight out of Ovid's *Metamorphoses* (1.466–71), but other vernacular poets besides Cino had referred to the two arrows in their poetry. Petrarch mentions the arrow of gold in *Sì come il padre del folle Fetonte*, v. 2: "quando prima sentì la punta d'oro."

together, fully blending their two worlds: he does not employ a simile (I am *like* Apollo) or a metaphor (I *am* Apollo) — he is *with* Apollo (*Rvf* 34.12–14):

> sì vedrem poi per meraviglia inseme
> seder la donna nostra sopra l'erba,
> et far de le sue braccia a se stessa ombra.

[So we will see a marvel together: our lady sitting on the grass and shading herself with her arms.]

Like Aurora in the sonnet exchange between Petrarch and Sennuccio del Bene, the female character (Daphne/Laura) in this sonnet — here even called "*our* lady" (*Rvf* 34.13; emphasis added) — possesses characteristics belonging to the classical world where Daphne originally appeared.[62] Their lady sits in the shade that her branches provide (*Rvf* 34.14), a reference to Daphne's transformation into a laurel tree (*Met.* 1.548–52).[63] The fact that both names are as good as absent in the *Canzoniere* (Daphne's name never appears, and Laura's only four times) facilitates the existence of this hybrid figure, who could be both or either.[64] Throughout the collection, Petrarch's "donna" shares many characteristics with the Ovidian Daphne: in addition to the metamorphosis into a laurel tree, Peter Hainsworth identified eight other elements from Ovid's account in the *Metamorphoses* that also define Laura, including her hair, as well as the woods and rivers in Thessaly that Petrarch transports to the Avignon region.[65] Petrarch sketches his lady with those fragments here and there — all fragments, as especially Nancy J. Vickers has pointed out: we never get a complete picture of Laura, definitely not in one poem.[66]

---

62 As Teodolinda Barolini pointed out, in this sonnet Petrarch establishes a temporal order ("or" [*Rvf* 34.7], "poi" [*Rvf* 34.8]) only to then cancel it. See "The Self in the Labyrinth of Time · *Rerum vulgarium fragmenta*," in Kirkham and Maggi, *Petrarch: A Critical Guide to the Complete Works*, 33–62, at 41. On Petrarch's manipulation of time throughout the *Canzoniere*, see Barolini, "The Making of a Lyric Sequence: Time and Narrative in Petrarch's *Rerum vulgarium fragmenta*," in Modern Language Notes 104 (1989): 1–38.

63 As much in Petrarch's poetry, this is not a rigid rule he applies in featuring his lady. For instance, as Santagata also pointed out, in the *sestina Giovene donna sotto un verde lauro* (*Rvf* 30) the lady and the tree are uncoupled in the opening verse: "a young lady under a green laurel" (Petrarch, *Canzoniere*, ed. Santagata, 169). Also in *Quel, che d'odore e di color vincea* (*Rvf* 337), "il mio signor ... et la mia dea" ("my lord and my goddess"), or Love and his lady sit together in the shade of the laurel tree (*Rvf* 337.4–8).

64 Peter R. J. Hainsworth, "The Myth of Daphne in the *Rerum vulgarium fragmenta*," Italian Studies 34 (1979): 28–44, at 36: "Laura oscillates between the human and the arboreal."

65 Hainsworth, "The Myth of Daphne," 30–33.

66 Nancy J. Vickers, "Diana Described: Scattered Woman and Scattered Rhyme," *Critical Inquiry* 8, no. 2 (1981): 265–79, at 266. Philip Hardie referred to the "absent

In the only explicit mention of Narcissus in the *Canzoniere*, in the sonnet *Il mio adversario in cui veder solete* (*Rvf* 45), Petrarch gestures toward this mixture of the clearly classical identifiers of the world created by Ovid and the present of his own writing:

> Il mio adversario in cui veder solete
> gli occhi vostri ch'Amore e 'l ciel honora,
> colle non sue bellezze v'innamora
> più che 'n guisa mortal soavi et liete.
>
> Per consiglio di lui, donna, m'avete
> scacciato del mio dolce albergo fora:
> misero exilio, avegna ch'i' non fôra
> d'abitar degno ove voi sola siete.
>
> Ma s'io v'era con saldi chiovi fisso,
> non devea specchio farvi per mio danno,
> a voi stessa piacendo, aspra et superba.
>
> Certo, se vi rimembra di Narcisso,
> questo et quel corso ad un termino vanno,
> benché di sì bel fior sia indegna l'erba.

[My adversary in which you often see your eyes, which Love and heaven honor, makes you fall in love not with his own beauty, sweet and delightful in more than mortal guise. Following his advice, lady, you have driven me away from my sweet abode: miserable exile, though I might not be worthy to stay where you alone are. But if I had been fixed there with firm nails, a mirror would not have made you harsh and proud about my harm, you who like yourself. For sure, if you remember Narcissus, this and that course lead to one end, even though the grass is not worthy of such a beautiful flower.]

The mirror ("specchio" [*Rvf* 45.10]) in which Laura admires herself is the poet's "adversary" (*Rvf* 45.1) — if he had obtained a firm position in her heart, the mirror would not have had that effect (*Rvf* 45.9–10). If the explicit mention of the

---

presences" of Ovid's Daphne in the *Canzoniere* in "Ovid into Laura: Absent presences in the *Metamorphoses* and Petrarch's *Rime sparse*," in *Ovidian Transformations: Essays on the 'Metamorphoses' and its Reception*, ed. Philip Hardie, Alessandro Barchiesi, and Stephen Hinds (Cambridge: Cambridge Philological Society, 1999), 254–70.

mirror, a key feature in previous lyric poems about Narcissus, was not enough to call up the Ovidian character,[67] Petrarch spells out Laura's self-love in the clearest narcissistic formulation: "you like yourself, harsh and proud about my harm" (*Rvf* 45.10–11), and makes Laura and Narcissus share the same quality: Laura is "superba" (*Rvf* 45.11), which matches Ovid's mention of Narcissus's "superbia" (*Met.* 3.354).[68] In the concluding verses, Petrarch drives home the point: he first explicitly brings to mind Narcissus (*Rvf* 45.11), and then, more cryptically, merges their paths in the present ("vanno" [*Rvf* 45.13]), writing that both Narcissus and Laura are going to end up the same way. The mention of the flower (*Rvf* 45.14) — Narcissus's final transformation — clarifies that this shared "termino" (*Rvf* 45.13) would mean their death. The previous lyric poems on Narcissus often mentioned the same key moments of the story (Narcissus staring at the reflecting pool or mirror, his folly, and his death) and compared Narcissus, losing himself in his self-love, to the vernacular poets, losing themselves in their love for their ladies.[69] By casting Laura and not himself in the role of the self-obsessed Narcissus, Petrarch crafts an analogy between his lady and Narcissus that is closer to Ovid's account than previous such comparisons in vernacular poems. This different identification leaves Petrarch room to add the conclusion of Ovid's account, Narcissus's transformation into a flower (*Rvf* 45.14), which is absent in those earlier vernacular poems on Ovid. Presented as a punishment in Ovid's account (*Met.* 3.406), the medieval

---

67 The mirror appears together with Narcissus in Bernart de Ventadorn's *Can vei la lauzeta mover*, Peirol's *Mout m'entremis de chantar voluntiers*, the anonymous *Aissi m'ave cum a l'enfan petit*, Rinaldo d'Aquino's *Poi li piace ch'avanzi suo valore*, Chiaro Davanzati's *Come Narcissi, in sua spera mirando*, the anonymous *Guardando la fontana il buo·Narciso*. These poems are discussed in more detail in Ch. 2.1.

68 In the commentaries on the *Metamorphoses*, similar terms are used: Arnulf of Orléans uses "arrogantia"; John of Garland, "cupidus gloria rerum"; the *Roman de la Rose*, "Narcisus tresorgueilleux"; and Giovanni del Virgilio, "gloria." Only Pierre Bersuire uses the same term as Ovid in the *Metamorphoses*, "superbia," but only once — the main term in his explanation of Narcissus is "gloria." See n. 70 for the full references to these passages. Petrarch features Narcissus also in the *Triumphus Cupidinis*, together with Echo (11.145–50). There Narcissus is called "il vano amador" ("the vain lover" [11.145]) and after his transformation "un bel fior" ("a beautiful flower") — as in *Il mio adversario in cui veder solete* (*Rvf* 45.14) — but one "senza alcun frutto" ("without any fruit" [11.148]). Echo's transformation into "un duro sasso asciutto" ("a hard, dry stone" [11.150]) is included in the *canzone Nel dolce tempo de la prima etade*, discussed further on in this section.

69 See the discussion in Ch. 2.2. For a discussion of the Narcissus simile in Petrarch's *Il mio adversario in cui veder solete* and Bernart de Ventadorn's *Can vei la lauzeta mover*, see Andrea Poli, "Bernart de Ventadorn in Petrarca," *Filologia e critica* 18, no. 1 (1993): 20–44, at 28–32. The shared mention of exile further tightens the connection between the two poems.

commentaries glossed this transformation with relative consensus: the flower renders Narcissus's pursuit (be it understood as arrogance, a love of earthly fame, or a focus on physical beauty) futile and temporary.[70] Petrarch does not go that far: the mention of the grass being unworthy of her beauty suggests her ultimate difference (*Rvf* 45.14).[71]

With Narcissus drawing all the attention to himself, it is easy to forget that his story features another character, another lover in addition to Narcissus: the nymph Echo, who had fallen for Narcissus but was rejected. With Laura featured in the role of Narcissus, the poet can take the place of Echo, as Giuseppe Mazzotta noted.[72] Like the nymph in Ovid's account, the poet is being ignored, driven away from his lady's presence. This second comparison is not as fleshed out in the poem as the one between Narcissus and Laura. But in this striking use of Narcissus, Petrarch seems interested in exploring roles newer than the ones the vernacular lyric poets had thus far assigned to themselves in their comparisons with the Ovidian character.

That is not to say that Petrarch was unfamiliar or unwilling to put forward the more traditional vernacular reading of Narcissus. As was the case for Pyramus and Thisbe, the greater importance of this Ovidian figure again lies outside the *Canzoniere*; this time in the *Secretum*, Petrarch's imagined dialogue between himself (Franciscus) and St. Augustine (Augustinus). Gur Zak has argued that the myth of Narcissus is the "focal point around which the entire dialogue revolves."[73] The struggle at the core of the dialogue, as Zak explained, is between two models of Narcissus, between St. Augustine's self-portrait of a corrected Narcissus and the "more fatalistic" portrayal of Narcissus from Ovid's

---

70 According to Arnulf of Orléans, Narcissus's self-love means that he prefers his own excellence to anything else; his death and transformation into a flower made this arrogant person useless like a flower (Ghisalberti, "Arnolfo d'Orléans," 209). John of Garland, on the other hand, interprets Narcissus's self-love as love for glory in the world, which, like the flower he turned into, will not last forever (vv. 163–66). Giovanni del Virgilio takes a similar stance, understanding Narcissus as a famous person whose love for his own shadow means that he relies too much on fame (Ghisalberti, *Giovanni del Virgilio*, 53). His transformation into a flower turns him into a fleeting object as well.

71 Giuseppe Mazzotta's reading of the conclusion is more negative: with the analogy between Narcissus and Laura collapsed, she will now "exist in the non-place of imagination." See "The *Canzoniere* and the Language of the Self," in *The Worlds of Petrarch* (Durham: Duke University Press, 1993), 58–79, at 66.

72 Mazzotta, "The *Canzoniere* and the Language of the Self," 67: "an emblem of the disembodied voice alluding to its own hollowness."

73 Gur Zak, "A Humanist in Exile: Ovid's Myth of Narcissus and the Experience of Self in Petrarch's *Secretum*," in Keith and Rupp, *Metamorphosis: The Changing Face of Ovid in Medieval and Early Modern Europe*, 179–98, at 180.

Metamorphoses, with the latter ultimately dominating.[74] Put in terms of the Ovidian tradition, in the descriptions of how the first-person (male) author relates to Narcissus in the *Secretum*, Petrarch draws on elements from both lyrical poetry (where vernacular poets compared themselves to Narcissus, and Narcissus's self-love to the love for their ladies) and the commentary tradition (where Narcissus's self-love stands for something negative to be corrected, be it arrogance, love for fleeting things, glory, physical beauty, and so on). When St. Augustine asks Petrarch if the story of Narcissus does not terrify him, his further explanation clarifies what this misguided love means in the *Secretum*: to be attracted to physical beauty only, to the "external appearance of the skin" (*Secr.* II.3.2). St. Augustine's point of view is found in the *Canzoniere* at times: for instance, in the realization that "cosa bella mortal passa et non dura" ("a beautiful mortal thing passes and does not last" [*Rvf* 248.8]). But ultimately, the conclusion of the *Secretum* is reminiscent of the final verse of the *canzone I' vo pensando* (*Rvf* 264), the opening poem of Part 2 of the *Canzoniere*. As noted before, Petrarch's verse "et veggio 'l meglio, et al peggior m'appiglio" (*Rvf* 264.136) translates Medea's statement (*Met.* 7.20–21). In the *Secretum*, Petrarch elaborates on the notion, but reaches the same conclusion (*Secr.* III.18.7):

> Fateor; neque aliam ob causam propero nunc tam studiosus ad reliqua, nisi ut, illis explicitis, ad hec redeam: non ignarus, ut paulo ante dicebas, multo michi futurum esse securius studium hoc unum sectari et, deviis pretermissis, rectum callem salutis apprehendere. Sed desiderium frenare non valeo.

> [I have to admit it; and I am hurrying now and eager to take care of the rest for no other reason than that, once I am done with this, I can return to these matters; I am not unaware, as you said a little earlier, that it would be much safer for me to go after this one pursuit and, without deviations, concentrate on the straight path to salvation. But I do not have the strength to control my desire.]

Petrarch thus uses the story of Echo and Narcissus in the *Secretum* to explore the importance of Narcissus to his own experience, but in the *Canzoniere* he is drawn to the figure of Echo to do this: in the previously discussed sonnet *Il mio adversario in cui veder solete* (*Rvf* 45), where the comparison between Laura and Narcissus turns the poet into Echo by analogy, and also in the *canzone Nel dolce tempo de la prima etade* (*Rvf* 23), where the poet is transformed

---

74 Zak, "A Humanist in Exile," 194–97.

into a voice, like Echo. This *canzone*, so rich in Ovidian material that it is also called the *Canzone delle metamorfosi*, embodies in many ways the fluidity that characterized the poems discussed up until this point — the fluid boundaries between the world of Ovid and the world of the poet, and the fluid and ambiguous identifications with Ovidian characters (sometimes the poet was like the Ovidian lover, at other times like the beloved; sometimes he identified with the male Ovidian characters, at other times with the female characters).[75]

The 169 verses of *Nel dolce tempo de la prima etade* pack a full range of Ovidian stories, with six transformations clearly modeled after Ovid's *Metamorphoses*, and a few more referred to in passing. This *canzone* might recall *Sì come il padre del folle Fetonte* for the density of Ovidian material (four Ovidian stories in sixteen verses), but Petrarch replaces the techniques he used in *Sì come il padre del folle Fetonte* to work with Ovidian with different poetic strategies in *Nel dolce tempo de la prima etade*. The poem only mentions a few names (Peneus, God, Jupiter),[76] and the similes have become metaphors: the poet is no longer *like* the Ovidian characters, he *becomes* them. The transformations that the poet describes in the *canzone* are easily connected to corresponding Ovidian stories, and confirmed by the many verbal echoes of Ovid's verses from the corresponding stories in the *Metamorphoses*. *Nel dolce tempo de la prima etade* has been singled out for its showy display of Ovidian sources,[77] and while no poem in the *Canzoniere* comes close to the amount of Ovidian material and the importance it gives to transformation, it should be noted that Petrarch's predominant technique to integrate Ovid's poem into this *canzone* — translations or paraphrases of Ovidian verses — is one that he employs in the entire collection.

---

75   Ovid is a constant presence in all discussions of the canzone *Nel dolce tempo de la prima etade*, and likewise, the *canzone* is mentioned in all writings on Petrarch and Ovid. See in particular Santagata, "La canzone delle metamorfosi (*R.v.f.* 23)," in *Per moderne carte*, 273–325; Sturm-Maddox's chapter "The Ovidian Subtext," in *Petrarch's Metamorphoses*, 9–38; Leonard Barkan, "Diana and Actaeon: The Myth as Synthesis," *English Literary Renaissance* 10, no. 3 (1980): 317–59, at 335–38; Albert J. Rivero, "Petrarch's 'Nel dolce tempo de la prima etade,'" *Modern Language Notes* 94, no. 1 (1979): 92–112; Annalisa Cipollone, "Ovidio nel Petrarca volgare," *Per leggere* 16 (2009): 157–74.

76   Petrarch mentions the river god Peneus, Daphne's father, here as a way to distinguish the world of the *Metamorphoses* and his own. He underlines that his transformation (unlike Daphne's) did not take place near the Peneus river, but near the Rhône, "a loftier river": "diventar due radici sovra l'onde / non di Peneo, ma d'un più altero fiume" ("to become two roots above the waves not of Peneus, but of a loftier river" [*Rvf* 23.47–48]). In *Amor, che viene armato a doppio dardo*, Cino refers to Daphne as "quella di Peneo," the daughter of Peneus (v. 6).

77   Santagata, *Per moderne carte*, 274.

Nel dolce tempo de la prima etade is the first *canzone* in the *Canzoniere*, a poem that Petrarch associated with his youth, but worked on for many years, as we learn from his notes in his sketchbook, the so-called *Codice degli abbozzi* (Vatican City, Biblioteca Apostolica Vaticana, MS Vat. lat. 3196).[78] The first stanza sets up the *canzone*: in language similar to the opening sonnet of the collection, *Voi ch'ascoltate in rime sparse il suono*, the poet looks back at an earlier time ("prima etade" [*Rvf* 23.1]; "primo giovenile errore" [*Rvf* 1.3]), and the negative attention he has drawn to himself ("io son facto a molta gente exempio" [*Rvf* 23.9]; "al popol tutto / favola fui" [*Rvf* 1.9–10]). In *Nel dolce tempo de la prima etade*, Petrarch eventually blurs the divide between past and present, clearly marked and maintained in *Voi ch'ascoltate*. But the *canzone* begins by retelling in a seemingly chronological order how the poet reached his current state: as the second stanza explains, he was transformed into a laurel after Love's attack, and then underwent five other transformations. The following chart (Table 11) lists the six major transformations in the *canzone* and their corresponding Ovidian stories.[79]

All these Ovidian characters were punished for some kind of transgression — of speech, vision, or love — just as the poet in *Nel dolce tempo de la prima etade* is punished for his violation. Ovid's Apollo provoked Cupid (Love) with derisive comments about his archery skills; Phaethon did not follow his father's guidelines; Battus broke a promise; Byblis fostered an improper love for her brother; Echo misled the goddess Juno with her speech; Actaeon should not have seen the goddess Diana bathing naked. As the chart on this *canzone* further illustrates, Petrarch's descriptions of his transformations are not neatly contained to one stanza per transformation, but spill over from one stanza to another. The element of transgression that all of Petrarch's transformations share, is mirrored in the formal structure of the *canzone*, where normally each stanza focuses on and develops only one specific idea or aspect.

The transformations that follow the first one into a laurel all contain an element of unfinishedness that seems to suggest that change is never final. In Ovid's *Metamorphoses*, almost all the transgressions led to death: Phaethon

---

78 Petrarca, *Trionfi, Rime estravaganti, Codice degli abbozzi*, ed. Pacca and Paolino, 842: "de primis inventionibus nostris" ("among our first inventions"). On the genesis of the *canzone*, see Dennis Dutschke, *Francesco Petrarca: Canzone XXIII from the First to Final Version* (Ravenna: Longo, 1977).

79 Peter Kuon noted in the sequence of the *canzone*'s transformations a movement from loss of identity to loss of every possible mode of expression (*L'aura dantesca*, 151). Francesca Southerden made a similar point in "Desire as a Dead Letter: A Reading of Petrarch's RVF 125," in *Desire in Dante and the Middle Ages*, ed. Manuele Gragnolati et al. (Oxford: Legenda, 2012), 185–207, at 192.

TABLE 11 The six major transformations in *Nel dolce tempo de la prima etade* (*Rvf* 23)

Transformation of the poet	Verses *Rvf* and stanza	Corresponding Ovidian character and story	Role in love story	Gender Ovidian character
"un lauro verde" (v. 39)	vv. 21–49 stanza 2–3	Daphne Apollo and Daphne (*Met.* 1.452–567)	beloved	female
"un cigno" (v. 60)	vv. 50–71 stanza 3–4	Cygnus Phaethon Cygnus (*Met.* 1.747–79, 2.1–400)	n/a	male
"un … sasso" (v. 80)	vv. 72–89 stanza 4–5	Battus Battus and Mercury (*Met.* 2.680–707)	n/a	male
"una fontana" (v. 117)	vv. 95–120 stanza 5–6	Byblis Byblis and Caunus (*Met.* 9.450–665)	lover	female
"voce" (v. 139)	vv. 136–46 stanza 7–8	Echo Echo and Narcissus (*Met.* 3.339–510)	lover	female
"un cervo solitario et vago" (v. 158)	vv. 147–60 stanza 8	Actaeon Diana and Actaeon (*Met.* 3.138–252)	lover	male

and Actaeon died, Byblis dissolved into a pool, Battus is forever a rock, as is Echo (a rock that still echoes what is being said). But Daphne's transformation into a laurel provided Petrarch with a more inconclusive transformation: post-metamorphosis she still acts in some respects like a human, Ovid suggests: "factis modo laurea ramis / adnuit utque caput uisa est agitasse cacumen" ("the laurel tree nodded with the branches that were just made and seemed to move the canopy like a head" [*Met.* 1.566–67]).[80] The transformed poet in *Nel dolce tempo de la prima etade* continues to live, too, and to change. So the poet was changed into a swan, but still retains some means of communication through his "estrania voce" ("strange voice" [*Rvf* 23.63]). He was changed into a rock, but

---

80   Another example from the *Metamorphoses*: the young girl Io still seeks contact with her family after her transformation into a heifer (*Met.* 1.639–50).

remains "quasi vivo et sbigottito" ("almost living and aghast" [*Rvf* 23.80]). The poet was turned into an echo, but one that can *decide* what to repeat, namely "Morte, et lei sola per nome" ("Death, and only her by name" [*Rvf* 23.140]). And in the description of the poet's transformation into a deer — "et in un cervo ... / ... mi trasformo: / et anchor de' miei can' fuggo lo stormo" ("and into a stag ... I am transformed: and I am still fleeing the pack of my dogs" [*Rvf* 23.158–60]) — the temporal marker "et anchor" and the present tenses ("mi trasformo" and "fuggo") bring the narration to the present of the poet's writing, after five previous transformations described in the past tense. Ovid's Actaeon got devoured by own hounds, but Petrarch excludes this fate by ending the final stanza of his *canzone* mid-chase.[81]

Petrarch thus presents a less definite model of metamorphosis, but maintains the sense of imminent danger that often characterizes the world of Ovid's *Metamorphoses*: in *Nel dolce tempo de la prima etade* the voice of the poet is constantly threatened.[82] The poet may not die like Ovid's Actaeon, but hears threats similar to the one that Diana made just before she turned Actaeon into a deer: "nunc tibi me posito uisam uelamine narres, / si poterit narrare, licet" ("now go tell around that you saw me without a veil, if you can" [*Met.* 3.192–93]). His lady or "dolce et acerba mia nemica" ("my sweet and bitter enemy" [*Rvf* 23.69]) told him: "Do not say a word about this" ("Di ciò non far parola" [*Rvf* 23.74]). But in the end, not having lost his life and his voice, the poet can and will continue to speak and write the *Canzoniere*.

Petrarch pushes the inconclusiveness of change even further in the *congedo*. After the six transformations described in great detail in the *canzone*, all with their own element of unfinishedness, Petrarch quickly glosses over three more in the *congedo*, three shapes Jupiter had taken on to conquer girls and boys: as a golden rain for Danaë, and as an eagle for Aegina and Ganymede (*Rvf* 23.161–66). At this point, Petrarch undermines the *canzone*'s chronology and questions all the changes that had occurred up until this point: he was never a rain cloud, but an eagle, but also ultimately never stopped being a laurel tree: "né per nova figura il primo alloro / seppi lassar" ("nor did I know how to leave the first laurel for a new shape" [*Rvf* 23.167–68]), basically cancelling all

---

81 On the figure of Actaeon in Petrarch's poetry, see especially Cynthia Nazarian, "Actaeon Ego Sum: Ovidian Dismemberment and Lyric Voice in Petrarch and Maurice Scève," in Keith and Rupp, *Metamorphosis: The Changing Face of Ovid in Medieval and Early Modern Europe*, 199–222; Vickers, "Diana Described"; Barkan, "Diana and Actaeon"; Lynn Enterline, *The Rhetoric of the Body from Ovid to Shakespeare* (Cambridge: Cambridge University Press, 2000), 99–110.

82 Petrarch includes that final scene, the hounds chasing and attacking Actaeon, in the *canzone Standomi un giorno solo a la fenestra* (*Rvf* 323.1–12).

previous transformations. Jupiter's ability to change shape brings to mind Cino da Pistoia's sonnet *Se conceduto mi fosse da Giove* (see Ch. 3.3), where the poet wishes to have the same ability as Jupiter: he would change ("muterei" [vv. 10, 13]) his lady and himself to animals and plants belonging to the world of the *Metamorphoses*.[83] Also in the sonnet *Poco era ad appressarsi agli occhi miei* (*Rvf* 51), a poem often referenced in discussions of *Nel dolce tempo de la prima etade*, Petrarch imagines to possess the same ability (*Rvf* 51.3–6):

> ... come vide lei cangiar Thesaglia,
> così cangiato ogni mia forma avrei.
>
> Et s'io non posso transformarmi in lei
> più ch'i' mi sia ...
>
> [... as Thessaly saw her change, so I would have changed every form of me. And if I cannot transform me into her more than I already have ...]

In *Nel dolce tempo de la prima etade*, however, it is not the poet who wishes to change himself into his lady (the laurel), but Love and his lady who change him into the tree: "i duo mi trasformaro in quel ch'i' sono, / facendomi d'uom vivo un lauro verde" ("the two of them transformed me into what I am, making me a green laurel from a living man" [*Rvf* 23.38–39]). Reversals — of role, of gender — characterize several transformations and identifications with Ovidian characters in the *canzone*, and generally in the *Canzoniere*. As noted in the chart on *Nel dolce tempo de la prima etade* (see above), Petrarch becomes three times a male Ovidian character (Cygnus, Battus, Actaeon) and three times a female Ovidian character (Daphne, Byblis, Echo). More importantly, he becomes three times the transformed pursuer (Byblis, Echo, Actaeon), but only one time the beloved, in the most important (first and final) transformation of the *canzone*: the laurel or Daphne.[84] Petrarch hints at this model of transformation in the *Secretum*, where he defends his love for Laura to St. Augustine in the following terms: "me, quantulumcunque conspicis, per illam esse.... Quidni enim in amatos mores transformarer?" ("however little I may seem to you, I am because of her ... Why would I not have turned into the habits of my

---

83   In the context of *Nel dolce tempo de la prima etade* Cino's sonnet *Amor, che viene armato a doppio dardo*, a sonnet about transformation and Apollo and Daphne, is mentioned more frequently. See, for instance, Santagata, *Per moderne carte*, 151–52.

84   The remaining two transformations of Cygnus and Battus are not connected to love and desire.

beloved?" [*Secr.* III.4.6–7]). This is not a concept or notion unique to Petrarch,[85] but surely a beloved one.[86]

Nel dolce tempo de la prima etade then becomes in several ways a microcosm of Petrarch's treatment of Ovidian material in the *Canzoniere*. In the *canzone* and in the collection, Petrarch explores desire through a variety of Ovidian stories, focusing within those stories on the experiences of both the lover and the beloved. Ultimately, though, he always comes back to the story of Apollo and Daphne, which is the final transformation of the *canzone* and the dominating one in the *Canzoniere*. In *Nel dolce tempo de la prima etade*, Petrarch re-creates the world of the *Metamorphoses* but also connects this hybrid world to the entire collection: the *canzone*'s transformations (based on Ovid's verses) occur in a landscape that does not differ from the familiar woods, streams, and meadows of the Avignon region featured in other poems of the *Canzoniere*.[87]

The particular imagery of these transformations is also not a feature of this *canzone* alone, but found throughout the *Canzoniere*. We have already seen that Petrarch's lady shares several features with Daphne pre- and post-transformation throughout the collection, and that the laurel tree is frequently featured. The "scorza" or bark (*Rvf* 23.20) that signaled the poet's transformation into a tree in *Nel dolce tempo de la prima etade* reappears in various other poems (e.g., *Rvf* 180.1–2 and *Rvf* 361.2). He is a rock again (e.g., *Rvf* 129.51 and *Rvf* 243.13); a deer again (e.g., *Rvf* 209.9–14); a pool again (e.g., *Rvf* 135.53). These returning transformations throughout the collection reinforce Petrarch's insistence in the *canzone delle metamorfosi* that no change is final. In the last poem of the *Canzoniere*, the *canzone* Vergine bella, che, di sol vestita (*Rvf* 366), Petrarch includes one last transformation that could have easily belonged in *Nel dolce tempo de la prima etade*: "Medusa et l'error mio m'àn fatto un sasso / d'umor vano stillante" ("Medusa and my error have made me a stone dripping vain humor" [*Rvf* 366.111–12]). In this concluding prayer to the Virgin Mary, Petrarch replaces the couple Love and his lady, who transformed the poet into a laurel tree in *Nel dolce tempo de la prima etade* (*Rvf* 23.38–39), with a new pair:

---

85   For instances of the same notion in other vernacular poems, see Santagata, *Per moderne carte*, 151–52.
86   In addition to the mentions in the *Secretum* and the *Canzoniere*, Petrarch describes the lover-beloved relationship in similar terms in the *Triumphus Cupidinis*: "so in qual guisa / l'amante ne l'amato si transforme" ("I know in what way the lover transforms himself into the beloved" [III.161–62]). For a psychoanalytical reading of this passage in the *Secretum* and the lover's transformation into the beloved in the *Canzoniere*, see Enterline, *The Rhetoric of the Body*, 92–95.
87   Petrarch perhaps best characterizes this hybrid world — Ovidian, but also very much his own — in his mention of Daphne's father, the river god Peneus. On those verses, see n. 76.

Medusa and the poet's own "error." The Virgin Mary is the proverbial rock in this final *canzone*: she is "stabile," the guiding star, the captain of the ship during a storm (*Rvf* 366.66–68). But the reference to yet another transformation brings the *Canzoniere*'s instability of identity and identification, most clearly expressed in *Nel dolce tempo de la prima etade*, back to the foreground: not only is the poet transformed again, but his lady now figures as Medusa.

Medusa made several appearances throughout the *Canzoniere*, a few times mentioned explicitly by name (*Rvf* 179.10 and *Rvf* 197.6), and implicitly through references to rocks, stones, and marble.[88] Any mentions of petrification and Medusa in Italian vernacular poetry bring Dante's *rime petrose* to mind (see Ch. 3.2). Unlike Petrarch, Dante never included her name in his poems. And while in the *petrose* she is clearly the antagonist, the ultimate harsh and icy lady who not only rejects but wants to destroy the lover, Petrarch's engagement with Medusa is more complex. Aileen A. Feng in particular stressed the "multifaceted Medusa" that Petrarch saw and the role this Ovidian character played in shaping Petrarch's self-fashioning as a poet beyond the *Canzoniere*.[89] In the *Canzoniere*, Petrarch maps some of Medusa's traits (filtered through Dante's *petrose*) onto his own lady.[90] Petrarch even finds ways to mirror his frequent puns on Laura's name and his transformation into a laurel tree in *Nel dolce tempo de la prima etade*. In the *canzone Di pensier in pensier, di monte in monte* (*Rvf* 129), the verse "pietra morta in pietra viva" ("a dead rock on a living rock" [*Rvf* 129.51]) is not only a pun on Petrarch's name (which contains the word "petra" or rock),[91] but also a variation of the model discussed earlier: the lover who transforms into the beloved — this time not into the laurel (his lady as Daphne), but into a rock (his lady as Medusa).[92] In the sonnet

---

[88] Aileen A. Feng pointed to the important distinction, originating in Ovid's *Metamorphoses*, between petrification into a rock (the effect that Medusa had on those who looked at her) and petrification into marble (the effect that Medusa's decapitated head in Perseus's hands had on those who looked at it), tracing Petrarch's use of both words. See "'Volto di Medusa': Monumentalizing the self in Petrarch's *Rerum vulgarium fragmenta*," *Forum Italicum* 46, no. 3 (2013): 497–521, at 498–500.

[89] Feng, "'Volto di Medusa,'" 499. The distinction pointed out in n. 88 is a good example of how Petrarch looked closely at the nuances in Ovid's story of Perseus and Medusa. Feng further analyzed Medusa as a "tool of self-aggrandizement" (516) in the *Familiares*, the *Africa*, and the *Collatio laureationis* (508–16).

[90] See especially Claudio G. Antoni, "Esperienze stilistiche petrose da Dante al Petrarca," *Modern Language Studies* 13, no. 2 (1983): 21–33.

[91] Remo Cesarini, "'Petrarca': Il nome come auto-reinvenzione poetica," *Quaderni petrarcheschi* 4 (1987): 121–37.

[92] As Marco Santagata noted, the image of the living stone is common in Latin poetry. See Petrarch, *Canzoniere*, ed. Santagata, 638–39.

Poco era ad appressarsi agli occhi miei (*Rvf* 51), a poem mentioned earlier for its use of transformation imagery, Petrarch shifts seamlessly from turning into Daphne (*Rvf* 51.3–6) into wanting to be petrified by Medusa (*Rvf* 51.7–14). When he expresses his jealously of Atlas (who was turned into a mountain by Medusa's gaze [*Met.* 4.631–62]), because of the relief such an end would mean (*Rvf* 51.12–14), a similar sentiment expressed in Ovid's exile letters comes to mind (*Ex Ponto* 1.2.34): "ille ego sum, frustra qui lapis esse uelim" ("I am one who in vain wants to be a rock").[93]

When Petrarch wrote about "Medusa and my error" in his final poem, was he thinking of Ovid's famous statement about the cause of his exile, "perdiderint ... me duo crimina, carmen et error" ("two crimes, a poem and a mistake, have ruined me" [*Tristia* 2.207])? Dante also alluded to this Ovidian verse in the account of his own exile in *Par.* 17 (see Ch. 4.2). But while Dante focused only on the potential damaging effect of his "carmen" and not any "error," Petrarch more closely follows Ovid's formulation in *Tristia* 2 by also identifying two causes for his Ovidian transformation. In the final *canzone* of the *Canzoniere*, Petrarch circles back to poems from the very beginning of the collection: initially, to the opening sonnet *Voi ch'ascoltate*, which, like the final *canzone*, couples the "error" of the past ("primo giovenile errore" [*Rvf* 1.3]) with the repentance the poet felt in the presence of his writing. But Petrarch also evokes the first *canzone Nel dolce tempo de la prima etade* (*Rvf* 23) and the instability of Ovidian transformation it so well described, which makes it impossible to interpret *Vergine bella* as the poet's final conversion at the end of the *Canzoniere*.[94]

Nel dolce tempo de la prima etade is also representative for the entire collection in its stylistic choices. As we have seen before, in the *Canzoniere* Petrarch abandons the simile, the rhetorical device that many vernacular poets before him repeatedly used to identify themselves with Ovidian characters, and instead uses metaphors and verbal traces that link his poetry with

---

93 On this letter, see Ch. 3.2.
94 For instance, Kenelm Foster, O.P., wrote: "Placing *Vergine bella* at the end of his book, [Petrarch] was well aware that the Muse of the *Canzoniere* as a whole was not Mary but Laura." See "Beatrice or Medusa," in *Italian Studies Presented to E. R. Vincent*, ed. Charles Peter Brand, Kenelm Foster, and Uberto Limentani (Cambridge: Heffer, 1962), 41–56, at 50. Patricia Berrahou Phillippy interpreted Medusa as the emblem of Ovidian transformation, and her presence in the final *canzone* as the return "to the realm of poetic metamorphosis rather than advancing toward ethical recantation." See "'Vergine bella': Palinode and Autobiography in Petrarch's *Rime sparse*," in *Love's Remedies: Recantation and Renaissance Lyric Poetry* (Lewisburg: Bucknell University Press, 1995), 61–91, at 82 and 86. On the scholarly tendency to treat Medusa as the emblem of Laura as a destructive force, initiated by Foster, see Feng, "Volto di Medusa,'" 497–98.

Ovid's as main ways to include Ovidian material.[95] But at a few points in the *Canzoniere* Petrarch still finds the simile the preferable mode of expression. The most noted in that respect is the madrigal *Non al suo amante più Dïana piacque* (*Rvf* 52) (included in full below), built around a comparison with Diana and Actaeon, a couple that also appeared in the *Canzone delle metamorfosi* (*Rvf* 23).[96] This madrigal immediately succeeds *Poco era ad appressarsi agli occhi miei* (*Rvf* 51), earlier discussed for its references to the story of Apollo and Daphne and transformation.

> Non al suo amante più Dïana piacque,
> quando per tal ventura tutta ignuda
> la vide in mezzo de le gelide acque,
>
> ch'a me la pastorella alpestra et cruda
> posta a bagnar un leggiadretto velo,
> ch'a l'aura il vago et biondo capel chiuda,
>
> tal che mi fece, or quand'egli arde 'l cielo,
> tutto tremar d'un amoroso gielo.

[Diana was not more pleasing to her lover, when by chance he saw her completely naked in the middle of the icy water, than the cruel mountain shepherdess was pleasing to me, when she started to wash a pretty veil that keeps her lovely blond hair away from the wind, so that she made me, now that the sky burns, completely tremble with a chill of love.]

In this poem, Petrarch returns to the tried-and-true formula of several lyric poets before him, who wrote that they or their ladies did something better and more than certain Ovidian characters who were famous for that something.[97] The starting point here is Actaeon's pleasure of seeing Diana bathing naked. The

---

95 On the simile in Petrarch's *Canzoniere*, see Claudia Berra, *La similitudine nei 'Rerum vulgarium fragmenta'* (Lucca: M. Pacini Fazzi, 1992). Berra listed all the similes with mythological (i.e., not exclusively Ovidian) references at 155–57. Worth mentioning is the sonnet *In tale stella duo belli occhi vidi* (*Rvf* 260), in which the poet praises the exceptional beauty of his lady, who outdoes — "Non si pareggi a lei" ("She cannot equal her" [*Rvf* 260.5]) — the classical beauties Helen, Lucretia, Polyxena, Hypsipyle, and Argea. In Ch. 2.1, I discuss several Occitan and Italian poems that use the simile in the same manner.

96 The sixth transformation of the *Nel dolce tempo*, the only one that Petrarch placed in the ongoing present, dealt with the same Ovidian material, but there is no consensus which poem preceded the other.

97 See Ch. 2.1 for a detailed discussion of this aspect.

poet outdoes Actaeon (the unnamed "lover" in the first verse) in this pleasure, but covers up the mistake — Ovid's word for what happened (*Met.* 3.142) — before it can occur: Diana is replaced by the "pastorella," who is not taking a bath naked but bathing a veil that will cover up her hair.[98] Both Petrarch's phrasing and my translation are deliberately ambiguous: because of the pun on Laura's name ("l'aura" [*Rvf* 52.6]) and the mention of hair (albeit not Daphne's/Laura's usual locks floating in the wind, but hidden under a veil [*Rvf* 52.5–6]), it is not clear whether the shepherdess is covering up her own hair or Laura's, or whether the shepherdess is Laura.[99] While Petrarch's mention of the veil evokes the commentary tradition ("integumentum" is one of the terms used to indicate that which covers up the true meaning of a passage), Petrarch does not present an allegorical or moral reading of the myth, like the medieval and Renaissance commentators who interpreted the story to be about the attraction of hunting, money, or usury.[100] Instead, the double layers in this poem are generic: as William D. Paden, Jr., explained, Petrarch lays classical material

---

98 Mazzotta pointed out that also the conditions of seeing the pastorella — "per tal ventura" (*Rvf* 52.2) — echoes the language and content of Ovid's account ("The *Canzoniere* and the Language of the Self," 69).

99 This ambiguity is not always addressed: for instance, Vickers, "Diana Described"; Mazzotta, "The *Canzoniere* and the Language of the Self"; and John Freccero, "The Fig Tree and the Laurel: Petrarch's Poetics," *Diacritics* 5 (1975): 34–40, all take this poem to be about Laura. I agree with William D. Paden, Jr. that the ambiguity about the identification seems deliberate. See "Aesthetic Distance in Petrarch's Response to the Pastourelle: *Rime* LII*,*" *Romance Notes* 16, no. 3 (1975): 702–7, at 705. Worth mentioning, however, is that in the previous version of the madrigal the verses 5–6 first referred to the sun and the wind: "fixa a bagnar el suo candido velo / ch'al sol e a l'aura el vago capel chiuda" ("intent to wash her white veil that keeps her lovely hair from the sun and the wind") — the fact that Petrarch in the final version only has "l'aura" has been considered a reason to identify the shepherdess as Laura. For such interpretations, see Laura Paolino, "Ancora qualche nota sui madrigali di Petrarca (*RVF* 52, 54, 106, 121)," *Italianistica* 30, no. 2 (2001): 307–23, at 308; and Vincenzo Dolla, "I madrigali del 'Canzoniere' (un'ipotesi di lettura petrarchesca)," *Esperienze letterarie* 1 (1976): 74–88, at 78–79. In both the original and changed verses I see Petrarch's intention to also include the story of Apollo and Daphne in this poem, be it through Apollo (Sol) and Laura in the first version ("al sol e a l'aura"), or just Laura ("a l'aura") in the final version.

100 For instance, Arnulf of Orléans focuses on the hunt (Ghisalberti, "Arnolfo d'Orléans," 208); Giovanni del Virgilio on money (Ghisalberti, *Giovanni del Virgilio*, 52); Pierre de Bersuire, among other things, on usury (Berchorius, *Reductorium morale, Liber XV, cap. ii–xv*, 65). Also Loredana Chines found little common ground with Giovanni del Virgilio's explanation of the myth, but pointed out Fulgentius's emphasis on the dangers of curiosity in "La ricezione petrarchesca del mito di Atteone," in *'Di selva in selva ratto mi trasformo': Identità e metamorfosi della parola petrarchesca* (Rome: Carocci, 2010), 43–54, at 51–54. Marcozzi discussed the figure of Actaeon in Petrarch's writings in *La biblioteca di Febo*, 241–45, with a similar point about the multiple meanings of "velo" at 242–43. On these

over the medieval genre of the *pastourelle* (poems about romances with shepherdesses), a genre Petrarch rarely turns to in the *Canzoniere*.[101] Moreover, the unexpected topic of Diana and Actaeon for this *pastourelle* is presented in an extended simile, a traditional feature of vernacular poetry, but used sparingly by Petrarch in the *Canzoniere*.

The shepherdess's veil, furthermore, comes straight from Ovid's account: Actaeon was punished for having seen Diana uncovered, "posito uisam *uelamine*" ("seen without *a veil*" [*Met.* 3.192]; emphasis added). His punishment (*Met.* 3.206–52) was included in *Nel dolce tempo de la prima etade*, where the poet is transformed into a deer, chased by his own hounds (*Rvf* 23.158–60). Replacing the uncovered naked female body with a veil covering up hair does not diminish the poet's pleasure (in fact, it is said to be greater than Actaeon's),[102] and in this way he avoids the punishment. Several scholars have pointed out the reversals and inconsistencies in the simile,[103] but that again is not unseen in comparisons with Ovidian characters in lyric poetry, which often are slightly altered or incomplete.[104] As Giuseppe Mazzotta highlighted, in the concluding verses of *Non al suo amante più Dïana piacque*, Petrarch returns to the beginning of the poem, describing the poet observing the shepherdess in similar terms as Diana in the opening comparison: "Dïana ... / ... *tutta* ignuda / ... *gelide* acque" (*Rvf* 52.1–3), "mi fece ... / *tutto* tremar d'un amoroso *gielo*" (*Rvf* 52.7–8; emphasis added).[105] This is not only another example of Petrarch's willingness to explore different roles within the same Ovidian story, but also another instance where Petrarch transfers elements from Ovid's world to his own. Unlike the sharp contrast that many vernacular poets drew in their Ovidian similes between the past experience of the Ovidian characters and the present of their own experience, Petrarch does not juxtapose the past of Actaeon looking at Diana ("vide" [*Rvf* 52.3]) with the present of his similar experience:

---

and other meanings of the veil in Petrarch's writing, see Loredana Chines, *I veli del poeta: un percorso tra Petrarca e Tasso* (Rome: Carocci, 2000), 15–40.

101   Paden, "Aesthetic Distance in Petrarch's Response to the Pastourelle," 705.
102   As Nancy Vickers pointed out in "Diana Described," 273, Petrarch's description of Actaeon's experience in the madrigal, "at one remove from his experience, safely permits and perpetuates his fascination."
103   Mazzotta, "The *Canzoniere* and the Language of the Self," 68; Vickers, "Diana Described," 273.
104   Several poets declared to be like Narcissus, but Narcissus's self-love becomes the poet's love for their lady; several poets declared to love their lady more than Pyramus loved Thisbe, but many left their death conveniently out of the equation. In Ch. 2.1, I discuss these comparisons in earlier lyric poems.
105   Mazzotta, "The *Canzoniere* and the Language of the Self," 68.

the shepherdess's effect on him originated in the past, "mi fece ... / ... tremar" (*Rvf* 52.7–8), even though he still feels it, "even now" (*Rvf* 52.7).

In *Non al suo amante più Dïana piacque*, time, genre, and identification are fluid: the madrigal resembles the medieval genre of the *pastourelle*, but Petrarch turned to classical Latin poetry, Ovid's story of Diana and Actaeon, for the content. His use of a classical simile brings earlier vernacular poems to mind that frequently relied on this rhetorical device to feature Ovidian characters, but Petrarch blurs past and present in the comparisons, as well as the usual clear indications of who is to being compared with whom, which such earlier poems with Ovidian similes always contained. Like other poems in the *Canzoniere*, most clearly in *Nel dolce tempo de la prima etade*, the madrigal renders time unstable — an instability mimicked in the ambiguous and reversible identifications with the Ovidian characters and world.

In *Mia benigna fortuna e 'l viver lieto* (*Rvf* 332), Petrarch employs the simile one last time to identify with classical characters. The poem is considered a *sestina doppia*, literally a double *sestina*, twice repeating the *sestina*'s formal structure of six stanzas with the same six same rhyme words shuffled around according to a fixed pattern — Petrarch explains this innovative structure in the verse "doppiando 'l dolor, doppia lo stile" ("doubling sorrow, doubles the style" [*Rvf* 332.39]). Already from the rhyme words "glad," "nights," "style," "rhymes," "weeping," "death" ("lieto," "notti," "stile," "rime," "pianto," "morte"), much can be gathered about the content: this is a poem about confronting the sadness caused by Laura's death and the struggle to write, make art, under such circumstances. Not surprisingly, then, Petrarch wishes to find classical doubles in Orpheus and Eurydice (*Rvf* 332.49–54):

> Or avess'io un sì pietoso stile
> che Laura mia potesse tôrre a Morte,
> come Euridice Orpheo sua senza rime,
> ch'i' viverei anchor più che mai lieto!
> S'esser non pò, qualchuna d'este notti
> chiuda omai queste due fonti di pianto.

[Now if I had such a sorrowful style that I could bring back my Laura from Death, as Orpheus did for his Eurydice without rhymes, then I would live more happily than ever! If this cannot be, may now one of these nights close these two springs of tears.]

The story of Orpheus and Eurydice, as we will see in the following section, runs through the *Canzoniere* — especially, but not exclusively, in its second part, after Laura's death. Its most complete appearance is found in the *canzone Standomi un giorno solo a la fenestra* (*Rvf* 323), the counterpart of *Nel dolce tempo* in the second part of the *Canzoniere*. The final of six visions (the poem is also known as the *Canzone delle visioni*) is Petrarch's fullest account of their story: an unnamed woman walks in the grass, is bitten by a snake, and dies — details that can only identify her as Eurydice (*Rvf* 323.61–72).[106] The *sestina doppia* deals with what happens after Eurydice's death.[107] Central is Petrarch's desire to duplicate the experience of Orpheus, who was given the chance to return to the underworld, and bring back his beloved from the dead: the only condition was not to look back. Petrarch's use of the conditional ("Or avess'io …" [*Rvf* 332.49]) reveals that he is skeptical; he knows how the story ends: Orpheus does look back, and loses Eurydice forever. But by not including their sad ending in the simile, Petrarch keeps at least the possibility alive. His language aims at repeating Orpheus's experience: "Laura mia" (*Rvf* 332.50), one of the few times her name is mentioned in the *Canzoniere*, and the only time with the affectionate "mia," is mirrored in the following verse as "Euridice … sua" (*Rvf* 332.51).[108] This final classical simile in the *Canzoniere* is probably the most consistent in its analogies among the collections: I and my Laura are like Orpheus and his Eurydice, both men are artists, both women are dead.[109]

In general, though, Petrarch's identifications with Ovidian characters in the *Canzoniere* are not that explicit and precise. Petrarch is far removed from the first generations of Italian poets, discussed in Ch. 2.1, who found that Ovid's stories offered clear-cut scenarios to illustrate their own situation: I am like this Ovidian male character, my lady is like that Ovidian female character, and

---

106   See Fredi Chiappelli's thorough reading of this stanza, "La strofa di Euridice," in *Studi sul linguaggio del Petrarca: La canzone delle visioni* (Florence: Leo S. Olschki, 1971), 139–83. On Orpheus and Eurydice in the *Canzoniere*, see especially Federica Brunori, "Il mito ovidiano di Orfeo e Euridice nel *Canzoniere* di Petrarca," *Romance Quarterly* 44, no. 4 (1997): 233–44; and Nicola Gardini, "Un esempio di imitazione virgiliana nel *Canzoniere* Petrarchesco: Il mito di Orfeo," *Modern Language Notes* 110, no. 1 (1995): 132–44.

107   On this passage, see also Jennifer Rushworth, *Discourses of Mourning in Dante, Petrarch, and Proust* (Oxford: Oxford University Press, 2016), 108–9.

108   Vergil also uses the phrase "Eurydicen … suam" (*Georg.* 4.490), as did Ovid (*Met.* 11.66) and Boethius (3.XII,50). Ovid refers to Eurydice in this way in his description of how the two reunite in the underworld after Orpheus's death: "Eurydicenque suam iam tuto respicit Orpheus" ("and Orpheus now safely looks back at his Eurydice" [*Met.* 11.66]). Moreover, as Brunori pointed out, Petrarch translates this Ovidian verse in the sonnet *Anima bella da quel nodo sciolta* (*Rvf* 305) about Laura's death, but reversed the roles: "omai tutta secura / volgi a me gli occhi, e i miei sospiri ascolta ("now in safety turn your eyes to me and listen to my sighs" [*Rvf* 305.7–8]). See "Il mito di Orfeo e Euridice," 240.

109   The concept of doubling is inherent to the story: Orpheus, after all, suffered a double loss, losing Eurydice twice — in Ovid's words, "gemina nece" (*Met.* 10.64).

so on. At the same time, in those straightforward identifications, the versatility of Ovid's stories already became apparent: for instance, depending on which vernacular poet was making the comparisons, Pyramus and Thisbe could represent both foolish love and fine love. Petrarch takes this much further in the *Canzoniere*: like Dante in his lyric poetry and in the *Commedia*, he ignores the gender divisions, and identifies himself with male and female Ovidian characters. Dante was most interested in the female experience when describing his similar situation as mistreated lover: for instance, his identification with Dido in *Così nel mio parlar vogli'esser aspro* (see Ch. 3.2). Petrarch instead draws on the fullest range of experiences that the *Metamorphoses* offers, often exploring both sides of Ovidian stories, male and female, lover and beloved: some of those instances are found throughout the *Canzoniere* (e.g., his identifications with both Apollo and Daphne all through the collection), others within the same poem (e.g., his shared features with both Actaeon and Diana in the madrigal *Non al suo amante più Dïana piacque*), still others between the *Canzoniere* and other writings (e.g., his identifications with Echo in the *Canzoniere* and those with Narcissus in the *Secretum*). As the *Canzone delle metamorfosi* best illustrates, identifications are incomplete and open to change and re-interpretation.

Especially in the sonnets *Amor, che viene armato a doppio dardo* and *Se conceduto mi fosse da Giove*, Cino da Pistoia replaced the prevalent Ovidian similes of the lyric poets before him with the re-creation of the world of the *Metamorphoses*, literally placing the characters from Ovid's poem next to himself, his friend, and their ladies. That, too, characterizes much of Petrarch's Ovidian poems in the *Canzoniere*. With a few notable exceptions, Petrarch abandoned Ovidian similes in the *Canzoniere*, replacing them with verbal echoes to well-chosen Ovidian stories and metaphors that turned the poet and his lady into Ovidian characters. Like Cino, also Petrarch is at times in the company of Ovidian characters, blending the literary past and present. Petrarch's identifications with Ovidian characters thus cannot be separated from the vernacular lyric tradition and the ways in which poets before him treated Ovidian material, even though the main characteristics of such earlier poems underwent several transformations in the *Canzoniere*. That Ovidian poems with more traditional features such as *Sì come il padre del folle Fetonte* were excluded from the collection underscores that in the *Canzoniere* Petrarch wanted to distinguish himself from previous treatments of Ovidian material. At the same time, several poems that were included in the collection still contain traces of such earlier treatments. In general, Petrarch's debt to the vernacular lyric tradition is not as visible as his use of Ovid's Latin text, since names of Ovidian characters and famous story lines clearly signal their Ovidian origin. But translations and paraphrases of Ovid's Latin verses make their way into the Italian verses of the *Canzoniere*, as they did in the *Commedia*: like Dante, Petrarch combines Latin and vernacular readings of Ovid in his poetry. Petrarch, in other words, draws on several literary traditions in creating his own unique approach to Ovidian characters in the *Canzoniere*. Its most distinguishing feature, the instability and variability of the identifications, reminds us that much in Petrarch's world — time, the self, change — is unstable and incomplete. This kind of Ovidian identification and transformation is far removed from the model St. Augustine presented in the *Secretum*, where he describes his own religious transformation or conversion in the statement, "transformatus sum in alterum Augustinum" ("I was transformed into another Augustine" [*Secr.* 1.5.5]) — his transformation was final. As noted earlier, Marco Santagata warned against interpreting the Ovidian transformations in the *Canzoniere* through an exclusively moralizing lens, and indeed, Petrarch's reading of Ovid has little in common with the straightforward and easy moral and religious interpretations proposed in the Latin commentary tradition on Ovid's *Metamorphoses*.

5.3   Metamorphosis as a Narrative Principle

Metamorphosis is a rich and fruitful metaphor in the critical writing about Petrarch's *Canzoniere*: it has been used to describe Petrarch's treatment of his sources,[110] the changes that his poems underwent from his notebooks to the *Canzoniere*,[111] and the internal journey of the poet and his own change.[112] Likewise, fragmentation — a concept already present in the collection's title *Rime sparse* or *Scattered Rhymes* — seems to capture essential and comprehensive traits of Petrarch's poetry: of his text, his voice, his collection's narrative. In this section, I examine the Ovidian inspiration for these two features: metamorphosis and fragmentation. I also place metamorphosis at the center of the discussion, but I demonstrate how Petrarch draws on many Ovidian works, and not solely the *Metamorphoses*.

The structure and form of Ovid's poems, especially the *Metamorphoses*, have long been a topic of discussion, beginning with Ovid's own comments. Already in the proem of the *Metamorphoses*, Ovid signaled that his own

---

110 See, for instance, Kuon, *L'aura dantesca*; and Sturm-Maddox, *Petrarch's Metamorphoses*.
111 See, for instance, Guglielmo Gorni, "Metamorfosi e redenzione in Petrarca: il senso della forma Correggio del *Canzoniere*," *Lettere Italiane* 30 (1978): 3–13.
112 See, for instance, Chines, *'Di selva in selva ratto mi trasformo.'*

writing could and should undergo change: "di, coeptis (nam uos mutastis et illa) / aspirate" ("gods, inspire this undertaking [since you have changed it as well]" [*Met.* 1.2–3]).[113] As pointed out in Ch. 4.4, Dante and Petrarch and their contemporaries most likely read "et illas" and not "et illa," but Ovid expressed his belief in the transformative powers of his art at various other points in his poems. For instance, in the opening letter of the *Tristia*, written later in exile, Ovid reframes the topic of his *Metamorphoses* — "forms changed into new bodies" ("IN NOVA ... mutatas ... formas / corpora" [*Met.* 1.1–2]) — stating that also the "face," the look of his own destiny should be counted among those changing bodies (*Tristia* 1.1.117–22):[114]

> sunt quoque mutatae, ter quinque uolumina, formae,
> nuper ab exequiis pignora rapta meis.
> his mando dicas, inter mutata referri
> fortunae uultum corpora posse meae;
> namque ea dissimilis subito est effecta priori,
> flendaque nunc, alio tempore laeta fuit.

> [There are also fifteen books on changing forms, stakes recently taken from my burial. I ask that you tell them that the look of my destiny can be added among those changed bodies. Because that look has all of the sudden become different from what was before: it now makes you cry, while it once caused joy.]

Further on in the *Tristia* (1.7), Ovid notes that the *Metamorphoses* was not published by its author, and, if permitted, he would have emended the mistakes of his "unfinished poem" ("rude carmen") (vv. 35–40) — another indication that Ovid wanted to make more changes to his epic.[115]

---

113   The proem of the *Metamorphoses* contains several phrases whose meaning changes as one reads on. For instance, the meaning of the first four words of the poem, the half-verse "IN NOVA fert animus" ("My mind turns to new things"), changes immediately after reading what follows, "mutatas dicere formas / corpora" [*Met.* 1.1–2]; the complete sentence now means: "My mind turns to talking about forms changed into new bodies." Stephen Wheeler listed all interpretative transformations of the proem in "Into New Bodies: The Incipit of Ovid's *Metamorphoses* as Intertext in Imperial Latin Literature," *Materiali e discussioni per l'analisi dei testi classici* 61 (2009): 147–60, at 149–52.

114   Alessandro Barchiesi and Philip Hardie, "The Ovidian career model: Ovid, Gallus, Apuleius, Boccaccio," in *Classical Literary Careers and their Reception*, ed. Philip Hardie and Helen Moore (Cambridge: Cambridge University Press, 2010), 59–88, at 76.

115   For a systematic study of the practice of revision in Ovid's oeuvre, see Francesca Martelli, *Ovid's Revisions: The Editor as Author* (Cambridge: Cambridge University Press, 2013). On

As a whole, the *Metamorphoses* follows a chronological narrative line ("from the very beginning of the world up until my own time" [*Met.* 1.3–4], as Ovid indicates in the proem), but it has always invited fragmentation: most of our modern-day editions divide the poem into stories, often introduced by titles for each story, a practice that goes back to the first commentaries on Ovid's *Metamorphoses*, which broke down the poem in similar ways (see Ch. 1.1). Moreover, Ovid also tested the structural boundaries of the epic genre — the division into books — by letting his stories run over from one book to the other, instead of presenting the neat conclusion normally found at the end of a book.[116] While most medieval commentaries on Ovid's *Metamorphoses* embraced the division into stories and structured their commentary by division, Matthew of Vendôme and Conrad of Hirsau, two disapproving critics of Ovid *tout court*, attacked Ovid's poem for its confusing structure.[117]

Ovid's interest in fragmentation and transformation is not limited to the structure and form of the poem. Since his version of a particular myth often became the dominant and best-known version, it is easy to forget that Ovid himself crafted his stories from a long tradition of writing about myth and transformation.[118] Change is the dominating principle in the *Metamorphoses*: in addition to the transformations of the narrative material that Ovid worked with and the actual physical changes that his characters undergo at the end of each story, Ovid also turned to style and genre, combining the epic conventions with features from other genres.[119] His attention to form and style stood out especially to the anonymous writer of the Vulgate Commentary, who, as Frank T. Coulson has pointed out, had a particular interest in discussing the

---

these examples from Book 1 of the *Tristia*, see Stephen Hinds, "Booking the Return Trip: Ovid and *Tristia* 1," *Proceedings of the Cambridge Philological Society* n.s. 31 (1985): 13–32.

116 An excellent example is the transition between Books 1 and 2 of the *Metamorphoses*, where Ovid cleverly combines form and content: the story of Phaethon runs from *Met.* 1.749–79 to *Met.* 2.1–400, and the break between the books covers Phaethon's journey to the palace of the Sun. For more on this transition, see Ch. 4, n. 48.

117 Marcozzi, "Petrarca lettore di Ovidio," 59–60.

118 G. Karl Galinsky's chapter on Ovid's "Inspiration, Tone and Theme" in *Ovid's 'Metamorphoses': An Introduction to the Basic Aspects* (Berkeley: University of California Press, 1975), 1–78 offers an excellent overview of this aspect of Ovid's writing. Also the six-volume edition of Ovid's *Metamorphoses* in the Fondazione Lorenzo Valla series, edited by Alessandro Barchiesi and commentary by Barchiesi (Books 1–4), Gianpiero Rosati (Books 3–6), Edward J. Kenney (Books 7–9), Joseph D. Reed (Books 10–12), and Philip Hardie (Books 13–15) (Milan: Mondadori, 2005, 2007, 2009, 2011, 2013, 2015), opens the commentary on each story with detailed notes on Ovid's sources.

119 Also in his other poems, Ovid often turned his attention to generic conventions. See, for instance, the programmatic opening poem *Am.* 2.1, discussed in Ch. 4.3.

poem's stylistic and formal aspects in his commentary.[120] Modern scholars of the epic also have studied these features of the *Metamorphoses*, identifying several episodes where Ovid experiments with complex narrative structures, mixes the generic conventions of epic and elegy, and offers new perspectives on existing narrative material.[121]

While Petrarch has little to say about the structure and the content of the *Metamorphoses* in his writings, his familiarity with the Ovidian tradition is well documented through his possession of some of Ovid's poems and commentaries on the *Metamorphoses*, his explicit references to Ovid's poems in his prose writings and reading notes, and through translations and imitations of Ovidian verses in his prose and poetry. Petrarch's knowledge of earlier vernacular poetry, which included several poems inspired by Ovidian material, is apparent in his own work. With such a wide range and variety of texts and approaches to Ovid's poems in his possession and on his mind, Petrarch saw remarkable diversity in Ovid's writings and diversity in the artistic responses to them. Most importantly, Petrarch saw that the form, content, and interpretation of stories and poems could always change, and used this principle, inherent to Ovid's works and the Ovidian tradition, to its maximum effect in creating his own narrative.

Any discussion about metamorphosis and fragmentation in the *Canzoniere* should start with the story of Apollo and Daphne, its fundamental Ovidian source text. Since over sixty poems from the collection refer to this Ovidian story in one way or another, we cannot write off Petrarch's interest in Ovid as solely a youthful endeavor.[122] As the chart documenting the location of its

---

120 See especially Coulson, "Literary criticism in the Vulgate Commentary on Ovid's *Metamorphoses*."

121 An excellent example is the competition between the Muses and the Pierides, which occupies much of Book 5 of the *Metamorphoses*. Gianpiero Rosati has called this entire passage "an essay on narrative technique, the most complex of the poem and probably of all classical literature" ("un saggio di tecnica della narrazione, il più complesso del poema, e probabilmente dell'intera letteratura greco-latina") in *Metamorfosi: Volume III (Libri V–VI)*, ed. Gianpiero Rosati, trans. by Giochino Chiarini (Milan: Fondazione Lorenzo Valla / Arnoldo Mondadori Editore, 2009), 177. The structure of the episode in the *Metamorphoses* is indeed complex: an unnamed Muse narrates the contest to Minerva in the first frame story, Calliope's long song provides a second frame story, which contains several more stories-within-stories. In the episode, Ovid switches from the generic conventions of elegy to those of epic poetry and back, and reinterprets the well-known story of the rape of Persephone. Stephen Hinds studied how Ovid turns to this same material in the *Metamorphoses* and the *Fasti* in *The Metamorphosis of Persephone: Ovid and the Self-Conscious Muse* (Cambridge: Cambridge University Press, 1987).

122 This count and the following chart build on the work on the myth of Apollo and Daphne in the *Canzoniere* by Hainsworth, "The Myth of Daphne in the *Rerum vulgarium*

excerpts in the *Canzoniere* clearly shows (included below), Petrarch does not follow the temporal sequence of Ovid's tale at all in the *Canzoniere*, moving from the time before Daphne's transformation to the post-metamorphosis world and back, often lingering in an ambiguous in-between, where it is not clear if Laura is already a laurel tree or not. In other poems, Petrarch uncouples Laura and Daphne, and his lady appears near a laurel tree. But all main narrative elements of the story of Apollo and Daphne are present in the *Canzoniere*.

TABLE 12   The distribution of Ovid's story of Apollo and Daphne in the *Canzoniere*

Petrarch *Rvf*	Ovid Met.	Context in *Metamorphoses*	Context in *Rvf*
5.12–14	1.557–59	Apollo declares the laurel to be his tree, his symbol	mention of Apollo's laurel leaves, in contrast with the poet's "presumptuous" human voice
	1.565	description of the beauty of the laurel's undying leaves	
6.1–4	1.502–3	description of Daphne's flight, "swifter than the lightest breath of air"	the poet chases his lady, also swift and flying away from him (like Daphne); his own running is called "slow"
	1.510–11	Apollo's request to escape slower, and his promise to then pursue slower	
22.34–36	1.530–42	Apollo hunts Daphne down	the poet hopes that his lady does not transform into a green forest to escape his arms, just as what happened when Apollo chased her
23.43–49 23.20	1.548–52	Daphne's transformation into a laurel tree	the poet's transformation into a laurel tree, not next to the Peneus (Daphne's father/river), but a "prouder" river (the Rhône)
34.7	1.564–65	description of the honor of the laurel's undying leaves	poet asks Apollo to defend the honored laurel leaves

fragmenta"; Sturm-Maddox, "The Ovidian Subtext"; and Marga Cottino-Jones, "The Myth of Apollo and Daphne in Petrarch's *Canzoniere*: The Dynamics and Literary Function of Transformation," in *Francis Petrarch, Six Centuries Later: A Symposium*, ed. Aldo Scaglione (Chapel Hill: University of North Carolina, 1975), 152–76.

TABLE 12 The distribution of Ovid's story of Apollo and Daphne in the *Canzoniere* (cont.)

Petrarch *Rvf*	Ovid Met.	Context in *Metamorphoses*	Context in *Rvf*
75.3	1.523	Apollo, god of medicine, realizes that he cannot heal himself	the poet is struck by his lady's eyes, and no herbs or magic art can heal him
90.1	1.529	description of the wind going through the hair of Daphne in flight	description of his lady's golden hair scattered in the wind
127.77–84	1.497	description of Daphne's hair, falling down her neck	two mentions of his lady's (golden) loose hairs falling down her neck, and floating in the wind
	1.542	Apollo breathes down on Daphne's loose hairs	
151.8	1.466–71	description of Cupid's two arrows (of gold and of lead), and their effects	Love gilds and sharpens his arrows
161.5–6	1.557–59	Apollo declares the laurel to be his tree, his symbol	mention of laurel leaves and their honor, and of their "twin" value (i.e., for poets and generals)
	1.560–63	the laurel is also the symbol of Roman generals	
	1.564–65	description of the honor of the laurel's undying leaves	
188.1–2	1.452	Daphne is called Apollo's first love	addressing the Sun (Apollo), the poet mentions his lady, "whom he loved first"
192.12–13	1.498–99	description of the spark in Daphne's eyes, similar to fire	description of the spark in his lady's eyes
197.2	1.452–73	Cupid goes after Apollo with his bow and makes him fall in love with Daphne, who escapes him	mention of Love piercing Apollo
206.10–11	1.468–71	description of Cupid's two arrows, of gold and of lead, and their effects: to fall in love (gold) and to flee love (lead)	"Let Love use the golden arrows on me, and those of lead on her"
325.57	1.502–3	description of Daphne's flight, "swifter than the lightest breath of air"	Fortune says that she can change the fate of men and is "lighter than the wind"

In the opening poems of the *Canzoniere*, Petrarch introduces Love, armed with arrows, attacking the poet. As illustrated at various points in this book, this is a common image in vernacular poetry — until the mention of the laurel in *Quando io movo i sospiri a chiamar voi* (*Rvf* 5), there is nothing specific that links Petrarch's poetry to Ovid's story of Apollo and Daphne yet. Throughout the *Canzoniere*, Petrarch inserts many elements from the tale that make the connection with Ovid undeniable, sometimes with verbal links to the Latin verses (see Table 12), but often not. In several poems, Petrarch's narrative matches Ovid's, but not always. In the last poem that clearly echoes the language of Ovid's story of Apollo and Daphne, the *canzone Tacer non posso* (*Rvf* 325), Petrarch goes back to an Ovidian verse describing how the pre-metamorphosis Daphne ran for her life, trying to escape Apollo, "faster than the wind" ("ocior aura" [*Met.* 1.502]). Petrarch mentions the same swiftness in the words of the unnamed Fortune, who in the *canzone* explained her control over people's affairs and how quickly they can turn: "et so far lieti et tristi in un momento, / più leggiera che 'l vento" ("and I know how to make people happy and sad in a moment, lighter than the wind" [*Rvf* 325.56–57]). But only in the very last poem that references the myth in the *Canzoniere* (and the fourth-to-last poem of the collection), the sonnet *Morte à spento quel sol ch'abagliar suolmi* (*Rvf* 363), do the symbolic language and imagery developed over the collection seem to come to a close. While the sun, one of Apollo's names, often signals the god in the *Canzoniere*, it is also frequently used as a stand-in for Laura (first in *Que' ch'infinita providentia et arte* [*Rvf* 4]). Such is the case in *Morte à spento quel sol ch'abagliar suolmi*, where Petrarch writes that the sun is extinguished ("spento" [*Rvf* 363.1]), indicating Laura's death. He further adds that also his laurel leaves (first introduced in *Quando io movo i sospiri a chiamar voi* [*Rvf* 5] and another signifier for Laura, for the poet's connection with her, and for poetry) are extinguished ("spenti" [*Rvf* 363.4]) as well.[123]

Petrarch did not consider Apollo's fight with Python (*Met.* 1.438–51) part of the story of Apollo and Daphne. The attack on Apollo and Daphne was revenge: after Apollo's victory over Python, a boastful Apollo mocked Love's archery skills. In response, Love went after Apollo and Daphne with his arrows to make him fall in love and her run away. As Petrarch's own manuscript containing the first four books of the *Metamorphoses* (London, British Library, MS Harley 3754) also shows, Petrarch separated the two stories in his reading: he wrote next to the passage on the battle with Python the gloss "phebus instituit

---

123   On the metaphor in general and Laura as the sun in the *Canzoniere*, see Peter Hainsworth, "Metaphor in Petrarch's *Rerum vulgarium fragmenta*," in *The Languages of Literature in Renaissance Italy*, ed. Peter Hainsworth et al. (Oxford: Clarendon Press, 1988), 1–18.

ludos phiteos" ("Phoebus founded the Pythian Games"), and added a new paragraph mark next to "primus amor" (the first verse of the actual story of Apollo and Daphne), writing "fabula daphnes" ("the story of Daphne" [fol. 162r]) in the margin.[124] Like in his manuscript, Petrarch kept the episode with Python separated from his extensive reading of the story of Apollo and Daphne in the *Canzoniere*, featuring it instead in the *rima estravagante Se Phebo al primo amor non è bugiardo* (Paolino 3a).

Se Phebo al primo amor non è bugiardo, part of an exchange with Ser Dietisalvi Petri di Siena, contains several features, including some undesirable qualities of Apollo, that Petrarch carefully keeps out of the *Canzoniere*. In the opening sonnet *El bell'occhio d'Appollo dal chui guardo* (Paolino 3), Ser Dietisalvi describes how Apollo at the sight of his lady ran off, and wonders what frightened him more: her perfect beauty or honesty.[125] In his reply *Se Phebo al primo amor non è bugiardo* (included in full below), Petrarch concludes that if Apollo had not given up on his first love Daphne, it must have been the resemblance between Petrarch's lady and Daphne that had caused Apollo's reaction:

> Se Phebo al primo amor non è bugiardo,
> o per novo piacer non si ripente,
> già mai non gli esce il bel lauro di mente,
> a la cui ombra io mi distruggo et ardo.
>
> Questi solo il può far veloce et tardo,
> et lieto et tristo, et timido et valente;
> ch'al suon del nome suo par che pavente,
> et fu contra Phiton già sì gagliardo.
>
> Altri per certo nol turbava allora,
> quando nel suo bel viso gli occhi apriste
> et non gli offese il varïato aspetto;

---

124 This image, together with a few more pages from MS Harley 3754, can be consulted in the Digital Catalogue of Illuminated Manuscripts of The British Library at http://www.bl.uk/catalogues/illuminatedmanuscripts/. In Petrarch's copy of the *Metamorphoses*, the beginning of this story is not marked by a larger initial or the inclusion of a rubric as in many other manuscripts of the *Metamorphoses*, including *figs.* 2 and 4 discussed in Ch. 1.1.

125 As Laura Paolino pointed out, Ser Dietisalvi's initial reference to the story of Apollo and Daphne shows that Petrarch's interest in this Ovidian story was well known. See Petrarca, *Trionfi, Rime estravaganti, Codice degli abbozzi*, ed. Pacca and Paolino, 660–61.

ma se pur chi voi dite il discolora,
sembianza è forse alcuna de le viste;
et so ben che 'l mio dir parrà sospetto.

[If Phoebus does not betray his first love, or does not regret it because of a new pleasure, the beautiful laurel, in whose shadow I destroy myself and am aflame, never leaves his mind. Only the laurel can make him fast and slow, happy and sad, timid and bold; as at the sound of her name it seems that he is frightened, while he was so powerful against Python. For certain no other love troubled him then, when you opened your eyes to see his beautiful face and his altered appearance did not offend them; but if she of whom you speak drained the color out of his face, perhaps there is some similarity in their looks; and I know that my words will seem suspect to you.]

This sonnet abounds with Ovidian references. Petrarch explicity refers to Apollo's fight against Python, contrasting Apollo's current feelings of despair with the vigor that he displayed earlier during this fight (v. 8). Moreover, Petrarch calls Apollo "Phebo" (which he rarely does in the *Canzoniere*),[126] the same name Ovid used, most famously in the opening verse of the story of Apollo and Daphne: "Primus amor Phoebi" (*Met.* 1.452). Following Ovid's example, also Petrarch's first verse mentions both "Phebo" and "primo amor" (v. 1). In the next verse, Petrarch mentions a possible "new pleasure" (v. 2), which retakes Apollo's "new fire" ("igne nouo") for Leucothoë, which Ovid describes further on in his poem (*Met.* 4.195). New love is a common trope in vernacular poetry; for instance, Laura Paolino noted a similar use of the expression "novo piacer" in Dante's sonnet *Cavalcando l'altr'ier per un cammino* (v. 12).[127] In Dante's letter to Cino da Pistoia (*Ep.* III), accompanying the sonnet *Io sono stato con Amore insieme*, he cites the same story of Apollo's "new fire" for Leucothoë to answer the question if the soul can move "from one passion to another" (see Ch. 3.3). While the "new love" trope is thus not new to vernacular verse, Petrarch is only explicit about Apollo's other love interests in this *rima estravagante*, not wanting to associate this characteristic of Apollo with the narrative of the *Canzoniere*.

---

126 Only in the sonnet *Quando dal proprio sito si rimove* (*Rvf* 41), Apollo is called "Phebo": "l'arbor ch'amò già Phebo in corpo humano" ("the tree … that Phoebus already loved in human form" [*Rvf* 41.2]).

127 Petrarca, *Trionfi, Rime estravaganti, Codice degli abbozzi*, ed. Pacca and Paolino, 661, note to vv. 1–3.

In the *Canzoniere*, Petrarch also shows more restraint in using the phrase "primo amor," which in *Se Phebo al primo amor non è bugiardo* describes Apollo's love for Daphne (v. 1), just like in Ovid's account ("Primus amor" [*Met.* 1.452]). Petrarch only uses it once, in the canzone *Amor, se vuo' ch'i' torni al giogo antico* (*Rvf* 270), a poem about his resistance to Love's continued attacks after Laura's death. There Petrarch uses the translation of the Ovidian phrase to describe his loss of Laura, his own "primo amor": "Indarno or sovra me tua forza adopre, / mentre 'l mio primo amor terra ricopre" ("in vain now you exert your force on me, while the earth covers my first love" [*Rvf* 270.44–45]). In contrast to the *rima estravagante Se Phebo al primo amor non è bugiardo*, where Petrarch packs the short poetic form of the sonnet with several obvious references to the Ovidian story of Apollo and Daphne, in the canzone *Amor, se vuo' ch'i' torni al giogo antico*, Petrarch is restrained in his use of Ovidian material related to Apollo. In the *canzone*, Petrarch describes the attraction of another woman via the intervention of Love — the "novo piacer" of *Se Phebo al primo amor non è bugiardo* (v. 2), which, as readers of Ovid's stories about Apollo in the *Metamorphoses* know, is soon to follow. But the other woman is (literally) a dead end in the *Canzoniere*, and ultimately Petrarch uses the Ovidian label of "primo amor" in the *Canzoniere* not only in the sense of "first," but also "best" and "only."[128] When in the sonnet *Almo Sol, quella fronde ch'io sola amo* (*Rvf* 188) Petrarch more loosely translates the Ovidian "primus amor," he does so underlining the primacy of his own love for Laura: "Almo Sol, quella fronde ch'io sola amo, / tu prima amasti" ("Noble Sun, the only branch that I love, you first loved" [*Rvf* 188.1–2]).

Se Phebo al primo amor non è bugiardo shares several features with another excluded poem, *Sì come il padre del folle Fetonte*, discussed in the previous section. The two poems (both part of sonnet exchanges) pack many references to Ovid's *Metamorphoses*; in the *Canzoniere* Petrarch is normally more

---

128 This *canzone* and the following sonnet *L'ardente nodo ov'io fui d'ora in hora* (*Rvf* 271) are often considered references to a new love interest — as especially Marco Santagata suggested, in the vein of Dante's "donna pietosa" in the *Vita nuova* after Beatrice's death. See *I frammenti dell'anima: Storia e racconto nel 'Canzoniere' di Petrarca* (Bologna: Il Mulino, 1992), 205–7. In the *canzone*, Petrarch resists the allure of a new love (Love's attacks are in vain, as the verses cited from the *canzone* above indicate); in the sonnet Petrarch seem more accessible, mentioning "un altro lacciuol" ("another snare" [*Rvf* 271.6]) and "di nova ésca un altro foco acceso" ("another fire kindled with new tinder" [*Rvf* 271.7]). Both poems end with death: with a final mention of Laura's death in *Amor, se vuo' ch'i' torni al giogo antico* (*Rvf* 270.106–8), which liberated the poet from Love's rule; and in *L'ardente nodo ov'io fui d'ora in hora* death liberates the poet "another time" ("un'altra volta" [*Rvf* 271.12]), leaving it unclear whether this refers again to Laura's death or the death of this new love interest.

restrained in his use of Ovidian references and verbal echoes, especially in the shorter poetic form of the sonnet. Like *Sì come il padre del folle Fetonte*, also this poem places the poets and their ladies in the same world as the Ovidian characters Apollo and Daphne. The laurel, which was always on Apollo's mind (v. 3), is the tree under which Petrarch now sits and suffers (v. 4). Especially in the last tercet, Petrarch experiments with this blending of both worlds, which characterizes many of his Ovidian poems in the *Canzoniere*. But in *Se Phebo al primo amor non è bugiardo* Petrarch spells out the comparison: "sembianza è forse alcuna de le viste" ("perhaps there is some similarity in their appearances" [v. 13]). As we just saw, other love interests only play a minimal role after Laura's death: there is no real place for other ladies in the *Canzoniere*, especially if they resemble Daphne/Laura.[129] Petrarch is also much subtler in creating a woman who is both Daphne and Laura,[130] without explicitly pointing out their "sembianza" (v. 13), as he does in *Se Phebo al primo amor non è bugiardo*.[131]

The story of Apollo and Daphne, in other words, dominates the *Canzoniere*, but entirely on Petrarch's terms: the references to the two Ovidian characters,

---

129   As Justin Steinberg pointed out, it is only in one of the *rime estravaganti*, *Donna mi vène spesso ne la mente* (Paolino 18), that Petrarch explicitly mentions his "donna" Laura (v. 1) together with the "other woman" ("altra donna" [v. 2]): "Nowhere else in his corpus does Petrarch come closer to challenging the exclusivity of his love for Laura." See "Dante *Estravagante*, Petrarca *Disperso*, and the Spectre of the Other Woman," in Barański and Cachey, *Petrarch & Dante*, 263–89, at 281. Also Marco Marcozzi listed *Se Phebo al primo amor non è bugiardo* among the poems (excluded from the *Canzoniere*) where the central focus is on Apollo's sensual love for Daphne, not on the virtues associated with her symbol, the laurel (*La biblioteca di Febo*, 253, and n. 293).

130   See, for instance, the sonnet *Poco era ad appressarsi agli occhi miei* (*Rvf* 51), discussed in the previous section.

131   A similar explicit comparison is found in another sonnet that was not included in the *Canzoniere*, *Sì mi fan risentire a l'aura sparsi* (Paolino 11). Petrarch describes his lady (the pun on Laura's name, "l'aura," is in the first verse) now appearing as a huntress (vv. 5–8), which reminds him of a passage in Vergil's *Aeneid* when the goddess Venus, also as huntress, appeared to Aeneas (*Aen.* 1.318–20): "Poi mi ricordo di Venus iddea, / qual Virgilio descrisse 'n sua figura, / e parmi Laura in quell'atto vedere" ("Then I am reminded of the goddess Venus, whose appearance Vergil described, and I seem to see Laura in those movements" [vv. 9–11]). Also in this tercet Petrarch spells out in no unclear terms the comparison between Laura and a classical character, even with the name of his source author. The sonnet *Né così bello il sol già mai levarsi*, also addressed to Sennuccio del Bene and included in the *Canzoniere* (*Rvf* 144), retakes the rhymes and hunting imagery of *Sì mi fan risentire a l'aura sparsi*, but the Vergilian reference to the goddess Venus is reduced to "nulla cosa mortal pote aguagliarsi" ("no mortal thing can equal" [*Rvf* 144.8]). On the use of classical material in both sonnets, see Steinberg, "Petrarch's Damned Poetry and the Poetics of Exclusion," 93–95, and 94, n. 23. On the cruder use of classical material in the *rime estravaganti*, see also Sturm-Maddox, *Petrarch's Laurels*, 4–6, who discusses these same poems.

often stand-ins and doubles of the poet and Laura through well-chosen translations and paraphrases of Ovid's verses, are many, but only from a reading of the *rime estravaganti* and the entire story in the *Metamorphoses* does it become clear how selective and curated Petrarch's seemingly abundant presence of Apollo and Daphne in the *Canzoniere* truly is.

The story of Orpheus and Eurydice receives a similar treatment throughout the *Canzoniere*: fragmented, unfinished, altered. As noted in the previous section, the two most explicit references to the story (references that include clearly recognizable narrative elements) are found in Part 2 of the *Canzoniere*: in the *Canzone delle visioni*, where the final vision consists of an unnamed Eurydice walking in the grass and being bitten by a snake (*Rvf* 323.61–72), and in a simile in the *sestina doppia Mia benigna fortuna e 'l viver lieto*, where the poet wishes that he too could recover his Laura from death, just as Orpheus was given the chance to bring back his Eurydice from the afterlife (*Rvf* 332.49–54). Petrarch first introduces Orpheus in the political *canzone O aspectata in ciel beata et bella* (*Rvf* 28), where he represents, together with Amphion, the power of the word (*Rvf* 28.68–69) — something his readers, Petrarch further remarks, would know from written sources ("leggendo" [*Rvf* 28.68]). Indeed, both Vergil and Ovid describe Orpheus's effect of his song on his audience.[132] But Petrarch's mention of written sources also points to the Latin commentaries on the myth, which all emphasize this feature of Orpheus. Pierre Bersuire, friend and correspondent of Petrarch, and the author of the *Ovidius moralizatus* (see Ch. 1.1), goes into great detail in his interpretation of this story, proposing Orpheus both as Christ and a sinner tempted by the devil.[133] The attraction to Eurydice in the latter reading is understood as one to temporal matters ("temporalia") — many commentators interpret Eurydice in this way, without explicitly framing this attraction within a Christian context as Bersuire did. Such a reading also entered the *Canzoniere*. For instance, in the sonnet *Poi che voi et io più volte abbiam provato* (*Rvf* 99), Petrarch writes that life on earth is almost ("quasi") like the meadow where Eurydice (unnamed in this sonnet) died (*Rvf* 99.5–8):

---

132   Petrarch's source is much more Vergilian than Ovidian, as Nicola Gardini illustrated in "Un esempio di imitazione virgiliana." Also in this instance, Petrarch shows little interest in moral interpretations of this Ovidian story (a point also made in Chines, 'Di selva in selva ratto mi trasformo,' 35–38).

133   Friedman, *Orpheus in the Middle Ages*, 126–32. Bersuire's contrasting readings of Orpheus in the *Ovidius moralizatus* serve as another reminder of the interpretative diversity that categorizes the commentary tradition on the *Metamorphoses*, at times even found within the same commentary.

> Questa vita terrena è quasi un prato,
> che 'l serpente tra' fiori et l'erba giace;
> et s'alcuna sua vista agli occhi piace,
> è per lassar piu l'animo invescato.
>
> [This earthly life is almost like a meadow where the serpent lies between the flowers and the grass, and if anything pleases our eyes, it is to leave our soul more enticed.]

Petrarch sustained such interpretations in his prose, connecting the story of Orpheus and Eurydice with that of Lot's wife in the Book of Genesis, another story where looking back had fatal consequences (Gen. 19). Others preceded Petrarch in connecting these classical and biblical accounts, among them Heloise and Abelard in their letters, a collection that Petrarch owned and annotated.[134] In a letter to pope Urban V, Petrarch unites the two turning points in these classical and biblical texts and clarifies their meaning (*Sen.* IX 1, 186):

> nec ignoras ut vel apud scriptores gentium Orpheus retro versus eductam ab inferis suam perdit Euridicen vel apud nostros Loth e Sodomis exeunti ut « salvet animam suam neque post tergum respiciat » imperatur; quod vel oblita vel descpiciens « uxor eius respiciensque post se in statuam salis versa » exemplum atque utile condimentum posteris liquit, quo in similibus salliantur, ne insipido rerum gustu ad ea que bene dimiserint animo aut oculis se convertant.
>
> [And you also know that Orpheus, according to the pagan writers, by turning around, lost his Eurydice whom he had taken out of the underworld, and that Lot, in our own Scriptures, was instructed upon leaving Sodom to "not turn his back in order to save his soul." But his wife, who

---

[134] The letters of Abelard and Heloise, with Petrarch's comments, are included in Paris, Bibliothèque nationale de France, MS lat. 2923, a late-thirteenth-century copy that came into Petrarch's possession between 1337 and 1343. On the letters and these comments, see de Nolhac, *Pétrarque et l'humanisme*, 2: 217–23; and Constant J. Mews, *The Lost Love Letters of Heloise and Abelard: Perceptions of Dialogue in Twelfth-century France*, trans. by Neville Chiavaroli and Constant J. Mews, 2nd ed. (New York: Palgrave Macmillan, 2008), 41–42. As Mews wrote, "Petrarch's fascination with Heloise is evident from the many comments that he appended to the margins of her letters in his manuscript" (42), but Petrarch did not comment on Heloise's mention of Lot's wife (fol. 16r). On the connection between Orpheus and Eurydice and Lot's wife, see Angelo Poliziano, *Poesie volgari*, ed. Francesco Bausi, 2 vols. (Rome: Vecchiarelli, 1997), 1: 10.

forgot or ignored this, "did look behind her and turned into a statue of salt." She left an example and a useful seasoning for posterity, so that people would be sprinkled with it in similar situations and because of an insipid taste of things would not turn their minds or their eyes to what they should rightly have left behind them.]

Similarly, in the *Secretum*, St. Augustine warns Petrarch not to be like Orpheus for the same reason: to not be attached to temporal matters (*Sec.* III.9.13).[135]

Even though in his prose Petrarch acknowledges the allegorical meaning of these stories and the example they set, his poetry shows that while he knows what is best, he follows the worst — paraphrasing the final verse of *I' vo pensando* (*Rvf* 264.136) — and keeps looking back. Notwithstanding the more obvious references to the story of Orpheus and Eurydice with names and narrative details, the main way in which the story runs through the *Canzoniere* are those repeated references to turning around and looking back. For instance, in the sonnet *Quand'io v'odo parlar sì dolcemente* (*Rvf* 143), Petrarch inserts the acts of turning and looking back in a tercet that started out describing his lady in distinctively Daphnean terms — the scattered hairs in the air are taken directly from Ovid's description of Daphne (*Met.* 1.529) — but then switches to the story of Orpheus and Eurydice when his lady turns around and he looks back (*Rvf* 143.9–11):

> Le chiome a l'aura sparse, et lei conversa
> indietro veggio; et così bella riede
> nel cor, come colei che tien la chiave.

[Her locks scattered by the wind, and I see her turning back; and so she returns beautiful in my heart, as one who holds the key.]

Even more obvious is the sonnet *Li angeli electi et l'anime beate* (*Rvf* 346) from Part 2 of the *Canzoniere*, which explicitly deals with Laura's death. In this imagining of Laura's arrival in heaven, Petrarch works with the same components — the lady turns around, the poet follows — but this poem is even more true to the story of Orpheus and Eurydice, for now the poet and his beloved are separated by death as well (*Rvf* 346.9–12):

---

135 The historical St. Augustine wrote about the example set by Lot's wife in *De civitate Dei* XVI.30.

> Ella, contenta aver cangiato albergo,
> si paragona pur coi più perfecti,
> et parte ad or ad or si volge a tergo,
>
> mirando s'io la seguo, et par ch'aspecti.
>
> [Glad to have changed her dwelling, she may be compared to even the most perfect souls, and from time to time she turns around to see if I am following her and seems to wait.]

Among the many phrases that Petrarch uses throughout the *Canzoniere* to describe the acts of looking back and turning around, his particular phrasing in this sonnet, "si volge a tergo" (*Rvf* 346.11), recalls the biblical account in the Book of Genesis, where God tells Lot's wife, "noli respicere post tergum" ("do not turn your back and look behind you" [Gen. 19:17]).[136] But while the language evokes the biblical episode, Petrarch's interpretation of this act is ultimately positive: the poet sketches out the conditions of his perfect reunion with his perfect lady. Petrarch, familiar with the moralizing and Christianizing interpretations of the story of Orpheus and Eurydice, expresses such views in his prose works, adding in the *Canzoniere* occasional glimpses of the temptation that Eurydice could represent. But mostly Petrarch charts his own interpretative path, where the main story line gets intertwined with references to other classical and biblical accounts.

Petrarch may turn to the stories of the *Metamorphoses* more often than to other Ovidian works, but several of the approaches identified in his treatment of the stories of Apollo and Daphne and Orpheus and Eurydice characterize Petrarch's use of Ovid's other poems as well. For instance, *Her.* 4 (Phaedra's letter to Hippolytus) is another Ovidian poem that is fragmented throughout the *Canzoniere*. In the letter, Phaedra confesses her love to her stepson Hippolytus; in the *Metamorphoses*, Ovid deals with the aftermath: Hippolytus's rejection, Phaedra's false but convincing accusation that Hippolytus raped her, and Hippolytus's subsequent exile (*Met.* 15.479–546). As we have seen in Ch. 2.2, Bertran Carbonel's *canso Aisi m'a dat fin'amor conoissensa* also drew on this letter — a letter full of tropes: the lover's hesitation to confess his love, the lover's difficulty or inability to express his feelings to his lady, Love commanding the lover to act. But Carbonel's poem featured the same sequence of actions

---

136   While in their accounts of the story of Orpheus and Eurydice Vergil and Ovid of course describe the acts of turning around and looking back, they do not use the phrase "post tergum."

described in the opening of Phaedra's letter (vv. 29–32), and explicitly indicated Ovid's writings as his source ("qu'ieu truep en l'escriptura / c'Ovidis dis" [vv. 29–30]) The entire passage from the *Heroides* is worth repeating here (*Her.* 4.7–14):

> Ter tecum conata loqui, ter inutilis haesit
> lingua, ter in primo restitit ore sonus.
> Qua licet et sequitur, pudor est miscendus amori;
> dicere quae puduit, scribere iussit amor.
> Quidquid Amor iussit, non est contemnere tutum;
> regnat et in dominos ius habet ille deos.
> Ille mihi primo dubitanti scribere dixit:
> "Scribe! Dabit victas ferreus ille manus."

[Three times I have tried to speak to you, three times my tongue was worthless, three times the words got stuck on the tip of my tongue. As much as it is possible, modesty should be mixed with love; love ordered me to write what is shameful to say. Whatever Love ordered, it is not safe to condemn; he rules and holds the law over the gods, our lords. He said to me when I first was in doubt to write: "Write! That cruel one will be overcome and surrender."]

In the *Canzoniere*, Petrarch works with the same material, but in the common way that narrative units in Ovid's poetry (be it an entire story in the *Metamorphoses* or an entire letter from the *Heroides*) are treated in the collection: divided over different poems, used where deemed fitting, combined with other sources, and appropriated to Petrarch's own narrative. He repeats Phaedra's stated inability to express herself (*Her.* 4.7–8) in the sonnets *Perch'io t'abbia guardato di menzogna* (*Rvf* 49) and *Più volte già dal bel sembiante humano* (*Rvf* 170).[137] The image of Love being in command, and especially of the poet's writing, is widely found in classical, vernacular, and theological literature, as we have seen in Ch. 4.3. But Petrarch's precise formulation in the opening verses of the sonnet *Più volte Amor m'avea già detto: Scrivi* (*Rvf* 93.1–2) connects his sonnet specifically with the sentiment expressed in Phaedra's letter (*Her.* 4.13–14):

---

137 These are the two poems where the expression of this notion comes closest to Phaedra's formulation in *Her.* 4; Marco Santagata mentions other examples in Petrarca, *Canzoniere*, ed. Santagata, 250.

Più volte Amor m'avea già detto: Scrivi,
scrivi quel che vedesti in lettere d'oro

[Several times Love had already said to me: "Write, write in letters of gold what you have seen."]

In the *sestina Là ver' l'aurora, che sì dolce l'aura* (*Rvf* 239), Petrarch portrays Love in the same way as Phaedra's letter does (*Her.* 4.12) — Love rules not only over humans, but also over gods: "Homini et dèi solea vincer per forza / Amor" ("Love often overcomes both men and gods with his powers" [*Rvf* 239.19–20]). Petrarch's treatment of his Ovidian source, moreover, also brings to mind the poetry of his vernacular predecessors. Like Bertran Carbonel and other Occitan and Italian poets before him, Petrarch points to written sources for this statement about Love: "come si legge in prose e 'n versi" ("as one reads in prose and in verses" [*Rvf* 239.20]).[138] And also like previous vernacular poets, Petrarch tests the validity of this statement with his own experience: "et io 'l provai in sul primo aprir de' fiori" ("and I experienced it when the flowers first bloomed" [*Rvf* 239.21]). Compare Petrarch's verses, for instance, with Dante da Maiano's statement in the sonnet *Amor mi fa sì fedelmente amare* (see Ch. 2.3): "D'Ovidio ciò mi son miso a *provare* / che disse ..." ("I have set myself to *test* what Ovid prescribed" [vv. 5–6]; emphasis added). Petrarch uses the same description of Love as ruler over gods and men in the sonnet *In mezzo di duo amanti honesta altera* (*Rvf* 115), an example of Petrarch's blending of the world of the *Metamorphoses* with that of the poet: the "two lovers" are Apollo and the poet, and together they see their lady and Love (vv. 1–4). Petrarch turns to the Ovidian phrase from the *Heroides* — describing Love as "quel signor ... / che fra gli uomini regna et fra li dèi" ("that lord who reigns over men and gods" (*Rvf* 115.2–3) — to further unite the poet ("men") and Apollo ("gods").

Many phrases from Ovid's poetry took on proverbial qualities, as we have seen at various points in this book, and Petrarch's poetry also provides several examples of this practice. In the *canzone Mai non vo' più cantar   com'io soleva* (*Rvf* 105), the verse "Proverbio « ama chi t'ama »   è fatto antico" ("The proverb 'Love those who love you' is an ancient fact" [*Rvf* 105.31]) technically retakes one of the concluding verses of Phaedra's letter: "sic numquam, quae te spernere possit, ames" ("So may you never love a girl who could despise you" [*Her.* 4.168]), but, as Petrarch indicates by calling it a "proverbio," the expression clearly already stood on its own. Also the *Fasti*, a minimal source in the *Canzoniere*, provided such a proverbial phrase: "fastus inest pulchris sequiturque superbia

---

138   See Ch. 2.2 and Ch. 2.3 for more examples.

formam" ("disdain is inherent to good-looking people, and arrogance comes with beauty" [*Fasti* 1.419]). In the *Canzoniere*, Petrarch shows the versatility of proverbs, isolated phrases that easily adapt to new contexts: when Laura is featured as a cruel lady, the Latin phrase from the *Fasti* becomes "et à sì egual a le bellezze orgoglio" ("and she has pride equal to her beauty" [*Rvf* 171.7]); when she is a force for good, the phrase is reversed: "e 'n humil donna alta beltà divina" ("and in a humble lady high divine beauty" [*Rvf* 213.4]).

Petrarch also finds in Ovid's *Tristia* and *Epistulae ex Ponto* several verses expressing the general suffering and malaise of an exile, which he then maps on the amorous topics of his poetry. For instance, in the verse "nec, quid agam, inuenio, nec quid nolimue uelimue" (*Ex Ponto* 4.12.45), written to a friend, Ovid declares that he does not know what to do or even what he wants. In the sonnet *S'amor non è, che dunque è quel ch'io sento?* (*Rvf* 132), this verse becomes the despair of a distraught lover: "ch'i' medesmo non so quel ch'io mi voglio" ("that I myself do not know what I want" [*Rvf* 132.13]). In the sonnet *In dubbio di mio stato, or piango or canto* (*Rvf* 252), Petrarch reflects on what his misfortune in love has done to him: "vivo ch'i' non son più quel che già fui" ("I live so that I am no longer what I was before" [*Rvf* 252.13]). This verse originates from a remark of Ovid to a detractor, asking why he attacks him, now that Ovid no longer is who he used to be: "non sum ego quod fueram" (*Tristia* 3.11.25). In a letter to Cotta Maximus, a friend and Roman senator whom he hoped could convince the emperor to revoke his exile, Ovid warned ("cavete") his friend not to end up in this hostile place: "denique, quae mecum est et erit sine fine, cauete, / ne sit inuiso uestra figura loco" ("Finally, make sure that your figure, which is with me and will be forever, is not in a hateful place" [*Ex Ponto* 2.8.63–64]). In the sonnet *Se voi poteste per turbati segni* (*Rvf* 64), Petrarch uses a similar phrase, now directed to his lady, asking her to change the feelings of hatred in her heart into feelings of love: "provedete almeno / di non star sempre in odïosa parte" ("at least make sure not to stay forever in a hateful place" [*Rvf* 64.13–14]). Throughout this book I have discussed several instances where Italian authors stripped the amorous tone from an Ovidian passage in the *Amores*, *Heroides*, or *Ars amatoria* and turned it into a gem of moral wisdom it never was in its original Ovidian context. In the passages from the *Canzoniere* discussed above, Petrarch does the reverse, adding the context of love to Ovidian verses that were once exclusively about exile: he reinterprets the feelings of alienation and distance captured in Ovid's exile letters to express similar feelings of the lover.[139]

---

139 As mentioned in Ch. 3.3, Catherine Keen has identified a similar practice in the love poetry of exiled poets: Cino da Pistoia and other exiled poets mapped the language of

Some of Ovid's exile letters are addressed to his wife, and thus literally combine the themes of exile and love. Petrarch turns to some of those letters in the *Canzoniere*. For instance, the sonnets *Se Virgilio et Homero avessin visto* (*Rvf* 186) and *Giunto Alexandro a la famosa tomba* (*Rvf* 187), as Vincenzo Fera first proposed, were modeled after an Ovidian letter written to his wife, *Tristia* 1.6.[140] In the letter, Ovid describes the consolation and joy that his wife's loyalty and support bring to him, comparing her not only to other women famous for the same qualities, but concluding that a better poet, the Maionian bard Homer, would have made her more famous than Penelope (vv. 21–22). Ovid adds that while his verses are rough and inadequate, at least they will make her live on forever in his poetry (vv. 35–36). The opening verses of Petrarch's sonnet *Se Virgilio et Homero avessin visto* indeed convey a similar message (*Rvf* 186.1–4):

> Se Virgilio et Homero avessin visto
> quel sole il qual vegg'io con gli occhi miei,
> tutte lor forze in dar fama a costei
> avrian posto, et l'un stil coll'altro misto:

> [If Vergil and Homer had seen that sun which I see with my own eyes, they would have concentrated all their efforts to give her fame, and mixed one style with another.]

In the following sonnet *Giunto Alexandro a la famosa tomba*, Petrarch repeats the sentiment (*Rvf* 187.9–11):

> Ché d'Omero dignissima et d'Orpheo,
> o del pastor ch'anchor Mantova honora,
> ch'andassen sempre lei sola cantando.

> [For she is most worthy of Homer and Orpheus or the shepherd that Mantua still honors, that they would sing forever only about her.]

---

exclusion, captivity, and exile (without reference to Ovid) on their love poetry, and addressed their lost cities with the language of desire. See Ch. 3.3, and n. 62 of that chapter. On Petrarch's readings of Ovid's exile poetry, see Keen's essay "Ovid's Exile and Medieval Italian Literature: The Lyric Tradition," in Miller and Newlands, *A Handbook to the Reception of Ovid*, 144–60, at 154–58, where she pointed out how Petrarch finds solace in the landscapes earlier exiled poets wanted to avoid.

140 Vincenzo Fera, "I sonetti CLXXXVI e CLXXXVII," *Lectura Petrarce* 7 (1987): 219–43, at 223–24.

Previous vernacular poets had often praised the exceptionality of their ladies, even compared them to famous women of antiquity, most notably in several of Chiaro Davanzati's poems (see Ch. 2.1). But here Petrarch looks closer at Ovid's example in the *Tristia*, who not only compares the ladies, but also the poets — evaluating what they are capable of doing with the subject of their writing. Like Ovid, Petrarch claims to be no Homer, and adds several more classical poets who would have been more successful in praising Laura in their poetry. The conclusion of Ovid's letter — the promise of immortality that his wife will ultimately achieve through his verses, as imperfect as they may be — is not found in Petrarch's sonnet, but the sentiment, to write his lady into literary immortality, is one that runs through the *Canzoniere*.

While Ovid's letter to his wife thus provided a model to write about Laura, Petrarch does not include Ovid in the list of poets who are mentioned for comparison. He copies Homer from Ovid's letter and pairs him with Vergil (*Rvf* 186.1 and *Rvf* 187.9–10) and Orpheus (*Rvf* 187.9); and finds Ennius more to be like him: unlike Homer and Vergil, they are poets who write "ruvido carme" ("inelegant song"), Ennius about Scipio Africanus, Petrarch about Laura (*Rvf* 186.12–13).[141] Here, as in the entire *Canzoniere*, Petrarch goes out of his way not to mention Ovid by name, despite the significant textual presence of the Latin poet.[142] In addition to *Tristia* 1.6, which provided the model for Petrarch's two sonnets, also the phrase "ruvido carme" is Ovidian: in the following exile letter, *Tristia* 1.7, Ovid uses the phrase to describe the *Metamorphoses* — a poem that, as Ovid tells us, his exile forced him to abandon, unfinished, rough ("rude carmen" [v. 39]), incomplete.[143] The connections between two consecutive letters in Ovid's *Tristia* (1.6 and 1.7) and the two consecutive sonnets in the *Canzoniere* (*Rvf* 186 and 187) provide a glimpse into Petrarch's process as reader and writer: while the two Ovidian letters share nothing in content — one is an ode to his wife (*Tristia* 1.6), the other about the *Metamorphoses* (*Tristia* 1.7) — Petrarch clearly read them together, in order, and elements from both letters make it

---

141   *Giunto Alexandro a la famosa tomba* ends on a similar note: in contrast with Homer, Orpheus, and Vergil, who would be outstanding and always praising her, Petrarch would be "tal che 'l suo bel nome adora, / ma forse scema sue lode parlando" ("one who adores her lovely name, but perhaps reduces her praise when he speaks" [*Rvf* 187.13–14]).

142   In contrast, Petrarch names Ennius frequently in his epic poem *Africa*, acknowledging his debt to the Latin poet.

143   Fera also mentioned the connection between the "ruvido carme" and *Tristia* 1.7 in "I sonetti CLXXXVI e CLXXXVII," 231, n. 45. See also the opening of this section, where this passage from *Tristia* 1.7 is mentioned as an example of how Ovid proposes to apply the theme of the *Metamorphoses* (change) to the interpretation of his poem itself.

into his two thematically linked sonnets, *Se Virgilio et Homero avessin visto* (*Rvf* 186) and *Giunto Alexandro a la famosa tomba* (*Rvf* 187).

In another letter addressed to his wife (*Ex Ponto* 1.4), Ovid imagines their reunion, both old and grey. At various points in the *Canzoniere* Petrarch addresses his aging body but unchanging love, in verses such as "Di dì in dì vo cangiando il viso e 'l pelo, / né però smorso i dolce inescati hami" ("From day to day my face and hair are changing, but I do not give up the sweetly baited hooks" [*Rvf* 195.1–2]), and "o colle brune o colle bianche chiome, / seguirò l'ombra di quel dolce lauro / ... / fin che l'ultimo dì chiuda quest'occhi" ("either with brown or with white hairs I will follow the shadow of that sweet laurel ... until the last day closes these eyes" [*Rvf* 30.15–18]). As Teodolinda Barolini and Nella Giannetto have argued, unlike any other lady in vernacular poetry before her, Petrarch's Laura also ages.[144] In the sonnet *Se la mia vita da l'aspro tormento* (*Rvf* 12), Ovid's letter to his wife seems the particular point of inspiration.[145] In this sonnet from the very beginning of the *Canzoniere*, Petrarch pictures Laura with "i cape' d'oro fin farsi d'argento" ("fine golden hair made silver" [*Rvf* 12.5]) — her aging rendered more explicit than in the opening verse of one of Petrarch's most famous sonnets, "*Erano* i capei d'oro a l'aura sparsi" ("her golden hair *was* scattered in the wind" [*Rvf* 90.1; emphasis added]). The poet imagines how only then he would finally find consolation in telling her all his "sufferings" ("mei martiri"):[146] "vi discovrirò de' mei martiri / qua' sono stati gli anni e i giorni et l'ore" ("I will reveal what have been the years and days and hours of my sufferings" [*Rvf* 12.10–11]). Ovid's letter first documents his own physical changes in age (*Ex Ponto* 1.4.1–8),[147] but then turns to his wife in verses containing the tenderness of conjugal love that could not exist in

---

144   Barolini, "The Self in the Labyrinth of Time," 49: "Petrarch's Laura does what no stilnovist or Dantean lyric love lady had done before her — she ages — and her aging, as in *Erano i capei d'oro a l'aura sparsi*, is a catalyst for the discourse of time, change, and multiplicity." See also Nella Giannetto, "Il motivo dell'amata incantuita nelle rime di Petrarca e Boccaccio," in *Miscellanea di studi in onore di Vittore Branca, II: Boccaccio e dintorni* (Florence: Leo S. Olschki, 1983), 23–49.

145   This connection between Petrarch's sonnet and Ovid's letter has, to my knowledge, not been noticed thus far.

146   Several scholars have pointed out how his verse retakes Francesca's "martìri" (*Inf.* 5.116). See, for instance, Feo, "Petrarca."

147   "Iam mihi deterior canis aspergitur aetas, / iamque meos uultus ruga senilis arat, / iam uigor et quasso languent in corpore uires, / nec iuueni lusus qui placuere iuuant, / nec, si me subito uideas, agnoscere possis: / aetatis facta est tanta ruina meae. / confiteor facere hoc annos, sed et altera causa est, / anxietas animi continuusque labor" ("Now the passing of the years has turned my hair white, and the wrinkles of an old man cut through my face; now strength and vigor languish in my broken body, the games that I liked in my youth do not entertain me anymore. If you were to see me all of a sudden, you would not

the *Canzoniere*. But all the other elements from Ovid's letter are present: Ovid imagines seeing his wife again after all those years of separation, and her hair has changed color. He wants to tell her about all his "sufferings" ("meos ... labores") and enjoy a talk he had never hoped for (*Ex Ponto* 1.4.49–54):

> o ego di faciant talem te cernere possim,
> caraque mutatis oscula ferre comis,
> amplectique meis corpus non pingue lacertis,
> et 'gracile hoc fecit' dicere 'cura mei'.
> et narrare meos flenti flens ipse labores,
> sperato numquam conloquioque frui.

[O may the gods let me see you like this, and place sweet kisses on your changed hair, and hold your tiny body in my arms, and say, "it is worry about me that made this body so thin," and through my tears tell you, also in tears, about all my sufferings, and enjoy a conversation that I never dared to hope would happen.]

Petrarch's attention never descends to Laura's aging body (Ovid's wife's "tiny body" [*Ex Ponto* 1.4.51] disappeared from Petrarch's sonnet, just like the conjugal kisses and embraces): her advanced age in the *Canzoniere* is only marked through the changing color of her hair, such a central feature of Petrarch's description of Laura's beauty. But Ovid's exile letters written to his wife — the perfect marriage of the themes of exile and love — provided Petrarch with ample verses fitting for the *Canzoniere*. The literal distance that separated Ovid and his wife became the distance and alienation Petrarch experiences from his beloved.

Petrarch's interest in the Ovidian concepts of fragmentation and metamorphosis is thus not limited to just his treatment of material from the *Metamorphoses*, the epic poem that embodies those concepts most fully. Also Ovid's amatory and exilic works offered passages and phrases that, similarly fragmented and altered, made their way into Petrarch's *Canzoniere*. The *Metamorphoses* remains Petrarch's main Ovidian source, as was the case for Dante in the *Commedia*. But while Dante included more stories and shorter passages, Petrarch was highly selective about which Ovidian characters and passages to include in the *Canzoniere*. The excluded poems or the *rime estravaganti* highlight Petrarch's careful curation in the *Canzoniere*: in several of the

---

recognize me; such is the ruin done to my life. I confess that the years have done this, but there is another cause: the anxiety of my mind and my continuous struggle").

rime estravaganti, Petrarch was explicit in his references to classical sources and went for quantity over quality; he spelled out the similarities ("sembianza" [*Se Phebo al primo amor non è bugiardo*, v. 13]) between his own situation and that of classical characters in ways that seem too heavy-handed for the *Canzoniere*. In contrast, in the *Canzoniere* Petrarch focused on just a few stories from the *Metamorphoses*, just a few Ovidian letters and poems: he blended them into individual poems of the *Canzoniere*, and fragmented them over the entire collection. Dante, too, fragmented certain episodes from Ovid's oeuvre over the *Commedia* (even though such global or programmatic readings were the exception), setting Ovidian material to his hand. The structure of the *Commedia*, however, is fundamentally different: a first-person account focused on what the pilgrim sees on his journey through hell, purgatory, and heaven. Ovid's verses helped give voice to what the pilgrim saw, what the pilgrim felt, and how other characters appeared. Petrarch's first-person account in the *Canzoniere* is, with the exception of the political poems, internal and introspective. And, more than any poet before him, Petrarch understood the manifold poetic possibilities that Ovid's poems, the Ovidian tradition, and the very Ovidian concepts of fragmentation and metamorphosis offered in crafting this personal narrative.

5.4 Conclusion

Petrarch's *Canzoniere* is, among many other things, a primer (albeit not the most accessible one) on the Ovidian tradition. Many of the works and genres discussed in Chapter 1 of this book, which charted the texts and contexts in which Italian readers during the thirteenth and fourteenth centuries could encounter Ovid, were integrated or re-interpreted in varying degrees in Petrarch's collection of poems. Petrarch integrates the commentary tradition on the *Metamorphoses*, the *volgarizzamento* of Ovid's works, the proverbial and "philosopher" Ovid of the anthologies and the treatises, and the many "filtered" Ovidian works — poetry inspired by Ovid's poems from late antiquity to Petrarch's days. His *Canzoniere* is also a testament to what Ovid and the Ovidian tradition meant to the Italian poets writing before Petrarch: in this chapter, I proposed readings of several Petrarchan poems as responses to how his predecessors integrated Ovidian material into their poetry. Petrarch's limited use of the simile featuring an Ovidian character in the *Canzoniere*, for instance, has been seen as a way to differentiate his *rime* from the traditional way in which Italian poets had featured Narcissus or Pyramus and Thisbe in their poems, explicitly comparing themselves and their ladies to these Ovidian characters (see Ch. 2.1). Petrarch's shifting identification with Ovidian characters (is he the Apollo or the Daphne of the story?) builds on some of Cino da Pistoia and Dante's poems, in which they tested out the boundaries of the similes in vernacular poetry (see Ch. 3.3). Petrarch's blending of the meadows of the *Metamorphoses* and the Vaucluse valley in the Avignon region was preceded by Cino's similar mixture of past and present in some of his sonnets (see Ch. 3.3). On the one hand, it is restricting to reduce Petrarch's Ovidian verses to an account of similarities and differences with his Italian precedessors, but on the other hand, this aspect of Petrarch's poetry is too often overlooked, since his frequent references to Ovid's Latin verses draw by far the most of the critical attention. And even though it is correct that any discussion of Petrarch and Ovid should start with Ovid's Latin poems, Petrarch's Ovid is multifaceted.

While Italian poets before Petrarch and Dante were eager to announce in their poetry that they were reading Ovid (see Ch. 2.3), Petrarch and Dante, whose poetry reveals a much broader and deeper familiarity with Ovid's poems, are reticent, to say the least, to commit Ovid's name to the page. Both poets relied heavily on the themes, characters, and words of Ovid's poems in their own poetry, but barely acknowledge him. Dante mentions Ovid twice: one time in *Inf.* 4, including him in the "bella scola" of classical poets in Limbo; the second time in *Inf.* 25, in much less favorable light, to silence him and announce that he writes about metamorphosis better than Ovid did. But even after that explicit denouncement, Ovid's verses never leave the fabric of the *Commedia* (see Ch. 4.2). Petrarch does not mention other poets often in the *Canzoniere*, but while other classical authors with lesser textual presence in the collection actually get their names mentioned, Ovid's name is remarkably absent. As we have seen throughout this book, Italian poets were drawn to Ovid and the Ovidian tradition — so rich, diverse, and versatile — for the many entry points they provided to address their own poetic topics and concerns. At the same time, "Ovidio," a name that could evoke, imply, and signify so much, from the wise and learned to the naughty and erotic, perhaps was kept out of the poetry of Dante and Petrarch, both much concerned with their poetic image, to not needlessly bring out all the shades of their versatile muse Ovid.

Bibliography

List of Editions

This list provides the full references of the primary source quotations in this volume. The text and the numbering (Roman or Arabic) of the listed editions are followed, unless otherwise noted. All translations are by the author, unless otherwise noted.

Alessio, Gian Carlo, ed. *Bene Florentini Candelabrum*. Padua: Antenore, 1983.
Alighieri, Dante. *La Commedia secondo l'antica vulgata*. Edited by Giorgio Petrocchi. 2nd rev. ed. 4 vols. Florence: Le Lettere, 1994. I use Arabic instead of Roman numerals for the canto numbers.
Alighieri, Dante. *Convivio*. Edited by Gianfranco Fioravanti and Claudio Giunta. In *Opere*. Vol. 2, *Convivio, Monarchia, Epistole, Egloge*, edited by Gianfranco Fioravanti, Claudio Giunta, Diego Quaglione, Claudia Villa, Gabriella Albanese, 3–805. Milan: Mondadori, 2014.
Alighieri, Dante. *De vulgari eloquentia*. Edited by Mirko Tavoni. In *Opere*. Vol. 1, *Rime, Vita Nova, De vulgari eloquentia*, edited by Claudio Giunta, Guglielmo Gorni, Mirko Tavoni, 1065–547. Milan: Mondadori, 2011.
Alighieri, Dante. *Epistole*. Edited by Claudia Villa. In *Opere*. Vol. 2, *Convivio, Monarchia, Epistole, Egloge*, edited by Gianfranco Fioravanti, Claudio Giunta, Diego Quaglione, Claudia Villa, Gabriella Albanese, 1417–1592. Milan: Mondadori, 2014.
Alighieri, Dante. *Monarchia*. Edited by Diego Quaglioni. In *Opere*. Vol. 2, *Convivio, Monarchia, Epistole, Egloge*, edited by Gianfranco Fioravanti, Claudio Giunta, Diego Quaglione, Claudia Villa, Gabriella Albanese, 807–1415. Milan: Mondadori, 2014.
Alighieri, Dante. *Rime*. Edited by Domenico De Robertis. Florence: SISMEL-Edizioni del Galluzzo, 2005. (Except for the sonnet of uncertain authorship *Nulla mi parve mai piú crudel cosa*, which is quoted from *Rime*. Edited by Gianfranco Contini, 266–67. Turin: Einaudi, 1939; rpt.1995.) For Dante's poems, I only give the *incipits* and not De Robertis or Contini's numberings.
Alighieri, Dante. *Vita nuova*. Edited by Donato Pirovano. In *Opere di Dante*. Vol. 1, *Rime, Vita nuova*, edited by Donato Pirovano and Marco Grimaldi, 1–289. Rome: Salerno, 2015. I use Arabic instead of Roman numerals for the chapter numbers.
Antonelli, Roberto, ed. *I poeti della Scuola siciliana*. Vol. 1, *Giacomo da Lentini*. Milan: Mondadori, 2008.
Aston, S. C., ed. *Peirol: Troubadour of Auvergne*. Cambridge: Cambridge University Press, 1953.
Bec, Pierre, ed. *Les saluts d'amour du troubadour Arnaud de Mareuil*. Toulouse: Edouard Privat, 1961.

Berchorius, Petrus. *Reductorium morale, Liber XV, cap. ii–xv: "Ovidius moralizatus."* Edited by Joseph Engels. Utrecht: Instituut voor Laat Latijn der Rijksuniversiteit, 1962.

Berchorius, Petrus. *Reductorium morale, Liber XV: Ovidius moralizatus, cap. i. De formis figurisque deorum. Textus e codice Brux., Bibl. Reg. 863–9 critice editus.* Edited by Joseph Engels. Utrecht: Instituut voor Laat Latijn der Rijksuniversiteit, 1966.

Biblia sacra iuxta vulgatam versionem. Edited by Robert Weber et al., 2nd rev. ed. Stuttgart: Württembergische Bibelgesellschaft, 1969.

Boas, Marcus, ed. *Disticha Catonis*, Amsterdam: North-Holland Publishing Company, 1952.

Boccaccio, Giovanni. *Trattatello in laude di Dante.* Edited by Pier Giorgio Ricci. In *Tutte le opere di Giovanni Boccaccio*, Vol. 3, *Amorosa visione – Ninfale fiesolano – Trattatello in laude di Dante*, edited by Vittore Branca, 423–538. Milan: Mondadori, 1974.

Boethius. *De consolatione philosophiae. Opuscula theologica.* Edited by Claudio Moreschini. Leipzig: Teubner, 2000.

Brugnoli, Georgius, and Fabius Stok, eds. *Vita Donatiana.* Rome: Typis Officinae Polygraphicae, 1997.

Carrega, Annamaria, ed. *Il gatto lupesco e Il mare amoroso.* Alessandria: Edizioni dell'Orso, 2000.

Cavalcanti, Guido. *Rime.* Edited by Roberto Rea and Giorgio Inglese. Rome: Carocci, 2011.

Coluccia, Rosario, ed. *I poeti della Scuola siciliana.* Vol. 3, *Poeti siculo-toscani*. Milan: Mondadori, 2008.

Contini, Giancarlo, ed. *Poeti del Duecento.* 2 vols. Milan: Riccardo Ricciardi, 1960.

Dante da Maiano. *Rime.* Edited by Rosanna Bettarini. Florence: F. Le Monnier, 1969.

Davanzati, Chiaro. *Rime.* Edited by Aldo Menichetti. Bologna: Commissione per i testi di lingua, 1965.

Delcorno, Carlo. *Giordano da Pisa e l'antica predicazione volgare.* Florence: Leo S. Olschki, 1975.

de Riquer, Martín. *Los cantares de gesta franceses: sus problemas, su relación con España.* Madrid: Editorial Gredos, 1952.

de Riquer, Martín. *Los trovadores: Historia literaria y textos.* Barcelona: Editorial Ariel, 1975.

Di Girolamo, Costanzo, ed. *I poeti della Scuola siciliana.* Vol. 2, *Poeti della corte di Federico II*. Milan: Mondadori, 2008.

Egidi, Francesco, ed. *Le rime di Guittone d'Arezzo.* Bari: Laterza, 1940.

Filippi, Rustico. *Sonetti amorosi e tenzone.* Edited by Silvia Buzzetti Gallarati. Rome: Carocci, 2009.

Gambino, Francesca, ed. *Canzoni anonime di trovatori e trobairitz.* Alessandria: Edizioni dell'Orso, 2003.

Gelli, Agenore, ed. *Fiore di virtù*. Florence: F. Le Monnier, 1856.
Geremia da Montagnone. *Epytoma sapientiae*. Venice, 1505.
Guinizzelli, Guido. *Rime*. Edited by Luciano Rossi. Turin: Einaudi, 2002.
Harvey, Ruth, and Linda Paterson, eds. *The troubadour 'tensos' and 'partimens': A critical edition*. 3 vols. Woodbridge: D. S. Brewer, 2010.
Hiltz, Sharon Lynne. *De amore et dilectione dei et proximi et aliarum rerum et de forma vitae – An Edition*. PhD diss., University of Pennsylvania, 1980.
Huillard-Bréholles, Jean-Louis-Alphonse, ed. *Vie et correspondance de Pierre de la Vigne*. Paris: H. Plon, 1865.
John of Garland. *Integumenta Ovidii: Poemetto inedito del secolo XIII*. Edited by Fausto Ghisalberti. Milan: Edizioni Principato, 1933.
Johnston, Ronald C., ed. *Les Poésies lyriques du troubadour Arnaut de Mareuil*. Paris: Librairie E. Droz, 1935.
Latini, Brunetto. *Il tesoretto (The Little Treasure)*. Edited and translated by Julia Bolton Holloway. New York: Garland Publishing, Inc., 1981.
Latini, Brunetto. *Tresor*. Edited and translated by Pietro G. Beltrami, Paolo Squillacioti, Plinio Torri, and Sergio Vatteroni. Turin: Einaudi, 2007.
Lavaud, René, ed. *Poésies complètes du troubadour Peire Cardenal (1180–1278)*. Toulouse: É. Privat, 1957.
Lazar, Moshé, ed. *Bernard de Ventadour, troubadour du XIIe siècle: Chansons d'amour*. Paris: C. Klincksieck, 1966.
Linskill, Joseph. *The poems of the troubadour Raimbaut de Vaqueiras. With an English Translation of the Poems and an Introductory Study*. The Hague: Mouton, 1964.
Lucan. *De bello civili Libri X*. Edited by D. R. Shackleton Bailey. Stuttgart: Teubner, 1988. I use Arabic instead of Roman numerals for the book numbers.
Maffia Scariati, Irene, ed. *La Corona di casistica amorosa e le canzoni del cosiddetto Amico di Dante*. Rome: Antenore, 2002.
Magnus, Hugo, ed. *Metamorphoseon libri XV, Lactanti Placidi qui dicitur narrationes fabularum Ovidianarum*. Berlin: Weidmann, 1914; rpt. New York: Arno Press, 1979.
Marti, Mario, ed. *Poeti del Dolce stil nuovo*. Florence: F. Le Monnier, 1969.
Monte Andrea da Fiorenza. *Le rime*. Edited by Francesco Filippo Minetti. Florence: L'Accademia della Crusca, 1979.
Nannucci, Vincentio, ed. *Petri Allegherii super Dantis ipsius genitoris Comoediam Commentarium*. Florence: Piatti, 1855.
Nannucci, Vincenzo, ed. *Ammaestramenti degli antichi latini e toscani raccolti e volgarizzati per fra Bartolommeo da San Concordio*. Florence: Presso Ricordi e Compagno, 1840.
Orosius, Paulus. *Histoires: contre les païens*. Edited and translated by Marie-Pierre Arnaud-Lindet. 3 vols. Paris: Belles Lettres, 1990–91.

Ovid. *Amores, Medicamina faciei femineae, Ars amatoria, Remedia amoris*. Edited by E. J. Kenney. Oxford: Oxford University Press, 1961; rpt. 1995. I use Arabic instead of Roman numerals for the book and poem numbers.

Ovid. *Epistulae Heroidum*. Edited by Henricus Dörrie. Berlin: Walter de Gruyter, 1971. I use Arabic instead of Roman numerals.

Ovid. *Ex Ponto Libri Quattuor*. Edited by J. A. Richmond. Leipzig: Teubner, 1990. I use Arabic instead of Roman numerals for the book numbers.

Ovid. *Fasti*. Edited by E. H. Alton, D. E. W. Wormell, E. Courtney. Leipzig: Teubner, 1988.

Ovid. *Metamorphoses*. Edited by R. J. Tarrant. Oxford: Oxford University Press, 2004. I use Arabic instead of Roman numerals for the book numbers.

Ovid. *Tristia*. Edited by John Barrie Hall. Leipzig: Teubner, 1995. I use Arabic instead of Roman numerals for the book numbers.

Petrarca, Francesco. *L'Afrique: 1338–1374*. Introduced and translated by Rebecca Lenoir. Grenoble: Éditions Jérôme Millon, 2002.

Petrarca, Francesco. *Canzoniere*. Edited by Marco Santagata. Milan: Mondadori, 1996; rpt. 2004.

Petrarca, Francesco. *De vita solitaria*. Edited by Marco Noce. Milan: Mondadori, 1992.

Petrarca, Francesco. *Le Familiari*. Edited by Vittorio Rossi and Umberto Bosco. 4 vols. Florence: Le Lettere, 1997.

Petrarca, Francesco. *My Secret Book*. Edited and translated by Nicholas Mann. The I Tatti Renaissance Library. Cambridge: Harvard University Press, 2016.

Petrarca, Francesco. *Les remèdes aux deux fortunes: 1354–1366 = De remediis utriusque fortune*. Edited and translated by Christophe Carraud. 2 vols. Grenoble: Éditions J. Millon, 2002.

Petrarca, Francesco. *Rerum memorandarum libri*. Edited by Marco Petoletti. Florence: Le Lettere, 2014.

Petrarca, Francesco. *Res seniles, Libri V–VIII*. Edited by Silvia Rizzo with the collaboration of Monica Berté. Florence: Le Lettere, 2009.

Petrarca, Francesco. *Res seniles, Libri IX–XII*. Edited by Silvia Rizzo with the collaboration of Monica Berté. Florence: Le Lettere, 2014.

Petrarca, Francesco. *Trionfi, Rime estravaganti, Codice degli abbozzi*. Edited by Vinicio Pacca and Laura Paolino. Milan: Mondadori, 1996.

Routledge, Michael J., ed. *Les poésies de Bertran Carbonel*. Birmingham: A.I.E.O., University of Birmingham, 2000.

Segre, Cesare, and Mario Marti, eds. *La prosa del Duecento*. Milan: Riccardo Ricciardi, 1959.

Seneca. *Naturalium quaestionum libros*. Edited by Harry M. Hine. Stuttgart: Teubner, 1996.

Squillacioti, Paolo, ed. *Le poesie di Folchetto di Marsiglia*. Pisa: Pacini Editore, 1999.

Statius. *Achilleide*. Edited by Gianfranco Nuzzo. Palermo: Palumbo, 2012.

Statius. *Thebais*. Edited by Alfredus Klotz. Leipzig: Teubner, 1973.

Strempel, Alexander. *Giraut de Salignac, ein provenzalischer Trobador*. Leipzig: Druck von August Hoffmann, 1916.

Sundby, Thor, ed. *Albertani Brixiensis Liber Consolationis et Consilii, ex quo hausta est fabula gallica de Melibeo et Prudentia, quam, anglice redditam et 'The Tale of Melibe' inscriptam, Galfridus Chaucer inter 'Canterbury Tales' recepit*. London: N. Trübner & Co., 1873.

Thilo, Georg, and Hermann Hagen, eds. *Servii Grammatici qui feruntur in Vergilii carmina commentarii*. Hildesheim: G. Olms, 1961.

Toja, Gianluigi, ed. *Arnaut Daniel: Canzoni. Edizione critica, studio introduttivo, commento e traduzione*. Florence: G. C. Sansoni, 1961.

Varvaro, Alberto, ed. *Rigaut de Berbezilh: Liriche*. Bari: Adriatica Editrice, 1960.

Vergil. *Opera*. Edited by R. A. B. Mynors. Oxford: Oxford University Press, 1969. I use Arabic instead of Roman numerals for the book and poem numbers.

Works Cited

Alfie, Fabian. *Dante's 'Tenzone' with Forese Donati: The Reprehension of Vice*. Toronto: Toronto University Press, 2011.

Alighieri, Dante. *La canzone montanina*. Edited by Paola Allegretti. Verbania: Tararà, 2001.

Alighieri, Dante. *De vulgari eloquentia*. Edited by Enrico Fenzi, with the collaboration of Luciano Formisano and Francesco Montuori. Rome: Salerno, 2012.

Alighieri, Dante. *De vulgari eloquentia*. Edited by Pier Vincenzo Mengaldo. Padua: Antenore, 1968.

Alighieri, Dante. *La Divina Commedia*. Edited by Enrico Mestica. Florence: R. Bemporad, 1921–22. https://dante.dartmouth.edu.

Alighieri, Dante. *La Divina Commedia*. Edited by Giuseppe Campi. Turin: Unione Tipografico-Editrice Torinese, 1888–93. https://dante.dartmouth.edu.

Alighieri, Dante. *La Divina Commedia*. Edited by Niccolò Tommaseo. Turin: Unione Tipografico-Editrice Torinese, 1944. https://dante.dartmouth.edu.

Alighieri, Dante. *La Divina Commedia*. Edited by Tommaso Casini and S. A. Barbi. Florence: G. C. Sansoni, 1944. https://dante.dartmouth.edu.

Alighieri, Dante. *Epistole*. Edited by Arsenio Frugoni and Giorgio Brugnoli. In *Opere minori*, edited by Pier Vincenzo Mengaldo et al. Milan: Riccardo Ricciardi, 1979.

Alighieri, Dante. *Epistole · Ecloge · Questio de situ et forma aque et terre*. Edited by Manlio Pastore Stocchi. Rome: Antenore, 2012.

Alighieri, Dante. *Paradiso*. Translated by Jean Hollander and Robert Hollander, with introduction and notes by Robert Hollander. New York: Anchor Books, 2007.

Alighieri, Dante. *Purgatorio*. Edited and translated by Robert M. Durling, with introduction and notes Ronald L. Martinez and Robert M. Durling. New York: Oxford University Press, 2003.

Alighieri, Dante. *Purgatorio*. Translated by Jean Hollander and Robert Hollander, with introduction and notes by Robert Hollander. New York: Anchor Books, 2004.

Alighieri, Dante. *Rime*. Edited by Domenico De Robertis. Florence: SISMEL-Edizioni del Galluzzo, 2005.

Alighieri, Dante, *Rime*. Edited by Domenico De Robertis. In *Le Opere di Dante Alighieri, Edizione Nazionale*, edited by the Società Dantesca Italiana. 5 vols. Florence: Le Lettere, 2002.

Alighieri, Dante, *Rime*. Edited by Gianfranco Contini. Turin: Einaudi, 1939; rpt. 1995.

Alighieri, Dante. *Rime della maturità e dell'esilio*. Edited by Michele Barbi and Vincenzo Pernicone. Florence: F. Le Monnier, 1969.

Alighieri, Dante. *Rime della 'Vita Nuova' e della giovinezza*. Edited by Michele Barbi and Francesco Maggini. Florence: F. Le Monnier, 1956.

Alighieri, Dante. *Rime giovanili e della 'Vita Nuova.'* Edited by Teodolinda Barolini. Milan: Rizzoli, 2009.

Alighieri, Dante. *Vita Nova*. Edited by Guglielmo Gorni. In *Opere*. Vol. 1, *Rime, Vita Nova, De vulgari eloquentia*, edited by Claudio Giunta, Guglielmo Gorni, and Mirko Tavoni, 745–1063. Milan: Mondadori, 2011.

Alighieri, Dante. *Vita nova*. Edited by Stefano Carrai. Milan: Rizzoli, 2009.

Alighieri, Dante. *Vita nuova*. Edited by Domenico De Robertis. Milan: Riccardo Ricciardi, 1980.

Alighieri, Dante. *Vita nuova*. Edited by Marcello Ciccuto. Milan: Rizzoli, 1984.

Allegretti, Paola. "La canzone 'montanina': Dante tra Ovidio e Melibeo." *Dante Studies* 124 (2006): 119–36.

Allen, Peter L. *Art of Love: Amatory Fiction from Ovid to the Romance of the Rose*. Philadelphia: University of Pennsylvania Press, 1992.

Antognini, Roberta. *Il progetto autobiografico delle 'Familiares' di Petrarca*. Milan: LED Edizioni Universitarie di Lettere Economia Diritto, 2008.

Antonelli, Roberto, ed. *I poeti della Scuola siciliana*. Vol. 1, *Giacomo da Lentini*. Milan: Mondadori, 2008.

Antonelli, Roberto, and Simonetta Bianchini, "Dal *clericus* al Poeta." In *Letteratura italiana*, edited by Alberto Asor Rosa. Vol. 2, *Produzione e consumo*, 171–229. Turin: Einaudi, 1983.

Antoni, Claudio G. "Esperienze stilistiche petrose da Dante al Petrarca." *Modern Language Studies* 13, no. 2 (1983): 21–33.

Ardissino, Erminia, ed. *Ovidio Metamorphoseos Vulgare / Giovanni Bonsignori da Città di Castello*. Bologna: Commissione per i testi di lingua, 2001.

Ascoli, Albert Russell. *Dante and the Making of a Modern Author*. Cambridge: Cambridge University Press, 2008.

Ascoli, Albert Russell. *"Favola fui": Petrarch Writes His Readers*, Bernardo Lecture Series, No. 17. Binghamton: Center for Medieval & Renaissance Studies, State University of New York at Binghamton, 2010.

Ascoli, Albert Russell. "Reading Dante's Readings: What? When? Where? How?" In *Dante and Heterodoxy: The Temptations of 13th Century Radical Thought*, edited by Maria Luisa Ardizzone, 126–43. Newcastle upon Tyne: Cambridge Scholars Publishing, 2014.

Aston, S. C. *Peirol: Troubadour of Auvergne*. Cambridge: Cambridge University Press, 1953.

Balbo, Andrea, and Giuseppe Noto, "I nomi dei classici latini nella poesia dei trovatori." In *'Tanti affetti in tal momento': Studi in onore di Giovanna Garbarino*, edited by Andrea Balbo, Federica Bessone, and Ermanno Malaspina, 11–40. Alessandria: Edizioni dell'Orso, 2011.

Barański, Zygmunt G. "L'*iter* ideologico di Dante." In *Dante e i segni: Saggi per una storia intellettuale di Dante Alighieri*, 9–39. Naples: Liguori, 2000.

Barański, Zygmunt G. "On Dante's Trail." *Italian Studies* 72 (2017): 1–15.

Barański, Zygmunt G. "The Roots of Dante's Plurilingualism: "Hybridity" and Language in the *Vita nova*." In *Dante's Plurilingualism: Authority, Knowledge, Subjectivity*, edited by Sara Fortuna, Manuele Gragnolati, and Jürgen Trabant, 98–121. Oxford: Legenda, 2010.

Barański, Zygmunt G., and Theodore J. Cachey, Jr., eds. *Petrarch & Dante: Anti-Dantism, Metaphysics, Tradition*. Notre Dame: University of Notre Dame Press, 2009.

Barber, Joseph A. "Il sonetto CXIII e gli altri sonetti a Sennuccio." *Lectura Petrarce* 2 (1982): 21–39.

Barchiesi, Alessandro. *Speaking Volumes: Narrative and Intertext in Ovid and Other Latin Poets*. London: Duckworth, 2001.

Barchiesi, Alessandro, and Philip Hardie, "The Ovidian career model: Ovid, Gallus, Apuleius, Boccaccio." In *Classical Literary Careers and their Reception*, edited by Philip Hardie and Helen Moore, 59–88. Cambridge: Cambridge University Press, 2010.

Barkan, Leonard. "Diana and Actaeon: The Myth as Synthesis." *English Literary Renaissance* 10, no. 3 (1980): 317–59.

Barney, Stephen A., W. J. Lewis, J. A. Beach, and Oliver Berghof, trans. *The 'Etymologies' of Isidore of Seville*. Cambridge: Cambridge University Press, 2006.

Barolini, Teodolinda. "Arachne, Argus and St. John: Transgressive Art in Dante and Ovid." *Mediaevalia* 13 (1989): 207–26.

Barolini, Teodolinda. "Canto XX: True and False See-ers." In *Lectura Dantis: Inferno: A Canto-by-Canto Commentary*, edited by Allen Mandelbaum, Anthony Oldcorn, and Charles Ross, 275–86. Berkeley: University of California Press, 1998.

Barolini, Teodolinda. "Dante and the Lyric Past." In *The Cambridge Companion to Dante*, edited by Rachel Jacoff, 14–33. Cambridge: Cambridge University Press, 1993.

Barolini, Teodolinda. *Dante and the Origins of Italian Literary Culture*. New York: Fordham University Press, 2006.

Barolini, Teodolinda. "Dante and the Troubadours: An Overview." *Tenso* 5, no. 1 (1989): 3–10.

Barolini, Teodolinda. *Dante's Poets. Textuality and Truth in the Comedy*. Princeton: Princeton University Press, 1984.

Barolini, Teodolinda. "The Making of a Lyric Sequence: Time and Narrative in Petrarch's *Rerum vulgarium fragmenta*." *Modern Language Notes* 104 (1989): 1–38.

Barolini, Teodolinda. "'Only Historicize': History, Material Culture (Food, Clothes, Books), and the Future of Dante Studies." *Dante Studies* 127 (2009): 37–54.

Barolini, Teodolinda. "The Self in the Labyrinth of Time · *Rerum vulgarium fragmenta*." In *Petrarch: A Critical Guide to the Complete Works*, edited by Victoria Kirkham and Armando Maggi, 33–62. Chicago: Chicago University Press, 2009.

Barolini, Teodolinda, and H. Wayne Storey, eds. *Dante for the New Millennium*. New York: Fordham University Press, 2003.

Bartolozzi, Vanni. "Ambiguità e metamorfosi nella sestina dantesca." *Romance Philology* 36 (1982): 1–17.

Bate, Keith A., ed. *Three Latin Comedies*. Toronto: Pontifical Institute of Mediaeval Studies, 1976.

Battaglia, Salvatore. "Piramo e Tisbe in una pagina di Sant'Agostino." In *La coscienza letteraria del Medioevo*, 51–61. Naples: Liguori, 1965.

Battistini, Andrea. "Lo stile della Medusa. I processi di pietrificazione in 'Io son venuto al punto de la rota.'" *Letture classensi* 26 (1997): 93–110.

Bec, Pierre, ed. *Les saluts d'amour du troubadour Arnaud de Mareuil*. Toulouse: Edouard Privat, 1961.

Beltrami, Pietro G. "Lirons-nous encore les troubadours, et comment?" In *L'Occitanie invitée de l'Euregio. Liège 1981 – Aix-la-Chapelle 2008: Bilan et perspectives, Actes du Neuvième Congrès International de l'Association Internationale d'Études Occitanes, Aix-la-Chapelle, 24–31 Août 2008*, edited by Angelica Rieger and Domergue Sumien, 101–20. Aix-la-Chapelle: Shaker Verlag, 2011.

Beneš, Carrie E. *Urban Legends: Civic Identity and the Classical Past in Northern Italy, 1250–1350*. University Park: Penn State University Press, 2011.

Bénéteau, David P. "Bartolomeo da San Concordio." In *Medieval Italy: An Encyclopedia*, edited by Christopher Kleinhenz, 1: 99–100. New York: Routledge, 2004.

Berra, Claudia. *La similitudine nei 'Rerum vulgarium fragmenta.'* Lucca: M. Pacini Fazzi, 1992.

Billanovich, Giuseppe. "'Veterum vestigia vatum' nei carmi dei preumanisti padovani: Lovato Lovati, Zambono di Andrea, Albertino Mussato e Lucrezio, Catullo, Orazio (*Carmina*), Tibullo, Properzio, Ovidio (*Ibis*), Marziale, Stazio (*Silvae*)." *Italia medioevale e umanistica* 1 (1958): 155–244.

Black, Robert. "Education." In *Dante in Context*, edited by Zygmunt G. Barański and Lino Pertile, 260–76. Cambridge: Cambridge University Press, 2015.

Black, Robert. *Humanism and Education in Medieval and Renaissance Italy: Tradition and Innovation in Latin Schools from the Twelfth to the Fifteenth Century*. Cambridge: Cambridge University Press, 2001.

Black, Robert. "Ovid in medieval Italy." In *Ovid in the Middle Ages*, edited by James G. Clark, Frank T. Coulson, and Kathryn L. McKinley, 123–42. Cambridge: Cambridge University Press, 2011.

Black, Robert. "Teaching techniques: the evidence of manuscript schoolbooks produced in Tuscany." In *The Classics in the Medieval and Renaissance Classroom: The Role of Ancient Texts in the Arts Curriculum as Revealed by Surviving Manuscripts and Early Printed Books*, edited by Juanita Feros Ruys, John O. Ward, and Melanie Heyworth, 245–65. Turnhout: Brepols, 2013.

Black, Robert, and Gabriella Pomaro. *La 'Consolazione della filosofia' nel Medioevo e nel Rinascimento italiano: libri di scuola e glosse nei manoscritti fiorentini / Boethius's 'Consolation of Philosophy' in Italian Medieval and Renaissance Education: Schoolbooks and Their Glosses in Florentine Manuscripts*. Florence: SISMEL-Edizioni del Galluzzo, 2000.

Bloom, Harold. *The Anxiety of Influence: A Theory of Poetry*. 2nd ed. Oxford: Oxford University Press, 1997.

Blumenfeld-Kosinski, Renate. "The Hermeneutics of the *Ovide moralisé*." In *Reading Myth: Classical Mythology and Its Interpretations in Medieval French Literature*, 90–136. Stanford: Stanford University Press, 1997.

Blumenthal, Wilfred. "Untersuchungen zur pseudo-ovidianischen Komödie *Pamphilus*." *Mittellateinisches Jahrbuch* 11 (1976): 224–311.

Boccia, Alessandro. "Stile allusivo e interpretazione testuale nell'epistolario di Pier della Vigna." In *Author and Authorship in Medieval Latin Literature: Proceedings of the VIth Congress of the International Medieval Latin Committee (Benevento-Naples, November 9–13, 2010)*, edited by Edoardo D'Angelo and Jan Ziolkowski, 85–100. Florence: SISMEL-Edizioni del Galluzzo, 2014.

Bonghi, Giuseppe, and Cono A. Mangieri, trans. *Proverbia quae dicuntur super naturam feminarum*. Biblioteca dei classici italiani, 2003. http://www.classicitaliani.it/duecento/Proverbia_Contini.pdf.

Bosco, Umberto. "La gara coi classici latini (canti XXIV–XXV dell'*Inferno*)." In *Altre pagine dantesche*, 93–108. Rome: Salvatore Sciascia Editore, 1987.

Brilli, Elisa. "Dante's Biographies and Historical Studies: An *Ouverture*." *Dante Studies* 136 (2018): 122–43.

The British Library. The Digital Catalogue of Illuminated Manuscripts. http://www.bl.uk/catalogues/illuminatedmanuscripts/.

Brock, Maurice, Francesco Furlan, and Frank La Brasca, eds. *La bibliothèque de Pétrarque: Livres et auteurs autour d'un humaniste*. Turnhout: Brepols, 2011.

Brownlee, Kevin. "Dante and Narcissus (*Purg.* XXX, 76–99)." *Dante Studies* 96 (1978): 201–6.

Brownlee, Kevin. "Ovid." In *Dante Encyclopedia,* edited by Richard Lansing, Teodolinda Barolini, et al., 666–68. New York: Garland Publishing, Inc., 2000.

Brownlee, Kevin. "Phaeton's Fall and Dante's Ascent." *Dante Studies* 102 (1984): 135–44.

Brownlee, Kevin. "The Practice of Cultural Authority: Italian Responses to French Cultural Dominance in *Il Tesoretto, Il Fiore*, and the *Commedia*." *Forum for Modern Language Studies* 33, no. 3 (1997): 258–69.

Brugnoli, Giorgio. "Forme ovidiane in Dante." In *Aetates Ovidianae: Lettori di Ovidio dall'Antichità al Rinascimento*, edited by Italo Gallo and Luciano Nicastri, 239–59. Naples: Edizioni scientifiche italiane, 1995.

Brugnoli, Giorgio. "L'Ovidio dell'esilio nell'esilio di Dante." *Linguistica e letteratura* 41, nos. 1–2 (2016): 13–35.

Brugnoli, Giorgio. "Paradiso XVII." *L'Alighieri* 5 (1995): 47–58.

Brugnolo, Furio. "Appendice a Cino (e Onesto) dentro e fuori la *Commedia*: Ancora sull'intertesto di Purgatorio XXIV 49–63." In *Leggere Dante*, edited by Lucia Battaglia Ricci, 153–70. Ravenna: Longo, 2003.

Brugnolo, Furio. "Cino (e Onesto) dentro e fuori la *Commedia*." In *Omaggio a Gianfranco Folena*, 1: 369–86. Padua: Editoriale Programma, 1993.

Brugnolo, Furio. "Il "nodo" di Bonagiunta e il "modo" di Dante: Per un'interpretazione di *Purgatorio* XXIV." *Rivista di studi danteschi* 9 (2009): 3–28.

Brunetti, Giuseppina. "All'ombra del lauro: nota per Cino e Petrarca." In *La lirica romanza del medioevo: Storia, tradizioni, interpretazioni. Atti del VI Convegno triennale della Società Italiana di Filologia Romanza*, edited by Furio Brugnolo and Francesca Gambino, 825–50. Padua: Unipress, 2009.

Brunetti, Giuseppina, and Sonia Gentili, "Una biblioteca nella Firenze di Dante: i manoscritti di Santa Croce." In *Testimoni del vero: Su alcuni libri in biblioteche d'autore*, edited by Emilio Russo, 21–55. Rome: Bulzoni, 2000.

Brunori, Federica. "Il mito ovidiano di Orfeo e Euridice nel *Canzoniere* di Petrarca." *Romance Quarterly* 44, no. 4 (1997): 233–44.

Buridant, Claude. "Nature and function of proverbs in jeux-partis." *Revue des sciences humaines* 163, no. 3 (1976): 377–418.

Burrow, J. A. *Medieval Writers and their Work: Middle English Literature 1100–1500.* 2nd ed. Oxford: Oxford University Press, 2008.

Burton, Rosemary. *Classical poets in the 'Florilegium Gallicum.'* Frankfurt am Main: P. Lang, 1983.

Busby, Keith, and Christopher Kleinhenz. "Medieval French and Italian literature: towards a manuscript history." In *The Medieval Manuscript Book: Cultural Approaches*, edited by Michael Johnston and Michael Van Dussen, 215–42. Cambridge: Cambridge University Press, 2015.

Cahoon, Leslie. "The Anxieties of Influence: Ovid's Reception by the Early Troubadours." *Mediaevalia* 13 (1987): 119–55.
Calenda, Corrado. "'Di vil matera': ipotesi esplicativa di una ipertrofia strutturale." In *Appartenenze metriche ed esegesi: Dante, Cavalcanti, Guittone*, 61–71. Naples: Bibliopolis, 1995.
Cameron, Alan. "An Anonymous Ancient Commentary on Ovid's *Metamorphoses*?" In *Greek Mythology in the Roman World*, 3–32. Oxford: Oxford University Press, 2004.
Capelli, Roberta. "The Arthurian Presence in Early Italian Lyric." In *The Arthur of the Italians: The Arthurian Legend in Medieval Italian Literature and Culture*, edited by Gloria Allaire and F. Regina Psaki, 133–44. Cardiff: University of Wales Press, 2014.
Capelli, Roberta. "Presenze arturiane nella lirica italiana delle origini (Pt. I)." *Quaderni di lingue e letterature* 31 (2006): 43–56.
Capelli, Roberta. "Presenze arturiane nella lirica italiana delle origini (Pt. II)." *Quaderni di lingue e letterature* 32 (2007): 17–27.
Carrai, Stefano. *La lirica toscana del Duecento*. Rome: Laterza, 1997.
Carruthers, Mary. *The Book of Memory: A Study of Memory in Medieval Culture*. 2nd ed. Cambridge: Cambridge University Press, 2008.
Cavalcanti, Guido. *Rime*. Edited by Roberto Rea and Giorgio Inglese. Rome: Carocci, 2011.
Cavalcanti, Guido. *Rime. Con le rime di Iacopo Cavalcanti*. Edited by Domenico De Robertis. Turin: Einaudi, 1986.
Cesarini, Remo. "'Petrarca': Il nome come auto-reinvenzione poetica." *Quaderni petrarcheschi* 4 (1987): 121–37.
Cestaro, Gary P. "'... quanquam Sarnum biberimus ante dentes ...': The Primal Scene of Suckling in Dante's *De vulgari eloquentia*." *Dante Studies* 109 (1991): 119–47.
Chambers, Frank M. *Proper Names in the Lyrics of the Troubadours*. Chapel Hill: University of North Carolina Press, 1971.
Chiappelli, Fredi. "La strofa di Euridice." In *Studi sul linguaggio del Petrarca: La canzone delle visioni*, 139–83. Florence: Leo S. Olschki, 1971.
Chiappelli, Luigi. "Appunti sul valore culturale dell'opera di Cino da Pistoia." *Bullettino Storico Pistoiese* 39 (1937): 31–39.
Chiarenza, Marguerite Mills. "Hippolytus' Exile: *Paradiso* XVII, vv. 46–48." *Dante Studies* 84 (1966): 65–68.
Chiarenza, Marguerite Mills. "Time and Eternity in the Myths of *Paradiso* XVII." In *Dante, Petrarch, Boccaccio: Studies in the Italian Trecento in Honor of Charles S. Singleton*, edited by Aldo S. Bernardo and Anthony L. Pellegrini, 133–50. Binghamton: Center for Medieval & Early Renaissance Studies, State University of New York at Binghamton, 1983.
Chines, Loredana. "La ricezione petrarchesca del mito di Atteone." In *'Di selva in selva ratto mi trasformo': Identità e metamorfosi della parola petrarchesca*, 43–54. Rome: Carocci, 2010.

Chines, Loredana. *I veli del poeta: un percorso tra Petrarca e Tasso*. Rome: Carocci, 2000.

Cioffi, Caron A. "The Anxieties of Ovidian Influence: Theft in *Inferno* XXIV and XXV." *Dante Studies* 112 (1994): 77–100.

Cipollone, Annalisa. "Ovidio nel Petrarca volgare." *Per leggere* 16 (2009): 157–74.

Clark, James G., Frank T. Coulson, and Kathryn L. McKinley, eds. *Ovid in the Middle Ages*. Cambridge: Cambridge University Press, 2011.

Clay, Diskin. "The Metamorphosis of Ovid in Dante's *Commedia*." In *Dante: Mito e poesia: Atti del secondo Seminario dantesco internazionale: Monte Verità, Ascona, 23–27 giugno 1997*, edited by Michelangelo Picone and Tatiana Crivelli, 69–85. Florence: Franco Cesati, 1999.

Clay, Diskin. "The Metamorphosis of Ovid in Dante's *Divine Comedy*." In *A Handbook to the Reception of Ovid*, edited by John F. Miller and Carole E. Newlands, 174–86. Chichester: Wiley-Blackwell, 2014.

Cnyrim, Eugen. *Sprichwörter, sprichwörtliche Redensarten und Sentenzen bei den Provenzalischen Lyrikern*. Marburg: N. G. Elwertsche Verlagsbuchhandlung, 1888.

Cohen, Gustave, ed. *La 'comédie' latine en France au XIIe siècle*. 2 vols. Paris: Société d'édition Les Belles-lettres, 1931.

Coluccia, Rosario, ed. *I poeti della Scuola siciliana*. Vol. 3, *Poeti siculo-toscani*. Milan: Mondadori, 2008.

Conte, Gian Biagio. *The Rhetoric of Imitation: Genre and Poetic Memory in Virgil and Other Latin Poets*. Ithaca: Cornell University Press, 1986.

Contini, Gianfranco. "Alcuni appunti su 'Purgatorio' XXVII." In *Un'idea di Dante: Saggi danteschi*, 171–90. Turin: Einaudi, 1976.

Contini, Gianfranco, ed. *Poeti del Duecento*. 2 vols. Milan: Riccardo Ricciardi, 1960.

Copeland, Rita. *Rhetoric, Hermeneutics, and Translation in the Middle Ages: Academic Traditions and Vernacular Texts*. Cambridge: Cambridge University Press, 1991.

Cornish, Alison. *Vernacular Translation in Dante's Italy: Illiterate Literature*. Cambridge: Cambridge University Press, 2011.

Cornish, Alison. "Vernacularization in context (*Volgarizzamenti* of Livy, Valerius Maximus, and Ovid)." In *Boccaccio: A Critical Guide to the Complete Works*, edited by Victoria Kirkham, Michael Sherberg, and Janet Levarie Smarr, 255–61. Chicago: University of Chicago Press, 2013.

Corti, Maria. "Le fonti del *Fiore di virtù* e la teoria della 'nobilità' nel Duecento." *Giornale storico della letteratura italiana* 136 (1959): 1–82.

Costa, Elio. "Il *Tesoretto* di Brunetto Latini e la tradizione allegorica medievale." In *Dante e le forme dell'allegoresi*, edited by Michelangelo Picone, 43–58. Ravenna: Longo, 1987.

Cottino-Jones, Marga. "The Myth of Apollo and Daphne in Petrarch's *Canzoniere*: The Dynamics and Literary Function of Transformation." In *Francis Petrarch, Six Centuries Later: A Symposium*, edited by Aldo Scaglione, 152–76. Chapel Hill: University of North Carolina, 1975.

Coulson, Frank T. "A Bibliographical update and corrigenda minora to Munari's catalogues of the manuscripts of Ovid's *Metamorphoses*." *Manuscripta* 38 (1994): 3–22.

Coulson, Frank T. "Literary criticism in the Vulgate Commentary on Ovid's *Metamorphoses*." In *Medieval Textual Cultures: Agents of Transmission, Translation and Transformation*, edited by Faith Wallis and Robert Wisnovsky, 121–32. Berlin: Walter de Gruyter, 2016.

Coulson, Frank T. "Newly Identified Manuscripts containing the *Summa Memorialis* on the *Metamorphoses* by Orico de Capriana." *Studi Medievali* 35 (1994): 817–22.

Coulson, Frank T. "Ovid's *Metamorphoses* in the school tradition of France, 1180–1400: Texts, manuscript traditions, manuscript settings." In *Ovid in the Middle Ages*, edited by James G. Clark, Frank T. Coulson, and Kathryn L. McKinley, 48–82. Cambridge: Cambridge University Press, 2011.

Coulson, Frank T. "Ovid's Transformations in Medieval France (ca. 1100–ca. 1350)." In *Metamorphosis: The Changing Face of Ovid in Medieval and Early Modern Europe*, edited by Alison Keith and Stephen Rupp, 33–60. Toronto: Centre for Reformation and Renaissance Studies, 2007.

Coulson, Frank T. "The *Vulgate* Commentary on Ovid's *Metamorphoses*." *Mediaevalia* 13 (1987): 29–61.

Coulson, Frank T., ed. and trans. *The Vulgate Commentary on Ovid's 'Metamorphoses' Book 1*. TEAMS Secular Commentary. Kalamazoo: Medieval Institute Publications, 2015.

Coulson, Frank T., ed. *The 'Vulgate' Commentary on Ovid's 'Metamorphoses': The Creation Myth and the Story of Orpheus*. Toronto: The Pontifical Institute of Mediaeval Studies, 1991.

Coulson, Frank T., and Bruno Roy. *Incipitarium Ovidianum: A Finding Guide for Texts Related to the Study of Ovid in the Middle Ages and Renaissance*. Turnhout: Brepols, 2000.

Crespo, Roberto. "Narciso nella lirica italiana del Duecento." *Studi di filologia italiana* 47 (1989): 5–10.

Da Imola, Benvenuto. *Comentum super Dantis Aldigherij Comoediam*. Edited by Giacomo Filippo Lacaita. Florence: Barbèra, 1887. https://dante.dartmouth.edu.

Davanzati, Chiaro. *Rime*, edited by Aldo Menichetti. Bologna: Commissione per i testi di lingua, 1965.

Davis, Charles. "Education in Dante's Florence." In *Dante's Italy, and Other Essays*, 137–65. Philadelphia: University of Pennsylvania Press, 1984.

Davis, Charles. "The Florentine *Studia* and Dante's 'Library.'" In *'The Divine Comedy' and the Encyclopedia of Arts and Sciences: Acta of the International Dante Symposium, 13–16 November 1983, Hunter College, New York*, edited by Giuseppe Di Scipio and Aldo Scaglione, 339–66. Amsterdam: John Benjamins Publishing Company, 1988.

Davisson, Mary H. T. "'Quid Moror Exemplis'?: Mythological "Exempla" in Ovid's Pre-Exilic Poems and the Elegies from Exile." *Phoenix* 47, no. 3 (1993): 213–37.

Della Terza, Dante. "The Canto of Brunetto Latini." In *Lectura Dantis: Inferno*, edited by Allen Mandelbaum, Anthony Oldcorn, and Charles Ross, 197–212. Berkeley: University of California Press, 1998.

De Marco, Giuseppe. "L'esperienza di Dante *exul immeritus* quale autobiografia universale." *Annali d'Italianistica* 20 (2002): 21–54.

De' Medici, Giuliana. "Le fonti dell'Ottimo commento alla *Divina Commedia*." *Italia medioevale e umanistica* 26 (1983): 71–125.

de Nolhac, Pierre. *Pétrarque et l'humanisme*. 2 vols. 2nd ed. Paris, Champion, 1907.

de Riquer, Martín. *Los trovadores: Historia literaria y textos*. Barcelona: Editorial Ariel, 1975.

De Robertis, Domenico. "Cino e le 'imitazioni' dalle rime di Dante." *Studi Danteschi* 29 (1950): 103–76.

De Robertis, Domenico. *Il libro della 'Vita nuova.'* Florence: G. C. Sansoni, 1970.

Desmond, Marilynn. ed. "Ovid in Medieval Culture." *Mediaevalia* 13 (1987).

Di Girolamo, Costanzo, ed. *I poeti della Scuola siciliana*. Vol. 2, *Poeti della corte di Federico II*. Milan: Mondadori, 2008.

Dolla, Vincenzo. "I madrigali del 'Canzoniere' (un'ipotesi di lettura petrarchesca)." *Esperienze letterarie* 1 (1976): 74–88.

Dragonetti, Roger. "Dante et Narcisse ou les faux-monnayeurs de l'image." *Revue des études italiennes* 11 (1965): 85–146.

Durling, Robert M. "'Io son venuto': Seneca, Plato, and the Microcosm." *Dante Studies* 93 (1975): 95–129.

Durling, Robert, and Ronald Martinez. *Time and the Crystal: Studies in Dante's 'Rime petrose.'* Berkeley: University of California Press, 1990.

Dutschke, Dennis. *Francesco Petrarca: Canzone XXIII from the First to Final Version*. Ravenna: Longo, 1977.

Dutschke, Dennis. "Il libro miscellaneo: Problemi di metodo tra Boccaccio e Petrarca." In *Gli Zibaldoni di Boccaccio: Memoria, scrittura, riscrittura. Atti del Seminario internazionale di Firenze-Certaldo (26–28 aprile 1996)*, edited by Michelangelo Picone and Claude Cazalé Bérard, 95–112. Florence: Franco Cesati, 1998.

Edmunds, Lowell. *Intertextuality and the Reading of Roman Poetry*. Baltimore: Johns Hopkins University Press, 2001.

Eisner, Martin. *Boccaccio and the Invention of Italian Literature: Dante, Petrarch, Cavalcanti, and the Authority of the Vernacular*. Cambridge: Cambridge University Press, 2013.

Eley, Penny, ed. and trans. *Narcisus et Dané*. Liverpool: University of Liverpool, 2002.

Eley, Penny, ed. and trans. *Piramus et Tisbé*. Liverpool: University of Liverpool, 2001.

Elliott, Alison G. "Accessus ad auctores: Twelfth-Century Introductions to Ovid." *Allegorica* 5 (1980): 6–48.

Elliott, Alison Goddard, trans. *Seven Medieval Latin Comedies*. New York: Garland Publishing, Inc., 1984.

Ellrich, Robert J. "Envy, Identity, and Creativity: *Inferno* XXIV–XXV." *Dante Studies* 102 (1984): 61–80.

Engelbrecht, Wilken. *Filologie in de Dertiende Eeuw: De 'Bursarii super Ovidios' van Magister Willem van Orléans (fl. 1200)*. PhD diss., Utrecht University, 2003.

Engelbrecht, Wilken. "Fulco, Arnulf, and William: Twelfth-Century Views on Ovid in Orléans." *The Journal of Medieval Latin* 18 (2008): 52–73.

Enterline, Lynn. *The Rhetoric of the Body from Ovid to Shakespeare*. Cambridge: Cambridge University Press, 2000.

Fantham, Elaine. "The Role of Evander in Ovid's *Fasti*." *Arethusa* 25 (1992): 155–72.

Farrell, Joseph. "Ovid's Virgilian Career." *Materiali e discussioni per l'analisi dei testi classici* 52 (2004): 41–55.

Favati, Guido. "Contributo alla determinazione del problema dello Stil nuovo." *Studi mediolatini e volgari* 4 (1956): 57–70.

Favati, Guido. *Inchiesta sul Dolce stil nuovo*. Florence: F. Le Monnier, 1975.

Feng, Aileen A. "'Volto di Medusa': Monumentalizing the Self in Petrarch's *Rerum Vulgarium Fragmenta*." *Forum Italicum* 47, no. 3 (2013): 497–521.

Fenzi, Enrico. "Ancora sulla *Epistola* a Moroello e sulla 'montanina' di Dante (*Rime*, 15)." *Tenzone* 4 (2003): 43–84.

Fenzi, Enrico. "Il mondo come patria: Da Seneca a Dante, *De vulgari eloquentia* I 6, 3." *Letture Classensi* 44 (2015): 85–95.

Fenzi, Enrico. "Le rime per la donna pietra." In *Miscellanea di studi danteschi*, 229–309. Genoa: Mario Bozzi, 1966.

Feo, Michele. "Petrarca." In *Enciclopedia Dantesca*. Rome: Istituto della Enciclopedia Italiana, 1973. http://www.treccani.it/enciclopedia/francesco-petrarca_(Enciclopedia-Dantesca)/.

Fera, Vincenzo. "I sonetti CLXXXVI e CLXXXVII." *Lectura Petrarce* 7 (1987): 219–43.

Fernández de la Cuesta González, Beatriz. *En la senda del 'Florilegium Gallicum': edición y estudio del florilegio del manuscrito Córdoba, Archivo Capitular 150*. Louvain-la-Neuve: Fédération internationale des instituts d'études médiévales, 2008.

Ferrara, Sabrina. "D'un bannissement subi à un exil revendiqué: la construction de l' 'exul' dans les *Épîtres* de Dante." *Arzanà* 16–17 (2013): 199–213.

Ferrara, Sabrina. "*Io mi credea del tutto esser partito:* il distacco di Dante da Cino." In *Cino da Pistoia nella storia della poesia italiana*, edited by Rossend Arqués Corominas and Silvia Tranfaglia, 99–112. Florence: Franco Cesati, 2016.

Ferrara, Sabrina. "Tra pena giuridica e diritto morale: l'esilio di Dante nelle *epistole*." *L'Alighieri* 40 (2012): 45–65.

Ferrari, Chiara. "Gender Reversals: Inversions and Conversions in Dante's *Rime Petrose*." *Italica* 90, no. 2 (2013): 153–75.

Ferretti, Matteo. "Per la 'recensio' e la prima diffusione delle 'Allegorie' di Giovanni del Virgilio." *L'Ellisse* 2 (2007): 9–28.

Filippi, Rustico. *Sonetti amorosi e tenzone*, edited by Silvia Buzzetti Gallarati. Rome: Carocci, 2009.

Fiorilla, Maurizio. *I classici nel 'Canzoniere': Note di lettura e scrittura poetica in Petrarca*. Padua: Antenore, 2012.

Foster, Kenelm. "Beatrice or Medusa." In *Italian Studies Presented to E.R. Vincent*, edited by Charles Peter Brand, Kenelm Foster, and Uberto Limentani, 41–56. Cambridge: Heffer, 1962.

Foster, Kenelm. "Dante in Great Britain, 1965." *Dante Studies* 84 (1966): 69–71.

Foster, Kenelm, and Patrick Boyde. *Dante's Lyric Poetry*. 2 vols. Oxford: Oxford University Press, 1967.

Fowler, Don. "On the Shoulders of Giants: Intertextuality and Classical Studies." *Materiali e discussioni per l'analisi dei testi classici* 39 (1997): 13–34.

Fratta, Aniello. *Le fonti provenzali dei poeti della scuola siciliana. I postillati del Torraca e altri contributi*. Florence: Le Lettere, 1996.

Freccero, John. "The Fig Tree and the Laurel: Petrarch's Poetics." *Diacritics* 5 (1975): 34–40.

Friedman, John Block. *Orpheus in the Middle Ages*. Cambridge: Harvard University Press, 1970.

Fumo, Jamie C. "Commentary and Collaboration in the Medieval Allegorical Tradition." In *A Handbook to the Reception of Ovid*, edited by John F. Miller and Carole E. Newlands, 114–28. Chichester: Wiley-Blackwell, 2014.

Galinsky, G. Karl. "Inspiration, Tone and Theme." In *Ovid's 'Metamorphoses': An Introduction to the Basic Aspects*, 1–78. Berkeley: University of California Press, 1975.

Gambino, Francesca, ed. *Canzoni anonime di trovatori e trobairitz*. Alessandria: Edizioni dell'Orso, 2003.

Gardini, Nicola. "Un esempio di imitazione virgiliana nel *Canzoniere* Petrarchesco: Il mito di Orfeo." *Modern Language Notes* 110, no. 1 (1995): 132–44.

Gargan, Luciano. *Dante, la sua biblioteca e lo Studio di Bologna*. Rome: Antenore, 2014.

Gargan, Luciano. "Per la biblioteca di Dante." *Giornale storico della letteratura italiana* 186 (2009): 161–93.

Gaunt, Simon. "Discourse Desired: Desire, Subjectivity, and *Mouvance* in *Can vei la lauzeta mover*." In *Desiring Discourse: The Literature of Love, Ovid Through Chaucer*, edited by James J. Paxson and Cynthia A. Gravlee, 89–110. Selinsgrove: Susquehanna University Press, 1998.

Gentili, Sonia, and Sylvain Piron, "La bibliothèque de Santa Croce." In *Frontières des savoirs en Italie à l'époque des premières universités (XIIIe–XIVe siècles)*, edited by Joël Chandelier and Aurélien Robert, 491–507. Rome: École française de Rome, 2015.

Gerber, Amanda J. "Rethinking Ovid: The Commentary Tradition." In *Medieval Ovid: Frame Narrative and Political Allegory*, 11–50. New York: Palgrave Macmillan, 2015.

Ghisalberti, Fausto. "Arnolfo d'Orléans: un cultore di Ovidio nel secolo XII." *Memorie del Reale Istituto Lombardo di Scienze e Lettere* 24 (1932): 157–234.
Ghisalberti, Fausto. *Giovanni del Virgilio espositore delle 'Metamorfosi.'* Florence: Leo S. Olschki, 1933.
Ghisalberti, Fausto. "Il commentario medioevale all' *'Ovidius maior'* consultato da Dante." *Rendiconti (Istituto lombardo di scienze e lettere, classe di lettere e scienze morali e politiche)* 100 (1966): 267–75.
Ghisalberti, Fausto. "L'enigma delle Naiadi." *Studi Danteschi* 16 (1932): 105–25.
Ghisalberti, Fausto. "Mediaeval Biographies of Ovid." *Journal of the Warburg and Courtauld Institutes* 9 (1946): 10–59.
Ghisalberti, Fausto. "La quadriga del sole nel 'Convivio.'" *Studi Danteschi* 18 (1934): 69–77.
Giancotti, Matteo. "La poesia del Duecento: 'Se Narcisso fosse vivo.' In *Il mito nella letteratura italiana*, edited by Pietro Gibellini. Vol. 1, *Dal Medioevo al Rinascimento*, edited by Gian Carlo Alessio, 97–123. Brescia: Morcelliana, 2005.
Giannetto, Nella. "Il motivo dell'amata incanutita nelle rime di Petrarca e Boccaccio." In *Miscellanea di studi in onore di Vittore Branca, II: Boccaccio e dintorni*, 23–39. Florence: Leo S. Olschki, 1983.
Gillespie, Vincent. "Part II: The Study of Classical Authors: From the twelfth century to c. 1450." In *The Cambridge History of Literary Criticism*. Vol. 2, *The Middle Ages*, edited by Alastair Minnis and Ian Johnson, 145–235. Cambridge: Cambridge University Press, 2008.
Ginsberg, Warren. *Dante's Aesthetics of Being*. Ann Arbor: University of Michigan Press, 1999.
Ginsberg, Warren. "Dante's Ovids." In *Ovid in the Middle Ages*, edited by James G. Clark, Frank T. Coulson, and Kathryn L. McKinley, 143–59. Cambridge: Cambridge University Press, 2011.
Ginsberg, Warren. "Dante's Ovids: Allegory, Irony, and the Poet as Translation." In *Chaucer's Italian Tradition*, 29–57. Ann Arbor: University of Michigan Press, 2002.
Ginsberg, Warren. "Ovidius ethicus? Ovid and the Medieval Commentary Tradition." In *Desiring Discourse: The Literature of Love, Ovid through Chaucer*, edited by James J. Paxson and Cynthia A. Gravlee, 62–71. Selinsgrove: Susquehanna University Press, 1998.
Giovanelli, Valerio. "Il mito di Apollo e Dafne e la tradizione esegetica delle moralizzazioni di Ovidio nel Canzoniere di Petrarca." *Carte italiane* 2, nos. 2–3 (2007): 23–34.
Giunta, Claudio. *La poesia italiana nell'età di Dante: La linea Bonagiunta-Guinizzelli*. Bologna: Il Mulino, 1998.
Giunta, Claudio. "Le rime di corrispondenza." In *Versi a un destinatario. Saggio sulla poesia italiana del Medioevo*, 167–266. Bologna: Il Mulino, 2002.
Glendinning, Robert. "Pyramus and Thisbe in the Medieval Classroom." *Speculum* 61 (1986): 51–78.

Gloria, Andrea, ed. *Volgare illustre nel 1100 e proverbi volgari del 1200.* Bologna: Forni, 1977.

Goldin, Frederick. *The Mirror of Narcissus in the Courtly Love Lyric.* Ithaca: Cornell University Press, 1967.

Gorni, Guglielmo. "Cino 'Vil ladro': Parola data e parola rubata." In *Il nodo della lingua e il verbo d'amore. Studi su Dante e altri duecentisti,* 125–39. Florence: Leo S. Olschki, 1981.

Gorni, Guglielmo. "Metamorfosi e redenzione in Petrarca: il senso della forma Correggio del *Canzoniere.*" *Lettere Italiane* 30 (1978): 3–13.

Grafton, Anthony, and Lisa Jardine. *From Humanism to the Humanities: Education and the Liberal Arts in Fifteenth- and Sixteenth-Century Europe.* Cambridge: Harvard University Press, 1986.

Graham, Angus. "Albertano da Brescia." In *Medieval Italy: An Encyclopedia,* edited by Christopher Kleinhenz, 1: 9–11. New York: Routledge, 2004.

Greene, Thomas M. *The Light in Troy: Imitation and Discovery in Renaissance Poetry.* New Haven: Yale University Press, 1982.

Grendler, Paul F. *Schooling in Renaissance Italy: Literacy and Learning, 1300–1600.* Baltimore: Johns Hopkins University Press, 1989.

Gura, David T. *A Critical Edition and Study of Arnulf of Orleans' Philological Commentary to Ovid's 'Metamorphoses.'* PhD diss., The Ohio State University, 2010.

Guthmüller, Bodo. *Ovidio metamorphoseos vulgare: Formen und Funktionen der volkssprachlichen Wiedergabe klassischer Dichtung in der italienischen Renaissance.* Boppard am Rhein: Boldt, 1981.

Guthmüller, Bodo. "Die *volgarizzamenti.*" In *Die Italienische Literatur im Zeitalter Dantes und am Übergang vom Mittelalter zur Renaissance.* Vol. 2, *Die Literatur bis zur Renaissance,* edited by August Buck, 201–54. Heidelberg: C. Winter, 1989.

Hainsworth, Peter R. J. "Metaphor in Petrarch's *Rerum vulgarium fragmenta.*" In *The Languages of Literature in Renaissance Italy,* edited by Peter Hainsworth, Valerio Lucchesi, Christina Roaf, David Robey, and J. R. Woodhouse, 1–18. Oxford: Clarendon Press, 1988.

Hainsworth, Peter R. J. "The Myth of Daphne in the *Rerum vulgarium fragmenta.*" *Italian Studies* 34 (1979): 28–44.

Hamacher, Johannes, ed. *Florilegium Gallicum: Prolegomena und Edition der Exzerpte von Petron bis Cicero, De oratore.* Bern: Herbert Lang, 1975.

Hardie, Colin G. "Dante's 'canzone montanina.'" *The Modern Language Review* 55 (1960): 359–70.

Hardie, Philip. "Ovid into Laura: Absent presences in the *Metamorphoses* and Petrarch's *Rime sparse.*" In *Ovidian Transformations: Essays on the 'Metamorphoses' and its Reception,* edited by Philip Hardie, Alessandro Barchiesi, and Stephen Hinds, 254–70. Cambridge: Cambridge Philological Society, 1999.

Harding, Catherine. "Visualizing Brunetto Latini's *Tesoretto* in early Trecento Florence." *Word & Image* 19, no. 3 (2003): 230–46.

Harvey, Ruth, and Linda Paterson, eds. *The Troubadour 'Tensos' and 'Partimens': A Critical Edition*. 3 vols. Woodbridge: D. S. Brewer, 2010.

Hawkins, Peter S. "Dante's Ovid." *Literature and Belief* 5 (1985): 1–12.

Hexter, Ralph J. "Literary History as a Provocation to Reception Studies." In *Classics and the Uses of Reception*, edited by Charles Martindale and Richard F. Thomas, 23–31. Oxford: Blackwell, 2006.

Hexter, Ralph J. "Medieval Articulations of Ovid's *Metamorphoses*: From Lactantian Segmentation to Arnulfian Allegory." *Mediaevalia* 13 (1987): 63–82.

Hexter, Ralph J. *Ovid and Medieval Schooling: Studies in Medieval School Commentaries on Ovid's 'Ars Amatoria,' 'Epistulae Ex Ponto,' and 'Epistulae Heroidum.'* Munich: Arbeo-Gesellschaft, 1986.

Hexter, Ralph J. "Ovid in the Middle Ages: Exile, Mythographer, Lover." In *Brill's Companion to Ovid*, edited by Barbara Weiden Boyd, 413–42. Leiden: Brill, 2002.

Hexter, Ralph J. "Ovid in translation in Medieval Europe." In *Übersetzung – Translation – Traduction: Ein internationales Handbuch zur Übersetzungsforschung / An international Encyclopedia of Translation Studies / Encyclopédie internationale de la recherche sur la traduction*, edited by Harald Kittel, Armin Paul Frank, Norbert Greiner, Theo Hermans, Werner Koller, José Lambert, and Fritz Paul, 2: 1311–23. Berlin: Walter de Gruyter, 2004.

Hexter, Ralph J. "Shades of Ovid: Pseudo- (and para-) Ovidiana in the Middle Ages." In *Ovid in the Middle Ages*, edited by James G. Clark, Frank T. Coulson, and Kathryn L. McKinley, 284–309. Cambridge: Cambridge University Press, 2011.

Hinds, Stephen. *Allusion and Intertextuality: Dynamics of Appropriation in Roman Poetry*. Cambridge: Cambridge University Press, 1998.

Hinds, Stephen. "Booking the Return Trip: Ovid and *Tristia* 1." *Proceedings of the Cambridge Philological Society* n.s. 31 (1985): 13–32.

Hinds, Stephen. *The Metamorphosis of Persephone: Ovid and the Self-Conscious Muse*. Cambridge: Cambridge University Press, 1987.

Hollander, Robert. *Allegory in Dante's 'Commedia.'* Princeton: Princeton University Press, 1969.

Hollander, Robert. "Dante and Cino da Pistoia." *Dante Studies* 110 (1992): 201–31.

Hollander, Robert. "Dante's 'dolce stil novo' and the *Comedy*." In *Dante: Mito e poesia: Atti del secondo Seminario dantesco internazionale: Monte Verità, Ascona, 23–27 giugno 1997*, edited by Michelangelo Picone and Tatiana Crivelli, 263–81. Florence: Franco Cesati, 1999.

Hollander, Robert. "Le opere di Virgilio nella *Commedia* di Dante." In *Dante e la "bella scola" della poesia: autorità e sfida poetica*, edited by Amilcare A. Iannucci, 247–343. Ravenna: Longo, 1993.

Holsinger, Bruce W. "Sodomy and Resurrection: The Homoerotic Subject of the *Divine Comedy*." In *Premodern Sexualities*, edited by Louise Fradenburg and Carla Freccero, 243–74. New York: Routledge, 1996.

Huygens, R. B. C., ed. *Accessus ad auctores. Bernard D'Utrecht. Conrad D'Hirsau. Dialogus super auctores*. Leiden: Brill, 1970.

Jacoff, Rachel. "Intertextualities in Arcadia: *Purgatorio* 30.49–51." In *The Poetry of Allusion: Virgil and Ovid in Dante's 'Commedia,'* edited by Rachel Jacoff and Jeffrey T. Schnapp, 131–44. Stanford: Stanford University Press, 1991.

Jacoff, Rachel. "Models of Literary Influence in the *Commedia*." In *Medieval Texts & Contemporary Readers*, edited by Laurie A. Finke and Martin B. Shichtman, 158–76. Ithaca: Cornell University Press, 1987.

Jacoff, Rachel, and Jeffrey T. Schnapp, eds. *The Poetry of Allusion: Virgil and Ovid in Dante's 'Commedia.'* Stanford: Stanford University Press, 1991.

Jennings, Lauren McGuire. "Ovid's *Heroides*, Florentine *Volgarizzamenti*, and Unnotated Song in Florence, Biblioteca Nazionale Centrale, II.II.61 and Magliabechiano VII 1040." In *Senza Vestimenta: The Literary Tradition of Trecento Song*, 133–58. Surrey: Ashgate, 2014.

Kay, Sarah. "Love in a Mirror: An Aspect of the Imagery of Bernart de Ventadorn." *Medium Aevum* 52 (1983): 272–85.

Kay, Tristan. *Dante's Lyric Redemption: Eros, Salvation, Vernacular Tradition*. Oxford: Oxford University Press, 2016.

Kay, Tristan. "Dido, Aeneas, and the Evolution of Dante's Poetics." *Dante Studies* 129 (2011): 135–60.

Kay, Tristan. "Redefining the 'matera amorosa': Dante's *Vita nova* and Guittone's (anti-)courtly 'canzoniere.'" *The Italianist* 29, no. 3 (2009): 369–99.

Keen, Catherine. "Cino da Pistoia and the Otherness of Exile." *Annali d'Italianistica* 20 (2002): 89–112.

Keen, Catherine. "Ovid's Exile and Medieval Italian Literature: The Lyric Tradition." In *A Handbook to the Reception of Ovid*, edited by John F. Miller and Carole E. Newlands, 144–60. Chichester: Wiley-Blackwell, 2014.

Keen, Catherine. "Sex and the Medieval City: Viewing the Body Politic from Exile in Early Italian Verse." In *Troubled Vision: Gender, Sexuality and Sight in Medieval Text and Image*, edited by Emma Campbell and Robert Mills, 155–71. New York: Palgrave Macmillan, 2004.

Keen, Catherine. "'Va', mia canzone': Textual Transmission and the Congedo in Medieval Exile Lyrics." *Italian Studies* 64, no. 2 (2009): 183–97.

Kenney, E. J. "Ovidius Prooemians." *Proceedings of the Cambridge Philological Society* 22 (1976): 46–53.

Kibler, William W., and Grover A. Zinn, eds. *Medieval France: An Encyclopedia*. New York: Garland Publications, Inc., 1995.

Kilgour, Maggie. "Dante's Ovidian Doubling." In *Dantean Dialogues: Engaging with the Legacy of Amilcare Iannucci*, edited by Maggie Kilgour and Elena Lombardi, 174–214. Toronto: University of Toronto Press, 2013.

Kleinhenz, Christopher. "Adventures in Textuality: Lyric Poetry, the 'Tenzone', and Cino da Pistoia." In *Textual Cultures of Medieval Italy*, edited by William Robins, 81–111. Toronto: Toronto University Press, 2011.

Kleinhenz, Christopher. "Cino da Pistoia." In *Medieval Italy: An Encyclopedia*, edited by Christopher Kleinhenz, 1: 225–27. New York: Routledge, 2004.

Kleinhenz, Christopher. "Perspectives on Intertextuality in Dante's *Divina Commedia*." *Romance Quarterly* 54, no. 3 (2007): 183–94.

Knoespel, Kenneth J. *Narcissus and the Invention of Personal History*. New York: Garland Publishing, Inc., 1985.

Kovacs, David. "Ovid, *Metamorphoses* 1.2." *The Classical Quarterly* 37, no. 2 (1987): 458–65.

Kuon, Peter. *L'aura dantesca: metamorfosi intertestuali nei 'Rerum vulgarium fragmenta.'* Florence: Franco Cesati, 2004.

Lansing, Richard H. *From Image to Idea: A Study of the Simile in Dante's 'Commedia.'* Ravenna: Longo, 1977.

Lateiner, Donald. "Mythic and Non-Mythic Artists in Ovid's *Metamorphoses*." *Ramus* 13 (1984): 1–30.

Latini, Brunetto. *Il tesoretto (The Little Treasure)*. Edited and translated by Julia Bolton Holloway. New York: Garland Publishing, Inc., 1981.

Latini, Brunetto. *Tesoretto: Riproduzione in facsimile del ms. Strozzi 146 conservato presso la Biblioteca Laurenziana*. Florence: Le Lettere, 2002.

Latini, Brunetto. *Tresor*. Edited and translated by Pietro G. Beltrami, Paolo Squillacioti, Plinio Torri, and Sergio Vatteroni. Turin: Einaudi, 2007.

Lazar, Moshé, ed. *Bernard de Ventadour, troubadour du XIIe siècle: Chansons d'amour*. Paris: C. Klincksieck, 1966.

Leach, Eleanor Winsor. "Ekphrasis and the Theme of Artistic Failure in Ovid's *Metamorphoses*." *Ramus* 3, no. 2 (1974): 102–42.

Ledda, Giuseppe. "*Paradiso*, XVII." In *Il trittico di Cacciaguida: lectura Dantis Scaligera, 2008–2009*, edited by Ennio Sandal, 107–46. Rome: Antenore, 2011.

Levin, Joan H. *Rustico di Filippo and the Florentine Lyric Tradition*. New York: Peter Lang, 1986.

Levin, Joan H. "Rustico Filippi." In *Medieval Italy: An Encyclopedia*, edited by Christopher Kleinhenz, 2: 992–93. New York: Routledge, 2004.

Levin, Joan H. "Sweet, New Endings: A Look at the Tornada in the Stilnovistic and Petrarchan Canzone." *Italica* 61, no. 4 (1984): 297–311.

Levine, Robert. "Exploiting Ovid: Medieval Allegorizations of the *Metamorphoses*." *Medioevo Romanzo* 14 (1989): 197–213.

Linskill, Joseph. *The Poems of the Troubadour Raimbaut de Vaqueiras. With an English Translation of the Poems and an Introductory Study.* The Hague: Mouton, 1964.

Lippi Bigazzi, Vanna. *I volgarizzamenti trecenteschi dell'Ars amandi e dei Remedia amoris.* 2 vols. Florence: Accademia della Crusca, 1987.

Livraghi, Leyla M. G. "Due usi di Ovidio a confronto in Cino da Pistoia lirico (*Se mai leggesti versi de l'Ovidi* & *Amor, che viene armato a doppio dardo*)." *Arzanà* 19 (2017): 9–22.

Livraghi, Leyla M. G. "Eros e dottrina nel sonetto dantesco *Io sono stato con amore insieme*." In *AlmaDante. Seminario Dantesco 2013*, edited by Giuseppe Ledda and Filippo Zanini, 67–85. Bologna: Edizioni Aspasia, 2015.

Lombardi, Elena. *The Wings of the Doves: Love and Desire in Dante and Medieval Culture.* Montreal: McGill-Queen's University Press, 2012.

Lorch, Maristella, and Lavinia Lorch. "Metaphor and Metamorphosis: *Purgatorio* 27 and *Metamorphoses* 4." In *Dante and Ovid: Essays in Intertextuality*, edited by Madison U. Sowell, 112–21. Binghamton: Medieval & Renaissance Texts & Studies, 1991.

Lund-Mead, Carolynn. "Dido Alighieri: Gender Inversion in the Francesca Episode." In *Dante & the Unorthodox: The Aesthetics of Transgression*, edited by James Miller, 121–50. Waterloo: Wilfrid Laurier University Press, 2005.

Maggini, Francesco. "Il 'Fiore di Rettorica.'" In *I primi volgarizzamenti dai classici latini*, 1–15. Florence: F. Le Monnier, 1952.

Magnus, Hugo, ed. *Metamorphoseon libri XV, Lactanti Placidi qui dicitur narrationes fabularum Ovidianarum.* Berlin: Weidmann, 1914; rpt. New York: Arno Press, 1979.

Mallette, Karla. "Rereading *Le Origini*: Sicilian Romance Poetry and the Language of Natural Philosophy." In *The Kingdom of Sicily, 1100–1250: A Literary History*, 65–83. Philadelphia: University of Pennsylvania Press, 2005.

Mann, Jill. "'He Knew Nat Catoun': Medieval School-Texts and Middle English Literature." In *The Text in the Community: Essays on Medieval Works, Manuscripts, Authors, and Readers*, edited by Jill Mann and Maura Nolan, 41–74. Notre Dame: University of Notre Dame Press, 2006.

Marcenaro, Simone. "Polemica letteraria e ironia nella lirica italiana del Duecento. Il caso di Cino da Pistoia." In *Parodia y debate metaliterarios en la Edad Media*, edited by Mercedes Brea, Esther Corral Díaz, and Miguel A. Pousada Cruz, 277–90. Alessandria: Edizioni dell'Orso, 2013.

Marcenaro, Simone. "Polemiche letterarie nella lirica del Duecento." *Revista de Filología Románica* 27 (2010): 77–99.

Marchesi, Simone. *Dante and Augustine: Linguistics, Poetics, Hermeneutics.* Toronto: University of Toronto Press, 2011.

Marchesi, Simone. "Distilling Ovid: Dante's Exile and Some Metamorphic Nomenclature in Hell." In *Writers Reading Writers: Intertextual Studies in Medieval and Early*

Modern Literature in Honor of Robert Hollander, edited by Janet L. Smarr, 21–39. Newark: University of Delaware Press, 2007.

Marchesi, Simone. "Epic Ironies: Poetics, Metapoetics, Self-translation (*Inferno* 18.1, *Purgatorio* 24.52, *Paradiso* 1.13)." *Dante Studies* 131 (2013): 101–17.

Marcozzi, Luca. *La biblioteca di Febo: Mitologia e allegoria in Petrarca*. Florence: Franco Cesati, 2003.

Marcozzi, Luca. "Petrarca lettore di Ovidio." In *Testimoni del vero: Su alcuni libri in biblioteche d'autore*, edited by Emilio Russo, 57–104. Rome: Bulzoni, 2000.

Marcozzi, Luca, ed. *Petrarca lettore: pratiche e rappresentazioni della lettura nelle opere dell'umanista*. Florence: Franco Cesati, 2016.

Marigo, Aristide. "Cultura letteraria e preumanistica nelle maggiori enciclopedie del Dugento: Lo 'Speculum' e il 'Tresors.'" *Giornale storico della letteratura italiana* 68 (1916): 1–42, 289–326.

Martelli, Francesca. *Ovid's Revisions: The Editor as Author*. Cambridge: Cambridge University Press, 2013.

Marti, Mario, ed. *Poeti del Dolce stil nuovo*. Florence: F. Le Monnier, 1969.

Martinez, Ronald. "Italy." In *A Handbook of the Troubadours*, edited by F. R. P. Akehurst and Judith M. Davis, 279–94. Berkeley: University of California Press, 1995.

Mazzotta, Giuseppe. "The *Canzoniere* and the Language of the Self." In *The Worlds of Petrarch*, 58–79. Durham: Duke University Press, 1993.

Mazzotta, Giuseppe. *Dante's Vision and the Circle of Knowledge*. Princeton: Princeton University Press, 1993.

McKeown, James C. *Ovid: Amores, Volume III. A Commentary on Book 2*. Leeds: Francis Cairns, 1998.

McLaughlin, Martin L. *Literary Imitation in the Italian Renaissance: The Theory and Practice of Literary Imitation in Italy from Dante to Bembo*. Oxford: Clarendon Press, 1995.

McMahon, Robert. "The Christian Scripture of Ovid's Narcissus in the 'Commedia.'" *Pacific Coast Philology* 20 (1985): 65–69.

McMahon, Robert. "Satan as Infernal Narcissus: Interpretative Translation in the *Commedia*." In *Dante and Ovid: Essays in Intertextuality*, edited by Madison U. Sowell, 65–86. Binghamton: Medieval & Renaissance Texts & Studies, 1991.

Meneghetti, Maria Luisa. "Intertextuality and Dialogism in the Troubadours." In *Troubadours: An Introduction*, edited by Simon Gaunt and Sarah Kay, 181–96. Cambridge: Cambridge University Press, 1999.

Meneghetti, Maria Luisa. *Il pubblico dei trovatori: ricenzione e riuso dei testi lirici cortesi fino al XIV secolo*. Modena: Mucchi, 1984.

Mews, Constant J. *The Lost Love Letters of Heloise and Abelard: Perceptions of Dialogue in Twelfth-century France*, translated by Neville Chiavaroli and Constant J. Mews. 2nd ed. New York: Palgrave Macmillan, 2008.

Minnis, Alastair. "Latin to Vernacular: Academic Prologues and the Medieval French Art of Love." In *Medieval and Renaissance Scholarship: Proceedings of the Second European Science Foundation Workshop on the Classical Tradition in the Middle Ages and the Renaissance*, edited by Nicholas Mann and Birger Munk Olsen, 153–86. Leiden: Brill, 1997.

Minnis, Alastair. *Magister amoris: The 'Roman de la Rose' and Vernacular Hermeneutics*. Oxford: Oxford University Press, 2001.

Minnis, Alastair. *Medieval Theory of Authorship: Scholastic Literary Attitudes in the Later Middle Ages*. 2nd ed. Philadelphia: University of Pennsylvania Press, 1988.

Minnis, Alastair, and A. B. Scott, eds. with assistance of David Wallace. *Medieval Literary Theory and Criticism c.1100 – c.1375: The Commentary Tradition*. Rev. ed. Oxford: Oxford University Press, 1992.

Mocan, Mira. *L'arca della mente. Riccardo di San Vittore nella 'Commedia' di Dante*. Florence: Leo S. Olschki, 2012.

Moevs, Christian. "Form." In *The Metaphysics of Dante's 'Comedy,'* 49–106. Oxford: Oxford University Press, 2005.

Moevs, Christian. "Pyramus at the Mulberry Tree: De-petrifying Dante's Tinted Mind." In *Imagining Heaven in the Middle Ages*, edited by Jan Swango Emerson and Hugh Feiss, O.S.B., 211–44. New York: Garland Publishing, Inc., 2000.

Monaci, Ernesto. "Le Miracole de Roma." *Archivio della Reale Società Romana di Storia Patria* 38 (1915): 551–90.

Monaci, Ernesto, ed. *Storie de Troja et de Roma, altrimenti dette Liber Ystoriarum Romanorum*. Rome: Società Romana di Storia Patria, 1920.

Monson, Don A. *Andreas Capellanus, Scholasticism, and the Courtly Tradition*. Washington: The Catholic University of America Press, 2005.

Moore, Edward. "Dante and Ovid." In *Scripture and Classical Authors in Dante*, 206–28. Oxford: Clarendon, 1896.

Moore, Edward. *Studies in Dante. First series: Scripture and Classical Authors in Dante*. Oxford: Clarendon, 1896.

Munari, Franco. *Catalogue of the MSS of Ovid's Metamorphoses*. London: Institute of Classical Studies in Conjunction with the Warburg Institute, 1957.

Munk Olsen, Birger. "Les classiques latins dans les florilèges médiévaux antérieurs au XIIIe siècle." *Revue d'histoire des textes* 9 (1979): 47–121.

Munk Olsen, Birger. "Les classiques latins dans les florilèges médiévaux antérieurs au XIIIe siècle." *Revue d'histoire des textes* 10 (1980): 115–64.

Munzi, Luigi. "Una inedita *Summa memorialis* delle *Metamorfosi* ovidiane." In *Dicti studiosus: scritti di filologia offerti a Scevola Mariotti dai suoi allievi*, 329–85. Urbino: Edizioni QuattroVenti, 1990.

Murray, K. Sarah-Jane. "Rewritings of Ovid." In *From Plato to Lancelot: A Preface to Chrétien de Troyes*, 48–83. Syracuse: Syracuse University Press, 2008.

BIBLIOGRAPHY 313

Navone, Paola, ed. *Albertano da Brescia, Liber de doctrina dicendi et tacendi. La parola del cittadino nell'Italia del Duecento*. Florence: SISMEL-Edizioni del Galluzzo, 1998.

Nazarian, Cynthia. "Actaeon Ego Sum: Ovidian Dismemberment and Lyric Voice in Petrarch and Maurice Scève." In *Metamorphosis: The Changing Face of Ovid in Medieval and Early Modern Europe*, edited by Alison Keith and Stephen Rupp, 199–222. Toronto: Centre for Reformation and Renaissance Studies, 2007.

Nighman, Chris L. The *Compendium moralium notabilium* Project. 2013-. http://web.wlu.ca/history/cnighman/CMN/index.html.

Noacco, Cristina, ed. *Piramo e Tisbe*. Rome: Carocci, 2005.

Nolan, Edward Peter. "Dante's Comedic Displacements of Ovid's Narcissus." In *The Influence of the Classical World on Medieval Literature, Architecture, Music, and Culture: A Collection of Interdisciplinary Studies*, edited by Fidel Fajardo-Acosta, 105–21. Lewiston: The Edwin Mellen Press, 1992.

O'Hara, James J. *Inconsistency in Roman Epic: Studies in Catullus, Lucretius, Vergil, Ovid and Lucan*. Cambridge: Cambridge University Press, 2007.

Olson, Kristina. "Shoes, Gowns and Turncoats: Reconsidering Cacciaguida's History of Florentine Fashion and Politics," *Dante Studies* 134 (2016): 26–47.

Ortiz, Ramiro. "La materia epica di ciclo classico nella lirica italiana delle origini." *Giornale storico della letteratura italiana* 85 (1925): 1–93.

Otis, Brooks. "The Argumenta of the So-Called Lactantius." *Harvard Studies in Classical Philology* 47 (1936): 131–63.

Ovid. *Metamorfosi: Volume I (Libri I–II)*. Edited by Alessandro Barchiesi and translated by Ludovica Koch. Milan: Fondazione Lorenzo Valla / Arnoldo Mondadori Editore, 2005.

Ovid. *Metamorfosi: Volume II (Libri III–IV)*. Edited by Alessandro Barchiesi and Gianpiero Rosati, translated by Ludovica Koch. Milan: Fondazione Lorenzo Valla / Arnoldo Mondadori Editore, 2007.

Ovid. *Metamorfosi: Volume III (Libri V–VI)*. Edited by Gianpiero Rosati, translated by Gioachino Chiarini. Milan: Fondazione Lorenzo Valla / Arnoldo Mondadori Editore, 2009.

Ovid. *Metamorfosi: Volume IV (Libri VII–IX)*. Edited by Edward J. Kenney, translated by Gioachino Chiarini. Milan: Fondazione Lorenzo Valla / Arnoldo Mondadori Editore, 2011.

Ovid. *Metamorfosi: Volume V (Libri X–XII)*. Edited by Joseph D. Reed, translated by Gioachino Chiarini. Milan: Fondazione Lorenzo Valla / Arnoldo Mondadori Editore, 2013.

Ovid. *Metamorfosi: Volume VI (Libri XIII–XV)*. Edited by Philip Hardie, translated by Gioachino Chiarini. Milan: Fondazione Lorenzo Valla / Arnoldo Mondadori Editore, 2015.

Ovid. *Metamorphoses*. Edited by R. J. Tarrant. Oxford: Oxford University Press, 2004.

Ovid. *The Poems of Exile*. Translated by Peter Green. Berkeley: University of California Press, 2005.

Ovid. *The Second Book of 'Amores.'* Edited with translation and commentary by Joan Booth. Warminster: Aris & Phillips, 1991.

Paden, William D., Jr. "Aesthetic Distance in Petrarch's Response to the Pastourelle: *Rime* LII." *Romance Notes* 16, no. 3 (1975): 702–7.

Pairet, Ana. "Recasting the *Metamorphoses* in fourteenth-century France: The challenges of the *Ovide moralisé*." In *Ovid in the Middle Ages*, edited by James G. Clark, Frank T. Coulson, and Kathryn L. McKinley, 83–107. Cambridge: Cambridge University Press, 2011.

Palgen, Rudolf. "Dante e Ovidio." *Convivium* 27 (1959): 277–87.

Panvini, Bruno. *Poeti italiani della corte di Federico II*. Naples: Liguori, 1994.

Panvini, Bruno, *Le rime della scuola siciliana*. Florence: Leo S. Olschki, 1962.

Panvini, Bruno. *La scuola poetica siciliana. Le canzoni dei rimatori non siciliani. Testo critico, interpretazione e note*. Florence: Leo S. Olschki, 1957.

Paolino, Laura. "Ancora qualche nota sui madrigali di Petrarca (*RVF* 52, 54, 106, 121)." *Italianistica* 30, no. 2 (2001): 307–23.

Paratore, Ettore. "Alcuni caratteri dello stile della cancelleria federiciana." In *Antico e nuovo*, 117–63. Caltanissetta: Salvatore Sciascia Editore, 1965.

Paratore, Ettore. "Il canto XXV dell'*Inferno*." In *Tradizione e struttura in Dante*, 250–80. Florence: G. C. Sansoni, 1968.

Paratore, Ettore. "Ovidio." *Enciclopedia dantesca*, edited by Umberto Bosco, 4: 225–36. Rome: Istituto dell'Enciclopedia Italiana, 1970–78.

Paratore, Ettore. "Ovidio e Dante." In *Nuovi saggi danteschi*, 47–100. Rome: A. Signorelli, 1973.

Pasquali, Giorgio. "Arte allusiva." In *Pagine stravaganti di un filologo*, 2: 275–82. Florence: Le Lettere, 1994.

Pasquini, Emilio. "Appunti sul carteggio Cino – Dante." In *Le rime di Dante. Gargnano del Garda (25–27 settembre 2008)*, edited by Claudia Berra and Paolo Borsa, 1–16. Milan: Cisalpino Istituto Editoriale Universitario, 2010.

Pasquini, Emilio. "Convenevole da Prato." In *Dizionario biografico degli Italiani* 28, edited by Alberto M. Ghisalberti, 563–68. Rome: Istituto dell'Enciclopedia Italiana, 1983.

Pasquini, Emilio. "Il mito dell'amore: Dante fra i due Guidi." In *Dante: Mito e poesia: Atti del secondo Seminario dantesco internazionale: Monte Verità, Ascona, 23–27 giugno 1997*, edited by Michelangelo Picone and Tatiana Crivelli, 283–95. Florence: Franco Cesati, 1999.

Pavlock, Barbara. *The Image of the Poet in Ovid's 'Metamorphoses.'* Madison: University of Wisconsin Press, 2009.

Pepin, Ronald E., trans. *The Vatican Mythographers*. New York: Fordham University Press, 2008.

Pertile, Lino. "Canto XXIV: Of Poetry and Politics." In *Lectura Dantis: Purgatorio. A Canto-by-Canto Commentary*, edited by Allen Mandelbaum, Anthony Oldcorn, and Charles Ross, 262–76. Berkeley: University of California Press, 2008.

Perugi, Maurizio. *Trovatori a Valchiusa: Un frammento della cultura provenzale del Petrarca*. Padua: Antenore, 1985.

Petrarca, Francesco. *Canzoniere*. Edited by Marco Santagata. Rev. ed. Milan: Mondadori, 2004.

Petrarca, Francesco. *Le postille del Virgilio Ambrosiano*. Edited by Marco Baglio, Antonietta Nebuloni Testa, and Marco Petoletti. 2 vols. Padua: Antenore, 2006.

Petrarca, Francesco. *Trionfi, Rime estravaganti, Codice degli abbozzi*. Edited by Vinicio Pacca and Laura Paolino. Milan: Mondadori, 1996.

Petrucci, Armando. "Le biblioteche antiche." In *Letteratura italiana*, edited by Alberto Asor Rosa. Vol. 2, *Produzione e consumo*, 527–54. Turin: Einaudi, 1983.

Pfeffer, Wendy. *Proverbs in Medieval Occitan Literature*. Gainesville: University Press of Florida, 1997.

Phillippy, Patricia Berrahou. "'Vergine bella': Palinode and Autobiography in Petrarch's *Rime sparse*." In *Love's Remedies: Recantation and Renaissance Lyric Poetry*, 61–91. Lewisburg: Bucknell University Press, 1995.

Picone, Michelangelo. "Dante e Cino: Una lunga amicizia. Prima parte: I tempi della Vita Nova." *Dante* 1 (2004): 39–53.

Picone, Michelangelo. "Dante e il mito di Narciso: Dal *Roman de la Rose* alla *Commedia*." *Romanische Forschungen* 89, no. 4 (1977): 382–97.

Picone, Michelangelo. "Dante e i miti." In *Dante: Mito e poesia: Atti del secondo Seminario dantesco internazionale (Monte Verità, Ascona, 23–27 giugno 1997)*, edited by Michelangelo Picone and Tatiana Crivelli, 21–32. Florence: Franco Cesati, 1999.

Picone, Michelangelo. "Dante, Ovidio e la poesia dell'esilio." *Rassegna europea di letteratura italiana* 14, no. 2 (1999): 7–23.

Picone, Michelangelo. "Dentro la biblioteca di Petrarca." In *La bibliothèque de Pétrarque: Livres et auteurs autour d'un humaniste*, edited by Maurice Brock, Francesco Furlan, and Frank La Brasca, 21–34. Turnhout: Brepols, 2011.

Picone, Michelangelo. "Ovid and the *Exul Inmeritus*." In *Dante for the New Millennium*, edited by Teodolinda Barolini and H. Wayne Storey, 389–407. New York: Fordham University Press, 2003.

Picone, Michelangelo. "L'Ovidio di Dante." In *Dante e la "bella scola" della poesia: autorità e sfida poetica*, edited by Amilcare A. Iannucci, 107–44. Ravenna: Longo, 1993.

Picone, Michelangelo. "Purgatorio XXVII: Passaggio rituale e *translatio* poetica." *Medioevo romanzo* 12, no. 2 (1987): 389–402.

Picone, Michelangelo. "Sulla canzone 'montanina' di Dante." *L'Alighieri* 42 (2002): 105–12.

Picone, Michelangelo. "La tenzone 'de amore' fra Jacopo Mostacci, Pier della Vigna e il Notaio." In *Il genere 'tenzone' nelle letterature romanze delle Origini*, edited by Matteo Pedroni and Antonio Stäuble, 13–31. Ravenna: Longo, 1999.

Picone, Michelangelo. "La teoria dell'*Auctoritas* nella *Vita nova*." *Tenzone* 6 (2005): 173–91.

Picone, Michelangelo. "La *Vita Nova* come macrotesto." In *Percorsi della lirica duecentesca: Dai Siciliani alla 'Vita Nova,'* 219–35. Florence: Cadmo, 2003.

Picone, Michelangelo. "La *Vita Nova* come *prosimetrum*." In *Percorsi della lirica duecentesca: Dai Siciliani alla 'Vita Nova,'* 237–48. Florence: Cadmo, 2003.

Pigman, G. W. III, "Versions of Imitation in the Renaissance." *Renaissance Quarterly* 33 (1980): 1–32.

Pirovano, Donato. *Il Dolce stil novo*. Rome: Salerno, 2014.

Pittaluga, Stefano. "Le *De tribus puellis*, 'comédie Ovidienne.'" *Vita Latina* 61 (1976): 2–13.

Pittaluga, Stefano. "Le *De tribus puellis*, 'comédie Ovidienne.'" *Vita Latina* 62 (1977): 2–14.

Pittaluga, Stefano. "Memoria letteraria e modi della ricezione di Seneca tragico nel medioevo e nell'umanesimo." In *Mediaeval Antiquity*, edited by Andries Welkenhuysen, Herman Braet, and Werner Verbeke, 45–58. Leuven: Leuven University Press, 1995.

Poli, Andrea. "Bernart de Ventadorn in Petrarca." *Filologia e critica* 18, no. 1 (1993): 20–44.

Poliziano, Angelo. *Poesie volgari*, edited by Francesco Bausi. 2 vols. Rome: Vecchiarelli, 1997.

Pollidori, Valentina. "Le rime di Guido Orlandi." *Studi di filologia italiana* 53 (1995): 55–202.

Pomaro, Gabriella. "Censimento dei manoscritti della Biblioteca di S. Maria Novella, Parte I, Origini e Trecento." *Memorie Domenicane*, n.s. 11 (1980): 325–470.

Possanza, Mark. "Editing Ovid: Immortal Works and Material Texts." In *A Companion to Ovid*, edited by Peter E. Knox, 311–26. Chichester: Wiley-Blackwell, 2009.

Powell, James M. *Albertanus da Brescia: The Pursuit of Happiness in the Early Thirteenth Century*. Philadelphia: University of Pennsylvania Press, 1992.

Quain, Edwin. "The Medieval Accessus Ad Auctores." *Traditio* 3 (1945): 214–64.

Quillen, Carol Everhart. *Rereading the Renaissance: Petrarch, Augustine, and the Language of Humanism*. Ann Arbor: University of Michigan Press, 1998.

Rackley, Sally A. "The Amatory Excerpts of Ovid in the *Florilegium Gallicum*: Evidence of the Knowledge of this Poet in the Twelfth Century." *Florilegium* 8 (1986): 71–112.

Rackley, Sally A. "The Excerpts from Ovid's *Heroides* in the *Florilegium gallicum*." *Manuscripta* 36, no. 2 (1992): 125–35.

Ramazzina, Antonella Miriam. "'Chantan volgra mon fin cor descobrir' e 'Poi li piace c'avanzi suo valore': due testi a confronto.'" *Medioevo Romanzo* 22, no. 3 (1998): 352–72.

Rand, Edward K. "Dante and Servius." *Annual Reports of the Dante Society* 33 (1914): 1–11.

Rea, Roberto. "Guinizzelli *praised and explained* (da *[O] caro padre meo* al XXVI del *Purgatorio*)." *The Italianist* 30 (2010): 1–17.

Richmond, John. "Manuscript Traditions and the Transmission of Ovid's Works." In *Brill's Companion to Ovid*, edited by Barbara Weiden Boyd, 443–83. Leiden: Brill, 2002.

Rieker, Jörg Rudolf, ed. *Arnulfi Aurelianensis Glosule Ovidii Fastorum*. Florence: SISMEL-Edizioni del Galluzzo, 2005.

Rivero, Albert J. "Petrarch's 'Nel dolce tempo de la prima etade.'" *Modern Language Notes* 94, no. 1 (1979): 92–112.

Robathan, Dorothy M. *The Pseudo-Ovidian 'De Vetula': Text, Introduction, and Notes*. Amsterdam: A. M. Hakkert, 1968.

Robson, Alan. "Dante's Reading of the Latin Poets and the Structure of the *Commedia*." In *The World of Dante: Essays on Dante and His Times*, edited by Cecil Grayson, 81–122. Oxford: Clarendon Press, 1980.

Roglieri, Maria Ann. "*Per Ovidio parla Amore, sì come se fosse persona umana* (V.N. XXV): The case for Ovid's figure of Amore in Dante's *Vita Nuova*." *Carte italiane* 2, nos. 2–3 (2007): 1–22.

Roncaglia, Aurelio. "Cino tra Dante e Petrarca." In *Colloquio Cino da Pistoia (Roma 25 ottobre 1975)*, 7–32. Rome: Accademia nazionale dei Lincei, 1976.

Roncaglia, Aurelio. "Precedenti e significato dello 'stil novo' dantesco." In *Dante e Bologna nei tempi di Dante*, edited by the Facoltà di lettere e filosofia, Università di Bologna, 13–34. Bologna: Commissione per i testi di lingua, 1967.

Roncaglia, Aurelio. "La tenzone fra Ugo Catola e Marcabruno." In *Linguistica e Filologia: Omaggio a Benvenuto Terracini*, edited by Cesare Segre, 203–54. Milan: Il Saggiatore, 1968.

Roncaglia, Aurelio. "Les Troubadours et Virgile." In *Lectures médiévales de Virgile. Actes du colloque de Rome (25–28 Octobre 1982)*, edited by École française de Rome, 267–83. Rome: École française de Rome, 1985.

Roos, Paolo. *Sentenza e proverbio nell'antichità e i 'Distici di Catone.'* Brescia: Morcelliana, 1984.

Rosemann, Philipp W., ed. *Mediaeval Commentaries on the 'Sentences' of Peter Lombard*. Vol. 3. Leiden: Brill, 2015.

Rossi, Luciano. "Canto XXIV." In *Lectura Dantis Turicensis: Purgatorio*, edited by Georges Güntert and Michelangelo Picone, 373–87. Florence: Franco Cesati, 2001.

Rossi, Luciano. "Maestria poetica e 'grivoiserie' nelle tenzoni Orlandi-Cavalcanti." In *Studi di filologia e letteratura italiana in onore di Gianvito Resta*, edited by Vitilio Masiello, 27–42. Rome: Salerno, 2000.

Rossi, Luciano. "Ovidio." In *Lo spazio letterario del Medioevo 2, Il Medioevo volgare*, Vol. 3, *La ricezione del testo*, edited by Piero Boitani, Mario Mancini, and Alberto Varvaro, 259–301. Rome: Salerno, 2003.

Rossi, Luciano. "I trovatori e l'esempio ovidiano." In *Ovidius redivivus: Von Ovid zu Dante*, edited by Michelangelo Picone and Bernhard Zimmermann, 105–49. Stuttgart: M&P, 1994.

Rotondi, Giuseppe. "Ovidio nel medioevo." *Convivium* 6 (1934): 262–69.

Rouse, R. H. "Florilegia and Latin Classical Authors in Twelfth- and Thirteenth-Century Orléans." *Viator* 10 (1979): 131–60.

Rushworth, Jennifer. *Discourses of Mourning in Dante, Petrarch, and Proust*. Oxford: Oxford University Press, 2016.

Sabbadini, Remigio. *Le scoperte dei codici latini e greci ne' secoli XIV e XV: Nuove ricerche col riassunto filologico dei due volumi. Edizione anastatica con nuove aggiunte e correzioni dell'autore a cura di Eugenio Garin*. Florence: G. C. Sansoni Editore, 1967.

Santagata, Marco. "La canzone delle metamorfosi (*R.v.f.* 23)." In *Per moderne carte: La biblioteca volgare di Petrarca*, 273–325. Bologna: Il Mulino, 1990.

Santagata, Marco. *I frammenti dell'anima: Storia e racconto nel 'Canzoniere' di Petrarca*. Bologna: Il Mulino, 1992.

Santagata, Marco. *Per moderne carte: La biblioteca volgare di Petrarca*. Bologna: Il Mulino, 1990.

Sartre, Jean-Paul. *War Diaries: Notebooks from a Phoney War, November 1939–March 1940*. Translated by Quintin Hoare. New York: Verso, 1999.

Savona, Eugenio. *Repertorio tematico del Dolce stil nuovo*. Bari: Adriatica Editrice, 1973.

Sayce, Olive. *Exemplary Comparison from Homer to Petrarch*. Woodbridge: D. S. Brewer, 2008.

Scarpati, Oriana. *Retorica del trobar: Le comparazioni nella lirica occitana*. Rome: Viella, 2008.

Schildgen, Brenda Deen. "Petrarch's Defense of Secular Letters, the Latin Fathers, and Ancient Roman Rhetoric." *Rhetorica* 11, no. 2 (1993): 119–34.

Schmitt-von Mühlenfels, Franz. *Pyramus und Thisbe: Rezeptionstypen eines Ovidischen Stoffes in Literatur, Kunst und Musik*. Heidelberg: C. Winter, 1972.

Schnapp, Jeffrey T. "Dante's Ovidian Self-Correction in *Paradiso* 17." In *The Poetry of Allusion: Virgil and Ovid in Dante's 'Commedia,'* edited by Rachel Jacoff and Jeffrey T. Schnapp, 214–23. Stanford: Stanford University Press, 1991.

Schnapp, Jeffrey T. "Dante's Sexual Solecisms: Gender and Genre in the *Commedia*." In *The New Medievalism*, edited by Marina S. Brownlee, Kevin Brownlee, and Stephen G. Nichols, 201–25. Baltimore: Johns Hopkins University Press, 1991.

Schnapp, Jeffrey T. "Trasfigurazione e metamorfosi nel *Paradiso* dantesco." In *Dante e la Bibbia: Atti del convegno internazionale promosso da "Biblia," Firenze, 26–27–28 settembre 1986*, edited by Giovanni Barblan, 273–94. Florence: Leo S. Olschki, 1988.

Schoonhoven, Henk, ed. *The Pseudo-Ovidian Ad Liviam de morte Drusi (Consolatio ad Liviam, Epicedium Drusi): A Critical Text with Introduction and Commentary*. Groningen: E. Forsten, 1992.

Scott, John A. "Cino da Pistoia and Dante Alighieri." In *Flinders Dante Conferences 2002–2004*, edited by Margaret Baker, Flavia Coassin, and Diana Glenn, 26–37. Adelaide: Lythrum Press, 2005.

Segre, Cesare. "Bartolomeo da San Concordio." In *Dizionario biografico degli Italiani*, edited by Alberto M. Ghisalberti, 6: 768–70. Rome: Istituto della Enciclopedia italiana, 1964.

Segre, Cesare. *Volgarizzamenti del Due e Trecento*. Turin: Unione Tipografico-Editrice Torinese, 1953.

Segre, Cesare, and Mario Marti, eds. *La prosa del Duecento*. Milan: Riccardo Ricciardi, 1959.

Selmi, Francesco, ed. *Dei trattati morali di Albertano da Brescia volgarizzamento inedito fatto nel 1268 da Andrea da Grosseto*. Bologna: Gaetano Romagnoli, 1873.

Simintendi da Prato, Arrigo. *Cinque altri libri delle Metamorfosi d'Ovidio volgarizzate da Ser Arrigo Simintendi*. Prato: Ranieri Guasti, 1848.

Simintendi da Prato, Arrigo. *I primi V libri delle Metamorfosi d'Ovidio volgarizzate da Ser Arrigo Simintendi da Prato*. Prato: Ranieri Guasti, 1846.

Simintendi da Prato, Arrigo. *Gli ultimi V libri delle Metamorfosi d'Ovidio volgarizzate da Ser Arrigo Simintendi da Prato*. Prato: Ranieri Guasti, 1850.

Singer, Samuel, ed. *Lexikon der Sprichwörter des romanisch-germanischen Mittelalters*. Berlin: Walter de Gruyter, 2001.

Singleton, Charles S. *The Divine Comedy. Inferno, 2: Commentary*. Princeton: Princeton University Press, 1990.

Slater, D. A. *Towards a Text of the Metamorphosis of Ovid*. Oxford: Clarendon Press, 1927.

Smarr, Janet Levarie. "Poets of Love and Exile." In *Dante and Ovid: Essays in Intertextuality*, edited by Madison U. Sowell, 139–51. Binghamton: Medieval & Renaissance Texts & Studies, 1991.

Smith, Nathaniel B. "The Lark Image in Bondie Dietaiuti and Dante." *Forum Italicum* 12 (1978): 233–42.

Southerden, Francesca. "Desire as a Dead Letter: A Reading of Petrarch's *RVF* 125." In *Desire in Dante and the Middle Ages*, edited by Manuele Gragnolati, Tristan Kay, Elena Lombardi, and Francesca Southerden, 185–207. Oxford: Legenda, 2012.

Sowell, Madison U., ed. *Dante and Ovid: Essays in Intertextuality*. Binghamton: Medieval & Renaissance Texts & Studies, 1991.

Sowell, Madison U. "Ovid in the Middle Ages." In *Medieval Italy: An Encyclopedia*, edited by Christopher Kleinhenz, 2: 813–14. New York: Routledge, 2004.

Stapleton, Michael L. *Harmful Eloquence: Ovid's 'Amores' from Antiquity to Shakespeare*. Ann Arbor: University of Michigan Press, 1996.

Stark, Caroline. "Dante's Narcissus." *Classical Outlook* 86, no. 4 (2009): 132–38.

Stark, Caroline. "Reflections of Narcissus." In *The Afterlife of Ovid*, edited by Peter Mack and John North, 23–41. London: Institute of Classical Studies, School of Advanced Study, University of London, 2015.

Steinberg, Justin. "Dante *Estravagante*, Petrarca *Disperso*, and the Spectre of the Other Woman." In *Petrarch & Dante: Anti-Dantism, Metaphysics, Tradition*, edited by Zygmunt Barański and Theodore J. Cachey, Jr., 263–89. Notre Dame: University of Notre Dame Press, 2009.

Steinberg, Justin. "Petrarch's Damned Poetry and the Poetics of Exclusion · *Rime disperse*." In *Petrarch: A Critical Guide to the Complete Works*, edited by Victoria Kirkham and Armando Maggi, 85–100. Chicago: Chicago University Press, 2009.

Stok, Fabio. "I *Fasti* di Ovidio tra Petrarca e Boccaccio." In *Ou pan ephemeron: scritti in memoria di Roberto Pretagostini offerti da colleghi, dottori e dottorandi di ricerca della Facoltà di Lettere e Filosofia (Vol. 1–2)*, edited by Cecilia Braidotti, Emanuele Dettori, and Eugenio Lanzillotta, 489–504. Rome: Edizioni Quasar, 2009.

Stroński, Stanisław. *Le troubadour Folquet de Marseille*. Kraków: Académie des Sciences: 1910.

Sturm-Maddox, Sara. "The Ovidian Subtext." In *Petrarch's Metamorphoses: Text and Subtext in the 'Rime sparse,'* 9–38. Columbia: University of Missouri Press, 1985.

Sturm-Maddox, Sara. *Petrarch's Laurels*. University Park: Pennsylvania University Press, 1992.

Sturm-Maddox, Sara. *Petrarch's Metamorphoses: Text and Subtext in the 'Rime sparse.'* Columbia: University of Missouri Press, 1985.

Sturm-Maddox, Sara. "The 'Rime Petrose' and the Purgatorial Palinode." *Studies in Philology* 84, no. 2 (1987): 119–33.

Szombathely, Gioachino. *Dante e Ovidio: Studio*. Trieste: Lloyd Austro-Ungarico, 1888.

Tarrant, Richard J. "The *Narrationes* of 'Lactantius' and the Transmission of Ovid's *Metamorphoses*." In *Formative Stages of Classical Traditions: Latin Texts from Antiquity to the Renaissance*, edited by Oronzo Pecere and Michael D. Reeve, 83–115. Spoleto: Centro italiano di studi sull'alto medioevo, 1995.

Tarrant, Richard J. "Ovid." In *Texts and Transmission: A Survey of the Latin Classics*, edited by L. D. Reynolds, 257–86. Oxford: Clarendon Press, 1983.

Tassi, Francesco, ed. *Delle storie contra i pagani di Paolo Orosio libri VII: Volgarizzamento di Bono Giamboni*. Florence: T. Baracchi, 1849.

Tesoro della lingua Italiana delle Origini. http://tlio.ovi.cnr.it/TLIO/.

Tilliette, Jean-Yves. "Savants et poètes du moyen âge face à Ovide: les débuts de l'aetas Ovidiana (v. 1050–v. 1200)." In *Ovidius redivivus: Von Ovid zu Dante*, edited by Michelangelo Picone and Bernhard Zimmermann, 63–104. Stuttgart: M&P, 1994.

Tobler, Adolf. "Proverbia que dicuntur super natura feminarum." *Zeitschrift für Romanische Philologie* 9 (1885): 287–331.

Todorović, Jelena. *Dante and the Dynamics of Textual Exchange: Authorship, Manuscript Culture, and the Making of the 'Vita Nova.'* New York: Fordham University Press, 2016.

Torraca, Francesco. Review of Oddone Zenatti's *Dante e Firenze: Prose antiche con note illustrative ed appendici*. In *Bullettino della Società Dantesca Italiana*, n.s. 10 (1903): 139–60.

Torri, Alessandro, ed. *L'Ottimo commento della Divina Commedia*. 3 vols. Bologna: Arnaldo Forni, 1995.

Toynbee, Paget, ed. and trans. *Dantis Alagherii Epistolae. The Letters of Dante*. Oxford: Clarendon Press, 1920.

Tronchet, Gilles. *La métamorphose à l'oeuvre: recherches sur la poétique d'Ovide dans les 'Métamorphoses.'* Leuven: Peeters, 1998.

Uguccione Pisa. *Derivationes*, edited by Enzo Cecchini and Guido Arbizzoni. Florence: SISMEL-Edizioni del Galluzzo, 2004.

Ullman, Berthold Louis. "Hieremias de Montagnone and his citations from Catullus." In *Studies in the Italian Renaissance*, 79–112. Rome: Edizioni di Storia e Letteratura, 1955.

Ullman, Berthold Louis. "Petrarch's Favorite Books." In *Studies in the Italian Renaissance*, 113–33. Rome: Edizioni di Storia e Letteratura, 1955.

Van Peteghem, Julie. "Dante lettore di Ovidio: Influssi ovidiani e riflessioni metaletterarie nella *Commedia*." *Studi Danteschi* 83 (2018): 149–71.

Van Peteghem, Julie. "Digital Readers of Allusive Texts: Ovidian Intertextuality in the *Commedia* and the Digital Concordance on *Intertextual Dante*." *Humanist Studies & the Digital Age* 4 (2015): 39–59.

Van Peteghem, Julie. *Intertextual Dante*. Digital Dante. New York: Columbia University Libraries, 2017. https://digitaldante.columbia.edu/intertexual-dante/.

Van Peteghem, Julie. "What is *Intertextual Dante*?" *Intertextual Dante*, Digital Dante. New York: Columbia University Libraries, 2017. https://digitaldante.columbia.edu/intertexual-dante-vanpeteghem/.

Varvaro, Alberto, ed. *Rigaut de Berbezilh: Liriche*. Bari: Adriatica Editrice, 1960.

Vazzana, Steno. *Dante e "la bella scola."* Rome: Edizioni dell'Ateneo, 2002.

Vazzana, Steno. "Ovidio è il terzo." In *Dante e "la bella scola*,*"* 123–47. Rome: Edizioni dell'Ateneo, 2002.

Velli, Giuseppe. "La memoria poetica del Petrarca." *Italia medioevale e umanistica* 19 (1976): 173–207.

Velli, Giuseppe. "Petrarca, Dante, la poesia classica: 'Ne la stagion che 'l ciel rapido inchina' (RVF, L) 'Io son venuto al punto de la rota' (*Rime*, C)." *Studi petrarcheschi* 15 (2002): 81–98.

Venturi, Luigi. *Le similitudini dantesche ordinate, illustrate e confrontate*. 3rd ed. Florence: G. C. Sansoni, 1911.

Vickers, Nancy J. "Diana Described: Scattered Woman and Scattered Rhyme." *Critical Inquiry* 8, no. 2 (1981): 265–79.

Villa, Claudia. "I commenti ai classici fra XII e XV secolo." In *Medieval and Renaissance Scholarship: Proceedings of the Second European Science Foundation Workshop on the Classical Tradition in the Middle Ages and the Renaissance*, edited by Nicholas Mann and Birger Munk Olsen, 19–32. Leiden: Brill, 1997.

Vinge, Louise. *The Narcissus Theme in Western European Literature up to the Early 19th Century*. Lund: Gleerups, 1967.

Volk, Katharina. "*Ille ego*: (Mis)Reading Ovid's Elegiac Persona." *Antike und Abendland* 51 (2005): 83–96.

Wallace, David. "Chaucer and Boccaccio's Early Writings." In *Chaucer and the Italian Trecento*, edited by Piero Boitani, 141–62. Cambridge: Cambridge University Press, 1983.

Wallace, David. *Chaucerian Polity: Absolutist Lineages and Associational Forms in England and Italy*. Stanford: Stanford University Press, 1997.

Wallace, David. "Chaucer's Continental Inheritance: The Early Poems and *Troilus and Criseyde*." In *The Cambridge Chaucer Companion*, edited by Piero Boitani and Jill Mann, 19–37. Cambridge: Cambridge University Press, 1986.

Wenzel, Siegfried. "Ovid from the pulpit." In *Ovid in the Middle Ages*, edited by James G. Clark, Frank T. Coulson, and Kathryn L. McKinley, 160–76. Cambridge: Cambridge University Press, 2011.

Wetherbee, Winthrop. "Ovid and Virgil in Purgatory." In *The Ancient Flame: Dante and the Poets*, 117–58. Notre Dame: University of Notre Dame Press, 2008.

Wetherbee, Winthrop. "The study of classical authors: From late Antiquity to the twelfth century." In *The Cambridge History of Literary Criticism*. Vol. 2, *The Middle Ages*, edited by Alastair Minnis and Ian Johnson, 99–144. Cambridge: Cambridge University Press, 2008.

Wheeler, Stephen M., ed. and trans. *Accessus ad auctores: Medieval Introductions to the Authors (Codex latinus monacensis 19475)*. TEAMS Secular Commentary. Kalamazoo: Medieval Institute Publications, 2015.

Wheeler, Stephen M. "Into New Bodies: The Incipit of Ovid's *Metamorphoses* as Intertext in Imperial Latin Literature." *Materiali e discussioni per l'analisi dei testi classici* 61 (2009): 147–60.

Whitbread, Leslie G. "Conrad of Hirsau as Literary Critic." *Speculum* 47, no. 2 (1972): 234–45.

Whitbread, Leslie G., trans. *Fulgentius the Mythographer*. Columbus: Ohio State University Press, 1971.

Wieruszowski, Helene. "Rhetoric and the Classics in Italian Education." In *Politics and Culture in Medieval Spain and Italy*, 589–627. Rome: Edizioni di storia e letteratura, 1971.

Wilhelm, James J. *Seven Troubadours: The Creators of Modern Verse*. University Park: The Pennsylvania State University, 1970.

Williams, Gareth D. *Banished Voices: Readings in Ovid's Exile Poetry*. Cambridge: Cambridge University Press, 1994.

Williams, Gareth D. "Representations of the Book-Roll in Latin Poetry: Ovid, *Tr.* 1, 1, 3–14 and Related Texts." *Mnemosyne* 45, no. 2 (1992): 178–89.

Witt, Ronald G. *In the Footsteps of the Ancients: The Origins of Humanism from Lovato to Bruni*. Boston: Brill, 2000.

Witt, Ronald G. *The Two Latin Cultures and the Foundation of Renaissance Humanism in Medieval Italy*. Cambridge: Cambridge University Press, 2012.

Witt, Ronald G. "What Did Giovannino Read and Write? Literacy in Early Renaissance Florence." *I Tatti Studies in the Italian Renaissance* 6 (1995): 83–114.

Zaccarello, Michelangelo. "Rimatori e poetiche 'da l'uno a l'altro stilo.'" In *Lectura Dantis Romana, Cento canti per centi anni, II. Purgatorio, 2. Canti XVIII–XXXIII*, edited by Enrico Malato and Andrea Mazzucchi, 712–44. Rome: Salerno, 2014.

Zaggia, Massimo, ed. *Heroides: volgarizzamento fiorentino trecentesco di Filippo Ceffi*. Vol. 1: *Introduzione, testo secondo l'autografo e glossario*. Florence: SISMEL-Edizioni del Galluzzo, 2009.

Zaggia, Massimo, ed. *Heroides: volgarizzamento fiorentino trecentesco di Filippo Ceffi*. Vol. 2: *I testimoni oltre l'autografo: ordinamento stemmatico e storia della tradizione*. Florence: SISMEL-Edizioni del Galluzzo, 2014.

Zaggia, Massimo, ed. *Heroides: volgarizzamento fiorentino trecentesco di Filippo Ceffi*. Vol. 3: *Le varianti di una tradizione innovativa e le chiose aggiunte*. Florence: SISMEL-Edizioni del Galluzzo, 2015.

Zaggia, Massimo, and Matteo Ceriana. *I manoscritti illustrati delle Eroidi ovidiane volgarizzate*. Pisa: Scuola normale superiore, 1996.

Zak, Gur. "A Humanist in Exile: Ovid's Myth of Narcissus and the Experience of Self in Petrarch's *Secretum*." In *Metamorphosis: The Changing Face of Ovid in Medieval and Early Modern Europe*, edited by Alison Keith and Stephen Rupp, 179–98. Toronto: Centre for Reformation and Renaissance Studies, 2007.

Zanni, Raffaella. "Una ricognizione per la biblioteca di Dante in margine ad alcuni contributi recenti." *Critica del testo* 17, no. 2 (2014): 161–204.

Zeeman, Nicolette. "In the Schoolroom with the *'Vulgate'* Commentary on Metamorphoses I." *New Medieval Literatures* 11 (2009): 1–18.

Ziolkowski, Jan M., and Michael C. J. Putnam, eds. *The Virgilian Tradition: The First Fifteen Hundred Years*. New Haven: Yale University Press, 2008.

Index Locorum

Abate di Tivoli
   Ai deo d'amore, a te faccio preghera   147
Aimon de Varennes
   Florimont   77
Albertano da Brescia
   De amore et dilectione Dei   36–37n82
   Liber consolationis et consilii   36–37, 36–37n82
Amico di Dante
   La pena che sentí Cato di Roma   109
Anonymous poems
   Aissi m'ave cum a l'enfan petit   81, 83–84, 87–88, 247n67
   L'amoroso conforto e lo disdotto   94–95
   Chi giudica lo pome ne lo fiore   93, 94n39
   Giamai null'om nonn-à sì gra-richezze   108, 110–12, 112n74, 216
   Lo gran valor di voi, donna sovrana   92–93n38
   Guardando la fontana il buo·Narciso   84, 86–87, 91, 243, 247n67
   Nulla mi parve mai più crudel cosa   153–54
   Poi di tutte bontà ben se' dispàri   108
Anonymous works
   Disticha Catonis   45, 112n75
   L'Intelligenza   231n30
   Il mare amoroso   96
   Pamphilus   238n48
   Proverbia quae dicuntur super natura feminarum   96–98nn42–43
Arnaut Daniel
   Chansson do·ill mot son plan e prim   214
Arnaut de Mareuil
   Mout eron doutz miei cossir   101, 216, 215–16n86
   Tant m'abellis e.m plaz   76, 92
Augustine, Saint
   Confessiones   141n43
   De civitate Dei   277n
Azalais de Porcairagues
   Ar em al freg temps vengut   101–2

Bartolomeo da San Concordio
   Ammaestramenti degli antichi   42–43, 43nn100–1, 44n103, 164, 164n82, 229n21
   Documenta antiquorum   44, 164n82
Bernart de Ventadorn
   Can vei la lauzeta mover   78–79, 78–79nn8–10, 84, 247n67, 247n69
   Conortz, era sai eu be   104, 104–5n59
   Tant ai mo cor ple de joya   79, 79n10
Bersuire, Pierre
   Ovidius moralizatus   225n5, 259n100
Bible
   Ad Hebraeos 13   229
   Book of Psalms
      Ps. 17   44n102
      Ps. 113 (*In exitu Israel de Aegypto*)   152n, 180
      Ps. 137   162n75
      Ps. 143   44n102
   Genesis 19   276, 278
   Gospel of John 15   165
Boethius
   Consolation of Philosophy   262n108

Carbonel, Bertran
   Aisi m'a dat fin'amor conoissensa   103, 215n86
Cardenal, Peire
   Sel que fes tot cant és   94
Catola, Uc
   Amics Marchabrun, car digam   98–99
Cavalcanti, Guido
   Di vil matera mi conven parlare   110, 117–19, 120n86, 132n21, 214, 216–17
   O tu, che porti nelli occhi sovente   147
   Poi che di doglia cor conven ch'i' porti   119
Cecco d'Ascoli
   Acerba   231n30
Cino da Pistoia
   Amor, che viene armato a doppio dardo   144–45, 144–45n, 147–49, 244, 250n76, 254n83, 263
   Amor che vien per le più dolci porte   113n76, 124, 199
   Dante, quando per caso s'abbandona   144, 149–50, 166

INDEX LOCORUM

Deh, quando rivedrò 'l dolce paese   109
Se conceduto mi fosse da Giove   144, 144n50, 148, 154, 166, 254, 263
Se mai leggesti versi de l'Ovidi   49, 51n127, 110, 112–14, 122, 124n, 144, 144n, 168, 216

Dalfi d'Auvergne
   Dalfi, sabriatz me vos   80
Dante
   Commedia
      Inferno
         Inf. 1   170n2
         Inf. 2   142n45
         Inf. 4   126, 181, 210, 210n75, 233, 287
         Inf. 5   141n43, 200n62, 201, 201n63, 242, 242nn56–57, 284n146
         Inf. 6   157, 183
         Inf. 7   169–70n2
         Inf. 10   183
         Inf. 15   165n84, 183
         Inf. 17   175n16, 189
         Inf. 18   188n43
         Inf. 24   135n25, 183
         Inf. 25   56n148, 59–60n157, 138n34, 197, 210, 210n75, 218–19, 287
         Inf. 27   195
         Inf. 30   175, 175n16, 176, 195, 208, 220
         Inf. 32   208
         Inf. 34   208
      Paradiso
         Par. 1   196–97
         Par. 2   197
         Par. 3   175n16, 209
         Par. 10   214, 214n85
         Par. 15   181, 183–85, 185n39
         Par. 16   181, 183, 185, 187, 189, 239
         Par. 17   181, 183–84, 188–89, 188n44, 191–94, 257
         Par. 18   181, 183
         Par. 20   78n8
         Par. 31   189
         Par. 33   169n2, 181, 198
      Purgatorio
         Purg. 2   152n, 180
         Purg. 7   60
         Purg. 8   183
         Purg. 11   183
         Purg. 21   204n68
         Purg. 23   195, 221
         Purg. 24   50, 183, 195, 198, 211, 211–12n78, 212, 213n83, 214, 214–15n85, 215, 217–19, 217n91, 218n92, 221
         Purg. 26   132n19
         Purg. 27   175n16, 200, 200n61, 201–3, 202–3n66, 205, 207, 242
         Purg. 28   195
         Purg. 30   203, 204n68, 205–6, 209
         Purg. 33   173, 175n16, 206, 242
   Convivio
      II XII 2   53n137
      II XII 4   54
      II XII 7   53n136
      IV XXIII 14   173–75
   De monarchia
      II VIII 3   201
      II VIII 4   201
   De vulgari eloquentia
      I VI 3   163, 171n
      II IV 3   58
   Epistulae
      Ep. II   160n71, 161–62
      Ep. III   151–52, 152n, 154–55, 161–62, 165, 177n22, 191n52, 196n, 197, 272
      Ep. IV   156, 159–61, 160n72
      Ep. V   160n71, 161–62, 191n52
      Ep. VI   160n71, 161–62, 191n52
      Ep. VII   160n71, 161–62, 191n52
      Ep. IX   162
   Rime
      Al poco giorno ed al gran cerchio d'ombra   133, 138–41, 139n35, 154
      Amor, da che convien pur ch'io mi doglia   156–59, 158n, 161
      Amor, tu vedi ben che questa donna   133, 136, 142

    Cavalcando l'altr'ier per un
        cammino 272
    Così nel mio parlar vogli'esser
        aspro 133, 141–42, 141–42n43, 263
    Io mi senti' svegliar dentr'a lo core 125,
        132
    Io sento sì d'Amor la gran
        possanza 157
    Io sono stato con Amore
        insieme 116n80, 150–51, 151n56,
        161, 272
    Io son venuto al punto della rota 133–
        36, 135nn, 136n27, 137n, 142
    Savere e cortesia, ingegno ed arte 115–
        17, 116n80, 128, 134, 210
    Tre donne intorno al cor mi son
        venute 147
    Vita nuova
        VN 1   125, 130, 130n16, 131
        VN 3   129n13
        VN 12   130n16
        VN 19   219
        VN 24   125, 129n13, 132
        VN 25   125–27, 129–34, 129nn12–13,
        130n16, 171n
        VN 28   130n16
        VN 30   129n13
Davanzati, Chiaro
    Come 'l fantin ca ne lo speglio
        smira 87–88
    Come Narcissi, in sua spera
        mirando 83n20, 84–87, 91,
        247n67
    Di lontano riviera 93
    Disidero lo pome ne lo fiore (D) 93, 95
    Lo disïoso core e la sperenza 93
    Madonna, lungiamente ag[g]io
        portato 93
    Or tornate in usanza, buona gente 108
    Ringrazzo amore de l'aventurosa 93
Dietaiuti, Bondie
    Madonna, m'è avenuto simigliante 78n8

Filippi, Rustico
    Oi amoroso e mio fedele amante 91–92,
        91n36, 202n65
Folquet de Marselha

    Chantan volgra mon fin cor descobrir 82,
        82n16, 83n21

Geoffrey of Vinsauf
    Poetria nova 127n5
Geremia da Montagnone
    Compendium moralium notabilium
        (*Epytoma sapientiae*) 32n86, 41,
        41n96, 42n97, 164n82, 229n21
Giacomo da Lentini
    Amor è uno disio che ven da
        core 120–21n87
    Dal core mi vene 89–90n32
    Io m'aggio posto in core a Dio
        servire 86n26
Giamboni, Bono
    Delle storie contra i pagani di Paolo
        Orosio 201n63
Giraut de Cabreira
    Cabra juglar 94
Giraut de Salignac
    En atretal esperansa 88, 92, 202n65
Guinizzelli, Guido
    Caro padre mëo, de vostra laude 109,
        120n86
    Omo ch' è saggio non corre leggero 109,
        120, 217
    Lo vostro bel saluto e 'l gentil sguardo 147
Guittone d'Arezzo
    Comune perta fa comune dolore 52,
        52n129
    De lui, cui di' ch'è morte 231n30
    Figlio mio dilettoso, in faccia laude 109,
        120n86

Heinrich von Morungen
    Mirst geschên als eime kindelîne 81n12

Isarn
    Vos qe amatz cuenda donn'e
        plazen 94–95

John of Garland
    Integumenta Ovidii 22, 24, 247n68,
        248n70

Latini, Brunetto
    Tesoretto 3–6

INDEX LOCORUM

Tresor
   1.160   39
   2.61–67   39n90
   2.84   164
Lucan
   Pharsalia
      Phars. 9.338–40   135, 135n25
      Phars. 9.488–89   135, 135n25
      Phars. 9.650–51   136, 136n28
      Phars. 9.700–33   109

Marcabru
   Amics Marchabrun, car digam   98–99
Matthew of Vendôme
   Ars versificatoria   127–28, 127n5
Monte, Andrea
   Sì come ciascun om può sua figura   87
Mostacci, Iacopo
   Solicitando un poco meo
      savere   120–21n87

Onesto da Bologna
   Assai son certo che somenta in lidi   48, 113
   Mente ed umìle e più di mille
      sporte   113n76, 124, 199
Orlandi, Guido
   Amico, i' saccio ben che sa' limare   117, 119,
      132, 132n21
   Per troppa sottiglianza il fil si rompe   132,
      132n21, 216–18, 217n90
Orosius, Paulus
   Historiae adversus paganos   201n63
Ovid
   Amores
      Am. 1.1   126
      Am. 1.8   36
      Am. 2.1   211n78, 212–14, 219, 221,
         266n119
      Am. 2.4   100
      Am. 2.9*b*   105
      Am. 3.8   213n81
      Am. 3.11   105, 106n61
   Ars amatoria
      1.1–2   6n6
      1.17   6n6
      1.475–76   104
      1.478   105
      1.653–58   195

      1.715–16   114
      1.729   242n57
      1.769–70   100
      2.93–95   204n69
      2.109–250   114n77
      2.145–46   42n97, 114
      2.152   42n97
      2.159–62   42n97
      2.161–65   102, 216
      2.177–78   42n97
      2.177–96   144
      2.229   42n97
      2.241–42   42n97
      2.276–80   42n97
      2.289–90   42n97
      2.293–94   42n97
      2.329   42n97
      2.340   42n97
      2.351   42n97
      2.357–58   42n97
      2.511–12   42n97
      2.743–44   6n6
      3.811–12   6n6
   Epistulae ex Ponto
      1.2   213n81, 257
      1.4   284–85
      1.7   158
      2.8   281
      4.3   213n81
      4.10   104–5n59
      4.12   281
   Fasti
      1.419   281
      1.479–96   163
      1.493–94   41n96, 163
      1.540   163n77
      2.241–42   38
      6.771–72   225, 228, 228–29n21
   Heroides
      Her. 1   31n60
      Her. 2   31n60
      Her. 3   31n60, 39n90
      Her. 4   98n43, 103–4, 278–79, 279n137,
         280
      Her. 5   31n60
      Her. 7   142, 142n47
      Her. 15   34
      Her. 16   34

Her. 17   34, 36
Metamorphoses
   Met. 1.1–4 (proem)   197, 221–22, 265, 265n113, 266
   Met. 1.5–88 (creation story)   40, 40n
   Met. 1.89–150 (the four ages)   195
   Met. 1.438–51 (Apollo and Python)   270
   Met. 1.452–567 (Apollo and Daphne)   47, 141, 147, 235, 237, 241–42n54, 244–45, 244n61, 252, 268–70, 272–73, 277
   Met. 1.568–746 (Io)   252n80
   Met. 1.747–79, 2.1–400 (Phaethon)   174, 184, 188–90, 190n48, 237, 252, 266n116
   Met. 2.680–707 (Mercury and Battus)   237, 252
   Met. 2.833–75, 3.1–27 (Europa)   242n55
   Met. 3.138–252 (Diana and Actaeon)   237, 252–53, 259–60
   Met. 3.316–38 (Tiresias)   97
   Met. 3.339–510 (Narcissus and Echo)   86–87, 96, 139, 139n38, 208–9, 237, 247, 252
   Met. 4.55–166 (Pyramus and Thisbe)   88–90, 92, 201–2, 204–7, 237–38, 242
   Met. 4.167–273 (Apollo, Leucothoë, and Clytie)   138–39, 138nn34–35, 139n35, 152–54, 272
   Met. 4.274–388 (Salmacis and Hermaphroditus)   210n75
   Met. 4.563–603 (Cadmus and Harmonia)   210n75
   Met. 4.604–803 (Perseus, Atlas, Andromeda, and Medusa)   135–36, 135n26, 136n28, 138, 237, 257
   Met. 5.341–661 (Persephone)   56n148
   Met. 6.424–674 (Tereus, Procne, and Philomela)   97–98n43, 149, 237
   Met. 6.675–721 (Boreas and Orithyia)   170n2
   Met. 7.1–452 (Medea and Jason)   169n2, 186–87, 230–31, 237–38, 249
   Met. 7.661–865 (Cephalus and Procris)   173
   Met. 8.152–235 (Daedalus and Icarus)   204n69
   Met. 8.611–724 (Philemon and Baucis)   149
   Met. 8.725–884 (Erysichthon)   195
   Met. 9.450–665 (Byblis)   237
   Met. 10.1–85 (Orpheus and Eurydice)   44, 204n69, 237, 262n109
   Met. 10.243–97 (Pygmalion)   237
   Met. 10.298–502 (Myrrha)   97, 195
   Met. 10.503–59 (Venus and Adonis)   225n8, 228, 228–29n21
   Met. 11.1–84 (the Maenads and the death of Orpheus)   204n69, 262n108
   Met. 12.210–535 (the battle of the Lapiths and Centaurs)   176
   Met. 13.399–428 (Hecuba and the fall of Troy)   169–70n2
   Met. 13.898–968 (Glaucus)   196
   Met. 14.75–222 (Aeneas's travels to Italy)   142
   Met. 15.60–478 (Pythagoras's speech)   187–88, 187n
   Met. 15.497–546 (Hippolytus)   191, 191n52, 278
   Met. 15.745–870 (Julius Caesar)   23
   Met. 15.871–79 (epilogue)   18
Remedia amoris
   vv. 1–2   129–30, 133
   vv. 127–30   35
   vv. 343–44   185
Tristia
   1.1   155–56, 166, 265
   1.3   158
   1.5   157
   1.6   282–83
   1.7   265, 282–83, 283n143
   1.8   142n47
   2   43n100, 160n71, 193, 225, 257
   3.11   158n, 281
   3.14   149

INDEX LOCORUM

    3.23   127n5
    4.1   158–59, 193, 201n75
    4.10   159, 193, 210, 213n81, 233
    5.7b   213n81
    5.11   160n71

Pallavillani, Schiatta
  Poi che vi piace ch'io deg[g]ia treguare 95

Peirol
  Dalfi, sabriatz me vos 80
  Mout m'entremis de chantar voluntiers 80, 84, 247n67

Petrarch
  Africa
    VI.65–70 239
  De remediis utriusque fortune
    I.27.26 234, 234n39
    I.69.40 234, 234n39
    II.67.10 229
  De vita solitaria
    II.XII 233, 233n37
  Familiares
    Fam. II.1 229, 229–30n23
    Fam. IV.15 227
    Fam. XVIII.16 230, 230–31n27
    Fam. XX.3 230, 230–31n27
    Fam. XXII.2 228n18
    Fam. XXIV.1 225–26, 228–29, 233
  Rerum memorandarum libri
    I 13 7, 232
    II 20 2, 234
    III 73 2, 233
  Rerum vulgarium fragmenta (Canzoniere)
    Rvf 1 236, 251, 257
    Rvf 5 235, 268, 270
    Rvf 6 268
    Rvf 12 284
    Rvf 22 140, 142n45, 268
    Rvf 23 247n68, 249, 250n76, 251–55, 257–58, 260, 268
    Rvf 28 275
    Rvf 30 245n63, 284
    Rvf 34 244–45, 245n62, 268
    Rvf 41 272n126
    Rvf 45 246–49, 247n68
    Rvf 51 254, 257–58, 274n130
    Rvf 52 258–59, 259n98, 260–61
    Rvf 55 238

Rvf 75 269
Rvf 90 269, 284
Rvf 93 279–80
Rvf 99 275–76
Rvf 105 280
Rvf 108 240
Rvf 112 240
Rvf 113 240
Rvf 115 244, 280
Rvf 127 269
Rvf 129 255–56
Rvf 132 281
Rvf 135 255
Rvf 143 277
Rvf 144 240, 274n131
Rvf 151 269
Rvf 161 269
Rvf 171 281
Rvf 179 256
Rvf 180 255
Rvf 186 282–84
Rvf 187 282–84, 283n141
Rvf 188 269, 273
Rvf 192 269
Rvf 195 284
Rvf 197 256, 269
Rvf 206 269
Rvf 207 238
Rvf 209 255
Rvf 213 281
Rvf 239 243n59, 280
Rvf 243 255
Rvf 248 249
Rvf 252 281
Rvf 260 258n95
Rvf 264 231n27, 231, 231n30, 238, 249, 277
Rvf 270 273, 273n
Rvf 271 273n
Rvf 287 240
Rvf 291 242n57, 243, 243–44nn59–60
Rvf 305 262n108
Rvf 323 253n82, 262, 275
Rvf 325 269–70
Rvf 332 243n59, 261–62, 275
Rvf 337 245n63
Rvf 346 277–78
Rvf 361 255

Rvf 362   242n57
Rvf 363   270
Rvf 366   255–56
rime estravaganti
   Donna mi vène spesso ne la
      mente   274n129
   Se Phebo al primo amor non è
      bugiardo   271, 273–74, 274n129,
      286
   Sì come il padre del folle Fetonte   239–
      43, 241–42n54, 242n57, 244n61,
      250, 263, 273–74
   Sì mi fan risentire a l'aura
      sparsi   274n131
Secretum
   I.5.5   264
   II.3.2   249
   III.4.6–7   254–55
   III.14.8   227n17
   III.18.7   249
Seniles
   VII 1   96, 229–30n23
   IX 1   186, 276
Trionfi
   Triumphus Cupidinis
      II.145–50   247n68
      III.20   239
      III.161–62   255n86
      IV.22–24   233
      IV.28–60   233
Pier della Vigna
   Amore, in cui disio ed ò speranza   89–90,
      92, 96
   Però ch'Amore non si pò
      vedere   120–21n87

Raimbaut de Vaqueiras
   Era·m requier sa costum' e son us   88, 90,
      92, 202n65
Rigaut de Berbezilh

Tuit demandon qu'es
   devengud'Amors   105, 216, 216n86
Rinaldo d'Aquino
   Amor, che m'à 'n comando   84n22
   Amorosa donna fina   84n22
   In gioia mi tegno tuta la mia pena   82n17
   Per fin amore vao sì
      allegramente   83–84n22
   Poi li piace ch'avanzi suo valore   82,
      84–85, 91, 247n67
   Venuto m'è in talento   83, 83n22
Rofian
   Vos qe amatz cuenda donn'e
      plazen   94–95

Seneca
   Quaestiones naturales
      V 18.2   136, 136n27
Sennuccio del Bene
   La bella Aurora, nel mio orizonte   244
Statius
   Achilleid
      1.473–75   204n68
   Thebaid
      8.320   229–30n23
      12.805–7   204n68
      12.816–19   204n68

Vergil
   Aeneid
      Aen. 1.1   212n80
      Aen. 1.318–20   274n131
      Aen. 2.692–704   184
      Aen. 4.365–67   142n47
      Aen. 4.522–32   142
   Eclogues
      Ecl. 6.3–8   212
   Georgics
      Georg. 4.490   262n108
      Georg. 4.525–27   203

Index of Manuscripts

Florence, Biblioteca Medicea Laurenziana
    MS Gaddi rel. 71 (*volgarizzamento Gaddiano*)   30–31
    MS Pluteo 36.12   175–76
    MS Pluteo 36.18   22, 65 (*fig.* 3), 68
    MS Redi 9   83
    MS San Marco 225   20–21, 24, 64 (*fig.* 2), 68, 190n48, 227n13
    MS Strozzi 146   3, 4 (*fig.* 1), 4n, 5, 7–8, 33
Florence, Biblioteca Riccardiana
    MS Riccardianus 489   29n55
    MS Riccardianus 624   24, 24n36, 66–67 (*figs.* 4 and 5), 68–69
London, British Library
    MS Add. 11967   21
    MS Harley 3754   226, 226n12, 270, 271n124

Milan, Biblioteca Ambrosiana
    MS P 43 sup.   172, 174n14
Munich, Bayerische Staatsbibliothek
    MS clm 7205   22n29
    MS clm 19475   26, 26n43
Naples, Biblioteca Nazionale di Napoli
    MS IV.F.3   21
Paris, Bibliothèque nationale de France
    MS lat. 2201   226
    MS lat. 2923   276n
    MS lat. 8500   226, 227n13
    MS lat. 14135   174n14
Siena, Biblioteca Comunale degli Intronati
    MS S.IV.11   30n57
Vatican City, Biblioteca Apostolica Vaticana
    MS Vat. lat. 3196 (*Codice degli abbozzi*)   251
    MS Vat. lat. 3793   50, 83, 109n70, 111n, 112n74

General Index

Abate di Tivoli   147
Abelard, Peter   276, 276n134
accessus ad auctores   8–9, 18, 26–28, 127, 179, 234
  on Ovid's works   22, 24n37, 26–28, 33, 47, 57, 116, 127–28, 130, 234
Achilles (character)   39n90, 204n68
Actaeon (character), in Petrarch   237, 251–54, 253nn, 258–62, 259n100, 260n102, 263
  see also Diana
Aegina (character)   253
Aimon de Varennes
  Florimont   77
Albertano da Brescia   34–37, 34–35n75, 39, 39n90, 164n83, 231n31
  De arte loquendi et tacendi   39, 39n90, 164n83
  Liber consolationis et consilii   35–38, 35n76, 36n82, 39n90
  Italian translations of   35n75, 36n78, 39n90
Alfie, Fabian   107n66, 218n91
Alighieri, Dante
  see Dante
Alighieri, Pietro   192, 192n53
Allegretti, Paola   158, 158n
Amico di Dante   109, 109n70
Amor, god of love
  see personification: of love
Anchises (character)   184
Andrea da Grosseto   35n76, 36n78, 37n82, 39n90
Andreas Capellanus   46, 46n112
  De amore   46
anthologies
  citations of Ovid in   9, 15, 33–34, 38, 43, 47–48, 98, 164, 166, 168, 171n6, 228–31, 286
  knowledge of Ovid via   35, 37, 43, 47–48, 51, 62, 73, 100–1, 106, 133, 143, 171, 177, 179, 181, 185, 220
  organization of   33, 34n72, 41, 185
  Petrarch's views on   227–28, 227n17
  see also compendia, florilegia

Antonelli, Roberto   50–51, 51n121
Apollo (character)   47
  in Cino da Pistoia   144, 146–48, 166, 244, 254n83
  in Dante   138, 141, 143, 151–54, 173–75, 189, 189n46, 190n48, 196n, 272
  in Ovidian commentaries and manuscripts   19n20, 24, 64–69
  in Petrarch   235–37, 241, 241–42n54, 243–45, 251–52, 255, 258, 259n99, 263, 267–75, 271n125, 274n129, 278, 280, 287
  see also Clytie, Daphne, Leucothoë, Phaethon, Python
Appel, Carl   79n9, 104, 104n59
Argea (character)   258n95
Arnaut Daniel   133, 211, 214, 215n85, 221
Arnaut de Mareuil   76, 92, 101–2, 102n56, 115, 216
Arnulf of Orléans
  commentary on the *Met.*   21–25, 27–28, 65, 67–68, 81n13, 174–76, 178, 224, 247n68, 248n70, 259n100
  see also commentaries: on the *Met.*
artes dictaminis   33
Ascoli, Albert Russell   15n3, 125n3, 131n18, 151n56, 155, 180, 236
Athamas (character)   175–76, 175n16
Augustine, Saint   141n43, 200n62, 225–26, 277n
  as character in *Secretum*   227, 248–49, 254, 264, 277
Aurora (character)   241–45, 242n57, 243n59
  see also Laura
authority, of the vernacular   6–8, 6n5, 30n57, 57n151, 61–63, 121, 126, 128–33, 131n18, 219
Avianus   45
Azalais de Porcairagues   101–2, 102n54, 102n56, 106, 115

Barański, Zygmunt G.   53n136, 127n7, 172, 179–80, 179nn
Barolini, Teodolinda   86n26, 100n50, 109n69, 116n80, 119n84, 132n19, 170, 172n7, 215n85, 245n62, 284, 284n144

GENERAL INDEX 333

Bartolomeo da San Concordio
   Ammaestramenti degli antichi   42–43,
      164, 229, 231n31
   Documenta antiquorum   42, 44
Battus (character), in Petrarch   237, 251–52,
      254, 254n84
Baudri of Bourgueil   46
Beatrice (character), in Dante   53, 53n136,
      125, 143, 160n71, 183, 189n46, 194, 196,
      200–9, 204n68, 242, 273n
Bene da Firenze
   Candelabrum   40, 40n93
   Summa dictaminis   40
Beneš, Carrie E.   30n57, 31n60
Benvenuto da Imola   217n91
Bernart de Ventadorn   78–81, 78–79nn8–10,
      83–84, 104, 104n59, 247n67, 247n69
Bersuire, Pierre   25–26, 47, 57, 225, 236n43,
      247n68, 259n100, 275, 275n133
   Ovidius moralizatus   25–26, 47, 57, 225,
      236, 275n133
   Reductorium morale   26
   Petrarch and   26, 225, 275
   see also commentaries: on the *Met.*
Bianchini, Simonetta   50–51, 51n121
Bible, citations from   14, 32n69, 35, 41, 43, 77,
      162nn74–75, 165–66, 229, 229–30n23,
      276–77
Black, Robert   17, 16–17n10, 17n13, 21, 27–28,
      40n, 47, 53n137
Bloom, Harold   59–60n157
Boccaccio, Giovanni   12, 57–58, 172n7
   Decameron   42
   Filocolo   210n76
   Trattatello in laude di Dante   57,
      57nn151–52
   as vernacular translator   29–30nn55–56,
      31
Boethius   53–54, 53n137, 262n108
   Consolation of Philosophy, Dante's reading
      of   53–54, 53n137
Bologna
   intellectual activity in   17, 24–25, 25n38,
      40, 42, 51, 53n136, 224, 224n3
   teaching of classics at the
      University   24–25, 224, 224n3
   see also Giovanni del Virgilio
Bonaventure, Saint

   four roles in bookmaking (*modus faciendi
      librum*)   14–15, 14n2, 15n3, 33, 35, 61,
      73, 106, 125
Boncompagno da Signa   17, 40
Bonsignori, Giovanni
   Metamorphoseos Vulgare   31–33, 31n61,
      32–33n69, 224, 236
books
   collecting of   34–35n75, 228
   source of knowledge   96–97n42, 97,
      104–6, 117
   see also libraries, Saint Bonaventure
Brownlee, Kevin   6–7, 170n3, 189n45,
      190n49, 209
Brugnoli, Giorgio   192n54, 193
Brunetti, Giuseppina   144–45n, 149, 149nn
Busby, Keith   8–9, 15n5
Byblis (character)   237, 251–52, 254

Cacciaguida (character), in *Commedia*   181–
      95, 183n, 185n39, 189nn46–47, 239
Cadmus (character)   154, 210n75, 219
Caesar (character)   23, 25, 127n5
Cahoon, Leslie   61, 100
Carbonel, Bertran   103–4, 106, 115, 215n86,
      216, 278, 280
Cardenal, Peire   94
Carmentis (character)   162–63, 229
Carruthers, Mary   55
Cassiodorus
   De anima   226
Cato the Elder   45, 96
Catola, Uc   98–99, 102, 105, 107
Catullus   41n95, 233
Caunus (character)   237, 252
Cavalcanti, Guido   74, 110, 117–21, 129n3,
      131–32, 147, 211, 214, 215n85, 216n89,
      217–18, 221
   see also personification: of love
Cecco d'Ascoli
   Acerba   231, 231n30
Ceffi, Filippo   30–32, 30n58–59, 224
   Pistole di Ovidio Nasone   30
Charybdis (character)   169–70n2
Chaucer   100, 210–11n76
   Troilus and Criseyde   210–11n76
Chiappelli, Fredi   262n106
Chiappelli, Luigi   51, 51n127

Christ   23, 25, 165, 197, 275
Ciacco (character)   157, 183
Cicero   7–8, 7n7, 17, 35, 38, 43, 51, 53–54, 96,
    225, 227n17, 228n18, 232–33
  De amicitia, Dante's reading of   53–54
  De inventione   38, 51
  teaching of rhetoric and   17
  translations of   38, 51
Cino da Pistoia   10–11, 51, 77, 108–9, 146n,
    244n61
  Dante and   124–25, 134, 144, 144–45n,
    149–52, 154–55, 161–62, 165–68, 171, 177,
    272
  metapoetic discussions and   112–14, 113n,
    124, 199, 218
  Petrarch and   125, 145n, 223, 244, 250n76,
    254, 254n83, 263, 287
  poetic re-creation of the *Met.*   134,
    145–49, 166–67, 244, 263, 287
  sonnet exchanges and   48–49, 54, 124,
    146–51, 199, 216, 218
  views on Ovid   49, 110–15, 120–22, 168,
    216, 216n88
  see also Apollo, Daphne, gender,
    identification
classical authors
  interest in, Florence   52
  interest in, medieval Italy   16–17n10, 50,
    125
  teaching of   24–25, 25n38, 224
  see also Bologna, Orléans, Padua
Claudian
  De raptu Proserpinae   45
Clymene (character)   152, 188–89
Clytie (character)   138–44, 138n33, 152
commentaries
  on the Bible   14, 61
  on the *Commedia*   29n55, 185n39,
    187–88, 192, 217–18n91
  on the *Met.*   9, 18–28, 48, 57, 172–78, 224,
    226, 236–37, 249, 286
    allegorical and moral readings   6,
      21n26, 22–23, 27–28, 47, 170, 174,
      178–79, 208, 224–25, 236, 259, 264,
      278
    catena format   22, 22n29, 68
    Christianizing interpretations   22–23,
      25–26, 47, 57, 170, 177–78, 225, 275,
      278

  interpretative diversity   18–19, 19n19,
    179–80, 247n68, 275n133
  nature of notes   18, 21, 23, 178
  placement of glosses   19–22, 21n25,
    24, 62, 68–69, 177–80
  structure and elements   20–26,
    64–69, 266
  see also Arnulf of Orléans, Giovanni
    del Virgilio, John of Garland, *Ovide
    moralisé*, Pierre Bersuire, pseudo-
    Lactantius Placidus, Vulgate
    Commentary
  on Ovid's other works   22
  on works in translation   28–30, 30n57,
    32–33, 38
compendia   15, 43, 51, 164, 166, 168, 229–30
concordance, of *Commedia*   55–56, 55n144,
    154n59, 181nn34–35, 211n78
  digital   181–82, 181–82nn, 189n45, 194,
    199n60, 210n75
congedo   156–57, 253
  use of, by exiled poets   156, 156n64
Conrad of Hirsau   26n43, 266
Conte, Gian Biagio   59, 59n155, 60n158
Contini, Gianfranco   88n29, 89–90n32,
    97n43, 108n67, 112n75, 138n34, 149, 153n
Convenevole da Prato   225n7
Copeland, Rita   46n110, 61
Cornish, Alison   19, 28n51, 29n52, 29n55,
    30n56, 32n64, 38n89
Costa, Elio   6
Coulson, Frank T.   16n8, 19, 19n20, 21n25, 23,
    23n32, 24n34, 24n36, 28n50, 175n16,
    266
Cupid (character)   251, 269
  see also personification: of love
Cygnus (character)   237, 252, 254, 254n84

Daedalus (character)   78n7, 96, 204n69
Dalfi d'Auvergne   80
Danaë (character)   253
Dandolo, Andrea   230
Dante   9–12, 29n55, 30, 33n69, 41n96, 48,
    50–60, 53n148, 55–59, 59–60n157, 63,
    74, 77, 78n8, 100, 100n50, 112, 114–17,
    116n80, 120, 125–45, 129n13, 147,
    149–222, 160n71, 162n75, 223–25, 229,
    231–34, 237, 239–40, 242, 256–57,
    263–65, 272, 285–87

GENERAL INDEX

Commedia   11, 25–26, 48, 54, 55n144, 56, 56n148, 60, 109n69, 113n, 125–26, 128, 131, 134, 138n32, 141–42n43, 143, 143n49, 145n, 152n57, 154, 157, 160n71, 167–222, 223–24, 231–37, 240, 242, 263–64, 285–87
Convivio   53–54, 53n136, 141n43, 173–75, 174n14
De monarchia   54, 201, 242n56
De vulgari eloquentia   41n96, 54, 58, 163–64, 163n78, 165n, 168, 229
Eclogues   24
Epistulae   150–52, 154–56, 159–62, 160n71, 161n, 164–66, 168, 272
rime petrose   10, 124–25, 133–45, 147, 154, 168, 171, 181, 256
Vita nuova   10, 54, 124–34, 125n3, 129nn12–13, 130–32nn16–19, 145n, 167–68, 171n, 219, 273n
biography   54, 54n141
   see also Boccaccio: *Trattatello in laude di Dante*
Christian rewritings of Ovid   128–29, 129n12, 170, 207, 207n, 221
education   52–54, 53n136, 57, 172n7
familiarity with Ovid's works in Latin   125, 181–98, 220–21
familiarity with vernacular Ovidian tradition   198–221
interest in classics   52–53, 57, 57n152, 124–34, 138, 167–68
possible consulted Ovidian commentaries   21, 24–26, 57, 172–80
use of central and peripheral elements from Ovid's works   10, 125, 134, 141–43, 171, 181, 183–84, 186–87, 189–90, 194
use of citations from Ovid   41n96, 52n148, 126–31, 133, 163–64, 168, 229
   see also Apollo, Cino da Pistoia, exile, gender, identification, Medusa, metapoetics, Narcissus, personification, Petrarch, Phaethon, simile
Dante da Maiano   110, 114–17, 120–22, 124, 128, 134, 168, 198, 216, 216n88, 234, 280
Daphne (character)   47, 141, 143
   in Cino da Pistoia   144, 146–49, 166, 244, 254n83

   in Ovidian commentaries and manuscripts   19n20, 24, 64–69
   in Petrarch   235–37, 241, 241–42n54, 243–45, 245–46n66, 250n76, 252, 254–59, 255n87, 259n99, 263, 267–75, 271n125, 274n129, 277–78, 287
   see also Apollo, Laura
Davanzati, Chiaro   83n20, 84–88, 85n24, 86n25, 87n28, 91–94, 108, 145, 199, 247n67, 283
David (biblical figure)   99
Dejeanne, Jean Marie Lucien   100
De' Medici, Giuliana   188n43
de Nolhac, Pierre   226, 232n33
desire
   see love
De Vetula   16
   see also Ovid: biography and lives
Diana (character), in Petrarch   237, 251–53, 258–61, 259n99, 263
   see also Actaeon
didactic literature   8, 16–17n10, 17, 22–23, 27–28, 33, 40, 44–45, 47–48, 75–77, 94, 98, 126, 128, 225, 231
   see also education
Dido (character)   141–44, 141–42n43, 142n47, 263
Dietaiuti, Bondie   78n8
Dietisalvi di Pietro   271, 271n125
Disticha Catonis   45, 96, 112n75, 126
dolce stil novo   10, 74, 77, 78n7, 109n72, 112, 113n, 119, 122, 124, 217–18, 232, 232n35
dreams and   124, 218
Durling, Robert   133n, 134, 136n27, 139, 141, 143, 202–3n66

Earthly Paradise
   see Garden of Eden
Echo (character)   22, 74, 77, 78n7, 81n13, 139, 139n38, 237, 247n68, 248–54, 263
education, in medieval Italy   8, 16–17n10, 17, 27–28, 42, 44, 47, 49, 51–54, 52n130, 53n137, 57, 75, 101, 122, 172n7, 224–25
   see also didactic literature, Ovid: and medieval education
Eisner, Martin   57n151
elegy   212, 267, 267n121
Engelbrecht, Wilken   21n26

Ennius   233, 283, 283n142
envoy
    see congedo
Enzo, King of Sardinia   50
epic poetry   6, 78n7, 126, 199, 212–13, 219, 266
    conventions of   199, 212–13, 219, 265–67, 267n121
Erysichthon (character)   195
ethics, as branch of philosophy in *accessus ad auctores*   8, 26–27, 47, 57, 128n10
Europa (character)   240, 242–43, 242n55
Eurydice (character)   203, 204nn68–69, 237, 261–62, 262n106, 262nn108–9, 275–78, 276n, 278n
    see also Orpheus
Evander (character)   162, 163n77, 229
Eve (biblical figure)   99
exile
    in Bible   162, 162nn74–75
    in medieval lyric poetry   155, 156n64, 161, 281–82n139
    in *or* of Dante   11, 54, 125, 144, 147, 154–67, 154n60, 160n71, 183–84, 187–88, 190, 191n52, 192–94, 192n54, 211, 213n83, 221, 229
    in *or* of Ovid   5, 11, 18, 104n59, 137–38, 142n47, 144, 154–59, 160n71, 162–66, 163n77, 191–93, 191n52, 192n54, 221, 223, 229, 233, 257, 265, 278, 281–85
        see also Ovid: *Epistulae ex Ponto, Tristia*
    in Petrarch   246, 247n69, 257, 281, 281–82n139, 285

Faba, Guido   17, 40
Fabius Maximus, Paullus   38, 38n87
Fantham, Elaine   163n77
Farinata degli Uberti (character), in *Commedia*   183
Farrell, Joseph   213, 213n82
Feng, Aileen A.   256, 256nn88–89, 257n94
Fenzi, Enrico   133n, 136, 165, 165n
Fera, Vincenzo   282, 283n143
Ferrara, Sabrina   160n71, 161n
Filippi, Rustico   51–52, 91, 91n36, 199, 202n65
Fiore di virtù   37n82, 39n90
florilegia
    see anthologies
Florilegium Angelicum   34

Florilegium Gallicum   34, 34n72, 36, 36n82, 41, 43, 102, 105n59, 106n61,164, 185n40, 187n, 228n21, 229
Floris et Liriopé   200n62
fol'amor
    see love
Folquet de Marselha   82, 83n21, 101n52, 108
Fowler, Don   55n143
Francesca (character), in *Commedia*   141n43, 200n62, 239, 239n50, 242, 242n57
Francesco da Colle   51
Fratta, Aniello   111n, 112nn
Frederick II, Holy Roman Emperor   49–51, 90
free will (*libero arbitrio*)
    see love
Fulgentius   18n15, 33n69, 226, 226n12, 236, 259n100
    Mythologiae   18n15, 226, 226n12

Ganymede (character)   253
Garden of Eden, in *Commedia*   195, 203, 205, 209, 242
Gargan, Luciano   54
gender, reversals of, in comparisons
    in Cino da Pistoia   147–48, 167, 223
    in Dante   134, 141n43, 142–43, 143n49, 154, 167, 223, 252, 263
    in *Nulla mi parve mai piú crudel cosa* (anonymous)   153–54
    in Petrarch   223, 252, 254, 263
Geoffrey of Vinsauf
    Poetria nova   127n5
Geremia da Montagnone
    Compendium moralium notabilium   36n82, 40–42, 41nn95–96, 42n97, 52n131, 164, 228–29n21, 229
Geta   45–46
Gherardo da Reggio   146–48, 244
Ghisalberti, Fausto   19, 24, 24n36, 27n46, 172–74, 173n10, 174nn13–14, 175, 177–78
Giacomo da Lentini   50, 86n26, 90n32, 120, 120–21n87, 218–19
Giamboni, Bono   201n63
Giannetto, Nella   284
Ginsberg, Warren   128, 170, 189n47
Giordano da Pisa   44

GENERAL INDEX 337

Giovanni del Virgilio   24–25, 32–33, 32–33n69, 47, 57, 81n13, 176, 224, 224n3
  Allegorie librorum Ovidii Metamorphoseos and *Expositio*   24, 81n13, 247n68, 248n70, 259n100
  Eclogues   24
  Dante and   24
  Petrarch and   224, 224n3
  see also Bologna, commentaries: on the *Met.*
Giraut de Salignac   88, 90n33, 92, 94, 199, 202n65
Glaucus (character)   196–97
Grafton, Anthony   27
Graham, Angus   34n75
Greene, Thomas M.   60–61
Guido da Montefeltro (character), in *Commedia*   195
Guido delle Colonne   30n59, 33n69, 50
Guidotto da Bologna
  Fiore di rettorica   32n66
Guinevere (character)   200n62
Guinizzelli, Guido   51, 74, 109, 120, 120n86, 132n19, 147, 217–18, 217n90
Guittone d'Arezzo   52, 77, 109, 120n86, 132, 132nn19–20, 138n34, 218–19, 231, 231n30

Hainsworth, Peter   245, 267–68n122, 270n
Harmonia (character)   210n75
Hecuba (character)   170n2, 176
Helen (character)   36, 76, 82n17, 93, 258n95
Heloise   276, 276n
Henry VII, Holy Roman Emperor   162
Henry of Settimello   46
Hermaphroditus (character)   154, 210n75
Hero (character)   76
Hexter, Ralph J.   5n3, 16n9, 17, 19, 19nn19–20, 21n26, 29n52, 62, 62n164
Hinds, Stephen   60n158, 265–66n115, 267n121
Hippolytus (character)   98n43, 103, 183, 191, 191n51, 191–92n52, 196, 278
Hollander, Robert   145n, 176n19, 183n, 186n, 214–15n85
Holsinger, Bruce   204, 204n68
Homer   100, 126, 129n13, 210, 233, 282–83, 283n141
  Odyssey   126

Horace   126, 128, 129n13, 134, 210, 228n18, 232
  Ars poetica   128
Hugh of Saint Victor   35
Hypsipyle (character)   258n95

Icarus (character)   78n7, 189n46, 204n69
identification, with Ovidian characters
  fluidity of
    in Cino da Pistoia   147–48, 166–67
    in Dante   141–42n43
    in Petrarch   11, 223, 246–50, 252, 254, 260–61
  see also gender, references, simile
imitation
  medieval theories of   57–58
  modern theories of   55, 59–62, 59n157, 60n158
  see also Gian Biagio Conte, Thomas M. Greene, Alastair Minnis, Giorgio Pasquali
L'Intelligenza   77, 231, 231n30
Io (character)   252n
Isarn   94–95, 199
Iseult (character)   76, 79–80, 79n10, 89, 90n32, 93, 92–93n38
Isidore of Seville
  Etymologiae   40n
Ivo, Frate   215n85

Jacoff, Rachel   143n49, 169n1, 170n3, 204, 204nn68–69
Jacopo da Leona   51–52, 52n129
Jacopo della Lana   218n91
Jardine, Lisa   27
Jason (character)   186, 186n, 194, 230–31, 237–38
Jean de Meun   210n76
Jerome, Saint   191n51
John of Garland   22–25, 28, 81n13, 224, 247n68, 248n70
  Integumenta Ovidii   22–24, 23n31, 28, 224
  see also commentaries: on the *Met.*
John of Genoa   127n5
Juno (character)   126, 175, 251
Jupiter (character)   32n66, 43, 127n5, 148, 189, 236, 241, 242n55, 243, 250, 253–54

Kay, Sarah   78–79n9

Kay, Tristan   141–42n43, 215n85
Keen, Catherine   155, 156n64, 281–82n139
Kilgour, Maggie   170
Kleinhenz, Christopher   8–9, 15n5, 107n66, 109n72, 152n, 180
Kuon, Peter   251n79

Lai de Narcisse   75, 83
Lancelot (character)   200n62
Lancia, Andrea   29n55, 30n56, 31, 31n60
Latini, Brunetto   3–8, 38–39, 51–52, 127, 138n34, 164–65, 176, 210, 229
   Rettorica   38, 51, 127
   Tesoretto   3–8, 4n, 33, 51, 138n34, 210
   Tresor   8, 38–39, 38n88, 39nn90–91, 51, 164–65, 164n83, 165n, 176, 229, 231n31
   as character in *Commedia*   51, 183
   as translator and commentator   38–39, 39nn90–91, 51, 164n83, 165, 165n, 231n31
Laura (character), in Petrarch   257n94, 259n99, 270n, 274n129, 281, 283–85, 284n144
   Aurora and   243, 243n59
   Daphne and   245, 245n64, 245–46n66, 259, 268, 274
   death of   247, 261–62, 262n108, 270, 273–75, 273n, 277
   name of   149n54, 243, 243n59, 245, 256, 259, 274, 274n131
   Narcissus and   247–49, 248n71
laurel   68, 242n54
   in Cino da Pistoia   146–47
   in Petrarch   235–36, 236n43, 241, 245, 245n63, 251–56, 268–70, 272, 274, 274n129, 284
Leander (character)   76
Ledda, Giuseppe   188n44, 189nn45–46
Leucothoë (character)   138, 151–54, 177, 177n22, 196n, 272
Liber catonianus   44–45, 47–48, 128
libraries
   access to   53–54, 167n87
   in Florence   52–53
   monastic   52
   see also studia
   of Frederick II   50
   of Petrarch   224, 224n2, 232, 232n33, 235
Livraghi, Leyla M. G.   144n

Lombardi, Elena   48n113
Lot (biblical figure)   276, 276–77nn
Lovato dei Lovati   41, 41n94, 46, 52n131
love   47, 76, 88–90, 92, 96, 98n43, 100–1, 103, 108, 125, 138–39, 165–67, 192, 195, 199, 202n65, 231, 235, 278
   conjugal   284
   cures for   116–17, 141, 147, 210, 216n88, 234
   death and   80, 84–85, 94–95, 114, 141–42n43, 200–1, 207, 220, 242, 247
   destructive powers of   79, 81–83
   exile and   155, 160–61, 160n71, 281–82n139, 285
   fine   83–84, 83–84n22, 93–94, 103, 122, 263
   fol'amor   81–82, 93, 122, 263
   free will and   114, 116–17, 151, 161n
   (in)experience and   48, 93, 113–14, 151, 234
   madness and   80–81, 94–95, 200, 220
   nature of   3, 6, 93, 98, 105–6, 115, 120–21, 239
   negative view of   78–79, 95, 98–99, 108
   new love interest   150–52, 271–74, 273n, 274n129
   nobility and   101, 216
   positive view of   94, 98
   powerlessness against   114–17, 134, 143, 151, 159, 161n
   sexual   41–42, 80, 274n129
   suffering and   49, 94, 185, 194, 238, 281
   unchanged   140–41, 153–54, 284
   unrequited   82, 96, 104, 140–41, 143, 153–54
   vanity and self-love   77–78, 80–82, 81n13, 85–86, 200, 207, 247, 248n70, 249, 260n104
   see also Narcissus
   wealth and   42, 101–2, 102n54, 216
   see also personification: of love
Lucan   24, 45, 59n157, 109, 126, 127n5, 128, 129n13, 134, 135n25, 136, 136n28, 210
   Pharsalia   126, 127n5, 128, 134–35, 135n25, 136, 136n28
Lucretia (character)   258

Macer   45

GENERAL INDEX 339

Maestro Adamo (character), in
  Commedia 220
Malaspina, Currado (character), in
  Commedia 183
Malaspina, Moroello 156, 159, 161–62
manuscripts
  see Index of Manuscripts
Marcabru 98–100, 99n46, 102–3, 105–7, 133
Marchesi, Simone 163n78, 204n69, 211n77,
  213n83
Marcozzi, Luca 224n2, 227, 227nn13–14,
  234n40, 235–36, 259n100, 274n129
Il mare amoroso 77, 96
Marti, Mario 114n77, 146n, 149
Martinez, Ronald 75–76n3, 133–34n23, 134,
  139, 141, 143
Martini, Simone 227
Mary, Virgin (biblical figure) 255–56,
  257n94
Matelda (character), in *Commedia* 195
Matthew of Vendôme 127, 127n5, 266
Maximian
  Elegies 45
Mazzotta, Giuseppe 127, 141n43, 248,
  248nn71–72, 259nn98–99, 260
McLaughlin, Martin L. 58
Medea (character)
  in Dante 169n2, 186, 186n, 194, 239
  in Petrarch 230–31, 231n28, 237–39, 249
Medusa (character)
  in Dante 134–38, 138n33, 142–43
  in Petrarch 237, 255–57, 256nn88–89,
    257n94
  see also petrification
Meneghetti, Maria Luisa 99n46, 107
Mercury (character) 237, 252
metapoetics
  in Dante 125–33, 210n75, 211–19, 221
  in Italian sonnet exchanges 109, 109n72,
    113n, 119–20, 119n85, 120n86, 124, 129
    Ovid's role in 109–10, 117–20
  in Ovid 210n75, 212–14, 219, 221–22,
    264–65, 267n121
Mills Chiarenza, Marguerite 191
Minerva (character) 267n121
Minnis, Alastair J. 15n3, 61
Miracole de Roma 38n85
misogyny 78, 96, 97n42, 108

Moevs, Christian 200nn
Monte, Andrea 87, 95
Moore, Edward 56, 56n148, 58, 59n155, 60,
  154n59, 181n34
Morgana (character) 92–93n38, 93
Moses (biblical figure) 162
Mostacci, Iacopo 120, 120–21n87
Muses (characters) 267n121, 225, 233
Mussato, Albertino 41, 41n94, 46, 52n131
Myrrha (character) 97, 195
myth, as theme of Ovid's poetry 5, 18,
  166–67, 194
  see also commentaries: on the *Met.*,
  Dante, Petrarch, and individual
  character names

Naiades (characters) 173, 173n10, 175n16
Narcissus (character) 75n1, 77–78
  in Dante 175n16, 198–99, 207–9, 220
  in medieval Italian poetry 78n7, 82–88,
    100, 122, 143, 147, 153, 166, 198, 209, 220,
    243, 247, 247n67, 260n104, 286
  in Occitan poetry 78–82, 78–79nn7–9,
    86–87, 91, 100, 104, 143, 147, 153, 166,
    198, 209, 220, 247, 247n67, 247n69,
    260n104, 286
  in Ovidian commentaries 22, 74–75,
    81, 81n13, 208, 247–49, 247n68,
    248n70
  in Petrarch 237, 243, 246–49, 247nn68–
    69, 252, 263, 286
  see also Bernart de Ventadorn, Chiaro
    Davanzati, Echo, *Il mare amoroso*,
    Peirol, Rinaldo d'Aquino
Navone, Paola 35n75
Nemesis (character) 77
Neptune (character) 169–70n2, 181, 198
Niobe (character) 137–38

Oedipus (character) 173, 173n10
Onesto da Bologna 48–49, 54, 113–15, 113n,
  120–21, 124, 145n, 199, 218, 218n92
Orbicciani, Bonagiunta 108–9, 120, 120n86,
  217–19, 217–18nn90–92
  as character in *Commedia* 183, 198, 211,
    217–19, 217–18nn91–92, 221
Orico da Capriana
  Summa memorialis 28, 28n50

Orlandi, Guido   110, 117–21, 119n83, 119–20nn85–86, 132, 132n21, 216–18, 216n89, 217n90
Orléans, as center of classical studies in France   21–23, 21n26, 34
Orosius, Paulus   201, 201n63, 242n56
Orpheus (character)   44, 181, 262n109
  in Ovidian commentaries   275, 275n133
  in Petrarch   237, 261–62, 262n106, 262n108, 275–78, 276n, 282–83, 283n141
  in Vergil   203–5, 204nn68–69, 262n108, 275n132, 278n
  see also Eurydice
Ortiz, Ramiro   78n7, 85n24, 87, 94n39
Otis, Brooks   20
Ottimo Commento   29n55, 187, 188n43, 192
Ovid
  Amores   5, 8, 27, 31, 35–37, 42, 100, 105, 106n61, 116, 127–28, 211n78, 212–16, 212n80, 219, 221, 226, 227n16, 281
  Ars amatoria   5–6, 6n6, 8, 18, 29, 31–32, 33n69, 42, 44, 91, 100, 102, 104–5, 114, 116, 121, 128, 193, 215–16, 219, 224, 226, 227n16, 233–34, 233n37, 281
  Epistulae ex Ponto   5, 16n7, 38, 137, 143, 158, 192, 226, 281
  Fasti   5, 16n7, 22n28, 31, 33n69, 34, 38, 38n85, 162–64, 163nn77–78, 226, 227n16, 228–29, 229n22, 267n121, 280–81
  Heroides   5, 16n7, 27, 30–32, 30n58, 31n60, 33n69, 34n72, 35, 39nn90–91, 97, 97–98n43, 128, 142–43, 142n47, 215–16, 219, 224, 226, 227n16, 279–81
  Ibis   5, 16n7, 31, 39, 39n91, 43, 46n112, 52n131, 226
  Medicamina faciei femineae   16n7, 42–43, 226
  Metamorphoses
    see commentaries: on the *Met.*, Index Locorum, Ovid: translations, and names of individual characters and poets
  Remedia amoris   5–6, 6n6, 8, 16n7, 29, 29n55, 31, 35, 36n78, 45, 47, 116–17, 121, 128–30, 129n12, 130n16, 131, 133–34, 168, 171n, 184–85, 185n40, 186, 194, 219, 224, 226, 227n16, 233–34
  Tristia   5, 16n7, 29n55, 43–44, 142n47, 154–59, 160n71, 165–66, 192–94, 213n83, 225–26, 233, 257, 265, 266n115, 281–83
  see also pseudo-Ovidian works
  as character   3–5, 210, 287
  as doctor   116, 116n79, 234
  as philosopher   4, 7–8, 33, 225, 230, 286
  as teacher of the poor   42, 102–3
  autobiography (*Tristia* 4.10)   193, 210n75, 233
  biography and lives   16, 26, 27n46
  considered lascivious   44, 225, 233, 233n37
  diversity of works   5n3, 7–8, 12, 18, 63, 73, 166–67, 221, 235, 263, 267
  love
    as authority on   5, 41, 45, 49, 103, 106–7, 109, 111–12, 119–20n85, 121–22, 126–27, 145, 154, 168, 198, 215–16
    as example for love poets   74, 110, 117–18, 121, 129, 216–17
    as teacher of   5, 6n6, 45, 102, 109, 112n75, 121, 155, 215–16
    questioned as authority on   107, 109, 119–21, 168, 198, 209, 215, 234
  medieval education and   17, 21–25, 27–28, 33–34, 40, 44–45, 47–48, 75, 101n52, 128, 225
    see also anthologies, Bologna, commentaries: on the *Met.*, didactic literature, education, *Liber catonianus*, Orléans
  reception   8–10, 12–13, 18, 62–63, 74, 172, 178
  translations
    entire works   5, 7, 9, 28–33, 29n54, 39n91, 46n110, 48–49, 61, 187–88, 188n43, 224–25, 286
    fragments, in poetry   56, 91, 128, 154, 170, 180, 182, 187–88, 188n43, 192–93, 212, 218–19, 221, 231, 237–38, 242, 249–50, 262n108, 263–64, 267, 273, 275, 277
    fragments, in prose   8, 36n78, 37n82, 38–39, 39n90, 42–44, 164–66, 164n83, 231n31
  transmission   5–17, 15n5, 46, 109, 119–21, 209, 215, 234

GENERAL INDEX 341

Ovide moralisé   25, 32, 46n110, 47, 57, 61, 75, 225, 225n4
Ovidius maior (*Ovidio maggiore*)   5–7, 6n4, 44, 226
   see also Ovid: *Metamorphoses*

Paden, William D., Jr.   259, 259n99
Padua, (proto-)humanism in   25n38, 41, 41n94
   see also Geremia da Montagnone, Lovato dei Lovati, Albertino Mussato
Pallavillani, Schiatta   199
Pamphilus   45–46, 96, 114n77, 238
Paolino, Laura   242n57, 259n99, 271n125, 272
Paratore, Ettore   90, 172, 175, 175n16, 177–78
Paris (character)   36, 76, 82n17
Parthenopaeus (character)   204n68
Pasquali, Giorgio   58, 58n154, 59n155, 60
Paul, Saint   40, 229, 229–30n23
Peirol   80–81, 83–84, 247n67
Peleus (character)   96
Peneus (character)   47, 68, 146, 250, 250n76, 255n87, 268
Perillos (character)   195
Persephone (character)   267n121
Perseus (character)   135–36, 138, 143, 237, 256nn88–89
personification
   in Dante   126–28, 130, 132–33, 219
   in *dolce stil novo* poetry   119, 124, 214, 217–18
   in Latini   3, 5
   in rhetorical manuals   40, 127–28, 217n7
   of love   103, 114, 146, 216
      in Cavalcanti   119, 132, 214, 217
      in Dante   125–26, 128, 132–33, 142, 147, 151, 159–61, 211–15, 219
      in Ovid   126, 128–31, 212–15, 219
      in Petrarch   231, 235, 254, 279–80
   of poems   156–57
Peter Lombard   14, 14n2, 61
   Book of Sentences   14, 61
Peter the Venerable   98
Petrarca, Gherardo   225n7
Petrarch   9–12, 31, 41, 43, 77, 125, 140, 142n45, 148, 149n54, 164, 164n83, 166–68, 223–87
   Africa   239, 239n50, 256n89, 283n142

Codice degli abbozzi
   see Index of Manuscripts, MS. Vat. lat. 3196
Collatio laureationis   256n89
De remediis utriusque fortune   229, 233, 235
De vita solitaria   225n6, 233, 235
Familiares   225–30, 225n4, 225n6, 228n18, 229–30n23, 230–31n27, 233, 256n89
Rerum memorandarum libri   232–34
Rerum vulgarium fragmenta (*Canzoniere*)   11, 56, 125, 148, 149n54, 166–68, 223, 231, 231n28, 233, 235–40, 237n, 240n52, 242n57, 243–46, 244n60, 245nn62–63, 248–64, 255n86, 256n88, 257n94, 258n95, 259n99, 262n106, 267–87, 267–68n122, 270n123, 274n129, 274n131
rime estravaganti   239–43, 239–40nn51–52, 273–75, 274n129, 285–86
Secretum   227–28, 248–49, 254, 255n86, 263–64, 277
Seniles   230n23, 276
Trionfi   232–33, 239, 247n68, 255n86
annotated copy of Ovid's *Met.*   49, 54, 226–27, 226n12, 270–71
as reader   164n83, 224–28, 224n2, 226n10, 228n18, 232, 232n33
citations from Ovid   225–31, 226n9, 227n14, 229–30n23, 231n27
Dante and   59, 63, 223, 223n, 225, 232, 232n34, 236–37, 239–40, 239n50, 242, 242n57, 256–57, 263–65, 272, 273n, 284n144, 285–87
diverse use of Ovidian material   239–40, 239–40nn51–52, 250, 263, 274n129, 274n131, 275, 285–86
familiarity with Ovidian commentaries   18n15, 25–26, 225–27, 236–37, 249, 259
familiarity with vernacular Ovidian tradition   237–50, 260–63, 286
first readings of Ovid   49, 54, 56, 225, 256
fragmentation of Ovidian works   223, 245, 264, 267–86
poetic re-creation of the *Met.*   243–46, 245n63, 250–51, 250n76, 255, 260–61, 263, 274, 280

translations and paraphrases of Ovid's
    verses   231, 237–39, 249–50, 262n108
  views on Ovid   225, 232–35
  see also Actaeon, Apollo, Cino da Pistoia,
    Daphne, Eurydice, exile, gender,
    identification, Laura, laurel, Medea,
    Medusa, Narcissus, Orpheus,
    Phaethon, Pyramus, simile
Petri di Siena, Ser Dietisalvi
  see Dietisalvi di Pietro
petrification
  in Dante   136–38, 143
  in Petrarch   252–53, 255–57, 256n88
  see also Medusa
Petrucci, Armando   15n4
Phaedra (character)   98n, 103, 191, 278–80, 279n
Phaethon (character)   127n5, 138
  in Dante   175n16, 183–84, 186, 188–91, 188–90nn44–49, 194, 196
  in Petrarch   237, 241, 251–52, 266n116
Philippe de Cabassole   225, 225n6, 229, 233
Philippe de Vitry   225n4
Philomela (character)   97n43, 149, 149n53, 237
Picone, Michelangelo   6, 56, 121n, 129n12, 130n16, 160n71, 172, 177–80, 177n25, 192, 207, 207n, 221n93
Pier della Vigna   50, 89–92, 91n35, 95, 120, 120–21n87, 199–200, 202n65
Pierides (characters)   267n121
Piramus et Tisbé   75, 75n2
Pliny   236n43
Poliziano, Angelo   276n
Pollio, Gaius Asinius   232
Polydorus (character)   176
Polyxena (character)   176, 258n95
Possanza, Mark   222
preaching, use of Ovid in   26, 40n, 42, 44n104–5, 47
  see also Bartolomeo da San Concordio, Giordano da Pisa, Pierre Bersuire
Procne (character)   97, 97–98n43, 149, 149n53, 237
Propertius   210n75, 212, 233
prophecy, in Commedia   38, 157, 184, 190, 192
prosopopoeia
  see personification

Proverbia quae dicuntur super natura
    feminarum   77, 96–98, 96–98nn42–43
pseudo-Lactantius Placidus
  Metamorphoseon narrationes
    (Narrationes)   20–22, 20n21, 20–21n23, 21n27, 47, 64, 68, 176–78, 177n22, 190n48, 226, 227n13, 236
  see also commentaries: on the Met.
pseudo-Ovidian works
  Consolatio ad Liviam de Morte Drusi   16, 16n9
  De pulice   30
  De vetula   16
  Halieutica   16, 226
  Nux   16, 29n55, 40, 40n
pseudo-Senecan works
  De remediis fortuitorum   164–66, 164n83
Pygmalion (character)   237
Pyramus (character)
  and Thisbe
    in Dante   143, 154, 166, 175n16, 198–209, 202–3n66, 220
    in medieval French and Latin literature   74–75, 75n2, 77
    in medieval Italian poetry   88–96, 98, 100, 122, 134, 145, 147, 153, 198, 202n65, 220, 237, 260n104, 263, 268
    in Occitan poetry   76, 88–95, 100, 122, 202n65, 220, 237, 260n104, 263, 286
    in Petrarch   237–43, 248, 263, 286
  see also Chiaro Davanzati, Pier della Vigna, Giraut de Salignac, Raimbaut de Vaqueiras, Rustico Filippi, Schiatta Pallavillani
Pythagoras (character)   188
Python (character)   68, 270–72

Quillen, Carol E.   229–30

Raimbaut de Vaqueiras   88, 90, 90n33, 92, 199, 202n65
Ramazzina, Antonella   82, 82n16, 83n21
reading
  descriptions of, in medieval literature   130–31, 200n62, 228n18
  memory and   55, 55n142, 59–60, 130–31, 192n53

of Ovid
  in "filtered" sources   45–47, 49, 59, 62, 286
  in fragmented, intermediary sources   18n15, 33, 34–35n75, 39, 39n91, 44–45, 48, 51, 62, 104–5n59, 127, 143, 164, 168, 179–81, 185, 192n53, 195, 220, 227–28
    see also anthologies, compendia, florilegia, Florilegium Gallicum
  in translation
    see Ovid: translations
  mentions of, in medieval literature   45, 49, 54, 99–107, 109–22, 112n75, 216, 225, 287
reception
  see Ovid: reception
references, in poetry
  hybrid combinations of literary figures and traditions   76, 92–93, 92–93n38, 96
  to animal world and nature   86n25, 96, 142, 142n47, 148–49, 199, 252, 254
  to Arthurian characters   76–77, 79–80, 79n10, 89, 90n32, 92–93, 92–93n38, 96, 200n62
  to biblical figures   75–77, 96, 99, 111–12, 208
  to Ovidian characters   10–11, 74–98, 100, 122, 134, 143–49, 152–53, 166–69, 169–70n2, 181, 181n32, 188–91, 194–209, 220, 223, 235, 237–64, 267–80, 285, 287
    see also gender, identification, simile, and individual character names
Rhamnusia   165
rhetoric
  manuals of   40–41, 44, 47, 51, 127–28
  teaching of   17, 40, 47, 50–51, 225n7
  see also Bene da Firenze, Boncompagno da Signa, Guido Faba
Richard of St. Victor   215n85
Rigaut de Berbezilh   86n25, 105–6, 110, 115–16, 216, 216n86
rime di corrispondenza
  see sonnet exchanges
Rinaldo d'Aquino   82–85, 82nn16–17, 83nn20–22, 87, 91, 93, 122, 247n67
Robson, Alan   21, 172, 176–78, 176n19

Rofian   94–95, 199
Roman d'Alexandre   74
Roman de la Rose   7, 15n3, 46, 74, 210n76, 247n68
Roman de Troie   74
Roncaglia, Aurelio   108n68, 145n, 211–12n78
Rosati, Gianpiero   266n118, 267n121
Rossi, Luciano   100–2, 120n85
Rotondi, Giuseppe   25

Sabbadini, Remigio   41n94, 192n53, 232n33
Sallust   232
Salmacis (character)   154, 210n75
Samson (biblical figure)   99
Santagata, Marco   231–32, 231n30, 236, 245n63, 256n92, 264, 273n
Satan (biblical figure)   208
Savona, Eugenio   78n7, 149
Sayce, Olive   75n3, 88n29, 92
Scheludko, Dimitri   105
Schiatta di Messer Albizo
  see Schiatta Pallavillani
Schrötter, Willibald   105
Scylla (character)   169n2
Semele (character)   151
Semiramis (character)   200–1, 201n63, 242n56
Seneca   8, 35, 35n75, 43, 106, 136, 136n27, 164–66, 225, 227n14, 232, 234, 234n40
  Quaestiones naturales   136, 136n27
  see also pseudo-Senecan works
Sennuccio del Bene
  Petrarch and   239–40n51, 240–41, 243–44n60, 244–45, 274, 274n131
Servius   33n69, 191n51, 213, 213n84
Severinus   228n18
simile
  in Dante   169, 169–70n2, 182–84, 182n37, 186–88, 188n44, 194–96, 199–200, 199nn, 202–3, 202n66, 207, 220
  in Latin epic poetry   199
  in medieval lyric poetry   10, 74–96, 86n25, 122, 125, 143, 166–67, 207, 220
  in Petrarch   235, 237, 240–43, 245, 247n69, 250, 257–58, 258n95, 260–63, 275, 286–87

see also gender, identification, references, and individual character names
Simintendi, Arrigo (da Prato)
   as first Italian translator of the *Met.*   31–32, 31n61, 188n43, 224, 236
Sinone (character)   220
Soffredi del Grazia (di Pistoia)   35n76, 36n78, 39n90
Sol (character)
   see Apollo
Solomon (biblical figure)   99, 111–12
sonnet exchanges   48–49, 74, 93, 95, 107–9, 107n66, 109n72, 113–23, 113n76, 120–21n87, 124, 128–29, 166, 198, 209, 211, 216–21, 245
Sordello   60
Sowell, Madison U.   6n4, 56, 169n1, 170n3
Spinola, Galeotto   230
Statius   20, 24, 45, 127n5, 204, 204n68, 230n23
   Achilleid   45, 204, 204n68
   Thebaid   127n5, 204, 204n68, 230n23
   as character in *Commedia*   204n68
Steinberg, Justin   239–40nn51–52, 274n129, 274n131
Storie de Troia e de Roma   37–38, 37–38nn83–85
Stroński, Stanisław   101n52, 105
studia (monastic schools of higher learning), in Florence   52, 52n130
   see also libraries
Szombathely, Gioachino   56, 169n1, 181n34

tenso   94–95, 98–99, 102, 105–7, 106n63
tenzone
   see sonnet exchanges
Tereus (character)   97n43, 237
Theodulus
   Ecloga   45
Thisbe (character)
   see Pyramus
Thyestes (character)   97–98n43
Tibullus   210n75, 233
Tiresias (character)   97
Todorović, Jelena   15n3, 125, 129n14
translation
   French into Italian   31n60, 32n64
   French into Latin   38
   Italian into Latin   31

   Latin into Italian via French   30–32, 32n64
   Occitan into Italian   78n8, 82, 82n16, 92
   see also Ovid: translations, *volgarizzamento*
Tristan (character)   76, 79, 79n10, 80, 89, 90n32

Uguccione da Pisa
   Derivationes   40n
Urban V, Pope   229–30n23, 276

Varro   232
Varvaro, Alberto   105
Vatican Mythographers   18n15, 21n27, 33n69, 226n12, 227, 236
Vazzana, Steno   56, 154n59, 181n34, 210n75, 211n78
Venus (character)   100, 274n131
Vergil   12, 24, 33n69, 40n, 45, 106, 108–9, 108n68, 111–12, 126, 128, 129n13, 134, 141–42, 141–42n43, 184, 199, 203–5, 204nn, 210, 212–13, 227, 228n18, 232–33, 262n108, 274n131, 275, 275n132, 278n, 282–83, 283n141
   Aeneid   30n57, 31n60, 126, 128, 142, 184, 191n51, 199, 204n68, 212n80, 213, 274n131
      preproemium (so-called)   213, 213n83
   Eclogues   212
   Georgics   203, 204n68, 205, 262n108
Vickers, Nancy J.   245, 259n99, 260n102
Vidal, Peire   108
vidas   101, 101nn51–52
Virbius (character)   191, 191n51
Virgilio (character), in *Commedia*   60, 143, 169, 189n46, 200–1, 203, 204n68, 205–6, 209
volgarizzamento (Latin to vernacular)
   common profile of Italian translators   31
   French vs. Italian approaches   32, 32n66
   inconsistencies and variation   19, 36n78, 37–38, 37n82, 43–44, 179
   Latin poetry into Italian   7–8, 19, 28–33, 28n51, 29n52, 31n60, 46
   Latin prose into Italian   30n59, 35n76, 36n78, 37–38, 37nn82–83, 42–46, 45n108, 51, 201n63

merits of the vernacular and   7, 30, 30n57, 31n60
see also Ovid: translations
Vulgate Commentary   23–24, 23n32, 66–69, 172–75, 178, 266
see also commentaries: on the *Met.*

Wallace, David   54n141, 210–11n76
Wilhelm, James J.   100
Witt, Ronald G.   17n10, 25n38, 29n52, 29n54, 35n76, 41, 41n94, 43, 127, 224n3

Zak, Gur   248

Printed in the United States
By Bookmasters